Building the Financial Found
the Euro

Building the Financial Foundations of the Euro

Experiences and Challenges

Edited by
Lars Jonung, Christoph Walkner and Max Watson

Routledge
Taylor & Francis Group
LONDON AND NEW YORK

Publications Office
Publications.europa.eu

Published by Routledge, 2008
Albert House, 1–4 Singer Street, London, EC2A 4BQ, United Kingdom

Routledge is an imprint of the Taylor & Francis Group, an informa business

ISBN 978-92-79-05295-8 (pbk)
ISBN 978-0-203-88635-9 (ebk)

Typeset in 10.5 on 12 pt Baskerville by
Taylor & Francis Books
Printed and bound in Great Britain by
CPI Antony Rowe, Chippenham, Wiltshire

Contents

Notes on contributors viii
Preface xiv

PART I
Overview 1

1 Introduction 3
LARS JONUNG, CHRISTOPH WALKNER AND MAX WATSON

2 Financial markets in the euro area: realizing the full benefits of integration 19
KLAUS REGLING AND MAX WATSON

PART II
Monetary integration: convergence and adjustment 27

II.1 Moving to monetary union 29

3 Catch-up, the transition to full participation in EMU and financial stability 31
IAIN BEGG

4 Adjusting to the euro 56
GABRIEL FAGAN AND VÍTOR GASPAR

5 Booms and busts: experiences with internal and external adjustment 84
REINER MARTIN AND LUDGER SCHUKNECHT

6 Financial stability in emerging Europe 111
PIROSKA M. NAGY AND RICHARD FOX

II.2 Living inside a monetary union 125

7 Adjustment in EMU: a model-based analysis of country experiences 127
SVEN LANGEDIJK AND WERNER ROEGER

8 Housing markets and adjustment in monetary union 161
PETER HOELLER AND DAVID RAE

PART III
Financial integration: convergence and adjustment 195

III.1 Setting the scene 197

9 Regional interest rates within a monetary union: lessons from the United States 199
JOHN LANDON-LANE AND HUGH ROCKOFF

10 Where does capital flow? A comparison of US states and EU countries 1950–2000 222
SEBNEM KALEMLI-OZCAN, BENT E. SØRENSEN AND BELGI TURAN

11 Declining home bias and the increase in international risk sharing: lessons from European integration 242
MICHAEL J. ARTIS AND MATHIAS HOFFMANN

III.2 Banking across borders 259

12 Economic integration and financial stability: a European perspective 261
GIANNI DE NICOLÒ AND ALEXANDER TIEMAN

13 Banking integration and co-movements in EU banks' fragility 281
ANDREA BRASILI AND GIUSEPPE VULPES

14 Challenges to banking stability in the EU: a survey 306
CHRISTOPH WALKNER

PART IV
Policy challenges 335

15 Financial supervision in Europe: a proposal for a new architecture 337
DIRK SCHOENMAKER AND SANDER OOSTERLOO

16 Cross-border banking: challenges for deposit insurance and financial stability in the European Union 355
ROBERT A. EISENBEIS AND GEORGE G. KAUFMAN

17 The search for the elusive twin goals of monetary and financial stability 404
CLAUDIO BORIO

Index 431

Contributors

Michael J. Artis is professor of economics at Manchester University, where he directs the Manchester Regional Economics Centre for the Institute of Political and Economic Governance. He is a Fellow of the British Academy and a Research Fellow of the Centre for Economic Policy Research in London. Recent previous appointments include a Professorship at the European University Institute, Florence, and a Senior George Fellowship at the Bank of England. His current research interests include regional economics, business cycle analysis and the analysis of risk sharing.

Iain Begg is a Professorial Research Fellow at the European Institute, London School of Economics and Political Science. His main research work is on the political economy of European integration and EU economic governance. His current projects include studies on the governance of EU economic and social policy, the EU's Lisbon strategy, the social impact of globalization and reform of the EU budget. He has undertaken a number of advisory roles, including being called as an expert witness on EU issues by the House of Commons Treasury Committee, the House of Lords European Communities Committee and the European Parliament.

Claudio Borio is currently Head of Research and Policy Analysis, Bank for International Settlements (BIS). He has been at the BIS since 1987, covering various responsibilities in the Monetary and Economic Department, including being the Head of the Secretariat that services two standing committees of senior central bank officials from the G-10 countries, the Committee on the Global Financial System and the Gold and Foreign Exchange Committee (now Markets Committee). He holds a PhD from Brasenose College, Oxford. Borio has published widely in the fields of monetary policy, banking, finance and issues related to financial stability.

Andrea Brasili is an economist in the Research and Strategy Unit of UniCredit Group where he holds the position of Head of the Economic Studies Section. Within UniCredit, he also worked in the Research Department of UniCredit Banca d'Impresa and as senior economist in the investment bank of the group. His research interests include macroeconomic themes linked to the analysis of business cycles, the analysis of the relationships between banks and non-financial corporations, applied econometrics.

Gianni De Nicolò is a senior economist in the Research Department of the International Monetary Fund. Before joining the Fund, he worked in the Division of International Finance at the Board of Governors of the Federal Reserve System, was assistant professor at Brandeis University and lecturer at the University of Rome 'La Sapienza'. He holds a PhD from the University of Minnesota. His main research interests include the modelling of systemic risk and its macroeconomic impact, the industrial organization of financial intermediation, and firms' financial structure and governance.

Robert A. Eisenbeis is currently Chief Monetary Economist at Cumberland Advisors. He recently retired as Executive Vice President and Director of Research at the Federal Reserve Bank of Atlanta. He has also held officer positions at the Board of Governors of the Federal Reserve System and Federal Deposit Insurance Cooperation (FDIC) and is now a member of the US Shadow Financial Regulatory Committee. His research has focused on banking and regulatory policy as well as monetary policy. He holds a BS degree from Brown University and Masters and PhD degrees from the University of Wisconsin Madison.

Gabriel Fagan is Head of the Monetary Policy Research Division of the European Central Bank (ECB). He was previously Head of the Econometric Modelling Division. Prior to joining the ECB he worked for the European Monetary Institute, the Committee of Governors of the EC Central Banks and the Central Bank of Ireland. His research covers a number of areas of macroeconomics, including forecasting techniques, macroeconomic modelling and monetary policy strategy.

Richard Fox is a Senior Director in Fitch Ratings' sovereign group. Prior to joining Fitch in 1997, he held a variety of posts in the public and private sectors including the Bank of England, HM Treasury, IMF and Midland Bank. In 1993 he moved to Standard Chartered Bank, where he provided economic advice and analysis for both the commercial and investment bank on country risk, portfolio management, business strategy and treasury and capital markets issues. He has a first class honours degree in economics from the University of Cambridge and an MSc in economics from the University of London.

Vítor Gaspar is Head of the Bureau of Policy Advisers, which provides policy and political advice to the President of the European Commission and the Commission Services on issues relevant to the President's agenda. Until January 2007, he was Special Adviser at the Bank of Portugal. Before that he served as Director-General Research at the European Central Bank, between 1998 and 2004. He has also been Director of Research at the Bank of Portugal and Director of Economic Studies at the Portuguese Ministry of Finance. He has authored and edited several books and published widely in scientific journals.

Peter Hoeller is Head of Country Studies IV Division in the Economics Department at the OECD in Paris. He joined the OECD in 1982. During his career at the OECD, he has headed several country desks. He also worked in the Policy Studies Branch of the Economics Department, focusing, inter alia, on issues relating to savings behaviour, pricing and climate change. He graduated at the University of Linz in Austria and was for several years a lecturer and researcher at this university. Prior to joining the OECD, he worked at a commercial bank in Vienna.

Mathias Hoffmann is Professor of International Trade and Finance at the University of Zurich. His research focuses on the macroeconomic aspects of international financial integration and on the link between asset markets and the macroeconomy more generally. Prior to arriving at Zurich, he was professor of economics at the University of Dortmund and a lecturer at Southampton University. Mathias Hoffmann is a fellow of CESifo and a visiting researcher at the Deutsche Bundesbank. He obtained his undergraduate education in economics and mathematics at WHU Koblenz, Brandeis and the University of Bonn and a PhD in economics at the European University Institute in Florence.

Lars Jonung is, since September 2000, a Research Adviser at DG ECFIN, European Commission, Brussels, dealing with macroeconomic issues. He was previously a professor of economics at the Stockholm School of Economics. His research is focused on monetary and fiscal policies, on monetary unions and exchange rate arrangements, and on the history of economic thought. Jonung has published several articles in major journals and books in English and Swedish.

Sebnem Kalemli-Ozcan is associate professor of economics at University of Houston and NBER fellow. She received a BSc degree from Middle East Technical University, Ankara, Turkey, in 1995, and a PhD in economics from Brown University, USA, in 2000. Her research agenda focuses on global linkages, financial markets, health and development. Her work has been published in major journals. She was selected as 2008 Duisenberg fellow of the European Central Bank based on her research on measuring the degree of financial integration within the European Union and the effects of this integration on financial stability and growth.

George G. Kaufman is the John F. Smith Professor of Economics and Finance at Loyola University Chicago and consultant to the Federal Reserve Bank of Chicago. Earlier he was an economist at the Federal Reserve Bank of Chicago and the John Rogers Professor of Finance at the University of Oregon. He has published widely on financial markets and institutions. Kaufman is co-editor of the *Journal of Financial Stability* and a founding editor of the *Journal of Financial Services Research*. He serves as co-chair of the Shadow Financial Regulatory Committee. Kaufman holds a PhD in economics from the University of Iowa.

John Landon-Lane is an Assistant Professor in the Department of Economics at Rutgers, the state university of New Jersey. His research includes work in econometric theory, applied macro-econometrics, growth and development and financial and economic history. He has published widely. His current research deals with the estimation of dynamic macroeconomic models. Prior to arriving at Rutgers University he worked at the School of Economics, the University of New South Wales. He has a Masters of Commerce from the University of Canterbury and a PhD from the University of Minnesota.

Sven Langedijk is an economist at the European Commission. He contributes to the development of the EU fiscal governance framework and the Stability and Growth Pact, and is a co-author of the Commission's annual report on *Public Finances in EMU*. Prior to joining the European Commission in 2001, he was a policy adviser in the Dutch Ministry of Finance. His research interests include fiscal policy coordination and adjustment dynamics in EMU. He was educated at the University of Leuven and the London School of Economics.

Reiner Martin is Head of the Convergence and Structural Analysis Section in the Directorate-General Economics of the European Central Bank. He focuses on euro area enlargement and economic developments in the EU Member States outside the euro area. Reiner Martin worked previously as Research Fellow at the Centre for European Policy Studies (CEPS) in Brussels and Deputy Head of Division at the German Federal Ministry of Economics in Bonn. He holds a PhD in economics from the University of Hamburg. His policy and research interests include nominal and real convergence within the EU as well as structural reforms in product and labour markets including labour mobility. He has published a number of books, papers and articles in these fields.

Piroska M. Nagy is Division Chief at the African Department of the International Monetary Fund, Washington DC. She worked previously as Senior Adviser at Fitch Ratings (where she wrote Chapter 6 in this volume with Richard Fox). She has also worked at the European Bank for Reconstruction and Development (EBRD), covering financial sector regulation and governance and banking sector systemic risk issues, as well as at the Research Department of the National Bank of Hungary. She holds an MSc in economics from the University of Budapest. Her policy and research interests include interlinkages between the financial sector and the macro-real economy, and macroeconomic policies in emerging market economies. She has published several books and papers in these fields.

Sander Oosterloo is a senior policy adviser at the Netherlands Ministry of Finance. Since 2002 he has been working on issues ranging from banking regulation and financial crisis management to the conduct of business issues and retail financial services. He obtained his PhD at the University of Groningen, and has written on institutional frameworks for financial stability, accountability of supervisory authorities, financial integration and challenges in EU supervision.

David Rae is a Senior Financial Analyst at the New Zealand Superannuation Fund, specializing in private markets and alternative investments. Prior to that he was Head of the European Union/Ireland desk at the OECD. At the OECD he worked on a range of country desks and in its macroeconomic analysis and research division. He has also worked as a research economist at New Zealand's central bank and at a private sector bank, the National Bank of New Zealand. He has degrees in physics and economics from University of the Waikato and the London School of Economics.

Klaus Regling became Director-General for Economic and Financial Affairs at the European Commission (DG ECFIN) on 1 July 2001. The main role of the Directorate-General is to foster European Economic and Monetary Union through economic surveillance and policy advice and by advancing economic policy coordination. Klaus Regling previously spent eleven years with the IMF in Washington and Jakarta, eleven years with the German Ministry of Finance and two years with the Moore Capital Strategy Group in London. He studied economics at the Universities of Hamburg and Regensburg.

Hugh Rockoff is a professor of economics at Rutgers University, the state university of New Jersey, and a Research Associate of the National Bureau of Economic Research. His main research has been on American monetary and financial history and wartime economics. He is currently working on a book on war and the American economy in the twentieth century. He was educated at Earlham College and the University of Chicago.

Werner Roeger is head of the Economic Modelling and Medium Term Studies Unit in the Directorate-General for Economic and Financial Affairs of the European Commission. He holds a PhD from the University of Freiburg. His work is focused on the application of structural economic models to the quantitative analysis of medium- and long-term policy issues. His research interests include nominal and real convergence within the EU, the effects of structural reforms in product and labour markets and fiscal policy. He has published in academic journals and books on these issues.

Dirk Schoenmaker is Director European Affairs, Competition and Consumer Policy at the Economics Ministry in the Netherlands. Before joining the Economics Ministry in 2008, he was Deputy Director, Financial Markets Policy, at the Ministry of Finance in the Netherlands. From 1996 till 1998, he served at the Banking Supervisory Policy Division of the Bank of England. He has been a research officer at the Financial Markets Group of the London School of Economics (LSE) and a visiting scholar at the IMF. Since 2004 he has served as part-time professor of finance, banking and insurance at the Vrije Universiteit, Amsterdam. He earned his PhD at the LSE. He has published on central banking, international banking and financial supervision.

Ludger Schuknecht is Senior Advisor in the Directorate-General Economics of the European Central Bank (ECB), where he contributes to the preparation of monetary policy decision making. He was previously head of the ECB's fiscal surveillance section which followed assignments at the World Trade Organization and at the International Monetary Fund. His recent research focuses on public expenditure policies and reform and the analysis of economic boom–bust episodes. He wrote *Public Spending in the 20th Century: A Global Perspective* together with Vito Tanzi.

Bent E. Sørensen is the Lay Professor of International Economics at University of Houston, having previously been affiliated with Binghamton and Brown Universities and the Federal Reserve Bank of Kansas City. He is a CEPR research fellow and his current empirical research focuses on macroeconomic aspects of financial integration and on models of consumption. A significant part of his research studies regions within countries as potential paradigms for perfectly integrated financial markets. His work, using regional data, has been published in major journals. He received his PhD in economics from the University of Copenhagen.

Alexander Tieman is an economist at the IMF's Monetary and Capital Markets Department. Prior to joining the Fund he worked at the Nederlandsche Bank (Dutch Central Bank) and in academia. His research focuses on financial stability, financial integration and cross-border banking issues in Europe, banking competition, and retail payment systems. In addition, he works on the development of credit risk modelling and stress testing. He has an MSc in econometrics and a PhD in game theory from the Tinbergen Institute/Free University, Amsterdam, the Netherlands.

Belgi Turan is a graduate student in the economics department at the University of Houston. Her research focuses on development economics and international macroeconomics. She received her MBA and BSc degrees from Middle East Technical University in Turkey.

Giuseppe Vulpes is an adviser in the Planning, Strategy and Research Area of the UniCredit Group. Previously he was an expert in macro-prudential analysis in the division Prudential Supervision of the European Central Bank. He has also worked as head of research at the Italian deposit insurance agency (Fondo Interbancario di Tutela dei Depositi). His research interests include financial stability, in particular the use of market indicators as monitoring devices for assessing banks' conditions, the analysis of the relationships between banks and non-financial corporations, and the determinants of banks' value creation.

Christoph Walkner works in the financial market analysis unit in the Directorate for Economic and Financial Affairs of the European Commission. He has published papers on corporate governance and EU banking integration. He has previously worked at Eurostat, the statistical institute of the European Commission, the Austrian Ministry of

Foreign Affairs and as a research assistant at the University of Vienna, the University of Business and Economics of Vienna and the University of Innsbruck.

Max Watson is a Fellow of Wolfson College, Oxford, and of the UK Institute of Financial Services, and an Associate Fellow of Chatham House (the Royal Institute of International Affairs). During 2003–7, he was an economic adviser to the European Commission, where he worked on the euro area and on financial issues in Eastern Europe. Previously, he spent some 20 years with the IMF, where he headed the International Capital Markets Division and the Debt Issues Unit, before being appointed a senior adviser on Europe and a Deputy Director of the Fund. His early career was spent in the Bank of England and at S.G. Warburg and Co., Ltd. He was educated at Cambridge and at INSEAD.

Preface

The growth and integration of financial markets is a central feature of today's international economy. As the euro area approaches its second decade, it is therefore timely to ask how changes in these markets have contributed to growth, adjustment and catching-up among present and prospective members of the euro area.

Experience in the past few years underscores that changes in the financial sector pose both opportunities and challenges for policy. So a key motive in reviewing recent trends is to distil policy lessons for the future, including for economies at an early stage of integration with the euro area. To shed light on these questions and promote discussion, this volume presents studies that explore different facets of financial market development and integration.

A common feature of the chapters in this volume is, by design, their focus on the economies that already belong to the euro area or are candidates to join it, and the contribution of financial markets in supporting ever-closer economic union in Europe. A second leitmotif is the challenges that cross-border integration presents for policy-makers, including in supervision and regulation. A recurring question is whether policy has kept pace with integration and is helping to realize its full potential.

The studies in this volume were originally presented at two conferences hosted by the Directorate-General for Economic and Financial Affairs of the European Commission (DG ECFIN) in Brussels. The first, 'Financial Stability and the Convergence Process in Europe', was held in October 2005, while the second, 'Adjustment under Monetary Unions: Financial Market Issues', took place in September 2006.

Contributions by discussants and by outside commentators greatly helped the authors in revising their contributions. At DG ECFIN, we would like to thank Klaus Regling, Director-General, Marco Buti, Deputy Director-General, and Jürgen Kröger, former Director of Economic Studies and Research, for their generous support for this project. We are also grateful to Michèle Devuyst and Bénédicte Herry for their secretarial support. We have benefited from the advice and views of Mary McCarthy and linguistic guidance from Sophie Bland.

Lars Jonung, Christoph Walkner and Max Watson
Brussels, February 2008

Part I

Overview

1 Introduction

Lars Jonung, Christoph Walkner and Max Watson

The introduction of the euro and the establishment of Economic and Monetary Union (EMU) have in a very short time changed the financial landscape of Europe. Major restrictions on financial flows across the borders of the Member States have been abolished, and exchange rate risks eliminated. The European Union, more broadly, is gradually being transformed into a single common financial market. This ongoing process is having far-reaching consequences. The financial transformation of Europe raises a number of issues concerning financial stability and fragility, financial supervision, risk sharing across capital markets, the transmission mechanism of monetary policy, and the character and speed of the adjustment process in the euro area – to name but a few.

The deep and far-reaching effects of financial integration in Europe have attracted increasing interest from researchers and policy-makers alike. The purpose of this volume is to make available some major contributions to this new field, as presented at the Annual Research Conferences of DG ECFIN in 2005 and 2006. Both these conferences dealt with financial aspects of the European integration process.

A major message emerging from the conferences and thus from this volume is that financial integration is a fundamental consequence of monetary unification as well as a necessary condition for making a monetary union work satisfactorily. In short, there is an important interaction between monetary and financial unification. They are closely related processes. In short, the euro causes financial integration and financial integration drives the euro project.

We consider this message in detail in the following account of the separate contributions.

In Chapter 2, 'Financial markets in the euro area: realizing the full benefits of integration', Klaus Regling and Max Watson present an overview of the issues considered in the volume. They explore the ways in which financial markets contributed to growth, adjustment and real convergence during the first decade of the euro, and ask how policy-makers can tap the full benefits that financial integration can bring. They emphasize the potential gains to be realized in terms of efficient adjustment to demand and supply shocks under monetary union, as well as the ways in which financial development and integration can support economic catching-up in present and future euro-area members.

Experience in the early years of the euro, they suggest, shows the financial sector playing a larger than expected role as a source and transmission channel of country-specific developments. This mainly occurred in connection with positive shocks in the form of lower risk premia, easier borrowing constraints and asset market booms – although economies did not always have policy frameworks in place to get the best out of these opportunities. Some of these developments – such as falling risk premia – reflected the initial gains of nominal convergence as the monetary union was created. But Regling and Watson consider that financial market influences on real activity will continue to be very important, and potentially benign, in the long run.

Particularly important under EMU is the continuing growth of cross-border risk sharing, since this 'insures' economies against country-specific shocks – thus helping to stabilize them, and indeed encouraging greater economic specialization. Catalysing stronger stabilization benefits through financial integration is especially valuable for euro-area economies, since other conventional cross-country stabilization mechanisms – such as labour mobility or fiscal transfers – play a less prominent role. The financial sector can also help to reallocate resources smoothly after shocks, and dampen the effect of localized credit crunches. More generally, an integrated and diversified financial sector can increase the resilience of the economy, provided policies – including financial supervision – are well designed and effective.

Several key messages for policy are seen to emerge from the early years of EMU. The first is the importance of making strides with fiscal consolidation during nominal convergence booms. Taking advantage of such booms to move strongly towards fiscal balance, or a modest surplus, has two benefits. It helps to moderate the course of country-specific booms (counterbalancing financial accelerator effects to some degree); and it also creates greater budgetary room for manoeuvre, which will be especially important if the country-specific boom is followed by a demanding adjustment period.

A second lesson from experience is the way financial channels have operated to support real convergence under EMU. Regling and Watson highlight work on this topic carried out by the Commission (and described in more detail later in this volume), pointing out that this is relevant also to future euro-area members.

A key finding is that economies undergoing real convergence stand to benefit greatly from the increased savings flows allowed by financial integration, but only if macro- and microeconomic policy frameworks are supportive. Given the speed with which financial integration is taking place, structural and institutional policy environments are particularly important in influencing patterns of resource allocation. Notably, there will be advantages if resources flow strongly to the traded goods sector, and other productive activities: this can underpin productivity growth, and may tend to moderate cycles in competitiveness and the current account. Strong productivity growth also eases any corrections in competitiveness, since it lessens the burden that has to be borne by nominal wage restraint. The public sector needs to support this process through good education and good investment. But in these and in other economies, vigilance is needed to make sure that the transitory revenue gains that occur during extended financial booms are not counted as permanent.

In sum, Regling and Watson note that financial integration can bring important gains in terms of growth, adjustment and convergence, including during economic catching-up. But this integration can also transmit adverse shocks more swiftly, or amplify policy errors. Thus financial markets bring opportunities that policy-makers may seize, rather than conferring automatic benefits. To foster growth and adjustment in the euro area, and to allow new members to share in its benefits, well-designed policies are crucial. These relate to fiscal policy, to the functioning of real sector markets, and to financial regulation and supervision. In all these domains, policy-makers need to internalize fully the opportunities and the challenges of deeper financial integration. EU policy frameworks, the authors emphasize, provide a benign setting to reap the benefits of such integration. And for economies already in EMU, the case for pressing forward in implementing those policies is all the more compelling.

In Chapter 3, 'Catch-up, the transition to full participation in EMU and financial stability', Iain Begg explores the challenges facing EU Member States in Eastern Europe as they navigate their approach to euro-area membership. He notes the impressive degree of real convergence they have already attained, but stresses that the remaining sizeable income gap vis-à-vis the EU average makes it especially important to ensure that policies for nominal convergence do not create serious tensions for a continued process of sustainable catching-up. A major change in monetary regime, he recalls, will have profound effects on the real economy and could imperil financial stability.

Begg focuses on three issues. First, there is the question whether the policy regimes required for euro adoption could constrain development – for example by limiting needed investment in public infrastructure. Second, policy-makers need to evaluate the implications of their pace of transition towards the euro in terms of the depth of shake-ups still required in the real economy. Third, while sound fiscal and monetary regimes should favour financial stability, the impact of changing patterns of capital inflows remains less clear. These issues are portrayed as a J-curve, featuring some potential upfront costs of pressing on to euro adoption, but major benefits down the line in terms of trade and stability benefits.

Begg considers that these factors may stack up differently in light of the varying economic characteristics of the eastern Member States. For small, open economies such as the Baltic States, he considers that the balance of advantage will tend to favour entering Stage III of EMU as quickly as possible. While their starting point in transition was inauspicious, they subsequently adopted regimes that have already transformed their macroeconomic policy performance and shaken up the supply side of the economy successfully. He sees analogies here with Ireland's very successful experience with real convergence and euro adoption.

Poland would be at the other end of the spectrum in terms of factors influencing the timing of euro adoption. It still faces significant challenges in tackling unemployment and handling further deep transformations in an economy still quite heavily based on rural activity. And like the Czech Republic, Poland has demonstrated its ability to manage a national currency successfully under inflation targeting. There is some analogy, Begg suggests, with the case of Spain. The experience of Spain, nonetheless, shows that the path to euro-area membership can be covered successfully in a much shorter time than observers had considered feasible, if current policies are right.

In conclusion, Begg evaluates the financial stability dimension of these challenges. Notwithstanding a degree of fiscal deterioration in some cases, he sees the core risk as lying in capital inflows, including sizeable EU cohesion transfers. The most obvious risk is vulnerability to a reversal of the more mobile forms of capital flows, and in this regard the switch from inflation targeting to ERM II will require careful handling. A further risk lies in asset bubbles or securities market disturbances. Payment systems and financial supervision will be particularly important, including effective relationships between supervisors and central banks in monitoring financial stability.

Amid the manifold and complex consequences of participating in a monetary union, Gabriel Fagan and Vítor Gaspar focus in Chapter 4, 'Adjusting to the euro', on the catalytic function of the financial dimension. Two main rationales underlie the key role of financial forces in shaping countries adopting the euro. First, compared with other economic aspects from euro-area participation, nominal interest rate convergence and financial integration are easy to document on the basis of available statistical information as both happened relatively fast.

Second, the available evidence indicates that the effects are large and significant. The authors argue that, for countries like Greece, Spain, Ireland, Italy and Portugal (hereafter referred to as 'converging countries'), one important aspect of the process of adjustment to participation in the euro area was associated with the convergence of high short- and long-term domestic interest rates to the relatively low levels prevailing in Germany. From the viewpoint of these countries, participation in the euro area entailed easier access to international financial markets, a fall in the risk premium combined with financial liberalization and financial integration.

Fagan and Gaspar first document stylized facts regarding the macroeconomic effects of interest rate convergence on the converging countries. Second, they examine the ability of simple macroeconomic models to explain the observed patterns of adjustment. Several stylized facts are highlighted. The convergence in interest rates has been associated with a sharp increase in household expenditures and a pronounced increase in household debt ratios in the converging countries. However, the expansion in expenditure does not seem to have been associated with noticeable effects on output or with sizeable effects on private sector productive investment. Instead, it has been allied with deterioration in the current account deficit and with the accumulation of sizeable negative net foreign asset positions. At the same time, the converging countries recorded inflation differentials which, under exchange rate stability followed by the adoption of the euro, implied significant real appreciation and loss of competitiveness, according to standard indicators.

Fagan and Gaspar develop an approach that relies on a model endowment economy setup, with traded and non-traded goods, to discuss the real exchange rate implications of changing the geographical patterns of world expenditure. Their setting allows the effects on the real exchange rate of changing expenditures patterns over time to be studied. Their model is able to account qualitatively for all the stylized facts reported above. However, with standard time-separable preferences, expenditure increases on impact and, immediately thereafter, its growth rate declines below the baseline. Moreover, the steady-state effects on the net foreign asset position seem implausibly large.

Chapter 4 shows that the introduction of external habit formation makes the model used more 'realistic'. The initial build-up in expenditure is more gradual and the size of effects on the steady state is much diminished. The conclusion is therefore that the model they adopt of a small, open, endowment economy, with habit formation and traded and non-traded goods, goes a long way towards explaining the adjustment process of the converging countries to the euro.

In Chapter 5, 'Booms and busts: experiences with internal and external adjustment', Reiner Martin and Ludger Schuknecht assess the implications of differing exchange rate strategies during financial cycles in industrialized and emerging market economies over the past twenty years. They make a key distinction between countries that made the external adjustment through a major change in the nominal exchange rate and those that adjusted mainly by re-orienting the economy without devaluation. In performing this analysis, the chapter focuses on real and financial sector transmission channels for shocks during a crisis, including the role of balance sheet risks. It is concerned with identifying empirical regularities rather than causality in these two cases.

Martin and Schuknecht examine a number of flow and stock variables that characterize the interaction between various transmission channels that contribute to boom–bust and crisis phenomena. Their findings confirm that real and financial channels interact in such episodes: indeed a cycle of deterioration and subsequent repair in sector balance sheets is an important driving force of the boom–bust cycle.

Martin and Schuknecht find somewhat similar patterns in industrialized and emerging market economies, while acknowledging that the latter may be more vulnerable to systemic risks and capital flow reversals. These common patterns feature a significant difference in the downturn and recovery path of countries depending on whether they used the real exchange rate as a main element in their adjustment strategy. Those cases that they term 'external adjusters' tended to experience more pronounced booms: greater overheating of demand, loss of competitiveness and private and public sector balance sheet vulnerabilities. The external adjusters' imbalances were initially more severe, causing steeper downturns, but their recoveries were also more rapid.

It is noted that some of the Member States that joined the EU in 2004 display either the early or the more advanced stages of a boom–bust cycle. However, data are less reliable in these countries than in the other industrialized economies, so such indications are tentative and at most can serve as a warning sign of potential challenges ahead.

Martin and Schuknecht note that their findings confirm many 'orthodox' messages about sectoral and systemic risks. These include the advantages of adopting preventive strategies, which can help avoid countries finding themselves experiencing the more acute crisis features of the external adjusters. Prudent monetary and wage policies may help moderate the scale of boom–bust cycles. Several lessons also emerge about the contribution of fiscal performance. In particular, fiscal policies should avoid stoking a boom, and here sound headline figures may be misleading due to transient revenue gains during a boom. Low initial public debt can also help by giving scope to socialize the costs and losses of a crisis.

The Maastricht criteria are noted to be well chosen from this angle of crisis analysis: they provide a significant amount of information about the sustainability of economic developments. However, experience across countries during boom–bust cycles also underscores the importance of monitoring balance sheet developments in the private sector, since these may play a major role over time in influencing economic outcomes.

In Chapter 6 'Financial stability in emerging Europe', Piroska M. Nagy and Richard Fox set out to apply an approach they had developed at Fitch Ratings to assess financial stability for the economies of Eastern Europe. This marries concepts of macro-prudential vulnerability developed by Claudio Borio and co-authors at the Bank for International Settlements (BIS) with banking sector systemic risks as captured by ratings of systemically important banks.

There are thus two strands to the analysis. The first is macro-prudential, and is based on a methodology to identify where excessive optimism about earnings and asset prices, compounded by strong capital inflows, may lead banks to underestimate risk over time. This builds on insights in the BIS literature, highlighting strong, simultaneous departures from trend in credit as well as asset prices and/or the real exchange rate. These developments are seen as potential forerunners of financial crises, to the extent the latter arise from procyclicality in the financial sector. The second strand in the authors' analysis is a conventional approach to assessing bank robustness. It is based on Fitch Ratings' assessment of banks, supplemented with an analysis that factors in common weaknesses across the banking sector. An insight is that stronger banking systems can better withstand macro-prudential shocks than weak ones.

Applying this methodology to advanced and emerging market economies, Nagy and Fox develop a matrix to categorize them along dimensions of macro-prudential risk and banking system strength. In the EU, only Luxembourg receives the highest score on both counts, but most 'EU-15' Member States are quite close to this ranking. Estonia is the only eastern Member State (or former transition economy) to rank alongside most EU-15 Member States. By contrast, Hungary receives a weaker ranking, due notably to macro-prudential risk and indirect foreign currency exposure in the banking system. In south-eastern Europe, Serbia is particularly weak, due to concerns about banking system robustness. Other economies that joined the EU in 2004 receive intermediate rankings, with weaknesses most frequently apparent in the field of banking robustness, at least when the assessment was made.

Nagy and Fox conclude that there are systemic risks building up in these latter economies, but they remain manageable for the time being. A particular concern is that those with weak banking systems could be vulnerable to even a small degree of macroeconomic stress: this, they see as a worry in south-eastern Europe and the CIS (Commonwealth of Independent States). Once the foreign ownership of banking systems is factored in, the risks of a classical banking crisis appear much lower. However, a 'growth crisis' cannot be ruled out, particularly where (as in some central European cases) fiscal positions are weak.

The policy recommendations of the authors for the eastern Member States are to strengthen fiscal positions and toughen prudential standards. On the prudential front, they emphasize risk management in areas such as indirect foreign currency exposure, recommending tools such as loan-to-value limits; marginal reserve requirements; and provisioning systems that build up levels of protection during periods of expansion.

In Chapter 7, 'Adjustment in EMU: a model-based analysis of country experiences', Sven Langedijk and Werner Roeger analyse adjustment dynamics in the euro area, using a dynamic stochastic general equilibrium (DSGE) model. This modelling approach is at present turning into a standard tool of macroeconomics. They start from the fact that, since the introduction of the euro, economic developments in the euro area have differed markedly amongst Member States. In particular, growth and inflation differences have been persistent thus affecting competitiveness and monetary conditions in the Member States. Another remarkable development in the early years of EMU is the emergence of substantial and persistent current account imbalances. To be sure, sustained differences in growth performance existed before the creation of monetary union.

Langedijk and Roeger identify some stylized macroeconomic facts in a sample of six euro-area countries that have experienced significant deviations of key macroeconomic variables from euro-area aggregates. These facts are then used to identify various shocks exogenous to their model, including entry-level shocks such as the convergence of exchange rate risk premia, the misalignment of entry parities and the further integration of financial markets, and 'steady-state' shocks such as debt ceilings, the growth rate of the population (especially growth in the household formation age groups), productivity growth, shifts in the structural employment rate, and shifts in preferences from tradables to non-tradables (services, housing). On the basis of the identified shocks, a number of simulations are carried out, providing insights into adjustment dynamics in the euro area.

The model simulations provide a fairly good match with actual growth and inflation performance of the euro-area economies. The main finding is that the diverging growth and inflation developments and current account shifts can largely be attributed to one-off adjustment to EMU (initial parities and exchange risk premium convergence) which broadly seems to have run its course. The absence of an exchange risk premium in EMU allows an increase in capital mobility resulting in a lower correlation between savings and investment. The model simulations show a persistent effect on the current account, which largely operates through a wealth effect. Differences in investment growth are the main cause behind growth differences after the establishment of EMU. Due to its non-tradable character, housing investment is the most responsive component of investment growth to changes in interest rates (risk premia).

In a number of countries some structural divergences are observed as well, related to total factor productivity and labour market developments. Due to differing factor productivity growth across countries, the link between inflation and competitiveness is not always strong. For example, high total factor productivity growth in the tradable sector in Ireland allows high inflation without deteriorating competitiveness. While the model matches the more short-lived (up to three years) divergences from the euro-area average rather easily with the standard entry-related shocks, some difficulties are observed in matching longer-term divergences. After the one-off adjustments in the wake of euro adoption, therefore, economic developments can be expected to be more symmetrical, mainly adjusting to a possible continuation of the series of consecutive supply shocks.

The model gives a somewhat benign picture of the adjustment process in the euro area, though the authors suggest that caution is warranted. A somewhat less rosy picture is possible if housing plays a larger role leading to endogenous build-up of excess demand, especially through wealth effects.

The central role of the housing market for adjustment inside the euro area is highlighted by Peter Hoeller and David Rae in Chapter 8 on 'Housing markets and adjustment in monetary union'. While they focus on adjustment mechanisms that limit or increase cyclical divergence in the first part of their chapter, the central part concerns the transmission of monetary policy via the housing market, which can be a source of resilience as well as a factor leading to prolonged divergence.

The authors argue that the main cost of joining a monetary union like the euro area lies in the implied loss of the instruments allowing for a sovereign setting of interest and exchange rates, making it potentially more difficult to adjust swiftly to shocks. Challenges depend on the frequency and nature of shocks hitting individual countries: the price or output response must be highest in the case of asymmetric economic shocks, which require substantially disparate monetary conditions within the euro area. In the case of symmetric shocks, by contrast, the loss of monetary autonomy is of lesser concern.

Even assuming symmetric shocks, however, a differing transmission mechanism among member countries would yield diverse outcomes in spite of uniform policy responses. Initial shocks might then perpetuate initially small inflation differentials over a significant period of time, eventually leading to heavy competitiveness losses and painful adjustment. This, in turn, could result in a prolonged period of sluggish economic performance reducing potential output growth due to low investment, loss of skills and labour market withdrawal.

Labour, product and financial market policies may play a significant role in hindering a rapid adjustment, and the commitments under the Stability and Growth Pact may limit the leeway for fiscal action to smooth the cycle. The authors discuss both the competitiveness and the interest rate channel by providing a model-based assessment as well as by looking at empirical developments within the euro area.

The central role of the housing market for the monetary transmission mechanism is highlighted in the second part of Chapter 8. Housing markets are important in the transmission of monetary policy and a high interest sensitivity is beneficial as it implies that monetary policy is more powerful in boosting or damping cyclical fluctuations overall in the euro area. However, the characteristics of housing and mortgage markets still differ widely across the euro area, leading to asymmetric behaviour of individual countries.

Hoeller and Rae highlight first the housing market's role in providing resilience in the face of an economic shock and offer then a detailed discussion on housing and mortgage market characteristics, and estimates for the marginal propensities to consume out of financial and housing wealth for differing countries. They discuss the economic implications of the existence of a complete mortgage market, focusing on the variety of mortgage products, as well as on the effects of specific regulatory frameworks for housing finance – ranging from tax incentives to land-use regulations and supervisory issues. Additional issues are explored in boxes, such as past empirical evidence for soft landings following the bursting of a housing bubble, and the advisability of a central bank response to house price booms.

When concluding, the authors stress that policy should neither hinder adjustment, nor exacerbate the cycle.

The chapter by Hoeller and Rae provides an important contribution to the assessment of the current state of housing markets worldwide and cautiously warns of slowdown or recession. Equally significant, by stressing the diversity of housing markets, this chapter sheds light on one of the most central transmission mechanisms within the euro area and allows therefore for a more profound understanding of the current forces dominating intra-euro-area adjustment.

In the literature on monetary unions, the proper policy response to asymmetric shocks plays an important role. Countries subject to severe asymmetric shocks are less likely to be candidates for a monetary union. Likewise, monetary policy-makers within a monetary union are faced with a delicate dilemma if the monetary union is subject to asymmetric shocks. To what extent are such shocks a challenge for monetary unification? How would a less than fully financially integrated monetary union respond to symmetric as well as asymmetric shocks? One way to answer these questions is to study the record of monetary unions other than the euro area, as John Landon-Lane and Hugh Rockoff do in Chapter 9, 'Regional interest rates within a monetary union: lessons from the United States'.

The authors look at the monetary and financial history of the United States from 1880 until today to arrive at some answers to the questions raised above and draw lessons for the euro area. They examine whether asymmetric shocks have constituted a challenge in the US monetary union, whether the problem of asymmetric shocks has changed over time, becoming more or less severe, and how US policy-makers have solved the challenge of asymmetric shocks.

The approach used in Chapter 9 is based on a number of steps. Landon-Lane and Rockoff make a distinction between three phases in the history of the US monetary union: first the period 1880–1913, when the United States did not yet have a central bank; second, the period 1914–43, the first years of the Federal Reserve system; and, third, the post-World War II era, when the federal funds rate emerged as the major instrument for monetary policy. The United States is split into four regions, the Northeast, the Plains, the South and the West.

Econometric and historical methods are used to identify various types of shocks. By shocks, the authors mean independent events that have shifted the supply or demand for funds and thus moved the interest rate and eventually impacted on the aggregate economy via the interest rate channel. They present a full account of all major shocks hitting the US economy, which shows that their econometric method is well designed to identify shocks.

The main result is that the US economy has been hit by a number of symmetric shocks impacting on the entire economy as well as asymmetric shocks impacting on only one region over the periods studied. Asymmetric regional shocks have been met in various ways, sometimes with measures designed specifically to have a regional effect, and sometimes being ignored by policy-makers.

In addition, the authors conclude that the problem of asymmetric shocks has diminished over time in the US monetary union. They explain this decline by the fact that the central bank – the Federal Reserve – gradually obtained control over regional interest rates, implying that the US currency union eventually evolved into a fully fledged financial union. They believe there is a lesson here for Europe: the faster European financial markets become integrated, the easier the task for the European Central Bank (ECB) will be as the problem of regional shocks will become less severe with financial integration.

Comparisons between the United States monetary union, the dollar area, and the European monetary union, the euro area, represent a fruitful way to evaluate European developments as illustrated by both Chapter 9 and Chapter 10, 'Where does capital flow? A comparison of US States and EU countries 1950–2000', authored by Sebnem Kalemli-Ozcan, Bent E. Sørensen and Belgi Turan. They study capital flows between states in the United States and between EU countries during the period 1950–2000 using an econometric approach.

They start from the question: where will capital flow? Different models give different answers. The standard reply based on simple neoclassical models is that capital shall move from rich regions or countries, which are capital-abundant, to poor regions and countries, which are labour-abundant and where the marginal product of capital is relatively high. This result, the 'downhill' pattern, assumes fully or near-fully integrated capital markets with no barriers to the flow of capital. However, a lack of good institutions such as lack of clear property rights may cause capital to flow the other way, 'uphill', that is from poor to rich countries.

Kalemli-Ozcan, Sørensen and Turan first examine the pattern of capital flows within the United States. They demonstrate that capital moved from rich northern states to southern states for about twenty years, during the 1950s and 1960s. They argue that this was part of a process of 'catch-up growth', resulting in income and output levels converging between the north and the south. This process eventually came to an end. Today, capital flows to states that are experiencing positive productivity shocks, commonly rich states. 'Catch-up growth' is thus a matter of history.

Next, the authors turn to the European integration process to examine where Europe stands relative to the United States, by comparing individual EU states with US states. Their econometric results suggest that EU is still in the 'catch-up growth phase', where the United States was in the 1950s and 1960s, with capital flowing from rich to poor states or regions. Capital is flowing to countries like Greece, Portugal and the new EU Member States, just as it did to Texas, Louisiana, Mississippi and Alabama in the decades after World War II. In their view, the catch-up process in Europe may be longer lasting than in the United States because financial market integration has not been completed in Europe, unlike in the US. Government regulations and institutions within the EU are still not fully geared towards complete capital market integration.

In the future, after the catch-up process and full financial market integration, Europe is likely to move to the phase where capital flows to regions and countries that experience positive growth and productivity shocks – such regions often have higher output than regions with low growth.

The phenomenon of international risk sharing has attracted considerable interest from researchers in recent years. The European integration process has served as an important source of inspiration as the rise of financial integration across borders in the European Union has fostered risk sharing and consumption smoothing. Deeper and more closely connected capital markets in the EU thus allow individuals to separate production and consumption decisions, in this way providing an insurance mechanism in the face of asymmetric shocks.

Starting from the fact that conventional consumption-based measures of risk sharing so far have had a hard time picking up the increase in international risk sharing, Michael J. Artis and Mathias Hoffmann, in Chapter 11, 'Declining home bias and the increase in international risk sharing: lessons from European integration', build on a novel approach to demonstrate that international consumption risk sharing has indeed increased. Their approach uses the information implicit in the levels of relative consumption and output. Their focus on relative levels – rather than on first differences of the data as in virtually all of the earlier literature – allows them to document longer-term trends in consumption risk sharing that earlier specifications have not been able to pick up.

Artis and Hoffmann claim that the increase in international risk sharing is economically significant. If regional evidence from a well-integrated economy such as the United States is taken as the benchmark, they conclude that international risk sharing has increased by between a third and half within a single decade in the EU. They also offer additional important results. First, they analyse the increase in international risk sharing with special reference to the experience of current EMU member countries. Second, they provide a detailed analysis of the channels through which improvements in international consumption risk sharing have come about, confirming that consumption risk sharing has improved equally in all industrialized countries. The level of consumption risk sharing reached among EU countries is higher and – possibly most interestingly – recent improvements have occurred through different channels. Among EU countries international capital income flows have become more important as a way to shield consumption from fluctuations in relative outputs, whereas in their entire panel of twenty-three industrialized countries, the ex post accumulation and decumulation of foreign assets remains the main channel of international risk sharing.

These findings are robust after controlling for other determinants of international risk sharing, in particular for the characteristics of the asset portfolios of the countries in their sample. They corroborate the finding that countries with lower home bias achieve more risk sharing, low risk sharing and portfolio home bias being twin puzzles separated at birth. They add to this the finding that countries with higher equity shares in their international portfolios share a larger portion of risk through capital income flows.

Artis and Hoffmann's results suggest that by the end of their sample period the possibly most important difference between EU Member States and other industrialized countries is that, in the late 1990s, capital income flows had taken over as the main driver of improvements in intra-European risk sharing. By the end of their sample, one-third of the risk sharing achieved through international financial markets was achieved through capital income flows. Outside Europe, this channel still plays virtually no role in risk sharing. While the sheer growth in intra-European risk sharing since the 1990s is already impressive, the patterns that emerge increasingly resemble those observed within national boundaries. EMU membership may make a difference not only to how much risk a country shares, but increasingly also to how it shares it. While it is too early to evaluate these trends conclusively, Artis and Hoffmann discuss the possibility that the creation of the euro in itself, and the associated elimination of exchange rate variability, is responsible for the emergence of their findings concerning increased risk sharing.

The economies of the Member States of the European Union are at present involved in a far-reaching integration process that is likely to impact on financial stability. In Chapter 12, 'Economic integration and financial stability: a European perspective', Gianni De Nicolò and Alexander Tieman explore the relationship between financial stability and the ongoing integration of Europe.

They note that increased real activity synchronization and financial integration can have both positive and negative consequences for financial stability. Integration of both the real economy and the financial system has differing effects. Increased synchronization of real activity may diminish the returns from cross-country diversification if the effects of shocks to a relevant set of economies become more similar, reducing the opportunities for diversifiable risks. On the other hand, financial integration may increase the returns to diversification by expanding financial markets and thus investment opportunities. In addition, stronger connections between intermediaries in different parts of the European Union may heighten the risk of them being subject to contagion in case of financial distress.

De Nicolò and Tieman set out to assess the existence and the potential magnitude of these countervailing effects. In their opinion, this knowledge is important for the monitoring of financial stability. If it emerges that increased synchronization of real activity and financial integration would result in a heightened potential for systemic risk in the financial system, then supervisors should place more emphasis on the monitoring of the systemic risk potential among institutions.

In order to determine the actual effects on changing financial intermediary risk due to increased real and financial integration, the authors first examine if and to what extent the synchronization of real activity and financial integration has actually progressed in Europe by applying a set of econometric tests. Second, they construct measures for the integration process that can be related to the risks that the financial system is exposed to. Their approach allows them to gauge whether the risk profiles of financial institutions taken as a whole as well as on a country-by-country basis have become more sensitive to estimates of a common component in real activity, and whether a proxy of financial integration has had any dynamic impact.

De Nicolò and Tieman find increased real activity synchronization since the early 1980s, increased financial integration and no evidence of a fall of risk profiles of banks and insurance companies in Europe. The data suggest also increased equity market integration starting in the early 1990s. Real and financial convergence has not improved the risk profiles of the financial system. While synchronization of real activity may have reduced the diversification benefits of cross-country investments, increases in financial integration are associated with a decline in financial institutions' risk profiles. The authors conclude that as the integration process may not necessarily lead to improved financial stability, enhanced monitoring of the interdependencies among financial institutions seems to be an important task for European supervisors as integration continues.

Growing financial integration within the EU raises a number of issues such as the degree to which commercial banks across the EU are subject to the same kind of shocks. This issue is addressed by Andrea Brasili and Giuseppe Vulpes in Chapter 13, 'Banking integration and co-movements in EU banks' fragility'. Co-movements in bank risks derive from the exposure to common shocks – relating to either macroeconomic shocks or common exposures to industries, countries, individual counterparts and interbank linkages. Using a sample of almost 100 small, medium-sized and large banks, Brasili and Vulpes analyse co-movements in the fragility of EU-15 banks and explore to what extent such movements have increased since the start of EMU.

Using a dynamic factor model, the authors provide a measure of co-movements in bank risk. Brasili and Vulpes construct a bank fragility indicator, which is decomposed into three components: an EU-wide factor, a country-specific component and a bank-level idiosyncratic element. In addition, they measure the influence of common macroeconomic shocks on their fragility indicator at the EU and the country level. The authors are also able to distinguish between short-term, cyclical and long-term co-movements in bank fragility.

There are reasons to believe that common shocks affecting EU banks have increased recently. First, European economies have become more integrated via trade linkages and via a common monetary policy for those Member States having adopted the euro. Second, bank inter-linkages in the euro area have significantly increased, stemming from direct cross-border interbank exposures, but also from indirect exposures, such as syndicated loans for large firms, derivatives and loan securitizations.

The econometric results by Brasili and Vulpes indicate that co-movements in bank fragility are significant at the EU-wide level and that the commonality of bank risk has increased since 1999. Around 42 per cent of the variance in bank risk is due to EU-wide shocks. The EU component is much larger for bigger banks, explaining in a number of cases more than 80 per cent of the observed variance in bank risk. Larger banks also act as an important transmission channel for shocks. Overall, the strong co-movements among larger EU banks indicate a two-tier system of banking integration, whereas smaller and medium-sized banks remain predominantly anchored in their national environments. Finally, the dynamics of EU banks' fragility is accounted for to a larger extent by banking sector specific factors than by macroeconomic shocks.

Growing bank integration as documented by Brasili and Vulpes provides a clear indication of a need for macro-prudential surveillance at the EU level. These findings also provide some guidance as to the way supervisory competences should be split between national and EU-wide authorities: the still large weight of idiosyncratic components found in the analysis suggests that banking supervision at national level remains important, but its scope should be limited to small and medium-sized banks. In contrast, a case can be made that the supervision of large banks should be subject to greater cooperation among EU supervisory authorities.

Chapter 14, 'Challenges to banking stability in the EU: a survey', by Christoph Walkner highlights the financial stability impact of EU banking integration. In economies where banks do not cross borders, the fate of the domestic economy is closely tied to that of its banks as an economic downturn affecting non-financial companies would also impinge on the profitability and stability of the country's banking sector. Foreign bank entry can have different consequences for financial stability, to the extent that foreign bank subsidiaries (or branches) may behave not as completely autonomous businesses but as part of a larger bank holding company. Another impact on stability derives from increased competition, which promotes efficiency but might lead to reduced profitability of domestically owned banks, rendering weaker banks more vulnerable to stress.

After surveying the literature on macro-financial stability, Walkner examines the progress to date of cross-border banking integration in the EU. He demonstrates contrasting developments within the pre-enlargement EU-15 and the recently acceded EU-10. Cross-border banking linkages are relatively uncommon among the EU-15, when compared to linkages between the EU-15 and EU-10, suggesting that integration in the EU banking sector has progressed further outside the EU regulatory framework than within.

Exploring this paradox, Walkner examines the more typical avenues for banking integration within the EU, namely organic growth through greenfield investments, cross-border mergers and acquisitions, and cross-border provision of banking services. He identifies various barriers relating to national considerations as well as legal and institutional factors. In turn, the factors responsible for the high level of foreign ownership in the banking sector of the EU-10 are considered.

The chapter concludes by examining the EU supervisory framework, which has been regarded until recently as a convenient means to facilitate market entry without the need for a major change in Member State arrangements. Walkner notes this is now subject to debate, and explores a number of proposals for improving EU supervisory arrangements by looking at macroeconomic stability risks deriving from cross-border banking integration in the EU.

While financial integration is progressing within the EU, regulatory structures are still largely nationally rooted, implying possibly suboptimal outcomes in terms of financial institutions' cost-efficiency, competition and financial stability. This topical issue is explored by Dirk Schoenmaker and Sander Oosterloo in Chapter 15, 'Financial supervision in Europe: a proposal for a new architecture'.

The authors start from a presumed trilemma in financial supervision, whereby a stable financial system and an integrated financial market would not fit together with national-based supervisory structures. They highlight two industry trends: first, increasing cross-border penetration and, second, the centralization of important business functions. While the vast majority of the EU credit institutions remain nationally oriented, pan-European banks are emerging with a sizeable cross-border presence. Indeed, the fourteen largest of those cross-border groups already account for almost one-third of total EU banking assets. The extent of cross-border penetration is especially large in the new Member States (those which joined the EU in 2004 or thereafter). The observed trend of increasing cross-border penetration is robust and confirmed by using several methodological approaches.

As for the second industry trend, the authors show that banks are increasingly starting to centralize important business functions. As a result, the organizational structure of international financial firms is moving from the traditional country model to a business line model with integration of key management functions. The growing integration and centralization of management functions, such as risk management, internal controls, treasury operations (including liquidity management and funding), compliance and auditing, greatly affect the scope of control for supervisory authorities.

Starting from these trends, Schoenmaker and Oosterloo ask if the current supervisory settings are sufficient to sustain financial stability. They note that in the current system a financial institution is authorized and supervised by its home country. Given the centralization of important business functions at the headquarters as well as the increasing cross-border penetration of banking groups, the scope of control of the home country authorities is expanding. However, home authorities are not responsible for financial stability in host countries, which remains the remit of the host country. Increasing banking integration therefore gives rise to cross-border spill-over effects or externalities as a home country supervisor might have suboptimal incentives for overseeing – for example – an external branch of a domestic bank which is small overall from the home country perspective, but large from the host country perspective. While the cost of supervising such a bank would rest with the home country, the benefits would mainly accrue to the host country.

In response to this newly emerging European financial landscape, Schoenmaker and Oosterloo present three policy options. These choices range from (1) keeping the status quo, but enhancing the cooperation between home and host authorities for both financial supervision and stability; (2) switching to a lead supervisory structure where the home authority would not only supervise the mother bank and its branches but also the bank's subsidiaries – though without becoming responsible for financial stability in the host country; to (3) a novel supervisory structure, combining features of home country supervision for locally focused banks from the present setting with a European structure for cross-border oriented banks. This option would also push crisis management up towards a European level, although the home country would still take a leading role.

Coming out in favour of the third option, the authors propose a European Financial Authority working in tandem with the national financial supervisors. Key elements would be decentralized day-to-day supervision close to financial institutions and centralized policy-making to foster a uniform execution of the supervisory function. The newly created system would be accountable to the European Parliament and the EU finance ministers meeting as the ECOFIN Council. Although fairly comprehensive, the proposal leaves the thorny issue of fiscal burden sharing open, i.e. which countries should bear the cost of a possible bail-out of a financial institution?

With the rise of cross-border banking conducted through foreign-owned banking offices in the EU, regulatory issues concerning these institutions in case of financial distress have attracted considerable interest in recent years. In Chapter 16, 'Cross-border banking: challenges for deposit insurance and financial stability in the European Union', Robert A. Eisenbeis and George G. Kaufman contribute to the discussion. They focus on developments within the European Union that may create financial stability problems like reliance upon the home country as the primary provider of deposit insurance and inadequate bankruptcy and closure policies.

Eisenbeis and Kaufman describe first the EU cross-border banking regulatory structure and discuss the agency problems that may arise in the supervision and regulation of cross-border banking institutions in the EU. After focusing on the problems of providing deposit insurance for institutions operating in such an environment and looking at issues concerning the payout from deposit insurance plans and resolving large bank failures, the authors proceed to suggest a four part solution designed to mitigate the negative externalities associated with banking failures.

Banks become insolvent when the market value of their assets falls below the value of their deposits and other debt funding. Claimants may experience both credit and liquidity losses in the resolution process. Credit losses occur when the recovery value of the bank as a whole or in parts falls short of the par value of its deposits or other debt on the respective due dates.

Liquidity losses may occur for two reasons. First, depositors and other claimants may not have immediate and full access to the par value of their insured claims or to the estimated recovery value of their *de jure* uninsured claims. In the case of insured deposits, the insurer must have both the legal ability and funding to provide eligible depositors with immediate and full access to their funds. In the case of uninsured claims, liquidity can be provided through advance payments based on the estimated recovery value of the assets in receivership. Second, qualified borrowers may not be able to utilize their existing credit lines immediately.

The authors' proposal is based on four rules or principles, each of them stressing the importance of prompt action: (1) prompt legal closure when the bank's equity capital declines to some pre-specified and well-publicized positive minimum greater than zero (legal closure rule); (2) prompt estimate of the recovery values and assignment of credit losses ('haircuts') to *de jure* uninsured bank claimants when equity is negative to avoid protecting *de jure* uninsured claimants; (3) prompt reopening (preferably the next workday) of failed bank through sale or creation of a temporary bridge bank with full depositor access to their accounts on their due dates at their insured or estimated recovery values and full performing borrower access to their pre-established credit lines; and (4) prompt re-privatization of new bank with adequate capital.

Eisenbeis and Kaufman argue that the adoption of the above four principles and the necessary infrastructure to make them work would minimize most of the agency problems, negative externalities, insurance fund losses, and coordination problems associated with the current cross-border banking development within the EU and elsewhere.

In the final chapter, 'The search for the elusive twin goals of monetary and financial stability', Claudio Borio explores challenges for monetary and supervisory authorities in a world where the major challenge of the great inflation of the post-war era has been eliminated. The main focus of his chapter is on the possibility that the 'elasticity' or 'pro-cyclicality' of economies may have increased, making financial crises possibly more likely. The author suggests that this requires adjustments in current policy regimes.

The reasons for a change in the financial dynamics of the economy are seen to lie in two underlying developments. First, financial liberalization may have made it more likely that financial factors act as drivers of economic fluctuations, including through boom–bust cycles in credit and asset prices. Second, monetary regimes featuring high central bank credibility and firm control over retail price inflation may have made it more likely that emerging imbalances will appear first in asset prices and only later in the prices of goods and services. Together, these factors can cause greater pro-cyclicality in the financial system and amplify fluctuations in the real economy.

Important steps were taken after the Asian crisis to address financial sector risks, Borio notes, notably measures to strengthen national financial systems, based on international standards and codes. Less has been done to probe financial dynamics and liquidity risks. There is a need to address this 'missing pillar' of the international financial architecture. To achieve this, the philosophy and operating procedures of prudential and monetary authorities would need to better capture the failure of private sector agents to measure the time dimension of risk, and especially of systemic risk.

To meet these concerns, Borio advocates closer cooperation between prudential and monetary authorities. This involves more than an exchange of information. It would require a shift in the approach of both sets of agencies. On the prudential side, there would be greater attention to risk in the financial system, as opposed to individual institutions. On the monetary side, it would involve greater concern with imbalances building over the medium term, even if near-term inflation is well under control.

Borio explores how these changes in prudential and monetary approach could be mapped to operating procedures, in order to manage systemic risk more effectively during periods of swings on financial risk perceptions. In the prudential field the main change would be to use instruments such as bank loan loss provisions in a manner that builds up cushions during periods of cyclical strength, and to reverse this process during downswings. Monetary authorities, meanwhile, would lengthen the policy time horizon in some inflation targeting regimes, internalizing medium-term risks.

Such a shift in the philosophy and operating procedures of official agencies, Borio acknowledges, involves non-trivial technical questions. More work would be needed, for example, on the relationship between credit, asset prices (especially real estate prices) and the real exchange rate. Moreover, a significant educational effort would be required. But an evolution along these lines would reduce the likelihood that systemic financial risks, building up over the medium term, might fall through the cracks of official policy preoccupations. This would enhance the stability of the real economy.

* * *

The work presented in this volume thus sheds light from different angles on a single core question: how well is financial integration supporting growth, adjustment and catching-up in economies that are members – or future members – of the euro area, and are policy-makers moving swiftly enough to realize its full potential? Market events since these chapters were written only serve to highlight the relevance of this question.

In pursuit of this theme, the authors adopt a range of perspectives – in terms of both the specific policy areas they explore and the analytical techniques they deploy. Their purpose is in part to stimulate debate and future research; and it would be against the spirit of our volume to impose a false synthesis or draw unduly simple conclusions.

Nonetheless, it seems fair, and helpful to the reader, to underscore at the outset a few of the leitmotifs that run through the volume, because these are indeed the issues that policy-makers need to weigh particularly carefully as they press forward in adapting the policy frameworks of the EU, and specifically of the euro area.

The primary theme running through these chapters is that the benefits conferred by financial market development and integration are not to be taken for granted. They do depend on well-designed policy frameworks. This is a core message.

The reasons for this lie in a number of inherent imperfections that the literature attributes to capital markets. Most fundamentally, markets are aware that policy-makers have limited capacity to accept turbulence in the real economy, and that they may therefore intervene to bail out markets and guarantee the public's assets.

But beyond this classic argument of moral hazard, several of the chapters also underline that markets respond sensitively and quickly to changes in policies and economic prospects, while real sector markets are typically more 'sticky'. Financial markets are also quick to arbitrage regulations. This means that times of economic change are among those when policy-makers need to pay special attention to the signals and incentives that they send to markets. The rapid financial integration now underway in the euro area, and across its borders, is certainly such a time.

The final chapters of the volume, in particular, communicate some sense of urgency. Markets have moved swiftly: have policy-makers been able to keep pace? The authors clearly believe some speeding up of reform is needed. They stress this in the case of cross-border regulation and deposit insurance. They also highlight it in connection with pro-cyclical macroeconomic policies. And in the final chapter the question is raised whether our failure to achieve financial stability alongside monetary stability requires a systematic stretching of our present monetary and supervisory approaches.

What seems beyond doubt to the authors, nonetheless, is the great potential gains to be tapped from ongoing financial integration. As Regling and Watson underscore in Chapter 2, these gains are even greater for the members of the euro area, since financial integration can help to foster risk sharing, and hence support stable growth and deeper specialization – and this especially in a monetary union where other adjustment mechanisms such as labour mobility remain to be fully developed.

More integration, not less, is thus the message of the authors. They do not have a temptation to throw sand in the gears of the markets as proposed by some commentators inspired by James Tobin. But they do believe that well-designed policy frameworks are crucial; and they press policy-makers to take this challenge in earnest. The prize is clear, in their view. It is to safeguard sustainable financial integration, and to allow the citizens of a widening euro area to tap the full benefits for growth, adjustment and catching-up that deeper financial integration can deliver.

2 Financial markets in the euro area

Realizing the full benefits of integration

Klaus Regling and Max Watson

How have financial markets contributed to growth, adjustment and real convergence during the first decade of the euro? And have policy-makers tapped the full benefits that financial integration can bring? Two recent research conferences organized by DG ECFIN stimulated a range of papers on these topics. A selection of the papers, assembled in the present volume, underscores how wide the potential benefits of financial integration can be, provided the macro- and microeconomic policy environment is right.

Most frequently, economists discuss the gains from financial integration and development in terms of their contribution to fostering economic growth. That is certainly a key dimension. However, a second dimension is important also, especially under monetary union. This is the role of financial markets in supporting economic adjustment. Financial integration contributes to this through risk sharing and income- and consumption-smoothing. In addition, it allows catching-up economies to tap external savings on a sizeable scale, and this too has been a key feature of experience under the euro and in Member States converging towards it.

The emergence of gains from financial integration, however, is far from automatic. The United States has been a monetary union for some two centuries, but full financial integration at the retail level is in many ways a product of the past few decades. The euro area, where other adjustment mechanisms such as labour mobility and fiscal transfers are much less prominent than in the United States, cannot afford such leisurely and intermittent progress! Indeed, the Financial Services Action Plan testifies to the EU's resolve in this regard, and the euro area economies are already benefiting strongly from ever-deeper financial integration.

Moreover, economic history underscores that well-designed macro- and microeconomic policies are crucial if financial integration is to yield its full benefits. This lesson has been most striking, perhaps, in the case of emerging market economies, which have specific vulnerabilities. But in all economies, growing and adaptive financial markets make a positive contribution only if policies are right. Financial markets enhance the gains under favourable policy frameworks; but in other circumstances they can serve rather to amplify distortions and policy weaknesses.

Indeed, the interaction between official policies and financial markets offers continually evolving lessons. In this sense, policy-makers everywhere are engaged in a learning process as they seek to influence expectations and embed stability in innovative global financial markets. This is true in terms of tapping the gains of market innovation, and it is true also in safeguarding financial stability without engendering moral hazard.

So policy-makers in the euro area face challenges at various levels in realizing the full benefits of financial integration, and these challenges are the subject of the present volume.

The first is a recognition challenge: appreciating the full importance of the role that financial markets play in the euro area. The second is the challenge of prudent policy management in the steady state of monetary union: assuring the preconditions for financial markets to help deliver sound resource allocation and economic stability. The third is a challenge specific to catching-up economies: learning the lessons from recent experience as countries approaching euro area membership navigate the rapids of nominal and real convergence. Last but not least, there is an implementation challenge: putting in place forcefully the elements of the EU's Financial Services Action Plan, and complementing it with additional actions to address remaining barriers to full integration.

The importance of financial market integration

Financial development can strongly support economic growth. Its key roles include transforming the maturity of savings, overcoming information asymmetries, fostering consumption-smoothing through the use of financial instruments, and diversifying risks. Financial integration, in turn, plays a key role in boosting financial development – in particular, through scale effects, greater systemic resilience and a broader expansion of risk sharing. The function of cross-border risk sharing is particularly important under monetary union, since it 'insures' economies against country-specific shocks – thus helping to stabilize them, and indeed encouraging greater economic specialization.

The impact of financial market developments on economic adjustment in the euro area was recently reviewed by the European Commission. This was one of the main themes in the *EU Economy Review* of 2006, which was dedicated to the issue of adjustment in the euro area. Among the key conclusions from this review were:

- growth and inflation differences and current account trends in the euro area have been driven to a notable extent by capital account and asset market movements, including during the processes of nominal and real convergence;
- asset markets have, at times, played an important role in amplifying real interest rate effects through changes in wealth;
- credit and asset price booms had sizeable but transient effects on budgets: the magnitude and reversibility of these effects was not always fully internalized by policy-makers when they assessed underlying fiscal positions;
- financial markets are still far from playing their full role in risk sharing and income- and consumption-smoothing. There also appears to be unexploited scope for mortgage market integration to dampen local real estate market cycles.

We would like to stress that the role of financial markets has been even more powerful than was anticipated when monetary union was conceived. Moreover, the full benefits of integration have yet to be fully exploited.

Financial markets as drivers of macroeconomic change

A few examples will illustrate the important role that financial integration has already played in influencing macroeconomic developments in the euro area. Six case studies of Member State experience in the *EU Economy Review* of 2006 highlighted different kinds of 'shocks' that affected growth, inflation and current account balances during the early years of monetary union, based on a two-country, three-sector dynamic stochastic general equilibrium (DSGE) model of the euro area. This model is described in detail in Chapter 7 in this volume.

The Member States selected for these studies were Germany, Spain, Ireland, Italy, the Netherlands and Portugal, since these experienced particularly striking divergences in growth, inflation and current account balances. In most of these cases, factors related to financial markets turn out to have played a major role in explaining these macroeconomic trends – together, of course, with real sector influences such as the after-effects of German unification, changes in TFP growth in the traded and non-traded goods sectors, and migration flows.

Specifically, a reduction in the exchange risk premium was an important influence on economic developments in a majority of these cases, and especially in Spain, Italy and Portugal. Changes in credit constraints played a significant role in four of the cases. In addition, financial market factors, together with real sector effects such as migration, were a key influence on housing demand – and this played a major role in all cases. Finally, when we consider the channels through which these factors operated, we find that house prices played a significant role, especially in Italy and the Netherlands (Table 2.1).

Experience in the early years of the euro thus highlights the role of the financial sector as a source and transmission channel of country-specific developments – in this case mainly through benign shocks in the form of lower risk premia and easier borrowing constraints.

It is important to reflect how far this experience is a guide to the future. After all, many of the initial shocks that predated or followed the creation of the euro are now tapering off, including the impact of nominal convergence in economies that had experienced high risk premia before the strengthening of macroeconomic policies and elimination of nominal exchange rate fluctuations.

Nonetheless, there are at least two reasons to think that financial market influences on country-specific developments in growth, inflation and current account balances may remain important:

1 Some countries (such as Ireland and Spain) until recently were experiencing strong asset market booms. It remains to be seen how the unwinding of booms will ultimately affect demands in these economies – although it is clear that housing demand in these cases has been responding to some permanent real sector influences, such as migration and rising income levels.
2 It remains to be seen how recent external shocks from conditions in global financial markets could impact the euro area in the period ahead. As in the early years of monetary union,

Table 2.1 Major financial market and asset price influences on growth, inflation and current account balances (1995–2005)

	Germany	*Spain*	*Ireland*	*Italy*	*Netherlands*	*Portugal*
Decline in exchange risk premium*	0	90	60	90	40	140
Easier credit constraints**	−2	24	21	7	22	25
Major impact of housing demand	Yes	Yes	Yes	Yes	Yes	Yes
House prices: major role in transmission				Yes	Yes	

Source: *EU Economy Review* (2006).

Notes:

* Exchange risk premium improvement (+) versus Germany: model values for 1995–8, in basis points.

** Rise (+) in household debt ratio to GDP 1999–2005, in percentage points.

the euro will protect its members from some shocks through the elimination of intra-euro area nominal exchange rate fluctuations. But in other ways shocks (for example to global exchange rates, risk premia or trade flows) could affect members differentially.

These considerations underscore the case for increasing the efficiency with which real sector markets adjust, and for ensuring prudent fiscal policies to enhance economic resilience. But they also highlight the importance of realizing the full benefits of financial integration in terms of its stabilizing role in the economy.

The stabilizing role of financial integration

Financial sector integration can greatly enhance the adjustment process under monetary union. The financial sector can help reallocate resources smoothly after shocks; dampen the effect of local credit crunches; and smooth incomes and consumption through the use of financial instruments and the cross-border holding of financial assets. More generally, a widely integrated and diversified financial sector should increase resilience at times of economic stress.

Experience in the United States underscores the benefits of financial integration for the adjustment process. When specific shocks affect output in a US state, almost two-fifths of the impact on incomes of firms and households is diversified away by cross-state asset holdings (Box 2.1). In the European Union, the equivalent effect has been estimated at only 10 per cent – although current research suggests it is on a rising trend. Also, as mortgage markets have become more integrated in the United States in recent years, some estimates suggest that this may have halved the scale of 'credit crunches' in local real estate cycles.

Catalysing stronger stabilization benefits through financial integration is particularly important for the euro area, since other cross-country stabilization mechanisms are less prominent. Labour mobility is lower than in the United States; and there are no sizeable fiscal transfers to smooth inter-country shocks. Even in the United States, some estimates suggest that financial integration plays a larger role than the federal government in smoothing income fluctuations following economic shocks. This contribution of financial markets is thus of key importance in the steady state of monetary union. These important issues are analysed in depth in Chapters 10 and 11 of this volume.

Box 2.1 The role of financial markets in risk sharing and consumption-smoothing

Financial markets can be compared with other institutional channels as a route for risk sharing. In particular, it is interesting to explore their significance relative to the more familiar route of the fiscal system, which shares risks through taxes and transfers. In the United States, the role of private risk sharing has been compared to that of fiscal transfers, and according to some estimates private risk sharing has an even greater impact. According to Asdrubali, Sørensen and Yosha (1996), 39 per cent of shocks to gross state product are smoothed by capital markets and 23 per cent are smoothed by credit markets. This compares with 13 per cent that are smoothed by the federal government. The remaining 25 per cent are not smoothed.

Thus the role of private risk sharing (and of financial markets more generally) in the United States is large relative to that of fiscal transfers.

As regards the euro area, at this stage it is difficult to assess the quantitative importance of this type of adjustment, in particular when comparing it with other types of adjustment processes. Available estimates for the period before adoption of the euro suggest that risk sharing through financial markets may have smoothed at least 10 per cent of shocks among EU Member States, but this proportion is considered to have been rising strongly since the late 1990s. As the EU budget is much smaller than the federal budget in the United States, and does not respond to cyclical swings, it is logical to assume that risk sharing through financial asset holdings could play by far the predominant role as financial market integration continues. More broadly, it is clear that risk sharing and resource reallocation through financial markets can play a critically important role in a monetary union where labour mobility is low and there is not a large federal budget. On this point see also Chapter 11.

The challenges of nominal and real convergence

A further feature of financial market experience since the introduction of the euro concerns the processes of nominal and real convergence. It is particularly important to analyse this experience carefully, so that future euro area members can benefit from it.

As we look back on the track record of euro area members that have been experiencing nominal and real convergence, several points deserve attention. The first point is the importance of using the opportunity of *nominal convergence booms*, when economic conditions are particularly propitious, as a period to achieve fiscal consolidation. During these booms, fiscal consolidation will also help moderate demand pressures on the economy. This strategy has the added advantage of ensuring fiscal room for manoeuvre for the future – which may be particularly valuable when a strong nominal convergence boom comes to an end.

In addition, the analysis in the *EU Economy Review* of 2006 sheds some light on the role of financial factors in *real convergence* experience in euro area members. While the DSGE modelling approach is not designed to capture long-run convergence effects, it does highlight differences in medium-term adjustment patterns, including through the impact of sectoral productivity shocks and through the relative role of financial and real shocks in stimulating demand. The most enlightening contrast is between Ireland and Portugal. In the former, successful real convergence was driven initially by very strong productivity growth in tradeables, in a setting of fiscal and wage restraint. The latter, by contrast, initially experienced a powerful consumption and housing boom, driven in large part by financial integration. This was not accompanied by strong productivity growth. Meanwhile, the authorities did not profit from these good times to consolidate the public finances – indeed there was an increase in the public debt. This boom did not lead to sustained real convergence: it was followed by a petering-out of growth.

One lesson from this experience is that economies undergoing real convergence stand to benefit greatly from the increased savings flows allowed by financial integration, but only if policies are well designed. Given the speed with which financial integration takes place, structural and institutional policy environments are particularly important in influencing patterns of resource allocation. There will be advantages if resources flow strongly to the traded goods sector, and other productive activities: this can underpin productivity growth, and may tend to moderate cycles in competitiveness and the current account. Strong productivity growth also eases any corrections in competitiveness under monetary union, since it lessens the burden that has to be borne by nominal wage restraint. The public sector needs to support this process through good education and investment – but, as during nominal convergence booms, it also needs to reduce its use of savings as imbalances in the private sector widen.

During real convergence, banking supervisors also need to be vigilant. This is a setting in which there is a quantum increase in the savings available to exploit high rates of return in under-capitalized economies, and it can trigger 'exuberance' – leading to distortions or fragility. As well as asset allocation, including in areas such as real estate, it can be important to monitor cross-border funding patterns – such as possible over-reliance on short-term cross-border bank funding, which could give rise to fragility risks. Under monetary union, economies do not experience 'external' financing constraints in the normal sense of the term; but patterns of current account financing, and the counterparts to current account imbalances, still provide valuable information to policy-makers about the sustainability of savings flows.

The circumstances of future euro area members, of course, vary greatly – and differ in many respects from their predecessors on the road to euro adoption. Among other factors, they typically lifted capital controls earlier than many existing members, and in some cases they have achieved already a substantial drop in risk premia. Some already have very sound fiscal positions. Financial sector catch-up is well underway, often from a modest starting-point.

So the relevance of past experience with nominal and real convergence will need to be interpreted carefully, on a case-by-case basis. Nonetheless, it remains a valuable policy resource for future euro area members to draw on, as they benefit from an expanded pool of savings in an open capital account setting – and also when their monetary autonomy either is, or soon will be, limited. It will be crucial that they achieve strong productivity gains to underpin income growth and to facilitate adjustment, so that the fruits of financial integration are reflected in sustained real convergence.

Realizing the full benefits of financial integration

For all members of the euro area, indeed, including those experiencing nominal and real convergence, the early years of monetary union highlight a number of policy priorities that are crucial in order to realize the full benefits of financial integration. These relate to fiscal policy, to the functioning of real sector markets and to policy frameworks that govern the financial sector itself. In all these domains, policy-makers need to internalize fully the opportunities and the challenges that relate to deeper financial integration.

In terms of *fiscal policy*, financial integration typically reduces the costs of borrowing and increases the ease with which deficits can be financed. In the euro area, risk premia on the public debt of some Member States have fallen significantly with the elimination of nominal exchange rate changes although there has recently been some reversal in certain cases. This puts the onus even more strongly on national policy-makers to exercise fiscal discipline within the broad framework of the Stability and Growth Pact. Strong national fiscal institutions can play an important role also in buttressing fiscal discipline, and the nature of these has been explored in recent reports on *Public Finances in EMU* by the European Commission.

Experience in the early years of the euro has highlighted the importance of achieving adequate fiscal consolidation in 'good times', a priority that is underscored in the reformed Stability and Growth Pact. Here, fiscal policy-makers need to pay careful attention to the impact of country-specific booms under monetary union. These call for particular prudence at times when asset prices are rising, the composition of GDP is tax-rich and estimates of potential output may be revised up prematurely. All these factors could contribute to overestimating underlying budget balances during boom periods, and thus could lead to pro-cyclical fiscal behaviour.

This issue of fiscal analysis during credit and asset price booms is far from unique to the euro area; but the experience since the late 1990s underscores that it is very important in this context. In particular, it is a mechanism through which there could be a mutually reinforcing interaction between financial market and fiscal pro-cyclicality. In other words, policy and market factors could amplify adjustment cycles in the economy, leading to unduly protracted swings in asset prices, output and inflation. This heightens the case for fiscal vigilance in 'good times'.

The management of the public finances is also key in fostering a healthy allocation of savings through well-judged tax and expenditure policies that support growth and avoid distorting activity. Indeed, integrated and adaptive financial markets make it all the more important to avoid fiscal distortions such as tax deductions or subsidies that favour specific purposes such as housing. And the public sector also needs to avoid triggering distortions through the impact of its wage-setting policies – including during the real convergence process.

The euro area environment also places special responsibility on policy-makers to ensure the efficient working of *product and labour markets*, and thus to create an environment in which the full benefits of financial integration can be tapped. This is important to foster growth, but the issue of adjustment to shocks is also of crucial importance. In particular, efficient real sector adjustment is the key to swift competitiveness adjustments after country-specific shocks. And the more efficiently product and labour markets function, the less national real interest rate effects will complicate the adjustment process.

Financial markets can play a key role in the adjustment process, but only if policy frameworks affecting the real sector provide the right environment.

Last but not least, *financial sector policies* need to drive integration forward, while ensuring that stability is not jeopardized. Policy-makers in the euro area have a special interest in proceeding rapidly with implementation of the EU's Financial Services Action Plan, given the adjustment benefits that integration can yield under monetary union. They will also stand to gain particularly strongly from measures to integrate the workings of mortgage markets, clearing and settlement arrangements, and deposit insurance. Vigilant competition policy at the EU level will be essential to ensure that efficiency gains are passed on to consumers.

Growing financial integration has implications for supervision. It is important that market participants and their supervisors internalize the changed nature of the country-specific adjustment process under monetary union, and take an appropriate medium-term view of the opportunities and risks that may accompany extended swings in output. There may be a need for close prudential surveillance during extended country-specific booms, in order to counter excessive risk-taking that could impair resilience during downswings. And, throughout the EU, cross-border supervision and crisis management need to keep pace with continuing market integration. And, as always, integrated and innovative financial markets tend to amplify both the opportunities and the challenges for policy-makers.

In all these policy domains, there is continuing potential for a positive and constructive interplay between policy initiatives at the EU-27 level and the frameworks needed for a well-functioning monetary union. The Stability and Growth Pact, the Lisbon Strategy and the Financial Services Action Plan are all EU-wide initiatives. They are, however, even more important for members of the monetary union in order for its full gains to be realized.

Where financial markets are concerned, in sum, the messages of the euro's first decade are clear. Financial integration can bring important gains in terms of supporting growth, adjustment and convergence in the euro area – and allowing new members to share fully in its benefits. But well-designed policies are needed to seize these opportunities. Here, the fiscal, structural and financial policies of the EU provide the essential framework for all of its members as they seek to realize fully the gains of financial integration. And for those that already participate in monetary union, the case for pressing forward strongly in implementing those policies is all the more compelling.

References

Asdrubali, P., B. Sørensen and O. Yosha (1996) 'Channels of interstate risk-sharing: United States 1963–90', *Quarterly Journal of Economics* 111(4): 1081–110.

EU Economy Review (2006) *Adjustment Dynamics in the Euro Area – Experiences and Challenges*, no. 6/2006 European Economy, European Commission, DG ECFIN.

Part II

Monetary integration

Convergence and adjustment

II.1

Moving to monetary union

3 Catch-up, the transition to full participation in EMU and financial stability

Iain Begg

Since the resolution of the Russian crisis of 1998, an event that had pronounced repercussions for several neighbouring countries, the growth rates of the recently acceded Member States of central and Eastern Europe (RAMs)[1] that joined the EU in 2004 have comfortably outpaced those of most of the EU-15. After the adverse shock of the early transition period when every country endured falling output and high inflation, most countries saw a bounce back in activity. This return of rapid growth in all the RAMs since the late 1990s (when, in addition to the Russian crisis, other asymmetric shocks of varying kinds had slowed growth) has resulted in an impressive degree of real convergence in GDP in recent years. Indeed, among the EU-15, only Greece and Ireland have had growth rates comparable with the RAMs since 2000 and, as Table 3.1 shows, the fastest growing RAMs have grown at four to five times the rate of the euro area as a whole. The convergence is consistent with what would be expected from the many studies triggered by the work of Barro and Sala-i-Martin (1992). However, as can be seen from Table 3.1, although the gap in GDP per head has narrowed, it remains substantial and bridging it will remain a challenge.

All the new members are expected to become full members of EMU, which will require them to fulfil the nominal convergence criteria. For some, current values for the relevant indicators suggest that there will be few problems in this regard, but for others a more extensive adjustment will need to occur. Nevertheless, for all the RAMs, the extent of the nominal adjustment they face to be eligible to move to stage 3 of EMU is not only manageable, but is also less than that which confronted some of the current members of the euro area at the time the Maastricht Treaty was signed as well as in the mid-1990s.

A successful transition to euro area membership will, though, entail far more than meeting the Maastricht criteria. A change of monetary regime, especially one as far-reaching as adoption of the euro, will have profound effects on the real economy and will also affect financial markets in ways that could imperil financial stability. Moreover, there are potential tensions between the catch-up process (real convergence) and the achievement of the nominal convergence criteria that could affect the political economy of how and when to seek full participation in EMU.

Financial stability[2] has been recognized as a crucial factor in promoting long-term growth and is, therefore, bound to be an issue in both catch-up and euro accession. Its importance has been underlined by the ECB (2005a) and is also evident in the increasing attention paid to it by the relevant authorities. That the RAMs are alert to the challenges of financial stability is evident from the increased emphasis it receives in the priorities of the respective national central banks. The Czech National Bank, for example, highlights on its web-site the fact that it 'commenced financial stability analysis in earnest when it defined the priorities of its economic research for the period 2003–4 and published the *Banking Sector*

Table 3.1 GDP levels and growth

Member State	*GDP per capita in PPS (EU-25=100)*			*GDP growth (%)*
	1995	*2000*	*2005*	*2000–6, cumulative*
Czech Republic	69.6	64.7	71.2	21.8
Estonia	33.9	41.5	53.0	43.3
Hungary	49.5	53.3	63.0	24.3
Latvia	29.8	35.4	46.1	53.7
Lithuania	34.1	38.4	50.2	49.7
Poland	40.7	46.1	48.6	22.2
Slovakia	68.4	73.1	79.9	32.1
Slovenia	44.5	47.8	55.6	22.7
EU-15, of which:	110.8	109.8	108.6	10.5
fastest growing (IRL)	99.0	126.3	136.4	35.5
slowest growing (DE)	119.2	111.7	106.2	4.8
euro area	110.8	109.8	108.6	9.1

Source: Ameco database.

Stability Report for 2003' and now publishes an annual financial stability report. Major causes for concern are the quality of prudential supervision, the potential for a rapid increase in consumer debt and how it might compromise macroeconomic stability, and the relatively under-developed banking sectors in the RAMs.

The next section of the chapter examines the challenges associated with acceding to stage 3 of EMU and in striking a balance between the long-term gains from EMU and the short-term risks to real convergence, highlighting the salience of financial stability. The following sections look at what is entailed in adjusting to EMU prior to accession (stage 2 adjustment) and once fully integrated (stage 3 adjustment). Next the links between real convergence and financial stability in the EMU context are appraised. Concluding comments complete the chapter.

The challenges of acceding to stage 3 of EMU

Strictly, the RAMs are in the same position as Sweden in having no opt-out from full participation in EMU. Instead, they initially had a 'derogation' from the obligation to participate fully in EMU. Given that the RAMs have to fulfil the standard Maastricht conditions which, in practice, include a minimum two-year participation in ERM II, the earliest any of them could have joined would have been in 2006, although it is important to note that all are expected to make the necessary effort, distinguishing them from the UK and Denmark, which are legally entitled to choose whether or not to join. Sweden, though, has already demonstrated that there is no real obstacle to staying out indefinitely and it looks as though some countries, notably the Czech Republic, intend to exploit this flexibility. Slovenia became the thirteenth euro area member in 2007, and was joined by Cyprus and Malta in 2008, while others, such as the Baltic countries, want to accede soon, whereas there are now signs that countries which were previously quite enthusiastic – Hungary, for instance – are now minded to proceed more cautiously, not least because it is confronted by awkward fiscal indicators.

Behind these positions lies a debate about the costs and benefits of early euro area accession, focusing especially on its implications for real convergence. The question is whether switching prematurely to the euro would endanger real growth, even if it is regarded as axiomatic that euro area membership confers longer-term benefits. This question goes beyond the simple approach of asking whether the new members are suited to join the euro area on the basis of conventional optimum currency area criteria by the intrusion of the element of timing. Orlowski (2005) describes how, during the 1990s, macroeconomic imbalances became quite severe in many of the central and Eastern European countries in the wake of real exchange rate movement and currency crises of various sorts and how severe action was taken to stabilize their economies in the aftermath of the initial shocks of transition. The approach to euro accession will inevitably involve a sequence of further steps in monetary policy and other policy areas. Orlowski spells out some of the challenges of optimal sequencing of shifts in the monetary policy regime in moving towards full participation in EMU. In advocating a form of direct inflation targeting as the appropriate regime for many countries, but with the expectation that once price stability is entrenched a greater focus can be put on exchange rate stability, Orlowski (2005: 223) notes that 'financial markets ought to be institutionally advanced in order to facilitate such a complex policy'.

As an analytic device for understanding the likely effects of acceding to, then participating fully in, monetary union, a useful concept is the 'j'-curve,[3] the essence of which is that there may be short-term costs of a change that produce a dip in performance (however measured), followed by an up-turn. It is important to stress that the change in question is a *counterfactual* in the sense that it need not imply absolute losses, so much as losses compared with what would otherwise have happened. Figure 3.1 illustrates it, showing that there is an expected trajectory for the economy in the absence of full adoption of the euro. Acceding to the euro area may cause a worsening of performance (GDP is the most obvious 'performance' variable, but not necessarily the only one), but then induces a superior performance.

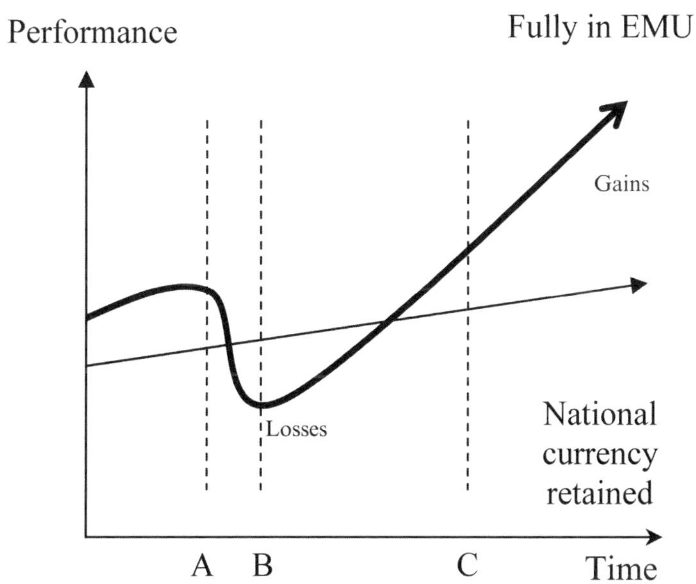

Figure 3.1 The euro membership 'j'-curve (trajectory of the economy).

Any such dip in performance will not necessarily arise prior to joining the euro area, though it may do for some prospective members, nor is it inevitable. Equally the experience of the first wave of membership points to two possible reasons for a 'j'-shaped trajectory. The first would be if the country has to engage in a significant fiscal consolidation or monetary tightening aimed at achieving the Maastricht criteria. In this case, there is likely to be an output loss prior to joining the single currency, although in many cases it is recognized that a fiscal tightening would have had to happen at some point, regardless of euro area membership. A second scenario is that the prospect of euro area membership can cause a 'convergence boom' if falling nominal interest rates, especially, trigger a surge in borrowing, but that unless policy corrects for this, the country may face increasing macroeconomic imbalances that require a post-accession tightening of policy. In other words the dip in the 'j' may arise after accession rather than before and if national policy-makers are slow to recognize the implications, they may face a more severe adjustment problem.

The crucial issues, especially from a political economy standpoint, are the depth of the dip in the 'j' and the time it takes for performance to revert to an upward trend (shown on the horizontal axis as the gap from point A to point B) then to return the economy to where it would have been in the absence of the shift to the euro (from point A to point C). A wide range of factors will influence these two transitions and thus how they bear on the decision, but it is also important to note that the relevant parameters will not be fixed at the outset and may, instead, vary quite substantially depending on specific policy choices or behavioural adaptations. In addition, behavioural adaptation may not only often be needed, but may also be under-estimated.

It is also important to recognize the extent of change taking place within the RAM economies as they continue to integrate and to consolidate their transition. The pace of these changes means that many of the attributes of these economies that might be appraised in determining whether they are a good 'fit' with EMU are themselves subject to change. Consequently, it will be especially difficult to establish whether, for example, optimum currency area (OCA) criteria assessed at any point in time can shed much light on the question of how rapidly to seek euro accession. Some recent literature has focused on the endogenous fulfilment of OCA criteria (for a summary, see De Grauwe and Mongelli 2005), with countries adapting as a result of joining the currency union. De Grauwe and Mongelli (2005) identify four areas in which endogeneities might follow from adhesion to a currency area, all of which contribute to the upward movement (from B to C in Figure 3.1) in the j-curve:

- effects attributable to the impact on economic integration, notably by accelerated price convergence and more intense trade with partner countries;
- the stimulation of financial integration and the resulting scope for financial flows to provide a form of automatic stabilization;
- convergence in susceptibility to shocks that lessen the probability of asymmetric shocks;
- encouragement of product and labour market flexibility.

De Grauwe and Mongelli (2005) posit three dimensions of optimality which they believe bear on the case for membership: the degree of economic integration among candidates for union, the flexibility of economies and the correlation (or symmetry) of incomes. They suggest that in the absence of closely correlated incomes, either strong integration or pronounced flexibility can be substitutes that still allow the microeconomic benefits of monetary integration to be realized, implying that any one can be traded off against either of the other two. They also point out that endogenous movements in the direction of optimality in the variables underlying any of the three dimensions will tend to improve the trade-off between any pair of variables, so that endogeneity becomes self-reinforcing.

However, it can be argued that because of their specific circumstances the cost–benefit calculus of early euro accession for the RAMs will depend crucially on how much of this 'endogeneity' can be achieved in advance of euro accession. Hence the issue is what might be called *anticipatory OCA endogeneity*, which can be defined as transformations of an economy that arise because of, but prior to, monetary integration. In one sense, the convergence trajectory embodied in the Maastricht convergence criteria presaged just such a process by stipulating the adaptation of nominal variables (and the influences on them), but the range of endogenous variables goes much further, and embraces variables that will shape the capacity to adjust within the monetary union and to 'live' successfully with it. Consequently, in appraising the conditions of the RAMs it is important to consider what is distinctive about them from an OCA perspective.

The new members as optimum currency area candidates

Much of the analysis of OCAs is predicated on the assumption that the countries that form the monetary union will all shape the resulting union, such that its characteristics represent some averaging of the individual economies. Clearly, if two countries are close to identical, their union will result in broadly the same configurations of relevant indicators and they will have little need to adapt. Identifying such pairs using OCA criteria is, indeed, aimed at minimizing this adaptation distance (see, for example, Bayoumi and Eichengreen 1997). At the outset, however, EMU did have to bring together economies with more disparate characteristics and the outcome is a mix that, at least for the largest economies, reflects some of their preferences, notably in institutional arrangements. Some of the euro area members, however, seemed to have used the common currency as a means of achieving a rapid paradigm shift, the most obvious cases being the conversion of the southern Member States from high- to low-inflation economies.

In time, the various pressures towards endogeneity should mean that all the members of the euro area should tend towards common attributes. Korhonen and Fidrmuc (2001) show that there were substantial changes over time among the current euro area members in the degree to which they can be considered convergent with Germany on OCA criteria. They also find that only Hungary and Estonia seemed at the time they were writing to be convergent with the euro area. In later work, these same two authors find, however, that the slowdown in EU-15 in the period 2000–2 led to increased heterogeneity in business cycles (Fidrmuc and Korhonen, 2004), so that there may be a cause for concern if current differences in growth rates between the RAMs and the core countries of the euro area persist.

For the RAMs, accession to the euro area will be on rather different terms from the current members, as they will be joining a monetary union in which all the common characteristics and institutional arrangements are settled. In other words, it is a 'take it or leave it' package, not one that will change to reflect their arrival other than in pretty marginal ways.[4] Moreover, because they are all, in GDP weight, small economies (even Poland would account for barely 3 per cent of an enlarged euro area GDP and in aggregate the eight new members add around 7 per cent to euro area GDP), the RAMs will make very little difference to the setting of monetary policy variables. Assuming the choice of interest rate is, approximately, the GDP-weighted average of the interest rates that would otherwise be set for individual Member States, for the needs of the RAMs to move the ECB repo rate by a quarter point (the smallest change that seems to occur) would imply that the rate required for the RAMs in aggregate should, in fact, be a full four percentage points above or below the rate that would be set.[5]

There is, moreover, a catch-22 at the heart of this argument. If the economic conditions in the RAMs are sufficiently divergent to sway the interest rate decision, the gap would be so big as to be alarming, yet it would only be accommodated by an interest rate decision that goes a tiny way towards the needs of the RAMs. In other words, if monetary policy is to be about right for the RAMs it will only be because they have engineered conditions that make it so, not because the ECB sets rates for their conditions.

One of the aspects of endogenous OCAs highlighted in the literature is that trade tends to expand because the common currency eliminates one source of uncertainty surrounding transactions with other countries. For small firms, especially, a threshold may be overcome and since the RAMs inevitably contain a preponderance of small firms, the effect may be especially pronounced for them. Yet Aglietta *et al.* (2003) note that the RAMs have successfully re-oriented their productive structures towards global markets without a common currency and that a key factor in doing so has been the balance struck between maintaining export competitiveness and containing inflation. They also argue that attempting to accede too rapidly to the euro could, by tipping the scales too far towards nominal convergence, upset this delicate balancing act and have an adverse effect on real convergence.

The contrary view has been well expressed by Leszek Balcerowicz, the then Governor of the National Bank of Poland, who stated in a speech to the 11th European Banking Congress in Frankfurt, on 23 November 2001, that early 'entry of the candidate countries into EMU would allow them to start reaping the related advantages (more price transparency, reduced transformation costs, stronger macroeconomic framework)' as quickly as possible and would help to consolidate the momentum towards structural reforms. The arguments about the optimal timing for full participation in EMU are thus, in some respects, more difficult to pin down than conventional OCA assessments.

The salience of financial stability

The risk that financial instability will have a damaging effect on the level and rate of growth of output is well known, and is by no means confined to under-developed countries. According to an ECB (2005a) study, the crises in Argentina (2001–2), Turkey (1999–2001) and Indonesia (1998) resulted in losses of 12–15 per cent of GDP, while Eichengreen (2004) cites evidence from the past 120 years that suggests that financial crises have 'cost' on average 9 per cent of GDP.[6] Moreover, the history of transition in the fifteen years since the demise of central planning in the economies of the RAMs has also seen various episodes of monetary and financial crises. Nor is the problem confined to less developed countries: major episodes of financial instability arose in the Nordic countries in the early 1990s. Jonung and Hagberg (2005) estimate that between the onset of the crisis in Finland in 1990 and the return to trend growth in 1994 there was a cumulative loss of real income of 26.4 percentage points. In the parallel crisis in Sweden, they estimate the cumulative loss to have been 13 percentage points. In both cases the financial dimension of the crisis was central.

Several issues arise in assessing the relationships between financial stability, full participation in EMU and the outlook for real convergence on the extent of the likely dip in the j-curve (from A to B in Figure 3.1).

1 As Issing (2005: 196) observes, 'monetary integration is more than just adopting a common currency; it also implies financial market integration'. Hence, the degree to which the financial markets of candidates for stage 3 of EMU are equipped to cope with the demands of integration will matter.
2 Consumer debt as a proportion of national income in the RAMs is well below the median for the EU-15 and would be expected to expand as they become more integrated into the EU (Tùma 2004). This is likely to have effects on asset markets and on the structures of bank balance sheets that could increase the risk of financial crises.
3 The experience of the RAMs in regulatory oversight and prudential supervision of financial intermediaries has been chequered, with a number of problems arising during the 1990s. Even if the framework now in place is regarded as sound, implementation also has to be taken into account and there will be a need for a phase of learning by doing, during which vulnerabilities may increase.
4 Ownership of major banks in most RAMs is now substantially in foreign hands. While this may be beneficial for risk spreading, there is also a danger that it will lead to lending policies that could exacerbate volatility in GDP if the parent banks make decisions not on the basis of circumstances in the host country, but on the basis of their overall markets.[7]
5 The intra-country dimension of real convergence also warrants attention, particularly in relation to asset markets. A characteristic of all the RAMs has been relatively more rapid growth and faster economic development in a small number of regions, usually the capital.

A central influence on the outlook for financial stability will be the choice of monetary regime. Golinelli and Ravelli (2005) identify a range of conditions for sound monetary policy (see Box 3.1). They claim that their 'findings provide strong support for the feasibility of an inflation targeting (IT) strategy in transition economies. This strategy may be adopted, in our view, as soon as the process of disinflation has been completed. In this perspective, IT emerges as the natural follower to a strategy of crawling band (as in Hungary and Poland), as well as to a strategy of exchange rate peg (as in the Czech Republic)' (Golinelli and Ravelli 2005: 198).

And what about real convergence?

Research on convergence has been far from conclusive and there are conflicting views on the degree to which economic cycles are, or will be, synchronized. Caselli and Tenreyro (2005) suggest four channels through which real convergence might occur:

- Solow-type growth reliant on their lack of capital and the consequent high marginal productivity of capital;
- technological catch-up;
- gains from trade in previously relatively closed economies;
- induced structural change in which there is a switch of resources from low- to high-productivity activities.

The competitive effects of the single market, arguably reinforced by monetary union, constitute a fifth mechanism not quoted by these authors which will also bear on structural adaptation. Together these effects can make a considerable difference to productive structures. Average productivity per worker in Spain was only 60 per cent of that in France in

Box 3.1 Preconditions for sound discretionary monetary policies

1 The central bank is independent of the government (and of all other macro agents).
2 Fiscal policy is sound and the financial position of the government is sustainable without recourse to monetization.
3 The economy is resilient and responsive to changes in interest and exchange rates.
4 Quantitative models of the inflation process and the transmission mechanism are available.

Additional preconditions for inflation targeting in emerging markets:

1 The central bank gives strong priority to the goal of price stability.
2 The goal of price stability is in close sight.
3 Exchange rate policy is not the main anchor (or intermediate target) of the disinflation policy – in particular, the pre-announcement of a rate of crawl no longer plays a central role in the strategy for disinflation.
4 The central bank has adopted an 'all-inclusive' information stance, looking at the determinants of inflation within a structured and broad analytical framework, without placing specific emphasis on the role of monetary aggregates.
5 Inflation forecasts have become the main intermediate target, and announcing the target is a credible anchor for inflation expectations.

Source: Golinelli and Ravelli (2005)

1950, but had converged to 90 per cent by 1970 (Caselli and Tenreyro 2005). Polish agricultural workers appear to achieve just 9 per cent of the productivity of their French counterparts compared with 40 per cent for manufacturing and 56 per cent for services. This suggests considerable scope for both between-sector resource reallocation and within-industry catch-up, though it will be a drawn-out process. The RAMs start with one advantage compared with their southern European counterparts of yesteryear, namely a relatively high level of human capital, though there may be a risk that the legacy from centrally planned days of a good education will erode and may be less suited to the contemporary knowledge-intensive economy.

Productivity growth and its links to labour costs are generally encouraging for the RAMs and the evidence is that nominal labour costs remain low, as can be seen from Table 3.2. EU accession can be expected to put upward pressure on nominal wage rates, but the data show that there remains considerable room for manoeuvre. Moreover, so long as productivity growth remains robust, it will offset nominal wage increases and some new members have an enviable record in this regard. Such higher productivity growth may reflect the lower starting point, especially of the Baltic States, and also the fact that their transition started later. Even bearing this in mind the productivity growth has been exceptional.

The findings of Brada *et al.* (2005) that the real output of the five new members they investigate is not very well co-integrated with France and Germany prompts them to advocate

Table 3.2 Labour costs in the new members and the EU-15 in 2003

	Hourly labour costs in Industry and Services €
EU-15 highest Sweden	28.56
EU-15 average	*22.19*
EU-15 lowest Portugal	8.13
RAMs	
Slovenia	8.98
Poland	4.48
Czech Republic	3.90
Hungary	3.83
Slovakia	3.06
Estonia	3.03
Lithuania	2.71
Latvia	2.42

Source: Eurostat.

caution in moving to full participation in stage 3 of EMU. They conclude that these 'economies would be well advised to retain some measure of policy autonomy to deal with productivity shocks whose magnitude and timing may continue to differ significantly from the shocks affecting the EU core. This is far from surprising given the extent of the transformations taking place and the very different phases in the macroeconomic performance of the new members. A data period that comprises an initial transformation recession, a phase of stabilization and phases of growth interrupted by supply or currency shocks is hardly a viable basis for estimation.

A further issue is how economic activity evolves within a Member State. There is a tendency across the EU for economic activity and dynamism to be most concentrated in capital regions, leading to possible spatial imbalances that, in turn, can give rise to macroeconomic imbalances. Although there are data lags that mean the most recent data relate only to the period before accession, the evidence nevertheless suggests that regional disparities are growing in the four larger new Member States. The remaining four (Slovenia and the three Baltic countries) are small, very open economies and, although there is also some evidence of disparities, it in a qualitatively different setting. In j-curve terms, spatial imbalance could result in a steeper initial dip and a slower recovery.

Paving the way: prior adjustment in stage 2 of EMU

It is easily forgotten that the current members of the euro area went through an extended apprenticeship before the start of stage 3 in 1999. Formally, the aim was to achieve a sufficient degree of nominal convergence such that prospective participants in stage 3 would not exhibit differences that would put undue strain on policy choices at the level of the euro area. Nominal convergence, however, was only part of the story, not least because it says little about the likely impact on the real economy, nor was it the only pathway to membership. In the debate around joining EMU at the time of the negotiation and ratification of the Maastricht Treaty, two schools of thought emerged about how to proceed. One, often referred to as the *economists'* perspective, favoured prior convergence by ensuring that the participants in the monetary union had similar inflation rates and other nominal indicators (Wyplosz 1997), an irony of this labelling being that it was most heartily endorsed by central bankers and little supported by academic economists.

The other school of thought – again with some irony – came to be known as the *monetarist* approach, in spite of being the one mainly espoused by academic economists of diverse persuasions. Its main thesis was that once countries entered a monetary union, economic agents would rapidly adapt their behaviour, a corollary of which is that their history would have only a marginal bearing on how they conducted themselves under EMU. The logic of this position was that a 'big bang' move to EMU would be the most attractive route, partly because it would avoid the potential damage to the real economy from an extended period of restraint aimed at achieving the required limits for the nominal indicators. In principle, this would mean a flatter j-curve with a smaller loss from the transition to EMU.

As noted above, for the RAMs the question is no longer the same. The rules are set and they have to conform, and the institutional structure of EMU is established. Consequently, being able to live with the EMU regime is now largely about the timing of different sorts of development. When the assessments of the current euro area members were done in 1998, the position was that all the contenders bar Greece comfortably passed the inflation and long-term interest rate tests, but for several an element of discretion had, in effect, to be used to enable them to pass the fiscal tests.[8]

A crucial question for the new members is the extent to which they are likely to be subject to the Balassa–Samuelson (BS) effect. This arises when high productivity growth in the traded sector leads to wage inflation in sheltered sectors because workers seek to maintain differentials, even if there is no corresponding productivity increase in the latter. For catching-up economies, the scope for productivity gains is substantial, especially if inward investment brings in substantial new capital. The outcome tends to be an appreciation in the real exchange rate. The magnitude and extent of such effects has been contested, with sharply varying estimates, although an authoritative study by Schadler *et al.* (2005) suggests that the effect will add in the range of 1–2 percentage points to consumer price inflation in the recently acceded states of central and Eastern Europe. The implication is that, to offset this effect, they will have to attain an underlying inflation rate in the traded sectors that is as low as that of the best performing euro area members in order to meet the Maastricht price inflation criterion.[9]

Price levels in the recently acceded Member States remain generally far below those of the euro area countries, though there has been notable convergence. According to the latest data in the Eurostat Structural Indicators database, prices in the euro area in 2006 were 103 per cent of the EU-27 average, while those in the new Member States ranged from a low of 44.8 per cent in Bulgaria to 75.3 per cent in Slovenia. In the six years from 2000 to 2006, the rate of price convergence was highest in Romania (up from 42.5 per cent to 57 per cent) and the Czech Republic (48.1 per cent to 61.5 per cent). In the other RAMs, the rate of convergence was lower, while in Latvia, Lithuania and Slovenia the relative price gap has been stable vis-à-vis the EU average. Asset prices, bearing in mind the experience of some of the current members of the euro area (notably Portugal and Ireland) may be a specific problem. Housing is the obvious concern, especially with the rapid growth in so many countries of housing loans, but share prices have gone up substantially in the RAMs, according to OECD data. Table 3.3 shows the rates of increase for selected countries up to July 2005.

Turning to budgetary ratios, six of the new members were found to have excessive deficits immediately following EU accession and Hungary was castigated again both in the spring and autumn of 2005 for inadequate efforts to abate the deficit. Reform fatigue may

Table 3.3 Rate of increase of stock market indices

Country or region	*Index, July 2005 (2000=100)*	*Rate of change over last 12 months, %*
Euro area	70.4	21.6
France	76.1	21.9
Germany	64.3	19.8
Italy	80.3	22.1
United Kingdom	81.1	20.3
Czech Republic	225.0	57.4
Hungary	226.4	70.8
Poland	137.3 (May)	12.1
Slovakia	547.3	126.3
Japan	75.0 (June)	0.1
US	108.6	14.7

Source: *OECD Main Economic Indicators.*

also be a factor complicating adjustment, especially with EU accession being sold as an economic opportunity. EU membership may, in addition, lead to some short-term fiscal problems, even though the sizeable allocations expected from the cohesion budget will result in net fiscal transfers to the new members. In particular, co-financing rules may oblige the new members to devote more public spending to public investment. Provided the investment in question is productive, it should underpin growth and thus generate greater fiscal resources in the medium term, but here again a short-term cost arises. The need to conform to environmental quality standards will potentially put pressure on public finances in the new Member States, although Hallett (2004) concludes that these fears have been exaggerated and that on balance EU accession will ease their fiscal positions.

Fiscal adjustment also contains a sting in the tail for the new members. The Maastricht ratios of 3 per cent deficit and 60 per cent debt were selected largely to ensure that a steady state could be maintained in the convergence process, assuming a 5 per cent trend growth in nominal GDP, values that were around the (then) EU-12 average at the time the criteria were set. Nominal growth at that rate would, in turn, be approximately 2.5 per cent real growth with 2 per cent inflation, or a similar combination of the two components.[10] A country growing at that rate with an initial debt of 60 per cent could sustain a 3 per cent deficit without increasing the debt ratio; if the deficit were held below 3 per cent, debt would decline. For the RAMs, however, the initial arithmetic is different. Real growth in recent years is well above the benchmark 2.5 per cent rate, as is inflation, while for several countries the debt ratio is well below 60 per cent. As a result, their deficits could remain some way above 3 per cent, without imperilling fiscal sustainability (as measured by indebtedness). Consequently, there is a risk that some countries will be obliged to rein in their deficits in a manner that would reduce aggregate demand and compromise public investment, yet not be necessary to contain public debt. Treaty change in this respect cannot be expected to happen, but it is evident that rapid fiscal consolidation could be damaging to real convergence.

The question of whether the new members would do well to retain the exchange rate as an instrument of adjustment in the early years of EU membership depends on the likely form of shocks. In essence, if shocks are financial or monetary, an independent exchange rate will be damaging, whereas if shocks mainly affect demand, then a relative price movement brought about by an exchange rate movement may be beneficial. A study by

Borghijs and Kuijs (2004) surveys the evidence on the experience of the Central and Eastern European countries (CEECs) in this regard and suggests that although the exchange rate may have been useful in dealing with real economy shocks in larger countries, in smaller economies it has not. They explore how useful exchange rates have been in resolving shocks in five CEECs and conclude that exchange rate variability has probably been unhelpful or even counterproductive.

There is also a significant risk of greater macroeconomic volatility from early membership of ERM II, a system that requires a fair degree of nominal convergence to be generally beneficial for its participants, but could prove to be damaging if exchange rates tend to diverge. At issue here is what is currently in place, as it could be argued that moving from a currency board to ERM carries little risk, whereas a country such as the Czech Republic which has an inflation-targeting monetary policy would be more vulnerable. A possible 'capital inflow stop' (Rostowski 2003) could trigger macroeconomic instability and thus a risk of currency depreciation, a solution to which would be to move rapidly to adopt the euro. The effect may be to damage the prospects for real convergence leading to an adverse outcome, especially if pressures for easy monetary policy create unsustainable short-term booms or at least tend to be pro-cyclical.

In addition, as Cihak and Holub (2003) point out, price convergence may be accelerated for reasons other than the conventional BS effect. If so, one of two problems for eligibility for stage 3 will arise, depending on the exchange rate regime in operation. For those that operate currency boards, the real appreciation will have to be accommodated by higher inflation, which could threaten achievement of the Maastricht inflation criterion during the period when convergence is being assessed. Arguably, this is exemplified by looking at inflation in Estonia in 2006, which was above the rate required to fulfil the convergence criteria, despite the exchange rate having been locked to the euro since 1999. Where there is nominal exchange rate flexibility, on the other hand, it will be the stability of the exchange rate that is threatened. A crucial issue, therefore, will be whether the 15 per cent ERM band or a much narrower band is applied in assessing the Maastricht exchange rate criterion.

Three approaches can be envisaged, all of which have differing implications for the conjunction of real convergence, financial stability and EMU accession, and thus the shape of the j-curve:

- a big bang approach aimed at acceding to full EMU at the earliest opportunity, perhaps occasioning a short, sharp fall in the j-curve – before or after accession – then rapid recovery;
- a longer period of acclimatization inside ERM II, but with the focus on a stable exchange rate, with less of a loss prior to accession, but a slower upturn;
- a sequencing approach in which the initial emphasis is on price stabilization (via inflation targeting) followed by a switch to the minimum period inside ERM II. Ideally managed, this could offer the most promising j-curve, or indeed avoid any downturn, whether before or after accession.

Links from financial stability to real convergence

The links between financial stability and real convergence likely to affect the RAMs operate through a variety of channels (see, for instance, Brouwer *et al.* 2003; Rostowski 2003). They include the stability of key macroeconomic variables and shifts in the policy frameworks affecting monetary policy and the exchange rate, the determinants of major financial flows, the character of the financial system and how it is evolving, and the regulatory environment for financial services. Macroeconomic mismanagement has long been recognized as a source of financial crises, in which inattention to price stability or imbalances in components of demand can lead to volatility in financial markets that precipitate problems.

Jiménez and Saurina (2005), in a statement that anticipates the problems being experienced in the fallout from the 2007 sub-prime crisis, note that there is a long history of banks succumbing to lending fervour in periods of relatively rapid economic growth and point out that mistakes are more likely during upturns than in periods of slower growth when banks exercise more caution. However, they also point out that the empirical support for the contention that rapid growth in lending is associated with higher credit risk is limited. They try to remedy this gap by investigating the relationship and find that there is a positive relationship between an increase in lending and future non-performing loans – an intuitively probable finding – but only with a fairly substantial lag. Their empirical work also demonstrates that it is the riskier loans extended in economic upturns that account for this phenomenon: as they put it, 'credit risk increases in boom periods although it only pops up as loan losses during bad times' (Jiménez and Saurina, 2005: 23). The current strong growth in the RAMs could, on this evidence, be a source of future problems.

Eichengreen (2004) makes the obvious, if telling, point that financial crises do not erupt in countries with rudimentary financial markets, and he suggests that the biggest problems are likely to be in emerging markets or transition economies. But Eichengreen also emphasizes the important links between financial development and productivity growth, and thus highlights an important trade-off that policy-makers have to optimize. Modernization of the financial sector is a necessary condition for real convergence, but it carries the risk that there will be a disruptive bout of financial instability. Eichengreen *et al.* (2003) point to three risks that tend to characterize emerging market economies:

- currency mismatch, which is characterized by short-term liabilities in an external currency while the assets and/or cash flow to service the debt are in the national currency;
- debt intolerance, which is an inability to manage the levels of debt that more developed countries can sustain;
- what they call 'original sin', the inability to borrow abroad the country's own currency, with the result that any external borrowing carries a currency risk.

Drawing the various influences together, Box 3.2 shows the range of possible effects of EMU accession on the banking sector.

Living with full EMU: stage 3 adjustment

Once fully in EMU, a country plainly has to adapt to the new regime and this, in turn, means rethinking the policy mix – in the broadest sense – because EMU changes the scope for using different policy instruments in adjusting the economy. Conventional demand management instruments operate in a very different manner and tend to be more constrained than for a single country,[11] so that more of the burden of any adjustment necessarily falls on supply-side policies, notably those that bear on the labour market. The high degree of trade integration between the new members and the euro area, as well as their relatively more flexible labour markets, mean that they may find it easier to 'live' with the euro than several of the current members. An inference is that stage 3 adjustment, part of which is the degree to which optimum currency area criteria are satisfied endogenously, will be more critical than stage 2 adjustment.

Box 3.2 Potential sources of disruption of banking in the move towards EMU

1 Macroeconomic instability affecting the lending and borrowing activity of the corporate and personal sectors, possibly exacerbated by volatility in interest rates. The processes can become self-reinforcing, for example if bad debts trigger a credit crunch by banks as they seek to shore up their balance sheets.
2 The impact of financial market liberalization which, in relation to the recently acceded Member States, will be particularly marked as they develop securities markets. Liberalization also tends to blur boundaries between market segments, with the risk of contagion between different types of financial services and increased complexity in assessing exposures.
3 Income growth that stimulates a willingness on the part of households to become more indebted, especially as the effective real interest rate is reduced.
4 Structural economic transformation affecting the supply side of the economy, with companies being taken over, rationalized or going out of business.
5 Political developments that affect credit risk.
6 The form and impact of any further privatization and how it bears on the recasting of regulation for particular industries.
7 Broader international trends in financial markets and the impact of these on financial integration at the global level.

The stage 3 challenges are, in part, about accommodation to the new policy environment, but also concern the dynamic effects of participation. In a Lucasian sense, EMU is a significant regime change that must be expected to transform a wide range of economic relationships. The implication is that past economic trends may not be a good indicator of how countries will fare once inside the euro area. In this regard, the record of the early years of the euro contains a number of surprises and, based on eight years of observations (hard data for 1999–2004 and forecasts for 2005–6), some lessons can be drawn. The travails of Germany, Portugal and Italy contrast with the apparent success of Spain, Finland and Ireland and, while it would be disingenuous to attribute these trends only to the single currency, can offer some insights.

Three overlapping, but distinct dimensions of adaptation are relevant. The first is macroeconomic acclimatization, which comprises a range of processes:

- rebalancing of the policy mix, given the switch to a firm monetary policy oriented to price stability, with fiscal policy expected to assume more of the burden of dealing with demand shocks – the macroeconomic rebalancing also includes learning to live with more constraints on fiscal flexibility;
- changes in the signals that guide the relationships between monetary and fiscal policy, and in how demand management interacts with the labour market;
- effects on nominal interest rates and thus on the burden of debt service that lead to a rebalancing of tax and spending, and may have distributive consequences by shifting demand from lenders to borrowers, a change that may also be regional in its incidence – such shifts may, in turn, have an effect on the banking industry, though whether they affect the risk of financial crises is hard to predict.

Second, there will be a shift in the dynamics of the labour market and how its different attributes affect the capacity for supply-side adjustment. An economy with a rigid labour market will find it more difficult to alter its competitiveness, because labour market adaptation occurs only slowly, and (as Germany, followed by France, has found since entering stage 3 of EMU) is highly contested. On the whole, however, the RAMs start from a more propitious position in that the extensive transformations that they have already undergone during transition have resulted in relatively freer labour markets than in many current euro area members.

Third, closer integration through monetary union induces longer-term effects. These include structural changes in the geography of economic activity caused by polarizing and agglomerating forces (see Neary 2001; and, for a perspective on policy issues, Baldwin *et al.* 2003). There will also be EMU-specific trends, such as a possible spatial concentration of financial services. One of the effects of EMU that was, arguably, under-anticipated has been the relatively rapid growth of intra-euro area trade, even though Rose (2004), especially, had pointed to it as a probable effect. Trade data show that the new members are generally more open economies than most EU-15 Member States, and also that their trade is now very largely with EU partners. This sort of trade pattern implies little need for adjustment.

A particular source of instability is capital inflows, which are likely to remain substantial in the new Member States, even though the major waves of privatization are now past. The experience of Ireland and Portugal also suggests that asset bubbles that could impinge on macroeconomic stability need to be anticipated and that dealing with a public investment boom (especially with a gearing-up of transfers from the EU Structural Funds) may be an issue.

Much has been written about the high level of employment in agriculture, notably in countries such as Poland. However, it is the share of primary activity (agriculture and fishing) in GDP that is, arguably, more revealing. In the euro area, the average in 2004, according to Eurostat data reported in the August 2005 issue of the ECB *Statistics Pocketbook*, was 2.2 per cent, with a range from 6.4 per cent in Greece to 1.1 per cent in Germany and just 0.5 per cent in Luxembourg. In the RAMs, the Baltic States have the highest ratios, peaking in Lithuania with 5.7 per cent, while most other countries are clustered around the 3 per cent mark (including Poland at 2.9 per cent). In general, manufacturing in the new member states accounts for a higher proportion of GDP than in the euro area: the highest share in 2004 was in the Czech Republic at 32 per cent and Slovenia at 30.2 per cent, with the median around 25 per cent, compared with 20.8 per cent in the euro area. However, the Irish manufacturing share is marginally higher than the Czech one, and Germany, Slovakia, Poland and Hungary have similar values around the 25–26 per cent mark.

In construction, the data suggest that it is the EU-15 'cohesion countries' that have the highest GDP shares, implying that receipts from the Structural Funds may have played a part. Most of the new members have a construction share close to the euro area average of 5.9 per cent, but higher than the three largest economies. The one area of economic activity where the new members are most distant from the euro area is finance and business, which accounted for 27.8 per cent of economic activity in 2004 in the euro area, but a spread from 12.1 per cent in Lithuania and 16.4 per cent in Poland to just over 21 per cent in Slovakia and Hungary.

These admittedly crude indicators suggest that, in terms of the broad structure of economic activity, the RAMs are not that different from the euro area. While the dependence on agriculture as a source of (plainly, low-quality) employment is much greater in the new

Member States, it would not take many years of relatively higher growth for the structures to converge with the euro area, at least at this highly aggregated level. Indeed, in the various broad sectors, the range among the twelve pre-2007 members of the euro area is such that, with the exception of finance and business, the RAMs would not appear to be out of place. More highly disaggregated data might tell a subtler story. However, to the extent that monetary policy tends to focus on the impact of interest rate changes on broad sectors, and on the distinctive transmission channels that bear on different sectors, there is no immediate cause for concern.

The value of the exchange rate on entry into EMU will also affect the shape of the j-curve by affecting competitiveness, influencing the trajectory of the economy in the short to medium run. Arguably, one of the problems confronting the Italian economy today is that its competitiveness declined progressively after accession to the euro because of the twin effects of low productivity growth and rising real wage costs. Consequently, for the new members 'getting the parity right will be another key part of the strategy', as Schadler *et al.* (2005: 9) note. Bulíř and Šmídková (2005) present potentially worrying evidence that the nominal exchange rates of some new members risk being overvalued, even within ERM II. They find that the Czech, Hungarian and Polish currencies were overvalued in 2003. Their simulation work suggests that, in contrast to the Slovenian Tolar, all three currencies would struggle to stay within the constraints of ERM II over the period 2004–10, based on their end-2004 exchange rates. Bulíř and Šmídková also suggest that the competitiveness of these three economies could be harmed if they try to meet the Maastricht criteria too soon, while Slovenia would have been well-advised to revalue before entering stage 3.

Several members of the euro area have struggled to conform to the fiscal rules and have found themselves in breach of the Stability and Growth Pact. It is, however, on the supply side of the euro area economies that problems have been most evident, although whether these can be attributed directly to EMU is doubtful. Labour market mismatch has been a feature in several countries, productivity growth has slowed and investment in R&D has been disappointing. These shortcomings have been extensively documented (see, for example, the Sapir report (Sapir *et al.* 2004) and the Kok report (Kok 2004)) and the 2005 relaunch of the Lisbon strategy is intended to offer a remedy. One sense in which these problems can be linked to EMU is that as fiscal consolidation has proceeded Member States have – as is so often the case – found it easier to cut public investment than consumption. Yet it also has to be pointed out that as nominal interest rates have declined there ought to have been greater incentives for the private sector to invest more. A second sense in which supply-side difficulties may have been affected by the shift to EMU is that the extended period of slow growth in certain Member States (partly associated with the transition to the euro during the 1990s) may have inhibited structural reforms. Such reforms are typically easier to push through when the economy is booming and the social and political costs of change can more easily be accommodated, whereas stagnation often entrenches defensive attitudes. For the RAMs, this diagnosis has a silver lining in that the extent of reform has already been considerable, with the result that some of the problems that characterize 'old' Europe – notably inflexible labour markets – have already been confronted, implying a lesser dip in the j-curve.

The financial system, monetary transmission and stabilization

Within the euro area, as with any currency zone, the central bank has to rely on the financial system for the transmission of monetary policy (Issing 2005). But if the financial system is underdeveloped there may be vulnerabilities that compromise its capacity to fulfil these functions. For similar reasons, any monetary policy decision (which, by definition, will be taken for the euro area as a whole) may lead to differentiated effects on the real economy of RAMs compared with the current members.

The ECB (2005a) notes the importance in the event of a financial crisis of private flows in resolving the problem. While official flows can play a useful catalytic role, especially where the country facing a crisis is classified as intermediate in credit ratings, they are shown not to be a reliable answer. The study also notes the obvious point that the involvement of domestic private sector creditors in dealing with a financial crisis has direct implications for the real economy which may aggravate the costs of the crisis. It follows that a robust system that minimizes the risks of such crises is a highly desirable attribute of an economy. A linked issue is the extent to which external rather than domestic private creditors are involved.

Brada *et al.* stress that even if monetary variables, such as the growth of base money or the interest rate, display convergence towards the euro area, the transmission mechanism to the real economy depends on the character of the financial system. They observe that

> even if the transition economies were to follow the monetary policies of the Bundesbank or, now, the European Central Bank (ECB), major changes in their financial systems could transform such policy into quite different results in terms of the growth of broader measures of the money supply, interest rates or inflation.
>
> (Brada *et al.* 2005: 253)

The financial sector in the RAMs

The financial legacy of transition, as well as current trends in the financial sector, will bear on the costs and benefits of euro area accession and on the prospects for adjustment, with both macroeconomic and microeconomic effects. Countries which have an overhang of external debt – Poland was one, although the reliefs granted by the Paris club eased the burden – face both a debt service and repayment outflows, whereas those (such as the Baltic States) which had the slate wiped clean at the start of the transition have an obvious advantage.

The extent of domestic credit is an important factor and one likely trend is that the indebtedness of consumers and the corporate sector will increase. Zdeněk Tùma, the Governor of the Czech National Bank, noted:

> in the acceding countries, bank credit to the domestic private sector typically has a ratio of 30 to 40 per cent of GDP, while the EU average is around 100 per cent of GDP. This difference is to a large extent natural, reflecting the lower GDP levels of the acceding countries, their history, and the recent weaknesses in their legal and institutional environments.
>
> (Tùma 2004: 2)

He goes on to make the point that higher debt is likely to be associated with greater risk of financial crises.

Although the bank credit to GDP ratio has risen substantially in nearly all the countries of central and Eastern Europe, the rate of increase has not been unreasonable, given the low starting-point. Indeed, actual stocks of lending are, in many cases, below what might be expected from the level of development of the country (Cottarelli *et al.* 2005). Three major shifts occurred during the 1990s: the need to write off the loans extended to state enterprises; privatization (mostly to foreign investors); and the building up of bank lending to the private business sector. Bank lending continues to dominate business finance (ECB 2005b). In 2003, the average lending to the private sector was around 35 per cent of GDP, compared with some 117 per cent in EU-15. An ECB (2005b) study attributes this low ratio to three factors:

- above all, the fact that private sector credit was largely absent under central planning, with the result that there was neither a developed banking system, nor experience among consumers or business in demanding credit;
- an uncertain legal environment that could have compromised debt enforcement;
- the fact that foreign-owned enterprises often relied on external sources of finance.

The ECB study also finds that the RAMs are – in keeping with experience elsewhere – progressively seeing an increase in the extent of financial intermediation. Although, by 2003, the average rose by six percentage points, to 35 per cent of GDP, from 29 per cent in 1995, the increase in private credit in some of the RAMs has been much more rapid and if the EU-15 average is seen as a benchmark towards which the new members will converge, the scope for a surge in credit is evident. This prospect raises a number of issues germane to financial stability. First, it implies that both lenders and borrowers will have to adapt their behaviour.

Recent data highlight the potential problems. Bank lending to the private sector in the RAMs has been growing rapidly in recent years, with growth of as much as 55 per cent in Lithuania in the year 2003 and 80 per cent in 2004. Lending to households grew more rapidly than to companies in seven of the eight RAMs (Slovenia is the odd one out), with growth in excess of 60 per cent during 2003 in Lithuania, Latvia and Hungary (ECB 2004). Figure 3.2 shows the trend for three of the RAMs for which comparable data are available. Much of this lending to households appears to have been for housing finance, raising the spectre of an unsustainable house price boom. In Hungary, for example, lending for house purchase rose more than six-fold in nominal terms between the beginning of 2002 and July 2005, while total lending to households 'only' quadrupled.[12] In Poland, the financial stability report for the first half of 2004 noted the sharp rise in lending to households, and the surge in housing loans associated with EU accession. Figure 3.3 shows the extent of the surge in house-related lending for the Czech Republic, Estonia and Hungary.

A second concern is that, as credit increases, the risk of credit induced effects on macroeconomic stability will also be increased, a change that may have repercussions for the monetary transmission mechanism. The speed with which credit expands – that is, slowly over many years, or rapidly as modern financial products are rolled out – will influence how this effect unfolds, as well as the trajectory towards stage 3 of EMU.

A third likely effect is that, as credit expands, the probability of defaults and bank failure will rise. The solution is not hard to state, namely to implement appropriate regulatory measures, notably assurance of capital adequacy, and to prevent trouble by well-designed prudential supervision. But it also has to be recognized that there is a learning process in developing such measures. Particular attention will need to be paid to how the financial system evolves and the degree to which the dominance of traditional banking is replaced by an increase in other forms of intermediation. Off-balance sheet risks have manifestly been a source of problems in EU-15 even before the 2008 credit crunch and represent one potential threat to financial stability in a rapidly changing financial environment.

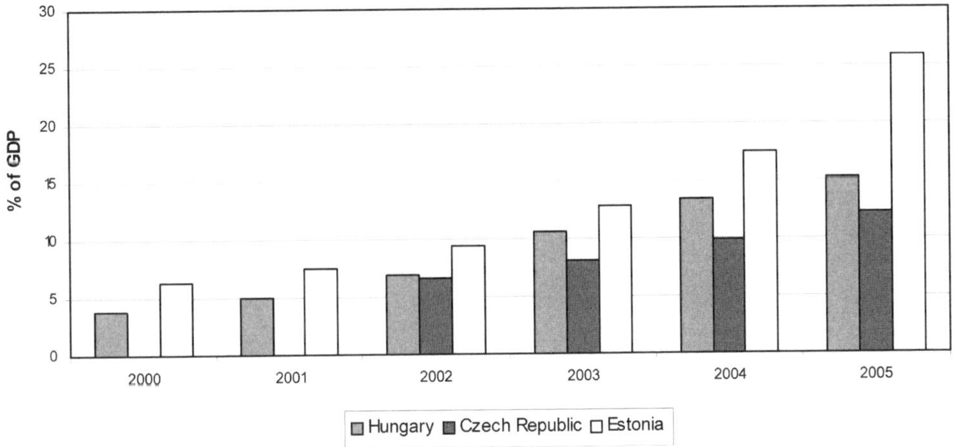

Figure 3.2 Bank lending to households, % of GDP.

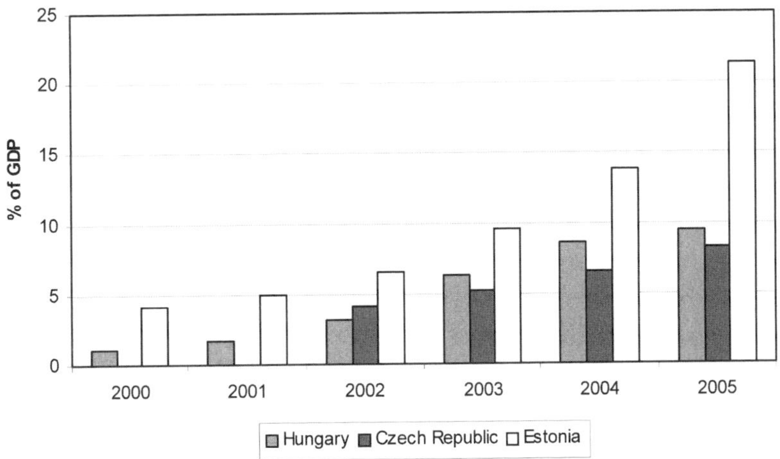

Figure 3.3 Bank lending to households for housing.

The ECB study also shows that stock market capitalization, at just under 20 per cent of GDP, is substantially below the EU-15 level (68 per cent), reinforcing the image of an under-developed financial sector. As part of the transition from central planning, most banks were privatized and there are now hardly any state-owned banks. Indeed, a large proportion of the banking system is now foreign owned, a fact that may help risk sharing in a way that is supportive of financial stability. Only in Latvia and Slovenia is the foreign share of bank assets under 50 per cent, while in three countries (Czech Republic, Slovakia and Estonia) it is close to 100 per cent. The ECB study shows that most of this foreign ownership takes the form of RAM banks being subsidiaries of foreign credit institutions.

More encouragingly, the ECB study shows that, on various indicators of solvency, the banking system in the RAMs is in reasonably good shape. Loans amounted to 49 per cent of assets in the RAMs in 2003, compared with 51 per cent in EU-15, while liquid assets were also sizeable. The robustness of these and other indicators does, though, have to be viewed with caution given the likely increase expected in financial intermediation in general and lending to households in particular. How banks themselves change as organizations will also be an issue. For example, there are unrealized economies of scale among the smaller banks in the RAMs (Fries and Taci 2005), implying scope for efficiency gains through consolidation.

All of these trends point to the probability of an increased sensitivity of the economy to possible interest rate shocks and, potentially, to an intensified risk of financial instability. Issing (2003: 22) maintains that 'a system definition of financial stability practically excludes a trade-off between monetary and financial stability', though he concedes that a short-term conflict may arise. But for economies in transition, it might be expected that the conflict could be more acute, especially if Balassa–Samuelson influences or measurement problems complicate the issue.

Concluding comments

Full participation in EMU promises to entrench macroeconomic stability, to accelerate the integration of financial markets and helps to assure financial stability, and to raise the volume of trade by eliminating currency risk as a form of barrier. The trouble is, though, that to attain these prizes an economy has to be in a position to exploit the opportunities afforded by accession to the euro area. Any doubts concern whether, having come through the process of transition during the 1990s, EMU imposes constraints on macroeconomic policy and would restrict flexibility by eliminating the exchange rate as a potential instrument of adjustment and shock absorber. These constraints could slow real convergence.

The question is not whether the stable macroeconomic policy that EMU assures is in the interests of economies in search of a long-term economic development strategy, but whether they are yet able to cope with it. In some respects, the Maastricht nominal convergence route to monetary union may be more demanding in the short term for the new members. They face greater pressures for public investment and may also have to confront demands from their citizens for an 'EU membership dividend' in social spending. Dealing with the consequences of real convergence in the form of a Balassa–Samuelson effect on the price level may also be challenging, since it could engender a conflict between price stability and exchange rate stability.

This chapter has emphasized that the challenges are about the speed with which different facets of economic change occur, and the ease with which behaviour and structures consistent with the single currency can be engendered. There cannot be an all-encompassing answer, and a range of trajectories along the j-curve can be envisaged. For the small open economies, the balance of costs and benefits will tend to favour entering stage 3 as quickly as possible. The Baltic economies exemplify this, since their record shows that despite entering transition in 1992 in an inauspicious position they have been able not only to adapt their macroeconomic variables rapidly, but also to shake up the supply side of the economy successfully. Ireland's experience may have some resonance for them.

Poland is a rather different story, for which Spain, a country that has been through a successful transition – albeit from a different form of totalitarianism – may offer a parallel. Like Poland, Spain saw a rapid rise in unemployment and had to contend with a sharply declining rural economy. The time span was longer and the distance that had to be travelled less, but the fact that Spain, as seen in 1991–2, let alone 1986 or 1975, has gone from being a marginal candidate for full participation in EMU to one of the more successful economies ought to be a source of encouragement for countries like Poland. Even so, von Hagen and Traistaru (2005: 166) suggest that Poland and the Czech Republic 'are the only two new member states for which a late entry makes sense, given that they have demonstrated the potential for an autonomous, stability-oriented monetary policy based on inflation targets'. Having analysed the congruence of shocks, Frenkel and Nickel (2002: 23) also conclude that their results 'support an entry into EMU for more advanced east central European states at the earliest possible date'.

In keeping with the overall themes of this volume, an important question is how financial stability bears on the decision, recognizing that it affects both the transition and how comfortable the RAMs find living with EMU. Some of the risks commonly associated with episodes of financial crisis can be played down. Macroeconomic policy, notably, seems unlikely to be a trigger for financial instability, notwithstanding the trend in some of the RAMs for fiscal deterioration. As Table 3.4 shows, with the possible exception of Hungary, all the EMU candidates meet or are within touching distance of the nominal convergence criteria, so that unless a maverick government comes to power and squanders these advantages in what would be a very cavalier manner, it is hard to see a breakdown of discipline. Central Bank independence and its corollary, a commitment to price stability, would, in any case, be likely to inhibit any such trajectory.

Of potentially more concern is the impact of financial flows. Here, a variety of flows come into play. The RAMs will, in all probability, continue to be attractive destinations for foreign investment. Flows of up to 4 per cent of GDP will also come from EU cohesion policy beyond 2006, so that the consolidation of EU membership will provide a net

Table 3.4 The Maastricht fiscal criteria: recent values and prospects

	Fiscal indicator	*Trend from 2000–3*	*Ratio in 2004, % of GDP*	*Forecasts for next years*	*Outlook for EMU accession*
Czech Republic	Deficit	High and worsening	−3.0	Excessive deficit	Comfortable
	Debt	Low but growing	37.4	Stable	
Estonia	Deficit	In surplus	+1.8	Staying in surplus	Veryfavourable
	Debt	Negligible	4.9	Lower still	
Latvia	Deficit	Low and stable	−0.8	Slight worsening	Favourable
	Debt	Low and stable	14.4	Stable	
Lithuania	Deficit	Low and stable	−2.5	Steady	Comfortable
	Debt	Low and stable	19.7	Stable	Favourable
Hungary	Deficit	Persistently high	−4.5	Remaining 'excessive'	Needs to fall
	Debt	Approaching 60% limit	57.6	Stabilizing	Too close to limit
Poland	Deficit	Creeping over 4%	−4.8	Slight improvement	Needs to fall
	Debt	Rising beyond 40%	43.6	Slight increase	Acceptable now
Slovenia	Deficit	Shrinking	−1.9	Steady	Comfortable
	Debt	Stable	29.4	Stable	
Slovakia	Deficit	Falling	−3.3	Worsening	Becoming awkward
	Debt	Falling	43.6	Slight increase	

Source: Derived from Eurostat *Euro Indicators News Release* 39/2005, 18 March 2005; and European Commission Spring 2005 Macroeconomic Forecasts.

Note: The Maastricht criteria are 3 per cent of GDP for the deficit and 60 per cent for debt.

stimulus that may, in addition, be targeted at a narrow range of sectors (especially construction and training). Together, these flows will warrant quite substantial deficits on other components of the current account of the balance of payments. With high current account deficits already in many of the RAMs in recent years, the risks of imbalance could be intensifying. A related issue is whether there are currency mismatches. Thus, a crucial question will be how stable capital flows can be and whether a vulnerability to withdrawal of the more mobile forms of capital might exist. In particular, the switch – when it occurs – from inflation targeting to exchange rate stability in the two years of ERM membership will require careful handling.

The whole gamut of regulatory considerations as they affect the financial sector is also likely to be a potential source of concern as the sector itself evolves. An anticipated shift towards securities' markets, and the interplay between foreign ownership and the structure of balance sheets is one aspect, but so too is the growth of consumer credit. While, in most cases, the fundamentals (such as capital adequacy) of the banking sector in the RAMs look pretty sound, the possibility of an asset bubble and lack of experience in regulating securities markets – especially if inevitable problems trigger a wider crisis – could be a challenge if change occurs rapidly. A first question in this regard is whether institutional capacity is able to keep pace, while a second is whether financial liberalization needs to be tempered. Policy implications include improving the underpinnings of the financial system, such as the efficiency of the payment systems or the application of accounting standards, and ensuring that the regulatory machinery takes sufficient account of the need for stability. It is also clear that the relationship between the central bank and the supervisory authority is key.

It is far from obvious that retaining control of monetary policy at the national level (more so for very small open economies) aids stabilization, especially if time inconsistency considerations apply. Instead, the very fact of an external constraint can facilitate the pursuit of policies that have the better long-term pay-off. In the short term, though, pressures on governments to favour real over nominal convergence and thus to avoid policies that have an immediate cost will be strong. A first political economy challenge, therefore, is to flatten and shorten the dip in the j-curve by a careful mix of policies. Second, the RAMs need to learn from the founding members of the euro area that stage 3 adjustment matters and to prepare accordingly. Third, living with EMU means that endogenous change has to take place, and that it is not enough to meet the nominal criteria. Especially where the risks of financial stability are most pronounced, some caution may be warranted about rapid euro area accession, though for many the reverse may be true, namely that euro membership will provide an effective safeguard against financial crises.

Overall, a reasonably sanguine view can be taken of the prospects for the RAMs to move successfully to full participation in EMU without compromising real convergence or risking financial instability.

Notes

1 Because of their different background and economic characteristics, this chapter does not discuss Cyprus and Malta, which acceded to the EU at the same time.
2 Not an easy concept to define, other perhaps than as an absence of financial crisis (discussion with Charles Goodhart).
3 Conventionally used to assess the sequence of effects of a currency realignment.
4 Decision-making in the ECB Governing Council will evolve to become a rotation system, and it may be that explicit voting, rather than the present approach of consensus, will be implemented, but it is doubtful whether this would actually alter the decisions taken.

5 Plainly, this is back-of-the-envelope arithmetic and the actual judgement would be a more refined calculation, but it is nevertheless pretty telling.
6 Eichengreen also notes that the loss of output in Argentina and Indonesia exceeded that in the US during the Great Depression, triggering massive economic and social changes. As he puts it, 'the social impact of financial crises can be enormous' (Eichengreen 2004: 10).
7 Heid *et al.* (2004) show that the response of German banks to the 1998 Russian crisis was to scale back their lending to emerging markets. In contrast, during the Asian crises, banks re-weighted their portfolios toward the emerging markets with the better macroeconomic prospects, without altering their overall lending. Heid *et al.* (2004: 15) also warn that 'banks should also be aware of the fact that a country's creditworthiness can deteriorate very fast when investors suddenly change their perceptions towards emerging markets altogether in the face of problems in one of the emerging market countries'.
8 Some of the strains that have since arisen in fiscal discipline can probably be traced to this fudging of the criteria.
9 Because the benchmark is the three best, rather than the euro area HICP (Harmonised Index of Consumer Prices) inflation rate, it is almost inevitable that the RAMs will have to achieve a rate below the euro area average, especially if larger members have higher rates. It could, thus, be a demanding test. Indeed, the decision to exclude Lithuania in 2006 at the same time as Slovenia was approved relied on an average of the three best that included two non-euro area members. Had the euro area rate been applied, Lithuania would have fulfilled the convergence criteria.
10 The calculation is multiplicative rather additive.
11 Though less so for the smaller, open economies.
12 Data from the Magyar Nemzeti Bank, *Monetary Balance Sheet Statistics*, available at http://english.mnb.hu/engine.aspx?page=mnben_statisztikai_idosorok.

References

Aglietta, M., C. Baulant and S. Moatti (2003) 'Les PECOs devant la tentation de l'euro', *Economie Internationale* 93: 11–36.

Baldwin, R., R. Forslid, P. Martin, G. Ottaviano and F. Robert-Nicoud (2003) *Economic Geography and Public Policy*, Princeton: Princeton University Press.

Barro, R. and X. Sala-i-Martin (1992) 'Convergence', *Journal of Political Economy* 100: 223–51.

Bayoumi, T. and B. Eichengreen (1997) 'Ever close to heaven? An optimum-currency-area index for European countries', *European Economic Review* 41: 761–70.

Borghijs, A. and L. Kuijs (2004) 'Exchange rates in central Europe: a blessing or a curse', IMF Working Paper No. WP/04/2, Washington, DC: IMF.

Brada, J.C., A.M. Kutan and S. Zhou (2005) 'Real and monetary convergence between the European Union's core and recent member countries: a rolling cointegration approach', *Journal of Banking and Finance* 29: 249–70.

Brouwer, H., R. de Haas and B. Kiviet (2003) 'Banking sector development and financial stability in the run up to EU accession', in J.J. Teunissen and M. Teunissen (eds) *Financial Stability and Growth in Emerging Economies: The Role of the Financial Sector*, The Hague: FONDAD.

Bulíř, A. and K. Šmídková (2005) 'Exchange rates in the new EU accession countries: what have we learned from the forerunners?', IMF Working Paper No. 05/27, Washington, DC: IMF.

Bundesbank (2003) 'Financial markets in central and East European countries before accession to the EU', *Deutsche Bundesbank Monthly Report*, July: 39–55.

Caselli, F. and S. Tenreyro (2005) 'Is Poland the next Spain', NBER Working Paper No. 11045.

Cihak, M. and T. Holub (2003) 'Price convergence to the EU: what do the 1999 ICP data tell us?', Czech National Bank Working Paper No. 2/2003.

Cottarelli, C., G. Dell'Ariccia and I. Vladkova-Hollar (2005) 'Early birds, late risers and sleeping beauties: bank credit growth to the private sector in Central and Eastern Europe and in the Balkans', *Journal of Banking and Finance* 29: 83–104.

De Grauwe, P. and F.P. Mongelli (2005) 'Endogeneities of optimum currency areas: what brings countries sharing a common currency closer together?', European Central Bank Working Paper No. 468.

Detken, C., V. Gaspar and G. Noblet (eds) (2005) *The New EU Member States: Convergence and Stability*, Frankfurt: European Central Bank.

ECB (2004) *Convergence Report*, available at: www.ecb.int/pub/pdf/conrep/cr2004en.pdf.

—— (2005a) 'Managing financial crises in emerging market economies: experience with the involvement of private sector creditors', Occasional Paper No. 32, Frankfurt: European Central Bank.

—— (2005b) *Banking Structures in the New Member States*, available at: www.ecb.int/pub/pdf/other/bankingstructuresnewmemberstatesen.pdf.

Eichengreen, B. (2004) *Financial Instability*, paper prepared for the Copenhagen Consensus meeting, 25–28 May 2004.

Eichengreen, B., R. Hausmann and U. Panizza (2003) 'Currency mismatches, debt intolerance and original sin: why they are not the same and why it matters', NBER Working Paper No. 10036.

Fidrmuc, J. and I. Korhonen (2004) 'The Euro goes east: implications of the 2000–2002 economic slowdown for the synchronization of business cycles between the euro area and CEEs', *Comparative Economic Studies* 46: 45–62.

Frenkel, M. and C. Nickel (2002) 'How symmetric are the shocks and the shock adjustment dynamics between the euro area and central and Eastern European countries?', IMF Working Paper No. WP/02/222, Washington, DC: IMF.

Fries, S. and A. Taci (2005) 'Cost efficiency of banks in transition: evidence from 289 banks in 15 post-communist countries', *Journal of Banking and Finance* 29: 55–81.

Golinelli, R. and R. Ravelli (2005) 'Monetary policy transmission, interest rate rules and inflation targeting in three transition countries', *Journal of Banking and Finance* 29: 183–201.

Hallett, M. (2004) 'Fiscal effects of accession in the new Member States' years', European Economy Economic Paper No. 203.

Heid, F., T. Nestmann, B. Weder di Mauro and N. von Westernhagen (2004) 'German bank lending during emerging market crises: a bank level analysis', Deutsche Bundesbank Discussion Paper Series 2: Banking and Financial Supervision No. 04/2004.

Issing, O. (2003) 'Monetary and financial stability: is there a trade-off?', BIS Papers No. 18 – *Monetary Stability, Financial Stability and the Business Cycle: Five Views*.

—— (2005) 'Introduction to the policy panel: EU enlargement and monetary integration', in C. Detken, V. Gaspar and G. Noblet (eds) *The New EU Member States: Convergence and Stability*, Frankfurt: European Central Bank, pp. 191–8.

Jiménez, G. and J. Saurina (2005) 'Credit cycles, credit risk, and prudential regulation', paper presented at the Österreichische Nationalbank, Banking and Financial Stability: A Workshop on Applied Banking Research, Vienna, April 2005.

Jonung, L. and T. Hagberg (2005) 'How costly was the crisis of the 1990s? A comparative analysis of the deepest crises in Finland and Sweden over the last 130 years', European Economy Economic Paper No. 224.

Kok, W. (2004) *Facing the Challenge: The Lisbon Strategy for Growth and Employment*, Report from the High Level Group chaired by Wim Kok, November 2004, available at: http://europa.eu.int/comm/lisbon_strategy/pdf/2004–1866-EN-complet.pdf.

Korhonen, I. and J. Fidrmuc (2001) 'Similarity of supply and demand shocks between the euro area and the accession countries', Austrian National Bank *Focus on Transition*, No. 2, pp. 26–42.

Neary, P. (2001) 'Of hype and hyperbolas: introducing the new economic geography', *Journal of Economic Literature* 49: 536–61.

Orlowski, L.T. (2005) 'Monetary convergence of the EU accession countries to the eurozone: a theoretical framework and policy implications', *Journal of Banking and Finance* 29: 203–25.

Rose, A.K. (2004) 'A meta-analysis of the effect of common currencies on international trade', NBER Working Paper No. 10373.

Rostowski, J. (2003) 'When should the central Europeans join EMU?', *International Affairs* 79: 993–1008.

Sapir, A., P. Aghion, G. Bertola, M. Hellwig, J. Pisani-Ferry, D. Rosati, J. Viñals, H. Wallace, M. Buti, M. Nava and P.M. Smith (2004) *An Agenda for a Growing Europe*, Oxford: Oxford University Press.

Schadler, S., P. Drummond, L. Kuijs, Z. Murgasova and R. van Elkan (2005) 'Adopting the euro in central Europe: challenges of the next step in European integration', IMF Occasional Paper No. 234, Washington, DC: IMF.

Tùma, Z. (2004) 'Euro adoption, acceding countries and financial stability', introductory speech to the conference on Euro Adoption in the Accession Countries: Opportunities and Challenges, Prague, 2 February 2004.

von Hagen, J. and I. Traistaru (2005) 'Macroeconomic adjustment in the new Member States', in Detken, C., Gaspar, V. and Noblet, G. (eds) *The New EU Member States: Convergence and Stability*, Frankfurt: European Central Bank, pp. 122–70.

Wyplosz, C. (1997) 'EMU: why and how it might happen', *Journal of Economic Perspectives* 11(4): 3–22.

4 Adjusting to the euro

Gabriel Fagan and Vítor Gaspar

Introduction[1]

Participation in a monetary union entails manifold and complex consequences. The issue is of particular importance in Europe, where fifteen EU Member States have already adopted the euro as their single currency.[2] Even disregarding the important fact that economic and political integration are co-determined and co-evolutionary, participation in the euro area affects trade and financial integration, business cycle synchronization and the patterns of specialization. It also affects institutions, and the structure and behaviour of product and labour markets (see Mongelli and Vega 2006 and references therein for comprehensive surveys of the relevant issues and available evidence). Moreover, macroeconomic adjustment to the prospect of participation in the euro area is a topical issue for the new Member States which joined the European Union in 2004.[3]

In this chapter, we will argue that for countries like Greece, Spain, Ireland, Italy and Portugal (which we will refer to as converging countries) an important aspect of the process of adjustment to participation in the euro area is associated with easier access to finance for domestic economic agents. The most evident aspect of such a process is the convergence of short- and long-term interest rates to the relatively low levels prevailing in Germany and other low interest rate European countries. Nevertheless, it is clear that, from the viewpoint of converging countries, participation in the euro area entails easier access to international financial markets and is also associated with the broader processes of financial liberalization and financial integration. In our view, the focus on the financial dimension of participation in the euro area can be justified by two considerations. First, compared with other effects from euro area participation interest rate convergence and financial integration are easy to document on the basis of available statistical information and happened relatively fast. Second, from a macroeconomic point of view, the effects are likely to be large and significant. As we document below, economic trends in the converging countries were significantly different from those registered in countries like Germany or countries more closely integrated with Germany like Belgium, the Netherlands, Finland, France, Luxembourg and Austria. In particular, we find that the convergence of interest rates has been associated with a boom in household expenditures accompanied by a sizeable build-up in household debt. This higher expenditure appears not to have had marked effects on output but instead to have been reflected in a deterioration in the current account balance and in the net foreign asset position and to have been accompanied by a notable appreciation of these countries' intra-euro area real exchange rates. In an earlier paper (Fagan and Gaspar 2005), we examined the effects of a permanent fall in interest rates in the context of a dynamic general equilibrium model of a small open economy, with traded and non-traded sectors and a number of frictions, such as adjustment costs for investment and sticky prices. Again, the results indicated a notable deterioration in the current account balance following the initial impulse. The response of output to the shock was found to be slow and gradual while the dynamics of the current account and prices were dominated by the pattern of consumption.

Blanchard and Giavazzi (2002) explore the implications of entry into the euro area for countries such as Portugal and Greece via financial and goods market integration. For this purpose, they use a two-period, two-country model. They modelled financial integration into the euro area as a decline in the exogenous risk premium in domestic interest rates, in the high interest rate country. Their main finding is that the fall in interest rates is associated with an increase in the current account deficit in borrowing countries, and with a wider cross-country dispersion of current account balances. While the framework provides powerful insights, a problem with the two-period setup is that it provides no information on the crucial aspect of the dynamics of the adjustment path, e.g. the persistence of current account deficits and the duration of convergence towards steady state equilibrium.

Against this background, we argue that standard intertemporal macroeconomic frameworks, even abstracting from the production side of the economy, can go a long way in explaining the key features of this adjustment process. Specifically, we consider the combination of a simple endowment economy model, with a household sector, modelled along the lines of Blanchard (1985) and Yaari (1965). Such a model is uniquely suited to illustrate the importance of intertemporal expenditure effects which we believe are crucial for the case at hand. We consider the case with two goods (traded and non-traded). We will argue that such simple variants are already capable of capturing most salient, qualitative features of adjustment, present in much more complicated intertemporal models. Specifically, in the two goods endowment economy, the fall in the opportunity cost of external financing leads to an initial increase in expenditure followed by slow adjustment to the new lower steady state as foreign debt accumulates. In our model, the real exchange rate (defined as the relative price of non-tradable goods) follows exactly the path of aggregate expenditure. In other words, it increases initially (there is real appreciation) followed by a gradual decline to a level lower than in the initial steady state.

The analysis we perform for the endowment economy with non-traded goods is in the spirit of Obstfeld and Rogoff (2005). They also use an endowment economy framework, with traded and non-traded goods to discuss the real exchange rate implications of changing expenditure patterns. They focus on the implications of relocating expenditure in the global economy. From changing geographical patterns of expenditure implications for real exchange rates follow. In this chapter, we focus instead on the implications for real exchange rates from different intertemporal patterns of expenditure, endogenously generated by changes in a country's access to external financing. In our analysis, we focus on the case of the small open economy which enters a monetary union. The economy faces an exogenously given traded-goods price (which for convenience we will keep constant) and an interest rate which is determined by the 'world' (or, more specifically, area-wide) interest rate plus an exogenous risk premium. The shock resulting from financial integration into the monetary union is modelled – following Blanchard and Giavazzi – as a reduction in this exogenous risk premium.

The basic version of the model which we employ has the undesirable feature that, following the shock of entry into the monetary union, consumption jumps immediately and by a substantial magnitude before slowly converging to its new steady state. This property is at odds with the rather gradual pattern of adjustment which can be seen in the data. The pattern observed in the data might be explained in a number of ways. First, expectations regarding the creation of the monetary union and the participation of particular countries evolved during the course of the 1990s in response to political and economic developments. Hence, modelling EMU entry as a sharp one-off event as is done in this chapter is a simplification. Second, for the countries we are examining, EMU represented a new regime, so that agents may have required time to learn about the new environment, a phenomenon which would be expected to lead to a gradual adjustment on the part of agents. Third, agents' expenditures may in any case be subject to an inherent sluggishness, reflecting various types of adjustment costs or habit persistence.

In order to obtain a realistic pattern of adjustment in a convenient and tractable way we extend the basic model by incorporating habit formation into the consumer's optimization problem. Here we take a variant of the simplest version of habit formation from Abel (1990), Campbell and Cochrane (1999) and Carroll, Overland and Weil (2000). In our setup, habits are 'external' or of the 'keeping up with the Joneses' variety, and depend on average consumption in the economy as a whole. It is documented in the literature that habit formation not only helps to explain the persistence in consumption but also contributes to sorting out a number of important empirical finance puzzles. Moreover, available empirical evidence (for example Gruber 2004) suggests that the addition of habit formation leads to a significant improvement in the empirical performance of intertemporal current account models such as the one employed in this chapter. While, following the pioneering work of Mansoorian (1993), the inclusion of habit formation in infinitely lived agent models is straightforward and widely used, its incorporation into a Blanchard–Yaari setup involves a number of additional complexities and is rarely employed in the literature. Examples are Obstfeld (1992) and Velculescu (2006), who incorporate habit formation into one-sector open economy models. The introduction of habit formation into our model changes the results in two important ways: first, and as expected, we obtain a gradual build-up of aggregate expenditure in the short to medium term; second, and more surprisingly, we derive smaller effects in steady state. The latter effect is also very helpful as the steady state predictions from the simpler formulation look implausibly large.

The chapter is organized as follows. In the next section, we review some stylized facts in order to motivate our analysis. Then, we present our model, after which we present numerical simulations for the case with traded and non-traded goods, contrasting results with and without habit formation. Concluding comments complete the chapter.

Some stylized facts

The creation of the monetary union in Europe in 1999 was preceded by a process of nominal convergence among the participating countries. In 1996, for example, nominal long-term interest rates ranged from a high of 14.5 per cent in Greece to 4.5 per cent in Germany. Today spreads between the highest and lowest Government bond yields are of the order of 30 basis points. Similarly, the highest–lowest spread in short-term interest rates amounted to 10.5 percentage points in 1996. Currently, this spread is effectively zero. Of course, a significant component of the convergence in nominal interest rates across countries reflected a convergence of expected inflation across countries. However, the evidence shows that real interest rates were also significantly affected. While reliable measures of real long-term rates at the country level are not available for this period, the evidence from measures of real short-term interest rates (nominal rates minus actual inflation) points to a significant convergence in the period leading to monetary union, although much less marked than in the case of nominal rates. In 1996, for example, real short-term rates in excess of 4 per cent were common in a number of current EMU member countries, while for other so-called core countries (or, in our preferred wording, reference countries) real short-term interest rates between 1 and 2 per cent were the order of the day. After the start of the single monetary policy real interest rate differentials reflected differences in inflation among participating Member States.

This evidence thus suggests those countries which experienced a decline in their interest rates as a result of the move to EMU experienced a significant and permanent reduction in the financing costs available to their domestic economic agents. This process happened rather quickly and also appears to have contained a large unanticipated element. For example, according to various EMU calculators, the probability that some of these countries would enter EMU in 1999 was judged by markets to be significantly below 50 per cent as late as 1996 (see, for example, Favero *et al.* 2000; Bates 1999).

What were the economic effects of the decline in interest rates on the countries concerned? A full country-by-country account would need to reflect, in a comprehensive way, the various shocks and country-specificities affecting the different economies over this period in order to disentangle the separate contribution of interest rate convergence from other shocks. One possible approach would be to carry out counterfactual simulations using macromodels of individual countries. A problem with this approach is that the results are heavily dependent on the model specification employed (Berben *et al.* 2004). An alternative approach would be to attempt to use country-specific VARs to identify the impact of the interest rate shock. However, this approach too has a number of limitations. VAR results are often sensitive to the chosen identification scheme and, moreover, it is not clear that it would be possible to identify shocks of the kind we are interested in – permanent changes in financing costs – using VAR methodologies. Moreover, given the unique nature of the EMU experiment, it is not at all clear that empirical estimates based on average behaviour over past data would give an accurate picture of the impacts involved.

In the light of these difficulties, we follow an alternative approach. Specifically, we rely on a more informal event study method which aims at identifying some broad stylized facts regarding the impact of interest rate convergence. We start by separating the euro area countries into two groups on the basis of the relative nominal and real interest rates prevailing in the mid-1990s. The first group comprises low interest rate countries: Germany, Belgium, France, the Netherlands and Austria.[4] In common with the usual parlance, we henceforth denote this group as core countries. The second group comprises countries which, initially, had relatively high interest rates: Spain, Ireland, Italy and Portugal.[5] We call this group the converging countries. We do not include Greece in this latter group since it entered the euro area only in 2001, some two years later than the other countries.[6] With a view to identifying pertinent general features of the data, and as far as possible reducing the effects of country-specific noise, we calculate, for each economic variable, a pair of time series based on arithmetic (equally weighted) averages within the groups. Then, with a view to controlling for the possible effects of common shocks across all countries, we compare the differences across these averaged country groups. Thus, the analysis will be based on the analysis of cross-group differences in the behaviour of the variables of interest. Clearly, both the cross-sectional and time dimensions of the data are too limited to allow for robust statistical analysis. While the approach helps to identify common features within the two groups of countries, there still remains a considerable heterogeneity of country experience, reflecting the fact that – as well as interest rate convergence – the countries were also subject to a range of country-specific shocks during the period. Some of the key stylized facts we identify in this chapter do not apply to the same extent in each country within the converging group. In this sense, the facts we identify have to be viewed as highly stylized, and representative of the group as a whole rather than necessarily applying to each individual country in each case. Nonetheless, we believe that taking this perspective on the data does yield some useful and novel insights into the effects of the interest rate convergence process. Details of the data sources are presented in Appendix 1.

On the basis of the information derived from these calculations, the following features of the data are highlighted as key stylized facts:

First, and unsurprisingly, there was clearly a convergence of nominal and real interest rates. Charts 1 and 2 show, respectively, the evolution of nominal short-term and long-term interest rates in the two country groups. Convergence is evident. As regards real interest rates, there are no reliable measures of long-term real interest rates for the countries concerned. We can, however, easily calculate real ex-post short-term interest rates. The relevant data is shown in Chart 3. Strong convergence in real rates across the two country groups occurred up to 1999 with the average differential close to zero compared to around

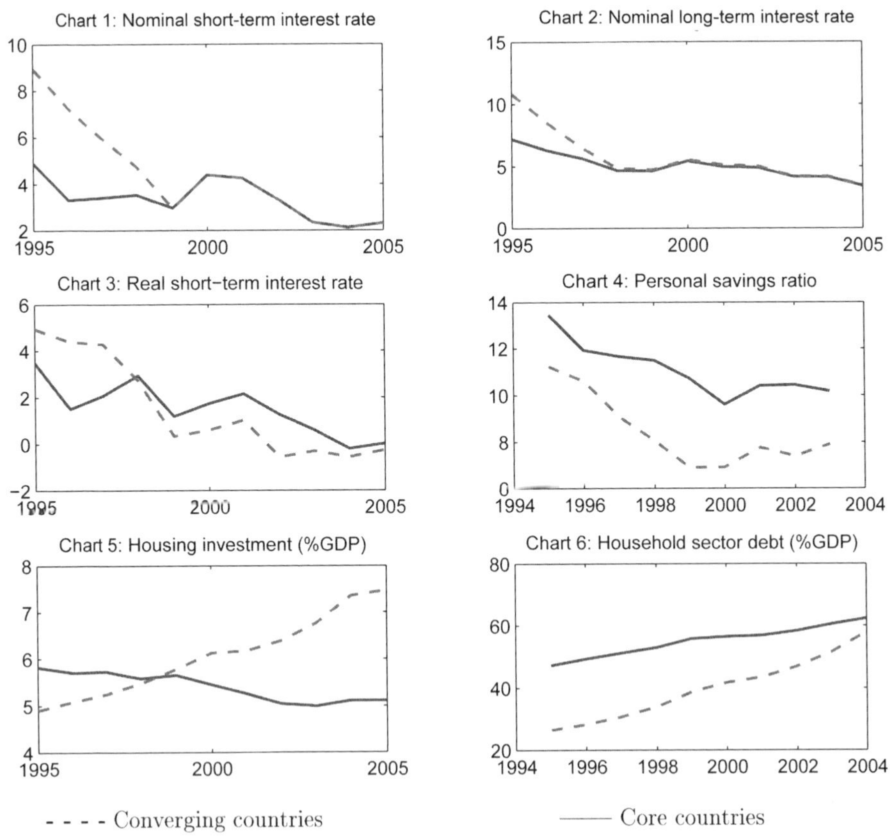

Charts 1 to 6

Note: The charts display averages for each variable and country group. 'Core countries' includes Austria, Belgium, France, Germany and the Netherlands. 'Converging countries' includes Ireland, Italy, Portugal and Spain.

290 basis points in 1996. With nominal short rates identical across countries following the move to monetary union, subsequent real interest rate differentials reflected inflation differentials. As a consequence, real interest rates in the converging countries fell below those in the core, and, from 2002 on, turned negative (see ECB 2003 for a further analysis of this phenomenon). In the analytical exercises carried out below the fall in interest rates will be the impulse triggering the subsequent adjustment of the economy.

We may summarize these remarks as our first stylized fact:

1 As part of the process of adjustment to participation in the euro area, a number of converging economies benefited from significantly lower nominal and real interest rates, with the former converging to those of the other participants in the euro area.

Second, a notable feature of the data is the marked difference across country groups in the behaviour of household expenditures (consumption plus housing investment). The converging countries experienced a boom in household expenditures. This was reflected in a more rapid decline in the household savings ratio (Chart 4) in the converging group. Housing investment (Chart 5) also boomed, rising as a share of GDP by 4 percentage points. In contrast, as a percentage of GDP, housing investment fell somewhat over this period in the reference countries.

2 Household expenditures increased significantly, leading to a fall in households' savings ratio.

Third, related to the previous point, there was a sharp rise in household indebtedness in the converging countries (Chart 6). Between 1995 and 2004, the ratio of household debt to GDP doubled, whereas in the reference group the increase was much more muted. It is interesting to note that initially, the level of debt to GDP in the converging countries was well below the level in the reference group. The resulting difference in credit growth thus led to a convergence in debt levels over the period (see ECB 2005a for further analysis).

3 Credit to households grew strongly, leading to a sharp increase in households' debt, converging to the levels prevailing in the reference countries.

Non-housing investment also rose in converging countries although its increase was less marked than in the case of housing investment. Up to 2000, non-housing investment rose in both country groups, driven mainly by cyclical factors, with the rise being more rapid in the converging group. Thereafter, this form of investment declined as a share of GDP at a broadly comparable rate in both groups (Chart 7).

4 Non-housing investment also rose in the converging countries relative to the core group, albeit less notably than housing investment.

Turning to output, over the whole period, GDP growth was around one percentage point higher in the converging countries. Surprisingly, growth differentials tended to narrow (see Chart 8) to levels which were low by historical standards. This conclusion is confirmed by the comprehensive review of developments in output growth across euro area countries contained in Benalal, del Hoyo, Pierluigi and Vidalis (2006).

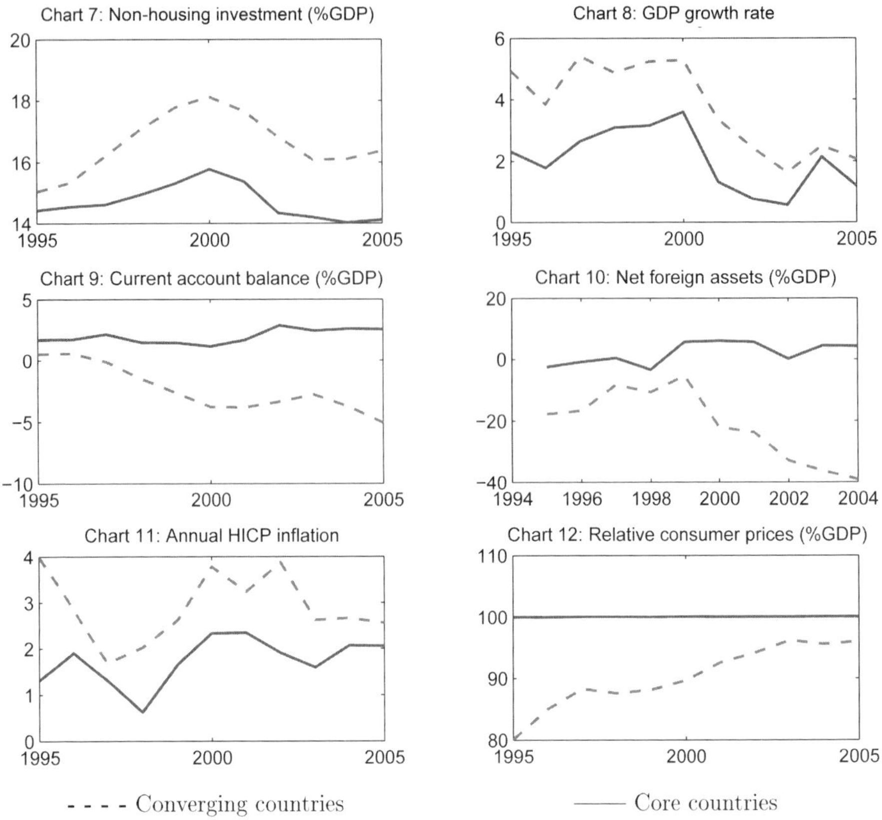

Charts 7 to 12
Note: The charts display averages for each variable and country group. 'Core countries' includes Austria, Belgium, France, Germany and the Netherlands. 'Converging countries' includes Ireland, Italy, Portugal and Spain.

5 Perhaps surprisingly, pronounced changes in GDP growth differentials are not a prominent feature of the data.

With relative output growth stable or declining and domestic demand rising vigorously in relative terms, there were notable differences in the behaviour of the current account balances and the evolution of net foreign assets across the two groups of countries (Charts 9 and 10). Over the whole period, the average current account balance was basically stable at a level of around 2 per cent of GDP in the reference countries. In sharp contrast, the current account balance in the converging countries declined steadily through the period, ending the period with a deficit of around 5 per cent of GDP. The increased dispersion of current account balances across the euro area, and the associated weakening of standard Feldstein–Horioka correlations, has been highlighted by Blanchard and Giavazzi (2002) as one of the key macroeconomic effects of the increased financial integration resulting from the creation of the euro.

This pattern in current account balances is also reflected in the evolution of net foreign assets. According to data presented in Lane and Milesi-Ferreti (2006) the ratio of net foreign assets to GDP in the reference countries increased slightly over the period 1995–2004. In contrast, in the converging countries, reflecting cumulated current account deficits, the net foreign asset ratio declined by over 30 GDP percentage points (see Chart 9).

6 Converging countries' current accounts turned into a large deficit position implying the accumulation of a substantial negative net foreign asset position during the period.

A striking feature of the data is the sharp and continuing appreciation of the real exchange rate of the converging countries vis-à-vis the core group. Our measure of the real exchange rate is based on Eurostat comparative consumer price indices shown in Chart 12. This shows relative consumer prices in the converging versus the core group. This is based on Eurostat data on comparative price levels. On this measure, the real exchange rate in 2005 was 20 per cent higher than its level in 1995. By definition, this appreciation reflected a persistent inflation differential between the two country groups (Chart 11). Inflation differentials in the euro area have been the subject of extensive study by both researchers and official organizations. The existing literature suggests that a number of factors are at play, including country-specific shocks, the effects of integration of goods markets resulting in price convergence, Balassa–Samuelson effects, cyclical divergences, inflation persistence and structural differences across economies which result in differential responses to external shocks (see ECB 2003 for a review of the various factors). However, the available evidence also suggests that interest rate convergence has played a prominent role (ECB 2005b).

7 Converging countries recorded sharp real appreciation.

Before summarizing our findings, it is useful to look in more detail at one of the most striking features, and one which will play a central role in the analysis below, namely the relative behaviour of the current account balances and particularly the sharp deterioration in the current account of the converging countries. A useful way of looking at this question is to examine the sectoral balances which constitute the counterparts of the current account. The standard national accounts identity which links the current account to savings and investment,

$$CA = S - I$$

may be further decomposed into

$$CA = (T - G) + (S_H - I_H) + (S_C - I_C)$$

This tells us that the current account surplus may be accounted for by three counterparts. The first is net lending by the government ($G - T$), or, in more usual parlance, the fiscal deficit. The second element is net lending by the household sector ($S_H - I_H$), which is the difference between gross savings by households and their investment expenditures (mainly on housing). The remaining component – which we calculate as a residual – is net lending by firms, defined in an analogous manner.

Chart 13 provides data on this decomposition for our two country groups. A first striking feature is that there was little difference across the country groups in the average fiscal balances which follow paths which are close to each other over the whole period under review. The different paths of the current balance are thus entirely reflected in differences

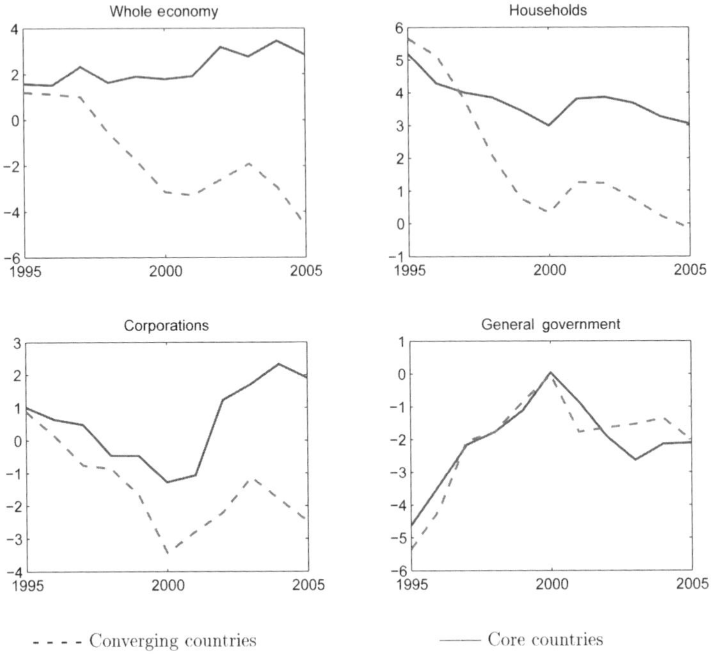

Chart 13 Net lending by sector (percent of GDP).

Note: The charts display averages for each variable and country group. 'Core countries' includes Austria, Belgium, France, Germany and the Netherlands. 'Converging countries' includes Ireland, Italy, Portugal and Spain.

in net lending of the private sector (both households and firms), with each component contributing to the relative deterioration of the current account in the converging countries.

At this stage, we summarize the main findings as follows. The process of interest rate convergence was accompanied by a boom in final expenditures of households (reflecting both standard consumption expenditure and housing investment) in the converging countries. This was accompanied by a sharp rise in the household debt ratio. Non-housing investment also increased in relative terms but the differences across country groups were not as sizeable. In contrast, fiscal balances were remarkably similar across the two groups of countries. Overall output growth differentials, however, did not increase. The boom in domestic expenditure fuelled by credit growth triggered a deterioration in the current account balance and a build-up of foreign debt. In addition, the converging countries experienced a sizeable real appreciation vis-à-vis the core group. Our evidence thus confirms the analysis of Lane, who points out that the convergence of interest rates 'generated rapid growth in lending and local housing booms in the favoured countries, with the sharp increase in demand contributing to inflationary pressures' (Lane 2006: 3).

Is it possible to explain these facts using an analytical, intertemporal general equilibrium model? Given that changes in overall economic activity do not appear to have been a dominant element in the adjustment to lower interest rates in the converging countries, we believe it is worthwhile to look at simple endowment economy models. Hence, the question we will try to answer in the remainder of the chapter is: given improved access to financing in converging countries reflected in lower interest rates facing agents, is it possible to use an intertemporal, endowment economy model to explain facts 2, 3, 6 and 7 (as stated above)? We will find that the answer is a qualified yes.

Blanchard–Yaari households in an endowment economy with habit formation

Demographics and insurance markets

Overlapping generations models are used to study aggregate implications from intertemporal optimization on the part of households. The most tractable model available in the literature is due to Blanchard (1985) and Yaari (1965). We will start this section following Blanchard (1985) and Blanchard and Fisher (1989) quite closely. In the model time is treated as a continuous variable. This assumption is made for analytical convenience only.[7] The model is based on two fundamental sets of assumptions. The first characterizes demographics. We assume a constant probability of death, independent of age, and denote it by ρ. Agents thus have the same life expectancy, regardless of their age. Due to this assumption the model is often referred to as a model of perpetual youth. It is convenient to work under the further assumption that population is constant over time. Thus, we assume that, each period, a new (large) cohort of people are born and that the size of such cohort is constant over time (and has always been so). If we, as a simplifying assumption, normalize the size of each cohort at birth to be ρ, it follows that the size of total population is normalized to one (which is convenient). In general, working out aggregate implications from intertemporal optimization on the part of households is very difficult in overlapping generations models. The reason is that households of different ages will differ not only in their accumulated wealth but also (given differences in life expectancy) in their propensity to consume out of wealth. Perpetual youth simplifies matters by doing away with the second complication, thus allowing for relatively simple aggregation across households. Moreover, the explicit allowance of births affects patterns of expenditure over time in interesting ways. The second fundamental set of assumptions relates to the availability of a perfectly competitive insurance annuities market. Given the demographic assumptions made, there is individual risk concerning the timing of death but no aggregate risk. Therefore, there is room for insurance. Specifically, the idea is that individuals will enter a contract with insurance companies stipulating that, in case of death, the insurance company will receive the individual's wealth. In exchange, the insurance company will pay the individual an amount equal to ρ times the amount of wealth in case of survival (competition ensures that such actuarially fair terms will be on offer).

We make two further simplifying assumptions. The first is that each period all agents, irrespective of age, receive an endowment, in the form of a constant flow of ω^T units of a traded good and ω^N units of a non-traded good. Both goods are non-storable. The traded good may be bought or sold on world markets at an exogenous world price, we, for convenience, set to unity. Agents may borrow from or lend at the interest rate r, which – given our open economy assumption – is exogenously given by the world interest rate plus an exogenous risk premium. In addition, as a further simplifying assumption, we postulate that preferences can be represented by a time-separable logarithmic utility function with θ denoting the intertemporal rate of time preference.

Let us start by writing down our demographic assumptions explicitly. Given the assumed constant mortality rate ρ the probability of dying at age t equals:

$$f(t) = \rho\, exp(-\rho t).$$

Given that $f(t)$ is the probability density function corresponding to dying at time t it is a standard matter to show that life expectancy is simply ρ^{-1}, which may be interpreted as the relevant economic horizon of economic agents. Given our assumption of mortality rates independent of age it is the case that this horizon is the same for all agents alive. For each individual household the timing of death is uncertain but we also assume that each age cohort has a sufficiently large number of individuals so that the law of large numbers exactly applies. In other words, in each period an exact ρ proportion of the population dies. It is this absence of aggregate risk that makes it possible to assume a perfectly competitive annuities market, offering actuarially fair terms to households.

In the remainder of this chapter, unless otherwise stated, we will use small caps to denote variables pertaining to individuals, while capital letters will be used for aggregate variables.

A representative household intertemporal problem

We are now ready to write down the problem of a representative household of cohort t. As in all standard applications of theory, households will maximize their expected utility. In our setting, with two goods, one traded good and one non-traded good, logarithmic preferences and habit formation, the household will maximize the present, expected discounted value of utility, which may be written as:

$$\max_{c_t^T, c_t^N} E_t \left[\int_t^\infty \log(c_s - \mu H_s) \exp(-\theta(s-t)) ds \right],$$

with c_s being given by a Cobb–Douglas composite of traded and non-traded goods:

$$c_s = \kappa (c_s^T)^\alpha (c_s^N)^{1-\alpha},$$

where t and s denote time, c_t^T and c_t^N denote, respectively, the consumption of traded and non-traded goods, H_s denotes the habit variable and θ is the subjective discount factor while κ is a parameter. Thus the instantaneous utility of the consumer depends not just on the level of consumption but rather on the level relative to some reference level, a 'normal' or habit consumption level (H_s). Since, in the model, the only uncertainty pertains to the timing of death, the objective of the household may be written more simply, using our demographic assumptions to calculate expected values, as:

$$\max_{c_t^T, c_t^N} \int_t^\infty \log(c_s - \mu H_s) \exp(-(\theta + \rho)(s-t)) ds.$$

Each household faces a budget constraint, which we may write in the form of accumulation of assets or, if negative, debts. Specifically:

$$\frac{df_t}{dt} = (r + \rho) f_t + p_t^T(\omega^T - c_t^T) + p_t^N(\omega^N - c_t^N).$$

The budget equation is intuitive. The individual household accumulates assets in accordance with the private rate of return on past assets, given by the sum of the interest rate with the compensation for the probability of death *plus* the sum of the value of endowment *minus* consumption expenditure. As we have indicated we will assume external habit formation so that the individual household takes the sequence of $[H_s]_{s=t}^{s=\infty}$ as given. In particular, in line with, for example, Carroll, Overland and Weil (2000), we assume that the stock of habit – which is common across consumers – evolves according to:

$$\dot{H}_t = \gamma(C_t - H_t),$$

where C_t is aggregate consumption. This equation implies that the reference habit level depends on a geometrically weighted average of current and past consumption in the economy, a form of 'keeping up with the Joneses'.

In what follows we will let p^T be the numeraire and set it to 1. Letting $z_t = p_t^T c_t^T + p_t^N c_t^N$ we can express the intratemporal first-order conditions for c^T and c^N as:

$$c_t^T = \alpha z_t$$

and

$$p_t^N c_t^N = (1 - \alpha) z_t$$

These expressions enable us to define a dual price index for aggregate consumption, p_t.[8] The budget constraint then becomes:

$$\frac{df_t}{dt} = (r + \rho) f_t + \omega^T + p_t^N \omega^N - p_t c_t.$$

Applying the maximum principle to solve the consumer's optimization problem, we obtain the following dynamic first-order conditions:

$$\frac{1}{c_t - \mu H_t} = \lambda_t p_t \qquad (1)$$

$$\dot{\lambda}_t = \lambda_t(\theta - r), \qquad (2)$$

where λ_t is the costate variable.

Letting $x_t = p_t c_t - \mu p_t H_t$ – a variable which may be described as nominal effective consumption – these first-order conditions together with the budget constraint and the transversality condition lead, after tedious but straightforward manipulation, to the individual household's consumption function:

$$x_t = (\theta + \rho)\left(f_t + \frac{\omega^T}{r + \rho} + \int_0^\infty y_s \exp(-(r + \rho)(s - t))ds \right)$$

where $y_t = p_t^N \omega^N - \mu p_t H_t$.

Aggregating across households we get:

$$X_t = (\theta + \rho)\left(F_t + \frac{\omega^T}{r+\rho} + \int_0^{\infty} Y_s \exp(-(r+\rho)(s-t))ds\right).$$

The corresponding equation of motion for the aggregate foreign asset position is:

$$\frac{dF_t}{dt} = rF_t + \omega^T + Y_t - X_t.$$

The dynamics of the aggregate economy

Aggregating the relations obtained in the previous subsection, and substantially working on the resulting equations, it is possible to obtain a system of equations describing the aggregate dynamics of the economy. The system consists of three differential equations and two additional definitional equations:

$$\dot{X}_t = (r - \theta)X_t - \rho(\theta + \rho)F_t \tag{3}$$

$$\dot{F}_t = rF_t + \omega^T - \alpha X_t - \alpha\mu p_t H_t \tag{4}$$

$$\dot{H}_t = \gamma(C_t - H_t) \tag{5}$$

$$X_t = p_t C_t - \mu p_t H_t \tag{6}$$

$$p_t = \phi^{\frac{1}{\alpha}} C_t^{\frac{1-\alpha}{\alpha}} \tag{7}$$

In deriving (4) we have made use of the market clearing condition for non-traded goods, $p_t^N \omega^N = p_t^N c_t^N = (1-\alpha)(X_t + \mu p_t H_t)$. (6) is a definition of aggregate nominal effective consumption. Equation (7) expresses the price index as a function of aggregate real consumption, with ϕ being a constant term which depends on ω^N, α and κ.[9]

Equations (3)–(7) may be reduced to a non-linear three-dimensional system of differential equations in $[Z_t, F_t, H_t]$, where Z_t is nominal consumption expenditure (i.e. $Z_t = p_t C_t$):

$$\dot{Z}_t = \frac{(\mu\gamma + r - \theta)Z_t - \mu\phi(\gamma + (r-\theta))Z_t^b H_t - \rho(\theta+\rho)F_t}{(1 - b\mu\phi Z_t^{b-1} H_t)} \tag{8}$$

$$\dot{F}_t = rF_t + \omega^T - \alpha Z_t \tag{9}$$

$$\dot{H} = \gamma\left(\frac{1}{\phi} Z_t^{1-b} - H_t\right) \tag{10}$$

where $b = 1 - \alpha$.

As far as we are aware, no analytical solution is available for this system so it will need to be solved numerically. Before doing so, however, it is useful to gain intuition about the functioning of the model by examining a number of simpler special cases. For these cases closed form analytical solutions can be derived, allowing for a detailed interpretation of the results. This we do in the next sections, starting with the simplest case: the single good case without habit formation.

Single good without habits

In this case we have $\mu = \gamma = \omega^N = 0$ and $\alpha = 1$. Under these assumptions, the system of differential equations (8), (9) and (10) can be reduced to:

$$\dot{C}_t = (r - \theta)C_t - \rho(\theta + \rho)F_t \tag{11}$$

and

$$\dot{F}_t = rF_t + \omega - C_t \tag{12}$$

This is the standard model discussed, at length, in Blanchard (1985) and Blanchard and Fisher (1989). (11) and (12) constitute two linear differential equations determining the dynamics of consumption and the net foreign asset position of the economy. The system is linear in C and F and $r < (\theta + \rho)$ is necessary in order for it to be saddle-path stable.[10] The dynamics of the system may be analysed by means of a standard phase diagram (Figure 4.1). In order to do so it is important to depict the locus, in the space (F_t, C_t), where $\dot{F}_t = 0$ and also the locus where $\dot{C}_t = 0$. It is possible to write those respectively as:

$$\dot{F}_t = 0 : C_t = \omega + rF_t \tag{13}$$

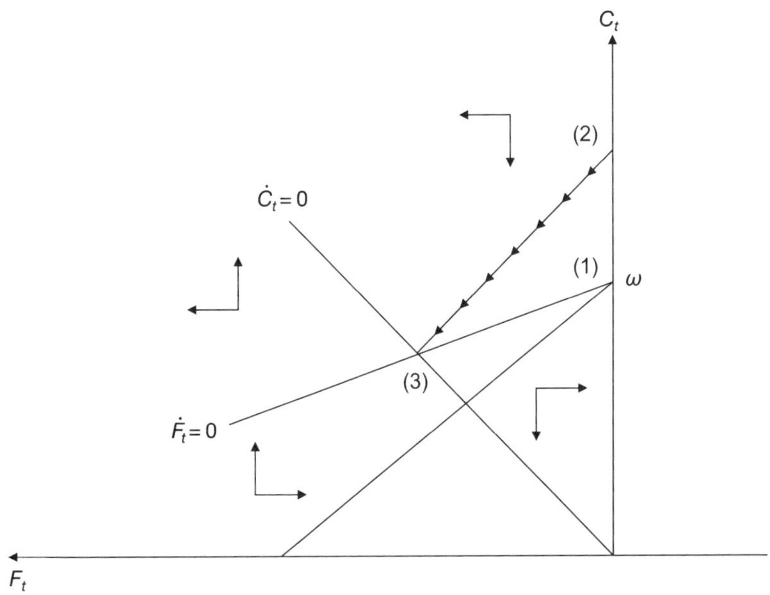

Figure 4.1 Dynamics of consumption and net foreign assets.

$$\dot{C}_t = 0 : C_t = \frac{\rho(\rho+\theta)}{r-\theta} F_t \tag{14}$$

We can solve (13) and (14) for the steady state values of the net foreign asset position and consumption as:

$$F = \frac{(r-\theta)}{(\theta+\rho-r)(r+\rho)}\omega \tag{15}$$

$$C = \frac{\rho(\theta+\rho)}{(\theta+\rho-r)(r+\rho)}\omega \tag{16}$$

Note that a positive level of consumption implies $r < \theta + \rho$, which is exactly the condition for saddle-path stability. In order to determine the impact of a permanent change in the interest rate on these two variables, we differentiate (15) and (16) with respect to r to obtain:

$$\frac{dF}{dr} = \frac{(r-\theta)^2 + (\rho+\theta)\rho}{[(\theta+\rho-r)(r+\rho)]^2}\omega > 0 \tag{17}$$

$$\frac{dC}{dr} = \frac{\rho(\rho+\theta)(2r-\theta)}{[(\theta+\rho-r)(r+\rho)]^2}\omega \tag{18}$$

Equation (17) shows that a fall in the interest rate will always lead to a decline in the steady state value of the net foreign asset position. The derivative in (18) will be positive provided $2r > \theta$, which will likely be the case in practice. Otherwise the implied rate of time preference would be such that the (negative) net foreign asset position would be enormous. Thus, in all relevant cases, a lower interest rate will lead to a decrease in steady state consumption.

We can illustrate the adjustment process in Figure 4.1. We start assuming that $r = \theta$ so that the initial value of the net foreign asset position is zero (as follows from (15)). The initial steady state position is labelled (1) in the figure. In the initial steady state it is clear that consumption is constant over time and equals the endowment (as may be verified from, for example, (16)).

When interest rates decline the locus, corresponding to an unchanging net foreign asset position, becomes more horizontal, turning around the point $C = \omega$. At the same time, the locus corresponding to unchanging consumption becomes visible in the figure as a negative sloped line in the left-hand side. Given the starting point it is clear that, in steady state, the net foreign asset position becomes negative (the country resorts to foreign debt) and consumption falls. However, on impact the net foreign asset position is predetermined while consumption is a jump variable. In our case consumption jumps immediately to the level $C = (\rho+\theta)/(\rho+r)\omega$ (see Figure 4.1, point 2). From such starting point consumption will monotonically decline and net foreign assets as well, until, eventually, the economy approaches the new steady state equilibrium (point 3 on Figure 4.1).

To repeat, the economy converges to a new steady state in which debt is higher than initially while consumption is lower. In short, what we see, in this simple example, is a form of consumption boom, as consumption significantly increases initially. Subsequently, it gradually declines until it reaches a steady state level lower than its initial level. It is important to note that the dynamics of adjustment is very slow. Specifically, the speed of adjustment is ruled by $r - \rho - \theta$, which is a very small number. For example if we were to consider a one percentage point drop in the cost of international financing (starting from $r = \theta$) and a life expectancy of fifty years, the half life of adjustment to the steady state would last for over twenty years. In our simple endowment economy, the pattern stems entirely from the dynamics of consumption and debt accumulation and by construction does not involve capital accumulation or capital adjustment costs.

It is warranted to stress that such a very simple model is apt to reproduce qualitatively many of the stylized facts described earlier. Expenditure does increase initially, savings decline and a persistent current account emerges, leading to a significant decline in the net foreign asset position. Therefore, the single good endowment model without habit formation already captures the essence of the intertemporal adjustment mechanism. The main limitations of the story have to do with the sudden initial jump in consumption and the extremely large predicted changes in the steady state net foreign asset position. Such enormous external debts have never been observed historically. In the next section we will see how habit formation helps along both these dimensions. In addition, since the model relates by construction to a single good economy, it has nothing to say about the real exchange rate, an important feature of the adjustment in the data, as was shown above.

Single good with habits

Now, for the purposes of exposition, let us introduce external habit formation into the economy while retaining the single good assumption. This is achieved by setting $0 < \mu < 1$ and $\gamma > 0$ while keeping $\alpha = 1$ and $\omega^N = 0$. The introduction of external habit formation changes significantly the dynamics of the economy. Specifically, the system of two equations (11) and (12) on p. 69 is replaced by the following system of three equations:

$$\dot{C}_t = (r + \mu\gamma - \theta)C_t + \mu(\theta - r - \gamma)H_t - \rho(\rho + \theta)F_t \tag{19}$$

$$\dot{F}_t = rF_t + \omega - C_t \tag{20}$$

$$\dot{H}_t = \gamma(C_t - H_t) \tag{21}$$

It is important to note that the equation describing the evolution of the net foreign asset position (20) is exactly as before (12). The main difference is given by the equation of motion for consumption. The implication is going to be a more gradual build-up of consumption, in response to the reduction in interest rates. More surprisingly, the introduction of habit formation leads to a reduction in the magnitude of the steady state impacts on consumption and the net foreign asset position. The intuition is discussed below. Both of these features of the model with habits help to better mimic the stylized facts reported earlier.

As before, in order to solve for steady state values we impose that $\dot{X}_t = 0$ for all state variables (C, F, H). It is clear from (21) that, in steady state, consumption will be exactly equal to the stock of habits. Thus, we don't need to worry about determining the steady state value of the stock of habits. Solving the system for C and F leads to:

$$C = \frac{\rho(\rho + \theta)}{\Delta}\omega \tag{22}$$

where $\Delta = -(1-\mu)r^2 + (1-\mu)r\theta + \rho(\rho+\theta)$. Similarly the expression for F may be written as:

$$F = \frac{(1-\mu)(r-\theta)}{\Delta}\omega \tag{23}$$

From (22) and (23) it may be verified that the expressions reduce, as expected, to the case without habit formation for the case $\mu = 0$. From these equations it is straightforward to derive the effect of a change in interest rates on steady state values. Specifically:

$$\frac{dC}{dr} = \frac{(1-\mu)(2r-\theta)\rho(\rho+\theta)}{\Delta^2}\omega \tag{24}$$

$$\frac{dF}{dr} = \frac{(1-\mu)(r-\theta)^2 + (\rho+\theta)\rho}{\Delta^2}\omega > 0 \tag{25}$$

Given that we have $0 < \mu < 1$, the first derivative in (24) will be positive provided that $2r > \theta$, the same condition as we had on p. 70. The fact that the term $(1-\mu)$ appears in the numerator of both equations makes it plausible that the introduction of external habit formation will contribute to mitigate the impact of interest rate changes on steady state values. This conjecture is confirmed by a more careful examination of the relevant expressions. The intuition for this result is as follows. In the model, the Euler equation of individual consumption implies that, when $\theta \neq r$, the consumption profile of an individual household will either be increasing over time (if $\theta < r$) or decreasing over time (if $\theta > r$). The consumer will therefore choose a path for consumption with this profile which satisfies his intertemporal budget constraint. In steady state consumption per capita is constant and, thus, $\dot{H} = 0$. When habits are introduced, the utility of the consumer depends on the difference between consumption and the level of habit, which in the steady state will be given by $\mu C > 0$, where C is aggregate consumption. This implies that, compared to the case without habits, they will prefer a flatter profile of consumption (i.e. they will not want their consumption to deviate 'too much' from average consumption in the economy). The flatter profile of consumption implies that households will acquire less debt over their lifetimes and thus, aggregating over cohorts, aggregate steady state net foreign debt will be lower. This is why steady state effects are reduced by habit formation. Of course, it is immediately intuitive that external habit formation will moderate the initial adjustment and spread it over time. The intuition here is even simpler since habits are a predetermined variable. Hence, external habit formation allows us to satisfactorily answer two of the reservations we have raised earlier.

Traded and non-traded goods without habits

We now consider a variant of the model with traded and non-traded goods but still disregarding habit formation. This corresponds to setting $\omega^N > 0$, $0 < \alpha < 1$ with $\mu = \gamma = 0$. Letting Z_t denote aggregate nominal consumption expenditure ($p_t C_t$), (8) collapses to:

$$\dot{Z}_t = (r-\theta)Z_t - \rho(\theta+\rho)F_t \tag{26}$$

The foreign asset accumulation (9) equation simplifies to:

$$\dot{F}_t = rF_t + \omega^T - \alpha Z_t \tag{27}$$

The equations (27) and (26) are analogous to the equations (12) and (11) that we obtained earlier for the single good case. The only difference is that consumption expenditure is measured in nominal terms and the coefficient α in the equation of motion of the net foreign asset position. This difference is immediately intuitive once we recognize that the relevant influence for the accumulation of foreign assets is given by the economy's net supply of tradable goods in world markets.

As before it is convenient to compute the steady state values of F_t and Z_t. In order to do so we follow exactly the steps we used in the earlier section and find the relation between F_t and Z_t that is compatible with unchanging values for each of the variables:

$$\dot{F}_t = 0 : Z_t = \frac{\omega^T}{\alpha} + \frac{r}{\alpha} F_t \tag{28}$$

$$\dot{Z}_t = 0 : Z_t = \frac{\rho(\rho + \theta)}{r - \theta} F_t \tag{29}$$

Equations (28) and (29) are analogous to the corresponding expressions in the previous section (with the qualification that α appears on the denominator of (28)). Solving the system for the steady state values of the variables F^* and Z^* allows us to write:

$$F^* = \frac{r - \theta}{(\theta + \rho - r)(r + \rho\alpha) - (1 - \alpha)r\rho} \omega^T \tag{30}$$

$$Z^* = \frac{\rho(\theta + \rho)}{(\theta + \rho - r)(r + \rho\alpha) - (1 - \alpha)r\rho} \omega^T \tag{31}$$

It may be verified that equations (30) and equation (31) reduce to the corresponding expressions (15) and (16) in case $\alpha = 1$ (i.e. when all goods are traded). We may now calculate the derivative of F^* and Z^* with respect to the interest rate, in order to obtain the response of the steady state values of the net foreign asset position and consumption to a change in interest rates. The result may be written as:

$$\frac{dF^*}{dr} = \frac{(r - \theta)^2 + \alpha\rho(\rho + \theta)}{[(\theta + \rho - r)(r + \rho\alpha) - (1 - \alpha)r\rho]^2} \omega^T \tag{32}$$

$$\frac{dZ^*}{dr} = \frac{\rho(\rho + \theta)(2r - \theta)}{[(\theta + \rho - r)(r + \rho\alpha) - (1 - \alpha)r\rho]^2} \omega^T, \tag{33}$$

where the derivatives are positive in the same conditions as before. Now for a given interest rate the dynamic system is linear and the conditions for saddle-path stability are easy to identify. The saddle path will be given by a straight line whose slope is determined by the value of the normalized eigenvector (see Appendix 2, and Figure 4.2). Given these preliminary remarks we can now continue and discuss the adjustment of the economy when faced with a reduction in interest rates.

We can illustrate the adjustment process in Figure 4.2. We start, as before, assuming that $r = \theta$ so that the initial value of the net foreign asset position is zero. The initial steady state position is labelled (1) in Figure 4.2. In the initial steady state it is clear that consumption is constant over time at the level $Z = \omega^T/\alpha$. As the interest rate declines, the locus corresponding to unchanging consumption becomes visible in Figure 4.2 as a negative sloped line in the left-hand side. Given the starting point it is clear that, in steady state, the net foreign asset position becomes negative (the country resorts to foreign debt) and consumption expenditure falls. However, on impact the net foreign asset position is predetermined while expenditure is a jump variable. In our case consumption jumps up immediately (see Figure 4.2, point 2).[11] From this starting point nominal consumption and net foreign assets will decline monotonically and the economy will approach the steady state equilibrium (point 3 on Figure 4.2). The adjustment is entirely analogous to the process described for the case of the simple endowment economy.

However, the version with non-traded goods allows us to discuss the relative price implications from the adjustment process. In the general case, the relative price of non-traded goods is determined by the supply and demand for these goods (see, for example, Neary 1988 for a compact exposition). In our case, since by assumption the supply of non-traded goods is fixed, then the price of non-traded goods is determined in a relatively straightforward manner by aggregate demand. To show this we note that the intratemporal first-order condition for non-traded goods implies that:

$$p_t^N C_t^N = (1-\alpha)Z_t,$$

while market clearing in the non-traded goods market requires:

$$C_t^N = \omega^N$$

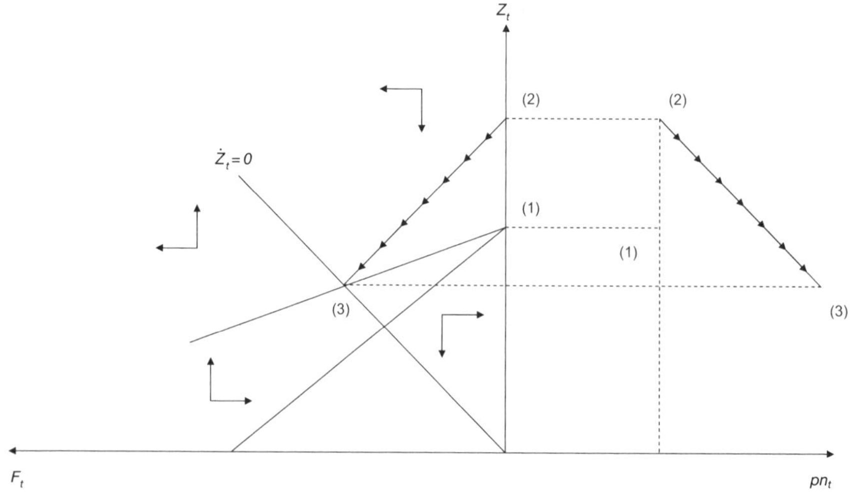

Figure 4.2 Dynamics of consumption, net foreign assets and the real exchange rate.

These two equations imply that:

$$p_t^N = \frac{(1-\alpha)Z_t}{\omega^N} \tag{34}$$

Since endowments are assumed constant over time (34) shows that there is a very simple linear relation between aggregate expenditure and the relative price of non-traded goods. Hence, in our simple setup, the real exchange rate jumps up on impact and subsequently depreciates very gradually, in line with the slowdown in domestic expenditure (see Figure 4.2). The new steady state value of the real exchange rate is lower (more depreciated) than in the initial steady state. This reflects the operation of a 'transfer effect' whereby the higher steady state level of foreign debt depresses domestic expenditure, leading to a lower non-traded goods price.

Numerical simulations for a two good economy

We now turn to the version of the model outlined on p. 68, equations (8) to (10), which includes both traded and non-traded goods as well as habit formation. We first analyse steady state effects, which are relatively straightforward. However, as regards dynamics, as far as we are aware, analytical solutions to this non-linear equation system are not available, so we examine the model's properties by use of numerical simulations. By way of comparison and in order to show the effects of habit formation, we compare results with the results obtained in the previous section (for a model with two goods but without habit formation). In the simulations reported below, the time period is annual.

Setting $\dot{X}$, $\dot{F}$ and $\dot{H}$ to zero, we can show that the steady state is given by

$$Z^* = \frac{\rho(\rho+\theta)}{\alpha\rho(\theta+\rho) - r(r-\theta)(1-\mu)}\omega^T$$

$$F^* = \frac{(r-\theta)(1-\mu)}{\alpha\rho(\theta+\rho) - r(r-\theta)(1-\mu)}\omega^T,$$

where, as before, $Z_t = p_t C_t$. We see immediately that when habit formation is suppressed (i.e. $\mu = 0$) we obtain exactly the same results as in the previous section. Differentiating these expressions with respect to r, we obtain:

$$\frac{dZ^*}{dr} = \frac{(2r-\theta)(1-\mu)\rho(\theta+\rho)}{[\alpha\rho(\rho+\theta) - r(r-\theta)(1-\mu)]^2}\omega^T$$

$$\frac{dF^*}{dr} = \frac{(1-\mu)\left(\alpha\rho(\theta+\rho) + (1-\mu)(r-\theta)^2\right)}{[\alpha\rho(\rho+\theta) - r(r-\theta)(1-\mu)]^2}\omega^T$$

The second expression is always positive while the first is positive for $2r > \theta$ (the same condition we had earlier). Comparing the expression for dZ^*/dr with the corresponding result for the case without habit, we see immediately that for $r < \theta$ it is smaller, i.e. the long-run response of consumer expenditure is less under habit formation. As regards foreign assets, consider the behaviour of the ratio F^*/Z^*. Clearly, the response of this ratio to changes in r is less under habit formation. Thus, to summarize, we obtain the same qualitative long-run effects from the decline in interest rates with and without habit formation. Following a fall in interest rates, expenditure falls while foreign debt rises in the long run. However, the magnitudes of the long-run effects are smaller under habit formation.

Turning to the dynamics, as in any numerical simulation exercise it is important to examine the sensitivity of the results for different parameter values. For this purpose, we linearize the system around the post-shock steady state and examine the dynamics of the linearized system over a wide grid of plausible parameter values.[12] The main results of this sensitivity analysis are as follows.

First, in all cases, the saddle-path property was satisfied. Thus, for every case, one of the roots had a positive real part while the remaining roots had negative real parts.

Second, in around 9 per cent of cases, the roots took the form of complex conjugates. Complex roots are typically associated with values of $\mu > 0.8$.

Third, in all cases, both real consumption (C) and nominal consumption (Z) jumped upwards on impact. The magnitude of the initial jump, however, varied greatly depending on the parameter values. In general the size of the jump in consumption is increasing in α but decreasing in μ, γ, r, ρ.

Fourth, the speed of adjustment to the steady state varied significantly across parameter sets. In particular, higher values of ρ – i.e. reduced life expectancy – are associated with more rapid adjustment in line with what we found earlier. Increases in the values of all of the other parameters also led to faster adjustment, though less strongly than in the case of ρ.

With this background, we now present simulations of the model. The shock we consider is a permanent reduction in the interest rate r from 5 per cent to 4 per cent. To implement the shock, we choose a set of parameters which we believe to be plausible. We begin with the intertemporal rate of time preference θ, which we set to 5 per cent. This specific choice is motivated by our desire to match data on net foreign assets. From the steady state results given earlier, we know that a rate of time preference equal to the interest rate implies a level of net foreign assets of zero. This is close to what we observe in the data for the converging countries prior to their entry into the monetary union. We assume a life expectancy of fifty years, corresponding to a ρ of 2 per cent, a standard value in the literature. We calibrate the parameter α to reproduce the expenditure share of traded goods at 30 per cent (so that $\alpha = 0.3$) which is in line with input–output evidence for the countries concerned. The price of traded goods is given in world markets and is chosen as the numeraire. The size of the endowment of traded goods is set to unity. The endowment of non-traded goods is set at a level such that the post-shock steady state price level is unity. In the case with habit formation there are two extra parameters to calibrate: μ and γ. Following the relevant literature we assume that $\mu = 0.7$ and $\gamma = 1$.[13] We also consider the case in which there is no habit formation, in which case we set $\mu = 0.0$ and $\gamma = 0.0$.

Starting from this initial position we consider a disturbance to the cost of financing of the economy in the world's financial markets. Specifically we consider a reduction of one full percentage point in the cost of external financing from 5 per cent to 4 per cent. As argued before, such reduction may be interpreted as reflecting a decline in an idiosyncratic risk premium in an uncovered interest rate parity condition or, more broadly, as reflecting a process of financial integration and financial liberalization, leading to easier access to financing for domestic economic agents.

The simulations presented are based on the system (8) to (10) on p. 68. Once these equations are solved, obtaining the equilibrium relative price of non-traded goods is straightforward, as is the computation of the dual price index, p_t. The system of differential equations is solved by using the MATLAB BVP4C routine, which employs collocation methods to solve two-point boundary problems for ordinary differential equations. The initial conditions for the two predetermined variables (F and H) correspond to the initial (pre-shock) steady state, while the value of nominal consumption (Z) at the terminal point is given by the post-shock steady state value.

The results are presented in Figure 4.3a (which shows the results for the first ten years) and Figure 4.3b (which shows the results for the first 100 years). The results are presented as deviations from baseline except for the current account and the net foreign asset position, which are presented as percentages of GDP. In both versions of the model – with and without habit formation – there is an increase in expenditure after the fall in the cost of external financing. This increased expenditure is financed through external debt, implying a current account deficit. The boom in expenditure leads – in the face of unchanged supply of non-traded goods – to an increase in the relative price of non-traded goods or, in other words, to an appreciation of the real exchange rate.

The difference between the two models in the short to medium term is clearly evident in Figure 4.3a. As expected, the response is more muted with habit formation and the initial increase in expenditure is spread over time, in accordance with an inverted U-shaped curve. The response of the current account is smaller, and, thus, the accumulation of

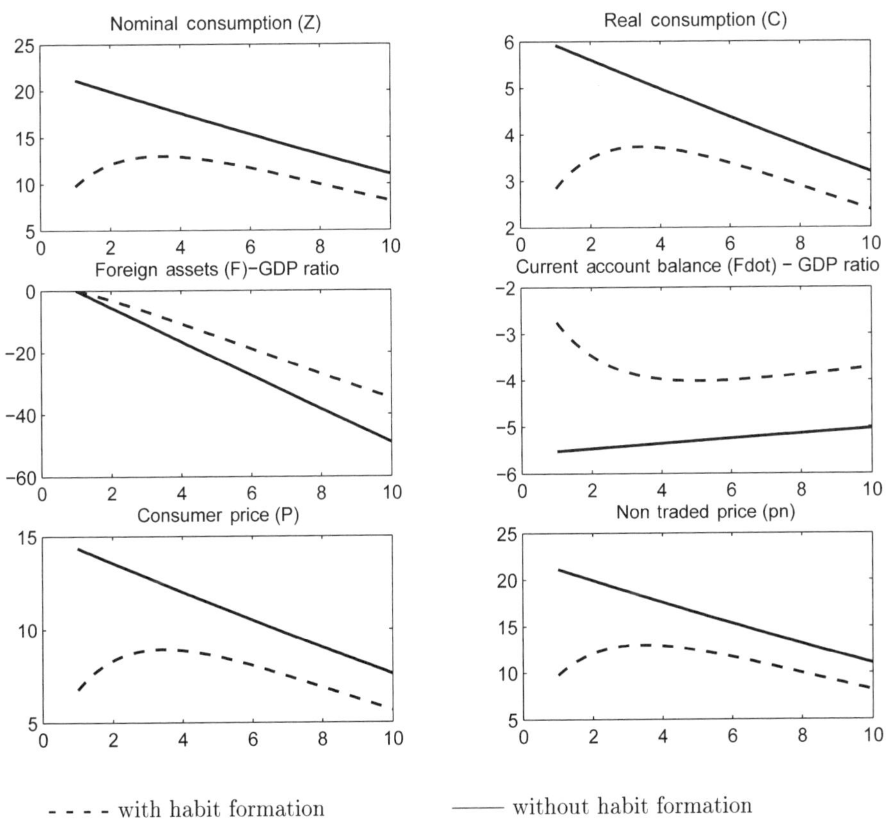

Figure 4.3a Simulated response to a fall in interest rates (first 10 years).

foreign debt slower. Since the effects on prices (and the real exchange rate) are basically proportional to aggregate expenditure the same remarks apply to prices. With habit formation the adjustment process looks much more realistic in the sense that the initial adjustment does not involve a large immediate jump in expenditure.

Moreover, there are also important differences concerning steady state results, as we would expect from the analytical results given earlier. Nevertheless, both versions of the model have in common that the adjustment process is very slow, as can be seen in Figure 4.3b. The reason is intuitive. Given the fall in the cost of external financing, interest rates are now lower than the households' rate of time preference. Thus, individual consumption expenditures will be declining over time. So, in order for aggregate consumption expenditures to be constant (in steady state) the level of consumption of newborns has to be sufficiently above the average consumption in the economy. This can only be the case after a sufficient accumulation of foreign debt has taken place, and this takes place only slowly.

For the case without habit formation, steady state results are very large. Specifically, for our parameter values, the model implies a steady state value of foreign debt (a negative net foreign asset position) equal to 550 per cent of GDP. Aggregate real consumption is 18 per cent lower in the new steady state. The relative price of non-traded goods falls by 50 per cent and, correspondingly, the true consumption price index falls by 38 per cent.

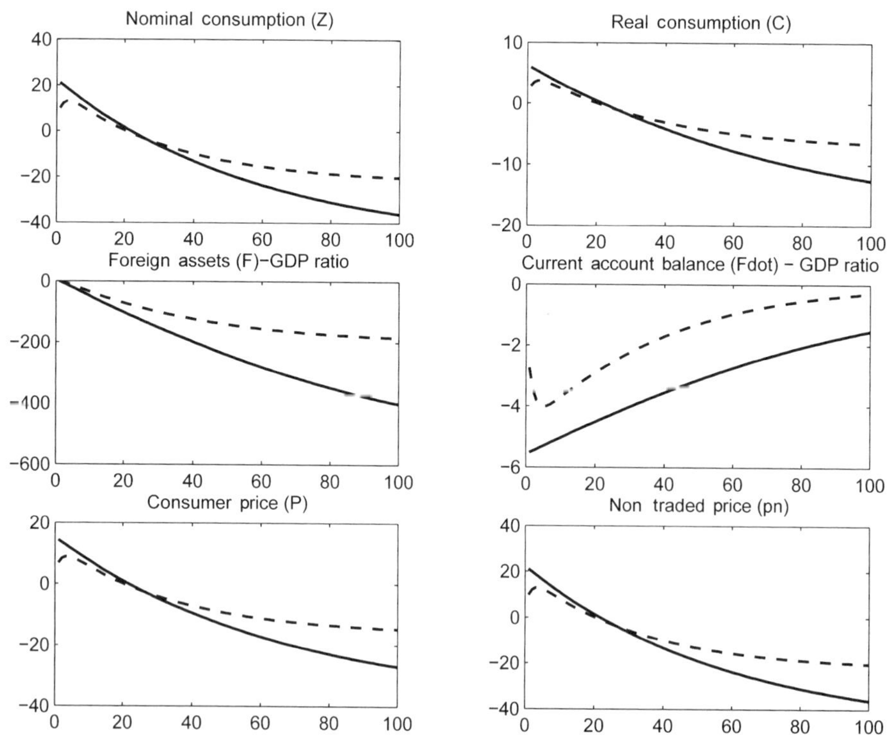

- - - - with habit formation —— without habit formation

Figure 4.3b Simulated response to a fall in interest rates (100 years).

With habit formation all the qualitative results are similar. However, habit formation makes all magnitudes much smaller. For example, the level of foreign debt with habit formation is reduced by almost a factor of three to 200 per cent of GDP. We think that these latter results are much more plausible.

Conclusion

In this chapter, we have argued that, for a number of countries, it is useful to look at the process of adjustment to euro area participation as involving a significant fall in the costs associated with international financing. The simplest way to think about such disturbance is as a fall in a country-specific risk premium leading to a drop in the relevant interest rate. It is, however, best to interpret it in broader terms, reflecting better conditions of access to financing for domestic economic agents, in part related to a process of financial integration and financial liberalization which accompany entry into the monetary union. In the chapter, we argue that the fall in the cost of financing was a common impulse affecting countries like Greece, Spain, Ireland, Italy and Portugal. In order to establish the relevant stylized facts we compare these converging countries with the remainder of the countries now constituting the euro area. In the chapter, we document that the process of adjustment in these economies shared a number of important common features. These include: an increase in aggregate expenditure and a fall in savings, the emergence of a significant current account deficit, an appreciation of the real exchange rate, and, finally, the accumulation of households' debt and of a negative net foreign asset position. Surprisingly no significant changes in the pattern of GDP growth differentials can be discerned in the data.

Hence we argue that it is possible to explain the observed patterns using a simple intertemporal general equilibrium model for an endowment economy. Specifically, we consider an economy constituted by Blanchard–Yaari households. We show that all the stylized facts can be qualitatively obtained in a simple endowment economy model with traded and non-traded goods. However, in versions with standard time-separable preferences, aggregate expenditure jumps instantaneously and the impact on the steady state net foreign asset position seems to be too large. We show that introducing external habit formation enables us to solve both problems. Therefore, we conclude that this version of the model goes a long way in explaining some important features of adjustment to the euro.

While the model seems to match the experience to date of the converging countries, its implications for the longer term are rather stark, implying a substantial build-up of foreign debt with the resulting implication of a sharp long-run fall in the real exchange rate as expenditures are curtailed in order to service the increased foreign debt burden. While the precise quantitative predictions for the long-run steady state may be taken with a grain of salt, nonetheless, it seems reasonable to assume that the initial boom in expenditures will be followed by a protracted correction to the new steady state.

Appendix 1: Data used in the section on 'Some stylized facts'

The main data source for the results presented above is the EU Commission's AMECO database. The codes for the series employed are as follows: nominal short-term interest rates (ISN), nominal long-term interest rates (ILN), household savings rate (ASGH), nominal housing investment (UIGDW), current account balance (UBCA), Harmonized Index of Consumer Prices (HICP), whole economy net lending (UBLA), general government net lending (UBLG), household net lending (UBLH), nominal GDP (UVGD) and real GDP (OVGD). Non-housing investment is calculated as the difference between total investment (UIGT) and housing investment.

The exceptions to the use of AMECO are as follows. Credit to households data came from the OECD Financial Balance Sheet databank (except in the case of Ireland, where the source was various issues of the *Central Bank of Ireland Quarterly Bulletin*). Data on net foreign assets are taken from Lane and Milesi-Ferreti (2006). Data on the Harmonized Index of Consumer Prices (HICP) were taken from Eurostat, while the data on relative consumer prices come from Eurostat's Comparative Consumer Price Level dataset and relate to price levels for final consumption by private households. For Portugal and Ireland, the data on net lending shown in Chart 13 are from the Banco de Portugal and the authors' own calculations, respectively.

Ratios to GDP were calculated by dividing the respective series (as described above) by nominal GDP. The variables for core countries were calculated by taking cross-country arithmetic means of the respective variables for Belgium, Germany, France, Austria and the Netherlands. Converging country variables were similarly calculated using data for Ireland, Italy, Portugal and Spain.

Appendix 2: Further results on the model with two goods and without habits

In this Appendix, we establish that consumption expenditures (Z_t) jump upwards following a fall in the interest rate. As is clear from Figure 4.2, this requires that the slope of the saddle path is more vertical than the slope of the $\dot{F} = 0$ locus (28). Thus, our task in the Appendix is to show that saddle-path stability implies the initial jump in consumption expenditures.

Let us start by noticing that the pair of equations (26) and (27) can be expressed in matrix form as:

$$\begin{pmatrix} \dot{Z}_t \\ \dot{F}_t \end{pmatrix} = \begin{pmatrix} (r-\theta) & -\rho(\theta+\rho) \\ -\alpha & r \end{pmatrix} \begin{pmatrix} Z_t \\ F_t \end{pmatrix} \begin{pmatrix} 0 \\ \omega^T \end{pmatrix}$$

Let

$$A = \begin{pmatrix} (r-\theta) & -\rho(\theta+\rho) \\ -\alpha & r \end{pmatrix}$$

Saddle-path stability requires that the determinant of A be negative, i.e.

$$r(r-\theta) - \rho\alpha(\theta+\rho) < 0$$

Let $\lambda_1 < 0$ denote the stable root of A. Then the solution of the model is given by:

$$\begin{pmatrix} Z_t - Z^* \\ F_t - F^* \end{pmatrix} = b \begin{pmatrix} v_{11} \\ 1 \end{pmatrix} e^{\lambda_1 t}$$

where b is a constant determined to match the initial value of the predetermined variable, $(v_{11}, 1)'$ is the normalized eigenvector associated with λ_1 and a star on the variable denotes the steady state value. The equation for the saddle path is therefore:

$$Z_t - Z_t^* = v_{11}(F_t - F^*)$$

and its slope is therefore v_{11}. Now v_{11} is determined by the solution of

$$\begin{pmatrix} (r-\theta-\lambda_1) & -\rho(\theta+\rho) \\ -\alpha & r-\lambda_1 \end{pmatrix} \begin{pmatrix} v_{11} \\ 1 \end{pmatrix} = \begin{pmatrix} 0 \\ 0 \end{pmatrix}$$

This implies that

$$v_{11} = \frac{r-\lambda_1}{\alpha} > 0.$$

Let η denote the slope of the $\dot{F} = 0$ locus (28). Clearly

$$\eta = \frac{r}{\alpha}.$$

We have then:

$$v_{11} - \eta = \frac{-\lambda_1}{\alpha} > 0$$

because, as noted above, $\lambda_1 < 0$. So the slope of the saddle path is greater than the slope of the $\dot{F} = 0$ locus, as required.

Notes

1 We are grateful to Marta Abreu, Chris Allsopp, Nuno Alves and an anonymous referee for useful comments. We also thank Ramon Adalid for excellent research assistance. The views expressed are the authors' own and do not necessarily reflect those of the European Central Bank (ECB), the Eurosystem or the European Commission.
2 Belgium, Greece, Spain, France, Germany, Ireland, Italy, Luxembourg, the Netherlands, Austria, Portugal and Finland. In January 2007 Slovenia became the thirteenth member of the euro area. Cyprus and Malta joined in 2008
3 Czech Republic, Estonia, Cyprus, Hungary, Latvia, Lithuania, Malta, Poland, Slovenia and Slovakia.
4 We do not include Luxembourg in our analysis due to difficulties with data availability.
5 We do not include Finland in either group. This reflects the fact that it only joined the EU in 1994 and the evolution of its economy over part of the period under review is heavily distorted by special factors (such as the recovery from the sharp recession recorded in the early 1990s).
6 We have replicated the analysis including Greece in the converging group. We find that the conclusions derived in this section are not sensitive to the exclusion of Greece. Details are available on request from the authors.
7 Frenkel and Razin (1996) present a discrete time version of the model. Many times when performing numerical simulation exercises a discrete time version of the model is used.

8 The formula for the dual price index is

$$p_t = \left(\frac{1}{\kappa}\right)\left(\alpha^{-\alpha}(1-\alpha)^{-(1-\alpha)}\right)p_t^{\alpha}p^{(1-\alpha)}.$$

9 This equation is derived from the formula for the dual price index, the first-order condition for non-traded goods consumption and the market clearing condition for non-traded goods. Specifically, $\phi = \alpha^{-\alpha}(1/\kappa)\left(\omega^N\right)^{\alpha-1}$.

10 The system has two corresponding eigenvalues $r+\rho>0$ and $r-\rho-\theta$. In order for it to be saddle-path stable the second eigenvalue must be negative $r-\rho-\theta<0$.

11 The fact that expenditure jumps upwards follows from the fact that the slope of the saddle path is greater than the slope of the line connecting the points of unchanging net foreign asset position given by (28) (see Appendix 2).

12 A total of just over 20,000 different cases were considered. The range of parameters considered was: $r \in [0.03, 0.07]$, $\rho \in [0.01, 0.05]$, $\alpha \in [0.1, 0.9]$, $\mu \in [0.1, 0.9]$, $\gamma \in [0.1, 1.0]$.

13 The value of μ is consistent with the values chosen by Christiano, Eichenbaum and Evans (2005) and Smets and Wouters (2003). In both discrete time models, the authors set $H_t = C_{t-1}$. Applied to our continuous time case, this corresponds to setting $\gamma = 1$.

References

Abel, A. (1990) 'Asset prices under habit formation and catching up with the Joneses', *American Economic Review* 40(2): 38–42.

Bates, D.S. (1999) 'Financial markets' assessment of EMU', *Carnegie–Rochester Series on Public Policy* 51: 229–69.

Benalal, J., J.-L. del Hoyo, B. Pierluigi and N. Vidalis (2006) *Output Growth Differentials Across the Euro Area Countries: Some Stylised Facts*, ECB Occasional Paper no. 45.

Berben, R.-P., A. Locarno, J. Morgan and J. Valles (2004) *Cross-country Differences in Monetary Policy Transmission*, ECB Working Paper no. 400.

Blanchard, O. (1985) 'Debt, deficits and finite horizons', *Journal of Political Economy* 93: 223–47.

Blanchard, O. and S. Fisher (1989) *Lectures on Macroeconomics*, Cambridge, MA: MIT Press.

Blanchard, O. and F. Giavazzi (2002) 'Current account deficits in the euro area: the end of the Feldstein–Horioka puzzle', *Brookings Papers on Economic Activity* 2: 147–86.

Campbell, J. and J. Cochrane (1999) 'By force of habit: a consumption-based explanation of aggregate stock market behavior', *Journal of Political Economy* 107(2): 205–51.

Carroll, C., J. Overland and D. Weil (2000) 'Saving and growth with habit formation', *American Economic Review* 90(3): 341–55.

Christiano, L., Eichenbaum, M. and Evans, C. (2005) 'Nominal rigidities and the dynamic effects of a shock to monetary policy', *Journal of Political Economy* 113(1): 1–45.

ECB (2003) *Inflation Differentials in the Euro Area: Potential Causes and Policy Implications*, Frankfurt: ECB.

—— (2005a) *ECB Annual Report*, Frankfurt: ECB.

—— (2005b) 'Monetary policy and inflation differentials in a heterogenous currency area', *ECB Monthly Bulletin*, May: 61–78.

Fagan, G. and V. Gaspar (2005) 'Adjusting to the euro: some issues inspired by the Portuguese experience', paper presented at the ECB workshop on What Effects Is EMU Having on the Euro Area and Its Member States?, June 2005; available at http://www.ecb.int/events/pdf/conferences/emu/sessionVI_Gaspar.pdf.

Favero, C., F. Giavazzi, F. Iacone and G. Tabellini (2000) 'Extracting information from asset prices: the methodology of EMU calculators', *European Economic Review* 44: 1607–32.

Frenkel, J. and A. Razin (1996) *Fiscal Policies and Growth in the World Economy*, Cambridge MA: MIT Press.

Gruber, J. (2004) 'A present value test of habits and the current account', *Journal of Monetary Economics* 51: 1495-507.

Lane, P. (2006) 'The real effects of European Monetary Union', *Journal of Economic Perspectives* 20(4): 47–66.

Lane, P. and G. Milesi-Ferreti (2006) *The External Wealth of Nations Mark II: Revised and Expanded Estimates of Foreign Assets and Liabilities, 1970–2004*, IMF Working Paper 06/69.
Mansoorian, A. (1993) 'Habit persistence and the Harberger–Laursen–Metzler effect in an infinite horizon model', *Journal of International Economics* 34: 153–66.
Mongelli, F. and J.L. Vega (2006) *What Effects Is EMU Having on the Euro Area and Its Member Countries?*, ECB Working Paper Series no. 599.
Neary, J.P. (1988) 'Determinants of equilibrium exchange rate', *American Economic Review* 78: 210–15.
Obstfeld, M. (1992) 'International adjustment with habit forming consumption: a diagrammatic exposition', *Review of International Economics International Economics* 1(1): 32–48.
Obstfeld, M. and K. Rogoff (2005) 'Global current account imbalances and exchange rate adjustments', *Brookings Papers on Economic Activity* 1: 67–146.
Smets, F. and R. Wouters (2003) 'An estimated dynamic stochastic general equilibrium model for the euro area', *Journal of the European Economic Association* 1(5): 1123–75.
Velculescu, D. (2006) 'Intergenerational habits, fiscal policy and welfare', *Topics in Macroeconomics* 4(1): 1–32.
Yaari, M.E. (1965) 'Uncertain lifetime, life insurance and the theory of the consumer', *Review of Economic Studies* 32: 137–50.

5 Booms and busts

Experiences with internal and external adjustment

Reiner Martin and Ludger Schuknecht

Introduction[1]

What have been the experiences with boom–bust episodes that have affected numerous industrialized and emerging market countries over the past 20 years before the onset of the financial turmoil in summer 2007? How has this experience been influenced by the exchange rate adjustment strategy? These are the first questions that this study tries to answer by deriving stylized facts on a number of boom–bust episodes. Many of these episodes have already been studied extensively on a country basis or from a regional perspective. But this study takes a more comprehensive, global view and looks at experiences and patterns across different country groups, including industrialized countries, emerging markets and a number of Central and East European EU Member States.

Moreover, our study analyses different adjustment strategies in the face of busts. It differentiates between those countries that experienced a (CPI-based) real effective exchange rate depreciation/devaluation during the bust, which we call 'external adjusters', and those that did not experience a devaluation, which we call 'internal adjusters'.

The study looks at the interaction of real and financial sector variables in boom–bust episodes where asset price cycles and their impact on private balance sheets constitute an important driving force. Volatility can be reinforced (or moderated) through domestic macroeconomic factors, competitiveness developments and the international financial environment. We derive stylized facts and some preliminary statistical analysis as regards the incidence and patterns of boom and bust episodes and their impact on the exchange rate strategy.

The study finds that boom–bust patterns are rather similar across industrialized and emerging countries. The former countries are perhaps less vulnerable but not immune to systemic risk with reversing international capital flows and busts turning into financial crises. Most importantly, we find that countries' different (exchange rate) adjustment experiences are correlated with the extent of macroeconomic imbalances and balance sheet deterioration:

- External adjusters tend to experience more pronounced booms with more overheating of demand, increases in prices and credit, loss of competitiveness and deterioration of (private, public and external) balance sheets than reported for internal adjusters.
- In busts, external adjusters tend to experience deep downturns and rapid recoveries as imbalances are initially more severe but, subsequently, also unwind more quickly. Internal adjusters tend to face less deep but more protracted downturns (and even deflation) as imbalances unwind more slowly and adjustment via the trade and credit channels takes more time.

What is the current situation of the Central and East European EU Member States? The analysis of these countries suggests that there are a few new CEE Member States that appear to be in the early stages of a boom, while there are some others that appear to be further along. But clear and definite conclusions cannot be drawn as yet, not least due to serious data problems. The experiences of boom–bust scenarios in other countries may nevertheless serve as an 'early warning' and may raise awareness of related policy challenges.[2]

The study has a number of shortcomings. The choice to discuss stylized facts for a large number of diverse countries comes at the expense of a more detailed analysis for the individual countries or regions. Furthermore, we do not analyse whether countries 'chose' a certain adjustment strategy or whether markets 'forced' them to do so (or a mixture of the two).[3] We are mainly interested in detecting patterns of cross-country experiences with booms and busts as depending on the different exchange rate adjustment experience. Moreover, we focus on the interaction of various transmission channels and different country groups but not on institutional and micro-structural issues.

The study is organized as follows. The next section discusses conceptual issues, including the discussion of exchange rate adjustment experiences, the relevant sectoral variables and transmission channels and the methodology for identifying boom–bust cycles. Then there is a section discussing experiences across different country groups, with subsections which report the experience of ten industrialized countries with boom–bust phases in the 1980s and 1990s, then turn to a small sample of emerging Asian market countries, before examining the recent experiences of Portugal and the Netherlands. The next section takes stock of the situation in CEE EU Member States. Concluding comments complete the chapter.

Conceptual issues

Transmission channels

Boom–bust episodes are empirical phenomena. There is not just one and only one theoretical framework that defines them and explains their emergence and evolution. There are different theoretical approaches and measurement tools. Nevertheless, there is a considerable literature that looks at boom–bust episodes primarily as a result of asset price 'cycles' that propagate into the real economy via the credit transmission channel (Bernanke *et al.* 1999; Bordo and Jeanne 2002; Borio 2008).[4] This channel also forms our conceptual basis for identifying boom–bust episodes. However, there are also three other propagation mechanisms or transmission channels which play a role in the evolution of booms and busts and which warrant a brief discussion: (2) the trade channel, (3) the international financial channel and (4) the fiscal channel.

As regards the first channel, the financial accelerator literature explains the emergence of boom–bust phenomena in the real and financial economy via asset supply rigidities and the *credit transmission channel.* When asset prices rise, the collateral value of the assets increases, which, in turn, stokes credit supply and demand. This in conjunction with wealth effects provokes further real demand, output and asset price rises. Asset supply increases and growth of debt cause this process to reverse at some point (putting pressure on prices and net worth), and the opposite, mutually reinforcing dynamics fuel the downturn of asset prices and the real economy.

The second channel worth referring to in this context is the *trade channel.* In a period of strong growth, a country may lose competitiveness via rising unit labour costs. This initially further boosts domestic demand and imports but it undermines the tradable goods sector and export growth. Over time the weakening effect from exports and the trade-competing sector start to dominate, employment is falling, so that growth weakens. In the downturn and especially if a devaluation of the exchange rate takes place, relative price adjustments result in the revival of import-competing industries which together with rising exports helps the economy to emerge from the downturn. If the exchange rate is not devalued, the full adjustment has to come through a reversal of unit labour costs and relative prices between tradables/non-tradables before the revival of exports and import-competing industries can set in.

The third channel is the *international financial channel*. Capital inflows in the boom/high growth period keep the exchange rate appreciated and imports cheap. Sudden stops of inflows and net capital outflows can exacerbate (if not trigger) the asset price bust and downturn of the real economy by choking domestic demand, increasing pressure on the exchange rate and on the banking system (see Calvo *et al.* 2004; Calvo *et al.* 2003; or Eichengreen and Choudhry 2005).

Much attention has been drawn to international capital flows exacerbating booms. They can give rise to significant short-term and foreign-currency denominated debt, coupled with insufficient reserves. If then the boom turns to bust, a reversal of capital flows may make the exchange rate untenable, which, in turn, exacerbates the effect of asset price declines on collateral value and non-performing loans and may even push the economy from 'bust' into a 'full-fledged' crisis. By contrast, the opposite case of countries experiencing capital inflows and pressure on their exchange rate to appreciate during bust phases has received much less attention. We will see below that this has been the experience of a number of countries whose currencies are considered safe havens, including Switzerland and Japan. In these instances, relative prices in the tradable/non-tradable goods sectors in the bust have to adjust internally even more strongly.

The role of public finances (or the *fiscal channel*) is little discussed in the boom–bust literature. Jaeger and Schuknecht (2004) point to revenue windfalls during booms that derive from asset-based taxes and from indirect tax revenue that is boosted by wealth effects on domestic demand. These windfalls can be very significant. They can create incentives of pro-cyclical policies in the boom if such windfalls are not recognized as such and spent. Fiscal policies can also be (forced to become) pro-cyclical in the downturn if the fiscal position at the beginning of the bust is weak and adjustment is needed to prevent destabilizing deficit increases. Jaeger and Schuknecht find significant evidence for such pro-cyclical policies in a study of industrialized country boom–bust episodes since the 1970s.

Fiscal policies can also exacerbate boom–bust experiences via indirect effects through other channels. The financing needs arising from large fiscal deficits can increase vulnerability via the international financial channel if such deficits raise the current account deficit and hence the vulnerability to 'sudden stops'. Fiscal policies can worsen imbalances via the competitiveness/trade and domestic financial channels if public wage and employment increases put pressure on unit labour costs and if these, in turn, stoke credit and asset price booms.

The previous references to interlinkages between the sectoral channels already point to the fact that vulnerabilities and risks need to be assessed from an intersectoral perspective. Or, in other words, we need to look at *systemic risks* and not just at sectoral ones. The literature has started to acknowledge the importance of analysing intersectoral linkages, especially via balance sheet vulnerability (Allen *et al.* 2002). Boom–bust phenomena that in some cases culminate in financial/balance of payments crises are intellectually interesting because of these very complexities. Moreover, they are economically relevant because of the significant adjustment needs and the large output and fiscal costs that can arise in protracted busts or deep crises (Watson 2005; Honohan and Klingebiel 2003; Bordo and Jeanne 2002; Calvo et al. 2003, 2004).

Identification of booms and busts

But when is there a boom and bust? There is by now a considerable literature that develops methodologies of identifying such phenomena. These include Bordo and Jeanne (2002), Jaeger and Schuknecht (2004) and Detken and Smets (2004) for defining boom and bust episodes in industrialized countries. For emerging markets busts could be proxied by financial crises as listed by Honohan and Klingebiel (2003) which include overt systemic financial crises and cases of financial distress where the net worth of the banking system is negative.

In this study, we look at (1) boom–bust episodes in industrialized countries since the mid-1980s as identified in Jaeger and Schuknecht (2004) and defined as phases of major and persistent upswings or downturns in asset price indices as derived by Borio, Kennedy and Prowse (1994);[5] (2) a number of Asian emerging market financial crises in the 1990s (as identified by Caprio and Klingebiel 2003), where anecdotal evidence suggests that crises were preceded by asset price booms; and (3) the situation of the CEE EU Member States, where in some cases strong growth is also coupled with anecdotal evidence of very significant asset price increases.

Internal versus external adjustment

When countries need to adjust in an environment turning from boom to bust as discussed above, they can either adjust through the exchange rate or the domestic price level or a combination of both. In this study we refer to *external adjusters* as those countries that allowed the nominal exchange rate to depreciate and (due to inflation differentials with trading partners being smaller than the devaluation) also experienced a depreciation of the real effective exchange rate. *Internal adjusters* are those countries that did not allow a depreciation or that experienced an appreciation of their real exchange rate through the depreciation of their trading partners. These countries had to correct real wage or tradable/non-tradable sector imbalances via domestic price adjustments while external adjusters primarily (though not necessarily exclusively) addressed imbalances through the exchange rate change.

We measure exchange rate developments via the real effective exchange rate that adjusts nominal exchange rate changes for CPI differentials for the weighted average of trading partners. This is a more appropriate measure than unit labour cost-based measures which already include wage-based internal adjustment.

Country and variable choice and 'road map' for discussion

Table 5.1 presents the countries we examine, the periods of booms and busts and the respective adjustment experience of each country. We apply a so-called case study approach. For all countries the first year of the bust (or the first year of financial crisis) is set as $t + 1$. Previous years cover the boom period and are counted backward. Following years cover the bust and financial crisis/post-crisis period respectively. We normally look at 12-year windows from $t - 6$ to $t + 5$ (unless $t + 1$ is so recent that data until $t + 5$ is not yet available). We also conduct Wilcoxon/Mann–Whitney tests to see whether differences in the means and variances of external and internal adjusters are 'significant'.

Table 5.1 Sample countries and relevant dates/episodes

Country		
I Industrialized countries, mid-1980s to early 1990s	*Boom*	*Bust*
'External adjusters'		
Australia	1984–9	1990–5
Canada	1985–9	1990–5
Finland	1986–9	1990–3
Italy		1991–7
Spain	1985–90	1991–5
Sweden	1986–9	1990–3
United Kingdom	1983–9	1990–4
'Internal adjusters'		
France	1986–90	1991–6
Japan	1979–90	1991–2002
Switzerland	1983–9	1990–6
II Asian emerging economies, late 1990s	*Bust = start of Asian crisis*	
Hong Kong ('internal adjuster')	1997	
'External adjusters'		
Korea	1997	
Thailand	1997	
Malaysia	1997	
III Industrialized countries, late 1990s to present ('internal adjusters')	*Boom*	
Netherlands	1993–2000	
Portugal	1995–2001	
IV Central and East European EU Member States	*Observation period*	
Bulgaria	All 1999–2006	
Czech Republic		
Estonia		
Hungary		
Latvia		
Lithuania		
Poland		
Romania		
Slovakia		

In order to derive stylized facts for the case studies we look at a number of stock and flow variables that are most representative of the economic sectors and transmission channels discussed above. As shown in Table 5.2, these include (1) output and demand related variables, (2) credit and asset price variables and private sector debt (domestic financial channel), (3) real effective exchange rate, unit labour costs and export/GDP (trade/competitiveness channel), (4) the current account and external financing patterns and external debt (international financial channel) and (5) public deficits and debt (fiscal channel). As will be seen, this matrix of variables can in reality not be discussed fully homogenously as there are significant data gaps. But it provides a road map linking the conceptual framework with stylized facts discussed on pp. 89–95.

As we put particular emphasis on exchange rate developments and the adjustment strategy, we will first distinguish external and internal adjusters according to their real effective exchange rate developments. The subsequent discussion starts from the presumption

Table 5.2 Sample countries and relevant dates/episodes

	Real (demand and supply)	*Domestic financial*	*Trade/external competitiveness*	*International financial*	*Fiscal*
Flow variables	Δ output/ consumption/ investment	Δ credit Δ asset prices	Δ real effective exchange rate/ unit labour costs/ exports/current account	External financing via FDI, portfolio and other investment	Deficit
Stock variables	Cumulative changes	Household & corporate debt	Cumulative changes	Cumulative changes	Public debt

of a certain sequencing in boom–bust episodes that also suggests a certain order of the sectoral discussion. Initially domestic financial and real variables seem to interact and produce a boom. We start with the discussion of real sector variables before proceeding to asset prices and domestic financial developments.[6]

The trade and competitiveness channel tends to contribute to ending the boom and is therefore discussed next. The international financial channel can already exacerbate the boom but since its greatest relevance is for emerging markets (e.g. sudden stops) it is discussed fourth. Although public finances can exacerbate or moderate boom–bust episodes, the government often picks up the tab (as losses are socialized) and, hence, this channel is discussed last.

Analysing past boom–bust episodes in industrialized and emerging economies

Boom–bust episodes in industrialized countries in the 1980s and 1990s

This section will look at case studies and stylized facts for 10 industrialized countries which experienced (asset price) boom–bust episodes in the late 1980s and 1990s.[7] As we are particularly interested in the external environment and exchange rate policies, we will present stylized facts for: (1) the seven countries that experienced a depreciation of their real effective exchange rate in the bust; they include the UK, Sweden, Finland, Australia, Canada, Italy and Spain – these external adjusters are mostly countries that had relatively fixed exchange rates in the boom but floated/devalued their currencies early in the bust; (2) the three countries that experienced an appreciation in the real effective exchange rate (CPI-based) in the bust; this group includes Japan, Switzerland and France (called internal adjusters) – two of the internal adjusters had floating currencies throughout the boom and bust (Japan and Switzerland). France maintained its peg to the DM (while widening the band) so that it experienced a relative appreciation as its main trading partners devalued.

To prepare the discussion of stylized facts across economic sectors from the angle proposed above, we look at *exchange rate developments* in the sample countries. Chart A1 shows that over the boom period, the ten countries experienced a (CPI-based) real effective exchange rate appreciation (REER) of roughly 10 per cent on average. This appreciation was more pronounced in the group of external adjusters, especially towards the end of the boom. Most interesting is the pattern during the bust: external adjusters show a strong depreciation in the REER as of the second/third year of the bust (when most sample countries actively devalued or floated their currencies). A continued, gradual appreciation was experienced by the internal adjusters.

As regards the *real economic environment*, Chart A2 shows the relatively strong growth performance in the boom of the late 1980s ($t-5$ to $t0$): 3–4 per cent real growth. In the bust ($t+1$ to $t+6$), growth not only fell rapidly but significant divergences across the two country groups emerged. Amongst external adjusters growth fell very rapidly. Growth on average was negative by $t+2$. This was followed by a sharp rebound in $t+3$ to $t+4$. Internal adjusters experienced a more gradual slowdown to near zero growth in $t+2$ and $t+3$. But the subsequent recovery was also much more gradual: average growth only recovered to 1–2 per cent by the end of the observation period. In more concrete terms, it reflects the experience of six years of very low growth in France and Switzerland and the very persistent weak growth performance of Japan.

Turning to demand composition, all countries experienced a strong consumption and investment boom where average growth rates exceeded output growth (hence contributing to growing external imbalances). In the bust, the picture reversed, with the result that cumulative positive departures from trend consumption and investment were balanced out or even overshot in the other direction in the bust.[8] Consumption and investment declines were even steeper in the group of external adjusters, in line with the picture for real output growth.

Turning to the *domestic financial environment*, Chart A3 illustrates the significant real estate price cycle that was experienced over the boom and bust phase across all countries. Note that price increases during the boom were somewhat more extreme for external as compared to internal adjusters. The real estate price cycle coincided with a distinct credit cycle where credit growth accelerated gradually until the end of the boom phase and decelerated sharply thereafter (Chart A4). The credit cycle was also more pronounced for the external adjusters.

The credit and real estate boom led to a considerable build-up of private sector debt in the boom that was (at least partly) reversed in the bust. However, good quality data for that period is only available for very few countries. Household and corporate debt ratios increased on average by 50 per cent during the boom. This increase was largest in Japan (from 140 per cent of GDP in 1980 to about 210 per cent of GDP in 1991). On the whole, this picture is consistent with the view that the asset price cycle in conjunction with the credit channel contributed to the emergence and evolution of boom–bust phases.

Inflation developments are also interesting and point to important problems in the policy mix for external adjusters (Chart A5). On the whole, inflation picked up rather gradually over the boom before declining in the downturn. But as regards the two country groups, external adjusters on average experienced significantly higher inflation than internal adjusters in the boom. While inflation differentials were relatively moderate on a year-to-year basis (inflation peaked in $t+1$ at 7 per cent for the average of external adjusters versus 4 per cent for internal adjusters), the differential accumulated over the years is nevertheless very significant. In the bust, external adjusters experienced continued inflation pressures partly as a result of significant exchange rate devaluations.

The different inflation performance in conjunction with the credit channel could be an explanation for the hammock-shaped pattern of protracted low growth experienced by internal adjusters during the bust that contrasts with the V-shaped pattern experienced by external adjusters. The high inflation rate of the external adjusters facilitated a rapid price adjustment in real estate markets without much of a nominal price fall (given that real estate prices tend to be nominally sticky). Low inflation countries, by contrast, experienced

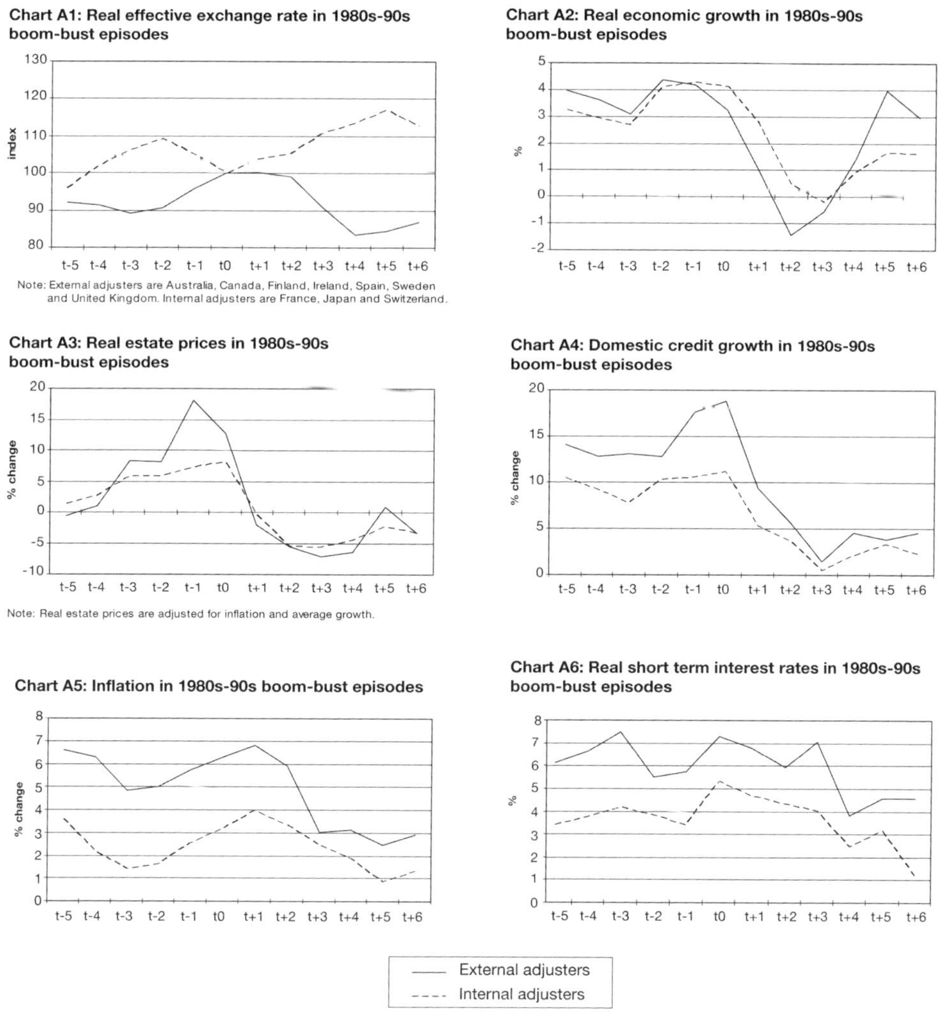

Charts A1–A6

a much more protracted housing market adjustment. The adverse effects of drawn-out house price adjustments via collateral effects on credit markets were, therefore, probably less pronounced but more persistent than in high inflation countries.

Interest rate policies at the time of the boom reflect the fact that external adjusters' monetary policies were geared at exchange rate targeting where high capital inflows kept interest rates less counter-cyclical than the strong demand (and asset price) boom might have otherwise suggested. Initially, interest rates also stayed high during the bust, first to defend the exchange rate and subsequently to fight inflationary pressures (Chart A6). Internal adjusters pursued somewhat more counter-cyclical policies and real interest rates rose more strongly in the boom while coming down gradually in the bust.

Turning to *competitiveness and the trade channel*, we find a strong divergence in competitiveness and trade developments over time and across country groups. We start with unit labour costs (ULC) which followed a very similar pattern as real and financial variables did

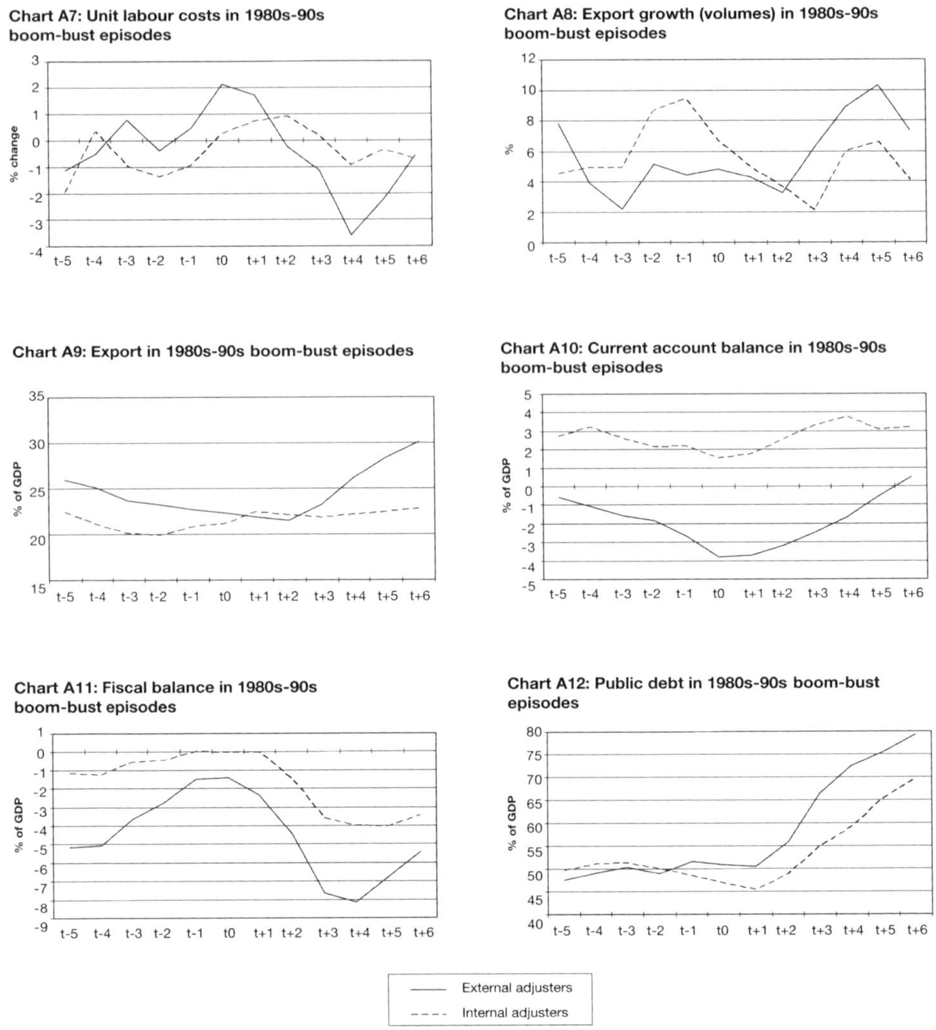

Charts A7–A12

before, with ULC growth increasing over the boom before declining significantly in the bust (Chart A7). The internal adjusters experienced a much more gradual trend of unit labour cost increases and decreases. External adjusters, however, first experienced significant ULC increases before experiencing a rather sharp reversal.

Real effective exchange rates and unit labour costs together are probably largely responsible for the emerging pattern of trade developments and, hence, the role of the trade channel. External adjusters experienced much weaker export growth than internal adjusters over the boom period (Chart A8). In the bust this relation reversed. Export volume growth increased strongly in the context of depreciation/devaluation while it remained more muted in countries pursuing internal adjustment. As a result export/GDP ratios were roughly flat over the boom and bust cycle for internal adjusters (Chart A9). For external adjusters, this ratio first declined in the boom before rising again in the bust. This supports the claim that competitiveness changes and the trade channel were much less relevant in the case of internal adjusters. This may be the second (and perhaps even more important) reason why the growth profile during the bust is that of protracted low growth (hammock) for internal adjusters than that of deep downturn followed by a rapid recovery (V shaped) for external adjusters.

Pulling the information from the real and external side together, we should find – and indeed this is confirmed in Chart A10 – that the current account balance (the counterpart to domestic savings and investment balance) deteriorates for the average of all countries in the boom before improving in the bust. This pattern is more distinct for external adjusters in the boom and bust due to stronger domestic demand growth in excess of output growth and competitiveness loss, slower export growth in the boom and a more distinct reversal of these trends in the bust. As regards the level of the current account balance, external adjusters on average report a deficit over the full cycle which increases strongly over the boom. Internal adjusters show a very modest deterioration in the current account in the boom and a moderate improvement in the bust, and overall levels remain positive throughout the cycle.

The *international financial channel* at first seems less relevant for this sample of countries where the volatility of capital flows is normally assumed to play a lesser role. Nevertheless given significant current account deficits in one group, the pattern of 'other investment flows' (bank lending etc.) for this group is worth looking at. The literature has identified exposure to short-term foreign capital as a main vulnerability that could lead to abrupt adjustment needs in periods of confidence loss ('sudden stops'). External adjusters experienced strong inflows in the boom (up to 3 per cent of GDP per annum) and strong outflows over the first three years of the bust (also up to almost 3 per cent of GDP). In this particular instance it is also worthwhile looking at individual countries in this group. The clearest sign of emerging market-type 'sudden stop' phenomena is visible for Finland and, in particular, Sweden. In the latter case, inflows of other investment amounted to 12.2 per cent of GDP in 1990 before reversing to −2.7 per cent in 1991 and staying negative until 1993. In these cases, anecdotal evidence also points to strong exposure to foreign-currency denominated debt in the private sector but firm data is hard to come by. Overall, this information suggests that the international financial channel may have played a significant role in the choice of adjustment strategy and the abruptness of adjustment (strong fall in growth) in at least some of these countries.

What role did *fiscal policies play*? First, fiscal variables reflect the revenue impact of the boom–bust cycle where revenue windfalls from capital gains related taxes boost fiscal accounts in the boom before reversing in the downturn. Consequently, the fiscal balance improves over the boom before deteriorating strongly over the bust (Chart A11). Again there is a difference in magnitude and levels in parallel with current account developments: internal adjusters experience better fiscal balances and a slower deterioration of fiscal accounts than external adjusters. The data also replicate the findings of Jaeger and Schuknecht (2004), who argue that political economy dynamics induce insufficient consolidation in the boom (the windfall is spent) and result in significant average deficits over the boom–bust cycles. In some (but not all) cases deficits reached magnitudes that required pro-cyclical consolidation to avoid macroeconomic destabilization.

The pattern of deficits and growth over boom–bust cycles determines public debt developments: debt goes down modestly in the boom before rising rapidly in the bust (Chart A12). Another way of interpreting this result is that the benefits of the boom are largely 'privatized' while the costs are 'socialized'. In some cases, this socialization was rather direct through bank and balance sheet support, e.g. in the cases of Sweden and Finland (Jonung and Stymne 1997; Eschenbach and Schuknecht 2004). In these countries, debt increased by 30 and 50 per cent of GDP, respectively.

While the chart illustrates well the sustainability risks from boom–bust episodes for external adjusters, it perhaps underemphasizes this risk for internal adjusters. Internal adjusters' debt dynamics look healthier at first but they also become very adverse over time and continue to remain adverse for longer as the adjustment period is more prolonged. Japan is the most extreme case in point.

Some simple *statistical tests* support the evidence as regards differences in the means and patterns over boom–bust episodes across the two country groups for most of the variables discussed above. Table 5.3 shows the results for Wilcoxon/Mann–Whitney tests for differences in the means of the two country groups ('populations') and tests of equal Variance (F-tests) for differences in the volatility of the series. Real effective exchange rates, credit, inflation, export shares and fiscal and external balances are found to differ significantly between internal and external adjusters. As regards real GDP and export growth, differences in means and volatility are not confirmed. This suggests that the main difference between the two groups is not the level and extremeness of the business and trade cycle per se while the more accentuated downturns and upswings in the groups of external adjusters is not picked up well with this test. The equal Variance test finds a significant difference in the amplitude of swings for the export share and the current account balance, and, perhaps even more importantly, for unit labour costs and (not quite statistically significant) real estate prices.

In summary, these stylized facts and statistical tests confirm the hypotheses expressed above: the domestic financial, trade and fiscal channels seem to contribute to the evolution of boom–bust episodes. Countries on average depicted the expected pattern of economic and financial developments. However, external adjusters were prone to experience more pronounced upswings with stronger asset price and credit growth, more competitiveness loss and unfavourable trade developments, external vulnerability due to cumulative external

Table 5.3 Wilcoxon signed ranks test for selected indicators, boom–bust episodes in industrialized countries in the 1980s and 1990s

	Wilcoxon/Mann–Whitney Eq. Variance (F-test) P-value	*Eq. Variance (F-test)*
REER	*0.00****	0.87
Real GDP growth	0.62	0.40
Real estate prices	0.84	0.14
Domestic credit growth	*0.09**	0.22
Inflation	*0.00****	0.77
ULC	0.89	*0.06*
Export growth (volumes)	0.98	0.61
Export, % of GDP	*0.002****	*0.002*
Current account balance, % of GDP	*0.00****	*0.03*
Fiscal balance, % of GDP	*0.003****	0.29
Public debt, % of GDP	0.26	0.16
Interest rate	*0.00****	0.77

Note: ***/**/* denotes significance at 1 per cent, 5 per cent and 10 per cent significance levels. Each series has 12 observations.

imbalances, and less favourable fiscal positions. In the bust, external adjusters experienced more pronounced troughs as competitiveness loss and balance sheet problems depressed demand. But once the currency was floated/devalued, growth also recovered more swiftly and forcefully, as exports rose and imports were being replaced by domestic output. The group of internal adjusters experienced fewer and smaller macroeconomic imbalances at the end of the boom, and economic and financial developments were less volatile. However, internal adjustment implied a more prolonged real and financial downturn.

While the findings clearly illustrate the intersectoral linkages that are at work, it is also important to point to systemic risks that can arise from their interplay. In Sweden, Finland and Japan, busts turned into financial crisis and both groups of countries were affected. Sweden and Finland also faced emerging market-type reversals of capital flows. They adjusted their exchange rate policy as part of the crisis resolution strategy. This strategy reinforced immediate adjustment needs in the real and financial sectors but also facilitated the emergence from the bust. Internal adjustment, pursued by Japan, did not prevent crisis but its emergence was delayed and its impact was felt in a more protracted manner.

Emerging markets: some experiences in South-east Asia in the late 1990s

When looking at boom–bust episodes from a global perspective, emerging markets are the second country group that it is most interesting to analyse. In some cases, countries experienced not just one but several (more and less severe) booms and busts over recent decades. In many cases, countries started with fixed exchange rates in the boom which proved unsustainable when 'good' times came to an end. In a number of countries, financial/balance of payment crises occurred at the turn from 'good' to 'bad' times.

Given that we have insufficient data on booms and busts in asset prices (beyond largely anecdotal references) but rather good data on incidences of financial crisis (Honohan and Klingebiel 2003; Caprio and Klingebiel 2002), we use this as criterion for selecting our sample countries and for determining the turning points from boom to bust under our case study approach. We focus on only a few 'Asian crises' in the past decade, namely Korea, Malaysia and Thailand (Asian 3). These countries floated/devalued their currencies and could hence be considered external adjusters. In addition, we examine the experience of Hong Kong, the only emerging economy of the region which should be considered an internal adjuster as it retained its currency board. These countries' experiences can be seen as particularly relevant from a European perspective as the level of development, policy and development strategies show some similarities with that of the CEE EU Member States.

We follow the same 'procedure' as on pp. 89–95 when going through the different transmission channels and indicator variables. The first bust/crisis year of 1997 is considered as $t+1$. Since all sample countries experienced booms and busts/crises at the same time, we can refer to 'real' years and we report data for the period 1991–2002 (which corresponds to the 12-year period of $t-5$ to $t+6$ in the previous section). However, even though data for these countries are better than for many other non-industrialized countries, the analysis is hampered by scarce data availability on certain key indicators. There is virtually no data on real estate prices and booms which from anecdotal evidence have played a significant role in several Asian countries. We have no comprehensive data on private sector indebtedness and even indicators of cost competitiveness are scarce and often not fully reliable. Hence the picture is sketchier than in the previous section.

Starting with *exchange rate developments* (i.e. the CPI-based REER), the pattern of developments in our sample of Asian financial crises economies is similar to that of industrialized country boom–bust episodes (Chart B1). The REER appreciated slightly in the boom preceding the bust/crisis. The bust/crisis starting in 1997 led to a drastic devaluation for the Asian 3. Thereafter, the REER appreciated again and some of the competitiveness gain was eroded. Hong Kong had the opposite experience, with the real effective exchange rate initially appreciating. Thereafter, appreciation in its major trading partners led to some correction, but on the whole the REER remained much higher than before 1997.

When looking at the *real sector*, we find confirmation of a strong economic upswing in the years before the bust/crisis (Chart B2). In particular, economic expansion of the Asian 3 was very fast, averaging 5–10 per cent annual real growth between 1991 and 1996. Hong Kong's economic growth was somewhat lower at around 5 per cent per annum. The bust/crisis led to a dramatic fall in growth especially in the Asian 3, and mostly in the first and second bust/crisis year before recovering. After a somewhat more moderate fall, growth remained more volatile and on average somewhat lower in Hong Kong.

When looking at *domestic financial conditions*, the Asian 3 experienced a pre-bust/crisis credit boom that is more extreme though, as a pattern, very reminiscent of the experiences in some industrialized countries (Chart B3). Evidence also points to deteriorating credit quality and growing non-performing loans in the pre-bust/crisis phase which contributed to later problems. Hong Kong also experienced strong credit growth but the magnitudes were more in line with industrialized country booms. In Hong Kong, real estate prices more than tripled in real terms between 1990 and 1997 (Chan *et al.* 2005).

In the downturn, the difference between adjustment strategies becomes fully apparent. Credit growth slowed strongly but remained positive in the Asian 3 while it became strongly negative in Hong Kong. This is consistent with a strongly contractionary effect through the credit channel as a real estate price decline of 40 per cent within two years and of almost 60 per cent within six years depressed collateral values dramatically. In this regard, Hong Kong's experience is much more extreme than that of the industrialized country internal adjusters of the early 1990s.

The significant difference between the Asian countries and external and internal adjusters among industrialized countries is also confirmed when looking at inflation developments (Chart B4). Hong Kong's inflation during the boom remained much lower and became negative in the aftermath of the bust/crisis. The 'brutal' internal adjustment process is reflected in negative price increases persisting for four years. The Asian 3 experienced a small blip in inflation after their devaluations but subsequently inflation came down to very low levels.

Arguably, the *competitiveness and trade channel* played a significant role in explaining this picture but there are some complications we need to make reference to. The Asian 3's export performance mirrors that of external adjusters among industrialized countries, albeit growth rates were on average much higher (Chart B5). Export growth came down in particular towards the end of the boom before it recovered after the devaluation. The adjustment of relative prices and regained competitiveness of the import-competing sector helped the post-crisis recovery. Hong Kong's export growth initially declined in tandem with the Asian 3 until 1996. However, it was much lower in the subsequent three years before internal adjustment could bear fruit.[9]

Real and trade developments are also reflected in current account data (Chart B6). The Asian 3 depicted again the pattern that was already typical for the external adjusters in the West – at least up to the devaluation: current account deficits were significant and growing (to −5 per cent of GDP in 1995/1996). During and after the bust/crisis, the current account took a turn which was much more dramatic than in our earlier sample countries.

Chart B1: Real effective exchange rate in Asian crisis countries

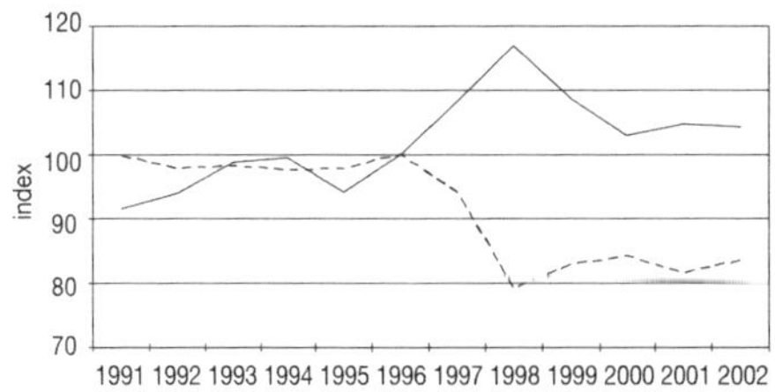

Chart B2: Real economic growth in Asian crisis countries

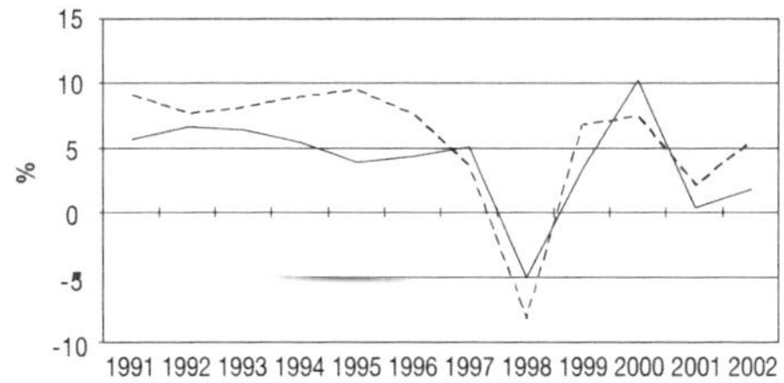

Chart B3: Domestic credit growth in Asian crisis countries

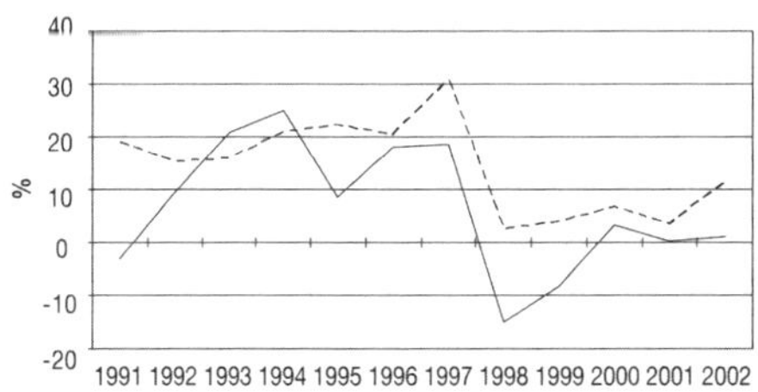

Chart B4: Inflation in Asian crisis countries

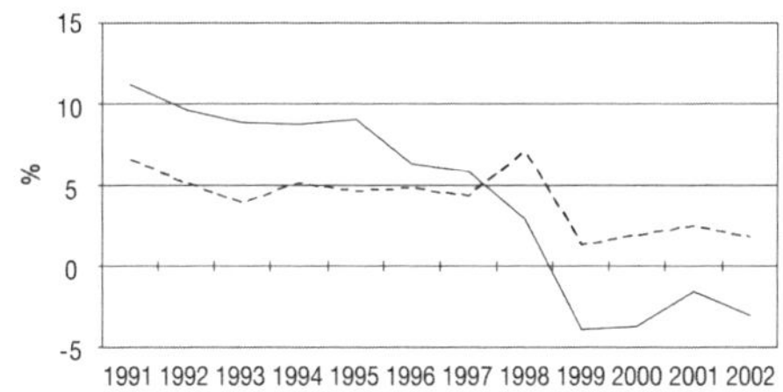

Chart B5: Export growth (volumes) in Asian crisis countries

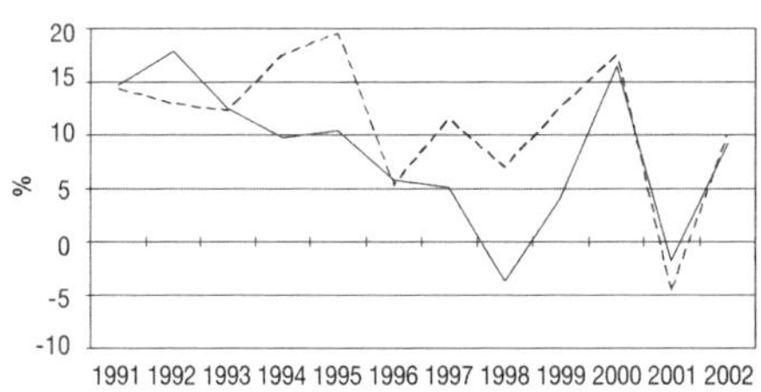

Chart B6: Current account balance in Asian crisis countries

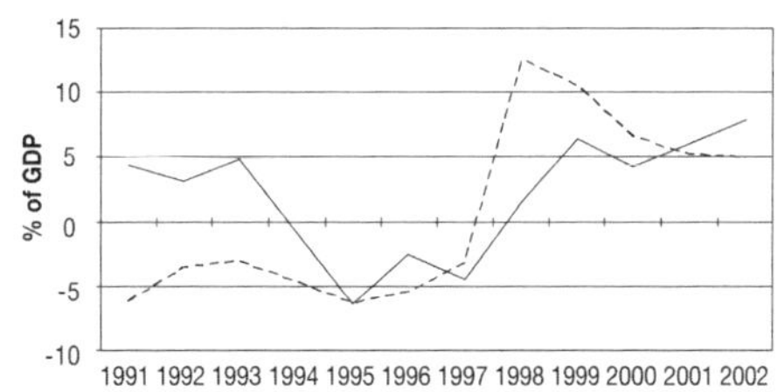

Chart B7: Portfolio and other investment in Asian crisis countries

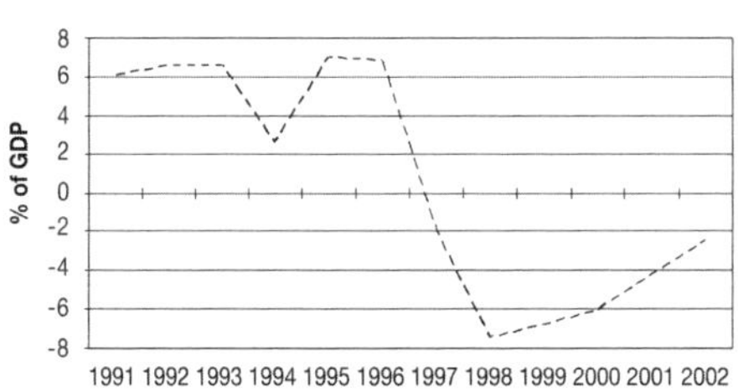

Chart B8: Fiscal balances in Asian crisis countries

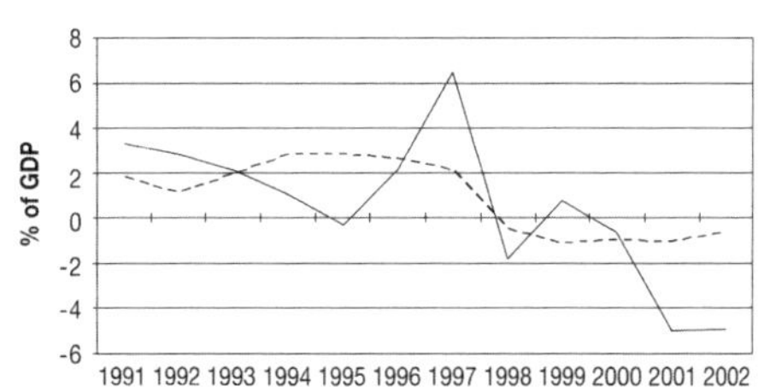

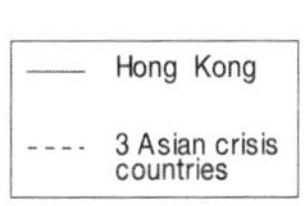

Charts B1–B8

The current account balance in the Asian 3 countries peaked at a surplus of over 10 per cent of GDP before coming down to 5 per cent of GDP by 2002. Hong Kong's experience was more consistent with that of the internal adjusters of the previous section. The external position was on average much more favourable in the boom with only two years of significant current account deficits. The recovery of the external balance was much slower than for the Asian 3.

In these (by global standards relatively small) economies the *international financial channel* and volatility in capital flows has been argued to be much more important than in industrialized countries when it comes to explaining booms and busts. Indeed, the Asian 3 experienced a huge swing in capital flows between boom and bust. Chart B7 shows that capital inflows of about 5 per cent of GDP of portfolio and other investment broadly financed the current account deficit until 1996. In 1997, capital flows became negative while the current account remained near a deficit of 5 per cent. As of 1998, the Asian 3 had reversed their current account position and were able to finance continued capital outflows. The situation of Hong Kong by contrast is unclear as no reasonable data is available for post-1996.

Finally, we take a quick look at *public finance* developments (Chart B8). Fiscal balances again show the same pattern as for industrialized country boom–bust episodes. But the starting point was much better for the Asian 3 (which experienced average surpluses in the boom). Fiscal balances deteriorated in all countries during the bust/crisis before they started recovering. Hong Kong's fiscal position in the boom on average was not better than for the Asian 3 but significant net assets of the government also helped prevent financial difficulties in the public sector.

In summary, the Asian (emerging market) booms and bust/crisis episodes in many ways show similar patterns to industrialized countries, although data availability at times hampers the analysis.[10] The same transmission channels seem to be at work even though in particular the international financial channel is likely to be much more important for emerging economies than for advanced countries. Reversal of capital flows can easily tip countries from a 'simple' bust into a full-fledged crisis when there are significant external liabilities – even when public debt is small. This again points to systemic risks that the interplay of the various transmission channels creates. External adjustment facilitated the emergence from bust/crisis.

The only country in South-east Asia that did not adjust its currency in the context of the Asian crisis was Hong Kong. Its internal adjustment strategy led to a somewhat more extreme adjustment experience than that of the internal adjusters in industrialized countries. At the end of the boom, external and fiscal positions were very favourable so that a full-fledged crisis could be avoided. The internal adjustment strategy implied deep relative price adjustment that manifested itself in several years of strong consumer and asset price deflation and low and volatile growth. However, this promoted balance sheet adjustment and the re-establishment of competitiveness.

Two case studies from recent years: the Netherlands and Portugal

From the perspective of the euro area and with a view to identify challenges for the CEE EU Member States, two more recent country experiences are worth discussing in more detail: the Netherlands and Portugal. In both countries, one could see 2000 as the last year of an asset price boom in conjunction with a period of rapid economic expansion and 2001 as the beginning of a period of low growth and other economic and financial developments that are akin to the busts of the early 1990s.[11]

Following the same approach as in the previous section (and assuming the same transmission channels and hypotheses), we look at stylized facts in these two countries and, when useful, compare them with euro area developments. Starting with exchange rate developments, both countries adopted the euro at the beginning of 1999. This means by definition that they chose the internal adjustment strategy for any eventual adjustment need. The data on real effective exchange rate developments illustrate that the two countries experienced similar REER developments over the boom to the internal adjusters in the previous section (Chart C1). Until 2000, the Netherlands and (to a lesser extent) Portugal experienced a depreciation of their CPI-based REER. Between 2000 and 2004, and with the end of the boom, the REER appreciated by 10 per cent in both countries (which was somewhat more than the euro area average).

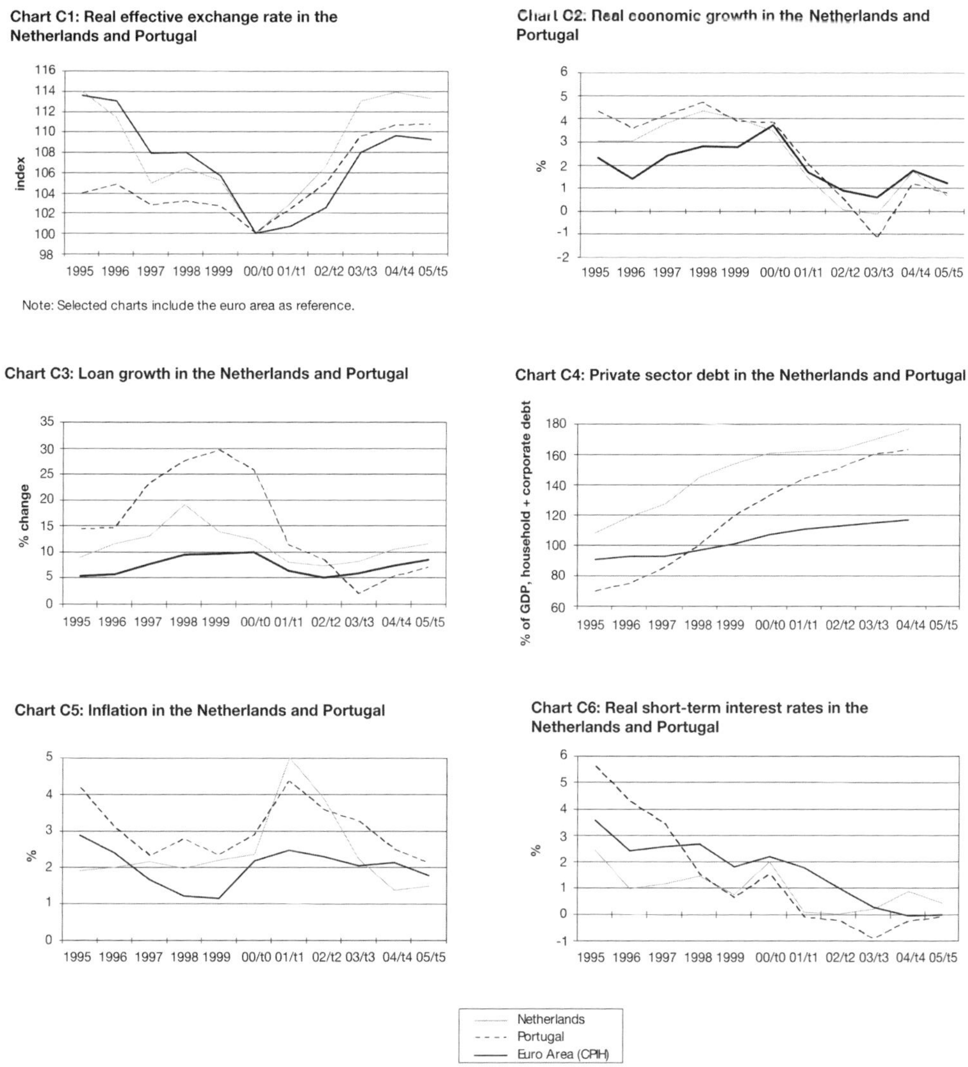

Charts C1–C6

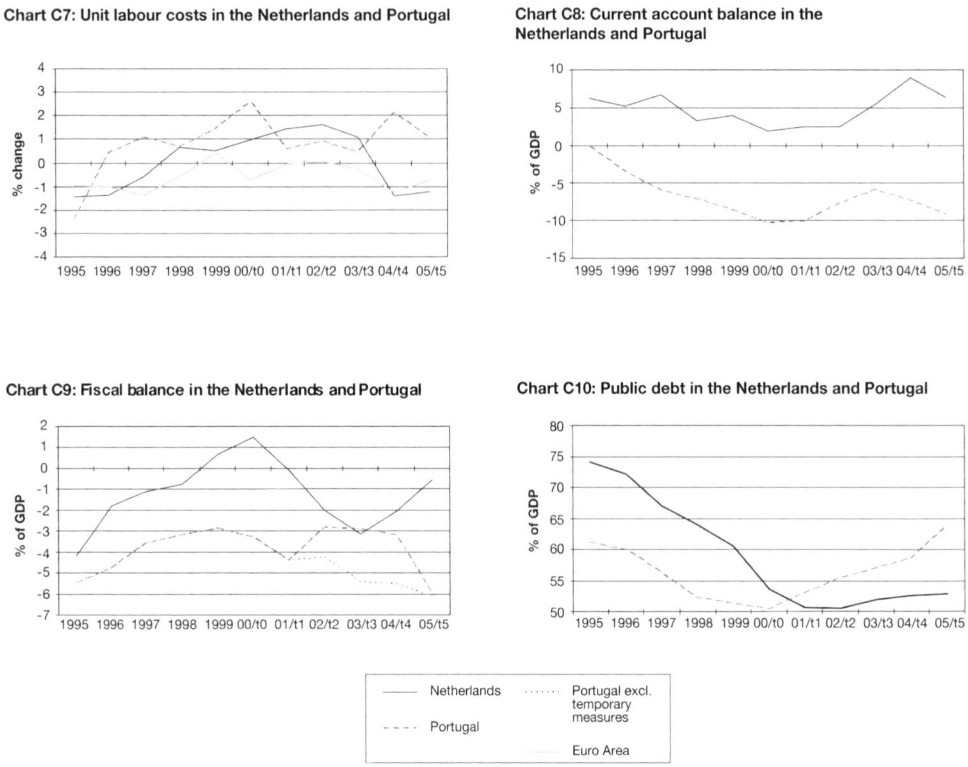

Charts C7–C10

Starting with the *real economy*, the boom–bust pattern is clearly visible in real economic growth figures as reported in Chart C2. The two countries experienced a strong boom between about 1995 and 2000: average growth reached nearly 4 per cent of GDP per annum. Since then growth first slowed down and briefly reached negative territory. Similar to the 1980s/1990s episodes, this pattern reflects a consumption and, even more importantly, investment boom in the two countries in the late 1990s which reversed in 2001.

When looking at the *domestic financial environment*, the earlier period was accompanied by a very strong stock and real estate price-cum-credit boom in the Netherlands. The inflation-adjusted stock market index, for example, increased five-fold between the early 1990s and 2000. It is not clear whether Portugal experienced a significant real estate price boom. Anecdotal evidence points to such an experience while the evidence from indicators is more mixed, which may also reflect measurement problems. However, the stock market boomed strongly in the late 1990s. Until 2001 loans in Portugal grew considerably more rapidly than in the Netherlands, although this can be partly explained by catching-up processes (Chart C3). The stock market boom came to an end in both countries in 2000 and indices fell by about 50 per cent within two years while the Netherlands real estate boom also faded out. In parallel, loan developments show a strong deceleration as of 2001.

The credit boom resulted in a dramatic deterioration of private sector balance sheets between 1995 and the early 2000s (for which there is good data available for euro area countries since 1995). This is illustrated in Chart C4. Dutch and Portuguese household and corporate debt increased very strongly over the 1995–2004 period to levels that were amongst the highest in industrialized countries and far above the euro area average.

Price developments in the two countries also exhibit a broadly similar pattern to previous boom–bust episodes (Chart C5). Inflation picked up especially towards the end of the boom, when it markedly exceeded the euro area average. Subsequently, inflation came down to levels relatively close to the euro area average of about 2 per cent. Despite these differences as compared to the euro area, inflation developments in the Netherlands and Portugal have still been more comparable to the experience of internal adjusters in the late 1980s and early 1990s.

The impact of monetary policy during the boom period was mildly expansionary in the Netherlands, where real short-term interest rates tended to fall until 1999, and strongly expansionary in Portugal, with a fall in real short-term interest rates by nearly five percentage points between 1995 and 1999 (Chart C6). This should be seen in the context of Portugal's nominal convergence process to the euro area. During the initial years of the bust, real short-term interest rates continued to fall in both Portugal and the Netherlands, thus playing a supportive role in the early phase of the internal adjustment process. Only from 2002 and 2003 onwards, respectively, the trend decline reversed, in line with the decline in inflation. Overall, however, real interest rates remained rather low in the Netherlands and Portugal.

Turning to *competitiveness and the trade channel*, unit labour costs grew rapidly during the boom (Chart C7). The depreciation of the REER may have compensated to some extent for the adverse effects until 2000, but thereafter it worked in the same direction. The reversal of the earlier competitiveness loss relative to the euro area started in 2004 in the Netherlands, while unit labour cost growth remained high in Portugal. In light of these figures it comes as no surprise that both countries' export performance also suffered in the course of the boom before it started to pick up again in 2004.

Current account developments of the two countries show a marked deterioration (Chart C8). But the Netherlands started from a significant surplus and the deterioration was less severe. As a result the current account remained in surplus at the height of the boom. This is very much in line with the pattern for internal adjusters displayed in earlier boom–bust episodes. Portugal reported a strong deterioration from balance in 1995 to a deficit of more than 10 per cent of GDP in 2000. This partly reversed until 2003 before deteriorating again thereafter. While the initial deterioration was roughly equally due to an increase in consumption and investment, developments in the following years featured a strong decline in investment that was partly 'eaten up' by a further decline in savings and an increase in consumption.

As regards *international financial vulnerability*, the magnitude of external imbalances for Portugal is reflected in rather dramatic capital flows. In fact, Portugal financed most of its current account imbalance via 'other (foreign) investment' which reflects mainly Spanish banks financing the Portuguese credit and demand boom.

In both countries, *fiscal balances* improved during the boom but this improvement was much stronger in the Netherlands than in Portugal (Chart C9). Portuguese public finances in fact already started to deteriorate in 2000. Revenue windfalls had largely been transformed into rising public spending in this country so that the fiscal deterioration in the bust started from an unfavourable level. By contrast, the bust-related worsening of the Dutch fiscal position started from a relatively favourable level.

Strategies also differed significantly in the downturn. Portugal undertook mostly one-off measures that stabilized headline deficits while masking a continuous further deterioration of the underlying balance. Chart C9, therefore, represents deficits both including and excluding temporary measures. The elimination of one-off measures brought the deficit to about 6 per cent of GDP in 2005. The Netherlands took drastic adjustment measures of about 4 per cent of GDP and the deficit breached the 3 per cent threshold in 2003 before improving again in the two subsequent years.

Public debt developments reflect deficit trends (Chart C10). The Netherlands used the good times for significant debt reduction and the following increase had not brought the debt ratio above the 60 per cent threshold again. Portuguese debt declined much less in the boom and then started rising rapidly again.

In summary, both Portugal and the Netherlands experienced an asset price, credit and real economy boom followed by a marked and sustained slowdown. Inflation in the boom was above the euro area average but differences remained rather contained and real interest rates were low during both the boom period and the subsequent downturn. However, private sector balance sheets and cost competitiveness declined in both countries during the boom and by 2005 had not yet improved (in particular in Portugal) so as to expect a rapid recovery via the trade and credit channel. There were also major differences between the two countries: the Netherlands was in a relatively favourable fiscal and external position at the end of the boom and determined action prevented major fiscal deterioration in the bust. The Portuguese 'party' of the 1990s left it with very significant imbalances where it appears that by 2005 most of them remained to be tackled.

The Central and East European EU Member States

Finally, we look at the recent experiences and economic situation of the eight Central and East European (CEE) EU Member States in the period 1999–2006.[12] The CEE countries can be broadly grouped into two separate sub-groups: (1) the three Baltic countries Estonia, Latvia and Lithuania plus Bulgaria (CEE4); and (2) the Czech Republic, Hungary, Poland, Romania and Slovakia (CEE5).[13] For the purposes of this chapter there are two key differences between these groups. The CEE4 are a group of (very) small open economies that decided early on in the transformation process to (largely) forgo active monetary and exchange rate policy and established currency boards instead. They can thus be considered as internal adjusters. The CEE5 countries are small to medium-sized open economies which, despite significant country-specific differences in their monetary and exchange rate policy, tend to make more active use of monetary and exchange rate policy instruments than the CEE4. However, ERM II membership and ultimately euro adoption imply for these countries that they will also have to ultimately move to an internal adjustment strategy (Backé *et al.* 2004; Schadler *et al.* 2005), although the timing of this transition process will again be country specific.

In line with the analytical framework used for the other country groups, we start our stock-taking exercise of the variables underlying the different transmission channels by first looking at *real effective exchange rate* developments in the CEE4 and the CEE5. Chart D1 shows a trend appreciation of the REER in both country groups. This is not surprising, given that these countries have been experiencing a real convergence process towards the euro area (and EU) average. However, the rate of appreciation was stronger in the CEE5 countries, whereas the appreciation trend flattened in the CEE4.

Real *economic growth* in the CEE5 countries was far below the growth rates of the CEE4. In fact, it was rather similar to growth rates experienced by industrialized countries during boom periods (Chart D2).[14] By contrast, the rate of economic expansion in the CEE4

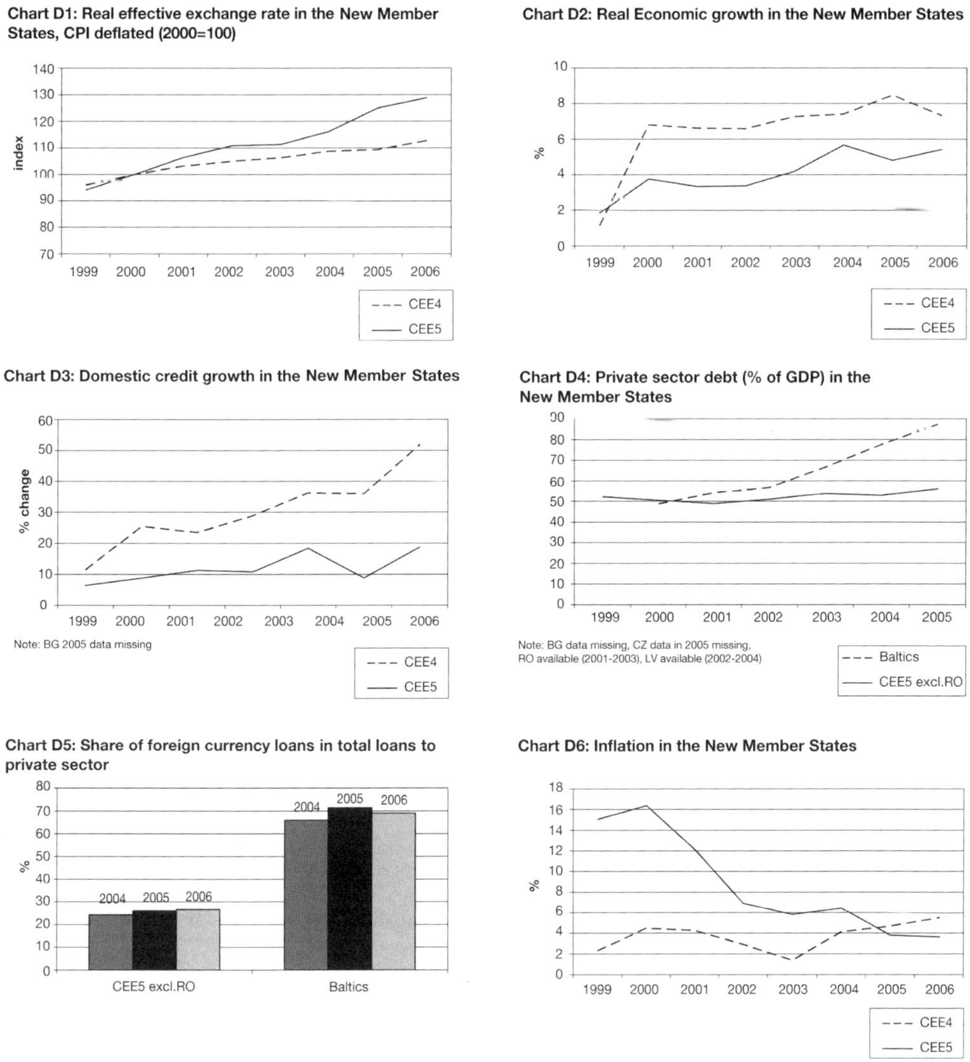

Charts D1–D6

countries was also very rapid. In fact, out of the country groups discussed in this chapter only the Asian emerging economies experienced similarly strong rates of economic expansion during their boom period until 1995. This similarity can also be observed for consumption and investment developments.

Analyses of the *domestic financial environment* in the CEE countries are unfortunately plagued by severe data problems.[15] However, the CEE countries have seen very buoyant credit growth. This applies in particular to the CEE4 (over 50 per cent in 2005) but also to some CEE5 countries (see Chart D3).[16] As a result, private sector debt-to-GDP ratios have begun to increase, especially in the Baltic countries. Although debt was still relatively low compared to the euro area average (see Chart D4 and Chart C4 for the euro area average) there are indications that the net financial position of non-financial corporations in the CEE

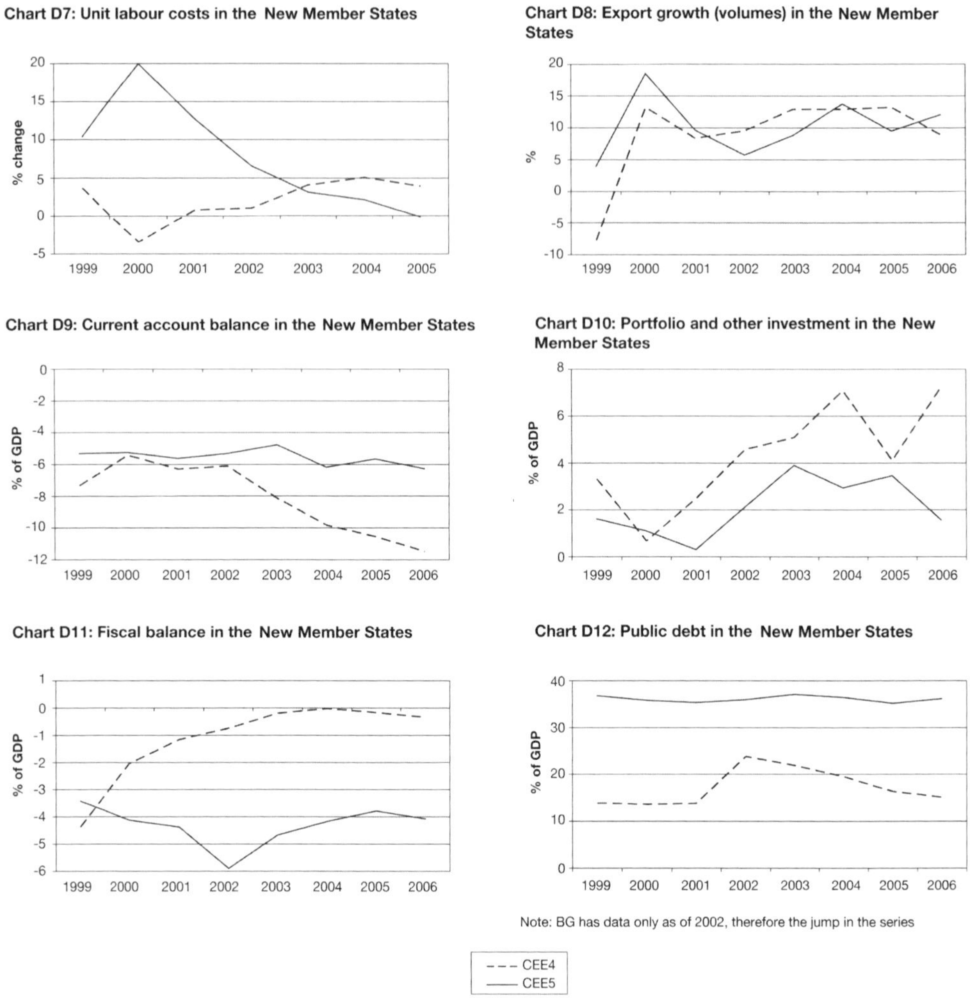

Charts D7–D12

countries became less advantageous than in the euro area (due to a less favourable asset position). Moreover, stock markets in the CEE countries have mostly experienced very fast growth in the recent past, and – although the data situation in this area is particularly weak – there is patchy evidence of strong house price increases in many CEE countries.

The very dynamic growth of credit is likely to have been influenced by the strong trend decline in real short-term interest rates observed in the CEE in general and particularly in the CEE4. In fact, real short-term interest rates in the CEE4 fell to levels below those seen in the groups of external and internal adjusters in the late 1980s. Furthermore, the share of foreign currency loans in per cent of total loans reached very high levels, in particular in the Baltic countries, where long-established currency boards and the associated perception of low currency risks make foreign currency loans with a lower interest rate particularly attractive (see Chart D5).[17] However, despite the at times considerable exchange rate volatility in the

CEE5 countries foreign currency loans also played a sizeable role in this group. This applies not only to euro-denominated loans but also to loans denominated in Japanese yen and Swiss francs.

Price developments in the CEE4 and the CEE5 from 1999 were characterized by a strong disinflation period in the CEE5 (strongly influenced by initially very high inflation in Romania) and relatively benign inflation between 1999 and 2003 in the CEE4 (see Chart D6). After 2004, however, inflation in the CEE4 picked up to levels above 5 per cent, well above the CEE5 and euro area average.

Turning to the *trade and international competitiveness channel*, unit labour cost increases in the CEE5 experienced a trend decline for a number of years largely due to very high gains in productivity (see Chart D7). However, although productivity increases in the CEE4 countries were also quite significant, ULC increased quite strongly in these countries from 2000. This is largely due to increasing wage growth, which in turn was related to emerging labour market bottlenecks in a very high growth environment.

Export growth was buoyant in both groups of CEE Member States from 2000, although the CEE4 experienced a slight decline in export volume growth (see Chart D8). Turning to the current account, however, both country groups showed persistent deficits during the entire observation period (see Chart D9). Moreover, current account imbalances in the CEE4 countries worsened considerably from 2002, reaching almost 12 per cent of GDP in 2006. Given that the CEE are catching-up economies, current account deficits are not surprising, also in view of the large investment needs of rapidly transforming economies. However, whereas the gap in investment growth between the CEE4 and the CEE5 averages closed, the current account gap widened significantly, suggesting that at least part of the CEE4's external imbalance originated from consumption rather than investment. In fact, these were the highest, persistent external imbalances experienced by any of the sample countries in this study.

Looking at the main sources of *international finance*[18] used to cover the external imbalances in the CEE countries, some similarities between the sub-groups emerge. Foreign direct investment (FDI) inflows were significant in the entire region, although they tended to decrease somewhat towards the end of the observation period. This can largely be explained by the trend decline in privatizations in these countries. By contrast, portfolio and other investment increased until 2003 in both country groups. Since then inflows into the CEE5 remained more or less constant or decreased in 2006. By contrast, these relatively volatile forms of international capital inflows reached almost 8 per cent of GDP in the CEE4 in 2004 and again in 2006 (see Chart D10).

Finally, turning to *fiscal developments* since 1999, public accounts in the CEE4 recovered steadily from the aftermath of the Russian crisis and remained at or close to balance from 2003 (see Chart D11).[19] However, despite very strong growth the CEE4 did not record fiscal surpluses. By contrast, fiscal balances in the CEE5 countries gradually deteriorated until 2002 and only the following years saw some moderate improvement. As a result, public debt in the CEE5 remained close to 40 per cent, still well below the EU average but well above the public debt ratio afforded by most emerging markets (Afonso *et al.* 2005) (see Chart D12).

Summing up, the CEE countries experienced a period of strong credit and asset price growth in conjunction with rapid economic expansion. On the basis of the stylized facts discussion for the period up to 2006 the emerging 'boom' in these countries appears more pronounced and advanced in the CEE4 while the CEE5 countries seem to be at an earlier stage.

Looking at the other sample groups discussed in this chapter, the external adjusters tended to experience more pronounced booms with more significant losses of external competitiveness and more pronounced external imbalances. By contrast, the internal adjusters among the CEE group of countries, i.e. the CEE4, appear to have been closer to a boom than the external adjusters, i.e. the CEE5. Great caution is needed, however, when interpreting this finding. First, the stylized facts do not allow a clear prediction of further development. The possibility cannot be excluded that the financial and economic expansion in the CEE5 countries will gain further momentum and catch up with the current situation in the CEE4. In addition – and even more importantly – boom periods do not need to turn into a bust but may as well lead to a more benign 'soft landing'.

Conclusions and policy implications

This study has derived stylized facts on and some preliminary statistical analysis of a number of boom–bust episodes. It has looked at different country groups (industrialized countries, emerging markets and the new CEE EU Member States) and at different adjustment strategies in the face of busts (external adjustment with real effective exchange rate devaluation versus internal adjustment without such devaluation).

The findings support the claim that real and financial variables interact in boom–bust episodes where asset price cycles and their impact on private balance sheets constitute an important driving force. The study also finds that boom–bust patterns are rather similar across industrialized and emerging countries. The former group is perhaps less vulnerable but not immune to systemic risk with reversing capital flows and busts turning into financial crises.

Most importantly, countries' different (exchange rate) adjustment experiences are correlated with the extent of macroeconomic imbalances and the degree of balance sheet vulnerability. Together with relatively loose fiscal policies, this stoked asset price and consumer price inflation and domestic demand. At the same time it reinforced competitiveness losses in the boom, which – when fortunes reversed – exacerbated the bust and the resulting adjustment needs. In those cases where the external adjustment was chosen and the exchange rate was devalued, this shift in policy first reinforced balance sheet problems in the private sector but then precipitated a rapid recovery. From this we conclude the following:

- External adjusters tend to experience more pronounced booms, with more overheating of demand, increases in prices and credit, loss of competitiveness and deterioration of (private sector, external and public) balance sheets than reported for internal adjusters.
- In busts, external adjusters tend to experience deep downturns and rapid recoveries as imbalances are initially more severe but, subsequently, also unwind more quickly. Internal adjusters tend to face less deep but more protracted downturns (and even deflation) as imbalances unwind more slowly and adjustment via the trade and credit channels takes more time.

What policy messages arise from these experiences? The study seems to confirm many 'orthodox' messages about sectoral and systemic risks:

- The more dramatic demand and financial excesses, competitiveness loss, and fiscal and external imbalances in the course of the boom, the more likely it seems that a country would be found in the group of external adjusters in the bust.

- Internal adjustment appears to be more prevalent when external and fiscal imbalances are small, and when credit growth, inflation and competitiveness loss are contained during the boom.
- Monetary policies and wage developments should not contribute to disequilibria in prices, demand or balance sheets. Fiscal policies should not stoke the boom. Low public debt would leave room for 'socializing' part of the losses in the bust if necessary. Fiscal policies have been more prudent on average in the group of internal adjusters but a number of country experiences have shown that sound headline figures in the boom are no panacea.

Stylized facts for the CEE EU Member States up to and including 2006 suggest that a few of them appear to be in the early stages of a boom while there are some others that appear to be further along. Although clear and definite conclusions cannot be drawn for the CEE EU Member States, not least due to the serious data problems for these countries that complicate, *inter alia*, a detailed examination of asset price developments and balance sheet vulnerabilities, the experiences of boom–bust scenarios in other countries may serve as an 'early warning' and may raise awareness of related policy challenges in the CEE countries. On the whole, they also confirm that the Maastricht convergence criteria provide important information to assess the sustainability of economic developments in EU Member States that aim at adopting the euro. However, balance sheet vulnerability in the private sector may be an additional factor to monitor. Whereas it is not part of the formal convergence assessment as specified in the EU Treaty, the country experiences reviewed in this chapter show that such imbalances may affect the indicators observed directly in the convergence process – although with a considerable lag and in a non-linear manner – and may provide early warnings on emerging boom–bust cycles.

Appendix: data and sources

Real effective exchange rate (REER): IMF/WEO database, Global Insight/World Market Monitor database and ECB

Real economy/demand channel

Real economic growth: OECD/OEO database and IMF/WEO database

Real private consumption: OECD/OEO database and IMF/WEO database

Real private investment: OECD/OEO and IMF/WEO database, European Commission/AMECO database and Eurostat

Total employment: OECD/OEO database and IMF/WEO database and European Commission/AMECO database

Domestic financial/credit channel

Asset price/real estate price indices: BIS, Hong Kong Monetary Authority

Credit: IMF/IFS database

Loans: ECB

Private debt: ECB

Real short-term interest: OECD/OEO

Inflation: OECD/OEO database and IMF/WEO database

Trade/competitiveness channel

Real unit labour costs: OECD/OEO database and IMF/WEO database, and Eurostat

Export volumes: IMF/WEO database

Import volumes: IMF/WEO database

Exports: IMF/WEO database
Imports: IMF/WEO database
International financial channel
Current account balance: OECD/OEO database and IMF/WEO database
Foreign Direct Investment: IMF/WEO database
Portfolio: IMF/WEO database
Other investment: IMF/WEO database
Fiscal channel
Fiscal balance (adjusted for one-off UMTS receipts): OECD/OEO database and IMF/WEO database
Public debt: OECD/OEO database

Notes

1 Valuable research assistance by Gerhard Schwab, Tobias Blattner and Ieva Rubene and editorial support by Sarah Whitehead, Saskia Schwaegermann and Stefanie Peuckmann is most appreciated. Comments by Antonio Afonso, Marcel Fratzscher, Lars Jonung, Hans Joachim Klöckers, José Marin, Philipp Rother, Livio Stracca, Max Watson and participants of the Second DG ECFIN Research Conference, European Commission, Brussels 6–7 October 2005, the IMF-EUR seminar in Washington on 29 June 2006 and the DG-Economics seminar of the ECB were very helpful. The views represented are those of the authors and not necessarily those of the ECB.
2 In addition, with respect to the CEE EU Member States it would be interesting to look at boom episodes that did *not* end in a bust period. Including such episodes and comparing them in a systematic way with the current situation in the CEE EU Member States is, however, beyond the scope of this chapter.
3 The 'choice' of adjustment strategy is to some extent endogenous given that larger imbalances ceteris paribus make internal adjustment more difficult/costly.
4 A somewhat different approach where frictions from adjustment costs to investment and monopolistic competition in the non-traded goods sector can generate boom–bust phenomena in dynamics general equilibrium modelling is applied by Fagan and Gaspar (2008).
5 Jaeger and Schuknecht (2004) construct boom and bust phases in real asset prices by following a dating method initially proposed by Harding and Pagan (2002), based on the so-called triangular methodology. This technique identifies the peaks and troughs of the asset price series (their turning points) whereby asset price indicators include stocks and real estate depending on their weight in the asset composition of an economy. They then calculate the duration of the period from trough to peak (the upswing) and from peak to trough (the downturn) and the amplitude of the asset price changes over these periods. By multiplying duration and amplitude, they arrive at a ranking of asset price upswings and downturns of which the largest quintile is referred to as boom–bust episodes. This enables them to separate booms and busts in asset prices from more normal asset price movements. The approach does not entail that a boom or a bust phase needs to be followed by another similar phase. The only exception in this list is Portugal, where no comparable asset price indicator is available.
6 The reverse order is also conceivable (see. e.g., Jonung *et al.* 2005) given that this is something of a 'chicken and egg problem'. However, the more 'conventional' ordering approach chosen in this study appeared to be a bit more reader-friendly.
7 For earlier studies, applying a stylized facts approach on these phenomena, see also Jaeger and Schuknecht (2004); Jonung, Schuknecht and Tujula (2005); and IMF (2000).
8 Jaeger and Schuknecht (2004) found that the average cumulative deviation from trend in booms and busts amounted to about 10 per cent for consumption and about one-quarter for investment.
9 Hong Kong's export growth reflects to a very significant extent re-exports which were positively affected by the export boom in those countries that had devalued. Hence the domestic export picture is probably less favourable.
10 This finding is also confirmed when conducting the earlier Wilcoxon/Mann–Whitney and variance tests on extended groups where Hong Kong is added to the group of internal adjusters and Korea, Malaysia and Thailand to the external adjusters.

11 While in the case of the Netherlands this is based on the Jaeger/Schuknecht methodology, in the case of Portugal asset price indicators were not available. The identification hence follows from the parallel experience of the stock market decline that started in 2000 in all industrialized countries and patterns of economic and financial developments discussed below.

12 Two other new EU Member States, Cyprus and Malta are not covered in this chapter given that asset price and financial market developments as well as real economic growth in these two countries have been rather subdued in recent years compared to the CEE countries. This makes a stock-taking exercise in view of possible boom and bust experiences due to the interaction of real and financial sector variables less meaningful.

13 Slovenia has not been included in either of these two groups. With regard to asset price and economic growth development it would fit into the CEE5 group of countries, but it follows an internal adjustment strategy. In fact Slovenia joined the euro area on 1 January 2007.

14 On growth prospects in the new central European EU Member States, see, e.g., Arratibel *et al.* (2007); European Commission (2004); or Wagner and Hlouskova (2002).

15 For a detailed overview of credit developments in the CEE countries, see Backé and Zumer (2005) or European Central Bank (2006a).

16 Cottarelli *et al.* (2003) do not see the recent evolution of bank credit in Central and Eastern Europe and the Balkans as troublesome. However, the results of their empirical work are based on developments only up to 2003.

17 Comparable recent data for Bulgaria and Romania are not available.

18 On international capital flows and the new Member States, see, e.g., Begg *et al.* (2003).

19 For a useful overview of fiscal developments in most CEE countries, see the ECB's Convergence Reports in 2006 (ECB 2006b; ECB 2006c).

References

Afonso, A., C. Nickel and P. Rother (2005) *Fiscal Consolidations in the Central and Eastern European Countries*, ECB Working Paper Series No. 473/2005.

Allen, M., C. Rosenberg, C. Keller, B. Setser and N. Roubini (2002) *A Balance Sheet Approach to Financial Crisis*, IMF Working Paper WP/02/210.

Arratibel, O., F. Heinz, R. Martin, M. Przybyla, L. Rawdanowicz, R. Serafini and T. Zumer (2007) *Determinants of Growth in the Central and Eastern European EU Member States – a Production Function Approach*, ECB Occasional Paper Series No. 61.

Backé, P. and T. Zumer (2005) 'Developments in credit to the private sector in Central and Eastern European EU Member States: emerging from financial repression – a comparative overview', in *Focus on European Economic Integration* 2/05, Oesterreichische Nationalbank: 83–109.

Backé, P., C. Thimann, O. Arratibel, O. Calvo-Gonzalez, A. Mehl and C. Nerlich (2004) *The Acceding Countries' Strategies Towards ERM II and the Adoption of the Euro: An Analytical Review*, ECB Occasional Paper Series No. 10.

Begg, D., B. Eichengreen, L. Halpern, J. von Hagen and C. Wyplosz (2003) *Sustainable Regimes of Capital Movements in Accession Countries*, CEPR Policy Paper No. 10.

Bernanke, B., M. Gertler and S. Gilchrist (1999) 'The financial accelerator in a quantitative business cycle framework', in J.B. Taylor and M. Woodford (eds) *Handbook of Macroeconomics*, vol. I, Amsterdam: Elsevier Science.

Bordo, M.D. and O. Jeanne (2002) *Monetary Policy and Asset Prices: Does 'Benign Neglect' Make Sense?*, IMF Working Paper WP/02/225.

Borio, C. (2008) 'The search for the elusive twin goals of monetary and financial stability', Chapter 17 in this volume.

Borio, C. and P. Lowe (2002) *Asset Prices, Financial and Monetary Stability: Exploring the Nexus*, BIS Working Paper No. 114.

Borio, C., N. Kennedy and S.D. Prowse (1994) *Exploring Aggregate Asset Price Fluctuations across Countries, Measurements, Determinants and Monetary Policy Implications*, BIS Economic Papers No. 40.

Calvo, G.A., A. Izquierdo and L.-F. Mejia (2004) *On the Empirics of Sudden Stops: the Relevance of Balance-Sheet Effects*, NBER Working Paper 10520.

Calvo, G.A., A. Izquierdo and E. Talvi (2003) *Sudden Stops, the Real Exchange Rate, and Fiscal Sustainability: Argentina's Lessons*, NBER Working Paper 9828.

Campos, N.F. and Y. Kinoshita (2003) *Why Does FDI Go Where It Goes? New Evidence from the Transition Economies*, IMF Working Paper WP/03/228.

Caprio, G. and D. Klingebiel (2002) 'Episodes of systematic and borderline banking crises', in D. Klingebiel and L. Laeven (eds) *Managing the Real and Fiscal Effects of Banking Crises*, World Bank Discussion Paper No. 428, pp. 31–49.

Chan, N., W. Peng and K. Fan (2005) 'A graphical framework for monitoring the property market in Hong Kong', *Hong Kong Monetary Authority Quarterly Bulletin*, March: 5–12.

Cottarelli, C, G. Dell'ariccia and I. Vladkova-Hollar (2003) *Early Birds, Late Risers and Sleeping Beauties: Bank Credit Growth to the Private Sector in Central and Eastern Europe and the Balkans*, IMF Working Paper WP/03/213.

Detken, C. and F. Smets (2004) 'Asset price booms and monetary policy', in Horst Siebert (ed.) *Macroeconomic Policies in the World Economy*, Berlin: Springer.

ECB (2004) *Convergence Report*, Frankfurt: ECB.

—— (2006a) 'Financial development in central, eastern and south-eastern Europe', *Monthly Bulletin*, November: 93–104.

—— (2006b) *Convergence Report May 2006*, Frankfurt: ECB.

—— (2006c) *Convergence Report December 2006*, Frankfurt: ECB.

Eichengreen, B. and O. Choudhry (2005) 'Managing capital inflows: Eastern Europe in an Asian mirror', paper presented at the Turkish Central Bank/Center for European Integration Studies Conference on Macroeconomic Policies for EU Accession, Ankara, 6–7 May.

Eschenbach, F. and L. Schuknecht (2004) 'Budgetary risks from real estate and stock markets', *Economic Policy*: 315–48.

European Commission (2004) *The EU Economy: 2004 Review*, Brussels: European Commission.

Fagan, G. and V. Gaspar (2008) 'Adjusting to the euro', Chapter 4 in this volume.

Finger, K. Michael and Ludger Schuknecht (1999) *Trade, Finance and Financial Crises*, WTO Special Studies 3.

Harding, D. and A. Pagan (2002) 'Dissecting the cycle: a methodological investigation', *Journal of Monetary Economics* 49: 265–81.

Honohan, P. and D. Klingebiel (2003) 'The fiscal cost implications of an accommodating approach to banking crises', *Journal of Banking & Finance*, 27: 1539–60.

IMF (2000) 'Asset prices and the business cycle', *World Economic Outlook*, Washington, DC: IMF, pp. 77–112.

Jaeger, A. and L. Schuknecht (2004) *Boom–Bust Phases in Asset Prices and Fiscal Policy Behavior*, IMF Working Paper WP/04/54.

Jonung, L. and J. Stymne (1997) 'The great regime shift: asset markets and economic activity in Sweden, 1985–93', in F. Capie and G. Wood (eds) *Asset Prices and the Real Economy*, London: Macmillan.

Jonung, L., L. Schuknecht and M. Tujula (2005) 'The boom–bust cycle in Finland and Sweden 1985–2000 in an international perspective', Economic Paper no. 237, Brussels: DG ECFIN; available at http://europa.eu.int/comm/economy_finance/publications/economic_papers/economicpapers237_en.htm.

Komulainen, T. (2004) *Essays on Financial Crises in Emerging Markets*, Helsinki: Bank of Finland.

Schadler, S., P. Drummond, L. Kuijs, Z. Murgasova and R. van Elkan (2005) *Adopting the Euro in Central Europe: Challenges of the Net Step in European Integration*, IMF Occasional Paper No. 234.

Sinn, H.W. (2004) *Ist Deutschland noch zu retten?*, Berlin: ECON.

Watson, M. (2005) 'Financial stability in macroeconomic surveillance: converging economies', mimeo, Brussels: DG ECFIN.

Wagner, M. and J. Hlouskova (2002) *The CEEC10s Real Convergence Prospects*, Centre for Economic Policy Research Discussion Paper No 3318.

6 Financial stability in emerging Europe

Piroska M. Nagy and Richard Fox

Introduction

The transformation of the financial sector in emerging market Europe and the main CIS countries (Kazakhstan, Russia and Ukraine)[1] has been one of the most dramatic in recent economic history. In the matter of a short decade and a half, emerging market Europe has transformed from a state-dominated mono-bank system that performed quasi-fiscal operations on behalf of the government into a reasonably effective, market-based system with many new competing banks providing increasingly sophisticated financial services. Financial intermediation, measured as domestic credit as a share of GDP, has increased from less than 25 per cent of GDP in 1990 to 54 per cent of GDP in 2004, albeit the levels are still much lower than what is seen in the euro area (117 per cent). Structural reforms started belatedly and the process is still incomplete in the CIS-3, but progress, led by Kazakhstan, is also clearly measurable in that region (Table 6.1).

The transformation, stabilization and consolidation of banking sectors in the context of an increasingly stable macroeconomic and increasingly market-friendly legal-regulatory environment have paved the way towards a very rapid domestic credit growth and financial deepening.[2] First there were the Cottarelli 'early birds' – countries where rapid credit growth had started first (Hungary, Croatia, Slovenia, etc.), but by 2005, credit boom was well underway in virtually all transition economies (Figure 6.1.)

As with any rapid credit growth period, concerns have emerged over systemic risk and financial sector stability. These are historically well justified: rapid credit growth has often led to serious banking sector stress and overt banking sector crisis in the last three decades, particularly in emerging markets (IMF 2004). Indeed, 'excessive' credit growth can lead to banking sector crisis through overstretched balance sheets with excessive risk taking, weakening portfolio quality and worsening efficiency. It may even result in a twin balance of payments and banking sector crisis, where banking sector stress eventually spurs a currency crisis in the context of fixed exchange rate regimes, which in turn deepens the banking crisis, activating a vicious spiral (Kaminsky and Reinhart 1999). When the boom ends in bust, recession sets in, with foreign exchange reserves depleted, and the exchange rate collapses. The drivers behind such credit growth can be excessive cyclical movements, which is generally characterized in the literature as market participants' inappropriate responses to changes in risks over time, i.e. market imperfections. A mechanism underpinning this is the so-called financial accelerator, where excessive optimism about future earnings boosts asset prices that in turn raise the value of collateral; capital inflows increase that finance credit growth to firms and households. In the downturn, asset prices and collateral values collapse, perceived risks increase and interest rates go up, making debt service increasingly difficult and eventually resulting in bank failures.

Table 6.1 Summary of financial sector transformation, 1989–2005

The 1989 start position	*2005 CEE*	*2005 CIS-3*
State ownership	Privatization is almost complete in most countries	Privatization is far from complete in Russia and Ukraine
Most banks are domestically owned 'pocket' banks, serving specific industry or client interest	Majority of banks owned by well-established foreign strategic investors; regulations limit connected lending	There is still significant 'pocket' banking with associated connected lending
Poor governance structure favouring insiders	Improving governance structure with tighter controls on related party transactions	Some improvement in governance but structure is still opaque. Weak governance is one of the biggest problems in Russia and Ukraine
Financial sector consisting only of commercial banks	Non-financial sector is emerging (insurance, mortgage banks, pension funds), but banks are still dominant	Non-financial sector is very small
Lack of medium- and long-term lending	Maturities extended	Still an issue
Little bank finance of enterprise investment or of household mortgages	Rapidly increasing bank finance of both households and firms	Rapidly increasing bank finance of both households and firms
Low financial intermediation	Rapidly increasing, albeit still relatively low	Rapidly increasing but still very low
Poor bank asset quality	Much improved thanks to balance sheet clean-ups, restructuring and privatization; risk management techniques more widely used	Improvements but still a problem
Banking supervision/ regulation does not exist	Regulatory framework being brought up to EU standards	Improvements but still rudimentary systems, except for Kazakhstan
Pervasive legal uncertainty	Significant legal reforms have taken place	Legal obstacles can still be a key obstacle to business

Against such bleak possibilities, how concerned should we be about financial sector stability in the rapidly growing banks of emerging market Europe? Research thus far has approached this question from two different angles: first, attempting to assess equilibrium credit levels in the region; and, second, analysing a similar experience of non-core euro area members in the run-up to European Monetary Union (EMU). The paper briefly reviews these two approaches and then proposes to use a new approach to assess financial sector stability we developed while working together at Fitch Ratings in 2003–4. The paper concludes with policy options to address the identified problems.

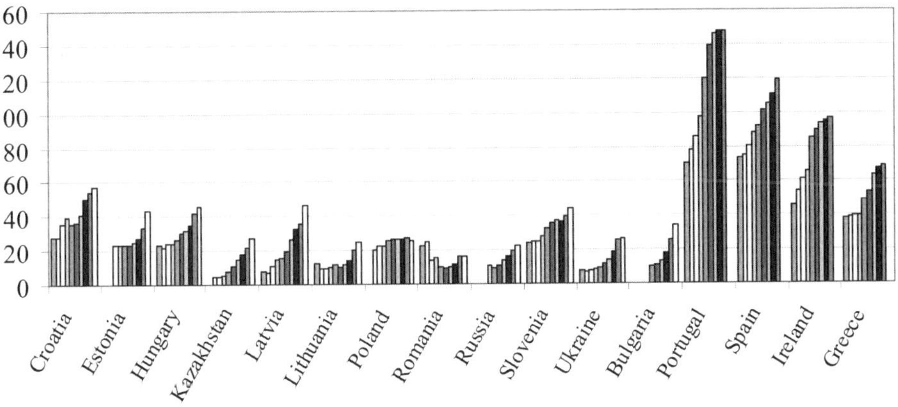

Figure 6.1 Ratio of private sector credit to GDP in emerging Europe, CIS-3 and non-core euro area countries, 1996–2004 (%).[1]

Sources: IFS and IMF country reports.

Note:

1 The Czech Republic and Slovakia are excluded because data contain the impact of ongoing debt write-offs, takeover of debt by various agencies and reclassifications through the past decade.

How concerned should we be about financial sector stability in emerging market Europe and the CIS-3?

Econometric evidence

Econometric analysis is constrained by lack of sufficient data series and structural breaks in them. Using out-of-sample estimations, Cottarelli *et al.* (2003) and Schadler *et al.* (2005) found that financial intermediation, measured as private sector credit as a share of GDP, was some 40–50 per cent below its equilibrium levels at end-2002. Cottarelli *et al.* (2003) estimated the equilibrium level of the private sector credit/GDP ratio for a panel of non-transition developing and developed countries for the period 1973–6. The ratio is related to public debt (to capture a 'crowding-in' effect of private sector credit over public sector credit), GDP per capita income (as a proxy for economic development), inflation, financial sector liberalization, bank entry requirements, accounting, and legal origin of the country (the 'German' model having a higher credit ratio). The resulting coefficients are then used to assess out-of-sample equilibrium level credit/GDP for transition countries. The results imply that credit levels in virtually all Central European and Balkan countries were considerably, on average 50 per cent, below their estimated equilibrium level at end-2002.

Schadler *et al.* (2005) follow a similar method, using an estimated dynamic (vector error correction) model for private sector credit growth for the panel of euro area members in 1991–2002. The model dependent variables include long-term interest rates on government bonds (proxy for cost of credit); and per capita income. The estimated impacts are quite large: a 10 per cent increase in per capita income raises the credit/GDP ratio by about 3 per cent in the long run; while a 1 per cent increase lowers it by two percentage points. The estimated parameters were again used to predict equilibrium values and dynamic adjustment paths to them for individual new EU Member States. The results were similar to those of Cottarelli *et al.*, indicating that actual private sector credit/GDP ratios were, on

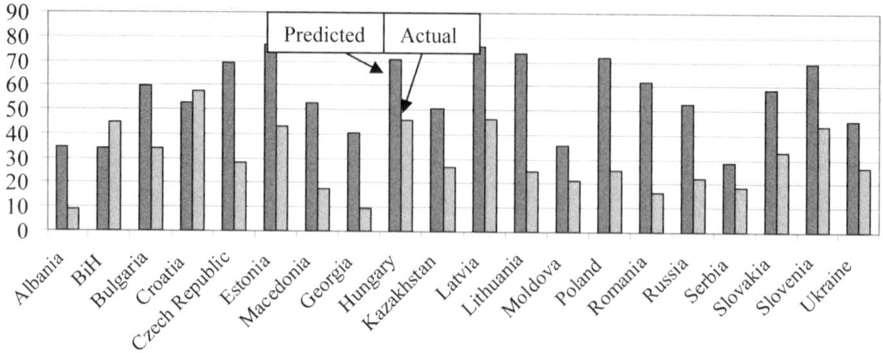

Figure 6.2 Actual and estimated 'equilibrium' level of credit in emerging Europe and CIS.
Source: EBRD (2005)

average, 41 per cent below their equilibrium level at end-2002. Schadler also found that real convergence-related private sector credit expansion in the near future is likely to bring very rapid credit growth. Their calculation of a dynamic trend path for private sector credit in the new EU Member States predicts annual credit growth rates of about 30–40 per cent in the coming years. This would still be lower than the rates seen in non-core euro-zone countries – Portugal, Spain, Ireland and Greece – in the run-up to the introduction of the euro.

Ongoing credit boom in emerging European markets thus mirrors genuine financial deepening. It is structurally driven, as these economies are moving toward their new long-term equilibrium. It is spurred by large differences in capital/labour ratios relative to the pre-enlargement EU-15, expectations of real exchange rate appreciation, in some cases still sizeable nominal interest rate differentials, and the ensuing capital inflows. It is likely to accelerate real sector convergence through investment financial and consumption smoothing.

While research thus far has focused on emerging market Europe, the ongoing financial deepening may not be simply a story of 'convergence play' to advanced Europe. It is probably a more general 'transition story'. A report by the EBRD (2005) found that using the parameters by Cottarelli *et al.* for out-of-sample estimations, private sector credit at end-2004 was below its equilibrium by about 50 per cent in the CIS-3 as well. The notable exceptions were Croatia and Bosnia-Herzegovina.

Lessons from historical experience

Non-core EMU countries – Greece, Ireland, Portugal and Spain – experienced a massive credit boom in the run-up to euro adoption (Figure 6.1). The countries' private sector credit/GDP ratio in the five years in the run-up to the adoption of the euro jumped by a staggering 41 percentage points of GDP on average. The credit expansion has continued to date, albeit at a reduced pace, with actual EMU membership having given perhaps an added impetus to the ongoing financial deepening.

Despite fears at the time about its sustainability, this decade-long credit boom has not produced spectacular financial sector or macroeconomic stress in the non-core EMU-4. None of these countries have experienced the feared possible negative consequences of rapid credit growth – deteriorating portfolio quality or clearly unsustainable macroeconomic imbalances ending in a spectacular bust. Capital adequacy has come under some pressure, especially in Portugal, but never slipped close to the 8 per cent Basel-minimum.

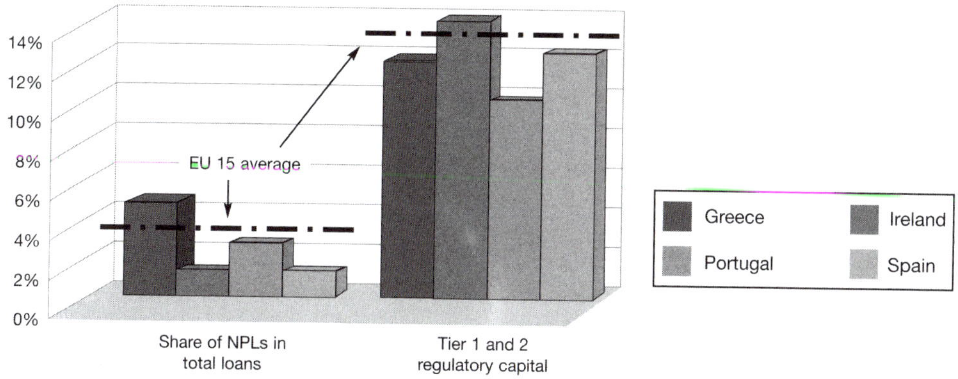

Figure 6.3 Share of non-performing loans in total loans and regulatory capital.
Sources: IMF country reports and ECB.

At the same time, bank portfolio quality has generally improved over the decade, with declining non-performing loans and improving provisioning. Efficiency has also improved. Profitability has been adequate, despite compression of interest rate margins under increased competition. Figure 6.3 shows that by end-2003, non-core EMU countries' portfolio quality and capital adequacy were broadly in line in the four non-core EMU countries with (pre-enlargement) EU-15 averages (marked by a dotted line).

On the macro side, the external current account worsened in all the four countries in the run-up to the euro, but even the worst performer, Portugal, has managed a subsequent adjustment (Figure 6.4). Currencies did not come under pressure even in the case of the belated Greek entry to the euro (the latter of course benefited from a large devaluation upon EMU entry). Fiscal balances improved strongly in all countries through 1999 (2000 for Greece) so as to meet the associated Maastricht fiscal criteria and qualify for the EMU. But fiscal policy relaxed afterwards, particularly in Greece and Portugal. However, Portugal had much stronger private sector credit growth than Greece and it is possible that the simultaneous overstretching of balance sheets of the government and the private sector and the subsequent necessary re-balancing by both may have contributed to an economic recession in 2003–4 and below-potential growth since then. The continued credit boom in the euro area could result in unwarranted real exchange appreciation (through relative prices and wages), thus loss of competitiveness, negatively impacting potential growth (European Commission 2005).

Assessment of banking sector stability

Against the backdrop of the consensus that the ongoing credit growth reflects shifts towards a new equilibrium and broadly reassuring recent historical episodes, what does banking sector stability look like today in emerging Europe and the CIS-3? To answer this question, we employ a novel banking sector systemic risk analysis (Fitch Ratings 2005a; 2005b). The approach combines evidence of macroeconomic vulnerability with an assessment of individual bank strength and systemic risk factors. The underlying idea is that while systemic vulnerability may increase either because the banking system becomes weaker or because macro-prudential vulnerability increases, strong systems are more likely to be able to absorb higher stress than weak systems. Therefore it is important to consider not only the macro-prudential and banking system strength factors alone but also their interplay.

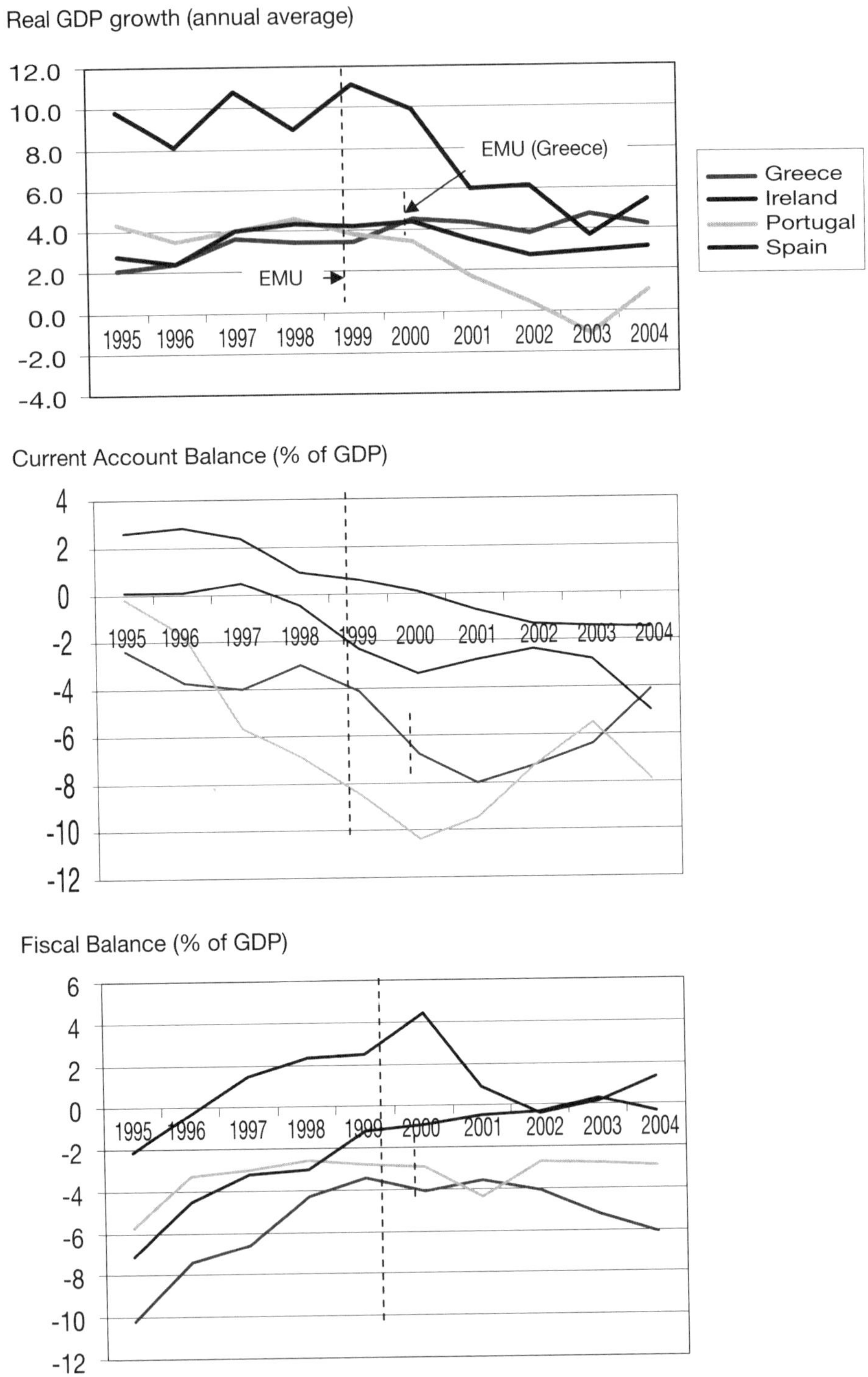

Figure 6.4 Macroeconomic performance in non-core EMU-4, 1995–2004.

The approach considers two main elements: a measure of banking system strength, the Banking System Indicator (BSI), and a measure of macro-prudential vulnerability, the Macro-prudential Indicator (MPI).

Banking System Indicator (BSI)

The BSI measures banking system 'quality' on a scale from A (very high quality) to E (very low quality). It starts from a measure of intrinsic banking system strength – the System Average Individual Rating (SAIR), derived from Fitch's bank Individual ratings. This is supplemented with a systemic risk assessment that identifies weaknesses common to most banks in a system and that have played a role in previous systemic banking crises.

Fitch's longstanding Individual bank ratings, which are internationally comparable, assess how a bank would be viewed in the absence of external support, whether from shareholders or the authorities. These ratings are designed to assess a bank's exposure to, appetite for, management of and capacity to absorb risk and thus represent Fitch's view on the likelihood that it would run into significant difficulties, such that it would require support.[3] In other words, the Individual rating expresses the risk of a bank failing.[4]

The system average Individual rating, or SAIR, is simply the average Individual rating of the system as a whole. It is an indication of the average risk of a systemically important bank failing. In most countries, Fitch rates banks accounting for a critical mass of the banking system (at least two-thirds of system assets and in most countries much more). The SAIR is an asset-weighted average of the Individual ratings of rated and systemically important unrated banks. (For unrated banks, an internal assessment of the Individual rating is used.) The SAIR does not therefore include all banks in the system, but it includes all those that are systemically important.[5]

By focusing on the Individual rating, this measure by definition excludes the impact of 'support'.[6] Support from a bank's institutional owners can have an important bearing on systemic risk. Foreign-owned banks, for example, may reduce systemic risk in a number of ways, either directly, by introducing better management and systems, or indirectly, by instilling confidence in a system that is otherwise seen as weak, as in many emerging markets. To the extent that foreign ownership enhances intrinsic bank strength, it will already be factored into the Individual rating. By contrast, if the bulk of the system is foreign owned and this is felt to bring benefits going beyond the impact on an individual bank, this is picked up by the systemic risk analysis, described next.

Failure of an individual bank will not always, or even often, trigger a systemic crisis. A supplementary element of the methodology therefore aims to identify specific systemic risks that either increase the chances of one bank's problems being transmitted to other banks or make the system as a whole vulnerable to an exogenous shock, such as the failure of a large corporate or a major devaluation.

Based on the literature in this area, combined with Fitch's own experience, causes of recent systemic banking crises have been grouped under nine headings:

- *Extensive inter-bank positions.* Inter-bank markets help efficient financial intermediation but under stress may become channels for transmitting liquidity problems, particularly when – as they often are – uncollateralized.
- *High borrower indebtedness.* High corporate and household debt may impair the borrowers' ability to service debt. For example, high corporate leverage was a key factor in the Asian crisis.

- *Foreign currency lending to borrowers without foreign currency resources.* Foreign currency lending to agents without foreign currency resources exposes both borrowers and banks to exchange rate risk, even if banks' overall foreign currency positions are matched.
- *High sovereign exposure.* Direct or indirect exposure to the sovereign, particularly where the sovereign is below investment grade, is a risk. The proportion of sovereign debt to total bank assets is generally less than 10 per cent in developed country banking systems and around 15 per cent in emerging markets. As well as direct lending, whether through credit or bonds, exposure to the sovereign may also be indirect, for example where there is extensive use of guarantees or government bonds as collateral. Previous episodes of forced lending to the government or pressure to change contractual terms are also considered, as was the case in Argentina prior to the 2001 sovereign default.
- *Lending concentration.* If many banks lend to a particular sector, industry, company or individual, its failure could trigger a banking crisis. The share of the 20 largest loans in bank portfolios can be a good indicator, which in a reasonably developed economy is less than 20 per cent. In a small undiversified economy the ratio may be naturally much higher, but still represent a risk.
- *Deposit concentration.* If deposits are highly concentrated, a sudden single deposit withdrawal can precipitate bank collapse.
- *Simultaneous existence of low capital, low liquidity and high share of demand deposits.* These three elements separately can be a source of weakness but not necessarily leading to bank failure. Yet when present together they increase the risk of systemic crisis if there is deposit flight and there is insufficient liquidity or capital.
- *Weak regulation or transparency and governance.* Weak governance is a proven cause of banking sector crises. Banking systems have also proved vulnerable to self-fulfilling crises emanating from financial contagion, fuelled by misinformation. The assessment of the regulatory system is also important, as it indicates the capacity to monitor bank performance, and help banks cope with financial stress.
- *Other factors,* such as off-balance sheet weaknesses. These may include widespread off-balance sheet operations (a reason for bank failures during the Asian crisis) or unprovisioned contingent liabilities.

Bank analysts assess each banking system according to the existence of these factors and the degree of concern. The focus is on weaknesses common to many or most banks in a system. It therefore goes beyond the identification of these risks in individual banks. This is important because the perspective of system-wide and individual bank risk can sometimes be very different. For example, large holdings of sovereign bonds may be a relative strength for an individual emerging market bank if there is a dearth of private lending opportunities. But if common to all banks, this represents a clear systemic risk in the event of a sovereign crisis or default. The weight Fitch attaches to the systemic risk assessment in compiling the overall Banking System Indicator is expected to increase over time as ways of measuring exposure to the various risks are refined and risk assessments consequently increase in comparability across countries.

Table 6.2 lists countries in emerging Europe in order of descending 'quality' of banking system, i.e. by descending Banking System Indicator (BSI).

Estonia is one of only five emerging nations[7] among Fitch-rated sovereigns with a Banking System Indicator of B (high quality). This puts it on a par with most developed country systems. The high score reflects the relatively high Individual ratings of its major banks (B/C) and low overall systemic weakness revealed by the Systemic Risk Analysis.

Three countries, all new EU entrants – the Czech Republic, Slovenia and Malta – have banking systems judged to be of 'adequate quality' (BSI C), on a par with some weaker developed country systems (e.g. Austria and Germany) but still relatively strong compared to most emerging markets. The assessment reflects bank Individual ratings which are at best 'adequate' (C), though the variation of Individual ratings in Slovenia is wider, ranging from B to C/D. Within each broad BSI category, countries are listed in descending order of Individual rating of the weakest bank in a system. Thus Malta is ranked weakest of these three BSI C category systems as the weakest systemically important Maltese bank attracts a D Individual rating. The systemic risk assessment in this category reveals modest overall weakness due to relatively high exposure to the sovereign, common lending concentrations (Malta and Slovenia) and shortfalls in regulation or transparency (Slovenia).

Half of all Fitch-rated emerging market banking systems fall into the BSI D or 'low quality' category. Hence, it is not surprising that a majority of Eastern European systems also fall into this category. However, the proportion of D-classed systems, at 70 per cent, is higher than in the more general emerging markets universe. The strongest banks in these countries attract a slightly weaker Individual rating than those of banks in countries with higher BSI categories and there is a wider dispersion of ratings resulting in a weaker

Table 6.2 Summary of Fitch's bank systemic risk model

Country	*Banking System Indicator (BSI)*	*Range of bank Individual ratings*	*Macro-prudential Indicator (MPI)*
Estonia	B	B/C	2
Czech Republic	C	C	1
Slovenia	C	B to C/D	1
Malta	C	C to D	1
Slovakia	D	C to C/D	1
Cyprus	D	C/D	1
Hungary	D	C to D	3
Croatia	D	C/D to D	2
Kazakhstan	D	C/D to D	1
Latvia	D	B/C to D/E	2
Lithuania	D	C to D/E	2
Bulgaria	D	C/D to D/E	2
Romania	D	C/D to D/E	1
Russia	D	C/D to E	2
Poland	D	C to D/E	1
Ukraine	D	D to D/E	1
Albania	*D/E*	...	*2*
Bosnia-Herzegovina	*D/E*	...	*2*
FYR Macedonia	*D*	...	*1*
Serbia	*E*	...	*2*
Memo items			
Portugal	B	B to C	2
Greece	B	B/C to C/D	2
Ireland	B	B	2
Spain	B	A to B/C	2
France	B	A/B to C/D	1
Germany	C	A/B to D	1
UK	A	A to C/D	2

Source: Fitch; EBRD for CEE countries, in italics.

average rating (SAIR). The strongest countries in this category are Slovakia and Cyprus, with the weakest major banks assessed C/D. Next come Hungary, Croatia and Kazakhstan, with the weakest systemically important banks having Individual ratings of D (weak). They are followed by Latvia, Lithuania, Bulgaria and Romania, where the weakest major banks are rated D/E. Russia has banks ranging from C/D to as low as E (serious problems). However, the weakest systems in this broad BSI D category are Poland and Ukraine, in both of which the average bank attracts a D Individual rating. Identified systemic risks are also noticeably higher amongst the weaker BSI D-rated banks.

Fitch's analysis does not currently extend to southeastern European countries. In its Transition Report 2005, the EBRD (2005) employs the Fitch methodology with some slight modifications and extends it to other EBRD transition countries. For individual bank ratings the EBRD uses its own assessment of individual bank strength and systemic risk factors. These countries are in the D to E categories; FYR Macedonia ranking D, and the rest D/E or E (Serbia). The latter captures systemic risks related to weak governance, loan concentration and large exposure to unhedged foreign exchange borrowers.

An EBRD analysis (EBRD 2005) also gives details on the specific systemic risk factors outlined earlier. It highlights that *transparency, governance and the quality of banking supervision* are key sources of concern in the CIS region and the CEE countries, but also in a few new and candidate EU members. But the quality of banking supervision differs widely among the three regions. The new EU Member States and candidates have broadly aligned their financial sector regulation and supervision with EU directives, although they are facing new challenges under Basel II. Meanwhile, supervision is less advanced and effective in the rest of the CEE and the CIS. *Concentration risks* are also significant in the undiversified economies in the CEE and CIS regions. A widely shared risk across the region is the *borrower exposure, particularly with regards to foreign currency lending* to agents without foreign currency earnings. This is a leading risk factor in the new and candidate EU members. A mitigating fact is when a country is making credible progress towards euro adoption, at which point the transfer risk will be eliminated, as may be the case for the Baltic countries. Also, there are countries where workers' remittances provide large and stable foreign exchange income for households (for instance in Bosnia-Herzegovina, Albania, Serbia and Montenegro). *High exposure to a sub-investment grade sovereign borrower* (directly, through holding government securities, or indirectly, through guarantees) is a source of risk in several of the CIS countries. Connected lending is a source of risk only in CIS countries, including Russia and the Ukraine.

Macro-prudential Indicator (MPI)

The MPI aims to identify circumstances which have preceded a majority of previous systemic crises. There are many such 'early warning' models. Fitch has chosen a model developed by Borio and Lowe (2002) for its simplicity and explanatory power. Borio and Lowe looked at deviations from trend of real credit to the private sector, the real exchange rate and real equity prices in 34 countries (21 industrial and 13 emerging markets)[8] over the period 1960–99. They found that where the ratio of credit to GDP and either the real exchange rate or real equity prices had risen significantly above trend, in up to 70 per cent of cases a banking crisis (broadly defined) had followed within three years. The model anticipated most major banking crises, including those in Latin America in the late 1970s and early 1980s, the Nordic countries, Japan and Australia in the early 1990s, Mexico in 1994 and Asia in 1997–8, with the exception of Korea and Taiwan.

Following the model, countries are assessed on a scale from 1 to 3, where 3 denotes high potential vulnerability to systemic distress, 2 moderate vulnerability and 1 low vulnerability. Such an assessment is made more difficult for emerging markets in Eastern Europe and the CIS, where relevant data has often been subject to major discontinuity and is sometimes quite short lived, making the identification of trends more problematic. Only one country – Hungary – shows high vulnerability to potential distress (MPI 3), with the ratio of private sector credit to GDP and the real exchange rate both significantly above trend in 2004. Foreign currency lending has been growing particularly fast. There are mitigating circumstances: the credit trend is sensitive to the starting point, while sharp increases in administered prices played an important part in the recent real exchange rate appreciation. There were also some signs of moderation in credit and exchange rate trends in 2005.[9] Macro-prudential trends also give cause for concern in the Baltics, Bulgaria, Croatia and Russia but these are designated only MPI 2 because concerns at this stage are only moderate. However, in many of these countries credit trends alone are sufficient to warrant close monitoring. In Russia, however, rapid credit growth is combined with strong real exchange rate appreciation, while in the Baltic countries strong lending growth has been accompanied by major stock market appreciation. Estonia's stronger banking system puts it in a better position to cope with any fallout – were this to materialize – and in all these countries, potential contingent liabilities are judged to be manageable because bank credit/GDP ratio remains fairly low. The median ratio is little more than 30 per cent outside the much more developed markets of Cyprus and Malta, where private sector credit by contrast is around 120 per cent of GDP. Potential contingent liabilities would therefore be much higher in these last two countries in the event of deterioration in credit quality. However, both countries are currently judged to have low vulnerability to macro-prudential risk (MPI 1). None of the CEE countries fall into the MPI 3 category.

Systemic risk matrix

A banking system may be vulnerable to systemic risk because it is intrinsically weak, as reflected in the BSI, either because individual banks are weak or because banks have common weaknesses that increase the vulnerability of the system as a whole. Or it may be vulnerable because rapid credit growth in conjunction with real exchange rate or asset price appreciation lays the system open to stress if and when these trends are reversed, as reflected in the MPI.

However, macro-prudential risks are of greater concern in weaker banking systems which are less able to absorb potential further weakening in balance sheets. In contrast, the stronger the intrinsic strength of the system, as reflected in the BSI, the greater the degree of macro-prudential stress it is likely to be able to absorb. For example, if macro-prudential concerns are manifested in deteriorating loan quality, stronger systems will be more able to absorb the higher provisions this is likely to entail, without the need for support. By contrast, the bursting of an asset price bubble, or a sudden devaluation, may well be sufficient to trigger a full-blown systemic crisis in a banking system that is already intrinsically weak.

This non-linear interplay of intrinsic system weakness and macro-prudential stress has led Fitch to present the results of its analysis in a systemic risk matrix. The strongest combination of outcomes – an intrinsically strong system with low macro-prudential concerns is A1, while the weakest combination, E3, reflects the combination of an intrinsically weak banking system and high macro-prudential vulnerability.

The systemic risk matrix in Table 6.3 includes the results for European emerging market countries and the CIS-3 group, and estimations made by the EBRD for CEE countries, along with the results for other sovereigns analysed by Fitch. Only Hungary appears to have a risk combination (D3) that would point to increased banking sector vulnerability and risks. Bulgaria, Croatia, Latvia, Lithuania and Russia appear to have weak systems with medium-level macroeconomic vulnerability (D2), which can also point to significant systemic risks. Cyprus, Kazakhstan, Poland, Romania and Slovakia also have weak systems but little macro-prudential tension. The Czech Republic, Malta, and Slovenia have stronger systems with few macro-prudential risks, indicating reduced risk of systemic crisis. Estonia has the strongest banking system in the region, which should help absorb macro-prudential stress (B2). According to EBRD analysis, CEE countries have weak systems with medium or low-level macroeconomic risks (D1 and D2, as well as E2 for Serbia).

Croatia and Bosnia-Herzegovina may need particular attention in the future if their credit growth starts to accelerate. It is so because, as shown earlier, econometric evidence indicates that they may have already reached their equilibrium domestic credit level. It does not mean that these countries should not see further increases in domestic credit, but the increases probably should be moderate, as they do not need 'catching up' to initial low credit levels.

Table 6.3 Bank systemic risk matrix

Banking system indicator	*Macro-prudential indicator*		
	1	2	3
A	Luxembourg, USA	Australia, Netherlands, UK	
B	Belgium, Bermuda, Canada, Chile, Denmark, France, Hong Hong, New Zealand, Norway, Saudi Arabia, Singapore, Sweden, Switzerland	*Estonia*, Finland, Greece, Ireland, Italy, Kuwait, Portugal, Spain	South Africa
C	Austria, Bahrain, *Czech Republic*, Germany, Korea, Malaysia, *Malta*, Mexico, Qatar, *Slovenia*, UAE	Iceland San Marino	
D	Benin, Brazil, Colombia, *Cyprus*, El Salvador, India, Indonesia, Israel, Japan, *Kazakhstan*, Lebanon, Oman, Panama, Peru, Philippines, *Poland*, *Romania, Slovakia*, Taiwan, Thailand, Turkey, *Ukraine*, Venezuela, *FYR Macedonia*	*Bulgaria*, Costa Rica, *Croatia, Latvia, Lithuania, Russia, Albania, Bosnia-Herzegovina*	*Hungary*
E	Argentina, Azerbaijan, Bolivia, China, Ecuador, Egypt, Tunisia, Uruguay, Vietnam	Dominican Republic Iran, *Serbia*	

Source: Fitch; EBRD (for Albania, Bosnia-Herzegovina, Macedonia and Serbia).

Conclusion on policy implications

This chapter has presented a methodology for financial sector stability assessment that combines macro-prudential indicators with indicators of banking system strength and systemic risk. Applying this methodology to emerging market Europe and the CIS-3, the chapter has found that (1) there are systemic risks building up in the two regions, but they appear manageable for the time being; (2) weak banking systems, i.e. in the D–E rating zone, can be vulnerable to even a small macroeconomic stress, and this is a concern particularly in CEE and the CIS-3; (3) there are concerns over foreign exchange exposures in many countries (Hungary); and (4) governance and transparency are weak in some of the CIS-3 and CEE countries where the ability of the regulatory system is also underdeveloped.

Should systemic risks lead over time to banking sector crisis, how would that crisis manifest itself? In the more advanced, new EU countries an overt 'classical' banking sector crisis might be less likely, given the relative strength of the sector, high foreign ownership, and relatively good supervision that is aligned with EU directives. But, just as in Portugal, the risks of overstretched balance sheets can ultimately lead to a protracted period of below-potential growth, particularly when fiscal policies are not flexible enough to make space for private sector growth. This is the case in the three largest new EU members, the Czech Republic, Poland and Hungary. Moreover, a particular risk related to borrowers with unhedged foreign exchange positions may be building up more rapidly when the date of euro adoption is slipping, as in the case of Hungary. In these cases, macroeconomic policies (fiscal and monetary policies) may be the best instruments to address signs of cyclical boom, accompanied by more extensive use of risk management/mitigation instruments (securitization, hedging, etc.). In the Baltic countries, tighter fiscal policies may need to be combined also with tighter prudential regulatory rules (such as strict loan-to-value limits, marginal reserve requirements, dynamic provisioning, etc.).[10]

In contrast, the banking sectors in Russia, Kazakhstan and Ukraine, and to some extent in the CEE countries, are still weak, making them more vulnerable to cyclical downturns. These countries may be more susceptible to an overt, 'classical' banking sector crisis that usually requires balance sheet clean-ups and ultimate government bailouts. But the size of the fiscal cost may be limited because the level of private sector credit in these economies is still low. Moreover, some of these countries have built up – and are likely to build further – sizeable foreign exchange reserves that can serve to fund such fiscal costs. In these economies, strengthening of banking supervision, addressing the identified systemic risks through prudential regulation, and market development (credit bureaus, stronger legal systems), etc. will have to be the priority.

Notes

1 Emerging Europe is defined to include the eight new EU members, the three candidate countries Bulgaria, Romania, as well as Croatia, and the Southern European transition economies.

2 Financial deepening is defined as a process whereby credit growth exceeds nominal GDP growth.

3 The principal factors used to evaluate Individual ratings are profitability and balance sheet integrity (including capitalization), franchise, management, operating environment and prospects. Consistency is an important consideration. Further details can be obtained at www.fitchratings.com, 'Bank Rating Methodology', May 2004.

4 Upon failure, either the bank defaults and goes into liquidation, or alternatively, and in recent years more frequently, the failure crystallizes the contingent liability that the bank represents either to its institutional owners or, more often than not, to the sovereign.

5 An alternative approach would be to focus on the weakest systemically important bank in the system, i.e. 'the weakest link'. While there is merit in such an approach, Fitch believes the resulting indicator would be more volatile and potentially misleading, for example where there is a wide distribution of banks in a system.
6 For a more extensive discussion of the concept of Support, see Fitch Ratings (2003).
7 The others are Chile, Kuwait, Saudi Arabia and South Africa.
8 USA, Canada, Japan, Australia, New Zealand, Austria, Belgium, Denmark, Finland, France, Germany, Greece, Ireland, Italy, Netherlands, Norway, Portugal, Spain, Sweden, Switzerland, UK, South Africa, Hong Kong, Indonesia, Korea, Malaysia, Singapore, Thailand, Taiwan, Argentina, Brazil, Chile, Mexico, Uruguay.
9 The results are based on data up to and including 2004.
10 For a good summary, see Hilbers *et al.* (2005).

Bibliography

Borio, C. and P. Lowe (2002) 'Assessing the risk of banking crises', *BIS Quarterly Review*, December: 43–54.

Cardenas, J., J. Graf and P. O'Dogherty (2003) 'Foreign banks entry in emerging market economies: a host country perspective', Bank for International Settlements.

Cottarelli, C., G. Dell'Ariccia and I. Vladkova-Hollar (2003) *Early Birds, Late Risers, and Sleeping Beauties: Bank Credit Growth to the Private Sector in Central and Eastern Europe and the Balkans*, IMF WP/03/213.

EBRD (2005) *Transition Report 2005*, EBRD.

European Central Bank (2004) *EU Banking Sector Stability*, November, Frankfurt: ECB.

—— (2005) *Banking Structures in the New EU Member States*, January, Frankfurt: ECB.

European Commission (2005) 'Public finance in EMU 2005'; available at www.europa.int.

Fitch Ratings (2003) 'Fitch Announces New Support Rating Methodology', April; available at www.fitchratings.com.

—— (2004) 'EMU Convergence Report 2004', July; available at www.fitchratings.com.

—— (2005a) 'Assessing Bank Systemic Risk: A New Product' and 'Bank Systemic Risk Report', July; available at www.fitchratings.com.

—— (2005b) 'EMU Convergence Report 2005', September; available at www.fitchratings.com.

Goldstein, M., G.L. Kaminski and C. Reinhart (2002) *Assessing Financial Vulnerability: An Early Warning System for Emerging Markets*, Washington, DC: Institute for International Economics.

Hilbers, P., I. Otker-Robe, C. Pazarbasiouglu and G. Johnsen (2003) *Assessing and Managing Rapid Credit Growth and the Role of Supervisory and Prudential Policies*, IMF WP/05/151.

IMF (2004) 'Are credit booms in emerging markets a concern?', in *World Economic Outlook*, April, IMF.

Kaminsky, G.L. and C.M. Reinhart (1999) 'The twin crises: the causes of banking and balance of payments problems', *American Economic Review* 89(3): 473–500.

Schadler, S., P. Drummond, L. Kuijs, Z. Murgasova and R. van Elkan (2005) *Adopting the Euro in Central Europe: Challenges of the Next Step in European Integration*, Occasional Paper no. 234, IMF.

II.2

Living inside a monetary union

7 Adjustment in EMU

A model-based analysis of country experiences

Sven Langedijk and Werner Roeger

Introduction[1]

In the run-up to the launch of the euro area, there were two broad schools of thought on how individual member countries would be affected by entry into the monetary union.[2] The discussion boiled down to two issues: first, the frequency and importance of idiosyncratic economic shocks to Member States leading to asymmetric developments; and, second, the effectiveness of adjustment to such shocks which depended on the relative strength of the stabilizing forces of competitive pressures and the destabilizing effects of the – generally pro-cyclical – real interest rates.

On the one side were those who believed that the member countries were too diverse leading to many important asymmetric economic developments. In their view, the common monetary policy would turn out to be pro-cyclical and destabilizing leading to protracted boom–bust cycles. Proponents of this view put the EMU project into question, considering that it implied economic instability resulting in inefficient resource allocation.

On the other side were those who believed that the single currency in itself would generate forces for greater economic integration and economic stabilization. The importance of increased trade competition and financial integration would in their view reduce the frequency and importance of asymmetric shocks. And when they occurred, competitive pressures would induce rapid and effective adjustment. EMU would be inherently stable and benefits of the monetary union would outweigh the costs in terms of the loss of the exchange rate and monetary policy.

Looking at the developments since the launch of the euro area, economic performances have differed markedly between Member States. Differences in price and wage inflation have been substantial, perversely affecting real interest rates in the national economies. Moreover, inflation differentials have been particularly persistent, also compared to the experience in the US. This persistence implies large shifts in measures of competitiveness and in particular real effective exchange rates. At the same time, substantial and persistent current account imbalances have emerged.

It is still difficult to arrive at precise estimates on the impact of the individual channels. We approach this issue by asking the question how well a standard DSGE model – which makes strong predictions about the stability of a monetary union provided that the Central Bank targets the area-wide inflation rate – can account for the stylized facts on growth, inflation and current account divergences in EMU. We identify shocks and estimate their order of magnitude by means of shock accounting. The analysis applies to both adjustment in the euro area on entry and adjustment in the euro area in its steady state. This framework allows us to assess shocks that trigger adjustment dynamics and to pinpoint which factors determine the speed of adjustment and the risk of overshooting. Models of this kind have been used by Fagan and Gaspar (2005) to study the current account developments and by Lopez Salido *et al.* (2005) to investigate inflation differentials in EMU. However, to our knowledge no attempt has been made so far to look at various developments and channels simultaneously.

The countries that we consider in the simulations are: Germany, Spain, Ireland, Italy, the Netherlands and Portugal. The Netherlands and Portugal, in particular, experienced high growth and overheating pressures towards the end of the 1990s and early 2000s. The subsequent slowdown was characterized by a drop in inflation, downward revisions of potential growth and a marked deterioration in the budgetary position. Other Member States have not seen a similar reversal in their economic fortunes. In Spain, economic growth and inflation continue to be above the euro-area average. These developments have been paralleled by high wage growth, booming asset prices and credit growth, and deteriorating current account balances. The experience of Germany in the euro area has been characterized by a protracted period of slow growth. This period of slow growth and lacklustre domestic demand has been accompanied by low inflation and wage growth and the regaining of competitiveness. Italy can be considered the 'odd man out' with a continuous loss in competitiveness coinciding with slow growth.

Stylized developments

Stylized fact 1: inflation differentials have narrowed but remain substantial and particularly persistent

From the early 1990s until the start of EMU, inflation differentials between euro-area Member States narrowed continuously (Figures 7.1 and 7.2). After some increase in 2000,

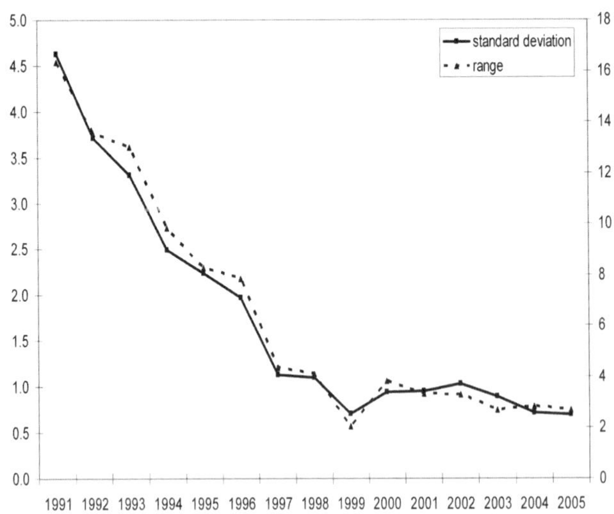

Figure 7.1 Standard deviation and range of inflation rates of the Member States of the eurozone (1991–2005).

Source: Commission services, own calculations.

Note: Dispersion of National Inflation Rates based on the National Consumer Price Index, 1991–2005. Standard deviation on the left scale, Range (= maximum minus minimum) on the right scale.

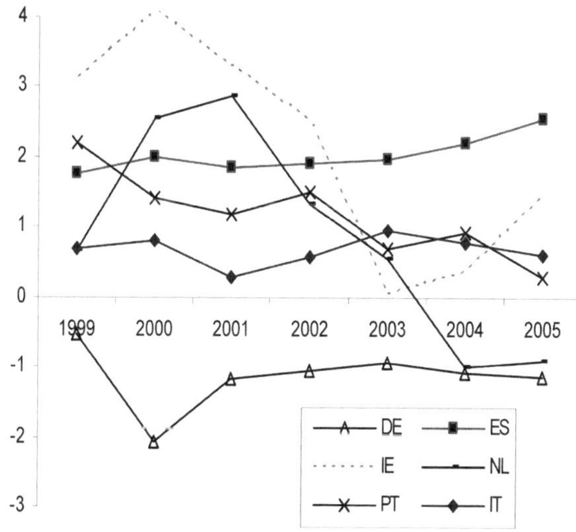

Figure 7.2 GDP-deflator minus euro-area average (1999–2005).
Source: Commission services.

the measures of inflation differentials stabilized. The substantial range and standard deviation as such may not be particularly remarkable. Looking at the deviations of inflation from the euro-area average in individual Member States, the persistence is notable. Germany has consistently shown the lowest rate of inflation, while Spanish inflation has continuously been two percentage points above the euro-area average. The resulting cumulative divergence of price level developments and its impact on competitiveness within the euro-area sparked political and research interest.

Stylized fact 2: differences in unit labour costs reflect very different productivity and wage trends

The dispersion in inflation rates is also broadly reflected in unit labour costs in the period 1999–2005 (Figure 7.3). Of the six Member States considered, only Germany witnessed unit labour costs increases below the euro-area average, due solely to nominal wage restraint. In the other countries, the underlying factors of the unit labour cost increase reflect quite diverse nominal wage and labour productivity developments. Nominal wages in general did not move in line with productivity advances. Especially in Portugal and Spain, negative labour productivity rates were accompanied by significant wage increases compared to the euro-area average.

Stylized fact 3: inflation dispersion was concentrated in the non-tradable sector, in particular building and construction

The different price developments are not spread homogeneously throughout the economy. Distinguishing between developments in the tradable and non-tradable sectors appears crucial to understand inflation persistence. The standard deviation and the range of average annual inflation rates was significantly larger in services, which represents to a large extent the non-tradable sector, than in goods, which are largely tradable (Table 7.1).

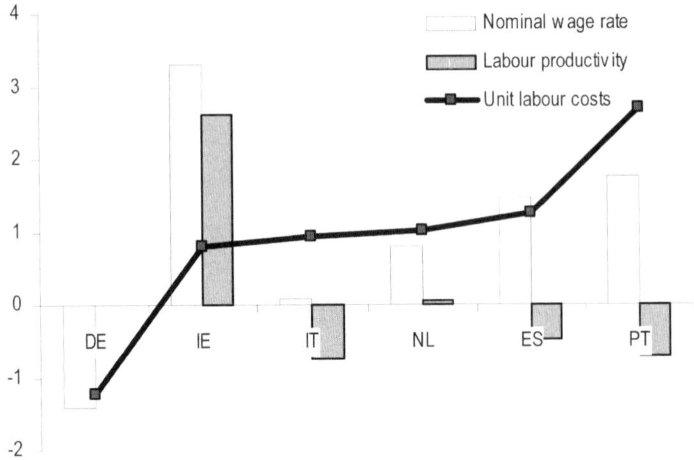

Figure 7.3 Average annual changes in unit labour costs, wages and productivity 1999–2005 (compared to euro-area average).
Source: Commission services.

A look at the price deflators for manufacturing, services, and building and construction shows similar developments (Figure 7.4). It also shows that there have been no reversals of relative price levels towards the euro-area average in the individual Member States highlighting the persistence of high or low inflation in the individual Member States. Figure 7.4 illustrates that the lower the tradable character of the sector is, the higher is the cumulative difference in price developments. In the manufacturing sector cumulative difference in price developments since 1999 ranged up to 14 percentage points, whereas this cumulative price deflator differential amounted to around 20 percentage points in the (largely) non-tradable service sector. The price deflator differential is even more pronounced in the building and construction sectors, where prices have increased 44 percentage points more in Spain than in Germany.

Stylized fact 4: housing price developments have been very marked and persistent

Deviations of housing price increases from the euro area average have been remarkable. Figure 7.5 (on the left-hand side) shows that there has been a reversal of fortunes only in the case of the Netherlands and Portugal, which saw relative price declines compared to the euro area after a period of buoyant growth. In the other Member States the persistence of the deviation from the euro-area average since 1999 is remarkable. Housing prices in Spain have grown at a continuously accelerating rate compared to the euro area, while in Germany the rate of price declines accelerated continuously.

Table 7.1 Average annual inflation rates (1999–2004)

	Standard deviation	*Range (max.–min.)*
Goods	0.6	1.2
Services	1.6	4.1

Source: Lane (2006).

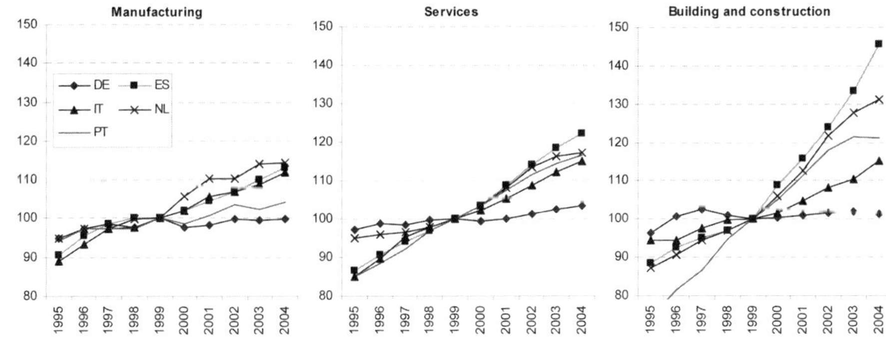

Figure 7.4 Price deflators for the sectors manufacturing, service and building and construction 1995–2004 (1999 = 100).
Source: Commission services.

Note: No data for Ireland available.

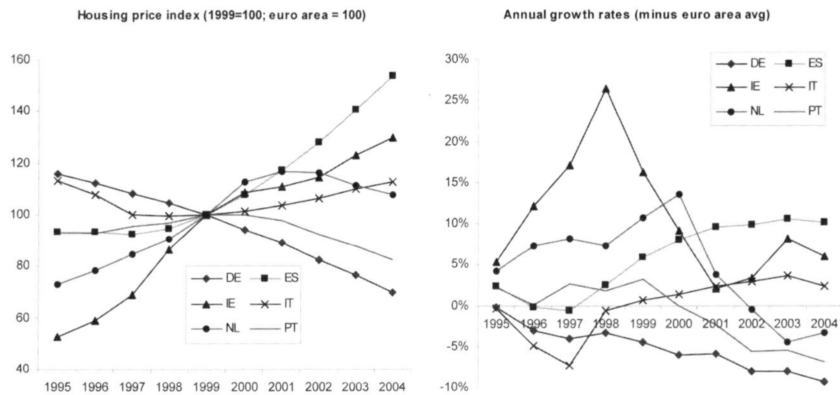

Figure 7.5 Housing price index and annual growth rates (compared to the euro area) 1995–2004.
Source: Commission services.

Stylized fact 5: current account imbalances have widened

The dispersion of current account positions within the euro area has widened significantly since the late 1990s. Figure 7.6 illustrates the development of the current account balances in the euro-area Member States through time from 1995 to 2004. In a context of free flow of capital (and no risk premia), one would expect countries with high growth potential to run current account deficits and low-growth countries to run surpluses as capital searches for the highest return if there are no risk premia. Figure 7.6 therefore depicts the development of the current account against the GDP per capita, which can be considered as a proxy for possible return on investment and scope for catching-up dynamics.

On the horizontal axis, GDP per capita is depicted (euro area = 100). The vertical axis represents the current account balance of euro-area Member States with the rest of the world minus the weighted euro-area average current account balance with the rest of the world.

In 1995 the correlation is still negligible. Only Austria and Germany have a current account deficit compared to the rest of the euro area. By 2002, only countries with a GDP per capita below the euro-area average have a significant current account deficit.

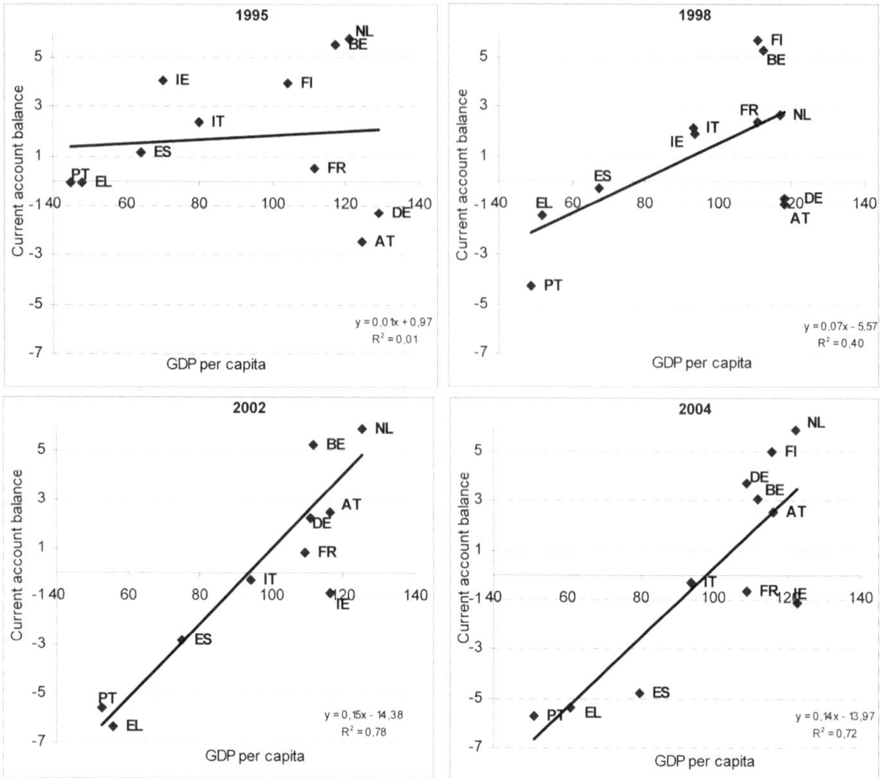

Figure 7.6 Current account balance (minus euro-area average) versus GDP per capita (euro area = 1). Source: Commission services.

A trend towards rising current account dispersion was also observed in economies worldwide. Still, while it is not a euro-area phenomenon, the deterioration in the net external asset positions in Portugal, Greece and Spain is unmatched in the OECD and by historical standards.

Stylized fact 6: exchange risk premia disappeared

Globalization, financial market developments and a search for return as nominal returns declined in a low-inflation environment may all have contributed to a global decline in the risk premia. The decline in the risk premia has been most pronounced in the euro-area Member States as the creation of the euro area eliminated exchange rate risk (Figure 7.7).

The DSGE model

The analysis of adjustment dynamics in the euro area is based on simulations with a two-country, three-sector model that distinguishes between tradables and non-tradables.[3] The tradable sector consists of agriculture and manufacturing, while the non-tradable sector is composed of construction and services. The model is a so-called New-Keynesian-DSGE model.[4] Consistent with the empirical evidence, we have introduced a number of nominal and real rigidities.[5] This makes the model partly forward and partly backward looking. The

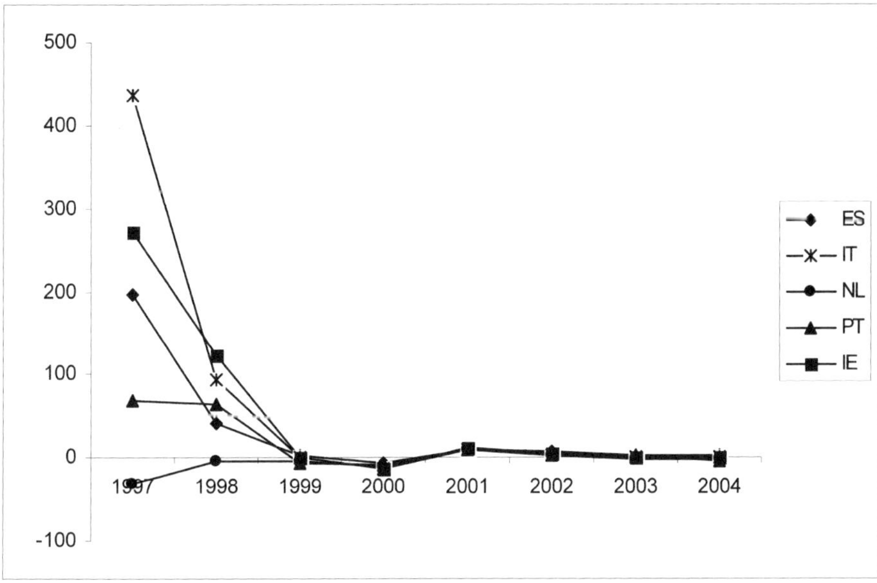

Figure 7.7 Exchange risk premia vis-á-vis Germany.
Notes: The exchange risk premium of country $C \in ES, IT, NL, PT, IE$ is calculated on the basis of an uncovered interest parity condition and defined as

$$rprem_t = (i_t^C - i_t^{DE}) + \frac{12}{j}\Delta j^{e^e_{t+j}}, j = 3.$$

For calculating the risk premium we use monthly data on interest rates (per annum) and exchange rates. The interest rates are 3 month money market rates. For the expected change in the exchange rate we use the log difference between the monthly exchange rate in $t + 3$ and t. Notice, instead of the expected exchange rate we use the realised rate. This is not very restrictive since we are only interested in the average risk premium over the year.

model can be calibrated to various country pairs. In the simulations on pp. 135–57, one country is analysed while the second country represents the aggregate of the rest of the euro area. The model is calibrated so as to respect the relative sizes of the countries.

In the short run nominal rigidities are important in the model, while in the medium and long run prices and wages adjust. For each permanent and temporary shock the model reaches a long-run equilibrium position that is consistent with external and internal balance. Internal balance is characterized by a constant employment rate and a constant ratio of consumption to GDP (savings rate), while external balance is characterized by a constant (not necessarily zero) ratio of net foreign assets to GDP and a constant real exchange rate.

Given the heterogeneous pattern of house price developments across the euro area, the model has been extended further by disaggregating the non-tradable sector into construction and 'other' non-tradables and by separating investment into housing and non-housing investment. The housing market boom in several Member States was accompanied by very strong credit expansion. The liberalization of the mortgage markets and increased competition between mortgage providers led to the introduction of new mortgage products that postpone loan redemption until maturity. These developments, also fuelled by the falling nominal interest rates at the end of the 1990s which increased the borrowing capacity of households, resulted in significant re-mortgaging and equity withdrawal that fed into private consumption expenditure in several Member States. The degree to which these developments affected lending practices differed among Member States. To capture the strong divergence in credit growth, special emphasis has been devoted to modelling the financial constraints of the household sector. To this end, the household sector has been divided into credit- and non-credit-constrained parts, which allows consideration of the effects of loosening credit constraints on the demand for housing.[6]

In a monetary union, with interest rates targeted at the union's average economic conditions, investment in individual member states could potentially respond strongly to domestic demand shocks. An increase in domestic inflation could boost domestic investment because of lower real interest rates. This mechanism could transform temporary demand shocks into long investment-induced cycles. An often used counterargument is that with a monetary union, the relevant real rate for investors is not necessarily the national rate but the union average real rate.

In the model, sectoral investment differs according to the degree to which sectors are exposed to foreign competition and to the mix of domestic and foreign capital used in their production. In other words, the investment decision is based on demand and cost factors and relative prices have different effects on both components entering the investment decision. While it is true that higher inflation can lower capital costs for firms if the nominal interest rate stays constant, DSGE models also stress a demand (or competitiveness effect) for investment. Besides capital costs, in their investment decisions, profit maximizing firms take into account the evolution of their own output price relative to those of their (foreign) competitors over the lifetime of the investment project, since this relative price determines current and expected demand. Since higher domestic inflation worsens the competitive condition of domestic firms, the demand effect works in the opposite direction to that of the cost effect. It can be a powerful stabilizing force especially if the elasticity of substitution between domestic and foreign goods is high. Obviously, the demand effect is greatest in the tradable sector, while it is much weaker in the non-tradable sector (including housing). In the DSGE model used for this analysis the following distinction is made between the tradable and non-tradable sectors concerning their exposure to foreign competition and to the composition of investment.

Composition of investment (costs)

It is assumed that investment in the non-tradable sector is largely domestically produced. Housing investment is undertaken by a domestic construction sector. The tradable sector uses both domestic and imported investment goods. Four factors determine the capital costs of a firm:

- physical rate of depreciation;
- corporate taxes;
- real interest rate: nominal interest rate minus the expected capital gain, expressed by the expected inflation rate of the capital aggregate used by the specific firm;
- the price of the investment good relative to the producer price of the investing firm.

Suppose the composition of investment of a particular sector, s, in country c is made up of a composite good of the currency union with shares proportional to the size of the union members, then the relevant real interest rate would be the nominal interest rate minus the expected inflation rate of investment goods in the currency union. However, even in this particular case, domestic inflation could still lower real capital costs, if the inflation in the domestic tradable sector exceeds investment price inflation. For the non-tradable sector, it is assumed that all investment is domestic (in particular for housing). Therefore, the real interest rate for investment in the non-tradable sector is defined as the union-wide nominal rate minus the expected inflation in the non-tradable sector.

Exposure to competition (demand)

Domestic firms in the tradable sector are exposed to competition from foreign firms in the tradable sector. Here we assume a high elasticity of substitution (between 2.5 and 7.0) between domestic and foreign tradables. The domestic tradable sector is also exposed to competition from domestic non tradables to the extent that domestic households and firms regard tradable and non-tradable goods as substitutes. Following the literature, we impose a low elasticity of substitution of 0.4. As a mirror-image, firms in the non-tradable sector are exposed to (weak) competition from the tradable sector.

As a result of these assumptions the model predicts that investment in the non-tradable sector should respond more strongly to demand shocks than investment in the tradable sector.

The model simulations allow us to systematically analyse the possible origins of sustained differences in economic variables in the euro area. Three origins of the divergences of the economic developments and their persistence are considered in the economic literature: (1) they can boil down to dissimilar supply conditions – as such, they do not need to hamper the smooth functioning of the monetary union; (2) they can be the result of one-off adjustment effects caused by the adaptation to the monetary union – after the completion of the initial adjustment their effects on growth and inflation will fade out; (3) a third possible source would be the occurrence of asymmetric shocks in EMU at its steady state. These can be due to common external shocks with different effects in the Member States due to differences in industrial structure and sectoral specialization, or to differences in geographical compositions of the trading partners.[7] They can also be due to movements in critical domestic variables.

Country dynamics

In this section we apply the model to Germany, Ireland, Italy, the Netherlands, Portugal and Spain, which have shown the largest deviation from the euro area in terms of growth, inflation and the current account. The goal of this exercise is to see whether this model can approximately match orders of magnitude of deviations of important macro aggregates from the euro-area average as well as account for the duration of these deviations. We don't have the intention of fitting the variables exactly. An exact fit is not possible since we base our analysis only on a very small set of exogenous shocks.

Table 7.2 shows the country-specific development ('shocks') on which we focus. First, on the supply side these are differences in total factor productivity (TFP) trends in the tradable and non-tradable sector. Second, related to the creation of EMU, changes in the exchange risk premia could be an important factor explaining some of the country-specific developments in the early years of EMU. Third, on the demand side, financial market liberalization and innovation have led to the introduction of new lending instruments which have effectively increased credit ceilings for housing investment of private households. Credit expansion has been particularly strong in Ireland, Spain, Portugal and the Netherlands. Apart from these

Table 7.2 Exogenous driving forces (1999–2003)

	Productivity tradables[1]	*Productivity non-tradables*[2]	*Risk premium vs Germany (basis points)*[3]	*Household debt*[4]
Germany	3.4	1.7	0	−2.0
Ireland	15.8	3.2	60	21.1
Italy	0.7	0.0	90	6.8
Netherlands	2.8	1.5	0	22.5
Portugal	2.0	0.5	140	24.8
Spain	1.8	0.1	90	23.8
Euro area	2.8	0.9		

Source: Groningen Growth and Development Centre (GGDC) sectoral data base, AMECO (the annual macro-economic database of the European Commission's Directorate General for Economic and Financial Affairs (DG ECFIN)).

Notes:
1 Primary production and manufacturing (average productivity per annum growth 1999–2003 in %).
2 Private services (average productivity growth per annum 1999–2003 in %).
3 Assumed values calculated over the period 1995–8. Ex post estimates from open arbitrage conditions give larger absolute values. However, these estimates are dominated by outliers and therefore likely to be biased upwards.
4 Difference between 2005 and 1999 as a % of GDP.

shocks we also take into account fiscal developments and some other country-specific shocks which will be explained in more detail in the respective country sections.

Germany

Stylized facts

Germany's growth performance (in per capita terms) (see Table 7.3) has been disappointing in the first few years after the creation of the euro area. However, after a particularly weak performance in 1999, the growth rate gradually caught up with the euro-area average. In 2004 and 2005, Germany slightly exceeded per capita growth in the euro area. The slow growth performance in the first years of the euro area is somewhat surprising given the above-average TFP growth, especially in the non-tradable sector. Most observers of the German economy attribute the sluggish growth to weak domestic demand, especially investment and construction. Consistent with the hypothesis of weak demand, inflation has been persistently below the euro-area average by about one percentage point per annum. Rising current surpluses (reaching close to 4 per cent of GDP in 2005) further support the view that Germany is facing a demand problem.

Shocks

In this section we explore how in the context of the model, specific demand and supply shocks hitting the German economy could have contributed to these growth and inflation trends. On the demand side there are various explanatory factors. Germany entered EMU at a slightly overvalued exchange rate and lost a negative risk premium vis-à-vis euro-area competitors associated with the reputation of the Deutschmark (DM).[8] Though these

Table 7.3 Economic development, Germany (relative to euro area)

Variables	*1999*	*2000*	*2001*	*2002*	*2003*	*2004*	*2005*
Growth rate of real GDP[1]	−0.69	−0.23	−0.20	−0.37	−0.17	0.51	0.04
Growth rate of private consumption[1]	−0.13	−0.36	0.40	−0.94	−0.21	−0.06	−0.84
Growth rate of investment[1]	−1.42	−1.99	−4.15	−4.61	−1.63	−2.48	−2.43
Labour productivity growth	−0.31	−0.10	0.44	0.34	0.40	−0.21	0.44
Employment rate[2]	−0.15	−0.13	−0.51	−0.99	−1.40	−0.90	−1.17
Inflation (GDP)	−0.51	−2.10	−1.18	−1.10	−0.98	−1.13	−1.29
Wage inflation	−1.45	−0.56	−1.04	−1.21	−0.79	−1.81	−1.71
Growth of terms of trade	0.55	−4.83	−0.13	2.11	1.02	−0.24	−1.52
Current account[2]	−0.47	−0.91	0.69	2.95	2.82	4.44	4.66

Source: Commission services.

Notes:
1 The growth rates of GDP and its components are per capita.
2 The employment rate and the current account are expressed as deviation from 1998 levels.

developments may also partly explain weak demand, most likely other more structural factors play a role as well. Probably weak demand for housing is also due to a correction of over-investment during the unification-induced construction boom in the mid-1990s. However, housing investment is not sufficient to explain the slowdown in investment; business investment has been particularly weak as well. A possible explanation advanced by Broadbent *et al.* (2004) is structural changes in the German banking system which could have increased capital costs for firms by 200 basis points.[9] This estimate appears high. The DSGE model replicates the low investment rate with a 30 basis point increase of capital costs. Low consumption growth is possibly due to precautionary savings in a context of uncertainty surrounding pension and labour market reforms and anticipation of future taxation to adjust public finance imbalances in the light of the ageing population. The observed high productivity growth in non-tradables could be a supply-side explanation for low inflation.

Simulation results

The loss of the risk premium bonus and the overvaluation can indeed explain some of the demand shortfall in the first two years (see Figure 7.8). Eliminating the risk premium reduces housing investment growth by about 1.5 percentage points in the first year and close to 1 per cent in the second year. Also the initial overvaluation had a temporary negative demand effect. However, it does not explain the sustained weakness of consumption and, even more striking, the low investment growth. Though housing is the investment category most affected by the elimination of the risk premium, a more permanent shock to housing is required in order to replicate the low growth of investment.[10] The negative housing shock does indeed explain a significant part of low growth in Germany (without a negative housing demand shock GDP growth in Germany would have been about 0.25 percentage points higher). But it only explains about 10 per cent of the inflation differential to the euro area. Low housing investment is also insufficient to completely explain low total investment. According to the model corporate investment should be boosted because of positive TFP trends. In order to account for a decline in corporate investment a shock to the required rate of return in the tradable sector is given (in the order of magnitude of 50 basis points). This has a powerful effect; it not only reduces investment but also helps to explain some of the weakness of consumption

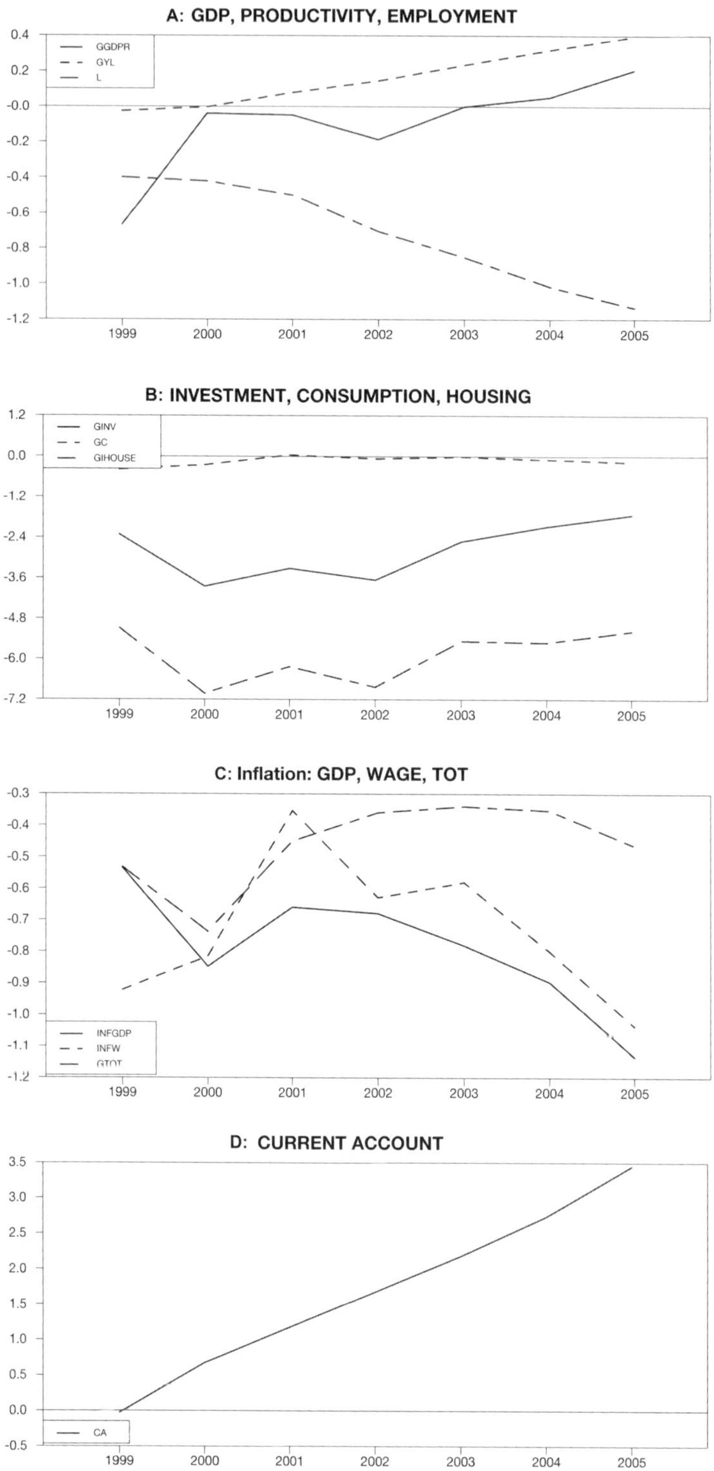

Figure 7.8 DSGE Results for Germany (deviation from euro-area average).

and adds another 0.25 percentage point reduction to the inflation rate. An additional demand shock is generated by rising transfers, financed by distortionary labour taxes.[11] The net effect on consumption growth is negative and adds another 0.25 percentage points to reducing the inflation rate in Germany in the period 2002–5. Finally, high productivity growth in non-tradables explains a negative inflation differential of about 0.33 percentage points.

Summing up

Shocks related to the creation of the euro area explain GDP and its components as well as inflation in the first two to three years. The rise in the risk premium also explains a lower permanent consumption level and a more permanent current account surplus (of about 0.6 per cent of GDP).

In order to match the model simulations with the data in recent years (since 2002) specific demand shocks must be given (especially shocks to housing investment and corporate investment in the tradable sector plus a fiscal shock to explain weak consumption growth). These demand shocks partially explain low inflation plus an increase in the current account surplus.

On the supply side, TFP growth of non-tradables is important for two features of the German data, namely first a gradual recovery of German growth and second low inflation.

Notice, no particular shock is given to the labour market. The demand shocks, especially housing and corporate investment, are sufficient to generate a decline of the employment rate in the order of magnitude as observed in the data.

Ireland

Stylized facts

Like no other country in the euro area, Ireland benefited from the ICT boom of the 1990s, which generated high rates of technical progress in the production of computers, semiconductors and telecom equipment. With a high ICT production share the Irish economy has exhibited very high growth rates of labour productivity (see Table 7.4). Productivity growth in the tradable sector of the Irish economy exceeded that of the rest of the euro area by about 13 percentage points per annum on average over the period 1999–2003. In recent years there have been some signs that the rate of technical progress is slowing down. However, other sectors of the economy have also scored above average in terms of productivity growth. In the non-tradable sector productivity growth has been two percentage points higher than the euro-area average over the same period. High productivity growth biased towards the tradable sector could at least partly explain the above-average Irish inflation rates (Balassa–Samuelson effect). The labour market may have been another factor adding to the persistence of inflation. The Irish employment rate increased throughout the 1990s. As the unemployment rate approached 4 per cent, some wage pressure emerged eventually and the unemployment rate finally stabilized at a low level. On the demand side two characteristic features may be observed. First, there is strong housing demand, with growth rates deviating from the euro-area average by about 10 percentage points per annum, and second government consumption (as a share of GDP) has increased at an above-average speed between 2000 and 2005. Despite high domestic growth and inflation above the euro-area average, the external balance has remained remarkably stable, with the current account surplus deteriorating by about two percentage points since the late 1990s.

Table 7.4 Economic development, Ireland (relative to euro area)

Variables	*1999*	*2000*	*2001*	*2002*	*2003*	*2004*	*2005*
Growth rate of real GDP[1]	5.97	3.49	2.30	3.33	2.31	0.84	1.27
Growth rate of private consumption[1]	3.21	3.58	1.54	0.67	0.93	0.95	2.21
Growth rate of investment[1]	8.67	2.54	−0.73	5.12	4.85	5.64	10.82
Labour productivity growth	3.25	2.95	2.72	3.98	2.03	−0.12	−0.75
Employment rate[2]	1.59	1.91	1.64	1.22	1.40	2.04	3.40
Inflation (GDP)	3.16	4.05	3.29	2.47	0.02	0.33	1.38
Wage inflation	1.99	5.57	4.83	2.47	3.32	3.42	3.21
Growth of terms of trade	−0.26	−1.11	0.38	0.96	−1.07	−0.33	0.37
Current account[2]	0.35	−0.36	−0.57	−0.99	0.00	−0.79	−1.04

Source: Commission services.

Notes:
1 The growth rates of GDP and its components are per capita.
2 The employment rate and the current account are expressed as deviation from 1998 levels.

In the last two years of our sample (2004 and 2005), the high growth of labour productivity came to an end in Ireland but employment growth has picked up once again. Also inflation has diminished very quickly in recent years, although wage inflation remains high. It is therefore somewhat puzzling that the employment rate and investment growth (both construction and equipment) have started to increase again.

Shocks

In the model the productivity trends in Ireland are implemented as supply shocks to tradables and non-tradables TFP such that the model replicates the productivity growth differential between Ireland and the rest of EMU as well as the productivity growth differential between the tradable and non-tradable sector in the Irish economy. After the year 2000 a negative wage shock is removed in order to replicate the end of wage moderation in Ireland. Some idiosyncratic demand shocks can also be identified. From 2000 to 2005 the share of government consumption in GDP increased by two percentage points, (compared to an increase below one percentage point in the euro area). There is also empirical evidence of liberalized mortgage markets allowing rising household debt. As in the case of Spain the housing boom is to some extent an autonomous demand shock fuelled by demographics and catching-up processes. Some attention is devoted to the last two years, where we can observe a decline in the growth rate of GDP and a fall in productivity growth below the euro-area average. Within the context of the model a possible explanation for a simultaneous drop in productivity and inflation could be a decline in TFP growth in the tradable sector. In order to make these two developments consistent with no fall in wage inflation, rising employment shares and continued investment growth (both construction and equipment), increased competition in the non-tradable sector must be assumed.[12]

Simulations

According to the model simulations (see Figure 7.9), the TFP shocks are the most important factors for explaining the productivity trend in Ireland and other stylized facts. Tradable sector TFP growth explains a productivity differential of about 2.5 per cent from 1999 to

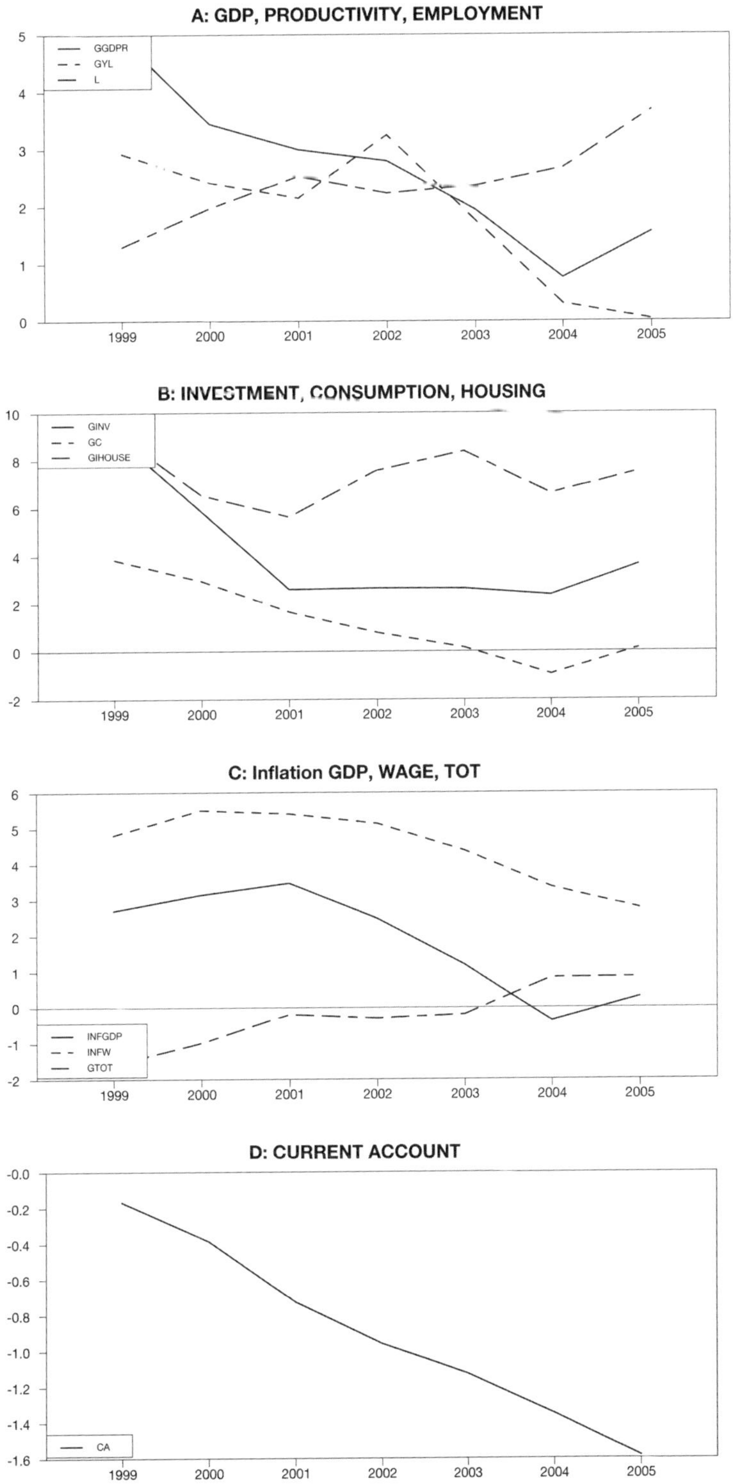

Figure 7.9 DSGE results for Ireland (deviation from euro-area average).

2003. Productivity growth in the tradable sector leads to (GDP) inflation with a certain lag (see standard simulation) via second round effects through wages and prices in the non-tradable sector. Eventually the inflation differential exceeds the productivity differential by about 30 per cent. Productivity growth in the non-tradable sector contributes to reducing GDP inflation. The stylized fact of falling inflation in recent years is generated by continued productivity gains in the non-tradable sector but falling productivity growth in tradables. According to the simulation results, the effect of increased housing demand on inflation has been relatively small (not exceeding 0.4 per cent on average in terms of explaining the inflation differential).[13] The relatively minor impact of house prices on inflation is not inconsistent with the fact that despite buoyant housing demand there has been a deceleration of inflation in recent years. Expansionary fiscal policy in Ireland helps to explain both the decline in the growth rate of investment and subdued growth in private consumption after 2000.

Summing up

The model accounts reasonably well for the decline in the growth rate of GDP (per capita) from around 5 per cent in 1999 to about 1 per cent in 2004–5 and a similar decline for productivity. The model also captures the evolution of employment.

Concerning prices and wages, the model explains the initially high inflation differential and its convergence to the euro-area average rate in recent years. The model is less successful in matching the terms of trade development, especially in recent years.[14]

Despite persistently high housing investment, the growth rate of Irish total investment has been declining from high levels in the late 1990s. This is roughly matched by the model. The model also generates a downward trend in consumption per capita, though it undershoots private consumption in 2004–5.

The model also replicates the overall decline in the current account; however, it fails to match the speed of its deterioration in the first years of the euro area.

Italy

Stylized facts

Persistently low growth of GDP per capita and moderate wage developments did not induce low inflation and improving competitiveness in Italy (see Table 7.5). On the contrary, unit labour costs and prices continued to increase faster in Italy than in competitor euro-area countries, resulting in a loss of competitiveness and export market shares. The current account gradually deteriorated over the whole period 1997–2005, in spite of weak domestic demand.[15]

Since 1999, consumption growth has been lacklustre and broadly in line with slow GDP growth. Investment growth has been supported somewhat by construction demand in view of accelerating housing prices. In recent years, investment growth turned negative again, mainly driven by falling equipment investment. After a sharp improvement in the run-up to 1999, the government budget balance has worsened considerably.

On the supply side, slow or even negative total factor productivity growth in both the tradable and non-tradable sectors largely explains the slow growth. In particular, in the more recent years under review, labour productivity growth was particularly low since employment growth remained robust in spite of the negative cyclical conditions and TFP growth literally collapsed.

Table 7.5 Economic development, Italy (relative to euro area)

Variables	*1997*	*1998*	*1999*	*2000*	*2001*	*2002*	*2003*	*2004*	*2005*
Growth rate of real GDP[1]	−0.20	−0.97	−0.52	0.30	0.54	−0.08	−0.61	−1.22	−1.15
Growth rate of private consumption[1]	1.95	0.83	−0.28	−0.22	−0.61	−0.22	−0.01	−1.20	−1.02
Growth rate of investment[1]	−1.06	−1.52	−2.61	1.36	2.00	5.46	−2.54	−0.15	−2.86
Labour productivity growth	−0.06	−0.45	−0.13	0.20	−0.58	−1.63	−1.82	−0.74	−0.91
Employment rate[2]	0.11	−0.48	−0.78	−0.84	−0.23	0.72	1.48	1.18	1.02
Inflation	1.19	1.06	0.47	0.60	0.61	0.82	1.04	1.02	0.34
Wage inflation	4.34	−2.43	−0.56	−0.20	0.31	−0.36	0.19	0.98	0.63
Growth of terms of trade[3]	1.04	3.42	2.73	2.55	3.71	3.36	2.34	3.36	3.81
Current account[2]	−0.19	−1.12	−2.03	−3.20	−2.77	−3.39	−3.96	−3.58	−4.13

Source: Commission services.

Notes:
1 The growth rates of GDP and its components are per capita.
2 The employment rate and the current account are expressed as deviations from 1996 levels.
3 The terms of trade are defined as export prices of the Member State relative to export prices of the rest of EMU.

Shocks

As did other Member States with a history of devaluations and high and volatile inflation, Italy benefited from a reduction in the exchange risk premium when entering EMU. A conservative estimate based on deviations from interest parity between the lira and the euro before 1999 suggests a risk premium of about 50 basis points was eliminated in the running-up phase to EMU. This provided a stimulus to domestic demand. However, other factors played in the opposite direction and contributed to the lacklustre growth performance. Fiscal retrenchment to qualify for the Maastricht criteria implied a drag on growth in 1997 and 1998. The most important shocks we consider in the case of Italy concern the continuous and accelerating reduction in TFP growth, both in the tradable and non-tradable sectors. A widespread view is that insufficient competition, especially in the service sector, low human capital accumulation, weak innovation and insufficient R&D expenditure are amongst the determinants of the marked slowdown in TFP.[16] In particular, productivity in manufacturing industry has stagnated since the mid-1990s, resulting in a significant and persistent differential in terms of unit labour costs with respect to the euro area, and a concomitant deterioration of the Italian competitive position. Furthermore, low productivity growth in manufacturing reflects a productive specialization in low-demand, low-technology sectors,[17] where the Italian industry is faced with strong competition from emerging producers. As a consequence, Italy has experienced a loss of market share amounting to more than 40 per cent in cumulative real terms since 1995. In addition, since 1992, the working-age population has been in decline in Italy.

Simulation

The reduction in the risk premium has a strong positive effect on domestic demand in 1997 and 1998. The risk premium reduction does not, however, feed into higher GDP in this last phase of the run-up to EMU as its effects are outweighed by the strongly contractionary effect of fiscal policy in that period such that GDP growth remains low (see Figure 7.10).

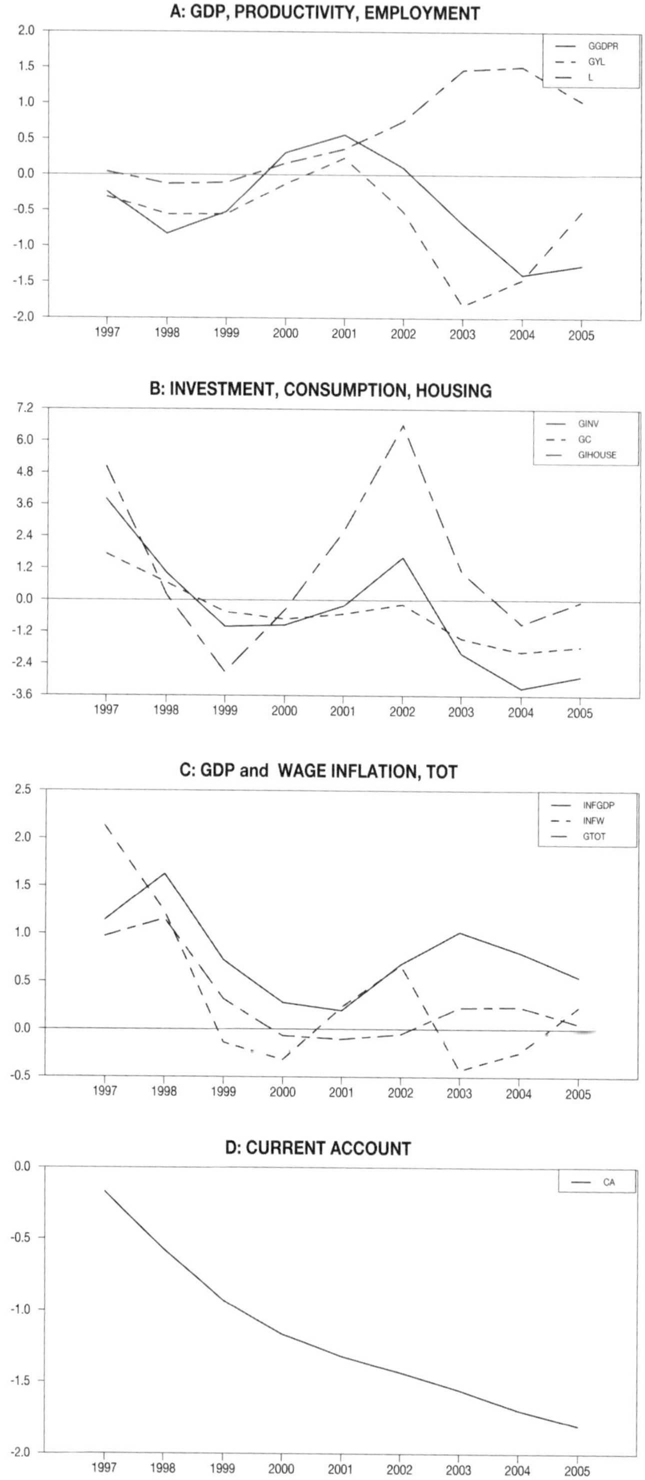

Figure 7.10 DSGE results for Italy (deviation from euro-area average).

The contribution of fiscal policy to GDP growth turns positive in 1999–2001 as the fiscal stance turns strongly expansionary. It remains slightly positive until 2003. Despite continued deterioration of the cyclically adjusted primary balances, the net effect of fiscal policy turns negative again from 2004, as the degree of crowding out of domestic demand generated in the model simulation exceeds the direct positive effect of net government demand.

From 2000 onwards, the increase in the employment rate through labour market reform and as a result of the negative TFP growth largely counters the effects of negative population growth on the GDP growth rate. A shift in demand towards housing together with loosening of lending constraints allowed increasing housing prices despite the unfavourable economic developments and underpinned construction investment.

The shocks to total factor productivity explain most of the low GDP growth and high inflation over the whole period considered. Especially from 2003 onwards, the cumulated effect of the TFP shocks weighs heavily on consumption and investment and reduces GDP growth by more than one percentage point per year. A shift in demand towards housing together with loosening of lending constraints helped (construction) investment.

The deterioration in the current account is largely explained by the reduction in the risk premium and the competitiveness effects of the negative TFP shocks.

Summing up

Shocks related to the creation of EMU do not explain GDP and its components nor inflation developments in Italy. The risk premium reduction did lead – as expected – to a deterioration of the current account; the anticipated higher growth rate did not, however, materialize.

By adding negative shocks to TFP, the development of the main variables can be matched. Structural challenges, feeding into negative total factor productivity shocks, thus seem the major factor behind persistently low growth and above-average inflation.

In addition, the fluctuations in GDP growth and its components seem to reflect to some extent fiscal policy behaviour: an initial sharp contraction, followed by strongly expansionary fiscal policy. From 2004 onwards, the crowding-out effect outweighs the direct expansionary effects of net government demand on GDP growth in the model simulations.

The Netherlands[18]

Stylized facts

In the second half of the 1990s, the Dutch economy consistently grew faster than most other euro-area countries (see Table 7.6). Annual real GDP growth outpaced the euro-area average by one percentage point in the period 1996–2000. High growth rates were fed by strong consumption and investment growth, in particular in construction. The strong growth period coincided with booming housing prices and a massive increase in mortgage debt. These developments, also fuelled by the falling nominal interest rates at the end of the 1990s, resulted in significant re-mortgaging and equity withdrawal that fed into private consumption expenditure. The Nederlandsche Bank estimates the annual spill-over effect of mortgage equity withdrawal on GDP growth via consumption expenditure at 0.5–1 percentage point in 1998–2000, turning to a negative contribution of around 0.5 percentage points in the period 2001–3 as equity withdrawal lessened.[19] As a result, household financial

Table 7.6 Economic development, the Netherlands (relative to euro area)

Variables	*1997*	*1998*	*1999*	*2000*	*2001*	*2002*	*2003*	*2004*	*2005*
Growth rate of real GDP[1]	1.10	1.20	0.71	−0.74	−0.82	−1.03	−0.72	−0.06	0.13
Growth rate of private consumption[1]	1.13	1.47	1.05	0.03	−0.93	−0.16	−1.62	−1.23	−0.65
Growth rate of investment[1]	3.95	−1.57	1.62	−3.62	−0.27	−3.07	−4.41	0.60	0.01
Labour productivity growth	1.04	0.77	0.37	−0.22	−0.97	−0.70	0.09	1.71	0.79
Employment rate[2]	1.53	1.99	2.41	2.25	2.51	2.29	1.66	0.37	−0.10
Inflation	0.66	0.19	0.70	2.52	2.84	1.27	0.51	−1.04	−0.17
Wage inflation	2.03	3.09	0.56	1.86	2.22	1.76	1.50	1.04	0.13
Growth of terms of trade[3]	0.79	−1.39	−0.48	3.71	0.28	−1.82	0.22	−1.06	0.49
Current account[2]	0.72	−2.33	−1.39	−0.54	−0.01	0.85	0.68	0.93	2.38

Source: Commission services.

Notes:

1 The growth rates of GDP and its components are per capita.

2 The employment rate and the current account are expressed as deviations from 1996 levels.

3 The terms of trade are defined as export prices of the Member State relative to export prices of the rest of EMU.

liabilities (as a percentage of GDP) in the Netherlands have almost doubled since 1990. On the supply side, employment and the labour share grew rapidly. Amidst symptoms of overheating, inflation peaked in 2000 and 2001 at more than two percentage points above the euro-area average. In 2001, a period of below-average growth set in in the Netherlands and inflation came down to below the euro-area average in the later years of the period under review.

Shocks

In the second half of the 1990s, the Dutch economy had an advantageous initial competitive position, reflected in an undervalued real exchange rate which exacerbated and prolonged the period of strong economic growth in the second half of the 1990s. The effects of the undervalued exchange rate were reinforced by a sharp increase in household debt as debt ceilings were increased and mortgage repayment requirements loosened.[20] Household debt has increased by about 30 per cent of GDP since the mid-1990s. The housing boom is to some extent an autonomous demand shock as dual-income households became more prevalent in the 1990s as female participation rates increased rapidly, increasing the mortgage borrowing capacity of households. A shock to debt financing and a housing demand shock are modelled to cover the increase in housing prices and indebtedness. Some fiscal shocks are given to reflect that a substantial part of windfall revenues was used to finance structural expenditure in the later phases of the upturn in the mistaken belief that these windfalls reflected sustainable revenue growth. In addition, data suggest that the Netherlands suffered from negative total factor productivity shocks at the end of the economic boom, which were reversed in the period 2003–5. As the Dutch guilder had been credibly linked to the DM for over a decade, the Netherlands did not benefit from the disappearance of an exchange risk premium with the entry into EMU. As the risk premium declined in most other euro-area Member States, this implies that we need to give a negative shock to the risk premium in the Netherlands (as compared to the euro-area average).

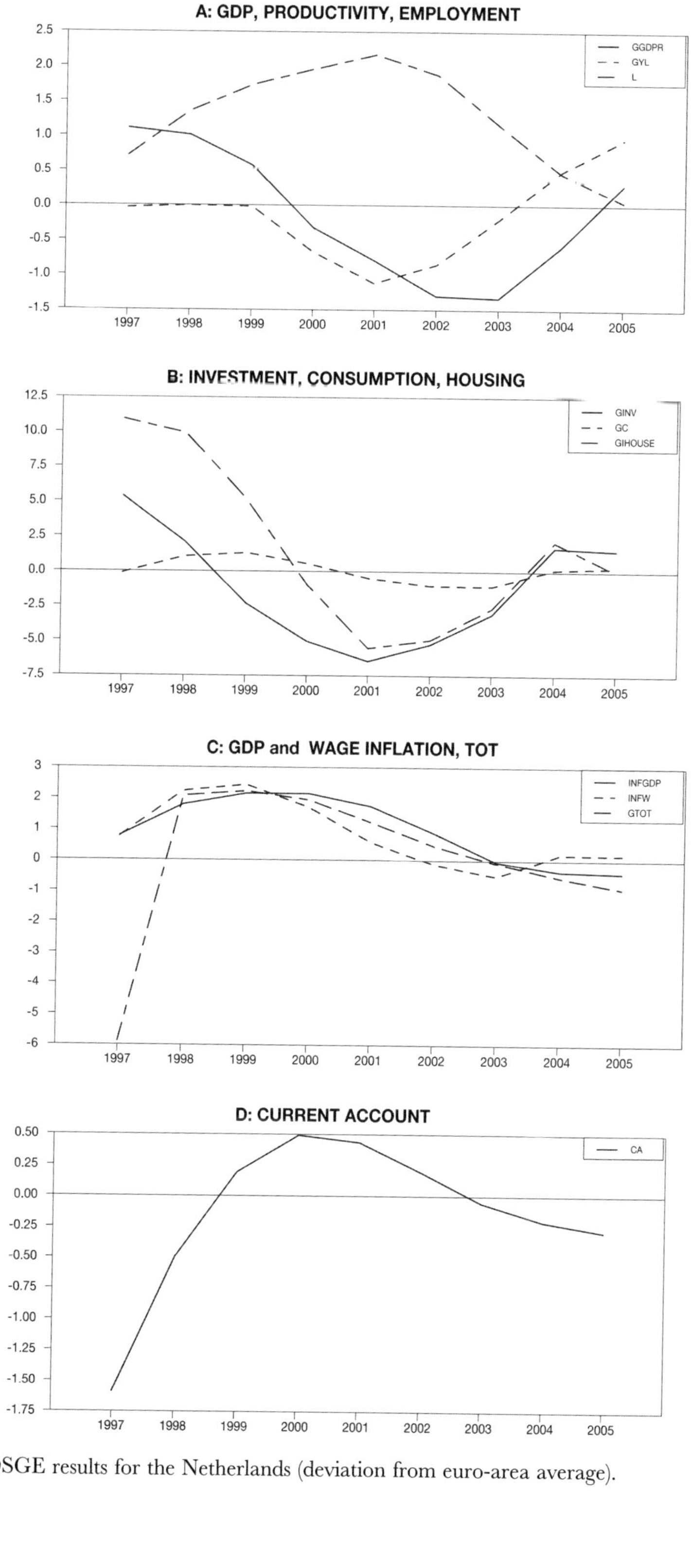

Figure 7.11 DSGE results for the Netherlands (deviation from euro-area average).

Simulation

The real exchange rate undervaluation at the entry into EMU can explain a large part of the high consumption and investment growth in 1997 and 1998 (see Figure 7.11). As the shock is given in the simulation in a single year – rather than built up gradually through wage moderation – it distorted the terms of trade development in 1997. The undervaluation led to increasing external and domestic demand, which resulted in price pressures. It explains up to 2.5 percentage points of the higher GDP level in the late 1990s.[21] Its effect was somewhat dampened by the loss of the negative risk premium compared to other euro-area Member States, which was associated with the credibility of the link to the DM. Since the late 1990s, prices and wages have grown faster in the Netherlands than in the rest of the euro area. Expansionary fiscal policy in the last phases of the long-lasting economic boom and strong consumption demand induced by the sharp increase in housing prices and wealth induced some overshooting dynamics.

A preference shift towards housing demand and raising of the debt ceiling together with pro-cyclical fiscal policy can partially explain high inflation and growth in the latter phases of the upturn, leading to overshooting of equilibrium price and wage levels, some overinvestment and strong employment growth, which put the unemployment rate below its equilibrium level. The booming housing market in particular stimulated consumer demand and further fuelled the build-up of imbalances until 2001–2. As the effect of these shocks faded out, consumption and investment dropped back to their baseline levels and the rate of inflation dropped below the euro-area average. The ending to the fiscal impulses and the subsequent fiscal tightening exacerbated the downturn. Together, the risk premium shock and the undervaluation of the real exchange rate explain the 2 per cent improvement in the current account balance over the period considered.

Summing up

The simulation of a shock to the real exchange rate in the run-up to EMU explains part of the high GDP growth and inflation in the first two to three years of the period considered.

The undervalued real exchange rate on entry into the euro area cannot explain the differences in the growth rate of housing investment and the extent of the consumption growth. This effect can be captured by assuming specific housing demand and debt financing shocks.

Portugal

Stylized facts

The Portuguese economy went through a boom in the running-up phase to EMU which started soon after the mid-1990s (see Table 7.7). GDP per capita growth exceeded that of the euro area until 1999. However since 2000 growth has dropped below euro average levels. High growth was accompanied by rising external imbalances. Somewhat surprisingly the current account deficit remains high despite the recent decline in GDP growth. The boom in the late 1990s was driven by extraordinary investment growth. Because of rising demand pressures, wage and price inflation exceeded the euro average by more than 5 and 2 per cent per annum, respectively, in the 1990s. In the meantime inflation differentials came down but so far they have not disappeared completely.

Table 7.7 Economic development, Portugal (relative to euro area)

Variables	*1997*	*1998*	*1999*	*2000*	*2001*	*2002*	*2003*	*2004*	*2005*
Growth rate of real GDP[1]	1.35	1.58	0.67	−0.21	−0.12	−0.39	−1.92	−0.94	−1.06
Growth rate of private consumption[1]	1.61	1.86	1.52	0.29	−0.84	0.19	−1.03	0.88	0.65
Growth rate of investment[1]	11.61	5.93	−0.01	−1.52	0.48	−2.01	−10.85	−1.44	−5.17
Labour productivity growth	0.94	1.12	1.06	0.73	−0.10	0.09	−1.12	−0.48	−0.37
Employment rate[2]	0.30	0.71	0.56	0.05	0.11	−0.22	−0.81	−1.12	−1.60
Inflation (GDP)	2.46	2.22	2.40	1.61	1.29	1.39	0.67	0.86	1.00
Wage inflation	5.94	4.62	2.84	4.25	2.74	1.80	0.82	0.35	0.99
Growth of terms of trade[3]	1.56	1.95	0.68	0.37	−0.47	0.20	−0.74	−0.11	−0.30
Current account[2]	−2.19	−3.24	−4.77	−6.61	−6.10	−4.06	−2.29	−3.65	−5.29

Source: Commission services.

Notes:
1 The growth rates of GDP and its components are per capita.
2 The employment rate and the current account are expressed as deviation from 1996 levels.
3 The terms of trade are defined as export prices of the Member State relative to export prices of the rest of EMU.

Shocks

We model the Portuguese development since 1997 by imposing specific demand and supply shocks. On the demand side there was an EMU-related shock, namely the abolition of the exchange risk premium at entry into EMU (100 basis points). Portugal also experienced financial market liberalization in the form of a reduction of credit constraints for housing investment. Finally one can observe a shift in demand from manufacturing to services. On the supply side a marked reduction in TFP growth in the non-tradable sector since the end of the 1990s can be identified. NAIRU (non-accelerating inflation rate of unemployment) estimates also suggest that there has been an increase in structural unemployment from about 5 per cent in 2000 to about 7 per cent in 2005.[22]

Simulation

According to the model the reduction of the risk premium was instrumental for the investment boom and the level shift of private consumption (consistent with the permanent income hypothesis) and caused the current account to decline by about five percentage points from 1997 to 2000. Consistent with the data, investment grows strongly in 1997 and 1998. There is, however, some overshooting of investment. After three years of strong investment, investment growth falls below euro-area average from 2000 onwards. From 2000 to 2002 investment growth is about 2 per cent below the euro-area average. The fall in the risk premium does not explain inflation persistence beyond the year 2000. In order to explain above-average inflation after 2000 four shocks seem relevant: (1) the decline in non-tradable TFP growth; (2) a rising debt ceiling; (3) an adverse wage shock; and (4) a shift in demand to non-tradables. Apart from being inflationary, the demand shocks also explain some other developments. The wage shock is important for capturing the trend reduction in the employment rate (relative to the euro area), which is, however, cushioned by the demand shift to non-tradables. Low TFP growth is the most important factor for low investment growth and also has a negative effect on employment. The reduction in the risk

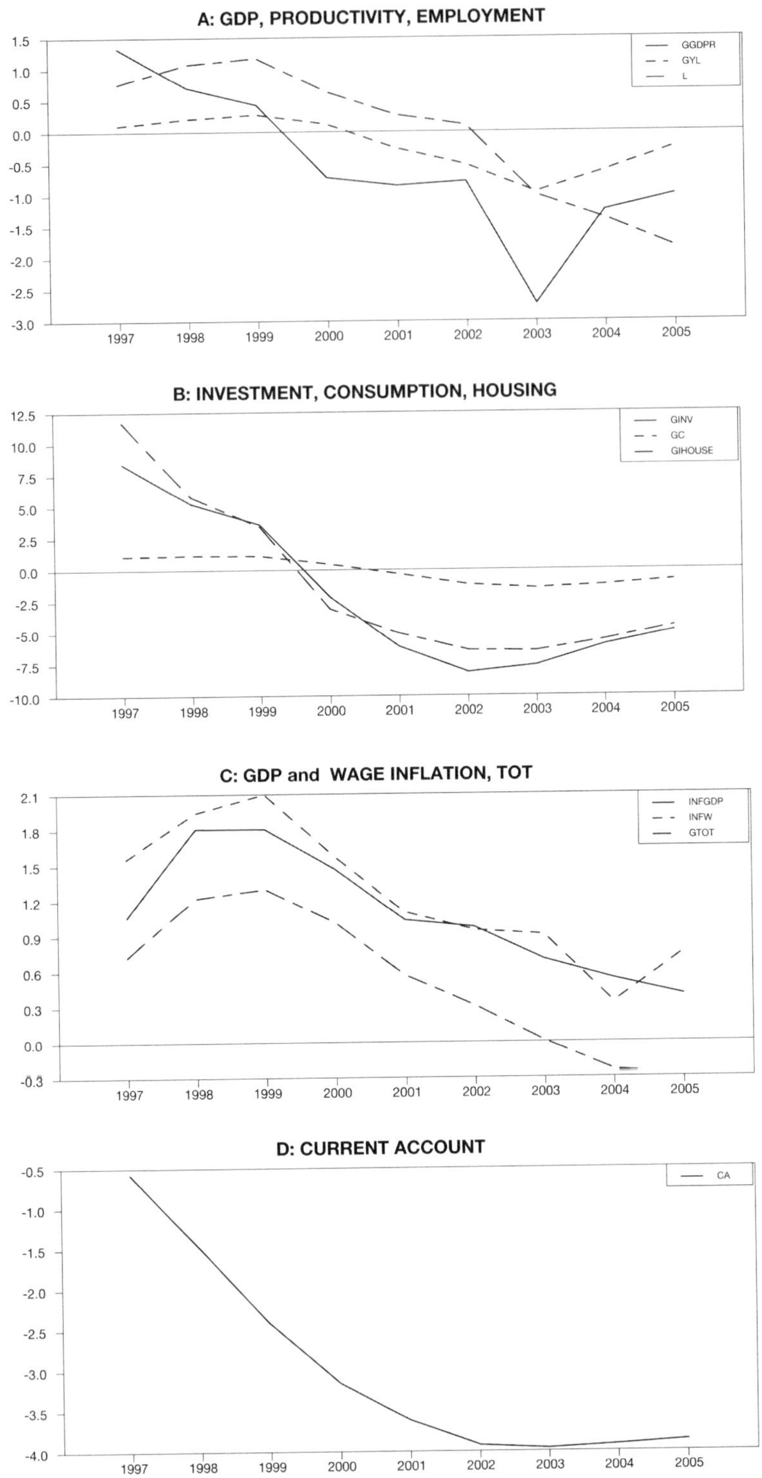

Figure 7.12 DSGE results for Portugal (deviation from euro-area average).

premium is the most important factor for explaining the persistent current account deficit. A non-negligible effect comes from a loosening of credit constraints. According to the model, increasing the debt ceiling for households has contributed about 0.5 per cent of GDP to the current account deficit in the most recent years and is the second most important factor for explaining the current account deficit.

Summing up

As can be seen from Figure 7.12, with these supply and demand shocks imposed, the model is capable of replicating some characteristic features of the Portuguese economic development since 1997, namely high growth in GDP and its components in the late 1990s, followed by a sustained negative growth differential since 2000; persistently positive (but declining) inflation differentials relative to the euro area; initially rising and then falling terms of trade growth; a rising current account deficit in the late 1990s which stabilized at high levels around 2000 and below-average productivity growth starting around the year 2000.

Spain

Stylized facts

In the running-up phase to EMU the currency risk premium of Spain declined and disappeared at the beginning of 1999. Starting in the 1990s the productivity performance in the non-tradable sector worsened relative to the euro area (see Table 7.8). These two developments are similar to those which occurred in Portugal. However, Spain differs from Portugal in a number of dimensions. The employment rate is still rising at an impressive pace. Since the beginning of the 1990s the participation rate has increased by 10 percentage points and the structural unemployment rate, which peaked at nearly 17 per cent in the mid-1990s, came down to 14 per cent in 1999 and has now reached a level of about 9 per cent. The increase in the employment rate is accompanied by a strong increase in the working-age population, mainly due to immigration. Second, unlike in Portugal the housing boom in Spain is continuing, possibly fuelled by high population growth, the age structure of the population and a boom in tourism (in particular an increasing number of holiday homes of foreigners). Because of high employment growth, GDP per capita has persistently been above the euro-area average, despite weak productivity growth. Investment growth has outpaced the euro-area average by roughly 4 per cent each year since the end of the 1990s. This is mostly due to housing investment (growth rate exceeds euro-area average by about 9 per cent). However, corporate investment in equipment has also shown strong growth in recent years. Inflation has permanently been high in Spain (about 2 per cent above the euro-area average). Wage inflation is, however, much more moderate, with a differential between Spain and the euro area below 1 per cent. High demand is also reflected in the current account balance. The current account deficit reached a level above 6 per cent in 2005.

Shocks

An important country-specific shock in the case of Spain is the reduction in the exchange risk premium when entering EMU. A conservative estimate based on deviations from

Table 7.8 Economic development, Spain (relative to euro area)

Variables	*1999*	*2000*	*2001*	*2002*	*2003*	*2004*	*2005*
Growth rate of real GDP[1]	1.41	0.49	0.71	0.58	1.01	−0.22	0.96
Growth rate of private consumption[1]	1.55	1.11	0.34	0.79	0.24	1.56	1.92
Growth rate of investment[1]	4.27	1.62	4.04	4.82	4.67	2.55	4.93
Labour productivity growth	−0.81	−1.46	−0.07	0.02	0.03	−0.98	−0.79
Employment rate[2]	1.10	2.09	2.49	2.82	3.42	3.88	4.97
Inflation (GDP)	1.77	2.03	1.79	1.88	1.93	2.16	2.69
Wage inflation	−0.45	0.35	0.96	0.74	1.06	1.18	0.25
Growth of terms of trade	−0.30	−2.95	2.15	3.13	1.29	0.19	0.79
Current account[2]	−1.50	−2.85	−3.08	−2.50	−2.93	−4.68	−6.23

Source: Commission services.

Notes:
1 The growth rates of GDP and its components are per capita.
2 The employment rate and the current account are expressed as deviation from 1998 levels.

interest parity between the peseta and the euro before 1999 suggests a risk premium of about 50 basis points was eliminated in the running-up phase to EMU. This provides a big stimulus to investment and consumption. Housing investment has also benefited from financial market liberalization, as shown, for example, by higher household debt (with an increase from 42.8 per cent (as a share of GDP) in 1999 to 64.5 per cent in 2005). However, other factors related to demographics, immigration and tourism also play a major role. In the simulation exercise all three types of housing shocks have been taken into account.[23] Spain differs from the rest of the euro area with respect to labour market trends. First, we allow for different population (of working age) trends and, second, we calculate negative shocks to the wage-setting rule such that the model replicates the increase in the employment rate. Another interesting structural development in the case of Spain is increased openness to foreign trade. While in the 1980s Spain was the country with the lowest import penetration (import share of 16.8 in 1980 versus 23.1 for France (second lowest) and 29.0 for the euro area), it has now overtaken France (30.6 for Spain versus 27.5 for France, 36.3 for the euro area). Following the empirical trade literature, increased openness is likely to increase competition in the tradable sector. In the simulations this is captured by a reduction in mark-ups in the tradable sector. Finally, we consider deviations in productivity growth in the non-tradable sector.

Simulation

The reduction in the risk premium has a powerful short-run effect on investment and consumption (see Figure 7.13). Consumption is increased by about 3 per cent in the first three years of EMU and has stayed at a higher level. Housing investment has responded vigorously to the reduction in the risk premium. Within the first two years it rose by about 8 per cent; however, afterwards housing investment gradually returns to baseline levels.[24] The risk premium can account for higher inflation between 0.5 and 1 per cent in the first four years of EMU; however, after four years the contribution of a lower risk premium to inflation is insignificant. Due to the level shift in demand, the risk premium shock has a rather long-lasting effect on the current account. It is the largest individual factor in explaining the current account deficit (and explains a deficit of 2.5 per cent in 2005). Other

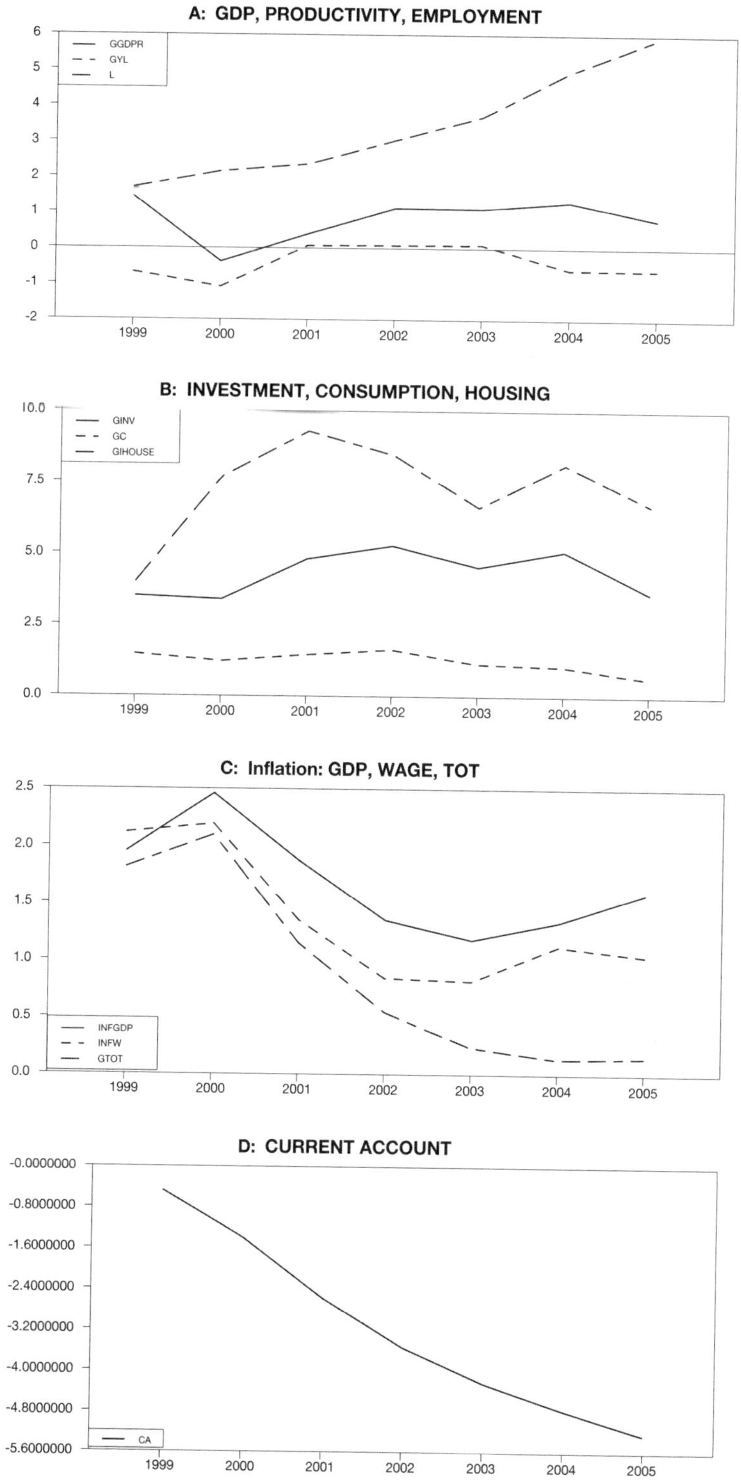

Figure 7.13 DSGE results for Spain (deviation from euro-area average).

structural factors (including the lifting of credit ceilings) have a more long-lasting effect on housing demand and on inflation (+0.4 per cent per annum in recent years). Other significant contributions to inflation derive from supply-side factors, namely low productivity growth in non-tradables and increased competition in tradables (the joint inflation effect is about 0.8 per cent per year between 2003 and 2005).[25]

Summing up

Shocks related to the creation of EMU explain GDP and its components as well as inflation in the first two to three years. The fall in the risk premium also explains a lower permanent consumption level and a more permanent current account deficit (of about 2.5 per cent of GDP).

The risk premium cannot explain sustained differences in the growth rate of housing investment. This can only be captured by assuming specific housing demand shocks. Increased housing demand can partially explain high inflation and a rising current account deficit in recent years.

On the supply side, low TFP growth of non-tradables and increased competition in tradables are important explanatory factors for inflation and the external balance in the Spanish economy.

The increase in the employment rate is only to a limited extent explained by the shocks considered. Both the population increase and increased competition contribute positively to employment. However, the bulk of the increase of the employment rate is generated by a shift in the wage-setting rule consistent with the observed decline in structural unemployment. Increased employment in Spain contributes significantly to housing demand, investment and private consumption.

A possible adjustment scenario for Spain and Germany

This section analyses how adjustment could take place in EMU after several years of asymmetric shocks. We analyse the cases of Spain and Germany, since these two countries experienced the largest asymmetric shocks with the strongest build-up of net foreign debt and assets, respectively, since the start of EMU. In the country simulations this process is driven by a sequence of asymmetric shocks. The question can be raised: what happens once these shocks stabilize? In this section we explore a scenario in which the exogenous variables stabilize gradually at their new levels at the end of 2007.

Adjustment in Spain

In the case of Spain the projection assumes that three country-specific developments came to an end by 2007 (see Figure 7.14). First, positive demand shocks to housing investment decline gradually and disappear at the end of 2007. Second, over the next two years, TFP growth in the non-tradable sector picks up and reaches similar growth rates as in the euro area. Third, positive labour market shocks (in the form of negative shocks to wages) gradually become smaller and disappear at the end of 2007.

Under these conditions the following stylized predictions are made by the model (notice all variables are in per capita terms and expressed as deviation from the euro-area average):

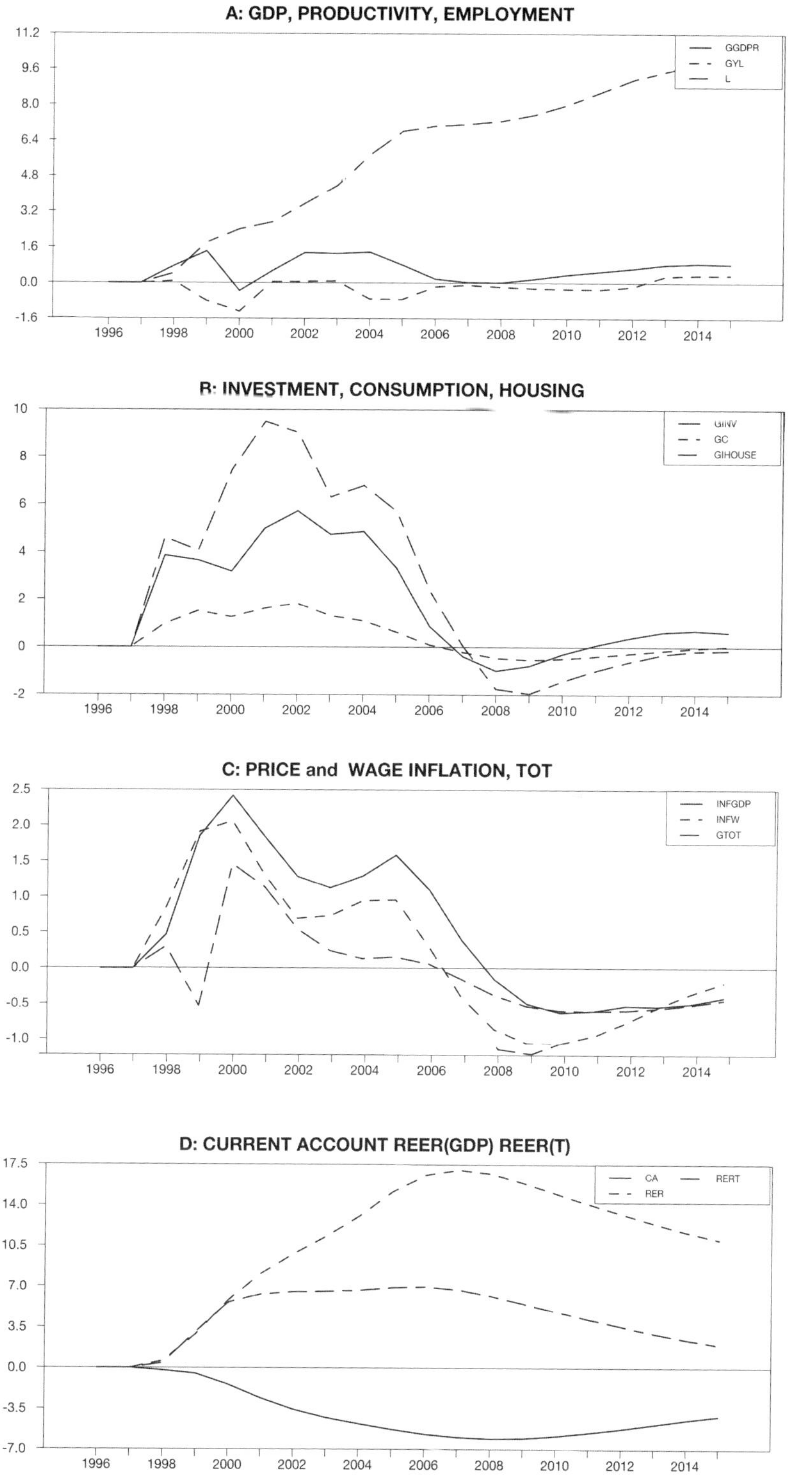

Figure 7.14 Adjustment in Spain.

- Investment demand (especially housing) declines strongly and undershoots euro-area investment growth (until 2011). The undershooting is more persistent in the case of housing investment.
- Growth of private consumption drops below the euro-area average (until 2015).
- Growth of GDP falls to the euro-area average rate.
- A continuous rise in the employment share prevents a strong fall in GDP per capita. There are two forces which drive up employment. First, wage inertia from previous negative wage shocks (labour market reforms) and, second, an income effect in labour supply. The prospect of declining real consumption and income increases labour supply.
- Inflation falls rapidly and reaches the euro-area average rate in 2008. However, inflation undershoots the euro-average inflation by about −0.5 to −1 per cent over several years. Wage inflation drops even more strongly.
- The adjustment of domestic demand and inflation first prevent the current account deficit from increasing further and cause a decline after 2009. However, the adjustment of the current account is rather slow. The real exchange rate in terms of tradables starts to fall in 2007, while the real exchange rate expressed in terms of the GDP deflator peaks in 2007 and starts declining in 2008.

This is a fairly orderly adjustment scenario. The following features are worth highlighting. Even though we are not assuming a collapse in housing investment, the fact that the boom is coming to an end will induce housing investment growth to undershoot. Inflation (especially wage inflation) also undershoots. Both features of the adjustment are similar to what happened in Germany at the end of the 1990s.

Adjustment in Germany

The scenario for Germany is based on three country-specific developments (Figure 7.15). First, demand for housing will not be subject to negative shocks any longer (phased out over a period of two years). Second, adverse shocks to corporate investment will fade out until the end of 2007. Third, the above-average growth of TFP in the non-tradable sector will slowly decline.

Under these conditions the following stylized predictions are made by the model.

- Investment demand (especially housing) picks up and growth of investment exceeds growth in the euro area after 2008.
- Growth of private consumption also increases but remains fairly subdued.
- Growth of GDP continues to exceed growth in the euro area (note that we still have above-average TFP growth in Germany in this scenario).
- Employment increases slightly but does not recover losses vis-à-vis the euro-area average over the period 1999–2005.
- Wage and price inflation increases gradually, however euro-area average rates of inflation are only reached after 2010.
- External adjustment is slow. The real exchange rate for tradables rises only slightly. This is because wages are not rising very strongly. The continued productivity improvements in the non-tradable sector contain labour demand and restrict any rise in wages.[26]

According to this scenario the outlook for Germany is rather promising for the coming years.

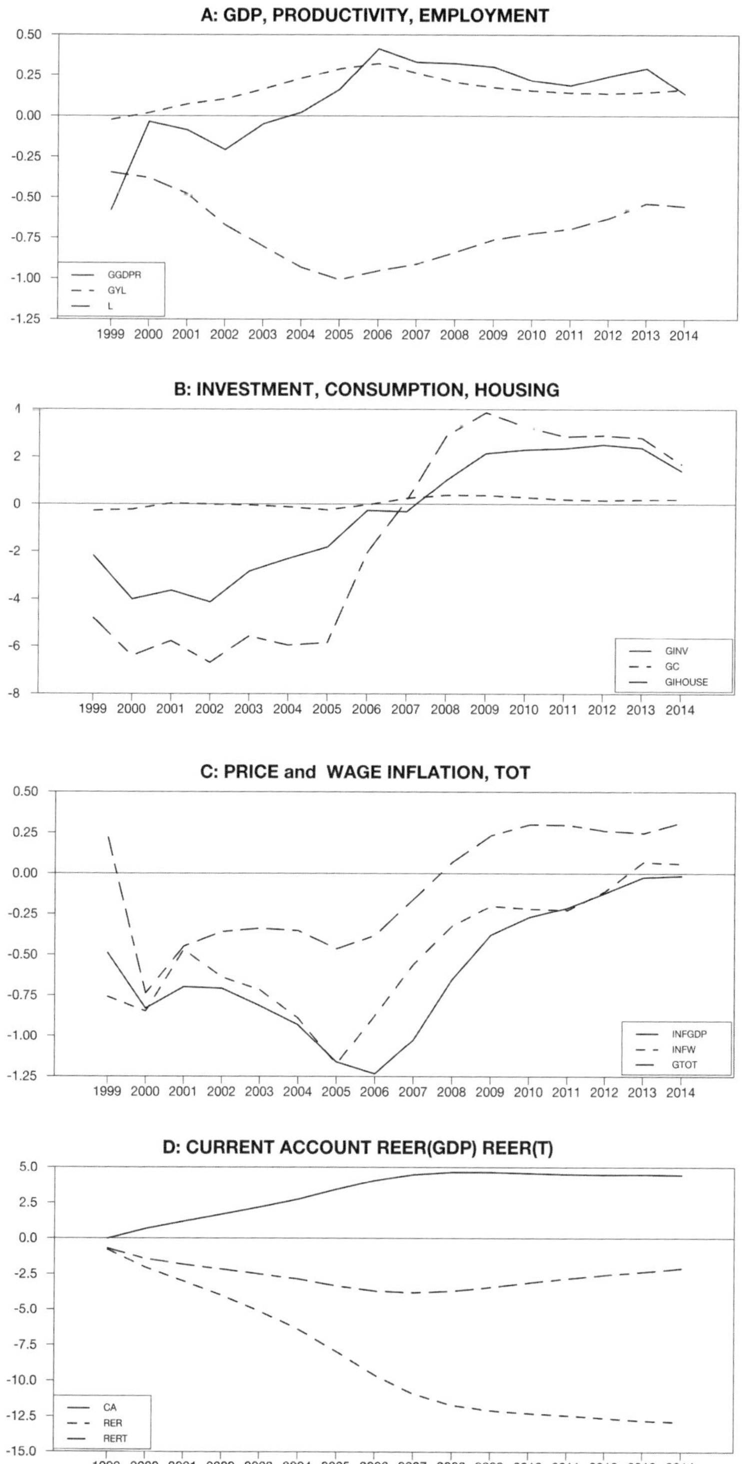

Figure 7.15 Adjustment in Germany.

Concluding remarks

This chapter has tried to explain some of the stylized facts of country dynamics in EMU. We have put special emphasis on the effects of changes in financial markets. The abolition of currency risk premia and increased capital mobility seem to have been an important driving force behind the current account dynamics. The absence of an exchange risk premium in EMU allows an increase in capital mobility, resulting in a lower correlation between savings and investment. The model simulations show a persistent effect on the current account, which largely operates through the wealth effect and housing investment. The risk premia convergence led to shifts from external to domestic demand in countries in which it declined (Ireland, Spain, Italy, Portugal), with the mirror-image in Germany.

The model simulations allow some benign and reassuring explanations of the economic divergence in the early years of EMU. To a significant extent they can be explained by the one-off shocks related to euro-area entry. After the one-off adjustment following the creation of the monetary union, economic developments apparently can be expected to be more symmetrical, though structural supply-side differences remain a source of growth differences.

Even though adjustment in EMU may be benign and rather efficient, return to baseline growth rates may imply significant changes over the years to come in some Member States. For example, a normalization of housing price increases may shave off excess demand in Spain, and will lead to lower consumption and investment growth and significantly lower growth and inflation. Also Germany may see a reversal of fortunes after a near decade of price/wage and current account adjustment.

Notes

1 This chapter presents in more detail a model analysis of adjustment experiences in EMU member states which appeared in the EU Economy Review 2006 (European Commission 2006). We are indebted to our colleagues in DG ECFIN for many helpful discussions. The views expressed in this chapter are those of the authors and should not be interpreted as those of the European Commission.

2 Lane (2006) provides a comprehensive survey of the issues at hand and reviews the evidence from the early years of EMU to investigate the performance of these hypotheses.

3 A more detailed model description can be found in Langedijk and Roeger (2007).

4 See, for instance, Smets and Wouters (2003).

5 Parameter values are taken from a DSGE model that was estimated for the euro area by Ratto, Roeger and In't Veld (2006).

6 In standard macro models (like QUEST, for example) households are usually divided into liquid ity and non-liquidity-constrained households. Liquidity-constrained households do not borrow at all but only consume current income. Housing investment is not modelled as a decision of the household sector but is part of the corporate investment decision. In this model we derive a housing investment equation explicitly from a decision problem of the household sector. Also, we allow all households to be able to borrow but assume that a fraction of households are credit constrained in the sense that existing collateral, in the form of the stock of housing wealth, puts a limit on the amount of period t borrowing. The price of housing consists of the price of land and the price of the house construction.

7 Differences in *industrial* structure may expose Member States differently to sectoral price and demand developments and sectoral competition from inside or outside the monetary union. When the industrial structure deviates strongly between Member States and a Member State has a high degree of sectoral specialization, the equilibrium real exchange rate may be affected if relative prices between sectors change. While real productivity is unaffected, the relative price change alters the value productivity in the sector. While each worker may produce the same output as before, the value of this output is reduced. Thereby equilibrium wages are reduced. Real wages have to decline to the new level of marginal value productivity, while sectoral adjustment takes place. The effects depend on the (perceived) persistence of the price shock.

8 Real effective equilibrium exchange rate estimates suggest that most of the real appreciation had disappeared at the end of the 1990s. For example, the estimates provided by Hansen and Roeger (2000) give an overvaluation in effective terms of 2 per cent.
9 This point is also made in the German country study. Broadbent *et al.* (2004) argue that German Banks have operated with relatively low margins in the past. However, financial market harmonization since EMU has made it easier to compare bank performance across countries in the euro area and Basel II is forcing German banks to reassess the risk of outstanding loans.
10 About two-thirds of the deviation results from a decline in the investment rate in Germany, while one-third is explained by an increase in the investment rate in the rest of the euro area. The investment shock decreases the value of housing relative to the value of consumption expenditure (excluding housing services) by about 5 per cent.
11 While most euro-area member states have lowered the share of transfers in GDP, this share has risen by about two percentage points in Germany since the mid-1990s. In the simulation an increase of one percentage point over the period 1999–2005 is assumed but a further increase by 2 per cent over the next decade is projected. This is less than the observed rate of increase since 1985 and conservative given the demographic pressure in Germany.
12 The recent development of manufacturing and services prices supports this view. Manufacturing inflation has increased sharply since the beginning of 2004 while service sector inflation has declined from about 7 per cent over the period 2000–3 to about 3.5 per cent over the period 2004–5 (see Irish Central Bank 2006). The Irish Central Bank attributes the decline in service prices at least in part to increased competition in home and transport insurance and the communications sector.
13 In the model, increased housing demand mainly leads to an increase in land prices and has less of an impact on construction because of wage equalization across sectors. There are also two offsetting effects. First, an increase in housing demand is partly compensated by lower demand for consumer goods. Second, a shift in the preference for houses increases labour supply and therefore has a dampening effect on wages. Finally, imputed rents are not considered.
14 The increase in the terms of trade as generated by the model results from an assumed reduction in TFP growth in the tradable sector.
15 Note that in the case of Italy we also considered the years 1997 and 1998 in the simulation, as these were characterized by strong fiscal consolidation which affected economic developments after the start of the euro area.
16 See, for instance, Banca d'Italia (2006).
17 See Larch (2005) and Monti (2005).
18 Note that in the case of the Netherlands we include the years 1997 and 1998 in the simulation, as demand pressures built up during this period which had repercussions in later years after the start of the euro area.
19 See Els *et al.* (2005).
20 The housing boom in the late 1990s was accompanied by a massive increase in mortgage debt, fuelled by a fiscal regime which permits virtually full tax deductibility of mortgage interest payments at the marginal tax rate. In combination with the liberalization of the mortgage market and increased competition between mortgage providers, this led to the introduction of new mortgage products that postpone loan redemption until maturity (concerns around 90 per cent of mortgages extended since 1995). Additionally, dual-income households became more prevalent in the 1990s, increasing the borrowing capacity of households.
21 Note that while the shock to the real exchange rate is given in a single year (1997), its building up (and unwinding) has been a gradual process.
22 In order to capture the strong decline of GDP growth in 2003 we impose two additional shocks, namely negative TFP shock in the tradable (primary) sector and a cut in government expenditures.
23 The last shock has been constructed as a residual shock to the model in order to replicate the divergent housing trend in Spain.
24 The effect of a reduction in the risk premium is an increase in the desired housing capital stock of private households. This is realized by initially rising investment, followed by a period of higher investment levels and a gradual return to the baseline level of investment.
25 An inflationary effect from increased competition in tradables sounds counterintuitive. Indeed, increased competition does not increase prices in the tradable sector but it increases wages, which in turn leads to higher inflation in the non-tradable sector.

26 The real exchange rate defined in terms of the GDP deflator remains on a downward trend because of the low inflation in the non-tradable sector.

References

Banca d'Italia (2006) *Annual Report for 2005 Assemblea generale ordinaria dei partecipanti*, Rome: Banca d'Italia.

Blanchard, O. (2006) *Adjustment with the Euro. The Difficult Case of Portugal*, MIT Working Paper No. 06–04.

Blanchard, O. and F. Giavazzi (2002) 'Current account deficits in the euro area. The end of the Feldstein–Horioka puzzle?' *Brookings Papers on Economic Activity* 2: 147–209.

Broadbent, B., D. Schumacher and S. Schels (2004) *No Gains without Pain – Germany's Adjustment to a Higher Cost of Capital*, Goldman Sachs Global Economics paper, No. 103.

Čech, Z. and J. Macdonald (2004) 'The "Celtic Tiger" learns to purr', *ECFIN Country Focus* 1(18).

Deroose, S., S. Langedijk and W. Roeger (2002) *Reviewing Adjustment Dynamics in EMU: From Overheating to Overcooling*, ECFIN Economic Papers, No. 198, Brussels: Directorate-General for Economic and Financial Affairs, European Commission.

Dhyne, E., L.J. Alvarez, H. Le Bihan, G. Veronese, D. Dias, J. Hoffmann, N. Jonker, P. Lünnemann, F. Rumler and J. Vilmunen (2006) 'Price changes in the euro area and the US: some facts from individual consumer price data', *Journal of Economic Perspectives* 20(2): 171–92.

Els, P.J.A. van, W.A. van den End and M.C.J. van Rooij (2005) 'Financial behaviour of Dutch households: analysis of the DNB Household Survey', in *Investigating the Relationship between the Financial and Real Economy*, BIS Papers, 22, Basel: Bank for International Settlements, pp. 1–40.

European Commission (2006) *The EU Economy: 2006 Review – Adjustment Dynamics in the Euro Area*, European Economy, No.6, Brussels: Directorate-General for Economic and Financial Affairs, European Commission.

Fagan, G. and V. Gaspar (2005) 'Adjusting to the euro area: some issues inspired by the Portuguese experience', mimeo, Banco de Portugal and ECB.

Hansen, J. and W. Roeger (2000) *Estimation of Real Equilibrium Exchange Rates*, DG ECFIN Economic Papers No. 144, Brussels: Directorate-General for Economic and Financial Affairs, European Commission.

Irish Central Bank (2006) *Quarterly Bulletin*, April.

Lane, P.R. (2006) *The Real Effects of EMU*, CEPR Discussion Paper No. 5556.

Langedijk, S. and W. Roeger (2007) *Adjustment in EMU: A Model-based Analysis of Country Experiences*, ECFIN Economic Papers No. 274.

Larch, M. (2005) 'Stuck in a rut? Italy's weak export performance and unfavourable product specialisation', *ECFIN Country Focus* II(9).

Lopez-Salido, D., F. Restoy and J. Valles (2005) *Inflation Differentials in EMU. The Spanish Case*, Banco d'Espagna Working Paper No. 0514.

Monti, P. (2005) *Caratteristiche e mutamenti della specializzazione delle esportazioni italiane*, Banca d'Italia Working Paper No. 559.

Ratto, M., W. Roeger and J. In't Veld (2006) 'Fiscal policy in an estimated open-economy model for the euro area', *Computing in Economics and Finance* 43, Society for Computational Economics.

—— (2007) *Fiscal Policy in an Estimated Model of the Euro Area*, ECFIN Economic Papers No. 266.

Smets, F. and R. Wouters (2003) 'An estimated dynamic stochastic general equilibrium model of the euro area', *Journal of the European Economic Association* 1(5): 1123–75.

8 Housing markets and adjustment in monetary union

Peter Hoeller and David Rae

Introduction[1]

Monetary union fosters integration by raising price transparency and reducing transactions costs. But it also implies the loss of the sovereign interest rate and exchange rate instruments. This is the main potential cost of joining a monetary union since it becomes more difficult to adjust swiftly to shocks. While price and output adjustment is necessary to absorb shocks, even relatively small inflation differentials that are perpetuated over time and become entrenched in expectations eventually lead to heavy competitiveness losses and painful adjustment. Moreover, sluggish growth for some time could reduce potential output growth due to low investment, loss of skills of the unemployed and withdrawal from the labour market. How high such costs are depends on the frequency and nature of the shocks that hit individual countries. The cost is highest if situations arise where substantially disparate monetary conditions would be called for in different countries due to economic disturbances that have uneven impacts across the area (asymmetric demand shocks). Moreover, the commitments under the Stability and Growth Pact may limit the leeway for fiscal action to smooth the cycle, while labour, product and financial market policies may hinder a speedy adjustment. In the case of demand shocks that affect all countries more or less equally (symmetric shocks), the loss of monetary autonomy implied by EMU is in principle of less concern, because the area-wide policy would tend to deliver monetary conditions that are appropriate for each country. However, this may not always be the case if the transmission mechanism differs across member countries, because then a uniform policy response would not yield uniform effects. Differences in housing markets and their effects on demand are, of course, important in this context.

This chapter first highlights factors that limit or increase cyclical divergence. It then reviews one policy area that is important in fostering a speedy adjustment to shocks: the transmission of monetary policy via the housing market, which can be a source of resilience as well as a factor leading to prolonged divergence. As a basic principle, policy should neither hinder adjustment nor exacerbate the cycle.

The major policy-related findings are:

- Following a positive cost or price shock, the boost to activity coming from lower real interest rates is quickly offset by competitiveness losses in small countries so that the output gap and inflation are back where they should be within a few years. The adjustment is considerably slower in larger countries that are less open to trade. However, asset bubbles are a cause of concern in the case of small countries as their limited overall weight means that the monetary stance is more likely to be out of line with their cyclical position.

- Backward-looking or extrapolative expectations in the housing market can be highly destabilizing. Some element of forward-looking or rational expectations can go a long way to anchoring the housing market. This emphasizes the importance of jawboning by policymakers in an attempt to talk down a market that is getting carried away.
- Housing markets are important in the transmission of monetary policy and a high interest rate sensitivity is beneficial as monetary policy is more powerful in dampening cyclical fluctuations overall in the euro area. However, the characteristics of housing and mortgage markets still differ widely across the euro area, leading to asymmetric behaviour of individual countries. These concern mainly differences in home-ownership rates, financial markets, taxation and supply constraints. Supply constraints and tax incentives to stimulate house ownership can exacerbate volatility in house prices and cyclical divergence.
- Moreover, in the absence of monetary policy and with fiscal policy constrained, it is important to have a financial system that can withstand asset bubbles. In this context, the pro-cyclicality of bank provisioning is of concern as it could lead to a credit crunch and reinforce a downturn. Prudential supervision across the area has become better co-ordinated, but still remains fragmented.
- Recent OECD surveys for Ireland, the Netherlands, Spain, Denmark and Finland have pointed to the need to ease supply constraints, to phase out fiscal incentives for housing, to reinforce prudential supervision and to reform social housing policies, which can have implications for migration.

The competitiveness and interest rate channels

Short-run (benign) price and output adjustment is necessary to absorb shocks. Inflation differentials should be allowed to rectify misalignments in real exchange rates, and the faster they unwind, the lower will be the sacrifice ratio, i.e. the amount of cyclical slack necessary to restore equilibrium in product and labour markets. Hoeller *et al.* (2002) provide a simple analytical framework to better understand the factors that hinder or help smooth adjustment in monetary union or that are likely to become more prominent with further EU integration:[2]

- Cross-country differences in demand pressures will lead to differences in inflation and labour cost developments, with real interest rates and competitiveness working in opposite directions. In this context it is critical whether real interest rate effects are strong relative to competitiveness effects. A relatively strong competitiveness effect implies rapid adjustment, while a relatively strong real interest rate effect implies a drawn-out adjustment. In a sluggish economy with lower inflation, for instance, rapid gains in competitiveness will boost foreign demand (crowding-in effect), while a strong effect of the higher real interest rate will hold back domestic demand (crowding-out effect).
- Wealth effects can be a double-edged sword. A greater ability to borrow against housing wealth can help smooth consumption by allowing households to borrow their way through a downturn. On the other hand, they can magnify cyclical divergences if households' expectations overshoot into 'irrational exuberance'. Despite reforms, the mortgage market still differs significantly across countries. In the United States, the United Kingdom and Australia, for instance, the ease and low cost at which housing equity can be withdrawn and mortgage loans refinanced at a lower interest rate have certainly played a role in the resilience of these economies to the negative shocks in recent years. But in Denmark mortgage market liberalization has helped fuel a substantial and not entirely warranted house price boom that has pushed the economy towards overheating.

Table 8.1 Real house prices are decelerating in some markets

	Per cent annual rate of change						
	1995–2000	*2001*	*2002*	*2003*	*2004*	*2005*	*2006*[1]
United States	2.3	5.0	5.2	4.5	7.8	9.6	7.3
Japan	−2.6	−3.4	−3.8	−5.2	−6.1	−4.6	−4.4
Germany	−1.6	−1.9	−3.3	−2.0	−3.8	−1.9	−2.0
France	2.1	6.0	6.2	9.4	12.6	13.2	10.9
Italy	−0.9	5.7	6.8	7.3	7.5	5.2	4.4
United Kingdom	8.2	6.8	14.6	14.2	10.4	3.4	2.3
Canada	0.0	2.0	7.7	6.5	7.5	7.6	9.1
Australia	3.5	6.5	15.3	15.0	4.1	−1.1	1.5
Denmark	6.7	3.4	1.3	1.1	7.9	15.6	22.4
Spain	2.6	6.5	12.9	16.4	14.8	10.9	6.9
Finland	7.8	−3.5	8.3	4.5	5.9	5.1	9.8
Ireland	17.6	4.1	5.6	11.4	9.1	9.4	11.7
Netherlands	11.6	5.6	4.3	2.4	2.9	3.3	3.1
Norway	9.3	3.9	3.6	−0.7	9.6	6.6	8.4
New Zealand	1.7	−0.8	6.6	17.3	15.2	11.1	6.7
Sweden	6.3	5.1	4.3	4.2	8.2	8.1	11.5
Switzerland	−2.5	0.9	4.0	2.3	1.5	−0.1	1.8
Euro area[2,3]	1.3	3.3	4.1	5.7	5.8	5.5	4.4
Total of above countries[3]	1.7	3.3	4.5	4.4	5.4	5.7	4.6

Source: Various national sources, see Table A.1 in Girouard *et al.* (2006a).

Notes:
1 First half of 2006 relative to first half of 2005.
2 Germany, France, Italy, Spain, Finland, Ireland and the Netherlands.
3 Using 2000 GDP weights.

Due to inflation differentials real interest rates have differed a lot across countries. Over the recent cycle, short-term interest rates were low in Ireland, Greece, the Netherlands, Portugal and Spain. But in Germany they were clearly very high, with France, Austria, Belgium and Finland in between. In some smaller economies that experienced a sharp decline in interest rates before entering monetary union the boost was compounded by a steep rise in house prices, especially so in Ireland and Spain. House prices also rose steeply in the Netherlands during the late 1990s and more recently in France, while they declined in Germany (see Table 8.1).

To be sure, there have been more factors than interest rates driving house prices. Over long periods of time, by far the most important factor is real per capita income, since higher incomes lead to greater consumption of all goods and services, including housing. Most econometric studies find that the long-run income elasticity of real house prices is between 1 and 2.[3] Strong income growth has been a key factor behind the house price booms in Ireland, Finland and Spain (see Figure 8.1). Demographic factors are also important. Population growth, often driven by immigration,[4] obviously drives up the demand for housing, as does a younger population. Portfolio adjustments have also played a role in some countries, where financial liberalization combined with a reduction in the interest rate risk premium have led households to increase their borrowing levels closer to international norms. The estimated response of house prices to interest rates varies substantially across econometric studies, but the average semi-elasticity from the studies reported in Girouard *et al.* (2006a) is around −3.5, i.e. a drop in real interest rates by one

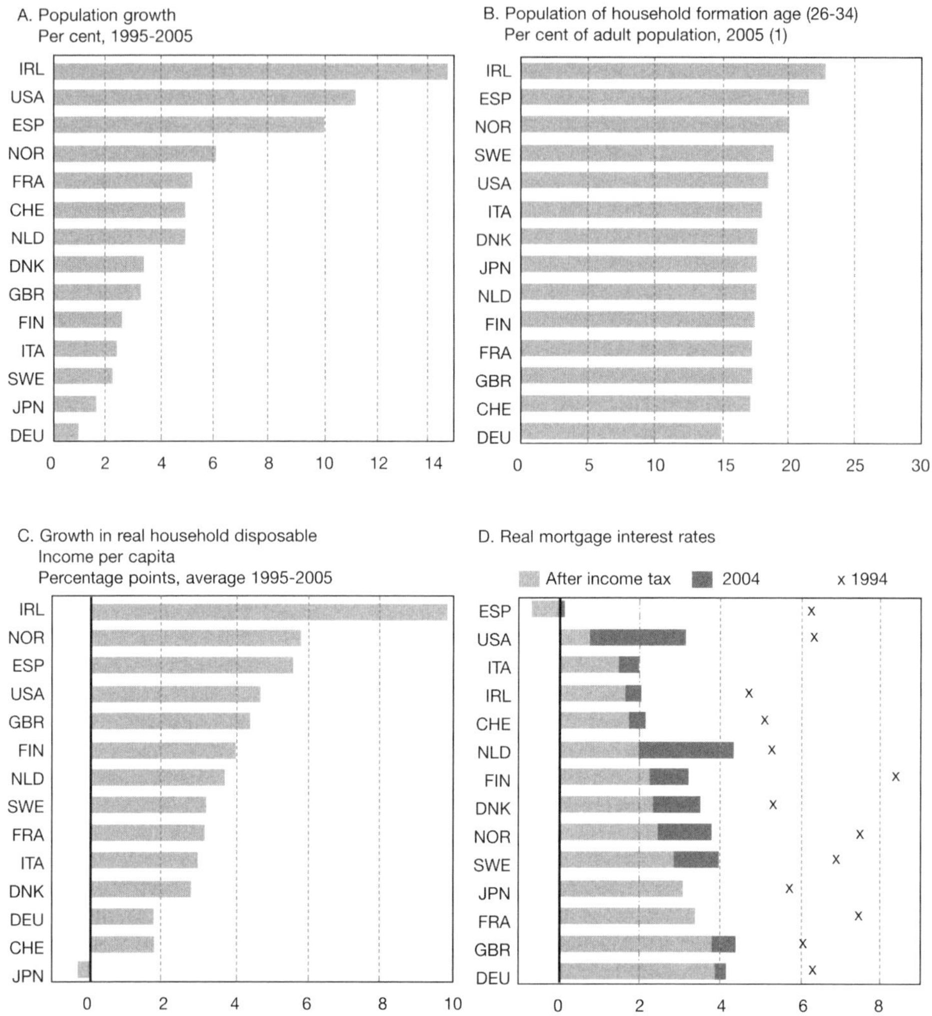

Figure 8.1 Forces shaping housing demand.
Source: OECD, Labour Force Statistics (2006), OECD Economic Outlook No. 79 database and Girouard *et al.* (2006a), for Panel B.

percentage point will raise real house prices by 3.5 per cent in the long run. This is not a large impact, but the effects of a temporary drop in interest rates can get amplified if expectations start to feed on themselves. The rise in house prices has brought forth an increase in supply, especially in Ireland and Spain (see Figure 8.2), leading to a construction boom that to some extent has generated its own economic momentum. The dynamics of house price developments depends critically on the elasticity of housing supply, which itself depends on incentives of municipalities to release land for building and the speediness of building approvals.

Equilibrating forces coming through external demand have helped to some extent (see Figure 8.3), but a key lesson from the early years of monetary union is that this balancing mechanism acts slowly. Fast-growing economies, and countries where wage gains outstrip

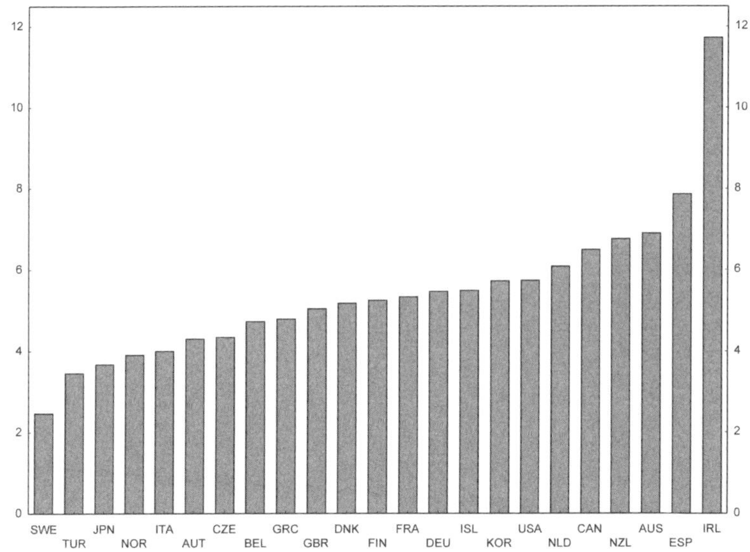

Figure 8.2 Housing investment share, % of GDP.
Source: OECD, National Accounts and Economic Outlook No. 79 database.

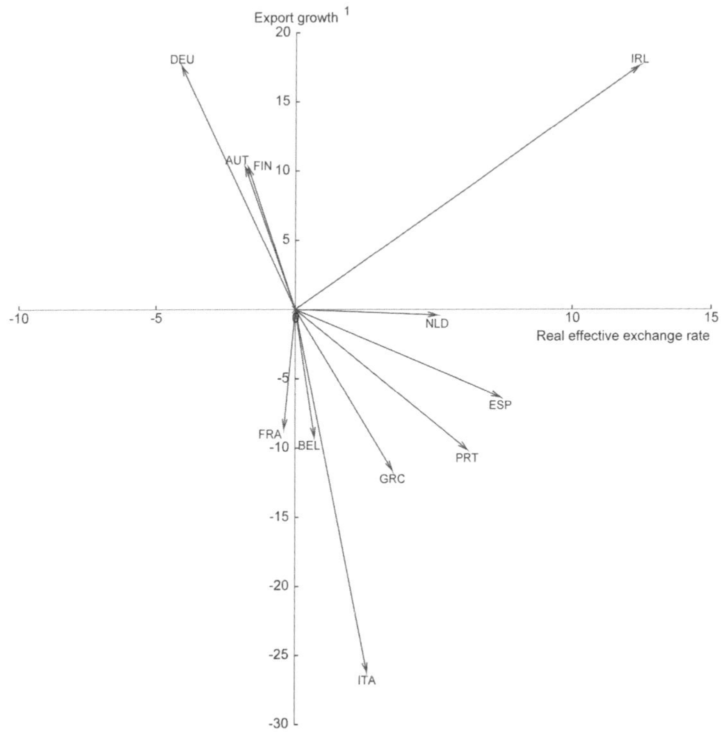

Figure 8.3 Real effective exchange rate and exports (cumulative change, 1999–2005).
Source: Eurostat and OECD, Economic Outlook database.

Note:
1 Excess over euro area average.

productivity, can maintain relatively high inflation for quite some time, putting exporters under pressure. Eventually they will hit a competitiveness wall, and job losses in export industries will put a brake on the more sheltered sectors. But because this feedback is delayed and out of sync with the driving forces of activity, it can lead to boom–bust cycles rather than stable growth. The housing market often plays a central role in magnifying these cycles. The initial impetus for growth in the domestic economy can be a normal convergence process, for example where income and price levels in Spain, Portugal and Greece catch up with the euro area average. However, if price level convergence is not backed up by strong productivity growth, competitiveness will suffer. This is why Ireland has done well on export markets despite substantial real exchange rate appreciation, while Portugal is struggling. Moreover, the convergence process is seldom one where countries land smoothly on their long-run equilibrium path and then settle down to grow at normal rates. Instead, theory[5] and evidence[6] show that countries can overshoot. This can be seen in new OECD data on unit labour cost levels (see Figure 8.4). Italy, Portugal and Spain used

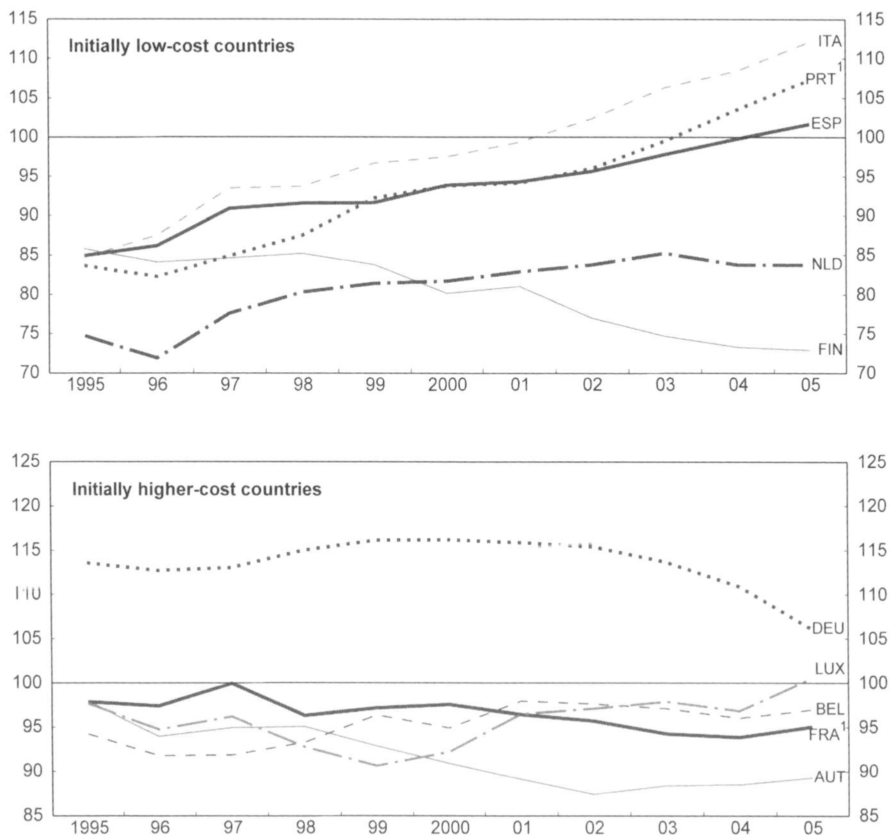

Figure 8.4 Relative unit labour cost levels in industry (euro area = 100).
Source: OECD, Main Economic Indicators – OECD online database and OECD Economic Outlook: Statistics and Projections – online database.

Note:
1 Extended using total-economy unit labour costs for Portugal (2003–5) and France (2005).

to have relatively low unit labour costs; Italy and Portugal have now overshot considerably, and on current trends Spain will follow suit shortly. It is not just the wealth effect of house prices that contributes to macroeconomic fluctuations; construction cycles can also be destabilizing, especially as in the past they have tended to end more with a bang than a whimper (see Box 8.1).

Box 8.1 Has there ever been a soft landing?

Residential investment cycles can be destabilizing in their own right. Between 1960 and 2004, 49 residential construction booms have occurred in 23 countries for which data is available (by construction, the latest peak that can be identified is 2002; the analysis here therefore omits the housing booms that are currently underway). In the cycles that have been identified, the average increase in real per capita residential investment from trough to peak is around 40 per cent. The largest occurred in Korea from 1973 to 1978 (where investment rose by 160 per cent). The trough-to-peak increase has exceeded 50 per cent in 16 cases.

The downturn that follows is usually rapid. On average, in the first year after the peak, 40 per cent of the increase during the trough-to-peak upswing is reversed, with another 40 per cent lost in the second year (see Figure 8.5). Investment stabilizes at that level for two years, before beginning to recover about five years after the peak. The spill-over effects to real activity are typically large. GDP growth declines sharply such that the output gap falls by nearly four percentage points from peak to trough in the years following the construction downturn. On average, the fiscal balance worsens by 2.5 percentage points of GDP and the unemployment rate rises by 2.5 percentage points. Surprisingly, a tightening of monetary policy is not always the trigger for the end of a construction boom. Of the 34 booms for which there is also data on short-term interest rates, monetary policy tightened before the investment peak only in a little over half of all cases.

There are noticeable differences between countries that had fixed exchange rates at the time and those that were either floating or devalued just after the peak. The size of the boom from trough to peak is larger in the fixed exchange rate case and the subsequent slump is longer – the trough of the investment cycle occurs two years after the peak when monetary policy is able to respond, but in the fixed exchange rate case investment is still falling after five years. Some real-world examples include Sweden and Finland in the late 1980s and early 1990s, where their downturns would have been even more severe if they had not devalued their currencies.

How common are soft landings? If a soft landing is defined as a relatively small reduction in the investment rate, they are not especially common. There have been only four cases where the decline in per capita residential investment has been smaller than one-third of the increase that occurred during the boom years (these are the Netherlands after 1978, Belgium after 1990, the United Kingdom after 1998 and Finland after 2000). Soft landings are more common if they are defined as gradual declines, i.e. where it takes at least three years to hit the trough. There have been around 20 of these. But all were comparatively deep declines. If a soft landing is defined as something that is *both mild and gradual*, there has not been a single case out of the 49 boom–bust cycles.

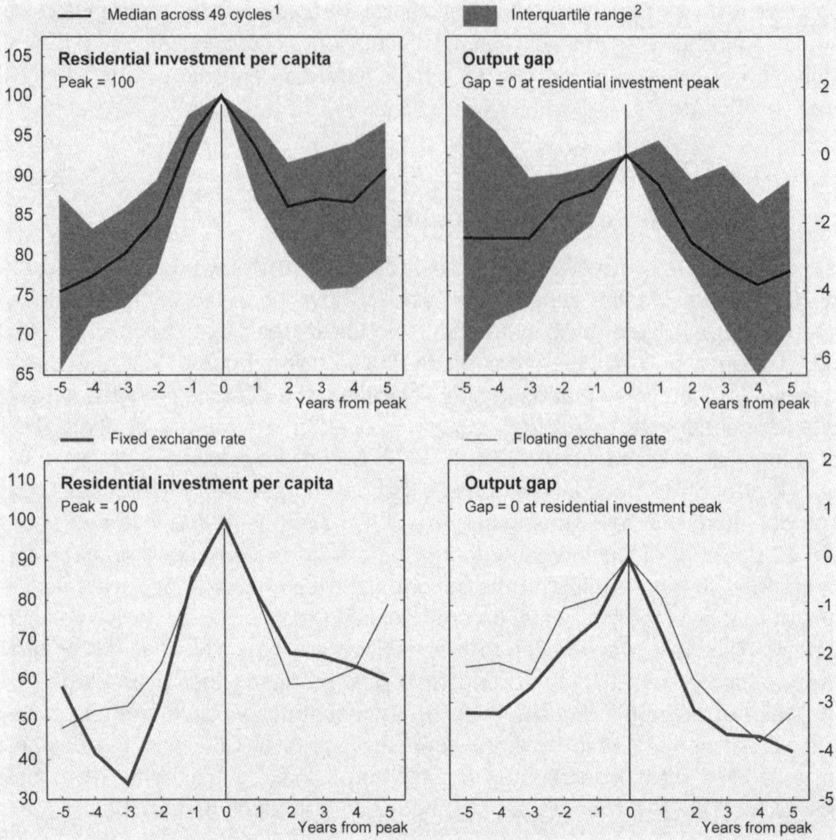

Figure 8.5 Has there ever been a soft landing?
Source: OECD (2005), Economic Outlook 79 database.

Notes:
1 In each cycle, real per capita residential investment is scaled so that the peak equals 100.
2 The shaded area shows the middle two quartiles (i.e. half the countries fall in this range).

Ahearne *et al.* (2005) conducted a similar exercise except that they looked at house price booms rather than construction cycles. They found that house prices are strongly pro-cyclical, and a recession typically follows a downturn in real house prices. Residential investment normally turns down about a year before house prices.

Source: Rae and van den Noord (2006).

Model simulations of the competitiveness and interest rate channels

These points are illustrated in more concrete terms with the help of model simulations. The model is described in detail in Appendix I. It can be thought of as a stripped-down version of the type of macro-econometric model commonly used by central banks. On the other hand, the housing channel is in some respects richer, and incorporates more modelling options than conventional models.

The conflict between the interest rate and competitiveness channels is illustrated in Figure 8.A1 in Appendix I. Two types of economies are compared: an open economy with a high trade exposure, such as Ireland, and a more closed economy, such as France. Each country faces the same positive price or cost shock. The initial jump in inflation has two impacts. The most important is a worsening in competitiveness that reduces exports and boosts imports. This obviously has a larger impact on the more open economy, which is why in the first two years output growth falls by considerably more than in the more closed economy. The second effect is a reduction in real interest rates. This provides an offsetting boost to business investment. It has a negligible initial impact on housing investment because, with forward-looking house price expectations, people realize that any rise in house prices will be short lived. The main difference between the relatively open and closed economies is how quickly the competitiveness channel drives inflation back to 2 per cent. In the open economy, the adjustment is largely complete after a few years whereas the cycles are much more protracted in the economy less exposed to trade because swings in inflation generate real interest rate effects that offset the comparatively weak trade channel. When they work at loggerheads, it takes longer for equilibrium to be restored. The key conclusion here is that a stronger competitiveness channel can create a bigger initial impact for this type of shock, but in general the economy will return to equilibrium more quickly.

The appendix also looks at how outcomes are affected by the expectations formation process and the strength of the wealth effect. Briefly, backward-looking or extrapolative expectations in the housing market can be highly destabilizing as temporary shocks are magnified and create large and long-lasting housing market bubbles that in turn lead to substantial swings in economic activity and inflation. The simulation with more weight on forward-looking or rational expectations shows cyclical responses that are considerably more dampened. Second, a strong wealth effect can lead to faster and smoother adjustment to equilibrium when housing market expectations are semi-rational (or forward looking to some degree), but when expectations are extrapolative the economy would be better off with a smaller wealth effect.

Other factors

We will not dwell in detail on the other factors that shape adjustment (see OECD 2006a for a more complete discussion). To summarize the main points, deep integration helps by giving greater opportunities for risk sharing across the monetary union. Flexible labour and product markets also help, but most euro area countries are not well placed in this respect. Cournède *et al.* (2005), for instance, show that when output is below potential, inflation falls by less in the euro area than in most other OECD countries, partly because of implicit pricing contracts and strategic interactions among firms. Nominal and real wage rigidities are affected by factors such as employment protection legislation and union coverage (EC 2005). Duval *et al.* (2007) finds that output gaps are more persistent where labour market and product market regulations are stringent, while high levels of household mortgage debt – which are more often found in deregulated mortgage markets – appear to speed up adjustment. The same factors can also magnify the initial impact of a shock, but Drew *et al.* (2004) show that from a welfare point of view the economy would be better off if it was flexible (delivering a short, sharp shock rather than a shallower but long-drawn-out adjustment) unless society puts a great deal of weight on inflation stabilization relative to output stabilization. In principle, labour mobility can act as a safety valve but in the European context it is unlikely to play an important role in the foreseeable future except perhaps in isolated cases such as Ireland and Spain. The only tool left is fiscal policy, but the need for fiscal consolidation rules fiscal action out in many countries.

Going forward, deeper integration in the European Union should boost trade integration and capital market linkages. Trade intensity and capital market linkages tend to be much larger among regions in a country than across countries. This means that there is less home bias, there are stronger capital market linkages and there is thus more risk sharing.

The European Union has, of course, aimed at deep integration via the single market, thus boosting trade and capital market linkages within the Union. So far, it has been fairly successful in implementing the single market for goods. Integration in other sectors has, on the other hand, still quite some way to go. Concerning financial services, which were further liberalized by the Financial Services Action Plan in recent years, progress towards better integration has been uneven across market segments, with retail banking and mortgage markets being among the least well-integrated areas. While market segmentation within the euro area is likely to be smaller than across the countries outside the Union, deep integration has still not been achieved across a variety of important market segments. A hard push to lower market segmentation would especially benefit the large euro area countries, both by reducing cyclical divergence, as it would raise the effectiveness of the competitiveness channel, and by leading to a more homogenous transmission mechanism.

The monetary transmission mechanism differs

Monetary policy affects output and inflation in many ways. The speed and strength of the monetary transmission mechanism can depend on the flexibility of wages and prices, exposure to trade outside the euro area, the size of equity holdings, whether equity ownership is spread widely across the population and whether it is tied up in pension funds, the stock of foreign assets and liabilities, the extent of relationship banking, corporate and household leverage rates, the size and diversification of banks, the structure of the economy (whether it is service intensive, for example), the extent of competition in banking and mortgage markets, regulations governing mortgages and consumer credit, and so on. In a sense, therefore, every country has a unique transmission mechanism, being strong in some areas but weak in others. This is why it is difficult to generalize about different monetary responses in, say, the large continental European countries compared with the smaller euro area members. Moreover, the transmission mechanism will change over time within an individual country. For example, the response to a rise in interest rates or the exchange rate in Finland or Sweden today would be radically different to 20 years ago when financial and corporate balance sheets were stretched to the limit. Thus, it may not be surprising that while the economic literature does find differences in the overall strength of the transmission mechanism across euro area members, the results do not point to *systematic* differences and instead depend heavily on the methods used and on which particular channel is being focused on.[7] Nevertheless, there are some fairly robust conclusions concerning the housing channel. Some of these are discussed below.

The housing market can be a source of resilience

Housing markets differ considerably across euro area countries and across the OECD, largely reflecting the extent of liberalization of the mortgage market, tax regimes and the extent to which house price changes feed through into residential construction. The feed-through can be small if planning restrictions are tight, even though higher house prices could strongly affect consumption via wealth effects. Housing markets are important in the transmission of monetary policy and a high interest sensitivity is beneficial as it implies that monetary policy is more powerful in boosting or dampening cyclical fluctuations overall in the euro area. Some housing and mortgage market differences are illustrated in Table 8.2

The strong transmission of monetary policy via the housing market channel is one of the major mechanisms that have helped in the United Kingdom to keep growth close to potential during the recent downswing. It has one of the most liberalized mortgage markets. Loan-to-value ratios are typically lower in continental Europe and transactions costs are higher. The latter are about 2 per cent of the purchase price in the United Kingdom, but much higher in Germany, Italy and France. In the large continental Europe countries, the lower degree of liberalization and lower level of transactions due to the higher transactions costs imply less mortgage equity withdrawal and fewer opportunities for consumption smoothing for liquidity-constrained households. On the other hand, they also imply lower volatility in house prices. By contrast, cycles in owner-occupied housing markets in some of the smaller euro area countries have produced swings in household wealth that in turn exacerbated the cross-country variation in economic activity.

Changes in house prices and private consumption are correlated in most countries, but to widely varying degrees. Housing wealth effects are strongest in the US, UK, Canada, the Netherlands and Australia and they are small in France, Germany and Italy. Consumption functions show a similar pattern (Catte *et al.* 2004): the marginal long-run propensity to consume out of housing wealth is between 0.05 and 0.08 (between 5 and 8 cents in the dollar/euro) for the first group of countries, but negligible in Italy and insignificant in France and Germany (see Table 8.3). These cross-country patterns are broadly confirmed in a range of

Table 8.2 Housing and mortgage market characteristics

	Residential mortgage debt (% of disposable income, 2003)[1]	*Typical loan-to-value ratios of new loans (%)*	*Typical loan term (years)*	*Variable interest rates (% of new loans, 2005)*[2]	*Securitization of mortgages*	*Home ownership rate (%, 2002)*[2]
Australia	120	90–100	25	84	Yes	70
Austria	–	–	20–30	–	–	56
Canada	77	70–80	25	29	Yes	66
Denmark	188	80	30	30	Yes	51
Finland	71	75–80	15–18	93	Limited	58
France	40	80	15	32	Limited	55
Germany	83	70–80	25–30	16	Limited	42
Ireland	106	70–100	20	85	Limited	77
Italy	20	50	15	78	No	80
Japan	58	80	25–30	22	No	60
Netherlands	208	87	30	36	Yes	53
New Zealand	129	–	–	33	–	65
Norway	24	70	15–20	–	No	77
Portugal	33	–	15	95	–	64
Spain	67	–	15	93	Yes	85
Sweden	98	80–90	<30	50	Limited	61
United Kingdom	105	75	25	35	Yes	69
United States	78	80	30	35	Yes	68

Source: *OECD Economic Outlook* Nos. 75 (2004), 78 (2005) and 80 (2006), Paris: OECD.

Notes:

1 2002 for Norway and Portugal, 2005 estimate for Ireland.

2 Or latest year available.

other studies, although not surprisingly different studies do throw up occasional country-specific anomalies.[8] Taken as a group, however, they deliver a relatively consistent message.

The size of the long-run marginal propensity to consume out of housing wealth is positively correlated with mortgage debt ratios across countries. Mortgage markets seem pivotal in translating house price swings into spending responses (see Figure 8.6, panel A). Mortgage debt ratios show large cross-country differences, with ratios being particularly high in Denmark, the Netherlands and the UK and low in France and Italy (see Table 8.2).

The influence of the housing market on consumption depends on the extent to which housing wealth can be accessed and, in particular, how easy it is for homeowners to borrow against housing wealth through mortgage equity withdrawal, defined as the increment to the mortgage debt less the amount used for residential construction. Indeed, the size of mortgage equity withdrawal is closely correlated with the impact of housing wealth on consumption (see Figure 8.6, panel B). The strong correlation suggests that it is liquidity constraints that matter in the countries that show a low correlation.

What explains the large country differences? Major factors are financial market characteristics, housing transactions costs and exemptions from capital gains taxes and a high rate of owner-occupancy (Catte *et al.* 2004).

Financial market characteristics can be summarized in an index of market completeness. Less regulated and more competitive markets offer a greater variety of mortgage products, serve a broader range of borrowers and apply lower mortgage interest spreads. They also provide second mortgages and mortgage equity release products. Indeed, for the few countries for which the completeness index exists, there is a strong correlation between the consumption sensitivity to changes in real house prices and this index (see Figure 8.7, panel A). There is also a close correlation with mortgage equity withdrawal (see Figure 8.7, panel B).

The composition of mortgages as between fixed and variable rates is also of crucial importance. In Germany, for instance, rates are typically at a fixed rate for 10 years and it is very difficult to refinance. In Finland, Ireland, Italy, Portugal and Spain, most loans are variable rate loans and interest rate changes feed through quickly into monthly service payments. In the United States, where most loans are fixed rate, penalty-free prepayment

Table 8.3 Short-term and long-term impact of financial and housing wealth on consumption

	Short term		*Long term*	
	Housing	*Financial*	*Housing*	*Financial*
Australia	0.02	–	0.07	0.03
Canada	0.03	0.03	0.06	0.04
France	–	–	–	0.02
Germany	–	0.01	–	0.02
Italy	–	0.01	0.01	0.01
Japan	0.01	–	0.01	0.07
Netherlands	0.02	–	0.08	0.06
Spain	0.01	–	0.02	0.02
United Kingdom	0.08	0.03	0.07	0.04
United States	–	0.02	0.05	0.03

Source: Catte *et al.* (2004).

Note: Estimated short-term and long-term marginal propensities to consume out of financial and housing wealth.

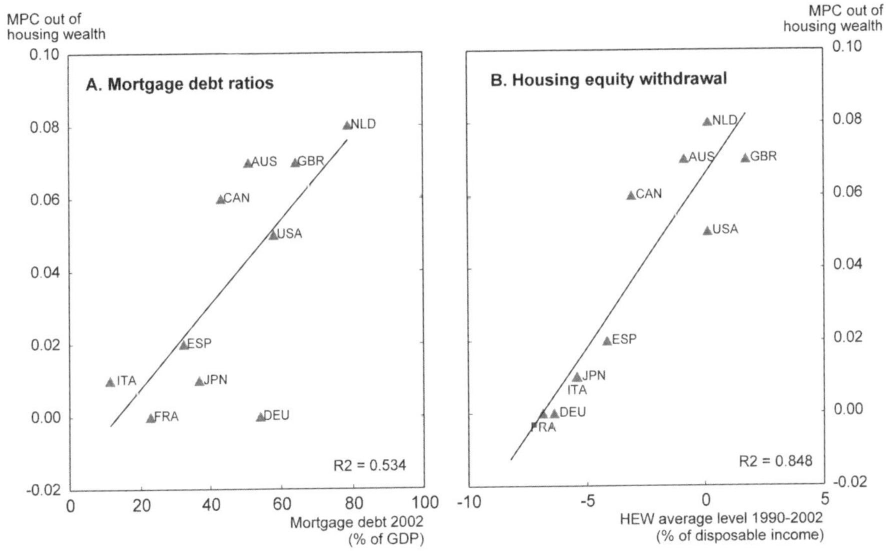

Figure 8.6 Leverage, housing equity withdrawal and the propensity to consume out of housing wealth.
Source: European Mortgage Federation; US Federal Reserve Board; Japan Statistics; UK Office for National Statistics; Bank of Canada; Bank of France; Statistics Canada; Bank of the Netherlands; Bank of Spain; ECB; Reserve Bank of Australia and OECD.

Note: MPC stands for marginal propensity to consume and HEW for housing equity withdrawal.

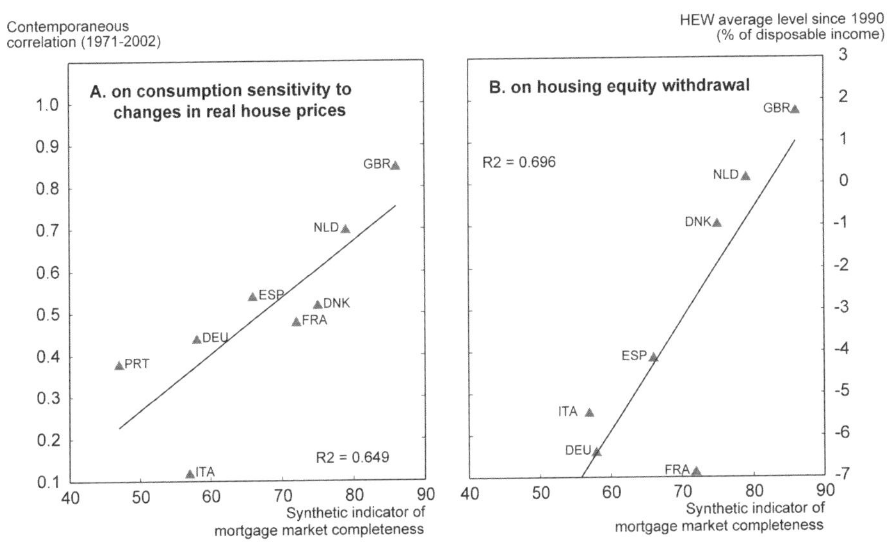

Figure 8.7 Effects of mortgage market completeness.
Source: Mercer, Oliver and Wyman (2003); US Federal Reserve Board; Japan Statistics; UK Office for National Statistics; Bank of Canada; Bank of France; Statistics Canada; Bank of the Netherlands; Bank of Spain; ECB; Reserve Bank of Australia and Catte *et al.* (2004), 'Housing Markets, Wealth and the Business Cycle', *OECD Economics Department Working Papers*, No. 394.

Note: HEW stands for housing equity withdrawal. The synthetic indicator of mortgage market completeness is presented in Table 5 of Catte *et al.* (2004).

options are common, as mortgage lending is largely funded through callable mortgage-backed securities (Green and Wachter 2005). The distinction between variable and fixed rates has become blurred by product innovation: mortgages can also have an initial period with fixed rates, where the interest rate can be fixed for another period after the initial fixed period, or move to a variable rate, while for mortgages with a capped rate, the variable interest rate paid by the borrower cannot rise above an agreed capped rate. And there are several more complex products (European Mortgage Federation 2006), which makes the classification into variable and fixed rate mortgages difficult. For instance, Denmark has a share of nearly 50 per cent of variable (adjustable) rate loans on the national definition, but only 30 per cent on the definition by the European Mortgage Federation, which is used in Table 8.2. Moreover, the share of variable and fixed rate loans in new loans can change quickly with a change in the yield curve. For instance, the United Kingdom, which tended to be a country with a high share of variable loans, has seen this share plummeting in recent years as the yield curve has flattened.

Two key indicators of the mortgage market's ability to provide access to financing are typical or maximum loan-to-value ratios and mortgage terms. Both are strongly correlated with the size of mortgage markets (see Table 8.2). Maximum ratios are above 100 per cent in the Netherlands and the UK and particularly low in Italy. The Italian case is striking as it has one of the highest home-ownership rates and one of the smallest mortgage markets (see Box 8.2). Concerning mortgage terms, equity withdrawal is easy in most English-speaking countries, the Netherlands and several Nordic countries. They are not widely marketed or not offered in France, Belgium and in southern European countries. Such differences partly reflect the legal protection of collateral, which seems weak in France, Belgium, Italy and Portugal, which have long legal procedures for repossessions.

Box 8.2 Why has the Italian mortgage market been so small?

Italy has one of the highest rates of home ownership and one of the smallest mortgage markets. Even more striking is the fact that households' ease in obtaining credit has differed a lot across local markets. Several studies have concluded that this has not been due to a low propensity of households to incur debt, but rather to a less developed credit supply. Liberalization of financial markets since the mid-1980s has led to the opening of many branches, a shift to the universal banking model and entry of foreign banks, and has raised competition and brought down interest rate spreads. Despite rapid growth in mortgage lending the market is still among the smallest in international comparison.

Casolaro *et al.* (2005) argue that inadequate formal and informal loan contract enforcement was a main factor, which has held back the development of the mortgage market. Time to decision in a trial and recovery of funds following a default has been very long, while social capital – the set of relationships that tie people together in a community – was also weak on average. Moreover, there was considerable variation across the Italian regions and low social capital and weak legal enforcement have tended to go hand in hand.

There are, of course, also other factors at play. For instance, information between borrowers and lenders is asymmetric. In most English-speaking countries specialized credit reference agencies report the credit histories of loan applicants and creditors share information. In some European countries, including Italy, such agencies are still in their infancy and information exchange on defaults and arrears is limited, so that information is potentially more asymmetric. In the presence of severe information problems, lenders protect themselves with larger down payments (Chiuri and Jappelli 2001).

Such credit market imperfections affect the age profile of home ownership, obliging young people to save and postpone a home purchase until later in life. Overcoming them will shift the ownership profile towards younger cohorts and prompt a temporary spurt in demand for home mortgages. Indeed, the indebtedness of young cohorts has become relatively high and there may be a cohort effect at play, with young, higher-debt cohorts replacing older low-debt cohorts over time (Girouard *et al.* 2006b).

Further liberalization and better integration of mortgage markets and lower transactions costs across the euro area countries would be beneficial from the point of view of economic efficiency. They would also strengthen the effectiveness of monetary policy, while at the same time reducing asymmetries in the transmission channel between countries.

Tax incentives, tight zoning and pro-cyclical bank provisioning tend to reinforce the cycle

However, cycles in owner-occupied housing markets can also produce swings in household wealth that in turn exacerbate the cross-country variation in economic activity. To the extent that housing cycles are asymmetric, i.e. not synchronized and/or very different in intensity across the monetary union, they also tend to intensify cyclical swings. The house price cycle stems from the relatively inelastic supply of housing, which results in strong movements in prices, which can be amplified or dampened by tax policy.

Tax incentives

The main purpose of any tax is to raise revenues, but the tax system is also used to promote various economic and social objectives. This is done by tax exemptions, preferential tax rates and special reliefs affecting incentives. Taken together these elements undermine tax neutrality and create distortions.

One issue in assessing housing taxation and tax neutrality is that housing is a special good: it can be either considered as an investment or as a consumption good. As housing provides a flow of services consumed by people, it should be taxed so that the costs of owner occupation and renting are equal. The tax advantage of homeowners is that they often do not pay taxes on the services (imputed rental income) provided by housing, while they are allowed to deduct the mortgage interest payments from income tax. According to the tax neutrality principle, the imputed rental income should be taxed, but homeowners should be allowed to deduct their mortgage interest payments and operating costs from this income. On the other hand, as an investment good housing should be taxed such that it would not distort incentives to invest in different assets. In this case, the additional tax advantage of investing in housing relative to other forms of investment is that capital gains from housing are often exempt from taxation. In practice, tax systems often violate the tax neutrality principle

Table 8.4 Taxation of residential property

	Imputed rental income taxed	*Tax relief on mortgages*		*Capital gains on housing assets taxable*	*Inheritance tax*
		Interest	*Principal repayments*		
Austria	N	Y (up to ceiling)	N	Y	Y
Belgium	Y (with fixed deduction)	Y (within limit)	Y (within limit)	Y (if sold <5 years) POOD are exempt	Y
Canada	N	N	N	Y (on 50% of gains) POOD are exempt	N (but subject to capital gains tax)
Denmark	N	Y	n/a	Y POOD are exempt	Y
Germany	N	N	N	Y (if sold <10 years) POOD are exempt	Y (lower than for financial assets)
Finland	N	Y (up to a ceiling)	n/a	Y POOD exempt if sold > 2 years	Y
France	N	N	N	Y POOD are exempt	Y
Ireland	N	Y	N	Y POOD are exempt	Y
Italy	N (for POOD)	Y (for POOD)	N	Y (50% for POOD)	Y (until 2001)
Netherlands	Y	Y	N	N	Y (above tax free threshold)
Norway	Y	Partly (as other interest expenses)	N	Y	Y
Spain	N (for POOD)	Y	Y	Y (exempt if reinvested)	Y
Sweden	Y	Y	N	Y (exempt if reinvested)	N
United Kingdom	N	N	N	Y POOD are exempt	Y
United States	N	Y (up to ceiling)	N	Y (until 2002) (deduction for POOD if held > 2 years)	Y (to be phased out)

Source: Catte *et al.* (2004); Baunkjoer (2004).

Note: POOD = principal owner-occupied dwellings.

between different forms of investment and housing tenure (see Table 8.4). Home ownership is often promoted by the deductibility of mortgage interest payments and the non-taxation of imputed rental income and capital gains.

Tax incentives that stimulate house ownership can exacerbate volatility in house prices. A tax system that contains generous incentives for house ownership not only results in a higher steady-state level of house prices (and an associated misallocation of resources), but may also result in greater volatility in house prices, as the tax incentive can increase the slope of the demand curve. The tax breaks for owner-occupied housing could act as a destabilizing force, to some extent offsetting the automatic stabilizing properties that are normally attributed to income taxation.

Van den Noord (2005) estimates the real financing cost of housing and the tax wedge between the market interest rate and the financing cost of housing investment. The real cost of financing is generally lowest in the smaller euro area economies, but is high in Germany. These tax incentives had been introduced to boost home ownership and to offset the high real cost of financing prior to the introduction of the common currency. Theory suggests that price variability of owner-occupied homes would be largest in countries where the tax breaks for owner-occupied housing are largest. Regressing the marginal effective tax wedges on owner-occupied housing in euro area countries on the variability of house prices (gauged by the standard deviation of the house price index) confirms this (see Figure 8.8, panel C).

An additional type of housing taxation is that on property values. This tax often raises revenue to finance local services provided by the municipalities, but may also accrue to central government. It can also be a means to tax gains from the increase in the value of property due to the changes in the zoning of land. Furthermore, a property tax may be considered as a tax on location. The property tax differs from the tax on imputed rental income as it does not involve taxation of the service income provided by housing and hence does not necessarily affect the tax neutrality between rental housing and owner occupation.

Maclennan *et al.* (1998) and Muellbauer (2005) argue that the taxation of residential property would help in dampening house price cycles since higher house prices have an immediate effect on tax payments and thus on households' income. Moreover, if households extrapolate house price rises into the future they will also anticipate the greater tax burden. This will lead to more cautious spending and portfolio decisions. But for the stabilization mechanism to work effectively, tax rates need to be high enough and property tax needs to be linked to current or recent house price developments throughout the house price cycle. However, the property tax take tends to be low in the euro area countries at typically well below 1 per cent of GDP (France being an exception with 2 per cent of GDP). This is because tax rates are low and in many countries property values are updated only with a long lag.[9] Taxation of residential property is close to 3 per cent of GDP in Canada, the United Kingdom and the United States.

Zoning regulations

The variability of house prices is likely to be higher if the supply of housing is price-inelastic and if the demand for housing is subject to large shocks. There is evidence that supply rigidities are indeed important (see Figure 8.8, panel A). The housing stock is given in the short run, while its long-run elasticity with respect to relative price changes is likely to depend mainly on the natural or policy-induced scarcity of urban land. For example, several studies (Swank *et al.* 2002 and EC 2006a) have found that in the United Kingdom tough local zoning regulations and a slow authorization process are among the reasons for

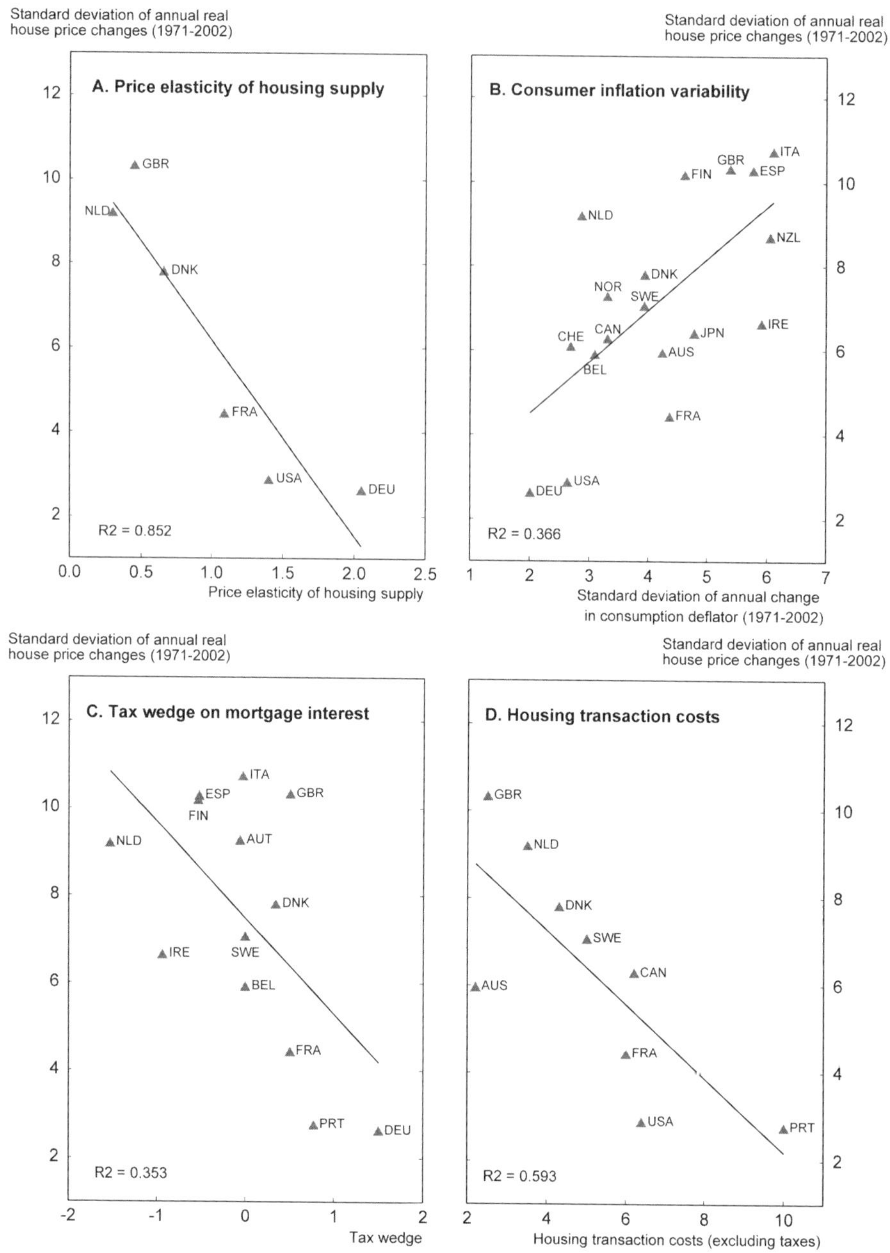

Figure 8.8 Real house price variability and selected explanatory variables.

Source: BIS and Quotable Value New Zealand for house price data; the Economist for data on housing transaction costs; Swank *et al.* (2002) for estimates of price elasticities of housing supply; Van den Noord (2005) for tax wedges on mortgage interest and OECD for data on consumer inflation variability.

Notes: In panel C, the tax wedge is defined as the difference between the after-tax and the pre-tax real interest rate on mortgage loans. It also incorporates the effect of property taxes. Thus, a low or negative tax wedge indicates a more favourable tax treatment of mortgage interest.

the rigidity of housing supply, and an important factor for both the trend rise of house prices and their high variability. The elasticity is also very low in the Netherlands, while it is relatively high in France, Germany and the United States.

While aggregate supply elasticities can shed some light on supply constraints, they say nothing about the underlying mechanisms. Economic analysis and evidence in this area are sparse for the euro area countries,[10] but the OECD country reviews shed light on the underlying mechanisms:

- In Finland, land prices have risen much faster than construction costs, an astonishing feature because Finland is sparsely populated and land is abundant around the metropolitan areas (Vartia 2006). This is partly explained by the slowness of the planning process, which allows for multiple possibilities to appeal decisions on local plans and building permits. More importantly perhaps, municipalities have a disincentive to allocate sufficient land for construction purposes, because they are responsible for providing costly infrastructure and also paying for schools, day care for children, health care and other services for new residents. Against this, the property tax rate on residential buildings is capped at 0.5 per cent and only provided 2 per cent of total municipal revenues in 2004.
- In Denmark, zoning regulations are tough and cumbersome and administrative procedures slow, and migration will increase net expenses of a municipality in the short run (Erlandsen *et al.* 2006). Moreover, in the Copenhagen area, the weak supply response is also related to insufficient infrastructure capacity, which raises commuting time and makes the development of new areas outside the capital less attractive.
- In the Netherlands, tough zoning regulations, especially in rural areas, are a major barrier to increased land supply, while building regulations are cumbersome and have grown in complexity. Moreover, the use of public enquiry procedures has increased, which delays the issuing of building permits (OECD 2004).
- Housing supply has reacted strongly in Spain to the surge in house prices, with the share of residential construction rising to 9 per cent of GDP in 2005, nearly double the EU average. Local governments, which control the supply of building land, face conflicting incentives. Municipalities are entitled to 10 per cent of the rezoned land and thus have an interest in keeping land prices high. On the other hand, they benefit directly from rezoning and thus have an incentive to approve new developments. On balance, the overall effect has increased the price of land, which is reinforced by the length and complexity of local planning procedures to build the required infrastructure (OECD 2006c).

Prudential supervision issues

Housing bubbles can be very costly. In Finland, the bursting of the housing bubble in the early 1990s led to a decline in GDP of more than 10 per cent and in Sweden of nearly 5 per cent, even though they greatly eased monetary policy and fiscal policy absorbed part of the shock (Eschenbach and Schuknecht 2002).[11] The question arises of who is in charge of avoiding asset bubbles and what can be done to avoid a heavy impact. There are arguments in favour of monetary policy at least leaning against the wind, if house prices rise strongly economy-wide, while others have argued that pricking a bubble is futile and potentially costly (see Box 8.3). This clearly leaves a heavy responsibility for the institutions that supervise the financial system. In the absence of a monetary policy at the national level and with fiscal policy constrained, it is important to have a financial system in place that is robust in the face of asset market bubbles.

Box 8.3 What should central banks do about house price booms?

The question of how central banks should respond to asset price booms remains hotly debated. Leaving aside the most extreme views (that there is no such thing as a bubble or that asset prices should form part of the price index and be targeted directly), the issue is whether central bankers should try to stop asset price bubbles developing even if there does not seem to be any threat to price stability over the medium term.

On one side are those who argue that central banks should not try to prick bubbles but should mop up afterwards (Posen 2003). The US Federal Reserve is in this camp. First of all, bubbles are hard to recognize. It is difficult to know whether an asset price or credit boom is justified by economic fundamentals such as a pickup in productivity growth or whether it reflects irrational exuberance by investors. Second, policymakers couldn't prick a bubble even if they were sure there was one. If a bubble is being driven by irrational expectations of higher returns, an extra 50 basis points on interest rates is unlikely to make much difference and the sort of increase in interest rates that would be required would risk driving the economy into recession. The implicit view is that the reaction to interest rate increases is discontinuous: no reaction to moderate increases, but financial collapse and recession following large increases. Third, the optimal policy is to cut interest rates aggressively after the bubble bursts. Policy should be asymmetric because the financial transmission mechanism through which asset prices affect economic activity is asymmetric: in a downswing, credit constraints and falling collateral values act as financial multipliers. Fourth, bubbles are harmful only when the financial system is fragile, but a problem of undercapitalized banks or poor supervision should be dealt with directly.

On the other side are those who believe that central banks should lean against asset price booms, even if it means that inflation undershoots its target for a while (Roubini 2006). By doing so, policymakers are taking out insurance against a costly boom–bust cycle, and tighter monetary policy is the insurance premium that must be paid. The main arguments are as follows. First, the problem of being unsure whether there is a bubble is no different in principle from the sort of uncertainty that policymakers face all the time. An optimal policy rule would still put weight on asset prices, although the weight would be less the greater is the uncertainty. Second, they dispute there being a discontinuous reaction to interest rate increases. In their view there are several examples where central banks have contributed to deflating asset price booms. Third, the type of boom can make a difference. Real estate busts are more costly than equity busts because bank-based financial systems, which are more exposed to real estate, tend to incur larger losses than market-based systems. A fourth argument is sometimes put forward – that an asymmetric policy creates a moral hazard problem for investors (the 'Greenspan put', in which the central bank implicitly underwrites the market).

Are current arrangements for cross-border supervision sufficient?

The IMF–World Bank Financial Sector Assessment Programmes found that the supervisory systems in the euro area (as well as EU) countries are of a higher and more even quality than in comparable countries (IMF 2006). However, there are still gaps between member country practices and the international standards and Assessment Programmes highlighted the need to meet new challenges, in particular those relating to cross-sector and cross-border financial integration. At the same time, the IMF (2006) also noted that the Assessment Programmes usually devote only limited resources to analysing cross-border issues, because they focus on individual countries. Cross-border issues have so far not come to the fore, because even in the countries where the housing market has turned, such as the Netherlands and Portugal, the effects on the financial system were benign. However, the current setup could be tested in the future.

Supervisory structures vary considerably across the euro area. The dominant forms of supervision at the national level are through separate entities for bank, insurance and securities supervision or through an integrated supervisor for all industries. In recent years, there was a trend towards adopting the single supervisor model (ECB 2006a). In some countries the central bank is responsible for supervision, in others an independent agency, while in a few, both are involved. Cross-border issues in the euro area are not tackled via a centralized supervisory authority, but via co-ordination and co-operation between the supervisory authorities. The European System of Central Banks (ESCB) is currently only peripherally involved, though it is charged with contributing 'to the smooth conduct of policies pursued by competent national authorities relating to the prudential supervision of credit institutions and the stability of the financial system' (Art. 105(5) of the Treaty Establishing the European Community).[12] It also fulfils a consultative and advisory role in the rule-making process. Concerning its tasks, the Banking Supervisory Committee assists the ESCB in the fulfilment of its tasks, by analysing matters of a macro-prudential nature, reviewing developments in the banking and financial systems, and promoting co-operation and exchange of information between central banks and banking supervisory authorities. On the other hand, the national central banks undertake the lender of last resort function and provide emergency liquidity assistance to financial institutions. They, and the national deposit insurance or national budget, bear the eventual cost of intervention. However, if liquidity assistance has consequences for monetary policy, the European Central Bank (ECB) will become involved.

The single market in banking is based on the harmonization of a minimum set of uniform banking regulations across the Union, mutual recognition of other regulations and policies and home-country control in supervision.[13] Banks can thus establish branches in other countries, without having to undergo a review by the regulators of the host countries. If a bank establishes a separately chartered subsidiary, the host country is responsible for supervision, though the supervision of the consolidated entity remains the responsibility of the home country. Co-operation among supervisors, which concerns information exchange, supervisory and crisis management procedures about cross-border activities, is achieved by 2003 and 2005 multilateral Memoranda of Understanding (MoU) between the supervisors, finance ministries and central banks in the EU. The 2005 MoU also includes arrangements for the development of contingency plans for the management of crisis situations, along with stress-testing and simulation exercises. The home-country approach and rising financial market integration should lead to regulatory competition, which in turn should lead to a less regulated and homogenous marketplace. However, it could also lead to problems and conflicts, if systematically important banks run into trouble.

First, agency problems can arise, as the incentives of regulators, deposit insurance providers and failure resolution entities are likely to be aligned with the residents of the regulators' home or host country, rather than with the interests of all customers of the financial institution. Risks may be shifted across the border as well as associated costs to taxpayers as regulators attempt to ingratiate themselves with constituent banks. Second, information problems arise, as foreign branches do not have meaningful balance sheets separate from the bank as a whole. This becomes critical, when foreign branches have a high share of the domestic market, as the host country is responsible for financial stability and the lender of last resort function. Third, home-country regulators may take insufficient account of externalities, so that a failure, and the way it is resolved, may affect the host country. Finally, the Memoranda of Understanding are only agreements and cannot be enforced under law. Regulators could thus take actions to benefit their own country's residents and institutions.

The EU arrangements for financial crisis management have been subject to a comprehensive review and may, of course, provide a coherent and flexible strategy for safeguarding financial stability. But the current fragmentation, information and incentive problems could raise systemic risks, the costs of financial instability and hinder the speedy resolution of the failure of a bank.

Bank provisioning tends to be pro-cyclical

In the absence of a monetary policy and with fiscal policy constrained, it is important to have a financial system in place that is robust in the face of asset market bubbles. If banks mis-assess risks during the business cycle, underestimating them in good times and overestimating them in bad times, the potential for credit and asset booms and busts is increased, thereby destabilizing the economy.

Over recent years, significant advances have been made in the measurement of credit risks. However, macroeconomic considerations still play only a small role in most approaches (Lowe 2002). And there is a risk that changes to the Basel II Capital Accord may lead to an even greater financial amplification of the business cycle.[14] Under the current Basel Accord, minimum capital requirements on a given portfolio are fixed and they typically become binding through a fall in a bank's capital following credit losses. Under the proposed system of risk-based capital, requirements would become binding through an increase in minimum requirements as loans migrate to higher risk classes (Jokipii and Milne 2006). Just when banks are most likely to record losses, the minimum capital requirements could themselves increase. From a macro-prudential perspective, the time dimension and the endogeneity of risk are important. Cushions should be built up in upswings to be relied upon in rough times. This would enhance an institution's ability to weather deteriorating economic conditions when access to external financing becomes more costly and constrained. Moreover, by leaning against the wind, it would reduce the amplitude of the financial cycle, limiting the risk of financial distress in the first place (Borio 2003).

Figure 8.9, which shows GDP growth and bank provisioning, highlights a pronounced pro-cyclical pattern for the euro area. Dobson and Hufbauer observe the following on forward loss provisioning:

> Banks are often reluctant to make adequate provision for their loan losses, and bank regulators are often hesitant about pushing banks to recognize losses before it becomes plain that borrowers are in trouble. No bank loan officer wants to admit she made a mistake, and few supervisors want to cry 'fire' when there is only smoke. As a consequence, published loan-loss provisions usually lag the eruption of a financial crisis. Hence, when the crisis strikes, banks typically have inadequate cushions of equity plus reserves to absorb the loss.
> (Dobson and Hufbauer 2001: 144)

They also observe that forward provisioning will require a change in tax laws so that loan-loss deductions can be taken in excess of historical experience. Current practice tends to permit deductions only for recognized problem loans.

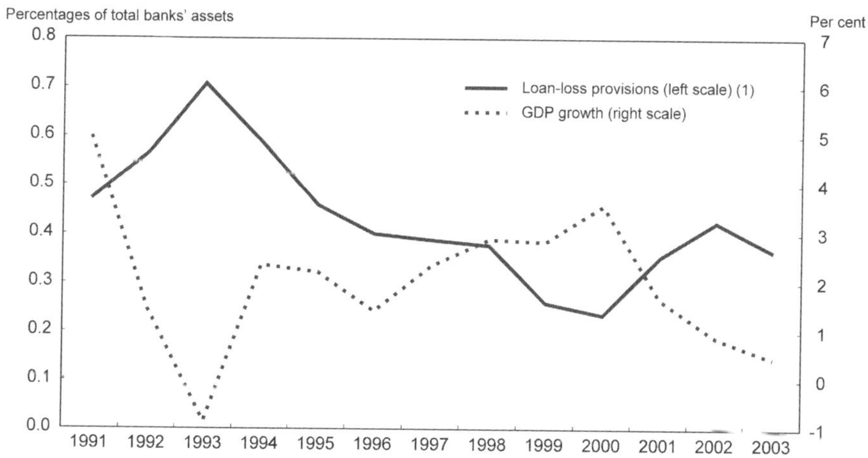

Figure 8.9 Bank provisioning is pro-cyclical.
Source: Bankscope, Eurostat, OECD and ECB calculations.

Note: Loan loss provisions data for 2003 have been inferred from data of the largest 50 banks for the first half of 2003.

Empirical work for Spain (Ayuso *et al.* 2004), Norway (Lindquist 2004) and for a large sample of European countries (Bikker and Metzemakers 2003; Jokipii and Milne 2006) tends to confirm this behaviour. These studies relate loan-loss provisions or the capital buffer to indicators of the economic cycle, like GDP growth, the output gap or the unemployment rate, while controlling for various bank-specific conditions, like loan growth, earnings and equity or capital ratios. They tend to find a negative relationship between the cycle and provisioning, though Jokipii and Milne (2006) also find a significant positive relationship for the countries that joined the Union in 2004 and for co-operative and small banks.

Spain has adopted a novel approach, by issuing a new loan-loss regulation in 2000. It obliges all deposit institutions to determine provisions based on default rates over the business cycle, rather than at a point in time. This forces banks to provide for bad loans during economic expansions by more than in the past, and thus avoids increased provisioning during recessions. While the new rule does not increase the overall level of provisions over the whole business cycle, it makes risk assessment more complex and requires a major effort of risk management by credit institutions. These have established their own risk management mechanisms to adapt to the new rule, while a standard management framework has been approved for those banks that do not have the technical capability to develop their own model (Fernández de Lis *et al.* 2001). The adoption of international accounting standards by the Union in 2004 obliged the Bank of Spain to change its provisioning framework, though it still contains a strong macro-prudential focus (Bank of Spain 2005).

What did the OECD recommend in its surveys?

The Spanish, Irish, Dutch, Finnish and Danish *Economic Surveys* included chapters or sections on housing markets in recent years.[15] Despite the rapid rise in prices in Spain, Ireland and Denmark, econometric work found some, but only limited, overvaluation of house prices, because fundamentals, like demographics or income gains, also rise rapidly, and income and interest rate elasticities are high. On the other hand, the supply elasticity is very low in the Netherlands.

The recommendations are actually very similar:

- Improve supply conditions by improving zoning laws (Spain, Finland and the Netherlands) and remove financial obstacles to new land developments (Denmark).
- Phase out tax breaks (Ireland, Finland, Spain, the Netherlands, Denmark).
- Raise property tax to fund local infrastructure (Ireland, Finland, Denmark).
- Encourage banks to be sufficiently prudent in their lending and loan-loss provisioning (Ireland, Spain already in place). Phase out the loan guarantee scheme in Finland. Remove legal barriers that block improved risk assessment (Denmark).
- Improve social housing policy (Ireland, Spain, Finland and the Netherlands, Denmark). Use vouchers or tenure-neutral housing benefits. Migration effect is of concern in Finland, Spain and the Netherlands.
- Remove rent controls (Denmark).

Appendix I: A model of a small country in a monetary union

This section describes the stylized model used for the simulations reported in the body of the chapter. It has a relatively standard form, and can be thought of as a stripped-down conventional macro-econometric model such as FRB-US (a macro-economic model of the US developed by the Research and Statistics Division of the Federal Reserve Board), the Bank of Canada's quarterly projection model (QPM) or the various country blocks of the Eurosystem's ESCB model. For simplicity, much of the richness of these models has been removed in order to concentrate on the salient features of the housing channel for monetary policy. On the other hand, the housing channel is in some respects richer, and incorporates more modelling options, than conventional models.

The model has two types of households: hand-to-mouth consumers who consume out of their current disposable income, and forward-looking consumers who consume out of their wealth. Equilibrium consumption (c^*) is a weighted average of the two types of households, where yd is real disposable income and W is real housing wealth (non-housing wealth is ignored as it will not play an important role in the discussion). In all the equations that follow, variables denoted by lower-case letters are in logs:

$$c^* = \alpha\, yd + (1-\alpha)[\beta W] + const.$$

The baseline version of the model assumes a strong wealth effect and few hand-to-mouth consumers by setting $\alpha = 0.1$. The parameter β is chosen to give a long-run marginal propensity to consume out of wealth equal to 0.05 while the constant term ensures that the wealth-to-consumption ratio equals 3 in equilibrium. Actual consumption is modelled by an error correction equation:

$$\Delta c_t = 0.1\Delta c_{t-1} - 0.25(c - c^*)_{t-1} + \delta_1 \Delta yd + \delta_2 \Delta W_t - \delta_3(r_t^H - 3)$$

In this equation, the short-run income and wealth elasticities can differ from and are typically larger than the long-run elasticities. r^H is the real interest rate for households (see below). Consumption also responds to the level of real interest rates (over and above its equilibrium value of 3 per cent). This term could equivalently be incorporated within the long-run part, but the distinction is irrelevant in this model where the equilibrium real interest rate is exogenous. In the baseline model, $\delta_1 = 0.1$ and $\delta_2 = 0.04$.

Residential investment, i^H, is consistent with a Q-theory formulation. It depends negatively on the real interest rate and positively on the ratio of house prices to consumer prices (plus a constant, which is not shown). In the long run, the investment-to-income ratio will be constant:

$$\Delta i_t^H = 0.3\Delta i_{t-1}^H - 0.2\left(i^H - y\right)_{t-1} - \chi_1\left(r_t^H - 3\right) + 0.05\left(p^H - p^C\right)$$

Non-residential (other) investment is similar, except it does not include the real house price term and uses the real interest rate faced by firms rather than households:

$$\Delta i_t^O = 0.3\Delta i_{t-1}^O - 0.2\left(i^O - y\right)_{t-1} - \chi_2\left(r_t - 3\right)$$

Exports and imports are modelled as error correction equations, depending on output (with unit elasticity), the real exchange rate and short-run dynamic effects. At a given real exchange rate (rer), exports and imports will be a constant proportion of output in the long run:

$$\Delta x_t = 0.2\Delta x_{t-1} - 0.5(x - y)_{t-1} - 0.5rer_{t-1} - 0.4\Delta rer_{t-1}$$

$$\Delta m_t = 0.2\Delta m_{t-1} - 0.5(x - y)_{t-1} - 0.5rer_{t-1} - 0.1\Delta rer_{t-1} + 0.25\Delta\log(Y_{t-1} + M_{t-1})$$

Employment is modelled as an Okun-type relationship (the employment gap being proportional to the output gap) augmented with a negative feedback from real wages to ensure a constant wage share in equilibrium (consistent with an underlying Cobb–Douglas production technology):

$$n_t - n_t^* = 0.33(y_{t-1} - y_{t-1}^*) - 0.5\left(w - p^C - y^*\right)_{t-1}$$

Consumer price inflation is determined by a Phillips curve, depending on expected inflation and the output gap. Expected inflation is a weighted average of the central bank's inflation target (2 per cent per annum) and past inflation. The coefficient $\phi_1 = 0.001$, which implies a sacrifice ratio consistent with those of a small economy in the INTERLINK model:

$$\Delta p_t^C = 0.5\Delta p_t^T + \frac{0.5(p_{t-1} - p_{t-5})}{4} + \phi_1\left(y_t - y_t^*\right)$$

Wages are determined by a similar equation, and are largely tied to consumer prices but are anchored to some extent by the inflation target. The coefficients assume a significant degree of real wage inertia. The output gap appears, but with a much smaller coefficient than in the consumer price equation, to reflect cyclical bargaining factors. An equilibrium-correction term also appears in order to tie down the level of real wages in the long run, although the adjustment speed is slow:

$$\Delta w_t = 0.2\Delta p_t^T + \frac{0.8(p_{t-1} - p_{t-5})}{4} + \frac{\phi_1}{10(y_t - y_t^*)} - 0.1\left(w - p^C - y^*\right)_{t-1}$$

Firms' inflation expectations, which feed into the business investment equation, are a weighted average of the average inflation rate over the past three years and the inflation target:

$$\pi_t^{e,B} = 0.2(2) + 0.8\left(\frac{100 \log \frac{p_t}{p_{t-12}}}{3}\right)$$

The real interest rate faced by firms is equal to the nominal rate (fixed at 5 per cent) minus expected inflation:

$$r_t = 5 - \pi_t^{e,B}$$

Expected house price inflation can take several forms. There are two backward-looking options, being functions of past house price inflation or consumer price inflation:

$$\pi_t^{e,H} = \frac{100\left(p_{t-1}^H - p_{t-13}^H\right)}{3} \qquad (a)$$

$$\pi_t^{e,H} = \frac{100\left(p_{t-1}^C - p_{t-13}^C\right)}{3} \qquad (b)$$

In the forward-looking option, rather than assuming perfect foresight at every point in time, we assume that households form an expectation of the *weighted average* of actual future house price inflation, where the weights decline geometrically over time. In this way, the infinite future is taken into account but with more weight being given to the near future. This reflects the assumption that people may be more confident in their forecasts over shorter horizons than longer horizons and that they may get the average inflation rate right but are not able to foresee the precise quarter-by-quarter profile. Medium-term expected house price inflation can be written thus:

$$\pi_t^{e,H} = (1 - \lambda) \sum_{i=0}^{\infty} \lambda^i E\left[\left(p_{t+i}^{e,H} - p_{t+i-1}^{e,H}\right) \times 400\right]$$

Shifting this equation forward by one quarter to solve for $\pi_{t+1}^{e,H}$, multiplying by λ and subtracting from the above equation gives the third option for expected house price inflation:

$$\pi_t^{e,H} = \lambda \pi_{t+1}^{e,H} + (1 - \lambda)\left(p_t^H - p_{t-1}^H\right) \times 400 \qquad (c)$$

This procedure is the forward-looking analog to the standard Koyck lag transformation. The advantage from a computational point of view is that all the forward-looking house price terms collapse down to a single one-period-ahead value. Lambda is set at 0.9, implying a median lead of around five years.

The three different formulations for expectations are nested in a single equation with weights that can vary. The baseline version of the model is purely forward looking, i.e. a weight of 1 on option (c) and 0 on options (a) and (b).

The real interest rate faced by households, which feeds into the consumption and dwelling investment equations, becomes:

$$r_t^H = 5 - \pi_t^{e,H}$$

Actual house prices depend on expected house price inflation as calculated above. It also depends on consumption growth (reflecting a consumption-driven asset price boom), real interest rates and an equilibrium correction term to ensure that real house prices are tied down in the long run.

$$\Delta p_t^H = \frac{\pi_t^{e,H}}{400} - 0.25\left(p_{t-1}^H - p_{t-1}^C\right) + 0.25\Delta c_t - \chi_3 r_t^H$$

Because this is assumed to be a small economy in the monetary union, nominal interest rates and the nominal exchange rate are fixed exogenously. The only other exogenous variables are government spending, potential employment, potential output and the foreign price level. The model includes standard identities for GDP, the output gap, housing wealth, the real exchange rate (measured in terms of the consumer price index, p^C), etc.

The parameters have been selected so that the model's responses to standard shocks are similar to those of the OECD's INTERLINK model. No attempt has been made to estimate them econometrically as this is a stylized model that deliberately abstracts from many features of the real world in order to focus on the issue at hand, namely the way in which the housing market can propagate shocks in a monetary union.

Illustrative simulations

The competitiveness and interest rate channels

The first simulation consists of an asymmetric price or cost shock. The consumer price level is assumed to increase by 1 per cent in the first quarter of the simulation. Two variants of the model are used: a small open economy, such as Ireland, is compared with a more closed economy such as France. The only difference between the models is the magnitude of trade relative to GDP. In the open economy, baseline exports and imports both equal 40 per cent of GDP, compared to 15 per cent in the more closed economy. House price expectations are assumed to be forward looking, and the wealth effect is 'switched on'.

The results are shown in Figure 8.A1. The initial jump in inflation has two impacts. The most important is a worsening in competitiveness that reduces exports and boosts imports. This obviously has a larger impact on the more open economy, which is why its output growth falls by considerably more in the first two years. The second effect is a reduction in real interest rates. This provides an offsetting boost to business investment. It has a negligible initial impact on dwelling investment because with forward-looking house price expectations, people realize that any rise in house prices will be short lived. The main difference between the relatively open and closed economies is how quickly the competitiveness

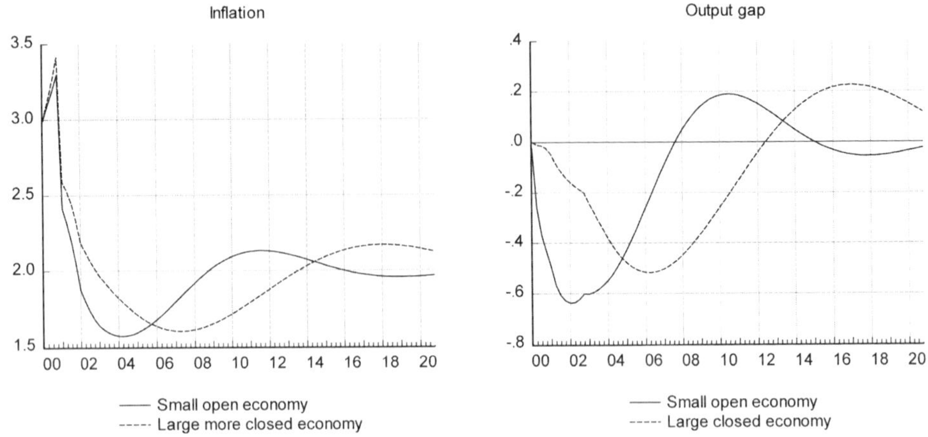

Figure 8.A1 Responses of different sized economies to a cost shock.

channel drives inflation back to 2 per cent. With a fixed exchange rate, the price *level* has to end up at baseline in the long run so that the real exchange rate returns to equilibrium, and therefore inflation has to undershoot the target level for a time. In the more open economy, this adjustment is largely complete after a few years whereas the cycles are much more protracted in the economy less exposed to trade. The main reason why the cycles last so long in this case is that the swings in inflation generate real interest rate effects that offset the comparatively weak trade channel. When they work at loggerheads, it takes longer for equilibrium to be restored. The key conclusion here is that a stronger competitiveness channel can create a bigger initial impact for this type of shock, but in general the economy will return to equilibrium more quickly.[16]

In the large-country case, spill-over effects to area-wide inflation may not be trivial and could induce a monetary policy easing. However, a decline in French inflation by 0.5 percentage points in the middle years of the simulation would reduce area-wide inflation by only 0.125 percentage points, which would be too small to trigger a noticeable monetary policy response.

The role of expectations

The second simulation consists of a negative demand shock. Consumption growth is reduced in the first four quarters of the simulation so that, if there were no offsetting or feedback effects, consumption would be 5 per cent lower after the first year. The first version of this simulation assumes that house price expectations are largely forward looking, as in the previous scenario. The second version has a mixture of backward-looking and forward-looking house price expectations; specifically, a 50:50 weight on options (a) and (c) above. The wealth effect is operating in both cases. As can be seen in Figure 8.A2, the response over the first two years is almost the same. The cycles die down quickly when house price expectations are relatively rational. However, backward-looking expectations tend to amplify the housing channel, leading to larger and longer-lasting swings in activity and inflation. For example, falling house prices lead to higher real interest rates in the housing market, further reducing residential investment, consumption and house prices themselves. It also cuts consumption through the wealth channel, which in turn is a further

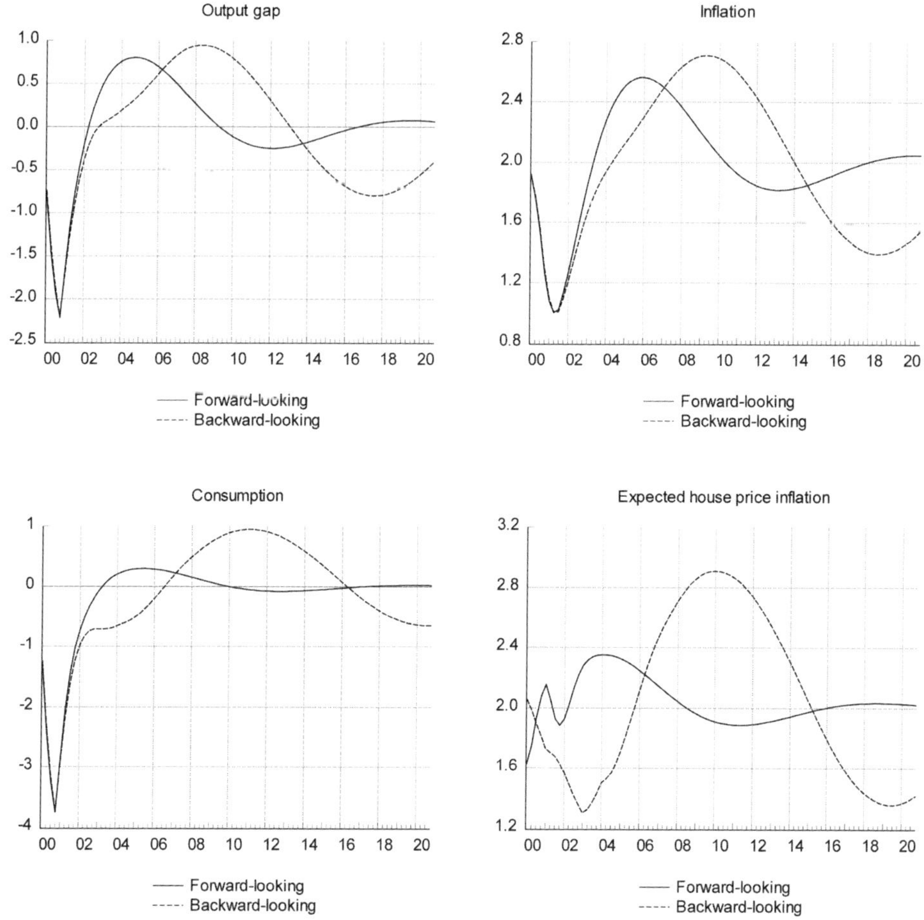

Figure 8.A2 Forward-looking expectations as a stabilizing force.

drag on consumer prices and house prices. Both channels feed on themselves, magnifying and prolonging the initial disturbance. The magnitude of these cycles will be larger when the feedback from the competitiveness channel is weaker.

The influence of wealth

The final scenario looks at how the wealth effect influences the response of the economy. This shock consists of a permanent increase in potential output of 5 per cent, phased in over five years. There are two simulations with the same (50:50) backward-looking expectations as above. One has the normal wealth effect on consumption, while the other sets the wealth effect to zero so that consumption is determined largely by current disposable income ($\alpha = 1$, $\delta_1 = 0.67$ and $\delta_2 = 0$). They are compared with a normal wealth effect and forward-looking house price expectations.

With forward-looking expectations, the housing channel ensures that the increase in consumption and output to their new equilibrium levels is faster and smoother. The reduction in inflation caused by the productivity jump leads to higher real interest rates, but

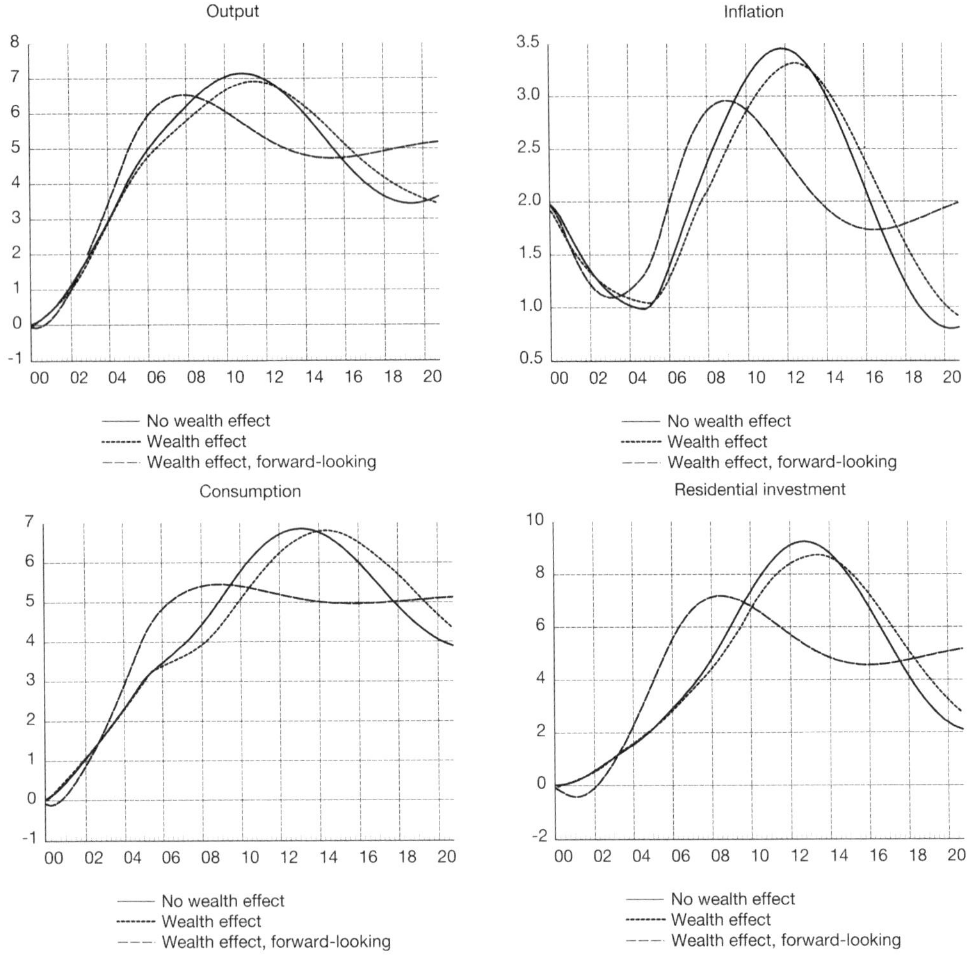

Figure 8.A3 Wealth effects with different expectations mechanisms.

this effect is muted when expectations are more forward looking. Consequently, housing investment rises more quickly. Comparing the simulations with and without a wealth effect (see Figure 8.A3), the difference is not large, but when expectations are partly backward looking, the economy would be better off without a wealth effect as the response is quicker and the cycles damp down faster. The combination of extrapolative expectations and a strong wealth effect can be destabilizing.

Notes

1 The authors are economists in the OECD's Economics Department. They would like to thank Sebastian Barnes, Pietro Catte, André Christophe, Nathalie Girouard, Felix Huefner and Vincent Koen for their useful comments and suggestions. Celia Rutkoski provided first-rate secretarial support.

2 Deroose *et al.* (2004) use a similar framework to simulate discretionary budgetary policy, greater labour and product market flexibility and stronger trade integration. See also EC (2006b) for a detailed assessment of the competitiveness and interest rate channels.

3 See Table 3 of Girouard *et al.* (2006a).
4 In some countries, however, a large proportion of the immigrant inflow have been construction workers themselves.
5 See, for example, Lane (2004).
6 See Sala-i-Martin (1996) and Weber and Beck (2005).
7 The most comprehensive review is the summary of studies undertaken by the Eurosystem's Monetary Transmission Network (Angeloni *et al.* 2004). Giuliodori (2005) finds that in those countries with more competitive mortgage markets and more efficient housing systems, house prices play an important role in the transmission of an interest rate shock to household consumer spending. The effect is very strong in the United Kingdom and still considerable in Sweden, Finland, Spain and the Netherlands.
8 See Kennedy and Andersen (1994); Henley and Morley (2001); Girouard and Blondal (2001); Iacoviello (2000); and HM Treasury (2003).
9 Linking property taxation to actual price developments is politically sensitive. Denmark, for instance, has frozen valuations and Sweden is currently planning to abolish the tax.
10 Much more is available for the United Kingdom (see, for instance, Barker 2006) and the United States (see, for instance, Glaeser *et al.* 2005 and Saks 2005).
11 In Finland, most of the credit losses came from corporate loans, while credit losses from housing loans were small. But households reacted to excess indebtedness and declining collateral values by accelerating the pay-back of loans, resulting in a rise in the saving ratio. This reduced domestic demand and increased the number of bankruptcies in the non-tradable sector and thereby the credit losses of banks. The total costs of the banking crisis are estimated at 8–10 per cent of GDP. The government provided the banks with around €16 billion. The net cost to the government was half of this amount (OECD 2006b).
12 Art 105(6) suggests that the ECB could be assigned supervisory powers in the future, except for insurance. There would thus be no need to reform the Treaty in this respect.
13 The following is mainly based on ECB (2006b), Gulde and Wolf (2005) and Eisenbeis and Kaufman (2006).
14 The pro-cyclicality could also diminish, as the awareness about the implications of an unduly pro-cyclical risk assessment has risen among both market participants and supervisors. Moreover, greater disclosure may become less tolerant and suspicious about risk assessments that change a lot over time and lead to substantial upgrades in good times.
15 Also recent UK surveys discussed housing market issues and the latest Economic Survey of Sweden includes an in-depth chapter on housing markets. Denmark, though outside the euro area, is included in this section, because its monetary policy shadows that of the ECB.
16 For a pure demand shock, by contrast, the initial impacts are not much different but the more open economy still comes back to equilibrium more quickly.

Bibliography

Ahearne, A., J. Ammer, B. Doyle, L. Kole and R. Martin (2005) *House Prices and Monetary Policy: A Cross-Country Study*, International Finance Discussion Papers, No. 841, Board of Governors of the Federal Reserve System, Washington.

Angeloni, I., A. Kashyap and B. Mojon (2004) *Monetary Policy Transmission in the Euro Area*, Cambridge: Cambridge University Press.

Ayuso, J., D. Pérez and D. Saurina (2004) 'Are capital buffers pro-cyclical?', *Journal of Financial Intermediation* 13: 249–64.

Bank of Spain (2005) *Financial Stability Report*, May, Madrid: Bank of Spain.

Barker, K. (2006) *Barker Review of Land Use Planning. Interim Report – Analysis*, London: HMSO.

Baunkjoer, C. (2004) 'Housing taxation', in M. Lujanen (ed.) *Housing and Housing Policy in Nordic Countries*, Nordic Council of Ministers, Arhus: Akaprintas.

Bikker, J.A. and P.A.J. Metzemakers (2003) *Bank Provisioning Behaviour and Procyclicality*, DNB Staff Reports, No. III/2003.

Borio, C. (2003) *Towards a Macroprudential Framework for Financial Supervision and Regulation*, BIS Working Papers, No. 128.

Casolaro, L., L. Gambacorta and L. Guiso (2005) *Regulation, Formal and Informal Enforcement and the Development of the Household Loan Market. Lessons from Italy*, Banca d'Italia Working Paper, No. 560.

Catte, P., N. Girouard, R. Price and C. André (2004) *Housing Markets, Wealth and the Business Cycle*, OECD Economics Department Working Papers, No. 394.

Chiuri, M. C. and T. Japelli (2001) *Financial Market Imperfections and Home Ownership: A Comparative Study*, CEPR Discussion Paper, No. 2717.

Cournède, B., A. Janovskaia and P. van den Noord (2005) *Sources of Inflation Persistence in the Euro Area*, OECD Economics Department Working Papers, No. 435, Paris.

Deroose, S., S. Langedijk and W. Roeger (2004) *Reviewing Adjustment Dynamics in EMU: from Overheating to Overcooling*, European Economy, Economic Papers, No. 198.

Dobson, W. and G.C. Hufbauer (2001) *World Capital Markets. Challenges for the G-10*, Washington, DC: Institute for International Economics.

Drew, A., M. Kennedy and T. Sløk (2004) *Differences in Resilience Between the Euro Area and US Economies*, OECD Economics Department Working Papers, No. 382, Paris.

Duval, R., J. Elmeskov and L. Vogel (2007) *Structural Policies and Economic Resilience to Shocks*, OECD Economics Department Working Papers, No. 567.

EC (2005) *Quarterly Report on the Euro Area*, March, Brussels: European Commission.

—— (2006a) *Quarterly Report on the Euro Area*, January, Brussels: European Commission.

—— (2006b) 'Adjustment Dynamics in the Euro Area: Experiences and Challenges', *EU Economy 2006 Review*, Brussels: European Commission.

ECB (2006a) *Recent Developments in Supervisory Structures in EU and Acceding Countries*, October, Frankfurt: ECB.

—— (2006b) 'The EU arrangements for financial crises management', *Financial Stability Review*, December, pp. 165–74.

Eisenbeis, R.A. and G.G. Kaufman (2006) 'Cross-border banking: challenges for deposit insurance and financial stability in the European Union', paper presented at the Third Annual DG ECFIN Research Conference on Adjustment under Monetary Union: Financial Market Issues, 7–8 September 2006. Chapter 16 in this volume.

Erlandsen, E., J. Lundsgaard and F. Huefner (2006) *The Danish Housing Market: Less Subsidy and more Flexibility*, OECD Economics Department Working Papers, No. 513.

Eschenbach, F. and L. Schuknecht (2002) *The Fiscal Costs of Financial Instability Revisited*, ECB Working Paper, No. 191.

European Mortgage Federation (2006) *EMF Study on Interest Rate Variability in Europe*, July, Brussels: EMF.

Fernández de Lis, S., J. Martinez Pagés and S. Saurina (2001) 'Credit growth, problem loans and credit risk provisioning in Spain', in *Marrying the Macro- and Microprudential Dimensions of Financial Stability*, BIS Papers, No. 1, Basel.

Girouard, N. and S. Blondal (2001) *House Prices and Economic Activity*, OECD Economics Department Working Papers, No. 279.

Girouard, N., M. Kennedy, P. van den Noord and C. André (2006a) *Recent House Price Developments: The Role of Fundamentals*, OECD Economics Department Working Papers, No. 475.

Girouard, N., M. Kennedy and C. André (2006b) *Has the Rise in Debt Made Households More Vulnerable?*, OECD Economics Department Working Papers, No. 555.

Giuliodori, M. (2005) 'The role of house prices in the monetary transmission mechanism across European countries', *Scottish Journal of Political Economy* 52(4): 519–43.

Glaeser, E., J. Gyourko and R. Saks (2005) *Why Have Housing Prices Gone Up?*, NBER Working Paper, No. 11129.

Green, R.K. and S. Wachter (2005) 'The American mortgage in historical and international context', *Journal of Economic Perspectives* 19(4): 93–114.

Gulde, A.-M. and H.C. Wolf (2005) 'Financial stability arrangements in Europe: a review', *Proceedings of OeNB Workshops* 4/2005, Austrian Central Bank.

Henley, A. and B. Morley (2001) *European House Price Volatility and the Macroeconomy: The Implications for European Monetary Union*, Aberystwyth: University of Wales, School of Management and Business.

HM Treasury (2003) *Housing, Consumption and EMU*, London: HMSO.

Hoeller, P., C. Giorno and C. de la Maisonneuve (2002) *Overheating in Small Euro Area Economies: Should Fiscal Policy React?*, OECD Economics Department Working Papers, No. 323.

Iacoviello, M. (2000) *House Prices and the Macroeconomy in Europe: Results from a Structural VAR Analysis*, ECB Working Paper No. 18, Frankfurt.

IMF (2006) 'Euro Area Policies: Selected Issues', *IMF Country Report* 06/288.

Jokipii, T. and A. Milne (2006) *The Cyclical Behaviour of European Bank Capital Buffers*, Bank of Finland Research Discussion Papers, No. 17.

Kennedy, N. and P. Andersen (1994) *Household Saving and Real House Prices: An International Perspective*, Bank for International Settlements Working Paper No. 20.

Lane, P. R. (2004) *Assessing Ireland's Price and Wage Competitiveness*, Economics Department, Trinity College, Dublin.

Lindquist, K. (2004) 'Banks' buffer capital: how important is risk?', *Journal of International Money and Finance* 23(3): 493–513.

Lowe, P. (2002) *Credit Risk Measurement and Procyclicality*, BIS Working Papers, No. 116.

Maclennan, D., J. Muellbauer and M. Stephens (1998) 'Asymmetries in housing and financial market institutions and EMU', *Oxford Review of Economic Policy* 14(3): 54–80.

Muellbauer, J. (2005) 'Property taxation and the economy after the Barker Review', *Economic Journal* 115(502): C99–C117.

OECD (2003) *Economic Survey of Spain*, Paris: OECD.

—— (2004) *Economic Survey of the Netherlands*, Paris: OECD.

—— (2006a) *Economic Survey of the Euro Area*, Paris: OECD.

—— (2006b) *Economic Survey of Finland*, Paris: OECD.

—— (2006c) *Economic Survey of Spain*, Paris: OECD.

Posen, A. (2003) 'It takes more than a bubble to become Japan', in A. Richards (ed.) *Asset Prices and Monetary Policy*, Sydney: Reserve Bank of Australia.

Rae, D. and P. van den Noord (2006) *Ireland's Housing Boom: What Has Driven It and Have Prices Overshot?*, OECD Economics Department Working Papers, No. 492.

Roubini, N. (2006) 'Why central banks should burst bubbles', *International Finance* 9: 87–107.

Sala-i-Martin, X. (1996) *Regional Cohesion: Evidence and Theories of Regional Growth and Convergence*, European Commission Economic Papers, No. 226.

Saks, R. (2005) *Job Creation and Housing Construction: Constraints on Metropolitan Area Employment Growth*, Finance and Economics Discussion Series, Federal Reserve Board, 2005–49.

Swank, J., J. Kakes and A.F. Tieman (2002) *The Housing Ladder, Taxation and Borrowing Constraints*, De Nederlandsche Bank Staff Reports, No. 9.

Van den Noord, P. (2005) 'Tax incentives and house price volatility in the euro area: theory and evidence', *Economie internationale* 101: 29–45.

Vartia, L. (2006) *Finland's Housing Market: Reducing Risks and Improving Policies*, OECD Economics Department Working Papers, No. 514.

Weber, A. and G. Beck (2005) *Price Stability, Inflation Convergence and Diversity in EMU: Does One Size Fit All?*, Frankfurt: Centre for Financial Studies.

Part III

Financial integration

Convergence and adjustment

III.1 Setting the scene

9 Regional interest rates within a monetary union

Lessons from the United States

John Landon-Lane and Hugh Rockoff

Introduction

This chapter uses econometric and traditional historical methods to look at the US monetary union in three distinct phases of its history: the period from 1880 to 1913, when the United States had a currency union but no central bank; the period from 1914 to 1943, when the newly created Federal Reserve had to meet a number of unexpected and difficult challenges; and the postwar era, during which the Federal Funds rate emerged as a dominant monetary instrument. At least since Mundell (1961) economists have recognized that monetary policy will normally be easier to formulate for a monetary union when all regions are experiencing the same kind of shock than when different regions are experiencing different kinds of shocks. If all regions, for example, are experiencing a housing boom that the monetary authority regards as dangerous, then the monetary authority may well choose a contractionary policy to combat the boom. Many monetary economists, of course, would recommend that the monetary authority ignore short-term shocks and instead focus on maintaining long-run price stability. Clearly, however, dealing with a situation in which all regions are experiencing the same type of housing boom, the case we refer to as a symmetric shock, will be easier than dealing with a situation in which one region is experiencing a housing boom while other regions are not, the situation we refer to as an asymmetric shock. If the monetary authority raised interest rates throughout the monetary union in order to slow the rise in housing prices in the one region experiencing a boom it might aggravate economic conditions in other regions.

Here we will explore US monetary history to see whether in fact asymmetric shocks have been a problem, whether the problem of asymmetric shocks has grown or diminished over time, and how the United States has coped with the problem of asymmetric shocks. We also discuss the evolution of banking regulation and its impact on the integration of capital markets throughout the period. Finally, we draw some lessons from the US experience for Europe.

We will try to identify regional shocks by looking at regional bank lending rates. These are the right rates to use because they reflect the actual conditions facing borrowers and lenders in each region of the United States. We will work with four regions: the Northeast, the Plains, the South and the West.[1] Figure 9.1 shows the basic bank lending rates in our four regions for the period 1880–2002. As you can see, there are a number of occasions in which rates diverge, presumably due to underlying shifts in the supply of or demand for bank loans. There is a clear tendency over the long run for the rates to converge, but even in recent decades, when the regional bank lending rates move closely together, there are periods of a year or more when the rates diverge.

To identify the locus of the shocks hitting the US economy we estimate a VAR model, described in the next section. In subsequent sections we compare the pattern of shocks

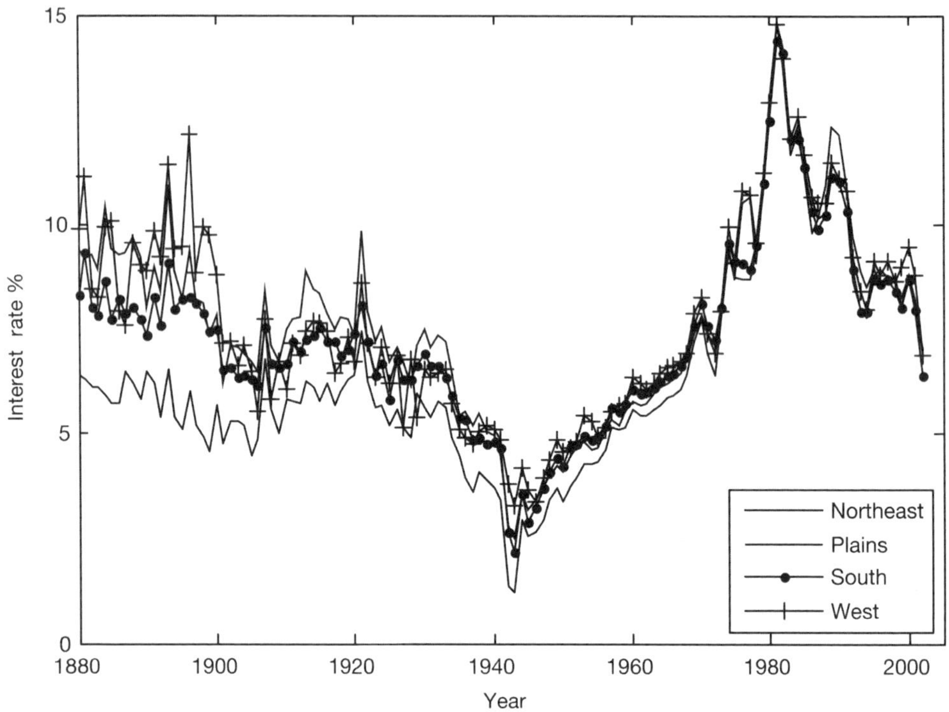

Figure 9.1 Regional interest rates (1880–2002).

uncovered by our econometric model with the shocks identified in traditional narrative histories of the American monetary system. For the most part our two sources reinforce each other: When our econometric model identifies a major shock we usually find a convincing story in the traditional literature, and vice versa. In a few cases our econometric results identify regional shocks that have not received much attention in the traditional literature, and suggest the need for further research.

In each case separately our attributions of particular interest rate shocks to particular events have to be considered tentative conjectures. It would take a great deal of digging to trace out the links that we hypothesize between, say, regional banking panics and regional bank lending rates. The cases do, however, add up and suggest that our identification of shocks makes sense.

In the end, it is clear that the US economy was struck repeatedly by both symmetric shocks – shocks hitting the core and the periphery – and by asymmetric shocks – shocks hitting only the core or the periphery, or opposed shocks hitting the core and the periphery. It is the latter pattern that creates the most difficult problem for an activist monetary policy agenda. It also appears that the problem of asymmetric shocks diminished in the postwar era.

The econometric exercise

To identify shocks more precisely, we estimated a VAR system that included a national interest rate (the commercial paper rate or the Federal Funds rate) and the bank lending rates in our four regions. We then used the VAR system to estimate the independent shocks hitting each region. In this section we provide an overview of our approach; in the following sections, which look in detail at sub-periods, we provide additional information about our methods and estimates.

We started with a simple model of the national and regional rates:

$$A_0 y_t = \mu + \sum_{j=1}^{p} A_j; y_{t-j} + u_t, \tag{1}$$

where y is a vector of interest rates and where $u_t \sim N(0, I)$. This system is assumed to be 'structural' in the sense that the shocks to each equation are mutually independent of each other and have some economic 'meaning'. The problem with this model is that we cannot estimate this system using ordinary least square (OLS) because each equation contains (depending on the exact makeup of A_0) endogenous variables.

We can, however, estimate the reduced form version of this model, which is:

$$y_t = c + \sum_{j=1}^{p} B_j; y_{t-j} + \varepsilon_t \tag{2}$$

where $\varepsilon_t \sim N(0, \Sigma)$. The relationship between the reduced form and the structural form is:

$$\begin{aligned} c &= A_0^{-1}\mu \\ B_j &= A_0^{-1}A_j, \ j = 1, \ldots p, \\ \Sigma &= A_0^{-1}A_0^{-1} \\ \varepsilon_t &= A_0^{-1}u_t \\ &\text{or} \\ u_t &= A_0\varepsilon_t \end{aligned} \tag{3}$$

The reduced form can be estimated consistently with equation-by-equation OLS. The problem, as usual, is going from the reduced form to the structural form. To identify the structural model, and hence identify orthogonal structural errors, we assume that A_0 is lower triangular, a common solution to the problem. This allows us to uniquely identify A_0 by noting that the variance–covariance matrix of the reduced form residuals (Σ) is the product of a lower triangular matrix and its transpose. This is the Cholesky decomposition. So we now have an estimate of A_0, which means we can uniquely identify the parameters that make up the structural VAR.

Thus to compute estimates of the structural residuals (shocks) we use:

$$u_t = A_0\varepsilon_t = P^{-1}\varepsilon_t \tag{4}$$

where P is the Cholesky factor (lower triangular) of Σ. The structural shocks that we identify have the following interpretation: the first shock is a shock to the national interest rate (commercial paper rate or Federal Funds rate). The next shock is a shock to the Northeast regional rate that is orthogonal to the shock identified that impacts the national rate. The third shock is a shock that impacts the Plains regional bank rate that is orthogonal to both the national shock and the Northeast regional shock. The fourth shock is a shock that impacts the South regional bank rate that is orthogonal to the national, Northeast and Plains shocks, while the last shock is a shock that impacts the West that is orthogonal to all the other structural shocks. Such an identification is convenient in that the peripheral shocks are orthogonal to the national or core shocks, which implies that large shocks that are identified in the periphery are not caused by crises emanating from the core.

This type of identification is sensitive to the ordering of our variables. The ordering we used was to order the core interest rates first (the national rate followed by the Northeast regional rate) followed then by the rates from the periphery. The ordering of the periphery is not so clear cut but we chose to order the Plains first, the South second and the West last. This ordering is a natural ordering for the early part of our sample but may not be the natural ordering later in the sample. We tested the sensitivity of our results by changing the ordering of the peripheral rates and found that our conclusions were not sensitive to how we ordered the peripheral rates.

The structural shocks that were identified were constructed to have unit variance. This is not the only approach we could have taken but normalizing the shocks to have unit variance is useful in determining which shocks were large. Clearly shocks bigger in magnitude than 2 are large shocks in a probabilistic sense (under the assumption of Normal errors). Under this normalization scheme we are therefore able to identify shocks to the core and peripheral bank rates as well as their relative magnitudes.

Before discussing the structural shocks that we identified using our procedure we first describe the models that we estimate and the general result we obtain. We found it useful to divide the long period shown in Figure 9.1 into three sub-periods: 1880–1913, 1914–43 and 1955–2002. These three periods neatly break the sample period into a period where the United States did not have a central monetary authority but was on the gold standard (1880–1913), a period where the United States had just obtained a central monetary authority (1914–43) and a period where the central monetary authority had been in existence for a long time (1955–2002).

The VAR model described in (2) can only be estimated consistently by OLS if all the variables in the model are stationary. If the regional interest rate series are all stationary, then we estimate (2) and use the identification restrictions described in (3) to identify the structural coefficients in (1). If the time series are non-stationary, then we test for cointegration to decide whether to estimate (2) in (a) first differences, in the case that there is no cointegration, or (b) as a vector error correction model, in the case where the time series are cointegrated.

Given the small sample size a battery of unit root tests were used. The tests used were the standard augmented Dickey–Fuller (ADF) test (Dickey and Fuller 1979), the GLS detrended version of the ADF test (ADF-GLS) (Elliot *et al.* 1996) and the ADF with a structural break (Perron 1989). All these tests have as their null hypothesis the hypothesis that the time series contains a unit root. Given the small sample size and the fact that these unit root tests are known to have small power, we also performed the unit root test suggested by Kwiatkowski *et al.* (1992), otherwise known as the KPSS test. This test has as its null hypothesis the hypothesis that the time series do not contain a unit root.

The results for these tests are reported in Table 9.1. In the first period (1880–1913) we find that there is little evidence that the time series contain a unit root. However, for the subsequent two periods we find evidence that all time series contain unit roots.

Table 9.1 Summary of unit root and cointegration tests

Unit root tests *Test*	*Commercial*	*Northeast*	*Plains*	*South*	*West*	*Federal Funds*
1880–1913						
ADF	0.00	0.01	0.03	0.62	0.11	
ADF-GLS	<0.01	<0.01	<0.01	>0.1	>0.1	
KPSS	<0.1	<0.05	>0.1	>0.1	>0.1	
Perron	<0.05	<0.05	<0.05	<0.05	<0.05	
1914–43						
ADF	0.44	0.85	0.44	0.92	0.36	
ADF-GLS	>0.1	>0.1	>0.1	>0.1	>0.1	
KPSS	<0.1	<0.05	<0.05	<0.05	>0.1	
1955–2002						
ADF	0.83	0.95	0.96	0.98	0.96	0.96
ADF-GLS	>0.1	>0.1	>0.1	>0.1	>0.1	>0.1
KPSS	<0.05	<0.05	<0.05	<0.05	<0.05	<0.05
Perron	>0.1	>0.1	>0.1	>0.1	>0.1	>0.1

Johansen cointegration tests

	Number of CI relationships				
Period	*None*	≤ 1	≤ 2	≤ 3	≤ 4
1914–43	0.59	0.77	0.88	0.93	0.98
1955–2002 (Commercial)	0.00	0.28	0.39	0.43	0.13
1955–2002 (Federal Funds)	0.00	0.30	0.74	0.65	0.41

Note: Values reported are p-values.

Given these results we proceed to test for cointegration using the method of Johansen (1988, 1992) with sample size corrected test statistic suggested by MacKinnon *et al.* (1999). These results (p-values) are also reported in Table 9.1 and they suggest that there is no evidence of cointegration in the second sub-period (1914–43) but there is evidence of one cointegrating relationship in the last sub-period (1955–2002). With these tests in mind we estimated a VAR in levels for the first sub-period, a VAR in first differences for the second sub-period, and a Vector Error Correction (VEC) model for the last sub-period (1955–2002).

Given that we have small samples in each of our sub-periods we used an information criterion approach to choose the lag length. We used the Schwarz Bayesian Information Criterion (SBIC) to choose the lag length for each sub-period as this information criterion consistently estimates the correct lag length if the true model is a VAR and does so for stationary and non-stationary models alike.

In all cases the SBIC was minimized for $p = 1$. It should be noted that the models being estimated are a DVAR, for the second sub-period, and a VEC, for the third sub-period. A DVAR and a VEC with one lag included are equivalent to a VAR in levels with two lags included. To be consistent across sub-periods we checked whether a VAR(2) in levels was appropriate for the first sub-period by performing a likelihood ratio test of whether the second lag of the endogenous variables are jointly 0 across all equations of the VAR. The result of this test was mixed in that the p-value of the likelihood ratio test was 0.06. Thus we could not reject the hypothesis that the coefficient matrix $B_2 = 0$ for a VAR(2) at the 5 per cent level but we could reject at the 10 per cent level. Given the small sample size and the fact that the penalty for adding extraneous variables is only a loss in efficiency, compared to the penalty for omitting a relevant variable being estimation bias, we decided to estimate a VAR(2) model for the first sub-period rather than a VAR(1). Thus we estimate a VAR(2) for the first sub-period, a DVAR(1) for the second sub-period, and a VEC(1) model for the third sub-period.[2]

We estimated each model and then used the estimates and the identification conditions described above to compute structural impulse response functions and variance decompositions. We do not report the individual estimation results here, for the sake of brevity, but these can be obtained from Landon-Lane and Rockoff (2006). We are more interested in the impulse response functions, the variance decompositions and the structural shocks as we think these are more natural objects to look at when considering the ability of the central monetary authority to pursue monetary policy over the time of the sample.

The impulse response functions are reported in Figures 9.A1–9.A4 in the appendix. The confidence intervals that are reported are calculated using the bootstrap method suggested in Lütkepohl and Krätzig (2004). The impulse response functions show that the national interest rate shock has a positive and significant impact on all regional rates in all periods and that for the second and third sub-periods this impact is permanent. This suggests that the markets were integrated in the sense that shocks that occurred in one region tended to reverberate through the system. Shocks to rates in the eastern financial markets did affect rates on the periphery. This is a natural definition of integration, although somewhat different, we should note, from the traditional definition in the literature on regional interest rates that identifies integration with convergence of interest rates in the long run. We also see that shocks to the periphery had some effect on other peripheral regions in the first two sub-periods.

The crucial question here is: does the central monetary authority have access to an instrument that dominates interest rates in the periphery? To get at this question we construct forecast error variance decompositions. The variance decompositions show the contribution of each structural shock to the non-forecastable components of each time series (i.e. the random component of each time series once we account for the trend, level and the relationship to past values of the series). Variance decompositions are more useful for this purpose than impulse–response functions because variance decompositions reflect the size and frequency of the shocks as well as their impact on other variables as described by the VAR equations. The impulse–response chart does not show the size or the frequency of the shocks, but merely what the effect of a standardized shock would be.

Table 9.2 reports the variance decomposition results for the three sub-periods. We see that there has been an increase over time of the dominance of the national shock. In the first sub-period the national shock did not have a great impact on some of the peripheral rates. This is particularly evident when we look at the effect of the national shock on the West bank rate. Here we see that the national shock only accounted for 10 per cent of the forecast error variance in the first period. In contrast the largest contributor to the forecast error variance in this period was the shock to the Plains and the West itself. This shows how the peripheral shocks were important in the early period. The Plains shock had a considerable effect on the South as well. By the second sub-period (1914–43) the national shock is starting to have a bigger effect on the periphery. Add the national shock to the Northeast shock and we see that it contributes a large proportion of the forecast error variance for the

Table 9.2 Variance decompositions

		1880–1913					*1914–43*				
		Shock to					*Shock to*				
	Period	*Commercial*	*NE*	*Plains*	*South*	*West*	*Commercial*	*NE*	*Plains*	*South*	*West*
Commercial	1	100.00	0.00	0.00	0.00	0.00	100.00	0.00	0.00	0.00	0.00
	2	81.68	3.53	9.84	0.00	4.94	88.79	3.22	5.12	0.98	1.89
	5	76.81	7.07	9.49	0.73	5.90	85.09	2.73	5.37	4.57	2.24
NE	1	53.26	46.74	0.00	0.00	0.00	0.64	99.36	0.00	0.00	0.00
	2	51.58	33.21	5.46	0.02	9.73	19.30	77.42	0.07	1.83	1.38
	5	45.96	29.36	6.28	1.75	16.65	20.28	74.15	1.30	2.41	1.86
Plains	1	36.39	12.69	50.91	0.00	0.00	10.19	68.39	21.43	0.00	0.00
	2	42.84	10.55	43.37	0.38	2.87	47.90	35.18	13.19	3.69	0.05
	5	41.62	10.94	33.37	0.32	13.75	48.34	32.56	13.90	4.51	0.70
South	1	16.06	19.44	50.17	14.33	0.00	0.15	69.07	2.07	28.71	0.00
	2	22.43	17.52	45.61	14.38	0.06	17.39	55.50	3.61	23.39	0.10
	5	26.60	12.01	48.61	8.30	4.48	17.79	54.52	3.49	23.04	1.15
West	1	2.90	3.50	37.06	6.63	49.92	3.37	43.58	7.51	2.12	43.42
	2	2.99	3.52	38.41	8.58	46.49	12.63	33.72	5.46	2.13	46.06
	5	9.90	4.63	44.48	7.14	33.85	14.66	24.99	5.11	8.45	46.80

continued on next page

Table 9.2 continued

		1955–2002 (Commercial)					1955–2002 (Fed Funds)				
		Shock to					Shock to				
	Period	Commercial	NE	Plains	South	West	Fed Funds	NE	Plains	South	West
Commercial/FF	1	100.00	0.00	0.00	0.00	0.00	100.00	0.00	0.00	0.00	0.00
	2	94.10	3.54	0.00	1.80	0.56	94.18	3.56	0.10	0.83	1.33
	5	83.13	12.34	0.02	3.38	1.12	82.09	13.50	0.54	1.58	2.29
NE	1	47.89	52.11	0.00	0.00	0.00	50.61	49.39	0.00	0.00	0.00
	2	64.12	34.45	0.04	0.80	0.59	64.29	33.08	0.32	1.54	0.77
	5	74.59	22.31	0.51	0.79	1.80	73.66	19.83	2.26	2.09	2.17
Plains	1	73.34	12.89	13.78	0.00	0.00	76.34	10.99	12.67	0.00	0.00
	2	87.47	5.18	6.39	0.51	0.45	88.46	4.33	6.43	0.08	0.70
	5	88.61	2.16	5.91	2.14	1.18	88.19	1.84	7.34	0.69	1.93
South	1	77.78	15.46	3.21	3.55	0.00	78.36	13.85	3.69	4.10	0.00
	2	91.68	5.70	1.42	0.93	0.27	90.88	5.15	1.99	1.45	0.52
	5	94.73	2.30	1.17	0.89	0.90	93.08	2.05	2.54	0.58	1.75
West	1	42.01	43.34	1.22	1.09	12.35	47.65	38.30	1.14	0.95	11.96
	2	65.46	26.11	0.99	1.42	6.01	67.61	23.21	1.45	2.37	5.36
	5	77.61	15.86	1.65	0.88	4.01	78.77	12.54	3.63	2.14	2.92

Notes: Each column in the table refers to the proportion of the forecast error of the model that is attributable to that shock. For example, if we look at the first sub-period, then 76.8 per cent of the error in forecasting the national interest rate in five periods time (in this case the commercial paper rate) is attributed to the shock hitting the national interest rate.

peripheral shocks. However, the 'own' shocks still appear to have a large impact on their own time series. By that we mean the Plains shock is impacting the Plains rate substantially, the South shock is impacting the South rate and the West shock is impacting the West rate substantially in this second sub-period (1914–43). It is only in the last sub-period (1955–2002) that we see that the national shock is clearly dominating all regional rates. The core shocks are clearly accounting for over 90 per cent of all forecast error variance in this last period.

What these results show is that over time the central monetary authority gained strong control over the regional rates in the periphery but that this did not happen overnight. What these results do not tell us, however, is the nature of the shocks that hit the core and the periphery during these periods and how these shocks affected the rates individually. To do this we look more closely at the identified structural shocks for each region and for each sub-period and use history to bring these shocks into focus. However, it should be noted that each regional shock is normalized to have unit variance, which is very useful for us to determine which shocks were large, but it should be remembered from the variance decompositions that the impact of the peripheral shocks on the actual regional interest rates has substantially diminished over time.

Before the Federal Reserve: 1880–1913

The Civil War (1861–5) divided the United States into three distinct currency areas. The Eastern part of the loyal states left the gold standard and adopted the greenback, a fiat paper money, as its monetary base. The South also left the gold standard, and adopted the Confederate dollar, a fiat paper money, as its monetary base. The Pacific Coast of the United States, however, remained on the gold standard: gold coins continued to circulate from hand to hand. In the East gold dollars were foreign exchange and sold at a premium in terms of the greenback dollar. In the West greenbacks were foreign exchange and traded at a discount (equal but opposite to the eastern premium) in terms of the gold dollar (Greenfield and Rockoff 1996). The United States even created a dual system of banks. National banks intended for the East were allowed to issue bank notes and deposits convertible into greenbacks. National Gold banks, however, intended for the West Coast, issued bank notes and deposits convertible into gold. This anomalous state of affairs – one country, two currencies – continued until the United States returned to the gold standard in 1879.

Thus our first sub-period (1880–1913) marks a distinct period in terms of the institutional history of the United States: there was a monetary union based on gold, but no central monetary authority. Figure 9.2 plots the structural shocks to the commercial paper rate (the national shock) and to the periphery (an average of the shocks in the Plains, the South and the West). A number of crises that have been pointed out by historians relying on traditional narrative methods also show up in our estimates of structural shocks.

(1) The mild panic of May 1884 is usually viewed as a New York-centred event. The liquidation of securities by foreign holders alarmed by railroad failures and the Bland–Allison Silver Purchase Act, it is said, led to large declines in share prices and loss of gold from bank reserves. The failure of a major brokerage house, Grant and Ward, on 8 May led to the failure of several banks and to what Elmus Wicker (2000) has referred to as an *incipient* panic. The prompt issue of clearinghouse loan certificates (a form of emergency currency issued by the private clearinghouse association) quickly brought the banking panic

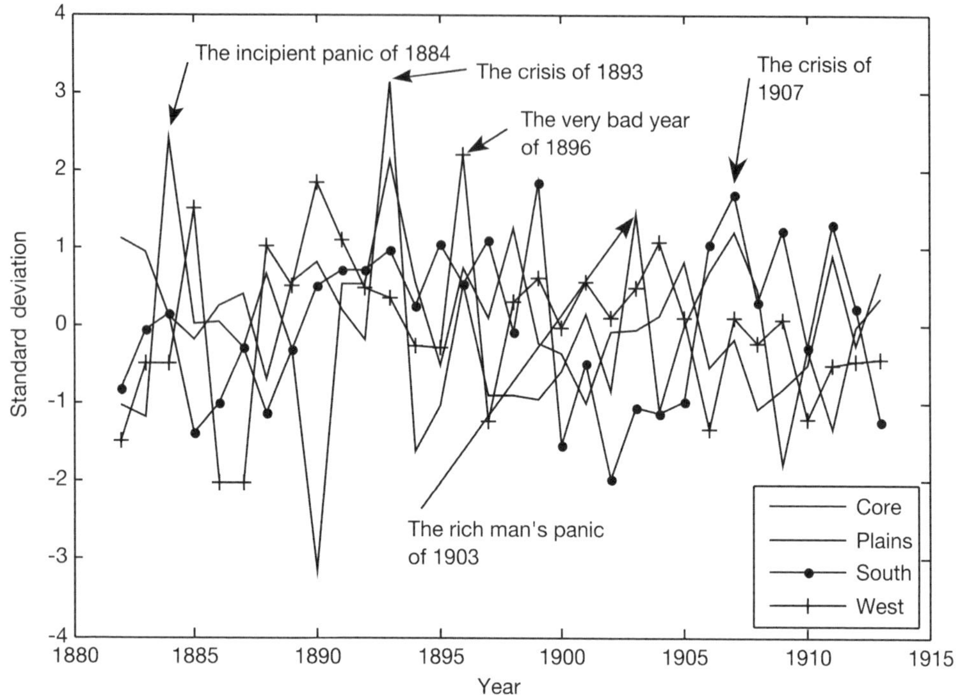

Figure 9.2 Shocks to regional and national interest rates (1882–1913).

to an end. Oddly enough this event shows up in our estimates as an asymmetric shock, but the region affected is on the periphery. The region affected according to our estimates was the Plains. We do not yet have a good explanation of the origins of this shock to the banking system of the Plains states or the relationship between this shock and the incipient panic.

(2) The severe Crisis of 1893 clearly stands out in our estimates as a major crisis resulting from symmetric shocks to the core and periphery. It makes sense, of course, that severe crises would be the result of multiple shocks.

In this case the multiple origins of the crisis have long been recognized by economic historians. Friedman and Schwartz (1963: 108–9) and subsequent writers provide an account of the Crisis of 1893 based on two negative shocks. First, there were fears about the willingness of the United States to maintain the gold standard based on the popularity of the free silver movement in the Midwest that was strong enough to produce legislation monetizing some silver. This fear produced an outflow of gold from the United States financed in part by the liquidation of foreign-owned stocks. The failure of a stock market favourite in May 1893 touched off a stock market crash, and soon triggered a banking crisis. The banking crisis was also produced by a wave of bank failures in the South and West, where silver was popular and fears about maintenance of the gold standard may not have been the crucial issue. These failures resulted from fears about the solvency of the banks produced by deflation, especially in agricultural prices. Friedman and Schwartz summarized the origins of the Crisis of 1893 thus:

> In short, two sets of forces were responsible for the two different drains: distrust of the Treasury's ability to maintain silver at parity with gold caused the external drain; distrust of the solvency of banks, particularly western institutions, caused the internal drain.
> (Friedman and Schwartz 1963: 108–9, fn. 28)

(3) The year 1896 also shows up in Figure 9.2 as a twin-shock crisis, with shocks hitting both the core and peripheral regions. However, 1896 is not included in the standard list of nineteenth-century crises.[3] The reason is that there was no banking crisis, in the sense that the banks suspended the convertibility of bank notes or deposits into gold, as happened in the standard 'crisis' years. However, 1896 was a very bad year for the US economy. After recovering incompletely from the previous recession, the economy reached a peak in December of 1895, according to the NBER chronology, and then entered a slide that lasted until June of 1897.[4] The rate of unemployment was high, and the Populist movement, which advocated radical economic reform, was at its zenith

(4) The stock market slide of 1903, sometimes referred to as the 'trust panic' or the 'rich man's panic', shows up on our chart as an asymmetric shock. The core was affected, but not the periphery.[5] This is the sort of event that often raises questions for monetary policy. Should the monetary authority respond to a slide in asset prices, with a general monetary instrument, say by lowering a target short-term interest rate, when the rest of the economy has not been affected?

(5) The severe crisis of 1907, which led to the appointment of the National Monetary Commission and to the establishment of the Federal Reserve System, however, was produced by symmetric shocks. Traditionally, financial and monetary historians discussed only one shock arising in New York, but our results suggest that there were also shocks on the periphery. New York had seen a rapid growth of Trust companies, financial institutions that operated as banks but were not subject to the strict regulations that applied to institutions with traditional state or national bank charters, and which were not members of the New York clearinghouse, the only institution capable of issuing emergency currency. The issue of clearinghouse loan certificates met the failure of several large commercial banks in autumn 1907. The failure of the Knickerbocker Trust Company, however, was not met in this way and it sparked a run on the Trust companies and eventually on the banking system as a whole, despite efforts to stem the panic by J.P. Morgan and the Federal Treasury. Speculative activities by the Trust companies, including an attempt to corner the copper market, are often seen as the root of the crisis.

We had expected to find a large peripheral shock hitting the West because recent research by Odell and Weidenmier (2004) attributes an important role to the San Francisco earthquake of 1906. Our rate for the West, however, does not show a large surge in 1907. There was a negative shock in the West in 1906, perhaps associated with a decline in economic activity produced by the earthquake, but not the surge in rates associated with rebuilding that we had expected to see.

Odell and Weidenmier (2004), however, see the earthquake working in a roundabout way. The fire in San Francisco that followed the earthquake destroyed much of San Francisco (assets equivalent to about 1 per cent of US GDP) and forced British insurers to pay out large amounts of gold. This created a drain on British banks that induced the Bank of England to raise its discount rate. The increase in the Bank of England's discount rate in turn produced an increase in rates in London and New York. The peripheral region that seems to have been hit hardest during the Crisis of 1907, by our reckoning, was the South. The traditional literature, however, as far as we are aware, has not identified a separate southern shock.

The Federal Reserve comes of age: 1914–43

The second segment we examined was the troubled period that included World War I, the 1920s and the Great Depression. The Federal Reserve, founded at the end of 1913, was just finding its way during this period. Figure 9.3 shows the shocks to bank lending rates during this period. Two episodes stand out: the surge in rates in all regions, except the South, in 1921, and the anomalous behaviour of rates in the South in the mid-1920s.

(1) The recession of 1920–1 was deep, although brief. One factor that intensified the contraction was the decision by the Federal Reserve to raise its discount rate. The rapid inflation experienced during World War I in the United States accelerated after the Armistice, and the Federal Reserve became concerned about the rise in prices and the possible loss of its gold reserves. In late 1919 the Federal Reserve began raising its discount rate in an effort to stem the tide. The last increase, from 4.75 per cent to 6 per cent, took place in January and February 1920. It was the largest increase in the history of the Federal Reserve. It is not surprising, therefore, that the Northeastern bank lending rate shows strong positive shock in 1921.

Our econometric machinery also identifies strong positive bank lending rate shocks in the Plains and the West in 1921. This matches with the traditional narrative histories of the recession. During World War I American farmers, especially wheat farmers, had borrowed heavily to expand production. After the war, as European producers came back into full production, agricultural prices fell, and economic and financial distress rose in American

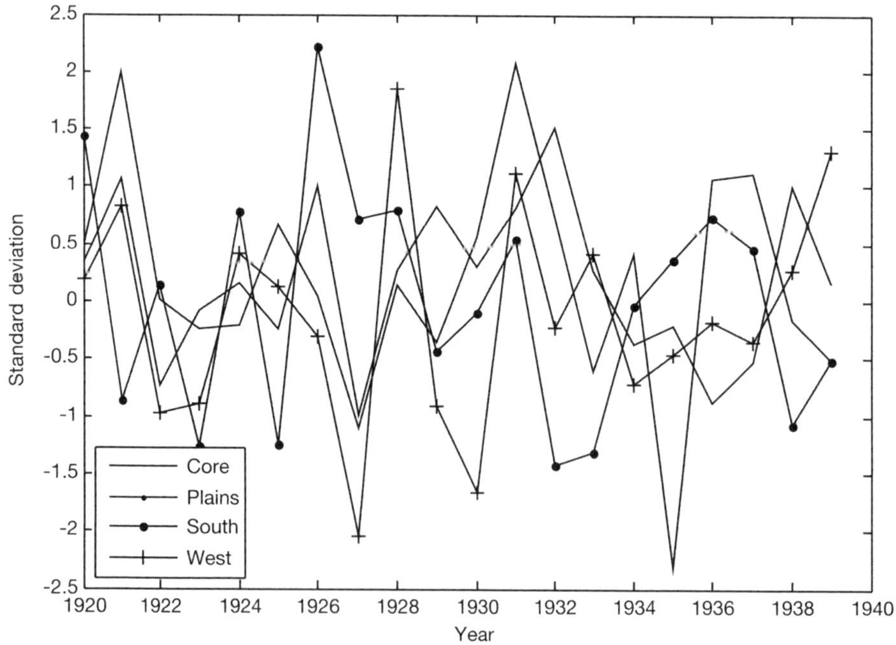

Figure 9.3 Shocks to regional and national interest rates (1920–1939).

agricultural regions. Livestock producers apparently had a particularly difficult time repaying loans (Meltzer 2003: 114–17).[6] One result of the crisis was that a World War I agency, the War Finance Corporation, was pressed into service to make loans to individuals and financial institutions in agriculture. This was, according to Gerald Nash (1959), an important precedent for the Reconstruction Finance Corporation and, more importantly for our purposes, the agricultural initiatives of the New Deal that established a system for agricultural lending.

The United States, to put it differently, was hit by two shocks, inflation and postwar readjustment in the agricultural sector, and so required two instruments to deal with them. A policy of high interest rates that might have been appropriate to deal with the inflation problem (although it was pushed too far even for that) was clearly the wrong policy to deal with the financial distress caused by the postwar agricultural readjustments. The US responded by developing a second instrument, loans to the agricultural sector by the War Finance Corporation, to deal with the second problem.

(2) The only event that we have identified that might explain the shock to southern bank lending rates in 1926 is the Florida land boom. The boom, which took place mainly in 1924 and reached a peak in late 1925 or early 1926, was a classic case of over-the-top real estate speculation: speculators trying to sell undeveloped swampland to unwary investors. Homer Vanderblue (1927a, 1927b) and Frazer and Guthrie (1995) provide excellent accounts of the economic dimensions of the boom. The Marx brothers catch the spirit of the boom in Coconuts (1929), their first movie. The boom was clearly a localized event, although it was sufficiently large to have an impact on the level of bank debits in the Atlanta Federal Reserve District (Matthews and Eckler 1928: 146). The collapse of the boom produced a localized banking panic and localized recession. The Federal Reserve did not respond either to the boom or to the collapse with changes to its interest rate policies. In the banking crisis that followed the bursting of the land bubble the Federal Reserve did extend aid to a few southern banks, but decided that most of the banks that suspended operations were small banks that had engaged in speculative behaviour and it was just as well if they closed permanently.[7] The Florida land boom, to sum up, was an asymmetric shock on the periphery. Contractionary monetary policies sufficient to stop the boom might have played havoc with the rest of the economy. The policy then was to let the boom burn out on its own. In the late 1920s the economy of Florida looked to be totally devastated. But, as Vanderblue (1927a, 1927b) recognized at the time, sooner or later, large-scale development would begin again.

(3) More has been written about the Great Contraction from 1929 to 1932 than about any other episode in American financial history. It is therefore worth looking at this short period in some detail. In neither 1929 nor 1930 is there any evidence of a dominating banking crisis – an increase in interest rates produced by a decline in loanable funds. The commercial paper rate and the western bank lending rates are hit by negative shocks, perhaps a decrease in the demand for funds produced by the recession that was intensified by the stock market crash of 1929. In 1930 the picture is mixed.

In 1931 we do see evidence of positive shocks to rates in all sections of the periphery. The Plains shock is about two standard deviations.[8] So in 1931 we have evidence of the banking panics reducing the supply of loanable funds and raising rates. This finding reinforces standard accounts of the banking crises of the early 1930s. The problem of banking panics began in the Plains and the West and then made its way east.

In 1932 the banking system of the United States was shut down by a series of 'banking holidays' in which state governors ordered the closing of the banks to protect their reserves and give panicky depositors time to calm down. New York was among the last states to succumb to the wave of holidays. The pattern of shocks to rates that we detect – first the periphery, then the Northeast – is consistent with the story of the bank holidays.

A great deal has been written about the failure of the Federal Reserve to respond appropriately to the unfolding catastrophe. Many theories have been offered about why the Federal Reserve failed to act more aggressively, from internal power struggles within the Federal Reserve, to mistakes about the appropriate indicators of monetary policy, to excessive concern about maintenance of the gold standard. Milton Friedman and Anna Schwartz have argued that policymakers could have followed the appropriate policy if they had heeded the ideas laid down in Bagehot's *Lombard Street* (1873). Figure 9.3 suggests that the regional pattern of shocks may have played a role in the failure of policymakers to recognize the crisis as one requiring action by the lender of last resort. First, until 1931 there is no clear indication in our data of the increase in rates that had marked earlier crises, such as the Crisis of 1893 and the Crisis of 1907. Policymakers who were looking for the sort of panic described by Walter Bagehot in *Lombard Street*, when bill brokers were scrambling for loans and willing to pay high interest rates, would not have found it. Rates were higher in 1931, but the shocks were greatest on the periphery. Again policymakers looking for a Bagehot-style crisis would have been looking for a panic in New York – after all, Lombard Street is in London, and the subtitle of Bagehot's great work was 'A Description of the Money Market' – but the problem was most acute on the periphery.

(4) One of the most controversial monetary actions undertaken in the 1930s was the Federal Reserve's decision in late 1936 and early 1937 to double legal reserve requirements for banks. Economic historians debate both the motives for the policy and the consequences for the economy. The central claim is Milton Friedman and Anna Schwartz's contention that the Federal Reserve action, although undertaken mainly to prevent a future inflation, contributed to the severe recession of 1937–8 (Friedman and Schwartz 1963: 543–5). Recently Allan Meltzer (2003: 490–534) has presented a detailed re-examination of the controversy sparked by the Friedman and Schwartz contention based on both the literature that developed in the intervening years and internal Federal Reserve documents. In the end Meltzer (2003: 521) agrees that the decision to double reserves did play a role, although other factors, including changes in fiscal policy, helped produce the recession.[9]

One of the reasons that policymakers at the time thought that the doubling of reserve ratios had not contributed to the recession is that short-term interest rates remained fairly stable. There were some upward movements in the commercial paper rate in 1937, but the rate remained under 1 per cent on an annual basis. It might be of interest, therefore, to see whether our apparatus, which is designed to detect shocks to rates, reveals anything of interest. As Figure 9.3 shows, our apparatus does pick out 1936 and 1937 as periods with positive shocks to rates, possibly the result of changes in lending policies by banks. But, as in the first recession in the 1930s, the shock seems to have occurred first on the periphery.

The postwar era: 1955–2002

We began in 1955 because this is when our data for the Federal Funds rate begins, and we wanted to use the Federal Funds rate, the rate at which banks lend reserves to each other on a short-term basis, as our core rate, because it has become the standard instrument of Federal Reserve policy. We also tried the commercial paper rate as the national rate, with very similar results.

The results for this period are displayed in Figure 9.4. Evidently, the most important shocks during this segment were the shocks hitting the Federal Funds rate. The two largest shocks occurred in 1973 and in 1979–81. Both resulted from attempts by the Federal Reserve to repress inflation. These episodes are well known and do not require extensive comment here. In 1974, after the lifting of the Nixon Administration's wage and price controls and other factors such as an expansionary monetary policy, inflation surged. The Federal Reserve Board decided to embark on a contractionary policy in order to reduce inflation and inflationary expectations. The 1979–81 shocks are the 'Volcker disinflation'. There was widespread agreement by 1979 that inflation and interest rates were 'out of control', and so the Federal Reserve under Paul Volcker adopted a contractionary policy.[10]

The shocks to the periphery are somewhat harder for us to identify. As shown in Figure 9.4, there were shocks to the Northeast in 1976, to the Plains in 1984 and to the West in 1999. The only one for which we can offer even a conjecture is the Northeast shock, which might be identified with the New York City financial crisis. Many New York City banks were affected by the threat to the city's solvency because they held New York City bonds. Eventually, a Federal loan helped resolve the problem. This is another example of a regional shock addressed by creating a new instrument, separate from the monetary authority, to deal with the problem. Neither of the alternatives, attempting to deal with the problem through a general increase in liquidity or allowing the problem to burn out without government intervention, was politically acceptable.

Although the regional bank lending rates continue to show the effects of asymmetric regional shocks in the postwar era, the importance of regional shocks appears to have declined. This can be seen best by looking at the variance decompositions of the variables.

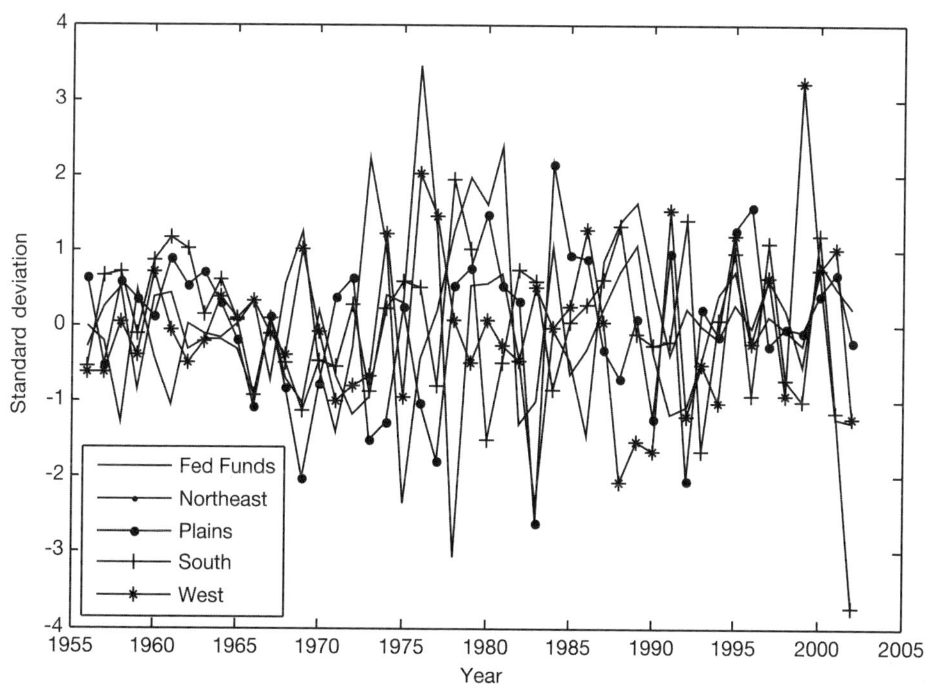

Figure 9.4 Shocks to regional and national interest rates (1955–2002).

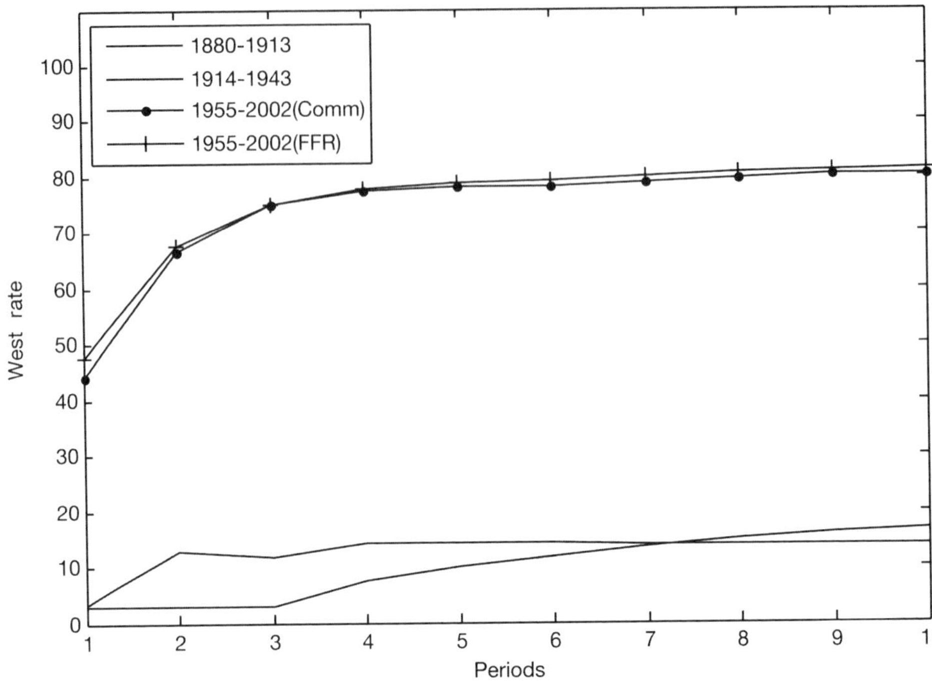

Figure 9.5 Variance decomposition of the effect of a shock to the national rate on the Western lending rate.

Figure 9.5, which is typical, shows the effects of the national rate on the West. In both 1880–1913 and 1914–43 shocks to the national rate (the commercial paper rate) explain very little of the variation in the Western bank lending rate. In fact most of the variation is accounted for by shocks hitting in the West. In 1955–2002, however, most of the variation, about 70 per cent, is accounted for by shocks to the commercial paper rate or the Federal Funds rate.

Summary and conclusions

In this chapter we use vector autoregressions to identify shocks to national and regional interest rates in the United States over the period 1880–2002. By shocks we mean independent events – shifts in the supply of or demand for loanable funds – that produced changes in interest rates that then reverberated through the economy. Our results lead us to a number of tentative conclusions:

(1) We find numerous examples of both symmetric shocks – shocks of the same type hitting both the core and the periphery – and asymmetric shocks – shocks hitting only one region, or opposite shocks hitting both regions. Not surprisingly, some of the most severe crises in US economic history, such as the Crisis of 1893 and the Great Contraction of 1929–32, appear to have been the result of multiple shocks hitting both the core and the periphery. We also find examples of asymmetric shocks, such as the 'rich man's panic of 1903', that seems to have affected mainly the Northeast, and the Florida land boom of the mid-1920s, that seems to have affected mainly the South.

(2) The problem of asymmetric regional shocks raises the issue of the appropriate number of policy instruments. In a number of cases the United States, for better or worse, addressed the problem of asymmetric shocks by devising alternative instruments to deal with them. Agriculture is the classic example, and the 1920–1 contraction the starting point. The United States faced what appeared to policymakers to be asymmetric shocks in the sense that they called for different responses, although they may not have thought of it in these terms: nationwide inflation, which called for higher interest rates, and an agricultural depression, which called for lower rates. In the end the solution was to raise the discount rate and reactivate the War Finance Corporation, a World War I agency, to provide loans to the agricultural sector. In later legislation in the 1920s and 1930s the commitment of the Federal government to the agricultural sector was strengthened. The extension of Federal loans to New York City in its fiscal crisis in the 1970s is a more recent example. In other cases, however, the United States followed a policy of simply allowing regional problems to burn out of their own accord. The Florida land boom, except for some loans to distressed banks, is an example from the 1920s.

(3) Although we find examples of asymmetric shocks throughout the period we examine, the problem of asymmetric shocks appears to have diminished over time, but this process took some time. One way of seeing this is to look at the variance decompositions of the vector autoregressions. In the late nineteenth century shocks to peripheral rates were a major source of the variance in the bank lending rates on the periphery. This remained true, although to a lesser degree, in the first half of the twentieth century. We still observe asymmetric shocks in the postwar era, but they are far less important than in earlier periods. Most of the variance in the rates on the periphery is now explained by shocks to the national rates.

(4) One reason that we observe smaller asymmetric interest rate shocks is probably the reform of the American banking system that began in the Great Depression and continued in the postwar years. A number of the shocks before the Depression resulted in part from local banking crises. Several factors – Federal Deposit Insurance, the growth of interstate branch banking, and a change in attitudes at the Federal Reserve toward local bank failures – have reduced the incidence of bank failures to a very low level, and have virtually eliminated local panics.

The lifting of the restrictions on intra- and interstate branch banking, moreover, allowed capital to flow more easily from region to region, reducing short-run fluctuations in regional rates. This is another reason why we observe interest rate shocks on the periphery becoming less important. The existence of nationwide branching systems, moreover, may have strengthened the 'leadership role' of the Federal Funds rate. The length of time it took to reform the American banking system, in other words, may be the reason why it took so long for the problem of asymmetric shocks to diminish.

We found that it took a long time for a fully integrated capital market with a single dominant monetary instrument to emerge in the United States. The main reason seems to have been the slow pace of interregional banking integration that was produced by the tendency of individual US states to jealously guard their regulatory powers. The restraints on cross-border banking were gradually overcome through state level agreements, rather than federal mandates. The lesson here may be that there is a role for leadership at the European level to achieve timely reforms in the banking sector, thus facilitating a quicker integration of European financial markets and simplifying the task of the central monetary authority.

Appendix

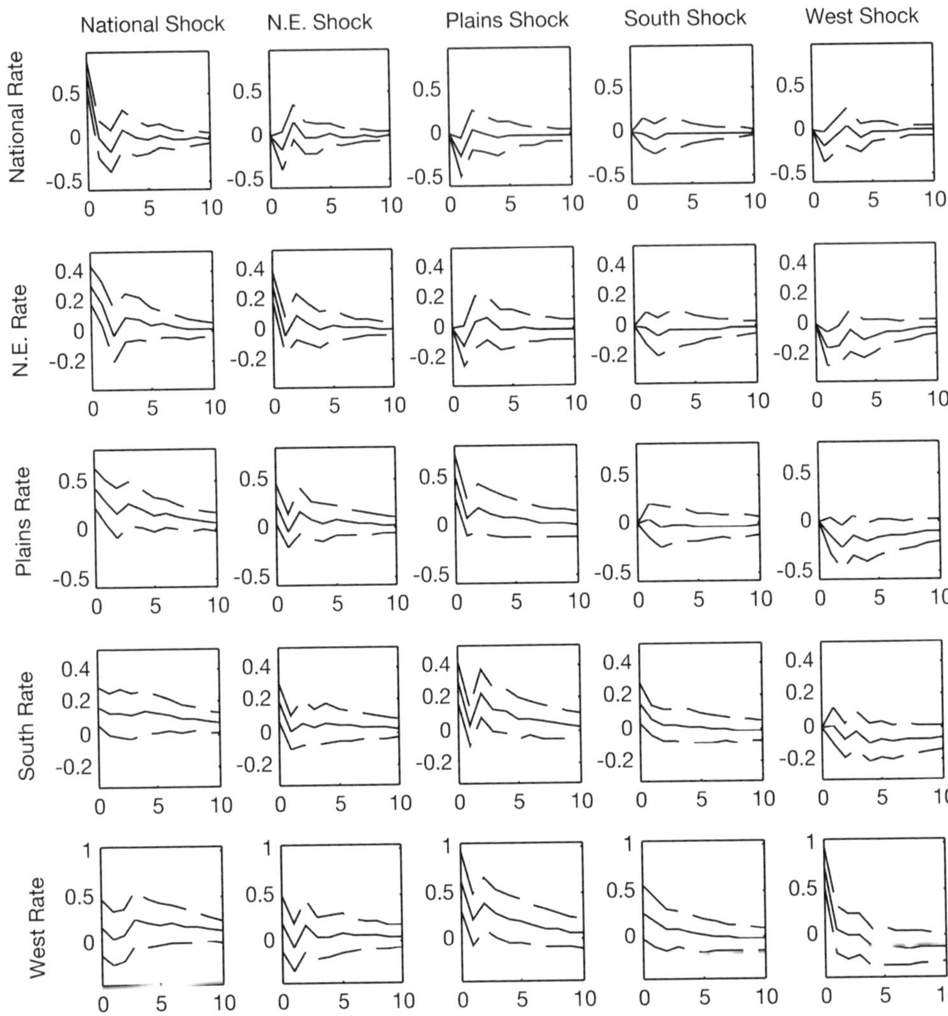

Figure 9.A1 Impulse response functions (1880–1913).

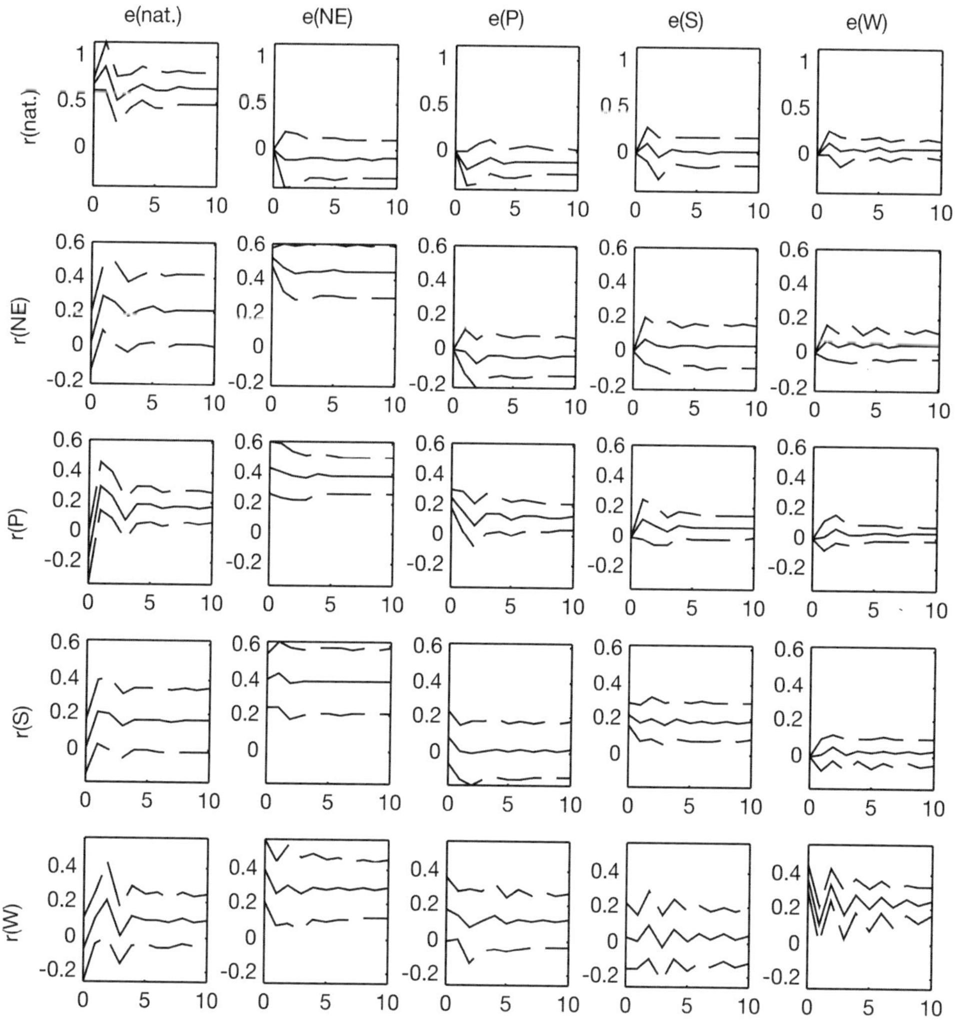

Figure 9.A2 Impulse response functions (1914–1943).

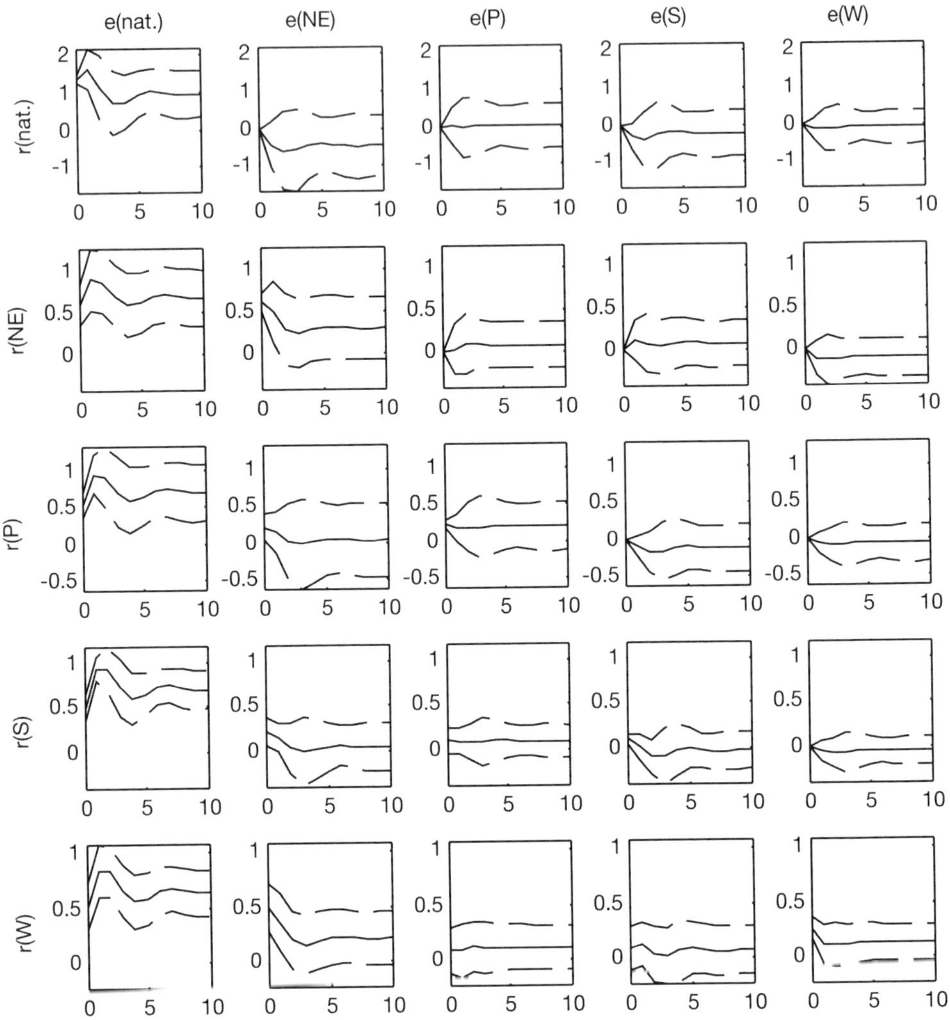

Figure 9.A3 Impulse response functions (1955–2002: Commercial rate).

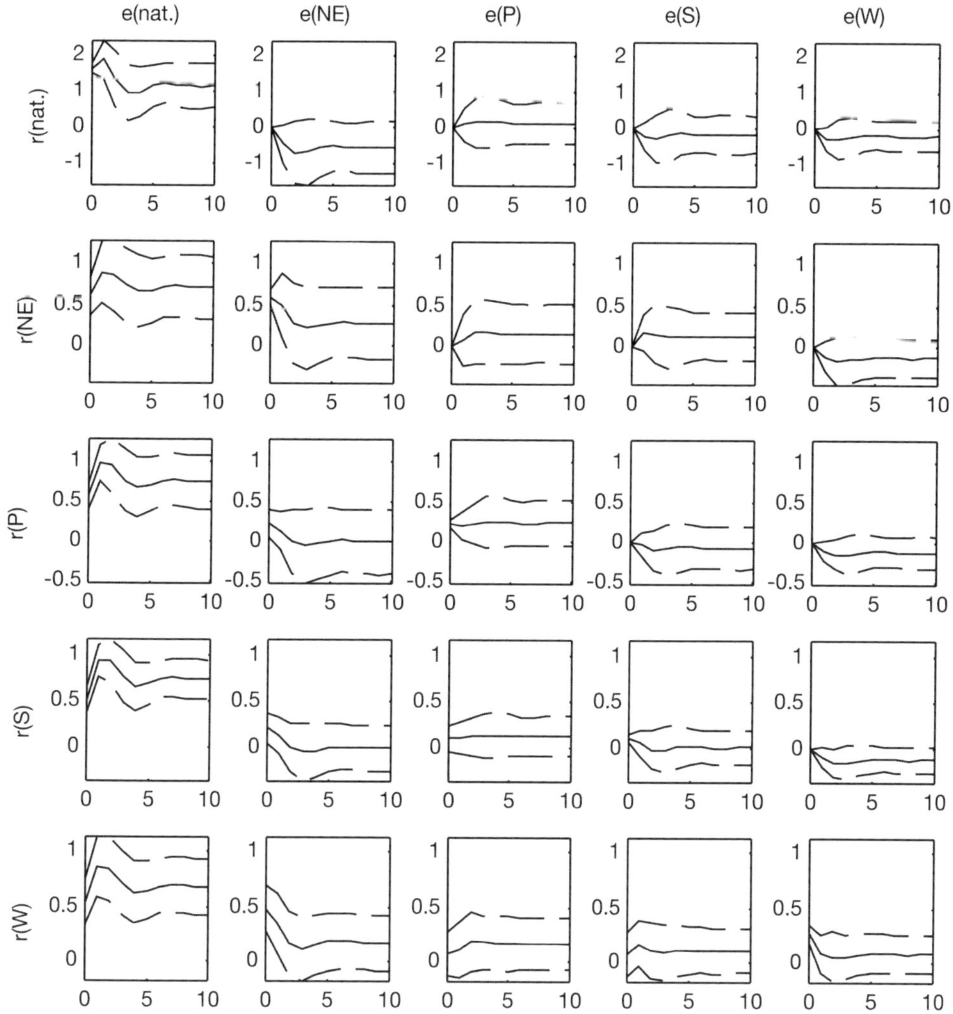

Figure 9.A4 Impulse response functions (1955–2002: Federal Funds rate).

Notes

1 The Northeast includes Maine, New Hampshire, Vermont, Massachusetts, Rhode Island, Connecticut, New York, New Jersey, Delaware, Pennsylvania, Maryland, Ohio, Indiana, Illinois, Michigan and Wisconsin. The South includes Virginia, West Virginia, North Carolina, South Carolina, Georgia, Florida, Alabama, Mississippi, Louisiana, Tennessee, Kentucky and Arkansas. The Plains includes Minnesota, Iowa, Missouri, Oklahoma, Texas, Kansas, Nebraska, North Dakota, New Mexico, Montana, Wyoming and Colorado. The West includes Arizona, Idaho, Utah, Nevada, California, Oregon and Washington.

2 The main results of this chapter are robust to the choice of lag length. Using different model selection criteria can lead to different model choices but in all cases that we have tried the main results always hold: the influence of the national shock on the periphery is getting stronger over time and the peripheral shocks have important effects in the first two periods but negligible effects in the last period.

3 The classic description of the monetary crises before the Federal Reserve is O.M.W. Sprague's *History of Crises Under the National Banking System* (1910), which was one of the monographs written for the National Monetary Commission. Sprague identifies four crises between the re-establishment of the gold standard in 1879 and the end of his period, 1910: (1) 'the panic of May 1884'; (2) the 'financial stringency in 1890'; (3) the 'crisis of 1893'; and (4) the 'crisis of 1907'.

4 http://www.nber.org/cycles.html/.

5 The term 'rich man's panic' later was also applied to the stock market crash in 1907.

6 Most agricultural prices seem to have tumbled in 1921. The price of wheat fell 62 per cent between 1920 and 1921; the price of cotton fell 81 per cent; and the price of hogs fell 53 per cent; while consumer prices were falling about 11 per cent. Cotton, however, seems to have bounced back a bit. By 1923 only the price of cotton had drawn even in real terms with the 1920 level (U.S. Bureau of the Census 1975, series E).

7 'National banks not involved', *New York Times*, 16 July 1926, p. 29.

8 To some extent the precise estimate of the shock in the Plains depends on our ordering of the regions which places the plains before the South and the West.

9 Friedman and Schwartz (1963: 541) also used language that left roles open for other factors in the story of the recession. Their claim was that Federal Reserve action had 'significantly intensified the severity of the decline and also probably caused it to occur earlier than otherwise'.

10 Romer and Romer (1989) identify a number of cases in the postwar era in which the Federal Reserve adopted a new policy in order to bring inflation under control. All of their episodes can be identified with Federal Funds rate shocks identified by our VARs.

References

Bagehot, Walter (1873) *Lombard Street: A Description of the Money Market*, London: H.S. King.

Dickey, D.A. and W.A. Fuller (1979) 'Distribution of the estimators for autoregressive time series with a unit root', *Journal of the American Statistical Association* 74: 427–31.

Elliott, G., T.J. Rothenberg and J.H. Stock (1996) 'Efficient tests for an autoregressive unit root', *Econometrica* 64: 813–36.

Frazer, William and John J. Guthrie (1995) *The Florida Land Boom: Speculation, Money, and the Banks*, Westport, CT: Quorum Books.

Friedman, Milton and Anna Jacobson Schwartz (1963) *A Monetary History of the United States, 1867–1960*, Princeton: Princeton University Press.

Greenfield, Robert and Hugh Rockoff (1996) 'Yellowbacks out west and greenbacks back east: Social-choice dimensions of monetary reform', *Southern Economic Journal* 62: 902–15.

Johansen, S. (1988) 'Statistical analysis of co-integration vectors', *Journal of Economic Dynamics and Control* 12: 231–54.

—— (1992) 'Determination of co-integration rank in the presence of a linear trend', *Oxford Bulletin of Economics and Statistics* 54: 383–97.

Kwiatkowski, D., P.C.B. Phillips, P. Schmidt and Y. Shin (1992) 'Testing the null of stationarity against the alternative of a unit root: how sure are we that economic time series have a unit root?', *Journal of Econometrics* 54: 159–78.

Landon-Lane, John and Hugh Rockoff (2006) *A Companion to 'The Origins and Diffusion of Shocks to Regional Interest Rates in the United States, 1880–2002'*, Rutgers University Economics Department Working Paper, 2006–8; available at http: //www.snde.rutgers.edu/Rutgers/wp/rutgers-wpsearch.html.

Lütkepohl, H. and M. Krätzig (eds) (2004) *Applied Time Series Econometrics*, Cambridge: Cambridge University Press.

MacKinnon, James G., Alfred A. Haug and Leo Michelis (1999) 'Numerical distribution functions of likelihood ratio tests for co-integration', *Journal of Applied Econometrics* 14: 563–77.

Matthews, Ada M. and A. Ross Eckler (1928) 'Regional business conditions: a study of bank debits', *Review of Economics and Statistics* 10: 140–55.

Meltzer, Allan H. (2003) *A History of the Federal Reserve*, Chicago: University of Chicago Press.

Mundell, Robert A. (1961) 'A theory of optimum currency areas', *American Economic Review* 51: 657–65.

Nash, Gerald D. (1959) 'Herbert Hoover and the origins of the reconstruction finance corporation', *Mississippi Valley Historical Review* 46: 455–68.

Odell, Kerry A. and Marc D. Weidenmier (2004) 'Real shock, monetary aftershock: the 1906 San Francisco earthquake and the panic of 1907', *Journal of Economic History* 64: 1002–27.

Perron, P.P. (1989) 'The great crash, the oil price shock and the unit root hypothesis', *Econometrica* 57: 1361–401.

Romer, Christina D. and David H. Romer (1989) 'Does monetary policy matter? A new test in the spirit of Friedman and Schwartz', *NBER Macroeconomics Annual* 4: 121–70.

Sprague, O.M.W. (1908) 'The American crisis of 1907', *Economic Journal* 18: 353–72.

—— (1910) *History of Crises under the National Banking System*, Washington, DC: Government Printing Office.

US Bureau of the Census (1975) *Historical Statistics of the United States, Colonial Times to 1970, Bicentennial Edition*, Washington, DC: Government Printing Office.

Vanderblue, Homer B. (1927a) 'The Florida land boom (Part I)', *Journal of Land and Public Utility Economics* 3(2): 113–31.

—— (1927b) 'The Florida land boom (Part II)', *Journal of Land and Public Utility Economics* 3(3): 252–69.

Wicker, Elmus (2000) *Banking Panics of the Gilded Age*, New York: Cambridge University Press.

10 Where does capital flow?

A comparison of US states and EU countries 1950–2000

Sebnem Kalemli-Ozcan, Bent E. Sørensen and Belgi Turan

Introduction

Standard neoclassical models predict that capital will move from regions where the marginal product of capital is relatively low to regions where it is relatively high.[1] Within a fully integrated capital market with no 'frictions', this implies that the capital stock will be highest in regions with the highest level of productivity. As shown by Blomstrom, Lipsey, and Zejan (1996) and Clark and Feenstra (2003), in a world of completely mobile capital the amount of physical capital installed in a country relative to the world average is fully explained by the relative level of total factor productivity.

In reality, the marginal product of capital may deviate from the return obtained by owners of capital, such as stock holders or direct owners, for numerous reasons. Risk-adjusted returns to investment may not be as high as suggested by simple neoclassical models for countries with low capital/labour ratios. Kraay and Ventura (2000) argue that low productivity countries' implied risk premiums on investment are quite high. Countries with low capital may also receive less foreign investment due to their low level of total factor productivity. Recent research shows a positive relation between capital flows and various proxies for productivity, such as good institutions (Alfaro *et al.* 2008), low cost of physical capital (Hsieh and Klenow 2007; Caselli and Feyrer 2007) and low risk of default (Gertler and Rogoff 1990; Reinhart and Rogoff 2004). As a result capital might flow 'uphill' from poor to rich countries rather than the opposite direction predicted by standard models. This observation was originally made by Lucas (1990) and recently discussed by Prasad *et al.* (2007) in the context of the 1990s globalization period. In a closely related paper, Gourinchas and Jeanne (2007) show that capital, on net, tends go to low growth, rather than to the predicted high growth countries.

The pervasiveness of deviations of country-level data from the predictions of simple neoclassical models is such that one may question whether such models are of any relevance in explaining capital flows. The disconnect between the models and the empirical evidence becomes more pressing in light of the recent global imbalances in capital flows – the answer to the question 'Where does capital flow?' is becoming of first-order policy importance.

In the United States and the EU, where capital markets are supposed to be fully integrated, laws and institutions are intended to secure the free flow of capital. Two of the co-authors of the present paper have studied the patterns of capital flows between US states (Kalemli-Ozcan *et al.* 2007) and between regions within the EU countries (Ekinci *et al.* forthcoming). These studies show that capital flows between regions *within* countries such as the United States and Germany are consistent with the predictions of neoclassical models while those *between* European countries are not. An important question is then why capital is not flowing as freely between EU countries as between regions and whether this appears to be a permanent pattern or whether EU countries are becoming more like US states.

We compare and contrast capital flows between US states with capital flows between EU *countries*. Specifically we ask: are EU countries becoming more like US states? When did this process start? Does it appear to be an accelerating process? Does it include all EU countries or certain subsets? We take a recent historical perspective and compare the integration of US capital markets since 1950 with that of EU countries since 1970. Our main goal is to highlight trends in financial integration and the direction of capital flows rather than systematically explore *why* integration may be imperfect.

In Europe, as well as in the United States, the northern countries and regions had high output and income levels early in the 20th century in comparison with their southern counterparts. In a setting of integrated markets capital should flow from capital-abundant regions in the North to labour abundant regions in the South, but for various reasons this did not happen. In Europe, capital flows between countries were severely curtailed after the outbreak of World War I. Following a slow recovery in the 1920s capital flows were cut off by the great depression and World War II, and markets were only slowly opened in the post-war period culminating with the Maastricht Treaty allowing for free movements of capital between EU countries. In the United States, no formal barriers to capital flows existed but for various reasons capital did not flow south in the early part of the century. Caselli and Coleman (2001) argue that this was an equilibrium outcome where low schooling combined with an agrarian economy that gave scant reward to education kept many states in the US South at a level of low average productivity.

In their model North and South are equally efficient at producing non-farm goods. However, atmospheric and soil conditions give the South a comparative advantage in farming. The two regions freely trade in the two goods, and all factors (other than land) freely move across regional borders. This leads to an optimum allocation of resources in which the production of farm goods is concentrated in the South. Per capita income in the South is then lower because the labour input for farm goods is mostly low-skilled workers. As the economy grows, these mechanisms push increasing fractions of successive cohorts of southern workers out of lower-wage farming and into higher-wage manufacturing, while at the same time increasing relative wages for those southern workers remaining in farming. Both these features of the structural transformation therefore lead to regional convergence in average labour incomes. We do not attempt to add to this discussion but document the patterns of capital flows that followed the removal of barriers whatever these were.

We find that the United States in the 1950s and 1960s was characterized by strong 'catch-up growth' in the South – consistent with the predictions of the simple neoclassical model. Income and output levels were converging to those of the North and capital was flowing from rich northern states to poorer southern states. However, we find no pattern of capital flowing to relatively poor states after the 1970s – if anything, capital flows to productive (rich) states within the United States. Our interpretation is that the 'catch-up' phase is over in the United States and capital now flows to states that are hit by positive productivity shocks. In this situation, where 'catch-up growth' is over, a state that has experienced a positive productivity shock will tend to be a high output state and, as a result, capital tends to flow to these high output states. For Europe, we find that capital has been flowing from the richer countries to the poorer countries since the 1970s, consistent with 'catch-up growth', with no signs yet of this 'catch-up' phase having run its course, except for the country of Ireland, which appears to be an outlier.

Our results can help understand the process of integration in Europe. 'Catch-up growth' in the United States roughly was over 20 years after World War II, while it appears that the process is going to take a while longer for Europe. There can be many reasons why this process has not yet come to an end, ranging from government policy, regulations and institutions broadly defined. We illustrate briefly that the level of financial integration is higher in countries with better institutions, measured as either an index of entry costs or an index of investor protection.

Comparing US states to EU countries

The model

Our model ignores adjustment costs and business cycle patterns and is intended to characterize the 'medium run'. Figure 10.1 illustrates the relationship between the capital stock and its marginal product (MPK) when output is determined by a Cobb–Douglas function and highlights how this relationship depends on the level of productivity within a small open economy framework. Let K be the country's capital stock and A be its productivity level. The MPK schedule shows how marginal product varies as the capital stock increases. For a given labour force, L, productivity, A, and depreciation (δ), an increase in the capital stock, K, reduces its marginal product due to the law of diminishing returns.[2] Under the small economy assumption the world interest rate is constant (assumed to be 0.06). The domestic capital stock is determined by the equation $MPK = R$. In Figure 10.1, the level of the capital stock is K_1 for the least productive of the two regions illustrated. Holding labour constant, the equilibrium level of the capital stock is higher in a country with higher productivity, such as the second country in Figure 10.1 with capital stock K_2. The equilibrium capital stock K_2 corresponds to the MPK schedule given by the dashed line where productivity is higher (assumed to be 1.5 times higher than the productivity level corresponding to the solid MPK line, i.e. $A_2 = 1.5A_1$).

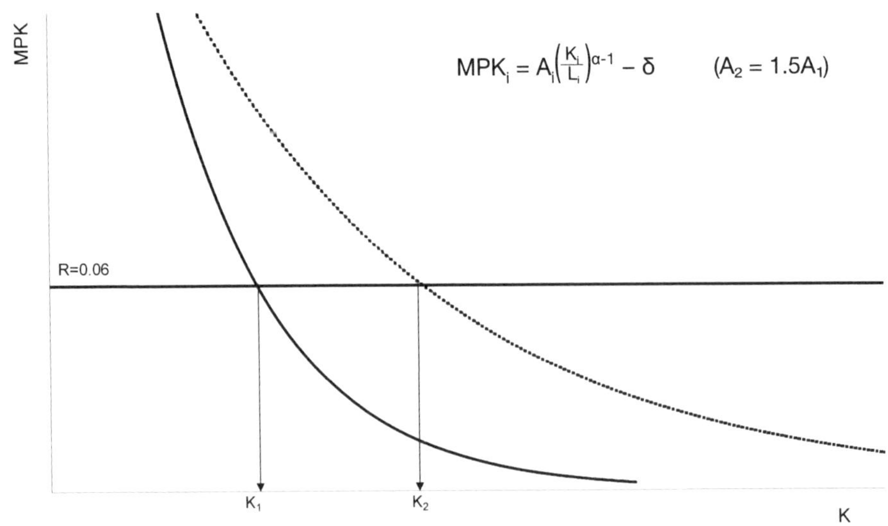

Figure 10.1 Equilibrium capital stock as a function of productivity.

Kalemli-Ozcan *et al.* (2007) show within a regression framework that capital in the United States tends to flow to fast growing states which also on average are high output states. They assume that each region's output is determined by a Cobb–Douglas production function where the level of 'productivity' differs across regions and is subject to occasional shocks that last for a number of years. Such shocks can be purely technological but can also be regulatory shocks or relative price shocks. For example, the return to capital in regions that specialize in oil-extraction is a function of the world oil price.

Under the assumption that capital adjusts to the equilibrium level within one period (a 'period' corresponds to, say, a decade in the data) following productivity shocks, this model predicts a positive relationship between capital flows and output growth. The mechanism is simply that productivity shocks lead to a higher growth and to a higher return to capital as shown in Figure 10.1. Capital flows in, until the equilibrium is reached where returns are equalized in all regions. Thus, we define integrated capital markets to include the condition that the return to capital is equated. We will call capital markets 'fully integrated' under the further condition that the ownership of capital is fully diversified. The model sketched in Figure 10.1 is deterministic, but we consider that an expository simplification of a model with uncertainty but no significant risk premia because of perfect diversification of capital ownership. Under this assumption, an increase in productivity in a region leads to an increase in output – gross domestic product (GDP) or its regional counterpart – but is associated with a lower increase in income of the region – gross national income (GNI). Why? Simply because the increase in productivity leads to a higher return to capital installed in the country and this capital is mainly owned by residents of other regions (assuming that each region is small compared to the total area under consideration).[3]

For countries, this prediction automatically translates into a positive relation between the current account (with sign reversed) and growth. For US states, we have approximate current accounts for 1953 and 1957 from Romans (1965), who painstakingly constructed estimates of saving and investment by state, but not for other years. However, past current account deficits will be reflected in current factor income payments (interest, dividends and profits) and an outflow of factor income will lower income relative to output. Hence, we use the ratio of output to income as our proxy for past capital inflows. The output/income ratio will be larger than one for debtor states which have been recipients of capital (we rescale it to be unity on average for each state) and smaller than one for creditor states who are receiving net capital income. Kalemli-Ozcan *et al.* (2007) show the ratio of output to income for a region can be expected to increase by about one-third the level of relative output growth in the previous period.[4]

A simple consequence of the above is that if all states start out at about the same level of output, then the states that are subject to relatively large increases in productivity will become states that will be debtors and at the same time will have a relatively high level of output. In other words, we expect states and countries – if the phase of 'catch-up growth' has come to an end – with relatively high output to be debtors.[5] In this chapter, we graphically verify the predictions that capital flows to high growth states or countries and we examine whether US states and European countries, respectively, appear to be past the 'catch-up phase'.

Results: US states

As in Kalemli-Ozcan *et al.* (2007), we use data from the Bureau of Economic Analysis (BEA). All nominal variables are converted into 2000 prices using the consumer price index. State-level GDP, denoted gross state product (GSP), is published by the BEA as part

Table 10.1 State 'current accounts' from Romans

	S–I in 1953 (per capita)	*S–I in 1957 (per capita)*	*S–I in 1953 (millions)*	*S–I in 1957 (millions)*
Alabama	−114	−629	−54	−319
Alaska	–	–	–	–
Arizona	−1226	−654	−170	−120
Arkansas	−576	−559	−159	−158
California	648	876	1231	2039
Colorado	216	−195	48	−53
Connecticut	1229	946	413	364
Delaware	2058	3970	112	276
Florida	542	956	278	682
Georgia	−29	−259	−16	−159
Hawaii	–	–	–	–
Idaho	−963	−754	−89	−79
Illinois	623	−19	876	−30
Indiana	−473	−1398	−307	−1033
Iowa	819	−68	334	−30
Kansas	−116	−688	−36	−239
Kentucky	−404	−280	−182	−134
Louisiana	−1316	−1472	−585	−748
Maine	247	247	35	38
Maryland	543	154	216	72
Massachusetts	982	1401	732	1127
Michigan	88	−342	93	−422
Minnesota	503	318	238	170
Mississippi	−110	−807	−36	−275
Missouri	847	502	528	343
Montana	−754	−533	−72	−58
Nebraska	778	−519	159	−118
Nevada	−595	−118	−18	−5
New Hampshire	1309	557	111	52
New Jersey	486	521	394	488
New Mexico	−1655	−1064	−194	−147
New York	1461	1790	3517	4783
North Carolina	−133	−205	−85	−146
North Dakota	−1292	−781	−122	−78
Ohio	−869	−531	−1157	−815
Oklahoma	30	−508	10	−189
Oregon	−48	−408	−12	−114
Pennsylvania	79	620	131	1109
Rhode Island	681	1195	86	166
South Carolina	−192	−447	−65	−166
South Dakota	149	−230	15	−25
Tennessee	−328	−275	−169	−154
Texas	−580	−1246	−750	−1844
Utah	−175	−1039	−20	−140
Vermont	408	130	24	8
Virginia	−63	−99	−35	−62
Washington	−173	−664	−66	−295
West Virginia	−909	−1470	−272	−442
Wisconsin	324	−42	176	−26
Wyoming	−1357	−1756	−61	−90

Notes: These data are from Romans (1965). S–I is the difference between state-level saving and state-level investment for the given years. All series are in 2000 prices. Romans' total investment estimates for each state are calculated by aggregating investment in manufacturing, mining, railroads, other transportation, public utilities, communications, agriculture and construction. He uses annual surveys for some industries and balance sheets of companies (railways, utilities, etc.) for others. For industries where neither is available, he imputes from aggregate investment figures utilizing state-level wages and salaries for that particular industry. His saving estimates are based on state-level data, when available, on currency and bank deposits, saving and loan shares, private insurance and pension reserves, consumer debt, securities loans, mortgages and bank debt, and involve a large number of imputations.

of the US state-level national accounts. GSP is derived as the sum of value added originating in all industries in the state; thus, it is exactly the state-level equivalent of GDP. GSP numbers are based on income generated in establishments and the main sources are industrial censuses such as the census of manufactures. GSP is available for the years 1977–2000. Previously published, but no longer updated by the BEA, GSP is available from 1963, but those data are not fully compatible with the data post-1977. Our main measure for income is state-level personal income (SPI), which is available from the BEA. SPI is based mainly on surveys of individual income.

The output/income ratio is our measure of the relative magnitude of net inter-state capital income flows to a state. If such flows are zero, the ratio is unity; if they are negative, the ratio exceeds unity; and if they are positive, the ratio is less than unity. The variables SPI and GSP contain aggregate (US-wide) components. These aggregate effects are not of interest to us in the context of inter-state capital mobility. To correct for this, we use the normalized output/income ratio:

$$\frac{Output}{Income_{it}} = \frac{\frac{GSP_{it}}{SPI_{it}}}{\frac{GSP_t}{SPI_t}},$$

where

$$SPI_t = \sum_i SPI_{it}\,,\quad GSP_t = \sum_i GSP_{it}$$

The ratio $Output/Income_{it}$ captures state i's output/income ratio in year t relative to the aggregate output/income ratio of the US states.

The main reason for this methodology is the unavailability of the state-level 'current accounts'. In Table 10.1, we display the 1953 and 1957 'current accounts' by state from

Table 10.2 State 'current accounts' and net capital income (dependent variable: log of average output/income)

	(1)	*(2)*	*(3)*	*(4)*
Sample	1963–70	1971–80	1981–90	1991–2000
States	47	47	47	47
Average saving minus investment	−0.09	−0.10	−0.08	−0.04
per capita 1953–7	(5.04)	(4.30)	(2.54)	(2.32)
R^2	0.51	0.50	0.29	0.19

Source: Kalemli-Ozcan *et al.* (2007).

Notes: 47 observations (missing data for Alaska and Hawaii; the outlier Delaware is left out). Average Output/Income is output divided by income (and normalized by US output/income), where output is gross state product (GSP) and income is state personal income (SPI), averaged over the relevant sample, given in 'Sample'. Average saving minus investment per capita 1953–7 is the difference between state-level saving and state-level investment per capita, averaged for the two years for which these data are available, 1953 and 1957. State-level investment and state-level saving are from Romans (1965) and used in thousands of dollars in 2000 prices in the above regressions. See Table 10.1 for the detailed explanations of state-level investment and saving estimates. A constant is included in all specifications. Heteroskedasticity robust t-statistics in parentheses.

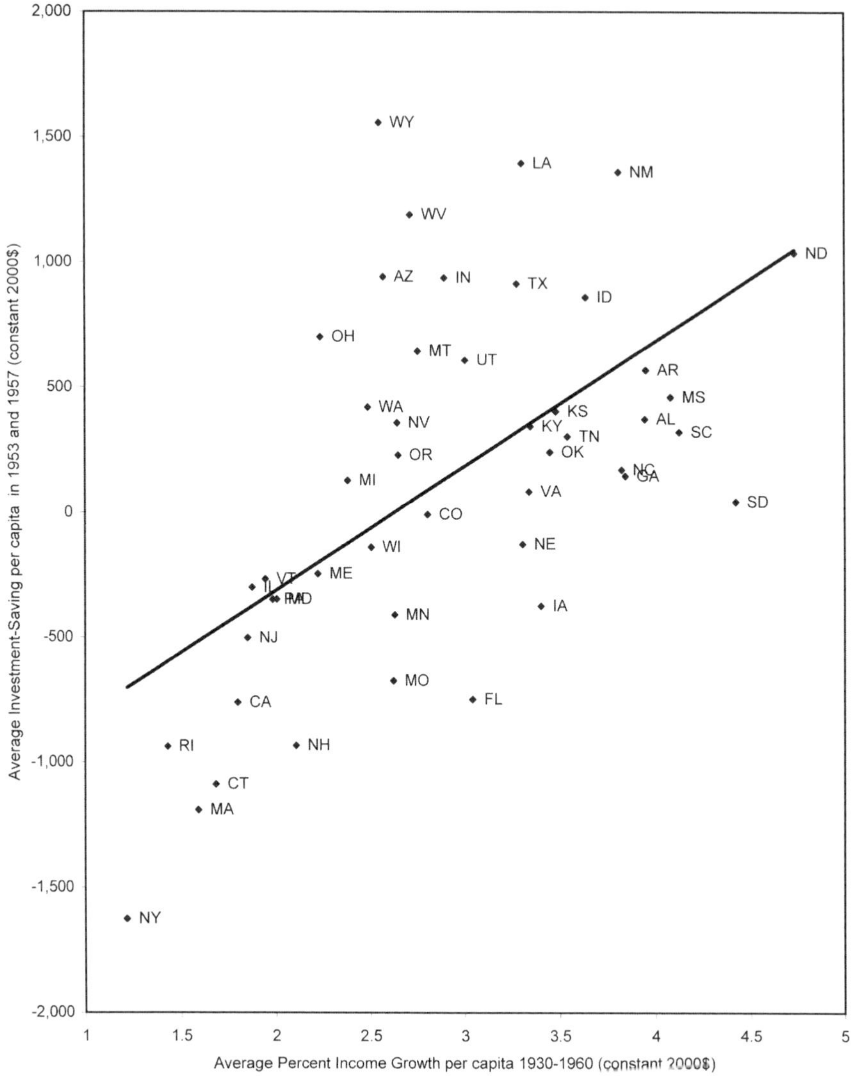

Figure 10.2 Capital flows and income growth before 1960, United States.

Romans (1965). More precisely, we display saving minus investment for these years. Those numbers clearly show that saving minus investment was very large and negative for southern states as well as for oil states. It is clear that during this period capital was flowing from the North and West to oil-rich states such as Texas and Louisiana, as well as to states in the Old South, such as Mississippi and Alabama, which were in the process of catching up. The states with large negative values of saving minus investment in the 1950s tend to be the states with high output/income ratios in the 1980s and 1990s.

We examine directly if the output/income ratio captures past 'current accounts' by regressing the output/income ratio averaged over 1963–70 on the average of 'current accounts' normalized by population for the years 1953 and 1957 (averaging may reduce measurement error). The results of this regression are displayed in the first column of Table 10.2 (see also

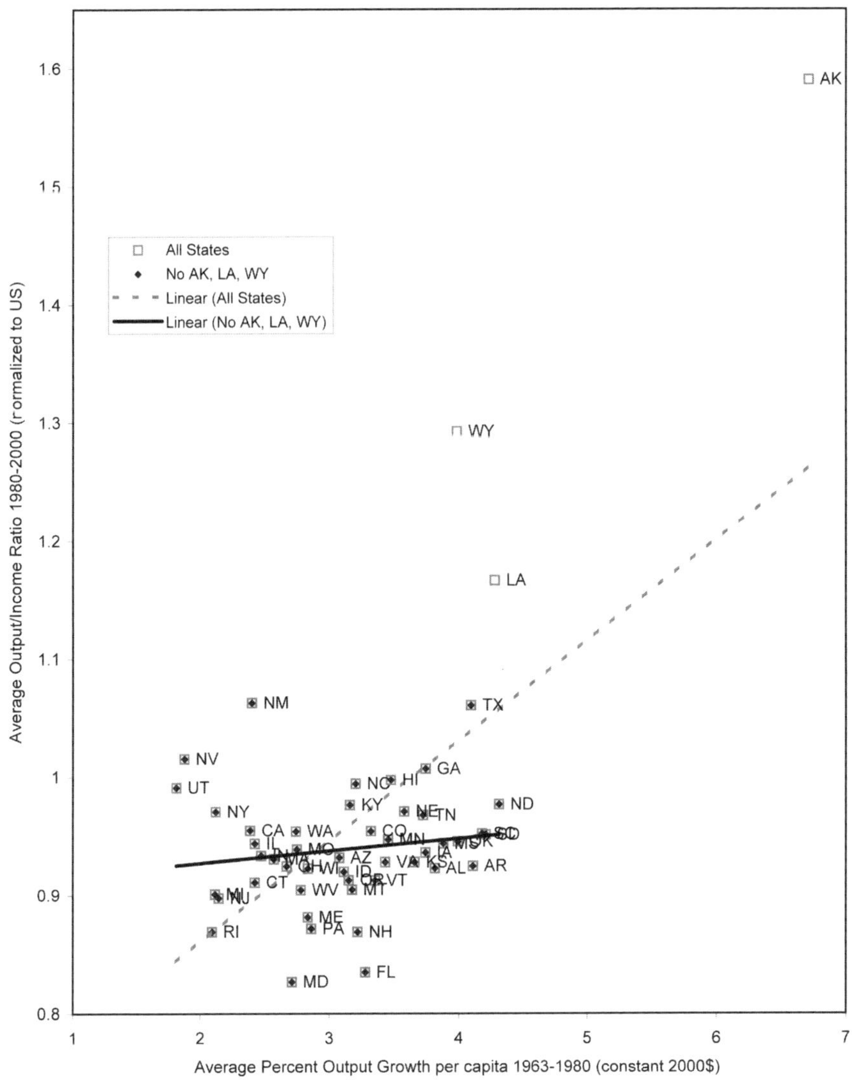

Figure 10.3 Capital flows and output growth after 1960, United States.

Kalemli-Ozcan *et al.* 2007). We find a highly significant value of the coefficient to the past 'current account' with an R^2 of 0.51. Clearly, there is a strong relationship between the output/income ratio and the 'current account' ten years earlier. In columns 2–4, we display the results for similar regressions for the decades of the 1970s, 1980s and 1990s. We observe a decline in explanatory power as we consider more recent decades but the 'current account' from the mid-1950s is still a significant determinant of the output/income ratio in the 1990s with an R^2 of 0.19.

Next we look at the predictions of the model. Figures 10.2–10.5 display the relation between the current account or output/income ratio in the late 20th century and previous period output and growth for the United States. As shown in Figures 10.2 and 10.3, throughout the sample period there is a positive relationship between capital flows and

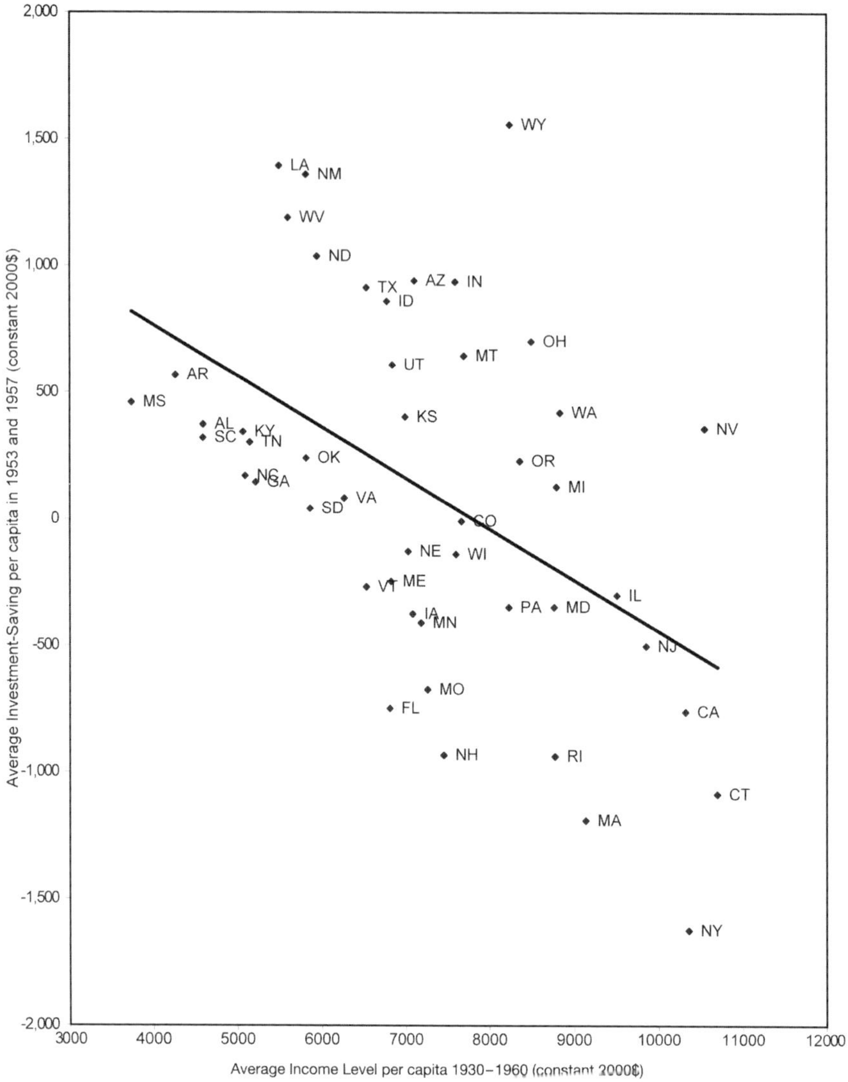

Figure 10.4 Capital flows and income before 1960, United States.

output growth, exactly as predicted by the model.[6] This shows that financial markets are well integrated within the United States.

Figure 10.4 demonstrates that in the early part of the century there is a negative relation between capital flows and income levels, whereas, as shown in Figure 10.5, in the latter part of the century this relationship turns to positive. Hence, there is evidence of 'catch-up growth' by southern states in the early part of the century, with the 'catch-up' phase being over in the latter part of the sample when capital starts flowing to high output states. The oil-states, Alaska (AK), Wyoming (WY) and Louisiana (LA), are clear outliers but even without them the pattern is visible. Barro and Sala-i-Martin (1991, 1992) documented that regional output levels (approximated by income levels) were converging in the early part of the 1900s. They interpret convergence in the context of a one-sector model with frictions to

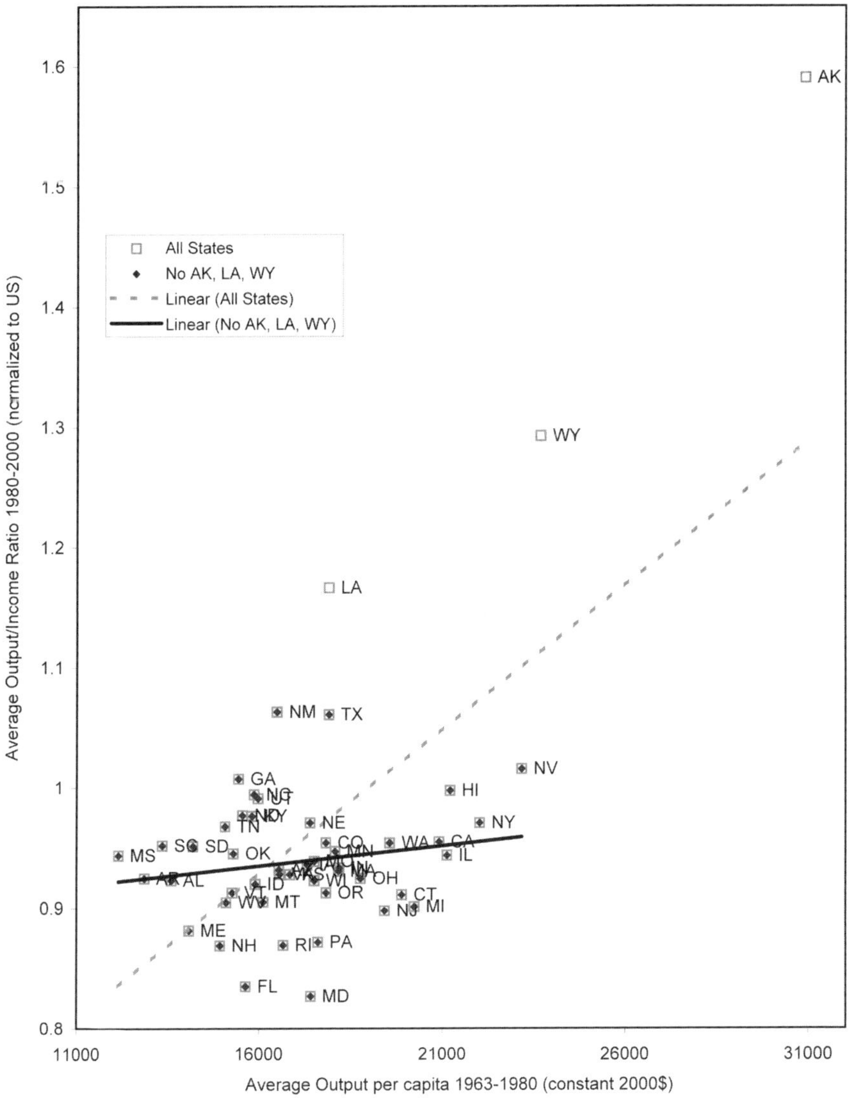

Figure 10.5 Capital flows and output after 1960, United States.

the movement of (physical or human) capital; when these frictions are removed convergence follows. The results in Figure 10.4 are consistent with convergence and further document that flows of capital to the poorer southern regions were reinforcing productivity growth in the South. However, we also consider our results consistent with the alternative view of Caselli and Coleman (2001) discussed earlier. They rely on a more complicated two-sector model in order to highlight the underlying reasons for convergence, but their model may – for the purpose of predicting the level and direction of capital flows – be approximated by a simple one-sector model as outlined in Figure 10.1.

How do European countries fit into this picture? This is the question that we are going to investigate next.

Results: EU countries

Figures 10.6–10.11 show that EU countries are still in the 'catch-up growth' phase. We investigate the 1970s, 1980s and 1990s separately and plot the average current account balances during these decades against output growth. We reverse the sign of the current accounts because we focus our discussion on capital inflows. Figures 10.6, 10.7 and 10.8 reveal a positive relation between growth and capital flows as the simple neoclassical model would suggest. A close look reveals that there is no relationship between growth and capital flows in the 1970s without Ireland, which shows that Europe was not well integrated in our sense. In the 1980s and 1990s financial integration increased and capital started flowing to high growth countries.

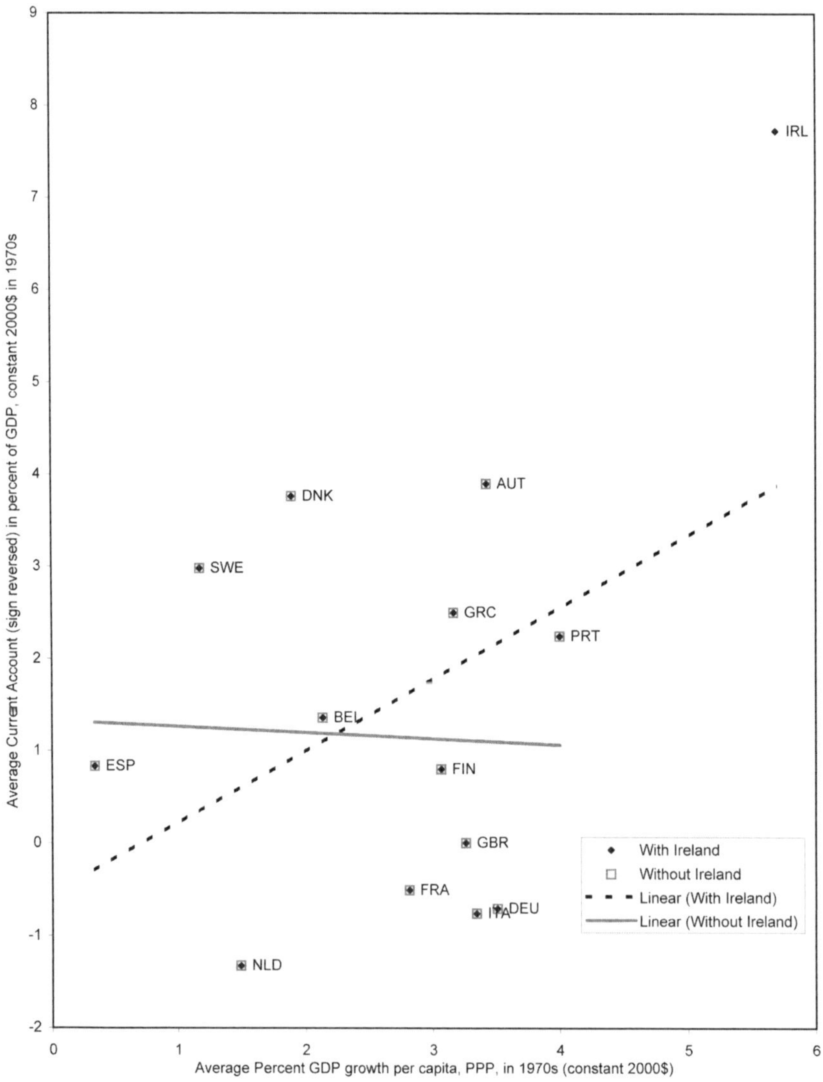

Figure 10.6 Capital flows and output growth in 1970s, European Union.

Figures 10.9, 10.10 and 10.11 reveal a negative relationship between the output level and capital flows with little change over time. This evidence suggests that the EU countries are still in the 'catch-up' phase.[7] Blanchard and Giavazzi (2002) consider the current account deficit of Portugal, which in 2001 reached 10 per cent of GDP, up from 2 per cent at the start of the 1990s. Greece is not far behind with a deficit of 7 per cent of GDP, up from 1 per cent in the early 1990s. This is not the first time that small member countries of the European Union have run large current account deficits. In the early 1980s, Portugal ran deficits of a different kind. Portugal then was still reeling from its 1975 revolution, from the loss of its colonies and from the second oil shock, and the government was running a large budget deficit. These deficits turned out to be unsustainable: between 1980 and 1987,

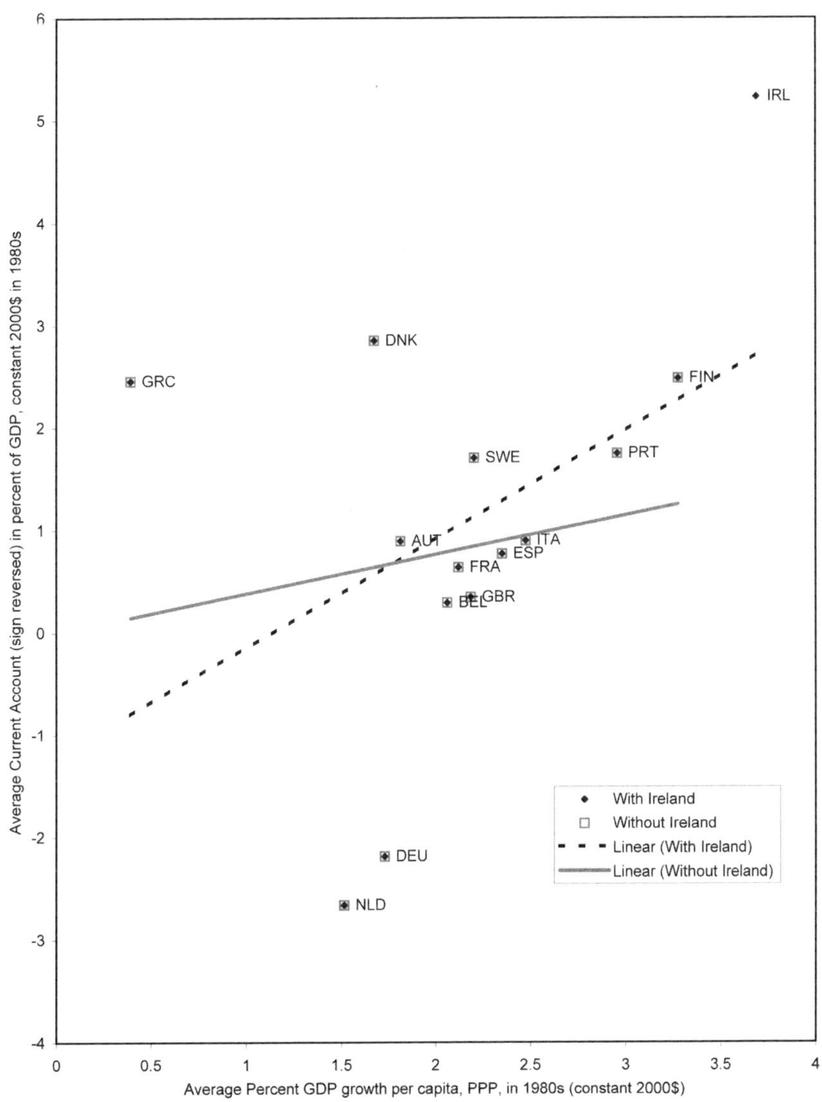

Figure 10.7 Capital flows and output growth in 1980s, European Union.

the escudo was devalued by 60 per cent and the current account deficit was eliminated. In contrast, Portugal today is not suffering from large adverse shocks; the official budget deficit has been reduced since the early 1990s. The fact that Portugal and Greece are each members of both the European Union and the euro area, and, in each case, the poorest members, suggests a natural explanation for these current account deficits. The deficits are exactly what theory suggests can and should happen when countries become more closely linked in goods and financial markets. If relatively poor countries have higher rates of return to capital, poor countries should see an increase in investment. If they further have high growth prospects, they should also see a decrease in saving according to permanent income theory. Thus, on both counts, poor countries should run larger current account

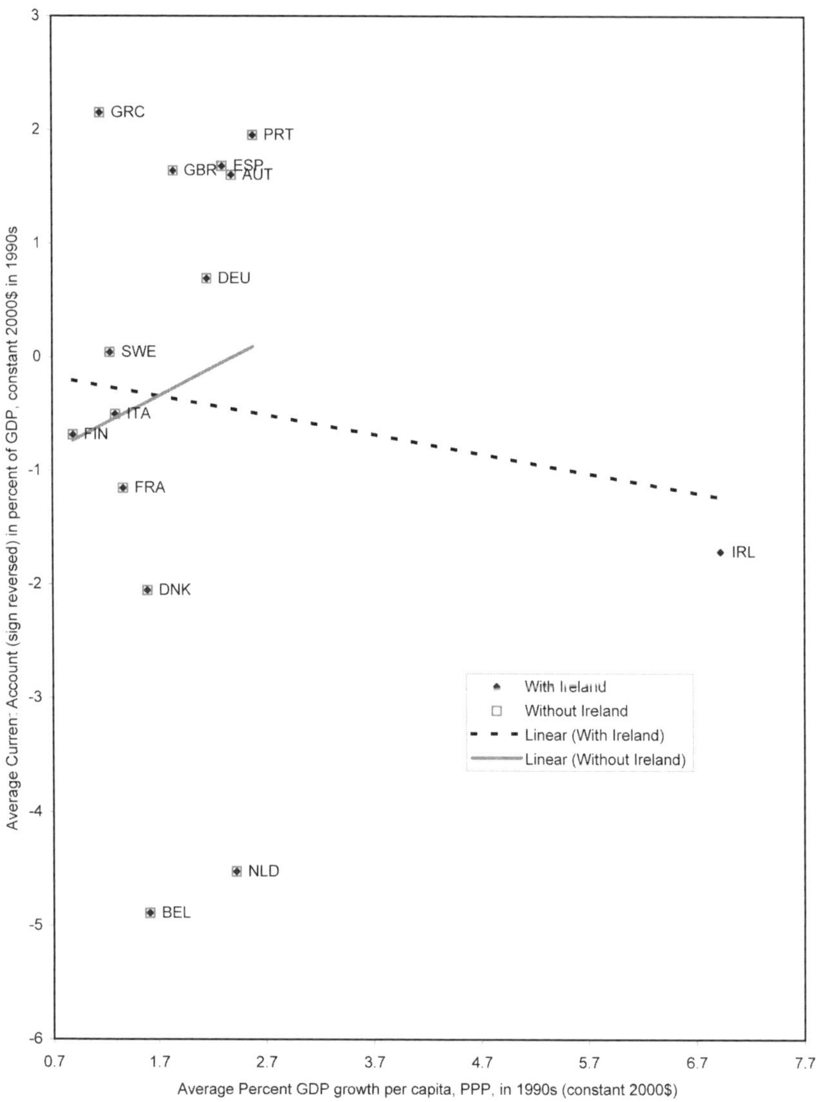

Figure 10.8 Capital flows and output growth in 1990s, European Union.

deficits. Symmetrically, richer countries should run larger current account surpluses. Blanchard and Giavazzi (2002) conclude that integration affects current account balances and the Feldstein–Horioka puzzle does not exist in Europe anymore.

Abiad, Leigh and Mody (2007) similarly show that, unlike the global sample, in Europe capital flows 'downhill' and capital flows have accelerated with increased financial integration and supported income convergence. They argue that Europe is the best place to test the relationship between financial integration and income convergence since the extent of financial integration within Europe is greater than in any other significant geographical region. They find a substantial flow of foreign capital from advanced countries to the new EU member countries of Central and Eastern Europe. Caselli and Tenreyro (2005) revisit

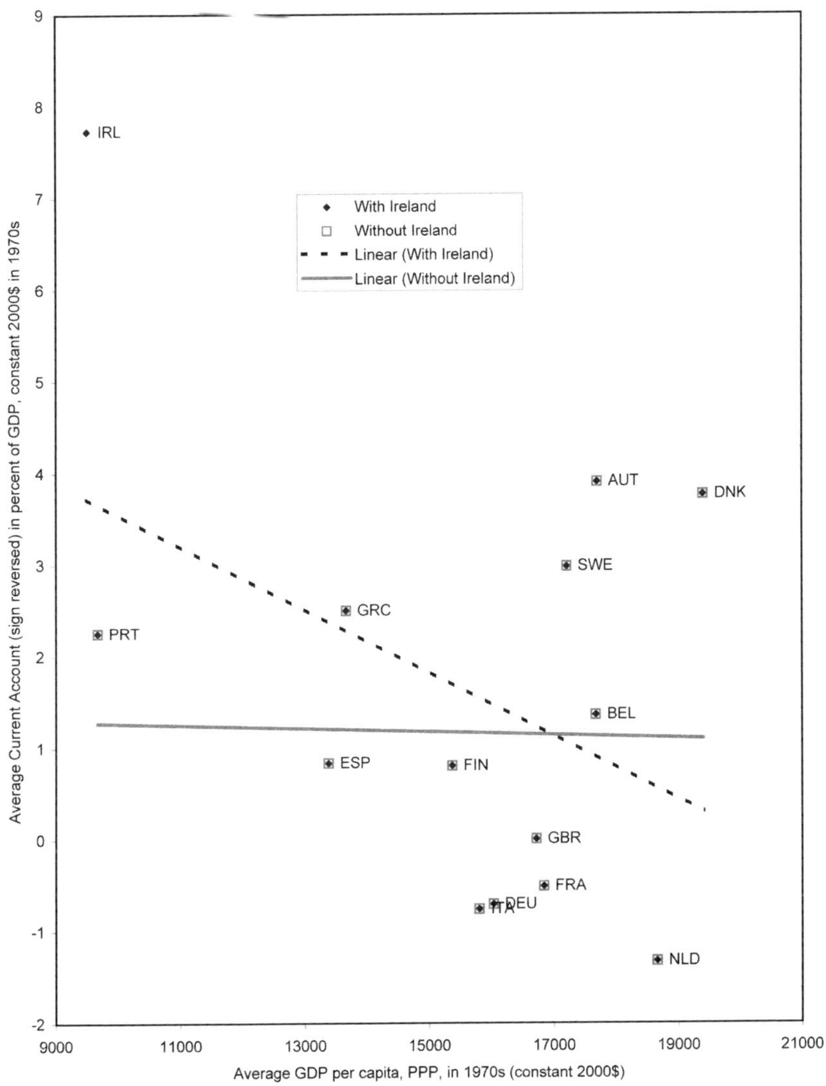

Figure 10.9 Capital flows and output in 1970s, European Union.

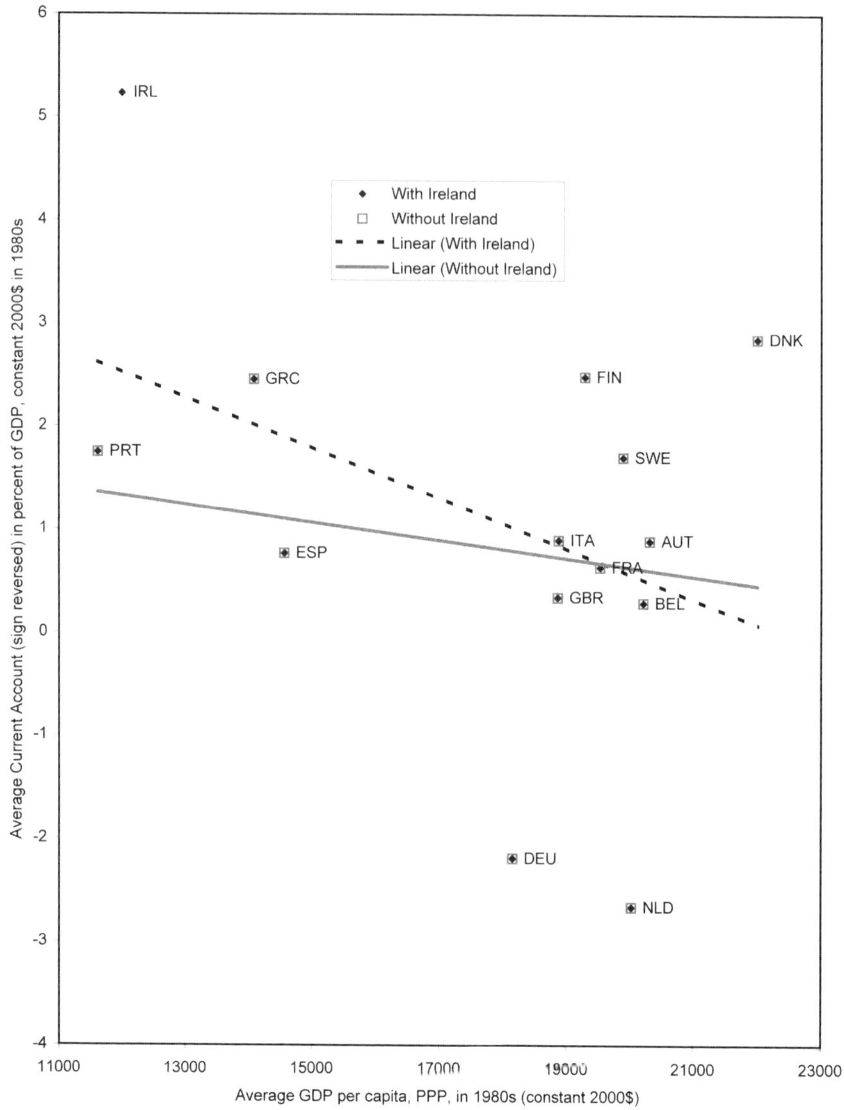

Figure 10.10 Capital flows and output in 1980s, European Union.

Western Europe's record of labour–productivity convergence. They find that the poorer Western European countries caught up with the richer ones through both higher rates of physical capital accumulation and greater total factor productivity (TFP) gains. These (relatively) high rates of capital accumulation and TFP growth reflect convergence along two margins. One margin (between industries) is a massive reallocation of labour from agriculture to manufacturing and services, which have higher capital intensity and use resources more efficiently. The other margin (within industries) reflects capital deepening and technology catch-up at the industry level.

Ekinci, Kalemli-Ozcan and Sørensen (forthcoming) investigate EU regions with a focus on capital flows between regions within countries. They find large net capital flows to high

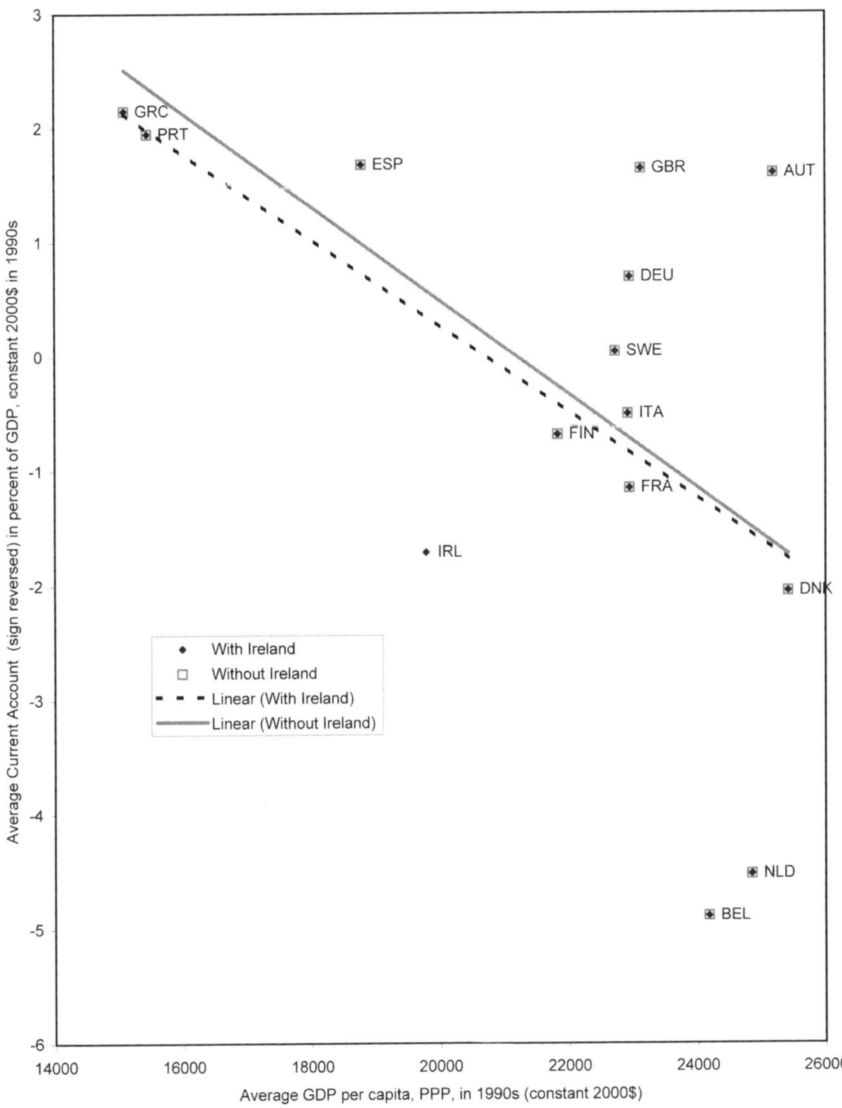

Figure 10.11 Capital flows and output in 1990s, European Union.

productivity regions within countries of northern Europe, whereas there is weak evidence for regions of southern Europe. They also find that European countries are far from fully integrated in the sense of both equal returns to capital and perfectly diversified ownership.

Capital flows and institutions

Countries

In this section, we provide simple suggestive evidence that institutions broadly defined are important determinants of capital flows. First we estimate an index that shows the degree of

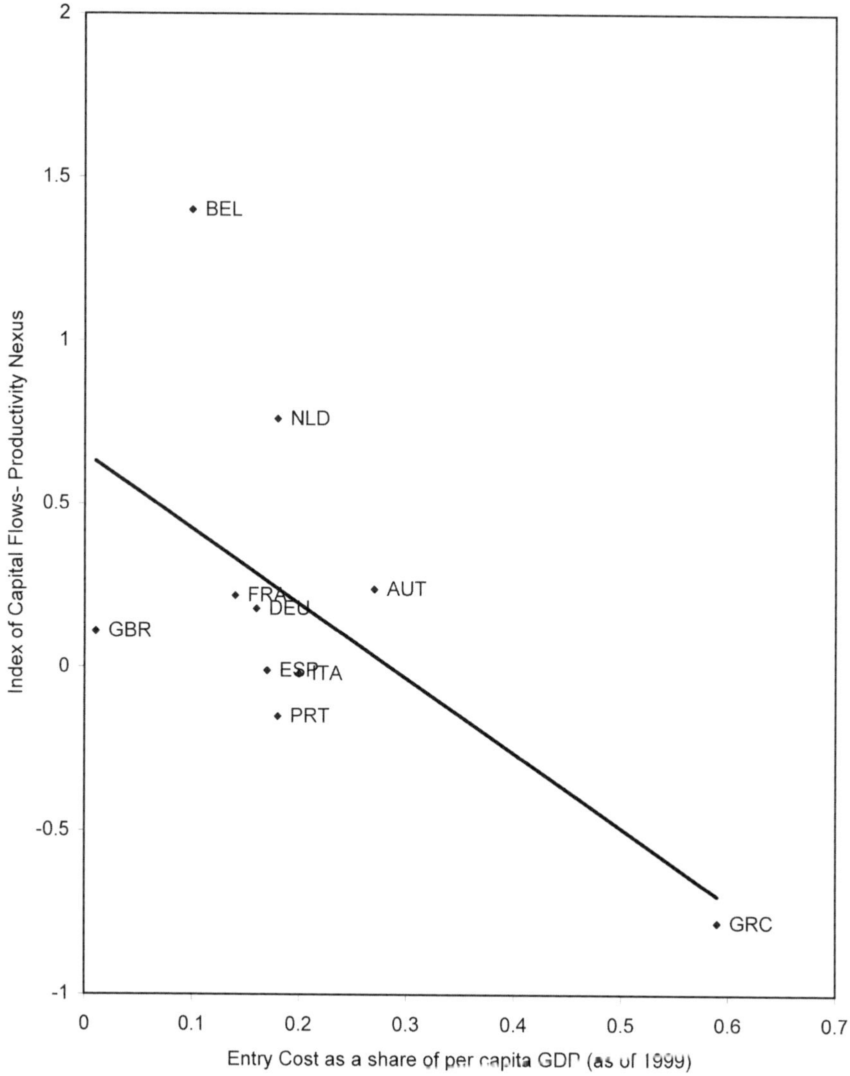

Figure 10.12 Capital flows and entry cost.

capital market integration. The index will be based on the responsiveness of capital income flows to productivity growth and derived from the model that is described in the section on 'The model' (pp. 224–25). Specifically, we examine whether the *change* in the output/income ratio is positive for regions with high growth using regression methods. As discussed before, intuitively, if capital ownership is fully diversified, the capital in a region will mainly be owned by non-residents. Assuming that the income share of capital is 0.33, a relative increase in growth should be associated with an increase in the ratio of output to income of about one-third the relative change in growth because a fraction 0.33 of the growth in output is generating capital income which is diffused over the whole EU.[8] Thus we interpret the slope coefficient from the regression of the *change* in the output/income ratio on regional growth as the *de facto* measure of financial integration.

The regression takes the form

$$\Delta\left(\frac{Output}{Income}\right)_i = \mu + \alpha\Delta\log GDP_i + e_i,$$

where $\Delta(\frac{Output}{Income})_i = \Delta(\frac{Output}{Income})_{i,2003} - \Delta(\frac{Output}{Income})_{i,1996}$ and

$$\Delta\log GDP_i = \log GDP_{i,1994} - \log GDP_{i,1991}.$$

The sample for growth and that for the output/income ratio are non-overlapping to prevent measurement errors in output appearing on both sides of the equality sign because that would create a spurious correlation between the left- and right-hand sides. GDP growth on the right-hand side is per capita and averaged over three years in order to minimize the impact of short-term fluctuations. The change in the output/income ratio is calculated for seven years,

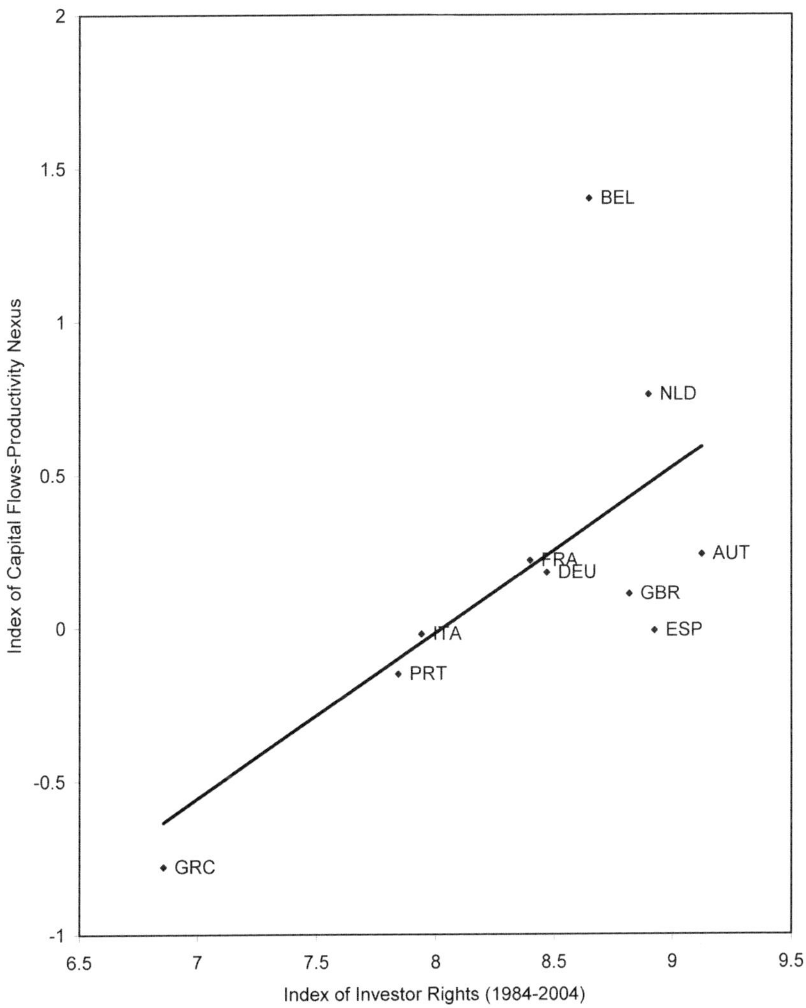

Figure 10.13 Capital flows and investor rights.

rather than one, in order to capture 'medium-run' changes. The regression estimate of α is equivalent to the slopes of the fitted lines in Figures 10.6–10.8 for the most recent sample we have available.

In Figure 10.12, we plot this capital flows–productivity index, i.e. the estimated value of α against the cost of entry from Djankov *et al.* (2002). There is a negative relationship between the two, indicating that capital does not fully flow from less productive to more productive countries within the EU if the countries involved have high business entry costs. Figure 10.13 plots the same measure against an index of property rights from the *International Country Risk Guide* (ICRG; Political Risk Services Group 2001) and it is evident that among the productive countries the ones with more investor rights and less corruption will receive more capital flows. Figures 10.12 and 10.13 suggest that financially integrated countries with good institutions obtain more flows than countries with worse institutions when hit by positive productivity shocks.

As noted above, Ekinci *et al.* (forthcoming) find large net capital flows to high productivity regions within countries of northern Europe, whereas there is weak evidence for regions of southern Europe. The differences in the findings for the northern and southern regions within countries are correlated with variables such as expropriation risk, government stability, and law and order. However, these variables do not fully explain the differences. In Italy and Spain, net income flows appear to be influenced significantly by patterns of government taxes and transfers. Ekinci *et al.* (forthcoming) also find that regions with high confidence and trust have a level of financial integration that is consistent with full integration.

Conclusion

Capital flows to regions where its marginal product is highest. When longstanding barriers to capital flows are removed, capital flows to relatively poor regions during a 'catch-up growth' phase, and when this phase is over it flows to regions with high productivity. Barriers to capital flows within the United States disappeared in the mid-20th century and for a period of time capital flowed from the wealthy northern states to poorer states in the old Confederacy. Today, US states are past the 'catch-up' phase and capital flows to states with positive productivity shocks – which tend to also be high output states. EU countries still appear to be in the 'catch-up' growth phase: within-EU capital flows to poor but fast growing countries such as Greece and Portugal.

Notes

1 Essential parts of this paper were prepared while Bent Sørensen stayed at the European Commission from 29 May to 6 June 2007 under the DG ECFIN Visiting Fellows Programme. He thanks the economists at the Commission for providing a stimulating research environment.
2 Note that the return to capital, α, is assumed to be 0.33.
3 This assumption holds to a first degree approximation for US states compared to the total United States and for EU countries compared to the total EU.
4 If the EU belonged to a fully integrated world market the ratio of output to income might increase by about one-third output growth but because we only want to examine the degree of integration among EU countries, we focus on relative output growth.
5 Note that Kraay and Ventura (2000) develop a model where investment risk is high and not diversified. An implication of their model is that the current account response to a productivity shock should be equal to the savings generated by the shock multiplied by the country's share of foreign assets in its savings portfolio. This implies that positive productivity shocks lead to deficits in debtor countries and surpluses in creditor countries.
6 Given that output data are not available before 1963, we use income instead on the X-axis for the pre-1960 period. We realize that this is contradictory to our key assumption in the model that

with perfectly integrated markets output and income will differ. However, income is highly correlated with output as long as labour income is not diversified and, with no other option available to us, we use income to illustrate our point.

7 We do not expect the model to fit perfectly at the country level because of its simplicity. For example, the assumption of a constant saving rate may be particularly heroic for countries which have, more or less, independent fiscal policies. Also, a country such as the Netherlands may have relatively high growth and high saving due to an aging population. We here focus only on the 'big picture' and do not attempt to reach a model with a better fit.

8 Full derivation of this result is shown in Kalemli-Ozcan *et al.* (2007).

References

Abiad, A.G., D. Leigh and A. Mody (2007) *International Finance and Income Convergence: Europe is Different*, IMF Working Paper 07/64.

Alfaro, L., S. Kalemli-Ozcan and V. Volosovych (2008) 'Why doesn't capital flow from rich to poor countries? An empirical investigation', *Review of Economics and Statistics* 90(2): 347–68.

Barro, R.J. and X. Sala-i-Martin (1991) 'Convergence across states and regions', *Brookings Papers on Economic Activity* 1991(1): 107–82.

—— (1992) 'Convergence', *Journal of Political Economy* 100(2): 223–51.

Blanchard, O. and F. Giavazzi (2002) 'Current account deficits in the euro area. The end of the Feldstein Horioka puzzle?', *Brookings Papers on Economic Activity* 2002(2): 147–86.

Blomstrom, M., R.E. Lipsey and M. Zejan (1996) 'Is fixed investment the key to economic growth?', *Quarterly Journal of Economics* 111(1): 269–76.

Caselli, F. and W.J. Coleman II (2001) 'The U.S. structural transformation and regional convergence: a reinterpretation', *Journal of Political Economy* 109(3): 584–616.

Caselli, F. and J. Feyrer (2007) 'The marginal product of capital', *Quarterly Journal of Economics* 122(2): 535–68.

Caselli, F. and S. Tenreyro (2005) *Is Poland the Next Spain?*, NBER Working Paper 11045.

Clark, G. and R. Feenstra (2003) 'Technology in the great divergence', in M.D. Bordo, A.M. Taylor and J.G. Williamson (eds) *Globalization in Historical Perspective*, Cambridge, MA: National Bureau of Economic Research Conference Report.

Djankov, S., R. La Porta, F. Lopez-de-Silanes and A. Shleifer (2002) 'The regulation of entry', *Quarterly Journal of Economics* 117(1): 1–37.

Ekinci, M., S. Kalemli-Ozcan and B.E. Sørensen (forthcoming) *Capital Flows within EU Countries: The Role of Institutions, Confidence and Trust*, NBER International Seminar on Macroeconomics 2007.

Gertler, M. and K. Rogoff (1990) 'North–South lending and endogenous domestic capital market inefficiencies', *Journal of Monetary Economics* 26(2): 245–66.

Gourinchas, P. and O. Jeanne (2007) *Capital Flows to Developing Countries: The Allocation Puzzle*, NBER Working Paper 13602.

Hsieh, C. and P. Klenow (2007) 'Relative prices and relative prosperity', *American Economic Review* 97 (3): 562–85.

Kalemli-Ozcan, S., A. Reshef, B.E. Sørensen and O. Yosha (2007) *Why Does Capital Flow to Rich States?*, NBER Working Paper 11301.

Kraay, A. and J. Ventura (2000) 'Current accounts in debtor and creditor countries', *Quarterly Journal of Economics* 115(4): 1137–66.

Lucas, R. (1990) 'Why doesn't capital flow from rich to poor countries?', *American Economic Review* 80(2): 92–6.

Political Risk Services Group (2001) *International Country Risk Guide*, New York: The PRS Group.

Prasad, E.S., R.G. Rajan and A. Subramanian (2007) 'Patterns of international capital flows and their implications for economic development', *Proceedings of the 2006 Jackson Hole Symposium*, 119–58.

Reinhart, C.M. and K.S. Rogoff (2004) 'Serial default and the "paradox" of rich to poor capital flows', *American Economic Review* 94(2): 53–8.

Romans, J.T. (1965) *Capital Exports and Growth among U.S. Regions*, Middletown, CT: Wesleyan University Press.

11 Declining home bias and the increase in international risk sharing

Lessons from European integration

Michael J. Artis and Mathias Hoffmann

Introduction[1]

The last decade has seen a virtual explosion of international cross-holdings of financial assets (see, e.g., Lane and Milesi-Ferretti 2003, 2007). It seems more than plausible that the gradual removal of portfolio home bias should lead to more efficient international risk sharing. From a macroeconomic perspective, a natural way to assess the welfare implications of better international portfolio diversification is to look at consumption-based measures of risk sharing. However, to date very few papers have been able to document that consumption risk sharing has actually improved along with the removal of portfolio home bias.

In this chapter, we first review this recent evidence that also includes some of our own work. We discuss why conventional consumption-based measures of risk sharing have a hard time picking up the increase in international risk sharing and we build on a novel approach suggested in Artis and Hoffmann (2006) to corroborate that international consumption risk sharing has indeed increased. This approach uses the information implicit in the levels of relative consumption and output. The focus on relative levels – rather than on first differences of the data as in virtually all of the earlier literature – allows us to document longer-term trends in consumption risk sharing that earlier specifications have not been able to pick up. We find that the increase in international risk sharing is economically significant: if regional evidence from a well-integrated economy such as the United States is taken as the benchmark, we find that between one-third and one-half of the lack of international risk sharing has vanished within a single decade.

The chapter first summarizes some of our previous analyses of portfolio holdings and capital income flows and risk sharing (Artis and Hoffmann 2006 and forthcoming). It is also closely related to Sørensen, Wu, Yosha and Zu (2007).[2] To our knowledge, these are so far the only papers to provide conclusive evidence that consumption risk sharing did indeed increase during the 1990s. In particular, SWYZ is the first to show that this increase in risk sharing is related to increased international portfolio diversification. Artis and Hoffmann (2006) establishes a similar result, but, in contrast to SWYZ, ours is based on international cross-holdings of assets; we find that countries with higher cumulated asset trade also share more risk.

Besides a synthesis of recent findings that we and others have obtained, we offer some important new results: first, we analyse the increase in international risk sharing with special reference to the experience of current EMU member countries. Second, we offer a detailed analysis of the channels through which improvements in international consumption risk sharing have come about. We confirm that consumption risk sharing has improved equally in all industrialized countries. But the level of consumption risk sharing reached among E(M)U countries is higher and – possibly most interestingly – recent improvements have occurred through different channels: among EU countries international capital income flows have become more important as a way to shield consumption from fluctuations in relative outputs, whereas in our entire panel of 23 industrialized countries, the ex-post cumulation and decumulation of foreign assets remains the main channel of international risk sharing.

These findings are robust once we control for other determinants of the patterns of international risk sharing and in particular so for the characteristics of countries' asset portfolios. We corroborate the finding that countries with lower home bias achieve more risk sharing – low risk sharing and portfolio home bias are twin puzzles separated at birth. We add to this the finding that countries with higher equity shares in their international portfolios share a larger portion of risk through capital income flows.

Our results suggest that by the end of our sample period that ranges from 1980 to 2004 the possibly most important difference between E(M)U and other industrialized countries is that, in the late 1990s, capital income flows took over as the main driver of improvements in intra-European risk sharing. By the year 2004, one-third of the risk sharing achieved through international financial markets was achieved through capital income flows. Outside Europe, this channel still plays virtually no role in risk sharing. While the sheer growth in intra-European risk sharing over the 1990s is already impressive, the patterns that emerge increasingly resemble those observed within national boundaries. EMU membership may matter for how *much* risk a country shares, but increasingly it also matters for *how* it shares it. While it is too early to evaluate these trends in a conclusive manner, we discuss the possibility that the creation of EMU itself and the associated elimination of exchange rate variability are responsible for the emergence of this pattern.

The remainder of this chapter is structured as follows: in the next section we review the theoretical rationale behind consumption-based measures of risk sharing. Then we document that simple risk sharing measures do not seem to have increased in the recent period of globalization and outline our alternative approach that is based on relative levels of consumption, income and output. In the subsequent section we then document patterns of international risk sharing for different country groupings, using an adaptation of the variance decomposition suggested by Asdrubali, Sørensen and Yosha (1996). Finally, we also relate these patterns to the structure of international portfolio holdings. Concluding comments complete the chapter.

Measuring consumption risk sharing

All consumption-based measures of risk sharing that we consider in this chapter are motivated by a benchmark model with complete markets. In the simplest complete markets model, marginal utility growth in country or region k equals the growth in the shadow price of consumption and is therefore equalized across countries:

$$\frac{u_k'(C_{t+1}^k)}{u_k'(C_t^k)} = \frac{\mu_{t+1}}{\mu_t} \tag{1}$$

where $u'(.)$ is the period utility function and C_t^k measures consumption in country k and μ_t is the shadow price of consumption. There are two related readings of this fundamental equation that have both found their reflections in the empirical literature. The first is that marginal utility growth should be perfectly correlated across countries. One branch of the literature therefore looks at consumption correlations. This line of research has encountered the now famous consumption correlation puzzle (Backus *et al.* 1992) that consists in the stylized fact that international consumption correlations are lower than the corresponding output correlations. Stockman and Tesar (1995) have argued that consumption is likely to be driven by preference shocks and subject to considerable measurement error so that low empirical consumption correlations could in principle arise even in complete markets. While this puzzle is an important stylized fact that calls for a theoretical explanation, the argument by Stockman and Tesar demonstrates that it is difficult to directly interpret consumption correlations as *measures* of risk sharing: the very fact that consumption correlations (as a measure of relative marginal utility) are lower than that of the underlying risks (i.e. output) would suggest that people use financial markets to destabilize their relative marginal utilities.

Our main focus in this chapter will therefore be on an alternative reading of equation (1) that has equally made a profound impact on the risk sharing literature: marginal utility growth in country k should be independent of country-specific risk variables. Since growth in the shadow price is common to all countries, the difference between marginal utility growth in two countries should be statistically independent of the relative endowment variables.

In order to obtain an estimable equation, specific assumptions on the form of the utility function are typically made. Under log-utility, the optimality condition can therefore be written as:

$$\mathbf{E}\left[\Delta c_t^k - \Delta c_t^* \mid \mathbf{X}_t^k\right] = 0$$

where $\mathbf{X}$ is a vector of idiosyncratic risk factors for country k, such as relative output growth, and the asterisked variable refers to a world average. Therefore, under full insurance, the regression

$$\Delta c_t^k - \Delta c_t^* = \mathbf{b}'\mathbf{X}_t^k + \varepsilon_t$$

should yield a coefficient of zero.[3] Specifically, many researchers, including Asdrubali, Sørensen and Yosha, as well as Hess and Shin (1998) and Crucini (1999) have used regressions of the form

$$\Delta c_t^k - \Delta c_t^* = \beta_u\left[\Delta y_t^k - \Delta y^*\right] + \varepsilon_t \tag{2}$$

where y^k is the logarithm of output in country k and the asterisk denotes the world average. We call this equation the basic risk sharing regression (RSR). Clearly, in a model with complete markets (and against the backdrop of the qualifications given above) the coefficient estimate of β_u should be zero or close to zero. The acknowledgement that real-world financial markets are likely to be incomplete in many ways has led researchers to adopt a more pragmatic approach in applied work. Rather than testing the null of complete markets, i.e. $\beta_u = 0$, Asdrubali, Sørensen and Yosha (1996) as well as Sørensen and Yosha (1998) have argued very convincingly that the coefficient β_u may be of interest in itself and that it should be interpreted as a *measure* of the deviation from the complete markets outcome. Applying this insight to US state level data, Asdrubali, Sørensen and Yosha find that roughly one-quarter of idiosyncratic output fluctuations remain uninsured. Conversely, Sørensen and Yosha (1998) show that among OECD countries, more than 70 per cent of idiosyncratic fluctuations remains uninsured. Hence, there is a lack of international consumption risk sharing when risk sharing within countries is taken as the benchmark.

In the next section, we examine this basic risk sharing regression in our international data set. In particular, we will focus on the way in which estimates of β_u have changed during the recent globalization period.

The increase in international risk sharing

Data

Our data are from the Penn World Table, release 6.2 (PWT 6.2) by Heston, Summers and Aten (2006) and range from 1960 to 2006. All data are in constant (1996) international prices. The countries included in our estimation are: (1) Canada; (2) the United States; (3) Japan; (4) Austria; (5) Belgium; (6) Denmark; (7) Finland; (8) France; (9) Germany (West); (10) Greece; (11) Iceland; (12) Ireland; (13) Italy; (14) Luxemburg; (15) the Netherlands; (16) Norway; (17) Portugal; (18) Spain; (19) Sweden; (20) Switzerland; (21) the United Kingdom; (22) Australia; (23) New Zealand.

Most of these countries are OECD countries and we will refer to them under this label. Since we are particularly interested in the role that European integration and monetary integration in particular may have played in allowing countries to share risk more efficiently, we also report results for EU and EMU member countries. Specifically, we consider the group of 15 EU countries as of 1996 (EU-15): Austria, Belgium, Denmark, Finland, France, Germany, Greece, Ireland, Italy, Luxemburg, the Netherlands, Portugal, Spain, Sweden and the United Kingdom; and the group of the 12 current (as of June 2006) EMU members (EMU-12).

We express all data in per capita terms. Rest of the World (RoW) aggregates are the OECD-wide average per capita values. Population data are also from the PWT. We will report results for two subperiods. The first subperiod ranges from 1980 to 1990 and covers a decade in which the momentum of formal liberalization of international capital markets increased apace. The second period covers 1990–2004. Considering this period should provide insights into the effects of the dramatic increase in net international asset positions that took place in particular in the 1990s (compare, for example, the data in Lane (2000) and Lane and Milesi-Ferretti (2001, 2006)). We refer to this latter part of our sample as the globalization period.

The impact of globalization on consumption-based risk sharing measures

Clearly, getting right the link between financial globalization – that undoubtedly *is* happening – and consumption-based measures of risk sharing is of the utmost importance if such measures are to inform policy discussions. Equally clearly, there is also a challenge from a theoretical perspective: the very raison d'être of financial markets is the allocation of consumption risk and in virtually all modern macroeconomic models the welfare gains from financial globalization will be a function of the variability of consumption.

But while basic risk sharing regressions have proven enormously useful in documenting a lack of risk sharing among countries, they have been much less successful in picking up the effects of financial globalization. Table 11.1 presents basic risk sharing regressions for the two subperiods 1980–90 and 1990–2004. We report results from two different estimation procedures: the first is simply panel ordinary least squares (OLS); in the second we account for potential heteroskedasticity by first running the risk sharing regression country by country. We then use the country-specific residual variance to weight the data for the second-stage regression. Only for the OECD do the regressions suggest a significant increase in risk sharing. This is clearly not the case for the two groups of European countries, the EU-15 and EMU-12. Rather to the contrary; here the estimates generally would even seem to suggest a decrease in risk sharing, even though the difference between subperiods does not generally appear significant.

One reason why the basic risk sharing regression may often fail to pick up the effects of financial globalization is that the risk sharing coefficient β_u will be a function not only of the degree of international diversification but also of the cross-sectional variability of output growth rates, their degree of synchronization and their relative persistence, i.e. of the underlying risks. In a world with complete markets, none of these parameters should matter: if $\beta_u = 0$, i.e. the correlation between relative output and consumption growth is zero, then no matter what the stochastic properties of relative output growth are, consumption will not react. But if there is *some* but not complete risk sharing, then the coefficient of the basic risk sharing regression can also be a function of the structure of business cycles, i.e. of the correlation structure of Δy^k and Δy^*.

For example, Crucini (1999) considers a model in which countries diversify their risk ex ante through trade in a set of Shiller securities, i.e. assets that pay a country's per capita output as a dividend (see Shiller 1993). Each country allocates its wealth between two assets: a world mutual fund of Shiller securities that pays world per capita output as its dividend and a claim to home output. In this model, income (GNP) growth in country k is a portfolio-weighted average of output growth rates at home and in the rest of the world:

$$\Delta inc_t^k = (1-\lambda)\Delta y_t^k + \lambda \Delta y_t^*$$

Table 11.1 Basic risk sharing regressions $(\Delta c_t^k - \Delta c_t^*) = const + \beta_u(\Delta y_t^k - \Delta y_t^*) + u_t^k$

	OLS	
	1980–90	*1990–2004*
OECD-23	0.83 (15.72)	0.64 (17.19)
EU-15	0.66 (9.56)	0.62 (14.63)
EMU-12	0.55 (7.14)	0.58 (13.33)
	Weighted least squares	
	1980–90	*1990–2000*
OECD-23	0.80 (16.82)	0.68 (19.70)
EU-15	0.66 (12.11)	0.65 (17.05)
EMU-12	0.61 (9.62)	0.63 (14.25)

Notes: Upper panel: OLS estimates; lower panel: weighted least squares: In a first stage, the risk sharing regression was run country by country. The country-specific residual variance is then used to weight the data in the second-stage panel regression. *t*-values in parentheses.

where Δinc^k denotes income growth and λ is the share of wealth invested in the world mutual fund. In this toy model, λ can be interpreted as the degree of diversification or of risk sharing and $1 - \lambda$ is a measure of the home bias. As we discuss in Artis and Hoffmann (forthcoming), in this model the basic risk sharing regression will only reveal the degree of diversification, i.e will uncover λ, if the representative consumer actually consumes her entire income, i.e. if $\Delta c^k = \Delta inc^k$. Then, it must also be that $\Delta c^* = \Delta inc^* = \Delta y^*$ so that the above reduces to:

$$\Delta c_t^k - \Delta c_t^* = (1 - \lambda)\left[\Delta y_t^k - \Delta y_t^*\right]$$

But the basic risk sharing regression (as equation (2)) will not generally correctly recover the lack of diversification. If λ is not equal to unity, optimizing consumers will generally seek to smooth their consumption further, e.g. by seeking to consume what is the permanent component of their income. Then, $\Delta c^k = \Delta inc^{kP}$, where the superscript denotes the permanent component.

It is well known that in a permanent income setting the response of consumption to current income critically depends on the degree of persistence of the underlying shocks. For example, if permanent output shocks trigger a positively serially correlated output response, then current consumption will be relatively more volatile than current income: since high current income predicts higher income tomorrow and since the shock is permanent it is optimal to destabilize consumption; current consumption will be more volatile than current income, so that

$$\Delta c_t^k - \Delta c_t^* = \phi(1 - \lambda)\left[\Delta y_t^k - \Delta y_t^*\right]$$

and $\beta_u = \phi(1 - \lambda)$ with $\phi > 1$ – the coefficient of the basic risk sharing regression will be biased upwards. Conversely, if shocks to income are temporary, then current income will be more volatile than consumption, so that $\phi < 1$, which biases β_u downward. In this case, the basic risk sharing regression would signal too much risk sharing.

As we argue in Artis and Hoffmann (forthcoming), the basic risk sharing regression is still likely to be a very useful tool in the sense that the biases in β_u seem relatively limited in any given subperiod that a researcher may wish to consider. In particular, differences in ϕ between, say, countries and regions can certainly not explain away the lack of international risk sharing. Still, gradual but secular changes in the structure of international business cycles, e.g. their variability and degree of synchronization, can over time affect ϕ and may therefore render long-range comparisons of estimates of β_u invalid.

In particular since the 1990s, financial globalization has led to ever larger cross-holdings of assets across countries; the home bias is eventually vanishing. In the toy model above, this is likely to have increased λ. But at the same time, the period since the 1980s has also seen huge changes in the structure of international business cycles. Stock and Watson (2005) have argued very forcefully that international business cycles have become much less volatile. Kose, Otrok and Whiteman (2003, 2005) show that they have also become more synchronized once one conditions on the presence of large negative shocks (such as the first and second oil shocks) that tend to be common across countries. As we argue in Artis and Hoffmann (forthcoming), the presence of large common shocks is likely to increase consumption correlations given the degree of international diversification. Since the beginning of the 1980s saw large common negative shocks that we did not experience in the 1990s, consumption correlations today may appear no higher than they were in the 1980s, even though globalization is likely to have affected them *ceteris paribus*. In a similar mould, Imbs (2006) provides cross-sectional evidence that countries with higher bilateral trade linkages have higher consumption correlations. Still, he finds the quantity puzzle (i.e. the fact that consumption correlations are lower than output correlations) persists because output correlations also increase with trade intensity. It is beyond the scope of this chapter to analyse these mechanisms in detail. What we wish to convey here is that the basic risk sharing regression may fail to pick up secular changes in risk sharing because it is highly susceptible to changes in the stochastic environment at the business cycle frequency. Here we illustrate this point by dissecting the basic risk sharing regression (2) into a sequence of cross-sectional regressions at each point during the sample period, i.e. we run

$$\Delta c_t^k - \Delta c_t^* = \beta_u(t)\left[\Delta y_t^k - \Delta y_t^*\right] + \varepsilon_t^k$$

for $t = 1980 \ldots 2004$.[4]

The first column of Figure 11.1 plots the sequence $\{\beta_u(t)\}_{t=1980\ldots2000}$ for the three groups: OECD, EU and EMU countries. As is apparent, the estimates of $\beta_u(t)$ are extremely volatile for all three country groups.

In spite of the huge volatility in the estimates, there seems to be an upward trend in risk sharing which can be teased out from the data, once we smooth the sequence of coefficients through HP-filtering.[5] These HP-trends are given by the smooth lines in the graphs. Indeed, it seems that there is a gradual increase in risk sharing. It is noteworthy, however, that for the OECD-23 this trend accelerates in the first half of the 1990s but flattens out thereafter. For the other two groups there is also a trend towards more risk sharing, but in particular for EMU countries most of the increase comes about in the first half of the 1980s, which seems odd if we take into account that financial integration even among EU and EMU countries is likely to have picked up speed only in the second half of the 1980s.

Though the findings here provide first evidence that risk sharing may indeed have increased, they underpin our earlier point that estimates of the basic risk sharing regression have a hard time uncovering the effect of identifying this increase head on. One possible reason that we have discussed is that these estimates are likely to be sensitive to the exact nature of shocks and in particular to changes in the stochastic environment that affect the correlation between consumption and output at business cycle frequencies. As a result, repeated cross-sectional estimates of the risk sharing coefficient $\beta_u(t)$ appear extremely volatile and even though these estimates do display a downward trend, they easily vary more over the business cycle than does the trend in $\beta_u(t)$ over the entire sample period.

A plausibly more direct approach that builds on our analysis in Artis and Hoffmann (2006) and that we also advocate here is to emphasize the low-frequency comovement of consumption and output by formulating the risk sharing regression in terms of relative levels rather than in relative differences. Hence, the regressions we will use in the remainder of this chapter are of the form

$$c_t^k - c_t^* = \beta_u^{LR}\left[y_t^k - y_t^*\right] + v_t^k + \text{constant}; \tag{3}$$

Here, the superscript '*LR*' is meant to emphasize that we think of this level risk sharing regression as picking up longer-term risk sharing.

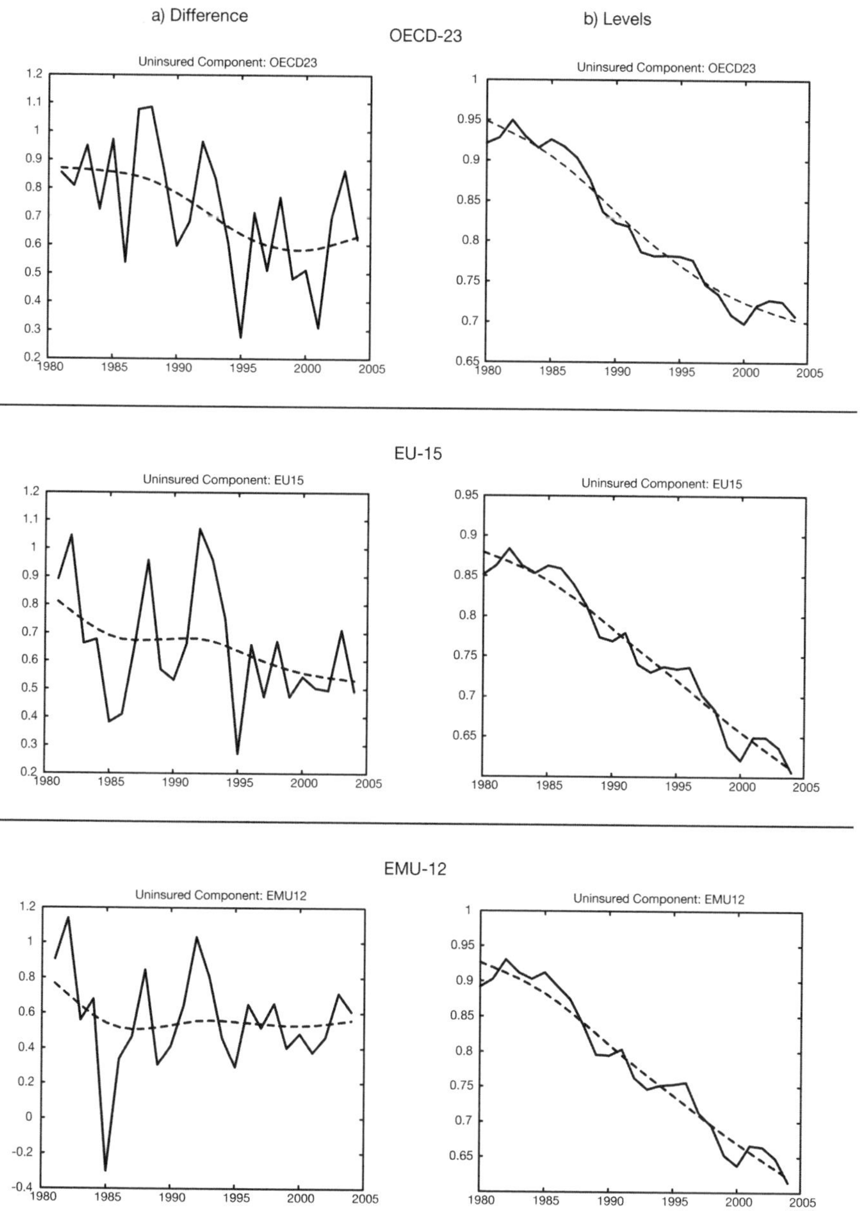

Figure 11.1 Cross-sectional risk sharing regressions 1980–2000.
Note: Dashed lines indicate HP-filtered trend values.

The estimation of this level risk sharing regression poses some interesting econometric issues, since relative consumption and output levels could be integrated variables. We discuss these issues in some more detail in the next section. For now, we provide a first demonstration of the potential usefulness of our approach by, again, dissecting the above regression into a sequence of cross-sectional regressions along the lines of the equation above. The second column of Figure 11.1 plots the sequences of $\{\beta_u^{LR}(t)\}$ thus obtained. For comparison, the smooth lines in the individual graphs reproduce the HP-trend of the sequence of basic risk sharing regressions. The first thing that is noteworthy is that for all three groups of countries the long-run risk sharing coefficient displays a clear downward tendency that is clearly discernible without having to resort to filtering techniques. As we would expect, this trend towards more risk sharing is somewhat more pronounced in the EU and EMU countries but follows the same overall pattern for all three country groups in that it kicks in in the second half of the 1980s to pick up speed throughout the 1990s.

Patterns of international risk sharing

We now turn to estimating the level risk sharing regressions as a panel relation. At the same time, we attempt to identify the channels through which the apparent increase in international risk sharing has come about. In so doing, we adapt the variance decomposition proposed by Asdrubali, Sørensen and Yosha (1996) to our level regressions here. This will allow us to identify two fundamental channels through which risk sharing can occur and which are also embodied in the simple theoretical framework that we discussed in the previous section. The first is the capital income flow channel; countries that have diversified by swapping assets *ex ante* will derive capital income flows from these assets. This will allow them to decouple their output from their income, their GDP from their GNP. We refer to this channel as the capital income flow or income smoothing channel. The second channel pertains to further smoothing of consumption *vis-à-vis* current income through asset accumulation or decumulation. We refer to this channel as the accumulation or consumption smoothing channel.

Following Asdrubali, Sørensen and Yosha, we gauge the role of the capital income flow channel by the comovement of international net factor income flows – given by the wedge between GDP and GNP – with home GDP fluctuations. This suggests a panel regression

$$gdp_t^k - gnp_t^k = \beta_K^{LR} gdp_t^k + u_t^k \tag{4}$$

where *gdp* and *gnp* denote the idiosyncratic relative component of the logarithm of GDP (output) and GNP (income) in country k, i.e. $gdp_t^k = \log(GDP_t^k/GDP_t^*) = y_t^k - y_t^*$ and $gnp_t^k = \log(GNP_t^k/GNP_t^*) = inc_t^k - inc_t^*$. Again, the superscript 'LR' is meant to distinguish the coefficient of this level regression from the one obtained from the analogous regressions in first differences.

We measure the contribution of the second channel by the comovement of saving or dissaving with GDP, i.e. we run regressions

$$gnp_t^k - cons_t^k = \beta_C^{LR} cons_t^k + \xi_t^k \tag{5}$$

where, in analogy to the above, $cons_t^k = \log(C_t^k/C_t^*) = c_t^k - c_t^*$ denotes log relative consumption.

Note that, by construction, the uninsured component of output risk is given by

$$\beta_u^{LR} = 1 - \beta_K^{LR} - \beta^{LR}$$

where β_u^{LR} is the coefficient of the panel version of the level risk sharing regression defined by (3) above and which for convenience we reproduce here using the more compact notation:

$$cons_t^k = \beta_u^{LR} gdp_t^k + v_t^k \tag{6}$$

We estimate the three equations (4), (5) and (6) by weighted panel OLS. To account for heteroskedasticity, we first run the above regressions country by country. We then weight all variables in the second-stage panel OLS regression by the standard deviation of the country-specific residual.

Estimation of the level regressions may, however, raise an additional issue because, unlike relative growth rates of consumption, income and output, relative levels may contain unit roots. But we note that even in the presence of unit roots the level risk sharing regressions (4)–(6) constitute long-run panel relations in the sense of Phillips and Moon (1999) and can, in principle, be estimated consistently by OLS. Since OLS may suffer from second-order bias due to potential simultaneity and serial correlation of the errors, we also experimented with a Panel Dynamic OLS estimator. Mark and Sul (2003) have forcefully argued for the use of this estimator not only on grounds of its simplicity but also because – unlike alternative methods such as Phillips and Moon's (1999) panel version of the fully modified OLS estimator – it is well suited for relatively small samples. The use of the Panel Dynamic OLS estimator yielded very similar results for all our specifications. In the remainder of the chapter, we therefore only report results obtained from plain panel OLS estimations.

Another important issue in estimating the above risk sharing regressions concerns the treatment of country-specific fixed effects. As argued in SWYZ, panel regressions in which country-specific effects are not controlled for can be thought of as capturing some notion of long-run risk sharing. In our setting, the level specification already is meant to capture long-run risk sharing. Still, as we argue in Artis and Hoffmann (2006), where we discuss this issue in considerable detail, the very notion of home bias implies that country portfolios are heterogeneous. For example, relative changes in asset prices can only affect a country's wealth in an asymmetric way if the size or composition of the country's portfolio is different from that of other countries. We think that this kind of heterogeneity is clearly interesting from a risk sharing perspective and should therefore not be removed up front. We therefore report results that are based on pooled regressions, i.e. in which no control for fixed effects has been included.

Table 11.2 presents the estimation results of the three level risk sharing regressions (4), (5) and (6) for the two subperiods 1980–90 and 1990–2004.

The first important observation is that risk sharing has indeed increased, in line with what we find from the repeated cross-sectional regressions in the previous section. EU countries and countries that later, in the 1990s, were to become EMU countries already in the 1980s shared more risk among themselves than the OECD average. Also the increase in risk sharing in Europe seems larger than for the OECD average, notably among EMU members. Note also that the group of future EMU countries started out from (slightly) less risk sharing than the EU-15 average in the 1980s but ended up sharing slightly (but significantly) more risk during the 1990–2004 period. This suggests that EMU membership, and the associated elimination of exchange rate risk along with the emergence of a common monetary policy, may in itself have led to better risk sharing – an issue to which we return on pp. 253–56.

Tabel 11.2 Channels of long-run risk sharing $x_t = const + \beta_X gdp_t^k + u_t^k$

		1980–90	*1990–2004*
OECD-23	β_K^{LR}	−0.05 (−9.55)	0.02 (4.16)
	β_C^{LR}	0.05 (2.78)	0.20 (13.54)
	β_U^{LR}	0.99 (58.64)	0.79 (49.32)
EU-15	β_K^{LR}	−0.06 (−7.10)	0.04 (9.71)
	β_C^{LR}	0.22 (18.61)	0.35 (46.47)
	β_U^{LR}	0.84 (59.33)	0.60 (64.77)
EMU-12	β_K^{LR}	−0.07 (−7.99)	0.05 (11.77)
	β_C^{LR}	0.18 (14.09)	0.37 (52.01)
	β_U^{LR}	0.89 (60.42)	0.58 (63.55)
Memorandum item		*Regression based*	*VAR based*
USA	β_K^{LR}	0.67	0.48
	β_C^{LR}	−0.16	0.08
	β_U^{LR}	0.51	0.44

Notes: The table reports estimates of the long-run (level) risk sharing regressions for the capital income flow ($x = gdp - gnp$, $X = K$) and the asset cumulation and decumulation ($x = gnp - cons$, $X = C$) channels as well as for the unsmoothed component ($x = cons$, $X = U$). The regressions were performed as a two-stage weighted least squares procedure along the lines described in Table 11.1. *t*-values in parentheses. The memorandum item contains a regression-based and a VAR-based estimate (at a 30-year forecasting horizon) of the long-run risk sharing channels for the US, 1963–90, taken from Table 1 (p. 791) and Table 2 (p. 793) in Becker and Hoffmann (2006).

It is important to put the increase in international risk sharing reflected by our estimates of β_u^{LR} into perspective. This increase in risk sharing is not only statistically significant, it is economically very important: the memorandum item in Table 11.2 shows that even in the US roughly 50 per cent of long-run idiosyncratic risk remains uninsured. So, if we depart from a world of complete risk sharing and consider instead the empirically much more relevant benchmark of a financially highly integrated economy such as the US, then the full extent of the increase in international risk sharing – and in particular of intra-European risk sharing – can be appreciated. Starting from an estimate of β_U^{LR} of more than 0.95 in the 1980s and going to 0.75–0.78 as in the OECD case then implies that *vis-à-vis* a realistic benchmark such as the federal states of the US – at least one-third, if not half of the previous 'lack of international risk sharing' has vanished within a single decade. This increase in risk sharing is even more impressive among the European countries in the sample: starting from around 0.85, these countries get stuck with just about 60 per cent of their idiosyncratic risk in the 1990–2004 period, implying that almost two-thirds of the risk sharing gap *vis-à-vis* the US has closed.

But while there is a clear increase in risk sharing, there seem to remain major differences in the way in which risk is shared at the international and at the regional levels. At the bottom of Table 11.2 we reproduce estimates of long-run risk sharing for the US obtained by Becker and Hoffmann (2006). Comparing our international estimates to these numbers reveals that at the international level all of the increase in risk sharing seems to come through asset accumulation and decumulation, whereas in the US most of the (long-run) risk sharing seems to be happening through capital income flows.

As is widely documented in the literature, the second half of the 1990s saw tremendous growth in portfolio cross-holdings, so, even though the sample period 1990–2000 is relatively short, the panel estimate could mask important changes in the relative role of the channels for risk sharing that might have occurred in the more recent past. In particular, the advent of European monetary union and the elimination of exchange rate risk are likely to have substantially affected the portfolio choice of European investors and may therefore also have changed the pattern of risk sharing.

In Figure 11.2 we investigate this issue, by presenting the estimates of time-slice (i.e. repeated cross-sectional) decompositions of the two channels into sequences $\{\beta_K^{LR}\}$ and $\{\beta^{LR}\}$ along the lines of our earlier decompositions of β_u^{LR} in Figure 11.1. Table 11.2 seems to suggest that the main difference between OECD countries and EMU or EU countries lies in how *much* risk they share, not so much in *how* they share it. However, the graphs in Figure 11.2 suggest that the time-average emphasized by our panel regressions does indeed hide as yet subtle but increasingly important differences in the pattern of risk sharing that started to emerge in the 1990s: in both the EU and EMU countries, capital income flows, starting from a very low (actually rather large negative) contribution to risk sharing in the 1980s, have grown to help smooth about 10 per cent of idiosyncratic output level risk in 2004. Given that 60 per cent of this risk remained uninsured at the end of the 1990s, this implies that one-quarter of the total risk sharing achieved between E(M)U countries is achieved through capital income flows. In fact, for the E(M)U, much of the growth in total consumption risk sharing in the most recent period seems to have been driven by the growth in capital income flows. For all three country groups, the accumulation/consumption smoothing channel has grown in importance but the curve described by $\beta^{LR}(t)$ seems to have flattened out somewhat in the second half of the 1990s, whereas for the EU and EMU countries, the rise in income flows only really starts after 1995.

Certainly, income smoothing through capital income flows has also increased on average in the OECD as a whole. But, first, the growth in $\beta_K^{LR}(t)$ is much more subdued – by the end of the sample period $\beta_K(t)$ barely exceeds 6 per cent – so that improvements in risk sharing seem to be driven mainly by a larger contribution of the asset accumulation channel. And, second (results not reported), we do not find any growth in the role of income smoothing over the 1980–2004 period, if we drop the EU or EMU countries from the OECD panel, which suggests that any growth in income flows we see in the larger group of OECD countries is ultimately driven by larger capital income flows among European countries.

Determinants of the pattern of risk sharing

We assess to what extent the rise in the contribution of capital income flows to risk sharing between EU and EMU countries is driven by country portfolio characteristics. Recent research (SWYZ) has started to document that the increase in international risk sharing can be associated with the decline in international portfolio home bias. In our own earlier work (Artis and Hoffmann 2006), we show that portfolio heterogeneity matters for the way in which risk is shared among countries. To the extent that EU countries hold different portfolios from other economies, this could possibly explain why the patterns of risk sharing differ between E(M)U and non-EU industrialized countries.

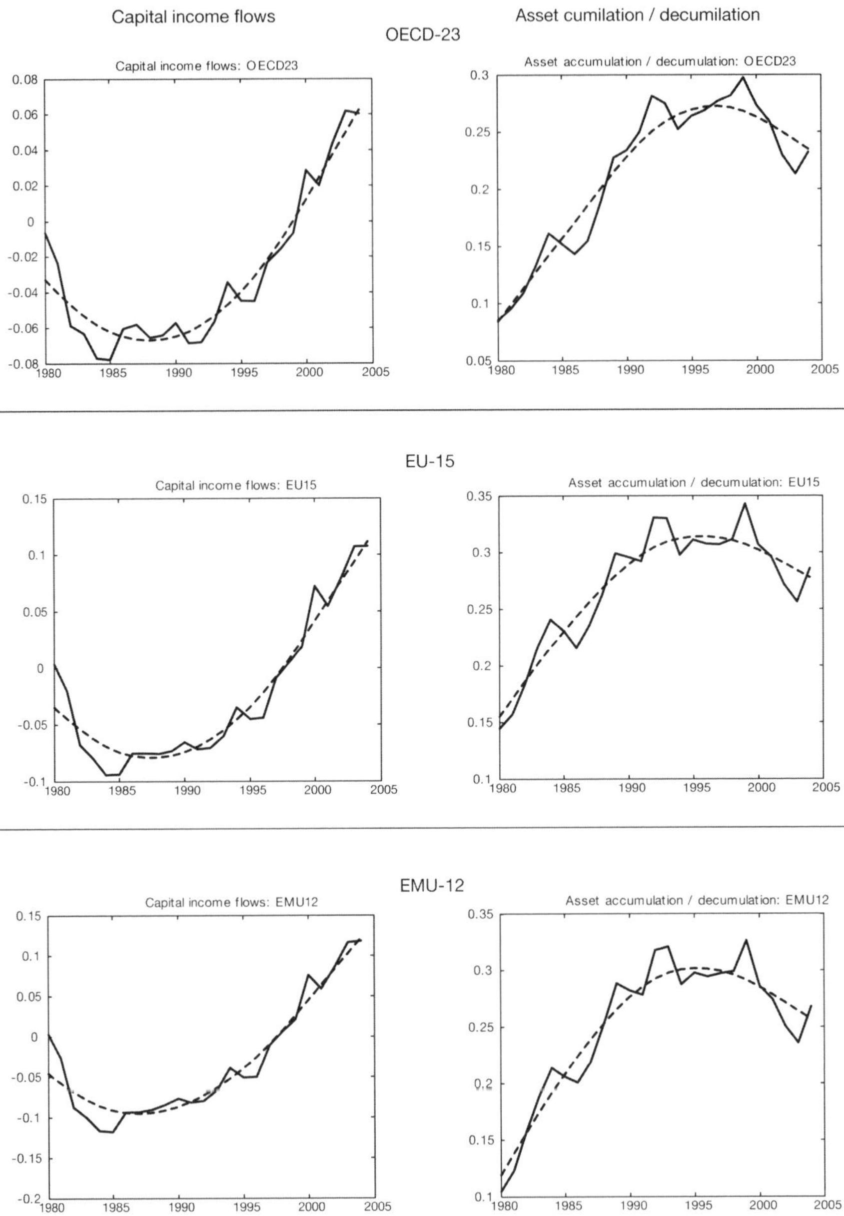

Figure 11.2 Cross-sectional level risk sharing regressions 1980-2000.
Note: Dashed lines indicate HP-trends.

To assess this issue, we extend SWYZ's and our own work by parameterizing the risk sharing coefficients β_K^{LR}, β^{LR} and β_U^{LR} as a function of both country portfolio characteristics and a time trend, so that

$$\beta_X^k(t) = \overline{\beta}_X + \kappa_X'(\mathbf{z}_k - \overline{\mathbf{z}})(t - t_0)$$

where $X = K, C, U$, $\overline{\beta}_X$ denotes average risk sharing through channel X, $\mathbf{z}_k$ is a vector of country characteristics and $\overline{\mathbf{z}}$ the vector of cross-country means of $\mathbf{z}_k$.[6] While we use period averages of country characteristics, so that $\mathbf{z}_k$ is not time-varying, we allow for time dynamics in β_X^k by interacting the country-characteristics with a deterministic trend term. In this way, we essentially proxy for a country-specific time trend in β_X^k. Plugging the above relation into (4)–(6) we then obtain a panel regression in which the elements of $(t - t_0)(\mathbf{z}_k - \overline{\mathbf{z}})$ are interacted with gdp_t^k and from which the coefficient vector κ_X can be estimated.

Our vector of country characteristics $\mathbf{z}_k$ includes two separate measures of international asset cross-holdings: the first, which we abbreviate as cat, is a measure of country k's cumulative asset trade (*cat*) relative to its total financial wealth. The second, called $eqshare$, is the share of equity in cumulative asset trade.[7] To assess the role of EMU membership in the extent and the pattern of risk sharing, we use an EMU membership dummy. Finally, we also include a pure time trend to capture the common time trend in risk sharing that we can think of as being driven by time variation in the cross-sectional mean $\overline{\mathbf{z}}$ and by other un-modelled common characteristics. This implies that we have

$$\mathbf{z}_k = \left[1,\ cat_k - \overline{cat},\ eqshare_k - \overline{eqshare},\ EMU^k - \overline{EMU}\,\right]'$$

To focus on recent developments, we present our results for the period since the start of EMU, i.e. for 1999–2004. Table 11.3 summarizes our findings.

For aggregate risk sharing, the results are very intuitive and confirm some of the earlier findings by SWYZ and ourselves: most importantly, countries with more asset trade (higher cat) share significantly more risk overall. The uninteracted part of the aggregate time trend tends to decrease risk sharing over the period, though. This could reflect the decline in world stock markets over that period that lowered the value of financial relative to real assets such as human capital and housing. It is possible that this relative increase in the value of virtually non-diversifiable assets could have resulted in a temporary decrease in aggregate risk sharing. Such an interpretation would also tie in with our finding that countries with relatively more equity trade share significantly less risk, an otherwise somewhat surprising

Table 11.3 Determinants of the pattern of risk sharing 1999–2004, OECD-23 countries

	1 Income smoothing	*2 Consumption smoothing*	*3 Uninsured*
$\overline{\beta}_x$	−0.007 (−0.20)	**0.30** (3.55)	**0.71** (8.03)
$t - t_0$	**−0.04** (−2.97)	−0.03 (−0.99)	**−0.07** (2.0824)
$cat_k(t - t_0)$	0.005 (1.88)	**0.02** (2.67)	**−0.02** (−3.29)
$eqshare_k(t - t_0)$	0.03 (0.50)	**−0.77** (−5.27)	**0.74** (4.90)
$EMU_k(t - t_0)$	**0.04** (2.57)	**−0.12** (−2.93)	*0.08* (1.86)
R^2	0.20	0.34	0.73
Memorandum item: level regression without IA-term, 1999–2004			
β_X^{LR}	**0.03** (2.0790)	**0.25** (6.1169)	**0.71** (16.6422)
R^2	0.03	0.22	0.67

Note: t-statistics in parentheses. Significant coefficients at the 5% and 10% levels are in bold and italics respectively.

result. Possibly, however, this effect could also be explained by the correlation between equity shares in country portfolios and the cumulated asset trade, which may make it somewhat difficult to isolate the effects of $eqshare$ and cat.[8] EMU membership *per se* as a point estimate is positive, which would suggest that EMU membership lowers risk sharing relative to the rest of the country group. However, this result is barely significant.

To our knowledge, results for the way in which portfolio characteristics affect the role of the individual channels of risk sharing have not been reported in the literature. We find that the common time trend is negative for both capital income flows and asset accumulation/decumulation, in line with our previous result that there was a downward 'trend' on risk sharing during this short sample period. The EMU dummy has a strongly positive effect on the contribution of capital income flows and a negative one on asset accumulation/decumulation. These two effects seem to cancel out; the net effect, as discussed previously, would barely seem significant. This reconfirms our point – already apparent from the earlier graphical results – that by the end of the 1990s EMU membership matters maybe less for how *much* risk an industrialized country shares than, increasingly, for *how* this risk sharing is accomplished.

Finally, by way of comparison, the lower panel of Table 11.3 also gives the estimates of β_X^{LR} for the period 1999–2004 obtained from a level risk sharing regression without interaction effects. These coefficients are very much in line with the estimates of $\overline{\beta}_X$ reported in the first line of the table. This fact, together with the substantial improvement in R^2 that we obtain through the interaction terms on the two channel regressions, i.e. for β_K^{LR} and β^{LR}, suggests that the three country characteristics we consider here – cumulative asset trade, the role of equity trade in international asset cross-holdings and EMU membership – do a reasonably good job in explaining country-specific trends in the patterns of international risk sharing since the inception of EMU.

Discussion and conclusion

International risk sharing increased in the 1990s. This chapter has shown that this increase is economically important and even more so in Europe than elsewhere. We have reported empirical findings to support the notion that intra-European risk sharing increasingly approximates the pattern observed in the US or more generally within countries; this is true maybe not so much for the actual extent of risk sharing – here there is still some way to go, even though one-third to one-half of the lack of international risk sharing seems to have vanished within a decade if the US is taken as a benchmark – but rather in the way in which risk gets shared, namely through more capital income flows due to *ex ante* swaps of equity.

It is interesting to link these findings to the more traditional approach of testing for long-run capital mobility between countries. A lot of this literature has built on Feldstein and Horioka (1980) by examining savings–investment correlations. In a recent study of European countries, Blanchard and Giavazzi (2002) document that savings–investment correlations have decreased in Europe and especially in the euro area. Our findings here complement this result from the perspective of the macroeconomic risk sharing literature: in particular, the rise of risk sharing through capital income flows is not only consistent with, but is ultimately a necessity for, the patterns in savings–investment correlations documented by Blanchard and Giavazzi to prevail. In the long run, for a country to decouple its savings from its investment will only be possible if the persistent current account imbalance is financed through non-zero net capital income flows.

While it is too early to tell what is at the source of this development, one plausible candidate is the elimination of exchange rate risk within the EU and among EMU countries in particular. The recent literature has emphasized the role of valuation effects for the size of international asset positions. As we have argued in our own recent work, portfolio heterogeneity is a precondition for such valuation effects to have an effect (either a stabilizing or destabilizing one) and we have shown that substantial international portfolio heterogeneity is required to explain why – at least at business cycle horizons – international income flows have remained relatively muted as international risk sharing has increased (Artis and Hoffmann 2006). As we know from recent research on global imbalances (most prominently Gourinchas and Rey 2007), valuation effects also work mainly through exchange rate adjustments. As argued in Hau and Rey (2006), such valuation effects can in themselves lead to frequent portfolio rebalancing if exchange rate risk cannot be fully diversified. The result is high turnover in equity markets: instead of holding foreign equity positions in order to reap dividend flows, investors rebalance their portfolio, by realizing foreign capital gains. For macroeconomic risk sharing that should imply that risk sharing takes place through cumulation and decumulation of assets rather than through capital income flows. However, to the extent that exchange rate variability gets eliminated, countries may then hold more homogeneous portfolios with less turnover so that risk sharing may take place through income flows rather than through continual sale and purchase of assets. The result should be a pattern of risk sharing as we see it within countries: lots of capital income flows. Possibly, what we start to see in European data is the reflection of these fundamental changes.

Notes

1 We are grateful to Lars Jonung, Jan van Lemmen and participants in the 2nd DG ECFIN Research Conference for their comments and suggestions.
2 We refer to this paper via the acronym 'SWYZ'.
3 Mace (1991), Cochrane (1991) and Townsend (1994) were the first authors to investigate regressions of this type in household-level data.
4 Asdrubali, Sørensen and Yosha (1996) demonstrate that the panel OLS coefficient β_u is a weighted time-average of the cross-sectional coefficients $\beta_u(t)$.
5 Our results reported here are based on a smoothness parameter of 100, but the results are not sensitive to this choice.
6 Since in this part of the chapter we are only dealing with level regressions, we simplify notation by dropping the superscript 'LR'.
7 Specifically, we construct cat as gross foreign assets relative to GDP, i.e. $cat_k = (A_k + L_k/Y_k)$, and cumulative equity trade as $ceqt_k = (A_k^{eq} + L_k^{eq})/Y_k$, where A_k and L_k are total gross foreign assets and gross liabilities, respectively, and A_k^{eq} and L_k^{eq} are gross foreign equity assets and liabilities. The equity share is then $eqshare_k = (ceqt_k/cat_k)$. Our data are based on Lane and Milesi-Ferretti's (2006) recently updated External Wealth of Nations data set.
8 Note that the size of the coefficient on $eqshare$ is owed to the fact that $eqshare$ is the percentage point deviation from the mean, whereas the other variables are measured in absolute deviations from their respective cross-sectional means.

Bibliography

Artis, Michael J. and Mathias Hoffmann (2006) *The Home Bias and Capital Income Flows between Countries and Regions*, CEPR Discussion Papers, No. 5691.

—— (forthcoming) 'Financial Globalization, International Business Cycles and Consumption Risk Sharing', to appear in *Scandinavian Journal of Economics*. An almost identical working paper version is available at http://papers.ssrn.com/abstract=1069601.

Asdrubali, P., P.E. Sørensen and O. Yosha (1996) 'Channels of interstate risk sharing: United States 1963–90', *Quarterly Journal of Economics* 111: 1081–110.

Backus, D., Kehoe, P. and Kydland, F. (1992) 'International real business cycles', *Journal of Political Economy* 100(4): 745–75.

Becker, S.O. and Hoffmann, M. (2006) 'Intra- and international risk sharing in the short-run and the long-run', *European Economic Review* 59: 777–806.

Blanchard, O. and F. Giavazzi (2002) 'Current account deficits in the EuroArea: the end of the Feldstein–Horioka puzzle?', *Brookings Papers in Economic Activity* 2: 147–209.

Cochrane, J.H. (1991) 'A simple test of consumption insurance', *Journal of Political Economy* 99(5): 957–76.

Crucini, M. (1999) 'On international and national dimensions of risk sharing', *Review of Economics and Statistics*, February, 81(1): 73–84.

Feldstein, M. and C. Horioka (1980) 'Domestic saving and international capital flows', *Economic Journal* 90: 314–29.

Gourinchas, Pierre-Olivier and Hélène Rey (2007) 'International financial adjustment', *Journal of Political Economy* 115(4): 665–703.

Hau, Harald and Hélène Rey (2006) 'Exchange rates, equity prices and capital flows', *Review of Financial Studies* 19(1): 273–317.

Hess, G.D. and K. Shin (1998) 'Intranational business cycles in the United States', *Journal of International Economics* 44: 289–313.

Heston, A., R. Summers and B. Aten (2006) *Penn World Table Version 6.2*, Center for International Comparisons at the University of Pennsylvania (CICUP), September.

Imbs, Jean (2006) 'The real effects of financial integration', *Journal of International Economics* 68: 296–324.

Kose, M. Ayhan, Cristopher Otrok and Charles. H. Whiteman (2003) 'International business cycles: world, region, and country-specific factors', *American Economic Review* 93(4): 1216–39.

—— (2005) *Understanding the Evolution of World Business Cycles*, IMF Working Paper No. 211/2005.

Lane, P.D. (2000) 'International investment positions: a cross-sectional analysis', *Journal of International Money and Finance* 19(4): 513–34.

—— (2001) 'Do international investment income flows smooth income?', *Weltwirtschaftliches Archiv* 137 (4): 714–36.

Lane, P.D. and G.M. Milesi-Ferretti (2001) 'The external wealth of nations: measures of foreign assets and liabilities for industrial and developing nations', *Journal of International Economics* 55: 263–94.

—— (2003) *International Financial Integration*, International Monetary Fund Staff Papers.

—— (2006) *The External Wealth of Nations Mark II: Revised and Extended Estimates of Foreign Assets and Liabilities, 1970–2004*, International Monetary Fund Working Paper No. 06/69.

—— (2007) 'A global perspective on external positions', in Richard Clarida (ed.) *G7 Current Account Imbalances: Sustainability and Adjustment*, Chicago: University of Chicago Press.

Mace, B. (1991) 'Full insurance in the presence of aggregate uncertainty', *Journal of Political Economy* 99 (5): 928–56.

Mark, N.C. and D. Sul (2003) 'Cointegration vector estimation by panel DOLS and long-run money demand', *Oxford Bulletin of Economics and Statistics* 65: 665–80.

Phillips, P.C.B. and H.R. Moon (1999) 'Linear regression limit theory for nonstationary panel data', *Econometrica* 67(5): 1057–111.

Shiller, R.J. (1993) *Macro Markets: Creating Institutions for Managing Society's Largest Economic Risk*, Clarendon Lectures in Economics Series, Oxford: Oxford University Press.

Sørensen, B.E. and O. Yosha (1998) 'International risk sharing and European monetary unification', *Journal of International Economics* 45: 211–38.

Sørensen, B.E., Y.-T. Wu, O. Yosha and Y. Zu (2007) 'Home bias and international risk sharing: twin puzzles separated at birth', *Journal of International Money and Finance* 26: 587–605.

Stock, James H. and Mark W. Watson (2005) 'Understanding changes in international business cycle dynamics', *Journal of the European Economic Association* 3(5), September: 968–1006.

Stockman, Alan C. and Linda L. Tesar (1995) 'Tastes and technology in a two-country model of the business cycle: explaining international co-movements', *American Economic Review* 85(1): 168–85.

Townsend, R.M. (1994) 'Risk and insurance in village India', *Econometrica* 62(3): 39–591.

III.2 Banking across borders

12 Economic integration and financial stability

A European perspective

Gianni De Nicolò and Alexander Tieman

Introduction[1]

Research on synchronization of real activity and financial integration in Europe has intensified in the past few years. Nevertheless, the implications of integration for financial stability remain largely unexplored. This chapter aims at contributing to filling in this gap.

Structural changes in the environment in which financial firms operate, such as increased real synchronization and advances in financial integration, may affect individual and system-wide risk profiles of financial intermediaries differentially (see De Nicolò and Kwast 2002; De Nicolò *et al.* 2004a). On the one hand, enhanced synchronization in real activity may *reduce* the benefits of cross-country diversification. If either the shocks hitting a set of economies (and the relevant borrowers) become more similar or the transmission mechanism of country-specific shocks becomes stronger, or both, then the pool of diversifiable (credit and market) risks available to intermediaries may shrink. On the other hand, financial integration may enhance diversification opportunities for *individual* intermediaries, which can rely on enlarged investment opportunities across activities and borders to enhance expected returns for the same amount of risk. Yet, a *set* of intermediaries may become less diversified as a whole if their exposures to the same risks increase, either by choice or because the sources of 'aggregate' risk have become more similar. Moreover, increased linkages among intermediaries through enhanced common exposures to financial markets may make their exposure to contagion more likely.

Disentangling these possibly countervailing effects on financial stability is the main task of this chapter. Accomplishing this task requires first assessing whether increases in real synchronization and advances in financial integration have indeed occurred, since the existing literature does not offer unequivocal answers. Second, it requires constructing measures of systemic risk, and relating them to outcomes of changes in real synchronization and financial integration.

With regard to real synchronization, several studies have attempted to identify a 'European business cycle', but research on the existence of such an object is still ongoing; as a result, few studies have focused on *changes* in real synchronization.[2] Moreover, this literature has dealt almost exclusively with fluctuations of GDP and/or industrial production growth rates. As our focus is on the impact of changes in real synchronization on the risk profiles of financial institutions through their portfolio choices, synchronization of *volatility* of growth rates of real activity may be as important as, if not more important than, synchronization in levels.

With regard to financial integration, recent studies have documented increased convergence in prices of money and bond markets, while noting the slower pace of price convergence in retail bank credit markets (Barros *et al.* 2005; Baele *et al.* 2004; Adam *et al.*

2002). However, the literature exhibits mixed results concerning the integration of equity markets. As stressed by Adjaouté and Danthine (2004), a difficulty in assessing integration lies in disentangling pricing effects from changes in fundamentals. Yet we view an assessment of advances in equity market integration as a robust gauge of advances in financial integration more generally, since equity markets are ones in which claims on a large variety of countries' investment opportunities are traded, and integration in such markets does not necessarily follow mechanically from cross-country convergence of interest rates.

We proceed in three steps. First, we assess cross-country convergence of the first *and* second moments of output growth. The consideration of second moments is novel, and turns out to be informative on the changing nature of common versus country-specific driving forces of the dynamics of real activity. Second, we test whether cross-country convergence of estimates of a discount factor used to price 'idiosyncratic' risks in equity markets has occurred, employing a version of the methodology introduced by Flood and Rose (2005). Finally, we document the dynamics of proxy measures of systemic risk based on data for a set of large European banks and insurance companies in the past 15 years. We test convergence in both levels and volatility of these dynamics, and assess whether the risk profiles of these financial institutions have become more sensitive to common real and financial shocks. In doing so, we view the sensitivity of financial institutions' risk profiles to common real and financial shocks as a useful metric to gauge the implications of increased synchronization in real activity and advances of financial integration through the overall exposure of intermediaries to 'common' market and credit risks.

Our investigation yields three main sets of results. First, we find evidence of increased synchronization in the dynamics of real activity since the early 1980s, in the form of declining trends in the cross-country dispersion in the mean *and* volatility of industrial production monthly growth rates. These declining trends are found after controlling for common shocks, whose magnitude has become smaller, and are mainly driven by business cycle synchronization. Second, we find evidence of increased equity market integration since the early 1990s, in the form of a declining trend in the cross-country dispersion of expected discount factors estimated in each of the European equity markets considered. Third, we find lack of evidence of a decline in risk profiles for European banks and insurance companies during the period 1990–2004. Importantly, we find that these risk profiles have converged, and that the sensitivity of bank risk profiles to both common real and financial shocks has significantly increased. An interpretation of these findings is that increased synchronization in real activity and advances in financial integration may have reduced the benefits of cross country diversification.

The remainder of the chapter consists of three sections. The first assesses synchronization in real activity, while the second considers integration of equity markets. Then the next constructs indicators of system-wide financial risk for a set of systemically important banks and insurance companies in a large set of European countries, and studies their dynamics. A further section assesses the sensitivity of our indicators of systemic risks to real and financial shocks. Concluding comments complete the chapter.

Synchronization of real activity

We gauge changes in synchronization of real activity by the evolution of the cross-country dispersion in the first *and* second conditional moments of seasonally adjusted monthly industrial production growth (IPG) for the 10 European countries for which we have complete data for the period from January 1961 to December 2004.[3] Subject to an important qualification detailed below, a downward trend in the dynamics of the *cross-country variance* of IPG *and* its country-specific volatility may capture increased synchronization in real activity, as this indicates increased correlation of the IPG series in the sample. As shown in Solnik and Roulet (2000), under the assumption that the data generating process for a sufficiently large set of variables is described by a factor model, the evolution of their cross-sectional dispersion is inversely related to their pairwise correlation. A statistical model for such dynamics is obtained as follows.

Let X_{it} denote IPG in country i at date t. X_{it} turns out well described by the following E(xponential)GARCH(1,1) model:

$$X_{it} = \alpha_{it} + \beta_i F_t + \gamma X_{it-1} + h_{it}\varepsilon_{it} \tag{1}$$

$$\ln(h_{it}^2) = a_{it} + b\varepsilon_{it-1}^2 + c\ln(h_{it-1}^2) \tag{2}$$

The term F_t in the mean equation (1) is a risk factor common to all countries. The variance equation (2) describes the evolution of country-specific volatility. As customary, the innovations ε_{it} are assumed to be independent and identically distributed (i.i.d.) and normally distributed with zero mean and unit variance.

We take a weighted average of IPG rates as a proxy measure of the *common component* of IPG rates. Thus, we set $F_t = \sum_i w_{it}X_{it}/N$. This common component is measured using the time-varying weights proposed by Lumsdaine and Prasad (2003), where $w_{it} \equiv \tilde{h}_{it}^{-1} / \sum_i \tilde{h}_{it}^{-1}$, and variances $\tilde{h}_{it}$ are obtained by estimates of model (1)–(3) without the common factor. This specification embeds the assumption that the relative conditional standard deviation is a measure of the degree of commonality of countries' real fluctuations.

Stock and Watson (2005) have documented a reduction in the volatility of G-7 business cycles, and argued that this has been associated with a reduction in the magnitude of common shocks. Have reductions in volatility and the magnitude of common shocks occurred in Europe? The answer is affirmative. Note that by construction, F_t is described by an EGARCH(1,1) model. As shown in Figure 12.1, the estimated conditional variance and the residuals of both series appear to exhibit a downward trend. Furthermore, we tested for such a downward trend by estimating the EGARCH model for F_t with a trend both in the mean and variance equations. As shown in Table 12.1, the coefficient of the time trend in the conditional mean and variance is negative and highly significant.

To obtain a model for the cross-country variance of IPG and its volatility, note that the conditional mean and variance of X_{it} are given by $m_{t-1}(X_{it}) \equiv \alpha_{it} + \beta_i E_{t-1}F_t + \gamma X_{it-1}$ and by $\text{var}_{t-1}(X_{it}) \equiv \beta_i^2\sigma_F^2(t) + h_{it}^2$ respectively. Assume that the coefficients $\{\alpha_{it}, \beta_i, a_i\}$ are distributed cross-sectionally with means $\{\alpha_t, \beta, a\}$ and variances $\{\sigma_{\alpha t}^2, \sigma_\beta^2, \sigma_a^2\}$, and that covariances among all these random variables, as well as that of X_{it-1} and F_t and each of these, are approximately nil. Under these assumptions, the *cross-sectional variances* of $m_{t-1}(X_{it})$ and h_{it}^2 are given by

$$\sigma_X^2(t) \equiv E(m_{t-1}(X_{it}) - Em_{t-1}(X_{it}))^2 = \sigma_{\alpha t}^2 + \sigma_\beta^2(E_{t-1}F_t)^2 + \gamma^2\sigma_X^2(t-1) \tag{3}$$

$$\sigma_{h^2}^2(t) \equiv E(h_{it}^2 - Eh_{it}^2)^2 = \sigma_{at}^2 + b^2\sigma_{\varepsilon^2}^2(t-1) + c^2\sigma_{h^2}^2(t-1) \tag{4}$$

Increased synchronization in real activity occurs if $\sigma_{\alpha t}^2$ and/or σ^2 exhibit a declining path. Note that a decline in $\sigma_X^2(t)$ exclusively driven by a decline in the magnitude of common shocks

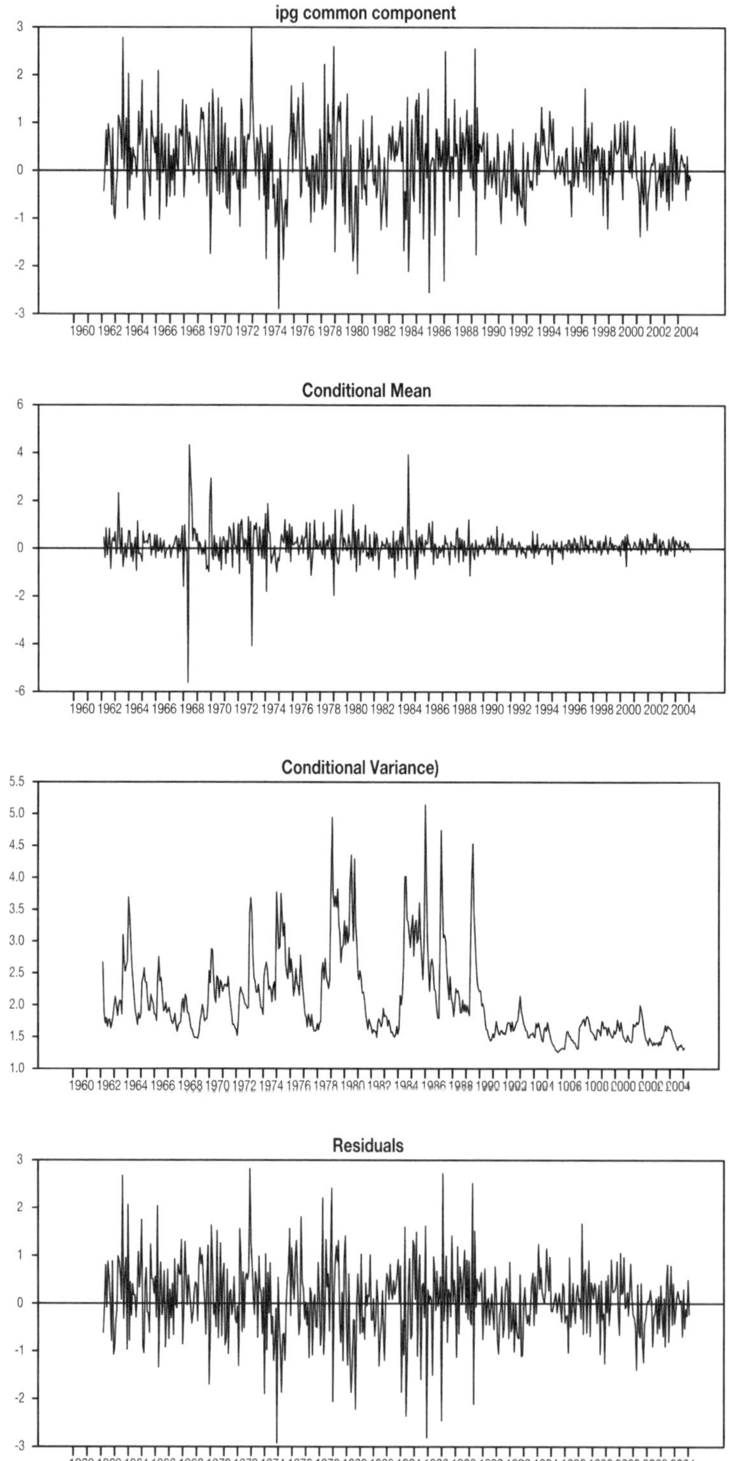

Figure 12.1 EGARCH estimates of IPG common component.

Table 12.1 EGARCH estimates for the common components of IPG

	Coefficients	*Standard error*	*t-statistic*	*p-value*
Mean equation ($F_t = A_0 + A_1t + A_2Ft - 1 + H_t\eta_t$)				
A0	0.33118	0.07129	4.64574	0.00000
A1	*−0.00057*	*0.00018*	*−3.22896*	*0.00124*
A2	0.03188	0.03612	0.88267	0.37741
Variance equation ($\log H_t^2 = B_0 + B_1t + B_2\eta_{t-1}^2 + B_3 \log H_{t-1}^2$)				
B0	−0.15833	0.19829	−0.79851	0.42457
B1	*−0.00267*	*0.00076*	*−3.51361*	*0.00044*
B2	0.38005	0.08970	4.23701	0.00002
B3	−0.12188	0.24345	−0.50065	0.61662

Notes: Figures in italic refer to the coefficients that are central in the analysis.

$((E_{t-1}F_t)^2)$ (which we have shown above has occurred) would *not* necessarily indicate increased integration, since disconnected economies hit by the same shock would exhibit the same decline.

We estimate the following counterpart of model (3)–(4):

$$\bar{\sigma}_X^2(t) = A_0 + A_1t + A_2(E_{t-1}F_t)^2 + A_3\bar{\sigma}_X^2(t-1) + H_t\eta_t \quad (5)$$

$$\log H_t^2 = B_0 + B_1t + B_2\eta_{t-1}^2 + B_3 \log H_{t-1}^2 \quad (6)$$

Two measures for $\bar{\sigma}_X^2(t)$ are used. The first one is the sample cross-sectional variance of IPG rates. The second one is the variance of *deviations* of IPG of each country from its own trend, obtained by applying the relevant HP filter.[4] This second measure is used to gauge the extent to which detrended and non-detrended dynamics differ. For both measures, we test whether A_1 and/or B_1 are negative.

Table 12.2 reports estimates of model (5)–(6). Both the trend coefficients in the mean equation (6) *and* the variance equation (7) are negative and significant. Moreover, the estimates of these coefficients remain virtually unchanged when the cross-sectional variance of *deviations* of IPG from trend is used. Most important, the relevant trend coefficients remain negative but become highly significant. This indicates that business cycle convergence is the primary driver of the decreasing dispersion of IPG rates. Notably, increased synchronization has occurred not only in the form of increased correlation of IPG fluctuations across countries, but also in terms of increased correlation of their (country-specific) volatilities.

To gauge the approximate timing of increased synchronization, we estimated model (1)–(2) for each country with dummies for different decades in both the mean and variance equations. As shown in Table 12.3, increased synchronization in the form of a decline in the cross-country variance of IPG rates started to occur in the early 1980s. By contrast, the cross-country dispersion in the variance of IPG volatility does not exhibit a decline. This result, coupled with the significant decline found earlier, suggests that convergence in volatility is either driven by a subset of countries in the sample or has occurred at different points in time in some countries, or both.

Summing up, synchronization in real activity appears to have increased since the early 1980s. It has been primarily driven by increases in business cycle synchronization, and is not the mechanical outcome of a decline in the magnitude of common shocks.

Table 12.2 EGARCH estimates for cross-country variances of IPG and detrended IPG

Mean equation: $\bar{\sigma}_X^2(t) = A_0 + A_1 t + A_2(E_{t-1}F_t)^2 + A_3\bar{\sigma}_X^2(t-1) + H_t\eta_t$

Variance equation: $\log H_t^2 = B_0 + B_1 t + B_2\eta_{t-1}^2 + B_3 \log H_{t-1}^2$

	Coeff	*Standard error*	*t-statistic*	*Signif*
Mean equation				
A0	5.832508368	2.292758087	2.54388	0.01096278
A1	*−0.007229695*	*0.004513876*	*−1.60166*	*0.10923082*
A2	2.918317416	0.859319970	3.39608	0.00068359
A3	0.085131670	0.084094149	1.01234	0.31137665
Variance equation				
B0	4.814365906	1.578460677	3.05004	0.00228812
B1	*−0.006901057*	*0.002589526*	*−2.66499*	*0.00769909*
B2	0.588642141	0.152287022	3.86535	0.00011093
B3	−0.026846689	0.203262590	−0.13208	0.89492192
Detrended				
Mean equation				
A0	5.303880223	0.950224807	5.58171	0.00000002
A1	*−0.006814521*	*0.001873768*	*−3.63680*	*0.00027605*
A2	7.069362688	3.455381054	2.04590	0.04076625
A3	0.233748490	0.069387844	3.36872	0.00075517
Variance equation				
B0	4.617319622	0.890776496	5.18348	0.00000022
B1	*−0.008062957*	*0.001681891*	*−4.79398*	*0.00000164*
B2	0.454190765	0.139146278	3.26412	0.00109803
B3	0.226598798	0.114381371	1.98108	0.04758215

Notes: Figures in italic refer to the coefficients that are central in the analysis.

Equity market integration

One difficulty in testing advances in equity market integration rests on disentangling pricing effects from the effects of fundamental shocks. Here we tackle this problem by using a version of the methodology proposed by Flood and Rose (2005) (FR henceforth), which exploits the pricing of 'idiosyncratic risk', as opposed to systematic risk. As detailed below, an advantage of this methodology is that it does not require taking a stand on a particular asset pricing model.

Consider the standard intertemporal asset pricing equation:

$$p_t^j = E_t(m_{t+1}x_{t+1}^j) = COV_t(m_{t+1}, x_{t+1}^j) + E_t m_{t+1} E_t x_{t+1}^j, \tag{7}$$

where p_t^j is the price of asset j at date t, E_t is the expectations operator, COV_t is the covariance operator conditional on information available at date t, and m_{t+1} is the rate used to discount the income x_{t+1}^j accruing to the holder of the asset at date $t+1$. Equation (8) can be rewritten as:

$$x_{t+1}^j = \delta_t(p_t^j - COV_t(m_{t+1}, x_{t+1}^j)) + \varepsilon_{t+1}^j, \tag{8}$$

Table 12.3 Country-by-country EGARCH estimates for IPG

Mean equation: $X_{it} = D60 + D70 + D80 + D9004 + \beta_i \bar{X}_t + \gamma X_{it-1} + h_{it}\epsilon_{it}$
Variance equation: $\ln(h_{it}^2) = D60 + D70 + D80 + D9004 + b\epsilon_{it-1}^2 + c\ln(h_{it-1}^2)$

	Mean equation				*Variance equation*			
	D60	D70	D80	D9004	D60	D70	D80	D9004
Austria	−0.02	0.36	0.13	0.36	0.76	−1.09	−1.15	−0.82
Belgium	0.09	0.02	0.06	0.13	−0.14	0.27	0.23	0.21
France	−0.01	0.24	0.07	0.07	1.27	−2.35	−2.72	−3.01
Germany	0.21	−0.07	0.03	0.04	0.44	−0.83	−0.58	−1.19
Greece	0.70	0.63	0.22	−0.04	0.51	−0.53	−0.30	−0.29
Italy	0.16	0.29	0.08	0.00	0.13	0.15	−0.21	−0.90
Netherlands	0.50	0.14	0.12	0.10	−0.17	0.44	0.91	0.62
Portugal	0.35	0.67	0.41	0.10	0.61	−0.56	−0.84	−0.89
Sweden	0.17	0.04	0.08	0.20	1.10	−1.68	−0.67	−2.30
UK	−0.01	0.04	0.07	−0.03	−0.83	1.59	1.00	0.40
Mean	0.21	0.24	0.13	0.09	0.37	−0.46	−0.44	−0.82
Variance	*0.06*	*0.07*	*0.01*	*0.01*	*0.40*	*1.28*	*1.15*	*1.34*

Notes: Figures in italic refer to the coefficients that are central in the analysis.

where $\delta_t \equiv 1/E_t m_{t+1}$ is the inverse of the expected discount factor (IEDF) and $\varepsilon_{t+1}^j \equiv x_{t+1}^j - E_t x_{t+1}^j$ is a prediction error orthogonal to information available at date t. If all assets traded in a given market are discounted at the same rate, then such asset market is said to be integrated.

As our focus is not on assessing integration per se, but *changes* in integration, we take the *dynamics* of the cross-country variance of estimated IEDFs across different equity markets as our measure of changes in integration. If markets become increasingly integrated, this variance should decline. If they moved towards perfect integration, this variance should converge to zero.

Estimates of IEDFs are obtained as follows. Let the time series vector Z_t denote the set of factors that capture *all* systematic components of (log) returns. Then, $p_t^j = p_{t-1}^j \exp(\beta' Z_t + v_t^j)$, where v_t^j is the idiosyncratic part of asset j return. Following FR, define the 'systematic price' $\tilde{p}_t^j$ as the value of p_t^j conditional on idiosyncratic information available at date t set to zero. Thus, $\tilde{p}_t^j \equiv p_{t-1}^j \exp(\beta' Z_t)$. Normalizing equation (8) by such price yields:

$$\frac{x_{t+1}^j}{\tilde{p}_t^j} = \delta_t\left(\frac{p_t^j}{\tilde{p}_t^j}\right) - \delta_t COV_t\left(m_{t+1}, \frac{x_{t+1}^j}{\tilde{p}_t^j}\right) + \varepsilon_{t+1}^j = \delta_t \exp(v_t^i) + u_{t+1}^j, \tag{9}$$

where $u_{t+1}^j \equiv \varepsilon_{t+1}^j - \delta_t COV_t(m_{t+1}, x_{t+1}^j/\tilde{p}_t^j)$.

Estimates of the IEDF δ_t can thus be obtained through regressions (9) by means of the following two-step procedure. In the first step, the 'systematic price' $\tilde{p}_t^j$ of value-weighted industry portfolios for each stock market is estimated by OLS, using the set of principal components of returns to factor out systematic risks. Their number is identified by standard statistical procedures. In the second step, returns are normalized with the estimated systematic price $\hat{p}_t^j$, and the IEDF estimates for each equity market and date are obtained by means of OLS cross-sectional regressions of the type:

$$\frac{x_{t+1}^j}{\hat{p}_t^j} = c_t + \delta_t \exp(v_t^i) + u_{t+1}^j \tag{10}$$

As stressed by Marshall (2005), the constant is needed to control for date-specific (aggregate) shocks that can still be embedded into the IEDF estimates. This estimation procedure was applied to the 13 sectoral portfolios and 9 countries for which monthly data from Datastream were available for the period from January 1975 to December 2004.[5]

All IEDF estimates exhibit correlation with future returns and first-order autocorrelation not significantly different from zero. They also exhibit high volatility, but standard tests reject the hypothesis of ARCH effects. It turns out that the dynamics of the IEDFs for country i at date t, denoted by M_{it}, is well represented by a simple random walk with drift. Thus, we gauge whether equity market integration has advanced by testing the significance of a time trend in the following equation for the cross-country variance of IEDFs, denoted by $\bar{\sigma}_M^2(t)$:

$$\bar{\sigma}_M^2(t) = A_0 + A_1 t + \eta_t \tag{11}$$

Table 12.4 reports estimates of (11), specified with a time trend as well as with a set of decade-long dummies. As shown in panel A, the trend coefficient is negative and significant. As shown in panel B, increased integration appears to have occurred approximately since the early 1990s. This is also confirmed by simple tests of differences in slopes associated with decade-long dummies. As shown in panel C, these results are further validated by estimated time trends for the IEDF for each country, since the cross-country variance of the decade-long dummies exhibits a decline from the early 1990s.

In sum, European equity market integration appears to have advanced since the early 1990s. This result is consistent with the conjectures advanced by Adjaouté and Danthine (2004), and with the finding of Baele *et al.* (2004), who document European stock returns and volatility as increasingly affected by 'common' European shocks.

Systemic risk and integration

Measures of systemic risk

Our indicators of systemic risk are distance-to-default (DD) measures of 'portfolios' of sets of publicly traded, systemically important European banks and insurance companies. These measures are based on the structural valuation model of Black and Scholes (1973) and Merton (1974) (BSM hereafter).[6] In the BSM model, the portfolio's equity is viewed as a call option on the portfolio's assets, with strike price equal to the current book value of total liabilities. When the value of the portfolio's assets is less than the strike price, its equity value is zero. The market value of assets is not observable, but can be estimated using equity values and accounting measures of liabilities.

Under the assumption that asset values follow a lognormal process, the DD of a *portfolio* of N firms (indexed by i) is given by:

$$DD_t = \frac{\ln(\frac{V_t^P}{L_t^P}) + (\mu_P - 0.5\sigma_P^2)}{\sigma_P},$$

Table 12.4 Dependent variables: cross-country variance of IEDFs and country IEDFs

	Coeff	*Standard error*	*t-statistic*	*Signif*
Panel A: $\bar{\sigma}_M^2(t) = A_0 + A_1 t + \eta_t$				
A0	0.238763917	0.032929671	7.25072	0.00000000
A1	*−0.000240336*	*0.000106836*	*−2.24957*	*0.02447599*
Panel B: $\bar{\sigma}_M^2(t) = D702 + D801 + D802 + D901 + D902 + D00 + \eta_t$				
D702	0.1727069830	0.0193907237	8.90668	0.00000000
D801	0.2497064481	0.0464092453	5.38053	0.00000007
D802	0.1860275694	0.0201381090	9.23759	0.00000000
D901	0.1888773756	0.0223010268	8.46945	0.00000000
D902	0.1544279148	0.0150023740	10.29357	0.00000000
D00	0.1431732182	0.0150554668	9.50972	0.00000000

Panel C: $EDF_i(t) = D702 + D801 + D802 + D901 + D902 + D00 + \eta_t$

	d702	*d801*	*d802*	*d901*	*d902*	*d00*
Austria	1.20645	1.10617	1.29210	1.16723	1.19304	1.20955
Belgium	1.13181	1.17612	1.22143	1.22645	1.17590	1.26687
Denmark	1.11991	1.27833	1.22076	1.23424	1.26985	1.15297
France	1.17015	1.19635	1.24437	1.28162	1.22491	1.20120
Germany	1.30347	1.25389	1.14590	1.15146	1.12503	1.13513
Ireland	1.05380	1.03319	1.27659	1.26040	1.28902	1.19700
Italy	1.30551	1.26973	1.27198	1.28658	1.34620	1.24998
Netherlands	1.20677	1.20968	1.23937	1.24176	1.25930	1.15309
UK	1.23885	1.25970	1.13021	1.20395	1.27444	1.26789
Mean	1.19297	1.19813	1.22697	1.22819	1.23974	1.20374
Variance	*0.00704*	*0.00684*	*0.00315*	*0.00221*	*0.00449*	*0.00252*

where $V^P = \sum_i V_t^i$ and $L_t^P = \sum_{i=1}^{N} L_t^i$ are the total value of assets and liabilities, respectively. The mean and variance of the portfolio are respectively given by $\mu_P = \sum_{i=1} w_t^i \mu^i$ and $\sigma_P = \sum_i \sum_j w_t^i w_t^j \sigma_{ij}$, where $w_t^i = V_t^i / \sum_i V_t^i$ and σ_{ij} is the asset return covariance of firm i and j. Thus, the 'portfolio' DD embeds the structure of risk interdependencies among firms. 'Default' at date $t+1$ occurs when $V_t^P < L_t^P$. Thus, the DD indicates how many standard deviations $Ln(V_t^P / L_t^P)$ has to deviate from its mean in order for default to occur. Since $V_t^P = L_t^P + E_t^P$, where E_t^P is the value of equity, declines in V_t^P / L_t^P imply declines in capitalization (E_t^P / L_t^P).

Lower (higher) levels of the 'portfolio' DD imply a higher (lower) probability of firms' joint failure. Since positive and negative variations in the DD of individual firms are allowed to offset each other, the DD of a portfolio is always higher than the (weighted) sum of the DDs of the individual firms.[7] As a result, the probability of 'failure' associated with the 'portfolio' DD is always lower than that associated with the actual probability of joint failures of sets of firms in the portfolio. Thus, the 'portfolio' DD can be viewed as tracking the evolution of a *lower bound* to the joint probabilities of failure of the firms composing a portfolio. For this reason, and because of the distributional assumptions underlying its derivation,[8] the portfolio DD measure is a *conservative* measure of systemic risk – that is, it is likely to *underestimate* systemic risk.

We constructed portfolios for all banks and insurance companies included in the relevant Datastream indexes during the period from January 1991 to December 2004.[9] The monthly

DD measures were estimated using the methodology described in Vassalou and Xing (2004). At each date, the value of asset, the return on assets and its volatility were derived using the option valuation formula of the BSM model, using one year of daily equity return data preceding the estimation date, and the accounting value of liabilities for the relevant year. This procedure was repeated for each month, and the relevant estimates were used to construct the 'portfolio' DD measures at a monthly frequency. As shown by Duan, Gauthier and Simonato (2004), this procedure yields maximum likelihood estimates of implied asset returns and volatility.

Trends in systemic risk

Figure 12.2 depicts the evolution of bank systemic risk measures and their trend computed applying an HP filter. Over the period 1990–2004, bank systemic risk does not appear to have declined.

One explanation of these dynamics rests on the changes in the composition of sources of income that have occurred during the period examined. European banks exhibited a substantial increase in noninterest income in the past decade (ECB 2004). As documented in De Nicolò *et al.* (2005a), the volatility of noninterest income growth was significantly larger than that of interest income growth at large banks since 1997. Moreover, the correlation between interest and noninterest income growth has been high (0.79 for the EU-15), indicating *decreasing* diversification benefits across traditional and nontraditional business lines. As banks' earnings have increasingly relied on income generated through financial market activity, most large banks have experienced significant increases in asset return volatility since the early 1990s. Substantial increases in capitalization and improvements in returns have occurred as well, but they have not been sufficient to offset increases in asset return volatility. Thus, large European banks may have supported higher-risk/higher-return investments with larger capital buffers. Yet risk-adjusted asset returns have not increased, and overall risk profiles have not declined. Using a different systemic risk metrics but a smaller sample of European financial institutions, Hartmann, Straetmans and de Vries (2005) provide further evidence consistent with our results.

These findings, and the attendant interpretation, do not characterize only European banks. A similar pattern appears to have characterized the evolution of risk profiles of US banks as well, as documented by De Nicolò, Hayward and Vir Bhatia (2004b) for US large complex banking groups, and by Stiroh (2004), Hartmann *et al.* (2005), Stiroh and Rumble (2006) and Houston and Stiroh (2006) for a large set of US bank holding companies, using different systemic risk metrics. Using a term aptly coined by Stiroh and Rumble, the 'dark side of diversification' has materialized for US banks as well during the same period.

The dynamics of systemic risk profiles for insurance companies is depicted in Figure 12.3. While in most European countries these dynamics are similar to those of banks, cross-country heterogeneity is more marked. In some instances, the systemic risk measures indicate that a decline has occurred recently.

Convergence of systemic risk measures

Hartmann *et al.* (2005) provide evidence of increased systemic risk in the 1990s for a set of large European (and US) banks in the form of increased correlation of measures of extreme realizations of bank stock excess returns. Unlike these measures, our measures of systemic risk are directly related to firms' joint probability of failures, since they take into account

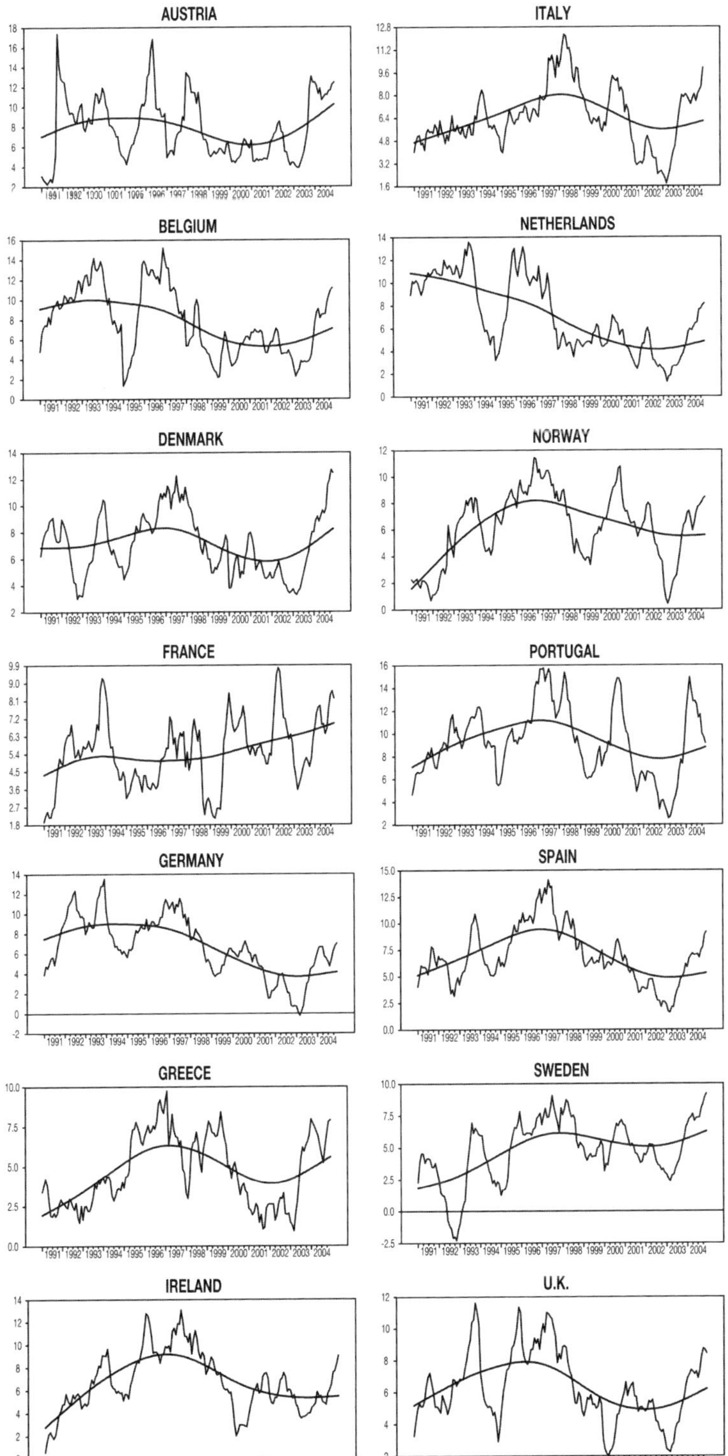

Figure 12.2 Bank DDs.

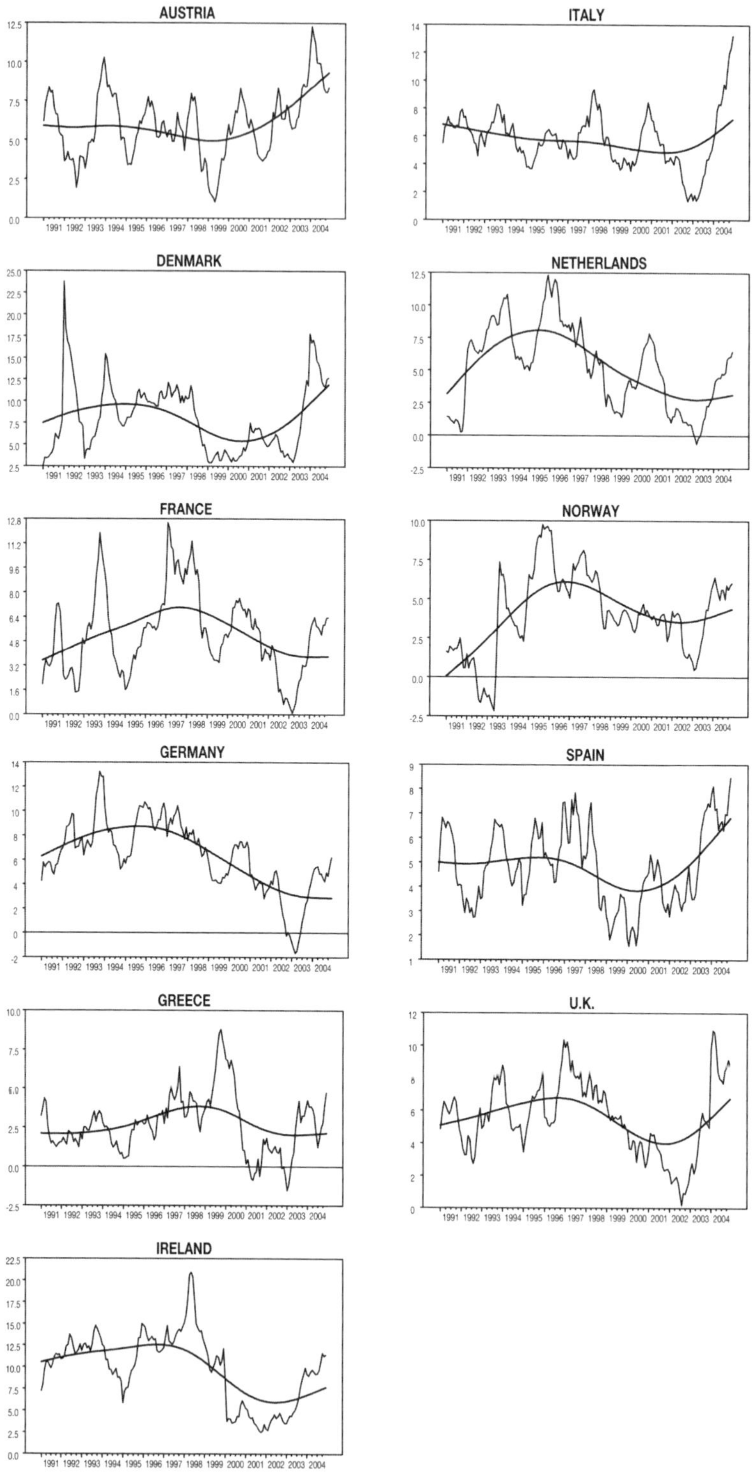

Figure 12.3 Insurance DDs.

not only the evolution of bank returns, but also their volatility and firms' capitalization. Do our measures of systemic risk point at increased correlation in the form of convergence? The answer is affirmative.

We test convergence in both levels *and* volatility of our systemic risk measures. Denote the sample cross-sectional variance of 'portfolio' DDs by $\bar{\sigma}^2_{DD}(t)$. We posit and estimate the following EGARCH-type model for $\bar{\sigma}^2_{DD}(t)$:

$$\bar{\sigma}^2_{DD}(t) = A_0 + A_1 t + A_2 Y_t^2 + A_3 \bar{\sigma}^2_{DD}(t-1) + H_t \eta_t \tag{12}$$

$$\log H_t^2 = B_0 + B_1 t + B_2 \eta^2_{t-1} + B_3 \log H^2_{t-1} \tag{13}$$

As remarked previously, assessing convergence requires controlling for the magnitude of common shocks, since financial firms operating in totally disconnected economies may exhibit increased comovements in their risk profiles just because the economies in which they operate are hit by the same shock. This motivates the introduction of a proxy measure of 'common' risks in the mean equation (12), which is simply measured by the average of each country financial sector DD, $Y_t = \sum_i DD_{it}/N$. Convergence in systemic risk profiles of the banks and insurance sectors is assessed by testing whether the coefficients A_1 and/or B_1 are negative.

Table 12.5 reports estimates of model (12)–(13). Bank systemic risk profiles exhibit convergence in both mean *and* variance, since the trend coefficients are negative and highly significant in both the mean and variance equations. These results provide strong support to the conjecture that risk interdependencies have increased remarkably. By contrast, insurance risk profiles do not exhibit convergence either in the mean or in the variance.

In sum, convergence in systemic risk profiles has occurred for banks, but there is no evidence that it has occurred for insurance companies.

The sensitivity of systemic risk measures to real and financial shocks

Have increased real synchronization and advances in financial market integration affected the dynamics of systemic risk profiles? We address this question by assessing whether the sensitivity of risk profiles of banks and insurance companies to both real and financial shocks common to all countries considered has significantly increased. The impact of such shocks is simply proxied by the common component of real activity estimated previously, and by a value-weighted index of European stock market returns.

An increased sensitivity of the dynamics of systemic risk profiles to the common component of real activity would indicate a greater impact of common real shocks to institutions' exposures, in part due to increased synchronization of real activity. Similarly, an increased sensitivity of these profiles to common financial shocks may be a result of increased financial integration. This is supported by our results on convergence in European IEDFs, as well as by the increased correlation of European stock market returns documented by Bekaert, Hodrick and Zhang (2005).

Changes in these sensitivities are gauged as follows. Let $\rho_t^i \equiv DD_{it} - DD_{it-1}$ denote *monthly changes* in the DD for banks and insurance sectors in country i. Standard tests for ρ_t^i reject ARCH effects for both banks and insurance companies. We estimate a version of the following simple model for ρ_t^i in each country:

$$\rho_t^i = \alpha + \beta_1(t) F_t + \beta_2(t) R_t + \gamma \rho^i_{t-1} + \varepsilon_t \tag{14}$$

Table 12.5 Dependent variables: cross-country variance of portfolios' DDs

Mean equation: $\bar{\sigma}^2_{DD}(t) = A_0 + A_1 t + A_2 Y_t^2 + A_3 \bar{\sigma}^2_{DD}(t-1) + H_t \eta_t$

Variance equation: $\log H_t^2 = B_0 + B_1 t + B_2 \eta_{t-1}^2 + B_3 \log H_{t-1}^2$

	Coeff	*Standard error*	*t-statistic*	*Signif*
BANKS				
Mean equation				
A0	2.130758233	0.796056529	2.67664	0.00743641
A1	*−0.004987358*	*0.001985143*	*−2.51234*	*0.01199330*
A2	0.005940051	0.003149941	1.88577	0.05932652
A3	0.858994960	0.039575910	21.70500	0.00000000
Variance equation				
B0	6.070978192	2.226300055	2.72694	0.00639254
B1	*−0.017596387*	*0.005921549*	*−2.97158*	*0.00296267*
B2	0.220411658	0.116434721	1.89301	0.05835703
B3	−0.224892329	0.226904246	−0.99113	0.32162055
INSURANCE				
Mean equation				
A0	1.103339887	2.667662223	0.41360	0.67916850
A1	*0.003887521*	*0.004944093*	*0.78630*	*0.43169399*
A2	0.057381532	0.021335058	2.68954	0.00715502
A3	0.719393328	0.103899125	6.92396	0.00000000
Variance equation				
B0	9.234640107	9.860517900	0.93653	0.34900198
B1	*−0.021483407*	*0.023667905*	*−0.90770*	*0.36403563*
B2	0.010679293	0.393523834	0.02714	0.97834998
B3	−0.470348664	0.936137459	−0.50244	0.61536123

Notes: Figures in italic refer to the coefficients that are central in the analysis.

where F_t denotes the common component of real activity estimated previously, and R_t denotes the Datastream European stock market index. Variables F_t and R_t are likely to capture distinct sources of real and financial shocks, since their contemporaneous correlation was only 0.06 during the entire period from January 1991 to December 2004.

We wish to test whether the coefficients $\beta_1(t)$ and $\beta_2(t)$ have increased. Given the short length of the sample, regressions (14) are simply estimated allowing these coefficients to differ for three periods approximately four years long: January 1991–December 1994, January 1995–December 1998 and January 1999–December 2004.

Table 12.6 reports regressions (14) for banks, where the coefficients for the three periods considered are denoted by β_{1j} and β_{2j}, $j = 1, 2, 3$, and the relevant indicator functions I_j, $j = 1, 2, 3$. The sensitivity of bank systemic risk measures to common shocks has increased in all countries but Austria, Greece, Italy and Norway, where it has remained approximately constant. In most cases, the relevant coefficients have turned from negative to positive, and significantly so. By contrast, the sensitivity of bank risk profiles to financial shocks has changed differently across countries, increasing in Austria, France, Germany, Greece, Italy, the Netherlands and Portugal, but decreasing in Belgium, Ireland, Norway, Spain, Sweden and the United Kingdom.

The results for insurance companies are similar to those for banks with respect to common real risks, but exhibit heterogeneity with respect to financial risks. As shown in

Table 12.6 Dependent variable: banks DDs changes

Models: (1) $\Delta\rho_t^i = \alpha + \beta_1(t)F_t + \beta_2(t)R_t + \gamma\rho_{t-1}^i + \varepsilon_t$

(2) $\Delta\rho_t^i = \alpha + \sum_{j=1}^{3} \beta_{1j}I_jF_t + \sum_{j=1}^{3} \beta_{2j}I_jR_t + \gamma\Delta\rho_{t-1}^i + \varepsilon_t^i$

	β_1	β_{11}	β_{12}	β_{13}	β_2	β_{21}	β_{22}	β_{23}
Austria	*0.22914*	*0.19882*	*0.24446*	*0.19005*	*3.06991*	*−2.58253*	*5.08501*	*4.14558*
t-statistic	1.12680	0.48277	0.74375	0.86648	0.90713	−0.31624	0.88052	2.02906
Belgium	*−0.05524*	*−0.14530*	*−0.18260*	*0.12222*	*6.79376*	*7.18137*	*6.00944*	*7.22582*
t-statistic	−0.44064	−0.83982	−0.48629	0.89236	3.71733	2.21134	1.41646	4.12920
Denmark	*0.18350*	*−0.02602*	*0.08777*	*0.50247*	*5.39206*	*11.29102*	*5.53111*	*1.83205*
t-statistic	1.72894	−0.21526	0.35315	2.98560	4.54716	5.23163	2.81885	1.05308
France	*−0.06485*	*−0.21530*	*−0.07057*	*0.06281*	*8.51009*	*6.23099*	*10.61516*	*7.25105*
t-statistic	−0.86576	−2.08099	−0.37863	0.58821	6.68370	2.43581	5.36341	4.64868
Germany	*0.00863*	*−0.08972*	*−0.12743*	*0.14603*	*6.01768*	*1.50707*	*5.94823*	*8.47721*
t-statistic	0.10507	−0.52650	−0.64834	1.93410	4.15413	0.24985	3.36277	5.78293
Greece	*0.00882*	*−0.10041*	*0.14396*	*0.02024*	*6.84393*	*4.94287*	*9.23776*	*5.07508*
t-statistic	0.10323	−0.90929	0.64083	0.15302	5.54959	2.61422	5.00959	2.54594
Ireland	*−0.08240*	*−0.26604*	*−0.08318*	*0.10216*	*5.67918*	*6.03562*	*5.79232*	*4.84149*
t-statistic	−1.01429	−1.88952	−0.49246	0.83259	4.19292	3.09929	2.26681	2.32658
Italy	*0.21024*	*0.25366*	*0.11337*	*0.17804*	*7.30423*	*2.14074*	*10.67059*	*7.15589*
t-statistic	2.50871	1.80220	0.77431	1.41244	6.47755	0.86133	7.00629	4.21428
Netherlands	*−0.02262*	*−0.23540*	*−0.03518*	*0.14693*	*5.91218*	*1.99414*	*6.59478*	*6.83980*
t-statistic	−0.26792	−1.62760	−0.16432	1.81176	4.79348	0.59233	3.15099	4.37547
Norway	*0.17415*	*0.20640*	*0.10871*	*0.18771*	*5.42550*	*5.60672*	*5.62960*	*5.31900*
t-statistic	1.95444	1.09798	0.72036	1.61691	4.36156	1.73398	2.78827	3.66942
Portugal	*0.14310*	*−0.14880*	*0.35741*	*0.23421*	*7.23641*	*2.33354*	*8.10958*	*7.98958*
t-statistic	1.55419	−1.09203	2.06801	1.41386	5.71466	0.82094	3.66198	4.03926
Spain	*−0.00595*	*−0.06114*	*−0.14175*	*0.15393*	*8.99014*	*10.51475*	*9.79983*	*7.39503*
t-statistic	−0.07638	−0.45176	−0.78550	1.52710	6.44645	2.56563	4.43565	4.20194
Sweden	*0.11139*	*−0.05850*	*0.01928*	*0.35596*	*5.62820*	*7.54971*	*6.35453*	*3.66768*
t-statistic	1.44782	−0.47774	0.11013	3.77615	4.85987	3.18056	2.92426	3.14802
UK	*−0.11513*	*−0.40599*	*−0.09382*	*0.15302*	*4.95129*	*5.10395*	*5.11531*	*3.94157*
t-statistic	−1.39310	−2.93993	−0.62166	1.18845	4.43553	2.00226	2.62350	2.81685

Table 12.7, the sensitivity of insurance systemic risk measures to common real shocks has increased in all countries but Austria, Denmark, Italy and the United Kingdom, where it has remained approximately constant. On the other hand, the sensitivity to financial shocks has increased in France, Germany, Italy and the Netherlands, but has decreased in Denmark, Ireland and Norway.

Summing up, we find a significant increase in the sensitivity of bank systemic risk profiles to real shocks. In no country have such sensitivities declined. We also find a significant increase in the sensitivities to financial shocks for institutions located in all large countries but Spain and the United Kingdom. The results for insurance risk profile mirror those for banks with regard to increased exposures to common real shocks, but exhibit heterogeneity with respect to common financial shocks. However, the sensitivity of insurance risk profiles to both common real and financial shocks has increased for most institutions located in the largest countries.

Table 12.7 Dependent variable: insurance DDs changes

Models: (1) $\Delta\rho_t^i = \alpha + \beta_1(t)F_t + \beta_2(t)R_t + \gamma\rho_{t-1}^i + \varepsilon_t$

(2) $\Delta\rho_t^i = \alpha + \sum_{j=1}^{3}\beta_{1j}I_jF_t + \sum_{j=1}^{3}\beta_{2j}I_jR_t + \gamma\Delta\rho_{t-1}^i + \varepsilon_t^i$

	β_1	β_{11}	β_{12}	β_{13}	β_2	β_{21}	β_{22}	β_{23}
Austria	*−0.07401*	*−0.13646*	*−0.02889*	*−0.05242*	*5.56877*	*4.79820*	*6.68891*	*4.74129*
t-statistic	−0.87164	−0.79823	−0.18099	−0.41560	3.93998	1.12355	3.95795	2.21433
Denmark	*0.35582*	*1.05606*	*0.12418*	*−0.00905*	*11.31496*	*28.15192*	*7.08159*	*8.84322*
t-statistic	1.32135	1.36990	0.52799	−0.04400	3.67787	1.89994	3.42040	2.21464
France	*−0.19178*	*−0.48789*	*−0.20667*	*0.08307*	*10.62458*	*8.60484*	*12.58048*	*9.19347*
t-statistic	−2.11906	−2.58970	−1.10573	0.89256	7.15602	2.15961	4.77712	5.59050
Germany	*0.02595*	*−0.03629*	*0.01163*	*0.08253*	*6.17503*	*4.73298*	*3.90193*	*9.01931*
t-statistic	0.29904	−0.18959	0.06824	0.84674	3.85809	0.77777	1.72722	6.90630
Greece	*−0.00128*	*−0.16637*	*0.31959*	*−0.05217*	*5.78269*	*4.96145*	*5.78071*	*5.30061*
t-statistic	−0.01313	−1.81309	1.48146	−0.33157	4.71844	2.88784	2.51895	2.65559
Ireland	*−0.00002*	*−0.12271*	*0.04893*	*0.09791*	*4.27298*	*5.76075*	*6.61989*	*0.92890*
t-statistic	−0.00143	−0.92617	0.13156	0.39044	2.58317	1.78139	1.97196	0.44966
Italy	*0.13099*	*0.12708*	*0.05859*	*0.12922*	*5.67917*	*0.60276*	*7.62463*	*6.70161*
t-statistic	1.99638	1.09772	0.50392	1.24325	4.58143	0.19621	3.87340	4.68354
Netherlands	*0.02564*	*−0.14301*	*0.01596*	*0.12346*	*5.43702*	*−1.57370*	*8.48470*	*5.82751*
t-statistic	0.30738	−1.06652	0.07301	1.42235	3.59210	−0.41880	3.98888	3.69937
Norway	*0.04063*	*0.00638*	*0.08005*	*0.08555*	*5.45010*	*8.69135*	*4.54006*	*4.48679*
t-statistic	0.46890	0.04253	0.41735	0.73726	4.95299	2.80595	2.57227	2.96369
Spain	*0.02762*	*−0.10887*	*0.12016*	*0.09305*	*5.97838*	*5.90317*	*7.39693*	*4.33736*
t-statistic	0.39628	−1.16996	0.75689	0.84544	5.60565	4.09959	3.59187	3.03786
UK	*−0.14484*	*−0.28911*	*0.17216*	*−0.19506*	*5.39866*	*7.48984*	*2.26799*	*6.49323*
t-statistic	−1.57067	−2.35482	0.66822	−1.30092	3.21487	3.25397	0.89055	2.04962

Conclusion

In this chapter we have assessed whether synchronization in real activity has increased and equity market integration has advanced, and have examined one dimension through which systemic risk profiles at large, systemically important European banks and insurance companies may have been affected by changes in real synchronization and financial market integration.

We found increased synchronization of real activity starting in the early 1980s, and increased integration in the equities markets starting in the early 1990s. We also found that our measures of bank systemic risk profiles have not declined over the last 15 years, and have converged both in levels and volatility. This evidence suggests that banks may have opted for investment strategies targeting higher-risk/higher expected returns.

Furthermore, we assessed whether the sensitivity of bank and insurance systemic risk profiles to common real and financial shocks have changed during this period. We found that for banks the sensitivity of risk profiles to common real and financial shocks has significantly increased in most countries. The sensitivity of risk profiles of insurance companies to common real shocks has significantly increased as well in most countries, while their sensitivity to common financial shocks appears to have increased only for institutions located in the large continental European countries.

Overall, these findings suggest that increased real synchronization and advances in financial integration may not have necessarily resulted in heightened financial stability. Thus, enhanced monitoring of increased interdependencies in risk profiles among institutions and through markets appears an important task European supervisors may face as integration progresses.

Appendix: Total assets, end-2004 (millions of euro)

Austria	
Banks	
BANK AU.CREDITANSTALT	145,680
ERSTE BANK	139,390
Insurance	
GENERALI HOLDING	10,430
UNIQA	15,125
WIENER STAEDT VZ	12,525
Belgium	
Banks	
ALMANIJ	259,629
DEXIA	349,463
FORTIS (BRU)	521,524
KBC BKVS.HDG.	225,587
Denmark	
Banks	
DANSKE BANK	248,949
JYSKE BANK	16,687
SYDBANK	10,453
Insurance	
ALM BRAND	2,897
CODAN	5,358
TOPDANMARK	4,516
France	
Banks	
BNP PARIBAS	905,001
CREDIT AGRICOLE	814,654
SOCIETE GENERALE	600,897
Insurance	
AGF-ASR.GL.DE FRN.	103,549
APRIL GROUP	419
AXA	440,744
EULER HERMES	5,716
FINAXA	4,973
SCOR	12,542
Italy	
Banks	
UNICREDITO ITALIANO	264,791
SAN PAOLO IMI	209,627
CAPITALIA	131,163
BANCA INTESA	273,181
BANCA MONTE DEI PASCHI	128,662
BCA.NAZ.LAVORO	78,111
Insurance	
CATTOLICA ASSICURAZIONI	14,773
FONDIARIA-SAI	31,381
GENERALI	252,542
MILANO ASSIC.	9,804
PREMAFIN-HLDG.DI PART.	31,493
Germany	
Banks	
BANKGESELLSCHAFT BERLIN	152,041
BAYER.HYPO-UND-VBK.	463,496
COMMERZBANK	419,674
DEUTSCHE BANK	836,368
Insurance	
ALLIANZ	958,579
AMB GENERALI HDG.	85,632
AXA KONZERN	38,438
AXA VERSICHERUNG	7,219
DBV-WINTERTHUR HOLDING	22,398
ERGO VERSICHERUNG	108,988
GERLING	4,327
HANNOVER RUCK.	30,615
KOELN.RUCK.	9,390
KOELN.VERWALT.GESELL.	69
MLP	2,378
MUNCH.RUCK.REGD.	203,501
WUESTENROT & WUERTT.	54,380
Greece	
Banks	
ALPHA BANK	32,917
BANK OF GREECE	32,810
BANK OF PIRAEUS	16,591
EFG EUROBANK ERGASIAS	31,760
EMPORIKI BK.OF GREECE	18,236
NAT.BK.OF GREECE	52,877
Insurance	
ETHNIKI GREEK GEN IN CO	1,621
Ireland	
Banks	
ALLIED IRISH BANKS	102,042
ANG.IR.BK.	34,305
BANK OF IRELAND	106,431
Insurance	
FBD HOLDINGS	1,394
Spain	
Banks	
BANCO ESPANOL DE CREDITO	66,257
BANCO POPULAR ESPANOL	62,522
BANCO SANTANDER CENTRAL HISPANO	569,795
BBV ARGENTARIA	306,218
Insurance	
CORP.MAPFRE 'R'	18,033
GRUPO CATALANA OCCIDENTE	3,536
Sweden	
Banks	
FNSPK. A	112,758

continued on next page

RAS	66,229
UNIPOL	32,201
Netherlands	
Banks	
ABN AMRO HOLDING	607,263
FORTIS (AMS)	521,524
Insurance	
ING GROEP CERTS.	866,201
Norway	
Banks	
DNB NOR	86,097
SPAREBANKEN ROGALAND	7,152
Insurance	
STOREBRAND	20,871
Portugal	
Banks	
BANCO BPI	26,166
BNC.ESPR.SANTO (BESCL)R	45,894
BNC.TOTTA & ACORES	28,824
BCP R	71,678
NORDEA BANK	262,523
SEB A	175,698
SVENSKA HANDBKN	149,071
UK	
Banks	
BARCLAYS	735,337
HBOS	623,776
HSBC HDG.	935,023
LLOYDS TSB GP.	394,145
RYL.BK.OF SCTL.	821,784
STD.CHARTERED	103,769
Insurance	
ADMIRAL GROUP	708
ALEA GP.HDG.(BERMUDA)	4,646
AMLIN	2,858
BEAZLEY	1,136
BENFIELD GROUP	6,052
BRIT INSURANCE HOLDINGS	3,563
CATLIN GROUP	2,437
CHAUCER HOLDINGS	1,074
COX IN.HOLDINGS	1,104
DOMESTIC & GENERAL GP.	474
HISCOX	2,269
JARDINE LLOYD THOMPSON	3,171
KILN	707
ROYAL & SUN ALL.IN.	28,279

Notes

1 We thank Robert Corker, Bob Flood, Ayan Kose, Til Schuermann, Boris Vujcic and participants in seminars at the IMF and the Universitat Pompeu Fabra, the DG-ECFIN 2005 Research Conference, the XIV Tor Vergata Conference, the 8th conference of the ECB-CFS Research Network on 'Financial Integration and Stability in Europe' and the Econometric Society European Meeting 2007 for comments and suggestions. Excellent research assistance by Marianne El-Khoury is gratefully acknowledged. The views expressed in this chapter are those of the authors and do not necessarily represent those of the IMF or IMF policy.

2 For recent reviews of the literature, see Stock and Watson (2005) and Kose *et al.* (2005). Persistence in business cycles heterogeneity within Europe is stressed by Artis (2003).

3 These countries are: Austria, Belgium, France, Germany, Greece, Italy, Netherlands, Portugal, Sweden and the United Kingdom. All results we obtain for first moments hold when we use quarterly GDP growth data instead of IPG data.

4 For data at monthly frequency, here and in the sequel we use the value of the smoothing parameter for the HP filter derived by Ravn and Uhlig (2002), equal to 129,600.

5 The sectors covered are: Banks, Insurance, Financials, Non-Financials, Basic Industries, Cyclical Consumer Goods, Cyclical Services, General Industrials, Information Technology, Non-Cyclical Services, Non-Cyclical Consumer Goods, Resources and Utilities. The countries are: Austria, Belgium, Denmark, France, Germany, Ireland, Italy, Netherlands and the United Kingdom. In all first-step regressions, the first two principal components were sufficient to capture common risks according to standard statistical criteria.

6 Risk measures obtained from structural models, such as the BSM model, have been shown to have predictive power for supervisory ratings, bond spreads and rating agencies' downgrades as well as actual defaults (see Krainer and Lopez 2001; Gropp *et al.* 2006; Arora *et al.* 2005; and Tarashev 2005).

7 This fact can be also seen as an implication of Jensen's inequality.

8 Recall that under the assumption that asset values follow a lognormal process, DD measures do not necessarily capture extreme events adequately. In addition, the simplifying assumption that the liability structure is composed of only equity and debt with fixed maturity for all firms, and no rollover of debt, may lead to underestimates of interest rate risks and other risks associated with contingent (derivative) liabilities.

9 As of end-2004, the Datastream indices included 63 banks and 53 insurance companies, whose identities and asset sizes are reported in the Appendix.

References

Adam, Klause, Tullio Jappelli, Annamaria Menichini, Mario Padula and Marco Pagano (2002) *Analyze, Compare and Apply Alternative Indicators and Monitoring Methodologies to Measure the Evolution of Capital Market Integration in the European Union*, report to the European Commission, Brussels: European Commission.

Adjaouté, Kpate and Jean-Pierre Danthine (2004) 'Equity returns and integration: is Europe changing?', *Oxford Review of Economic Policy* 20(4): 555–70.

Arora, Navneet, Jeffrey R. Bohn and Fanlin Zhu (2005) *Reduced Form versus Structural Models of Credit Risk: A Case Study of Three Models*, Moody's KMV White Paper, February, New York: Moody's.

Artis, Michael J. (2003) *Is There A European Business Cycle?*, CESifo Working Paper Series No. 1053, Munich: CESifo.

Baele, Lieven, Annalisa Ferrando, Peter Hördahl, Elizaveta Krylova and Cyril Monnet (2004) 'Measuring financial integration in the euro area', *Oxford Review of Economic Policy* 20(4): 509–30.

Barros, Pedro Pita, Erik Berglöf, Paolo Fulghieri, Jordi Gual, Colin Mayer and Xavier Vives (2005) *Integration of European Banking: The Way Forward*, CEPR, MED 2.

Bekaert, Geert, Robert J. Hodrick and Xiaoyan Zhang (2005) *International Stock Return Comovements*, NBER Working Paper No. 11906, Cambridge: NBER.

Black, F. and M. Scholes (1973) 'The pricing of options and corporate liabilities', *Journal of Political Economy* 81(3): 637–54.

De Nicolò, Gianni and Myron Kwast (2002) 'Financial risk and consolidation: are they related?', *Journal of Banking and Finance* 26(5): 861–80.

De Nicolò, Gianni, Phillip Bartholomew, Jahanara Zaman and Mary Zephirin (2004a) 'Bank consolidation, internationalization and conglomeration: trends and implications for financial risk', *Financial Markets, Institutions & Instruments* 13(4): 173–217.

De Nicolò, Gianni, Peter Hayward and Ashok Vir Bhatia (2004b) *U.S. Large Complex Banking Groups: Business Strategies, Risks and Surveillance Issues*, IMF Country Report 04/228, July, Washington, DC: International Monetary Fund, pp. 72–86.

De Nicolò, Gianni, Robert Corker, Alexander Tieman and Jan Willem Van-derVossen (2005a) *European Financial Integration, Stability and Supervision*, IMF Country Report 05/266, August, Washington, DC: International Monetary Fund, pp. 113–46.

De Nicolò, Gianni, Alexander Tieman and Robert Corker (2005b) *Large Banking Groups and Financial System Soundness*, IMF Country Report 05/116, March, Washington, DC: International Monetary Fund, pp. 102–11.

Duan, Jin-Chuan, Genevieve Gauthier and Jean-Guy Simonato (2004) 'On the equivalence of the KMV and maximum likelihood methods for structural credit risk models', unpublished, Toronto: University of Toronto.

ECB (2004) 'Accounting for the Resilience of the EU Banking Sector', *Monthly Bulletin*, April, Frankfurt: European Central Bank.

Flood, Robert and Andrew Rose (2005) 'Estimating the expected marginal rate of substitution: a systematic exploitation of idiosyncratic risk', *Journal of Monetary Economics* 52(5): 951–69.

Gropp, R.E., J. Vesala and G. Vulpes (2006) 'Equity and bond market signals as leading indicators of bank fragility', *Journal of Money, Credit and Banking* 32(2): 399–428.

Hartmann, Philipp, Stefan Straetmans and Casper de Vries (2005) *Banking System Stability: A Cross-Atlantic Perspective*, Working Paper No. 527, September, Frankfurt: European Central Bank.

Houston, Joel F. and Kevin J. Stiroh (2006) 'Three decades of financial sector risk, U.S. financial holding companies', July, unpublished, New York: Federal Reserve Bank of New York.

Kose, Ayhan, Christopher Otrok and Charles Whiteman (2005) *Understanding the Evolution of World Business Cycles*, IMF Working Paper 05/211, November, Washington, DC: International Monetary Fund.

Krainer, J. and J.A. Lopez (2001) *Incorporating Equity Market Information into Supervisory Monitoring Models*, FRBSF Working Paper 2001–14, San Francisco: Federal Reserve Bank.

Lumsdaine, Robert L. and Eswar S. Prasad (2003) 'Identifying the common component of international economic fluctuations: a new approach', *Economic Journal* 113, January: 101–27.

Marshall, David (2005) 'Comment on estimating the expected marginal rate of substitution', *Journal of Monetary Economics* 52(5): 971–79.

Merton, Robert.C. (1974) 'On the pricing of corporate debt: the risk structure of interest rates', *Journal of Finance* 29(2): 449–70.

Ravn, Morten O. and Harald Uhlig (2002) 'On adjusting the Hodrick–Prescott filter for the frequency of observations', *Review of Economics and Statistics* 84(2): 371–6.

Solnik, Bruno and Jacques Roulet (2000) 'Dispersion as cross-sectional correlation', *Financial Analyst Journal* 56(1): 54–61.

Stiroh, Kevin J. (2004) 'Diversification in banking: is noninterest income the answer?', *Journal of Money, Credit and Banking* 36(5): 853–82.

Stiroh, Kevin J, and Adrienne Rumble (2006) 'The dark side of diversification: the case of U.S. financial holding companies', *Journal of Banking and Finance* 30(8): 2131–61.

Stock, James H. and Mark W. Watson (2005) 'Understanding changes in international business cycle dynamics', *Journal of the European Economic Association* 3(5): 968–1006.

Tarashev, Nikola A. (2005) *An Empirical Evaluation of Structural Credit Risk Models*, BIS Working Paper, No. 179, July, Basel: Bank for International Settlements.

Vassalou, M. and Y. Xing (2004) 'Default risk in equity returns', *Journal of Finance* 59(2): 831–68.

13 Banking integration and co-movements in EU banks' fragility

Andrea Brasili and Giuseppe Vulpes

Introduction[1]

The aim of this chapter is to analyse co-movements in the fragility of EU-15 banks, and verify to which extent such co-movements have increased over time, following the completion of Monetary Union, the introduction of the euro and the process of European banking integration.

Essentially, co-movements in bank risk derive from the exposure to common shocks, which may come from different sources. They may be related to common macroeconomic shocks, but they may also stem from common exposures to industries, countries or individual counterparts, as well as from interbank linkages (see Upper and Worms 2002; Gropp *et al.* 2006b).

There are several reasons to believe that common shocks affecting EU banks may have increased. First, as regards common macro shocks at the EU-wide level, there seems to be sufficient evidence showing their relevance. Forni and Reichlin (2001), among others, show that the variance in output growth displayed by individual EU countries is largely explained by a European component. Second, as the process of banking and financial integration in Europe has progressed bank linkages have also risen. Hence, while retail banking has remained a largely domestic business, there has been a considerable growth in a number of segments that may have increased the sources of common shocks to which EU banks are exposed. Think, for example, of cross-border interbank exposures, which in the euro area have significantly increased since 1998 (Hartmann *et al.* 2003; Galati and Tsatsaronis 2001). To give an idea of such growth, note that as of December 2005 euro area monetary financial institutions (MFIs) cross-border interbank loans in the EU were 40 per cent of total interbank loans, up from 26 per cent at the end of 1997. Another example is represented by euro area MFIs' cross-border securities holdings, whose growth has been even higher and whose share of the total has more than doubled since 1999 (from less than 40 per cent at the end of 1998 to 84 per cent at the end of 2005). But one could also mention the growth in other segments of business, e.g. syndicated loans, derivatives and country exposures, which may increase the degree of commonality in banks' risk.

Clearly, a growth in co-movements in banks' fragility has consequences in terms of systemic stability, since it increases the likelihood of widespread banking crises. Indeed, as argued by De Nicolò and Tieman (in Chapter 12 in this volume), Stiroh (2004) and Stiroh and Rumble (2006), among others, financial integration may enhance diversification opportunities, thereby improving banks' risk profile. However, this could be true only for individual intermediaries, while the system as a whole may actually become less diversified if its exposure to the same sources of risk increases. This has far-reaching policy implications as regards the lender of last resort function in the EU single financial market (Schinasi and Teixeira 2006), but it may also have important implications for the structuring of banking supervision in Europe, e.g. the split of supervisory competencies between national and supranational or pan-European authorities. Indeed, finding robust evidence of growing linkages between the fragility of banks located in different national jurisdictions increases the extent of cross-border externalities, which is a typical argument in favour of a supervisory authority at EU level (Schoenmaker and Osterloo 2005). Certainly, such an outcome would increase the scope for supervisory co-operation among domestic authorities. This would be especially true if such interconnectedness is related not only to common macroeconomic shocks but also to growing EU-wide banking system specific factors.

Against this backdrop, we provide a measure of co-movements in bank risk by means of a dynamic factor model (Stock and Watson 2002; Forni *et al.* 2000), which allows us to decompose an indicator of bank fragility, the distance to default (DD) (Gropp *et al.* 2004), into three main components: an EU-wide, a country specific and a bank-level idiosyncratic component.

In addition, we measure the influence of common macroeconomic shocks at EU and country level on our fragility indicator. By removing the effects of such common macro shocks we identify a banking sector specific source of fragility which is in turn decomposed into the three components specified above.

A further contribution of our chapter is that, analysing the data in the frequency domain, we are able to distinguish between short-term, cyclical and long-term co-movements in bank fragility. Whereas the former might be related to large shocks or, eventually, some sort of contagion, the latter might be associated with common cyclical shocks or the fact that banking sectors are becoming increasingly similar (or integrated).

While the idea of co-movements in economic and financial variables is not new in the economic literature (see Sargent and Sims 1977) and has recently gained renewed interest, to our knowledge applications to the banking sector are more limited. Indeed, the most recent work has been devoted to measuring co-movements in economic variables, like GDP or inflation, in the context of the business cycle analysis, but there is also a vast literature regarding co-movements in financial variables (see, for instance, among others, Fama and French 1993; Emiris 2002).

Hawkesby, Marsh and Stevens (2003, 2005) provide an application to the banking sector. These authors analyse co-movements in equity returns for a set of US and European large complex financial institutions (LCFI) by using several statistical techniques amongst which is a static factor model. They find a high degree of commonality between asset price developments of most LCFIs. However, their results also show that there is still significant heterogeneity between sub-groups of LCFIs, e.g. according to geography. Increased interconnectedness among banks is also found by De Nicolò and Kwast (2002), who notice a significant rise in stock price correlation for a set of large US banks, which they partly attribute to consolidation in the financial sector. Increased exposure of financial institutions to common shocks is also found in the contribution by De Nicolò and Tieman (Chapter 12), which is very close to ours, as it is based on the same measure of risk, the distance to default (albeit applying a different methodology in gauging the degree of commonality in financial intermediaries' risk). The authors, focusing on a set of large European banks and insurance companies, look at the dynamics of the risk profiles of these institutions and analyse their sensitivity to common shocks in real activity and to a measure of financial integration. They find that the risk profiles of these intermediaries have converged during the past 15 years, and that this convergence is to a large extent related to increased synchronization in real economic activity among European countries, which offsets the diversification benefits coming from financial integration.

The analysis of co-movements in risk is also quite connected to credit risk's portfolio analysis. In both cases, in fact, the focus is on default correlations. Within this context, Nickell and Perraudin (1999), for UK banks, and Lehar (2003), for a sample of international banks, examine bank fragility in a portfolio perspective. To this end, they derive banks' default probabilities from observable market data based on the option pricing theory (similarly to us), and calculate the risk of simultaneous weakness in several banks by considering asset return correlations.

Our approach is different from that followed in the papers mentioned above, since we consider the propagation mechanism of common shocks, which, ultimately, are the sources of asset and default correlation. In other words, this means that different banks may be hit by the same shock but with different time delays (and leads), which allows for bank-level heterogeneity. Indeed, this is one of the main advantages of using a dynamic factor model, which enables the exploitation of much more information than, for instance, a static factor model. In addition, we are able to measure the relative contribution of EU-wide, domestic and idiosyncratic shocks to bank risk, which is the main focus of this chapter.

Our results highlight the fact that co-movements in bank fragility are not negligible at the EU-wide level. Further, it appears that the commonality in bank risk has been significantly increasing since 1999 and that such rise is largely related to the increased relevance of an EU banking system specific component rather than common macroeconomic shocks. Moreover, by analysing co-movements in the frequency domain, we find out that common EU-wide shocks are more relevant at cyclical and/or long-term frequencies, which is in line with the increasing integration in the EU banking system (Cabral *et al.* 2002). However, we notice that co-movements at very high frequencies (i.e. in the very short term) are relevant when one concentrates on large banks, which is consistent with some recent results on bank contagion in Europe (Gropp *et al.* 2006b).

The chapter is structured as follows. We start by describing the methodology underlying our fragility indicator and the data used. We then perform some basic descriptive analyses in order to provide first rough evidence of how EU banks' fragility is interconnected. These descriptive analyses constitute the premises for our dynamic factor model, whose description and results are then reported. Then in the next we assess the role of common macroeconomic shocks at national and EU-wide level in explaining the dynamics of banks' fragility. Concluding comments and an outline of possible lines for future research complete the chapter.

The fragility indicator and the data

The fragility indicator

We use the distance to default (DD) as an indicator of bank fragility. The DD is a Merton-based (i.e. option pricing) indicator derived from the Black and Scholes formula (see KMV 2003).

More specifically, assuming that the market value of a firm's assets follows a stochastic process of the type

$$\ln V_A^T = \ln V_A + \left(r - \frac{\sigma_A^2}{2}\right) \cdot T + \sigma_A \cdot \sqrt{T} \cdot \varepsilon,$$

which expresses the time path of the asset value given its current value (V_A) and a stochastic disturbance normally distributed with zero mean and unit variance ($\varepsilon \approx N(0,1)$).

From this, indicating with D the value of the firm's liabilities, we can define the distance from the default point as follows:

$$d = \ln V_A^T - \ln D = \ln V_A + \left(r - \frac{\sigma_A^2}{2}\right) \cdot T + \sigma_A \cdot \sqrt{T} \cdot \varepsilon - \ln D \Leftrightarrow$$

$$\frac{d}{\sigma_A \cdot \sqrt{T}} = \frac{\ln\left(\frac{V_A}{D}\right) + \left(r - \frac{\sigma_A^2}{2}\right) \cdot T}{\sigma_A \cdot \sqrt{T}} + \varepsilon$$

This yields the formula for the distance to default, which is defined as the number of standard deviations that a firm is from the default point.

$$DD \equiv \frac{d}{\sigma_A \cdot \sqrt{T}} - \varepsilon = \frac{\ln\left(\frac{V_A}{D}\right) + \left(r - \frac{\sigma_A^2}{2}\right) \cdot T}{\sigma_A \cdot \sqrt{T}}$$

We decided to use the DD as a fragility indicator since it represents a measure of bank risk with some desirable properties. In particular, Gropp *et al.* (2004, 2006a) show that this indicator encompasses most elements of bank risk (asset returns, volatility – i.e. asset risk – and leverage) and constitutes a measure not affected by the presence of explicit or implicit safety nets. Further, this indicator, being based on stock market information, is inherently forward looking and available more frequently than traditional balance-sheet indicators (in principle, it can be calculated on a real-time basis). More importantly, the authors show that this measure is more capable than other market indicators of bank fragility (e.g. subordinated bond spread, or stock returns) of predicting a material deterioration in a bank's condition (up to 18 months in advance). Hence, the DD may represent a useful indicator to monitor bank fragility that may complement the information provided by other sources (e.g. balance sheets).

However, the same authors also highlight some limitations of the DD indicator. In particular, the distance to default can be sensitive to trading irregularities which could be particularly high for banks with low trading volumes (typically small banks or banks in a troubled situation). In the context of this work this could mean biasing our results towards not finding evidence of co-movements in the fragility of EU banks.

It follows from the formula that the basic ingredients for the calculation of the DD are V_A and σ_A. They can be calculated from observable market value of equity, V_E, equity volatility, σ_E, and the value of liabilities D, by solving the following system of two equations:

$$V_E = V_A \cdot N(d_1) - D \cdot e^{-rT} \cdot N(d_2)$$

$$\sigma_E = \left(\frac{V_A}{V_E}\right) \cdot N(d_1) \cdot \sigma_A,$$

where

$$d_1 = \frac{\ln(\frac{V_A}{D}) + \left(r + \frac{\sigma_A^2}{2}\right)}{\sigma_A \cdot \sqrt{T}}$$

$$d_2 = d_1 - \sigma_A \cdot \sqrt{T}.$$

We solved the system of two equations by using the generalized gradient method to yield the values for V_A and σ_A. As observable market value of equity, V_E, we employed the end of week equity market capitalization from Thomson Financial Datastream. The equity volatility, σ_E, was estimated by taking the standard deviation of weekly equity returns in a rolling one-year window (i.e. 52 weeks). The total liabilities, D, are obtained from the banks' published accounts, and as risk free rates we used the interest rates on the one-year asset swap. Finally, the maturity of the debt, T, was set to one year, which is a common benchmark assumption without any specific information about the maturity structure of the debt.

Once we had obtained the DDs for each bank in the sample, we calculated their log first difference, $\ln(\Delta DD)$ at weekly and monthly frequencies,[2] in order to partly reduce the noise (which is especially high in financial markets data) that may affect weekly changes but also to better distinguish the short-term from the cyclical and long-term components of co-movements in bank risk.

The sample of banks

The initial sample of banks considered in the work is represented by 160 listed banks for which stock market data (stock price and market capitalization) and debt are available during the period from November 1994 to December 2004.

We estimated the dynamic factor model by using a balanced panel. Hence, we had to delete a number of banks for which data were not available for the whole sample period. We ended up with a sample of 99 banks incorporated in EU-15 countries (new-accession EU countries are not represented), with 529 weekly observations per bank. The list of banks, with their total assets and country of incorporation, is reported in Table 13.1.

The banks in the sample are relatively large (the average asset size amounts to slightly more than EUR 100 billion), but there is also a substantial presence of small to mid-sized banks. Note in this regard that the median size equals €25 billion. The largest bank in the sample is Deutsche Bank (end-2002 total assets of about €760 billion), while the smallest is Union Financière de France Banque, with only €186 million of total assets.

The distribution of the banks by country highlights the relatively high presence of Italian banks (19 banks), while some large countries are relatively underrepresented (there are only 8 French and UK banks). The reduced size of the sample for some countries may constitute a problem when estimating the country component of bank fragility. However, given the approach followed in estimating the dynamic factor model (i.e. the procedure suggested by Stock and Watson 2002), the fact of having a large T should preserve the significance of our results (at least as far as the EU-wide component is concerned).[3] Moreover, since our main interest relies on the estimate of the relevance of the EU-wide component, the fact that the measurement of the national component might be distorted by small sample size problems should not constitute a major issue. Nevertheless, this caveat should be borne in mind when interpreting the results obtained in the work.

Table 13.1 List of banks in the sample

No.	*Bank name*	*Country of incorporation*	*Total assets (€ millions)**
1	Bank für Tirol und Vorarlberg AG	Austria	5,712
2	Bank für Kaernten und Steiermark AG-BKS	Austria	3,733
3	Investkredit Bank AG	Austria	13,479
4	Oberbank AG	Austria	9,689
5	Fortis Bank	Belgium	377,728
6	KBCBank NV	Belgium	208,501
7	Baden-Wuertt. Bank	Germany	26,058
8	Bankgesellschaft Berlin AG	Germany	173,599
9	Bayerische Hypo- und Vereinsbank AG	Germany	678,340
10	Commerzbank AG	Germany	421,809
11	DePfa Deutsche Pfandbriefbank AG	Germany	180,899
12	Deutsche Bank AG	Germany	758,256
13	DVB Bank AG	Germany	9,389
14	Eurohypo AG	Germany	225,833
15	HSBC Trinkaus & Burkhardt KGaA	Germany	11,049
16	IKB Deutsche Industriebank AG	Germany	36,336
17	Vereins- und Westbank AG	Germany	21,232
18	Württembergische Hypothekenbank AG	Germany	29,253
19	Danske Bank A/S	Denmark	235,870
20	Fionia Bank	Denmark	2,341
21	Jyske Bank A/S	Denmark	20,633
22	Ringkjobing Bank	Denmark	400
23	Roskilde Bank	Denmark	1,147
24	Spar Nord Bank	Denmark	4,269
25	Sydbank A/S	Denmark	8,990
26	Vestjysk Bank A/S	Denmark	997
27	Banco Atlantico	Spain	9,720
28	Banco de Andalucia	Spain	4,978
29	Banco de Castilla	Spain	2,572
30	Banco de Credito Balear	Spain	1,134
31	Banco de Galicia	Spain	2,272
32	Banco de Valencia	Spain	6,618
33	Banco de Vasconia	Spain	1,860
34	Banco Español de Crédito SA, BANESTO	Spain	49,510
35	Banco Guipuzcoano SA	Spain	5,044
36	Banco Pastor SA	Spain	8,870
37	Banco Popular Español SA	Spain	41,899
38	Banco Santander Central Hispano	Spain	319,030
39	Bankinter	Spain	22,542
40	Banco Bilbao Vizcaya Argentaria SA	Spain	274,934
41	Alandsbanken Abp - Bank of Aland Ltd	Finland	1,813
42	OKOBank - OKOOsuuspankkien Keskuspankki Oyj	Finland	12,709
43	Sampo Plc	Finland	25,094
44	Banque de la Réunion	France	1,496
45	BNP Paribas	France	710,305
46	Crédit Foncier de France	France	43,857
47	Crédit Agricole d'Ile-de-France	France	18,537
48	Natexis Banques Populaires	France	133,400
49	Société Générale	France	501,265
50	Sophia Austria	France	3,407

Table 13.1 (continued)

No.	*Bank name*	*Country of incorporation*	*Total assets (€ millions)**
51	Union Financière de France Banque	France	
52	Alpha Bank AE	Greece	
53	Bank of Attica SA	Greece	
54	Piraeus Bank SA	Greece	
55	EFG Eurobank Ergasias SA	Greece	
56	Egnatia Bank SA	Greece	
57	Emporiki Bank of Greece SA	Greece	
58	General Bank of Greece SA	Greece	
59	National Bank of Greece SA	Greece	
60	Allied Irish Banks plc	Ireland	
61	Bank of Ireland	Ireland	
62	Banca Fideuram SpA	Italy	
63	Banca Intesa SpA	Italy	
64	Banca Lombarda e Piemontese SpA	Italy	
65	Banca Nazionale del Lavoro SpA-BNL	Italy	
66	Banca Popolare di Intra	Italy	
67	Banca Popolare di Lodi	Italy	
68	Banca Popolare di Milano SCaRL	Italy	
69	Banca popolare dell'Emilia Romagna	Italy	
70	Banche Popolari Unite - BPU Banca	Italy	
71	Banco di Sardegna SpA	Italy	
72	Capitalia SpA	Italy	
73	Credito Bergamasco	Italy	
74	Credito Emiliano SpA	Italy	
75	Credito Valtellinese SCarl	Italy	
76	Fineco Group SpA	Italy	
77	Mediobanca SpA	Italy	
78	Reti Bancarie Holding SpA	Italy	
79	San Paolo IMI	Italy	
80	UniCredito Italiano SpA	Italy	
81	Kredietbank SA Luxembourgeoise KBL	Luxembourg	
82	ABN Amro Holding NV	Netherlands	
83	ING Bank NV	Netherlands	
84	Kas Bank NV	Netherlands	
85	Banco BPI	Portugal	
86	Banco Totta & Açores, SA	Portugal	
87	BANIF SGPS SA	Portugal	
88	Banco Comercial Português, SA	Portugal	
89	Banco Espirito Santo SA	Portugal	
90	Skandinaviska Enskilda Banken AB	Sweden	
91	Svenska Handelsbanken	Sweden	
92	Abbey National Plc	United Kingdom	
93	Barclays Bank Plc	United Kingdom	
94	HBOS plc	United Kingdom	
95	HSBC Bank plc	United Kingdom	
96	Royal Bank of Scotland plc	United Kingdom	
97	Schroders Plc	United Kingdom	
98	Singer & Fried.	United Kingdom	
99	Standard Chartered Plc	United Kingdom	

Note: * As of end-2002.

Preliminary descriptive analyses

In order to provide first rough evidence of co-movements in bank fragility we conducted a set of preliminary descriptive analyses, as basic premises to our dynamic factor model.

Contemporaneous correlation analyses

We first looked at the contemporaneous correlation in the weekly and monthly changes in banks' DDs. We considered the monthly changes in order to partly reduce the noise (which is especially high in financial markets data) that may affect weekly changes. The correlations were calculated for the sample of 99 banks considering the entire period, and the periods before and after 1 January 1999 in order to check whether corresponding with the start of the EMU there has been a rise in the degree of co-movements between the fragility of EU banks. Of course the choice of the break-point in the sample is purely arbitrarily, but without any further reference as to where to fix it, the EMU starting date becomes a quite natural candidate. It is also clear that finding an increase in correlations between the two sub-periods does not necessarily mean that it has been 'caused' by the EMU process. Nevertheless, such a correspondence would certainly be of some interest, e.g. for research purposes. Results are summarized in Table 13.2.

In general, correlations in bank risk appear rather low on average (6 per cent for weekly changes, up to 14 per cent in the case of monthly changes). Distinguishing between correlations among banks belonging to the same country (domestic correlation) and correlations among banks from other countries (cross-border correlation), it appears that the average domestic correlation, albeit still low, is dominant over the cross-border one: while the average domestic correlation stands at 14 per cent (23 per cent for the monthly changes), the cross-border one equals only 5 per cent (12 per cent for monthly changes). Note, however, that the distinction made is not appropriate because part of what has been labelled domestic correlation may be due to EU-wide shocks. This is one of the reasons why a factor model is particularly useful, since it yields components of banks' fragility which are mutually orthogonal.

Splitting the sample in the two sub-periods there seems to be a slight increase in average pairwise correlations: taking the weekly changes the average correlation equals 4 per cent in the period before 1999, while it goes up to 8 per cent. A similar finding is obtained with the monthly changes.

Nonetheless, these results are not surprising as small and mid-sized banks are largely affected by developments in their country of incorporation or by idiosyncratic shocks. Further, as will be shown in the next section, contemporaneous correlations may not fully capture the transmission of shocks between banks.

Table 13.2 Mean correlations in EU banks' DDs

		Weekly changes			*Monthly changes*		
		Total	*Domestic*	*Cross-border*	*Total*	*Domestic*	*Cross-border*
All banks	All sample period	0.06	0.14	0.05	0.14	0.23	0.12
	1995–8	0.04	0.12	0.03	0.11	0.20	0.10
	1999–2004	0.08	0.16	0.07	0.15	0.26	0.14
Large banks	All sample period	0.17	0.27	0.16	0.35	0.44	0.34
	1995–8	0.10	0.24	0.08	0.21	0.35	0.19
	1999–2004	0.24	0.28	0.23	0.42	0.47	0.41

We moved then to look at the correlation in bank fragility among a set of large banks, defined somewhat arbitrarily as those with total assets as of end-2002 above €100 billion (28 banks belonging to 9 EU countries).

In this case, the average correlations appear significantly larger considering both the weekly (17 per cent) and the monthly changes (35 per cent): in both cases they are, in fact, above the standard threshold $\pm 2/\sqrt{T}$ (where T is the number of observations) denoting statistically significant correlations. Further, there seems to be a material increase in the average correlation in the post-1999 period: taking the weekly changes, the mean correlation goes up to 24 per cent from 10 per cent in the first part of the sample. It is worth noting that the observed increase is largely owing to cross-border correlations, which rise to 23 per cent in the post-1999 period from 8 per cent in the first sub-sample.

Correlations increase significantly between the two sub-periods also when the monthly changes are considered (from 21 per cent to 42 per cent). Even in this case the rise can be noticeably attributed to cross-border correlations (41 per cent in the post-1999 period from 19 per cent in the earlier part of the sample).

Looking at average correlations, though, may not fully reveal the degree of commonality in bank risk among EU banks. Indeed there could be large pairwise correlations which are then offset by low or even negative correlations. For the analysis of co-movements in bank fragility (and for financial stability purposes) it might thus be relevant to consider the distribution of such pairwise correlations. One can, in fact, think that even relatively few large correlations between the level of risk of banks incorporated in different countries might be sufficient to cause significant cross-border co-movements in bank fragility. Figures 13.1–13.4 report the frequency distribution of pairwise correlations between the changes in banks' DDs in the two sample-periods distinguishing among domestic and cross-border correlations as specified above. The figures reinforce the finding previously highlighted of

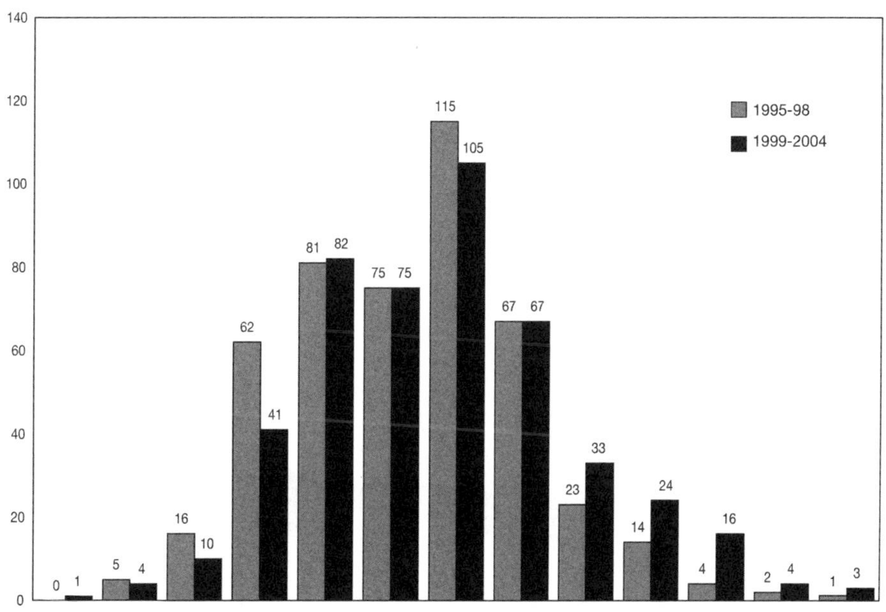

Figure 13.1 Frequency distribution of domestic pairwise correlations (weekly DD changes).

strengthened interconnectedness in the level of risk of EU banks. For example, taking the weekly changes (Figures 13.1 and 13.2) we do observe a large increase in the number of statistically significant pairwise positive correlations (namely greater than $\pm 2/\sqrt{T}$): the number of such significant correlations stands at 1,516 out of 4,851 (i.e. 99*98/2) in the post-1999 period versus 646 in the pre-1999 sample. Adopting a criterion of economic significance, e.g. considering correlations greater than or equal to 50 per cent (which are, indeed, very large if one takes weekly DD changes), we obtain a similar outcome: the number of economically significant correlations increases from 7 in the 1995–8 time interval to 48 in the 1999–2004 period. Again, we do find a large increase in the number of statistically and economically significant correlations at the cross-border level. The frequency distribution of correlations on monthly DD changes (Figures 13.3 and 13.4) tells a pretty similar story.

To sum up, the results of the correlation analysis in DD changes provides first evidence of the fact that co-movements in bank fragility at the EU-wide level are not negligible, especially when one concentrates on large banks. In addition, the commonality in bank risk appears to have significantly increased since 1999 even at the cross-border level.

Correlations at leads and lags

As a second step we looked at correlations at several leads and lags. This constitutes the basic premises for the dynamic factor model developed in the next section. Indeed, one motivation for the use of a dynamic factor model instead of a static one is the fact that not only are common shocks contemporaneous, but there exists a propagation mechanism of such shocks which follows a more complex dynamic, which implies the existence of first- or higher-order auto-correlations and cross-correlations. In addition, this enables the heterogeneity among banks in the propagation of common shocks to be taken into account.

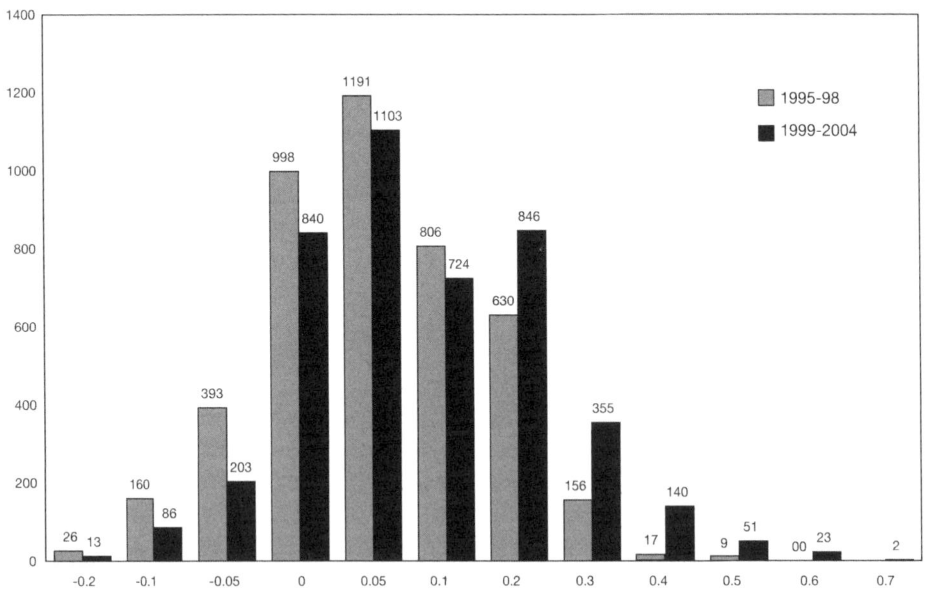

Figure 13.2 Frequency distribution of cross-border pairwise correlations (weekly DD changes).

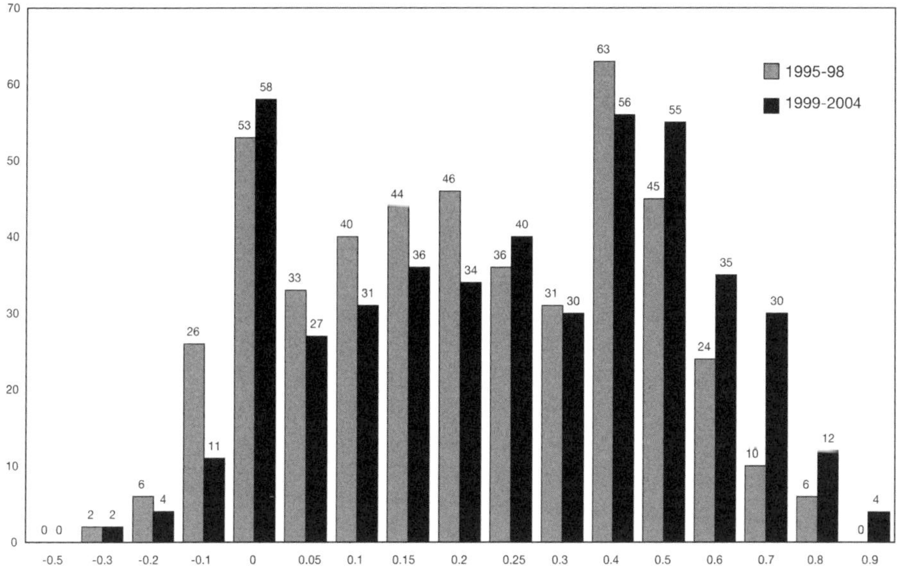

Figure 13.3 Frequency distribution of domestic pairwise correlations (monthly DD changes).

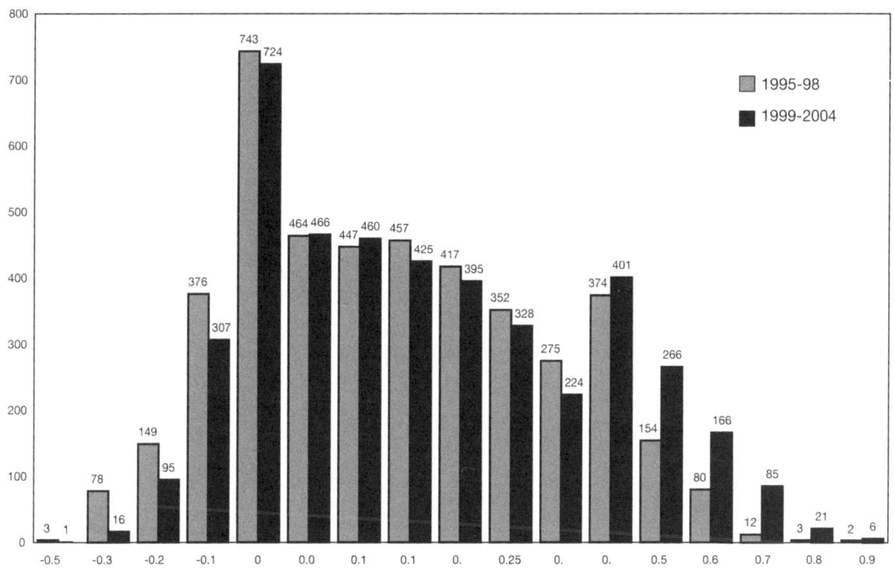

Figure 13.4 Frequency distribution of cross-border pairwise correlations (monthly DD changes).

As before, it is perhaps more interesting to focus on the distributions of the computed pairwise correlations at several leads and lags in weekly and monthly DD changes (we considered 8 leads and lags for the weekly changes and 3 leads and lags for the monthly changes). Tables 13.3 and 13.4 report the count of the statistically and economically significant correlations.[4] It shows that the number of such correlations is material, suggesting that including lead and lag changes in the factor model may increase its explicative power.

Table 13.3 Number of statistically significant correlations in DD changes at several leads and lags*

		Positive correlations		*Negative correlations*	
		Total	*of which cross-border*	*Total*	*of which cross-border*
Weekly changes					
Lead	1	1035	867	100	88
	2	714	584	90	86
	3	403	353	91	82
	4	317	276	84	68
	5	382	329	63	58
	6	327	277	87	75
	7	335	271	88	83
	8	316	278	85	77
Lag	1	953	761	99	88
	2	728	574	73	70
	3	362	298	85	77
	4	295	251	102	89
	5	398	354	75	71
	6	358	320	70	63
	7	377	326	66	59
	8	368	332	74	60
Monthly changes					
Lead	1	1344	1093	57	53
	2	743	639	71	66
	3	560	491	88	77
Lag	1	1384	1131	63	62
	2	808	731	59	53
	3	583	526	78	63

Note: * Statistically significant correlations are those above and below the threshold $\pm 2/\sqrt{T}$.

Taking, for example, the lag 1 for the weekly DD changes we find 953 statistically significant positive correlations, around 20 per cent of the total pairwise correlations. Further, around 80 per cent of these correlations (i.e. 761) are among banks incorporated in different EU countries. Indeed, considering leads and lags in the DD changes appears to be relevant to highlight the transmission of common shocks at the cross-border level especially between large and mid-sized banks. To illustrate we report, as an example, the cross-correlations between a large Italian bank (Capitalia) and a medium-sized Spanish bank (Banca Pastor): Figure 13.5 shows that correlations at lags 1 and 2 in the weekly DD changes are significantly higher than the contemporaneous one (equalling, respectively, 44 per cent and 25 per cent versus 17 per cent).

Dynamic correlations and cohesion

Further interesting insights may come from the analysis of dynamic correlations and cohesion which represent two measures of correlation in the frequency domain proposed by Croux, Forni and Reichlin (2001). Essentially, these measures highlight the frequencies at which cross-correlations between variables are more relevant. Thus, they help in saying whether co-movements are related to common short-term dynamics or if they reflect common cyclical shocks or more long-term tendencies.

Table 13.4 Number of economically significant correlations in DD changes at several leads and lags*

		Positive correlations		*Negative correlations*	
		Total	*of which cross-border*	*Total*	*of which cross-border*
Weekly changes					
Lead	1	16	12	1	0
	2	1	0	0	0
	3	2	0	0	0
	4	2	1	2	1
	5	3	3	0	0
	6	0	0	1	1
	7	2	1	0	0
	8	0	0	1	1
Lag	1	15	6	2	1
	2	4	2	2	2
	3	4	4	2	2
	4	0	0	2	1
	5	3	3	2	2
	6	1	1	0	0
	7	0	0	0	0
	8	2	2	2	2
Monthly changes					
Lead	1	17	1	0	0
	2	2	2	0	0
	3	1	1	0	0
Lag	1	20	4	0	0
	2	0	0	0	0
	3	0	0	0	0

Note: * Economically significant correlations are those above and below the thresholds ± 0.3 and ± 0.5 for weekly and monthly changes respectively.

Taking two zero-mean real stochastic processes x and y, the dynamic correlation can be defined as follows:

$$\rho_{xy}(\lambda) = \frac{C_{xy}(\lambda)}{\sqrt{S_x(\lambda) \cdot S_y(\lambda)}},$$

where $S_x(\lambda)$ and $S_y(\lambda)$, for $-\pi \leq \lambda \leq \pi$, are the spectral density functions of x and y, and $C_{xy}(\lambda)$ is the co-spectrum.

Along the same line, the cohesion is a synthetic measure of dynamic correlation when there are more than two variables. It simply equals the weighted average of dynamic correlations between all pairs of series.

In our case, we calculated these measures by using a Bartlett kernel with window width at T. Spectra, cross-spectra, dynamic correlations and cohesion have then been computed on 128 equally spaced points.[5]

In Figure 13.6 we report the cohesion on weekly changes, for the two sub-periods 1995–8 and 1999–2004.[6] These figures clearly show the increase in co-movements between the two periods. In addition, we notice that co-movements are concentrated mainly at low frequencies: i.e. bank risk co-moves in the long-term or at cyclical frequencies.

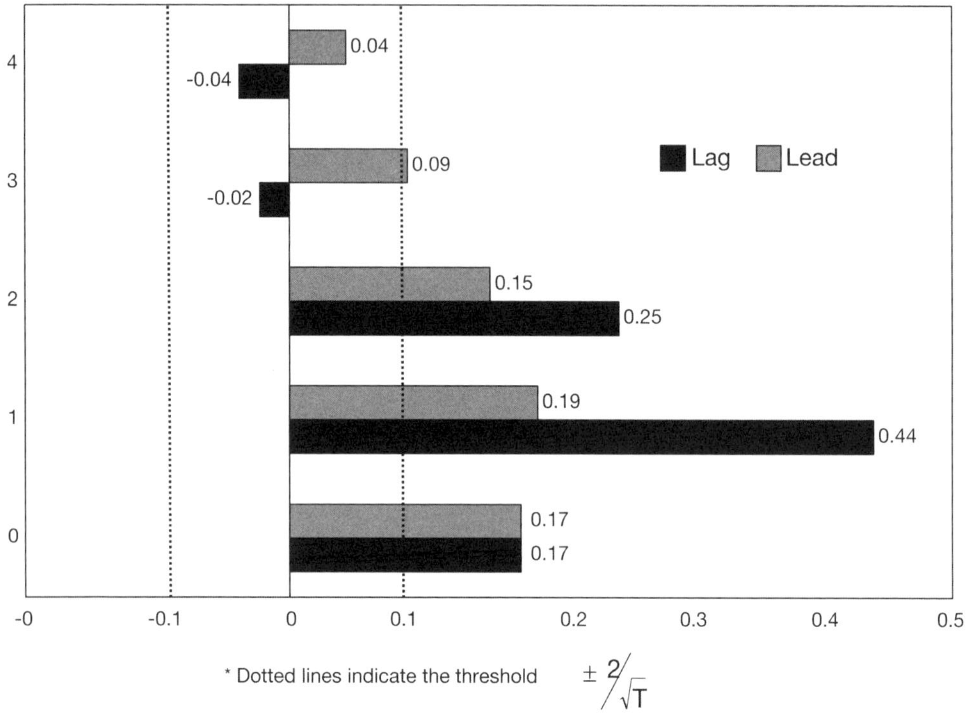

Figure 13.5 Cross-correlogram in weekly DD changes between Capitalia (Italy) and Banco Pastor (Spain).*
Note: * Dotted lines indicate the threshold $\pm 2/\sqrt{T}$.

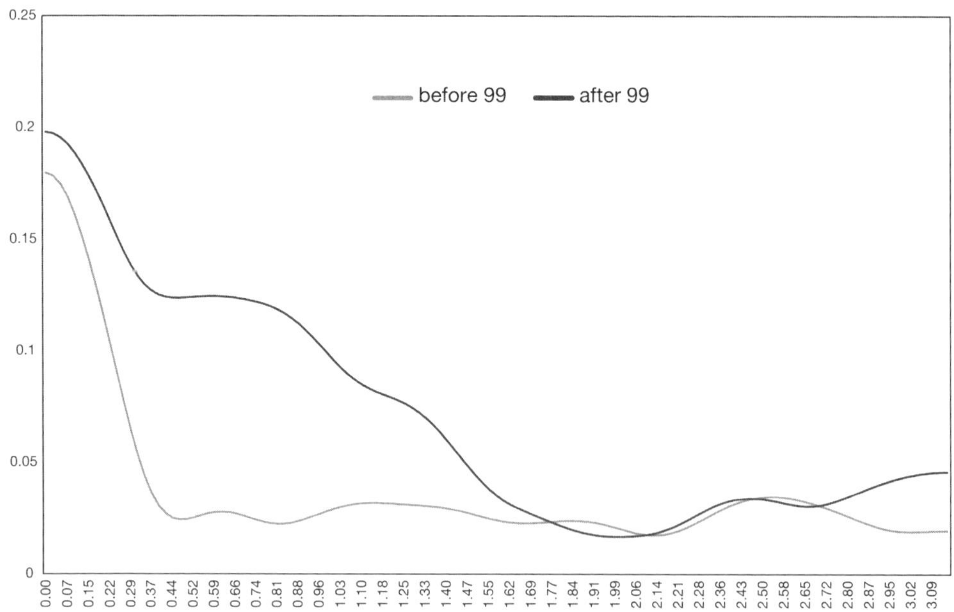

Figure 13.6 Cohesion in weekly DD changes.

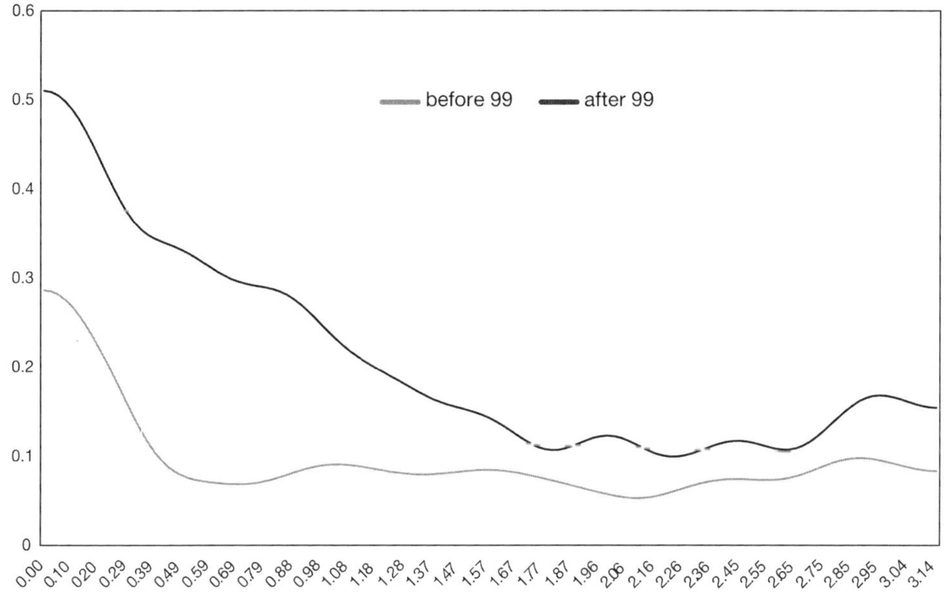

Figure 13.7 Cohesion in weekly DD changes (sample of 28 large banks).

Finally, we ran the exercise for the sample of 28 large banks (Figure 13.7). The results highlight the larger commonality among this set of banks found in the simple correlation analysis. For this set of banks we also notice a spike in the cohesion calculated on weekly DD changes at a frequency corresponding to a period of two weeks. This result also highlights the difference between the weekly and the monthly DD changes: while weekly DD changes tend to stress co-movements on a very short-term basis, the monthly changes appear more suitable to reflect co-movements related to common cyclical shocks or stemming from common long-term tendencies.

To sum up, the analysis on cohesion tends to suggest that cyclical and long-term co-movements in bank risk are more relevant than those at very short-term frequencies (i.e. high frequencies), which is coherent with the increasing integration in the EU banking system (Cabral *et al.* 2002).[7] There is also some evidence of co-movements in the very short term for large banks. This seems to suggest that in case of common shocks large banks are hit first. Perhaps more importantly, this result could also be indicative of some form of contagion hitting large banks, whose source might be worth investigation in future research.

The dynamic factor model

Model description and estimation procedure

Our basic assumption is that the bank fragility indicator (DD) can be decomposed into three main components: an EU-wide, a country specific and a bank specific (i.e. idiosyncratic) component. These three components are, by definition, mutually orthogonal.

Following Forni and Reichlin (2001) and denoting with DD_t^{ij} the distance to default of bank i incorporated in country j, we assume that the changes in the DDs can be decomposed as follows:

$$\Delta(DD_t^{ij}) = E_t^{ij} + N_t^{ij} + I_t^{ij},$$

where E_t^{ij}, N_t^{ij} and I_t^{ij} are the EU-wide component, the national component and the bank-level component, respectively. Each component can, in turn, be written as a linear combination of unit variance shocks, which are uncorrelated at all leads and lags. Thus,

$$E_t^{ij} = a^{ij}(L) \cdot e_t$$

$$N_t^{ij} = b^{ij}(L) \cdot n_t^j$$

$$I_t^{ij} = c^{ij}(L) \cdot i_t^{ij},$$

where a^{ij}, b^{ij} and c^{ij} are polynomials in the lag operator L, while e_t, n_t^j and i_t^{ij} are the EU-wide, the national and the bank specific shocks, respectively.

In order to better clarify the model it is important to underline the fact that those we have labelled EU-wide shocks refer to shocks that hit all the banks in the sample irrespective of the origin of the shock. Hence, they could be global shocks, but they may well be domestic (or even bank specific) shocks that then spread to banks incorporated in other countries. In other words, what we are interested in is the propagation mechanism of shocks to bank fragility rather than where they originate.

The model entails the estimation of the three unobserved components, which is done through a sequential procedure. More specifically, the EU-wide component is first estimated by means of an approximate dynamic factor model à la Stock and Watson[8] (2002) applied to all banks in the sample, which can be written as follows (in matrix notation):

$$\Delta(DD_t) = \Lambda F_t + \varepsilon_t$$

The matrix Λ contains the loadings, $F_t = (f_t, f_{t\pm1} \ldots, f_{t\pm q})$ is the matrix of common factors, while ε_t is the matrix of residuals, which in the first step of the procedure is a bundle of the national and idiosyncratic components (i.e. everything which is not common at the EU-wide level). The national component is, in turn, isolated from the idiosyncratic one by running the dynamic factor model on these extracted residuals for groups of banks incorporated in the same country.

As noted, while the estimation of the EU common factor should not constitute a major problem, the size of the sample (i.e. the number of cross-sections/banks) for some countries might not be sufficient to consistently estimate the country component of bank fragility. However, given that the focus of this chapter is on measuring the weight of the EU component this should not constitute a major issue.

Once the three components have been estimated and given their orthogonality, the decomposition enables the calculation of the contribution of each component to the variance of the DD changes.

As regards, in particular, the estimation of the dynamic factor model here employed, it requires a number of choices to be made. The first is the number of factors to be used in estimation, the second is the potential inclusion of lags in the observed series, and the third is the inclusion of leads and lags of the factors in the estimation of the common components.

While the first can be made on the basis of the modified information criteria proposed in Bai and Ng (2002), the second and the third have been performed by Stock and Watson

(2002) on the basis of the forecasting ability contribution of the model. In our case we choose on the basis of the amount of variance in the idiosyncratic component (trying to minimize it). Being not particularly interested in forecasting, but rather in the inherent dynamic structure of the data, we investigated whether there are advantages in using a two-sided interval (leads and lags for the extracted common factor). After preliminary estimations, a final set-up with one factor (using the Bai and Ng criteria), no lags in data, and three leads and lags in the factors has been chosen for the weekly DD changes.[9] For the monthly changes the Bai and Ng criteria identified two factors and one lead and lag in the factors.

The model's results

In Table 13.5 we report the average across banks of the variance explained by the three components for all countries and a set of selected countries in the two sub-periods 1995–8 and 1999–2004.

Our results show that the degree of commonality is quite clearly growing. The EU-wide and national components altogether have gone up to 32 per cent since 1999, from 28 per cent in the period 1995–8 in the case of weekly DD changes. Further, the increase in commonality is in large part due to the EU-wide component, which rises to 19 per cent since 1999 from 10 per cent before 1999.

Table 13.5 Variance decomposition of DD changes (average variance explained by each extracted component)

		Weekly changes		*Monthly changes*	
		1995–8	*1999–2004*	*1995–8*	*1999–2004*
All countries	EU-wide	0.102	0.188	0.336	0.526
	National	0.180	0.134	0.492	0.191
	Idiosyncratic	0.718	0.678	0.172	0.282
Italy	EU-wide	0.078	0.288	0.349	0.624
	National	0.167	0.074	0.467	0.113
	Idiosyncratic	0.755	0.638	0.184	0.263
Spain	EU-wide	0.117	0.202	0.333	0.513
	National	0.189	0.091	0.527	0.199
	Idiosyncratic	0.694	0.707	0.140	0.288
Germany	EU-wide	0.079	0.180	0.334	0.524
	National	0.191	0.078	0.486	0.158
	Idiosyncratic	0.730	0.742	0.180	0.318
France	EU-wide	0.066	0.216	0.341	0.547
	National	0.208	0.099	0.493	0.139
	Idiosyncratic	0.726	0.685	0.166	0.315
UK	EU-wide	0.173	0.207	0.337	0.531
	National	0.148	0.108	0.507	0.204
	Idiosyncratic	0.679	0.685	0.156	0.265
Large banks	EU-wide	0.167	0.339	0.329	0.687
	National	0.200	0.120	0.510	0.114
	Idiosyncratic	0.634	0.541	0.161	0.199

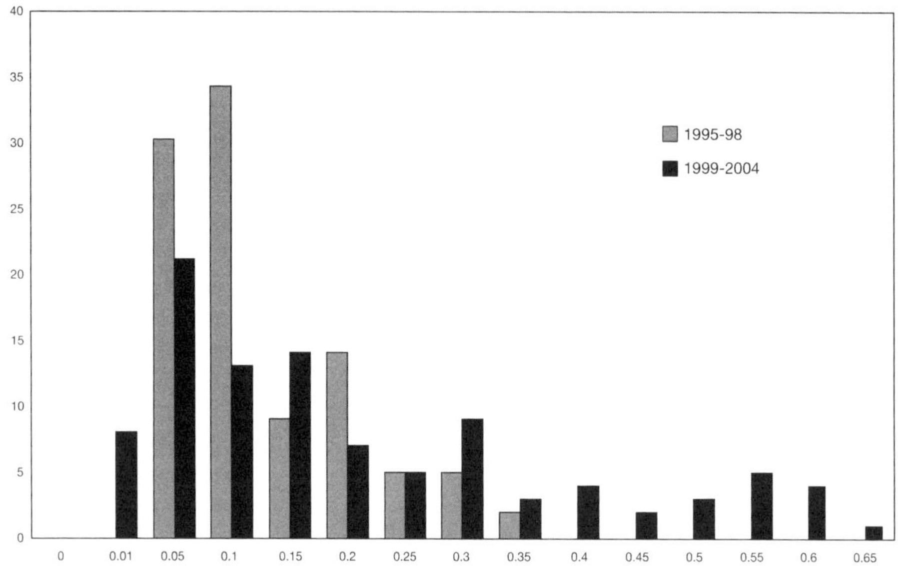

Figure 13.8 Frequency distribution of the variance explained by the EU component (weekly DD changes).

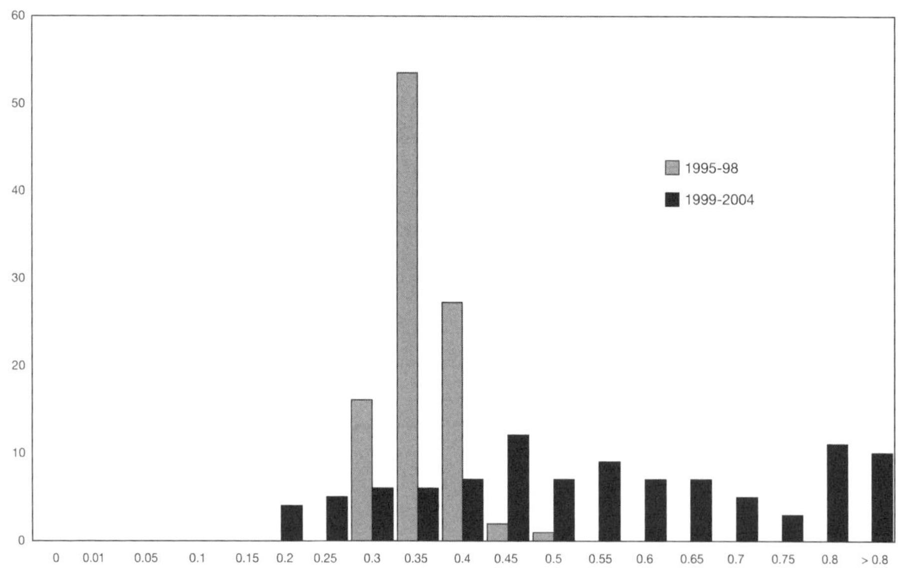

Figure 13.9 Frequency distribution of the variance explained by the EU component (monthly DD changes).

Co-movements in bank fragility appear much larger when monthly changes are considered. In such a case, in the post 1999-period, the EU-wide component explains 53 per cent of the variance in monthly DD changes (up from 34 per cent in the pre-1999 period). Even in this case the increase in the EU-wide component comes at the expense of the domestic one (down from 49 per cent to 19 per cent). There is also a significant reduction in the share of variance explained by the idiosyncratic component when we move from weekly to monthly

Table 13.6 Variance decomposition of weekly DD changes (selected sample of 28 large banks)

Bank name	*Country*	*1995–8*			*1999–2004*		
		EU-wide	*National*	*Idio-syncratic*	*EU-wide*	*National*	*Idio-syncratic*
Commerzbank	DE	0.173	0.417	0.411	0.623	0.171	0.207
Banco Santander Central Hispano	ES	0.185	0.055	0.76	0.582	0.131	0.286
Banca Intesa	IT	0.097	0.07	0.833	0.561	0.122	0.317
BBVA	ES	0.265	0.051	0.684	0.56	0.118	0.321
BNP Paribas	FR	0.081	0.714	0.205	0.55	0.221	0.228
ING	NL	0.29	0.061	0.649	0.534	0.072	0.394
Capitalia	IT	0.084	0.297	0.619	0.515	0.077	0.408
San Paolo-IMI	IT	0.079	0.147	0.774	0.505	0.018	0.478
Société Générale	FR	0.165	0.61	0.224	0.486	0.262	0.252
Fortis Bank	BE	0.309	0.091	0.6	0.484	0.281	0.235
Deutsche Bank	DE	0.205	0.463	0.333	0.442	0.153	0.405
Barclays	UK	0.314	0.112	0.574	0.389	0.094	0.518
UniCredito Italiano	IT	0.18	0.141	0.679	0.375	0.046	0.579
ABN Amro Holding NV	NL	0.16	0.042	0.798	0.354	0.133	0.512
KBC Bank NV	BE	0.261	0.188	0.551	0.348	0.361	0.291
Skandinaviska Enskilda Banken AB	SE	0.178	0.036	0.786	0.308	0.078	0.614
Royal Bank of Scotland	UK	0.157	0.307	0.535	0.29	0.105	0.605
Bayerische Hypo- und Vereinsbank AG	DE	0.162	0.327	0.51	0.275	0.194	0.531
HBOS - MARKET VALUE	UK	0.153	0.177	0.669	0.243	0.279	0.478
Natexis Banques Populaires	FR	0.063	0.099	0.838	0.227	0.046	0.726
HSBC Holdings Plc	UK	0.279	0.106	0.615	0.16	0.048	0.792
Abbey National Plc	UK	0.185	0.195	0.62	0.149	0.173	0.678
Standard Chartered Plc	UK	0.078	0.177	0.745	0.138	0.033	0.829
Bankgesellschaft Berlin AG	DE	0.081	0.051	0.868	0.127	0.054	0.818
Svenska Handelsbanken	SE	0.213	0.03	0.757	0.102	0.035	0.863
Danske Bank A/S	DK	0.162	0.344	0.493	0.093	0.004	0.903
DePfa Deutsche Pfandbrief Bank AG	DE	0.084	0.262	0.655	0.047	0.052	0.901
Eurohypo AG	DE	0.021	0.019	0.96	0.011	0.003	0.986

changes in the DDs. This probably reflects the reduction in noise implied in the monthly changes versus the weekly changes.

Looking at the results by country, we find that all countries share the increase in co-movements in the two sub-periods. Considering weekly DD changes, the largest increase is found in Italy (more than 20 per cent), while in Germany the EU-wide component (18 per cent in the post-1999 period) is the smallest (albeit higher than the average for the whole sample). Similar findings are obtained with the monthly DD changes.

The increase in the weight of the EU-wide component clearly appears from Figure 13.8, which displays the frequency distribution of the variance explained by the EU-wide component in the two sub-periods (weekly DD changes). While before 1999 the percentage of banks with a variance explained by the EU-wide factor of more than 30 per cent was only 2 per cent, after 1999 such percentage goes up to about 22 per cent. Moreover, for

Table 13.7 Variance decomposition of monthly DD changes (selected sample of 28 large banks)

		1995–8			*1999–2004*		
Bank name	*Country*	*EU-wide*	*National*	*Idio-syncratic*	*EU-wide*	*National*	*Idio-syncratic*
Fortis Bank	BE	0.348	0.561	0.092	0.876	0.043	0.080
Banco Santander Central Hispano	ES	0.346	0.577	0.078	0.852	0.027	0.121
Commerzbank	DE	0.350	0.583	0.067	0.848	0.031	0.121
San Paolo-IMI	IT	0.260	0.413	0.327	0.842	0.036	0.122
Banca Intesa	IT	0.379	0.421	0.200	0.841	0.051	0.108
Deutsche Bank	DE	0.350	0.595	0.054	0.833	0.049	0.118
BBVA	ES	0.327	0.549	0.125	0.811	0.050	0.139
ING	NL	0.336	0.423	0.241	0.795	0.019	0.186
UniCredito Italiano	IT	0.329	0.564	0.107	0.793	0.039	0.168
BNP Paribas	FR	0.352	0.568	0.081	0.788	0.088	0.125
ABN Amro Holding NV	NL	0.306	0.479	0.215	0.787	0.048	0.165
Capitalia	IT	0.361	0.461	0.179	0.783	0.087	0.129
Skandinaviska Enskilda Banken AB	SE	0.307	0.372	0.321	0.783	0.027	0.191
KBC Bank NV	BE	0.345	0.579	0.077	0.777	0.123	0.100
Barclays	UK	0.296	0.513	0.191	0.763	0.071	0.166
Société Générale	FR	0.352	0.596	0.052	0.763	0.091	0.146
Royal Bank of Scotland	UK	0.327	0.586	0.088	0.694	0.117	0.189
Bayerische Hypo- und Vereinsbank AG	DE	0.293	0.434	0.273	0.686	0.139	0.176
Svenska Handelsbanken	SE	0.285	0.464	0.252	0.675	0.108	0.217
Abbey National Plc	UK	0.339	0.545	0.116	0.609	0.146	0.245
Natexis Banques Populaires	FR	0.391	0.483	0.127	0.550	0.141	0.309
Standard Chartered Plc	UK	0.313	0.581	0.106	0.530	0.231	0.239
HBOS - MARKET VALUE	UK	0.337	0.553	0.110	0.493	0.281	0.226
Danske Bank A/S	DK	0.345	0.572	0.084	0.458	0.133	0.408
DePfa Deutsche Pfandbrief Bank AG	DE	0.346	0.588	0.066	0.456	0.167	0.377
Eurohypo AG	DE	0.268	0.175	0.557	0.448	0.201	0.351
Bankgesellschaft Berlin AG	DE	0.290	0.504	0.206	0.371	0.383	0.246
HSBC Holdings Plc	UK	0.332	0.541	0.127	0.337	0.251	0.412

10 banks in our sample more than 50 per cent of the variance in weekly DD changes is explained by the EU-wide factor. These are clearly those labelled as large banks (total assets higher than €100 billion). Indeed, Table 13.5 makes it clear that the increase in commonality is largely explained by this set of banks: for them the average variance explained by the EU-wide common factor goes from 17 per cent in the period 1995–8 to 34 per cent in the period 1999–2004. For some of these banks the EU-wide common factor explains a figure close to or even higher than 50 per cent of the variance in weekly DD changes (see Table 13.6).

These results are even more striking when monthly changes are considered. In particular, Figure 13.9 shows that, in the post-1999 period, for 21 banks the share of variance explained by the EU-wide component is larger than 75 per cent. A similar finding reported in Table 13.7 referred to the sample of large banks.

Sources of co-movements in banks' fragility: the role of common macro shocks

The model

In the previous section we showed that the commonality in the level of risk of EU banks is clearly increasing and that such a rise is largely due to the EU-wide component. It is also clear, however, that a proportion of the co-movements in banks' fragility may stem from common macro shocks both at the national and EU-wide level. It might thus be interesting to make a further step and investigate the role of such macro shocks in explaining the dynamics of our fragility indicator. To this end we resort again to a factor model and assume that the DD of each bank can be decomposed into the following mutually orthogonal components:

- a common macroeconomic EU-wide component
- a country specific macroeconomic component
- a residual component.

In other words, with this procedure we cleanse the dynamics of the DDs of those influences that may come from macroeconomic shocks. In this way, and provided that the common macro shocks are properly identified, we yield a residual component that could be interpreted as a banking system specific source of risk.

Hence, denoting with DD_t^{ij} the distance to default of bank i incorporated in country j, we assume that the changes in the DDs can be decomposed as follows:

$$\Delta(DD_t^{ij}) = macroEU_t^{ij} + macroN_t^{ij} + e_t^{ij}$$

In turn, similarly as was done in the previous section, the residual of the previous equation – the banking sector specific source of risk – can be further decomposed into an EU-wide banking sector, a domestic banking sector and a bank specific (or idiosyncratic) component, i.e.

$$e_t^{ij} = EU_t^{ij} + N_t^{ij} + I_t^{ij}$$

In order to identify the common macro shocks we took a set of macroeconomic variables at country level, available on a monthly frequency, as industrial output (with sector breakdown), consumer and producer prices (with product and sector breakdown), business and consumer confidence indicators, interest rates, exchange rates (nominal and real effective), stock market indexes, etc., for a total of over 700 series. We then ran a factor model on the complete set of macro variables to extract the EU-wide common macro factors. Subsequently, we estimated the common macro factors at national level by running the factor model for each country on the residuals of the first step. For each bank in the sample we then regressed the monthly DD changes on the EU-wide and national common macro factors (which are by definition orthogonal). As we said, the residuals of these regressions should represent the banking sector specific sources of risk. Finally, we applied the sequential procedure used in the previous section in order to decompose the banking sector specific source of risk into the EU-wide, domestic and bank specific (or idiosyncratic) components.

Table 13.8 Variance decomposition of monthly DD changes

	1995–8	*1999–2004*
EU macro factors	0.30	0.24
Domestic macro factors	0.11	0.08
Banking sector specific factors	0.59	0.68
EU-wide	0.20	0.34
Domestic	0.29	0.14
Bank specific (idiosyncratic)	0.09	0.20

In order to remove the influence of macro shocks from the dynamics of the fragility indicator, we tried to include as many macro factors as possible. Once again we used the Bai and Ng modified information criteria to choose the number of factors and we ended up with nine and five factors at the EU-wide and country level, respectively.

Results

The results of this exercise (summarized in Table 13.8) show that the dynamics of monthly DD changes can only in part be accounted for by macro factors. They explain on average in the entire sample period 34.3 per cent of the dynamics in monthly DD changes. The variance explained by EU common macro factors seems to dominate over the national one, since on average they account for 25.2 per cent of the total variance in banks' DDs versus 9.1 per cent for domestic macro factors. Taking the two sample periods we do observe a larger share of variance explained by the common macro factors in the first part of the sample (41 per cent), whilst in the period 1999–2004 the share of variance accounted for by the residuals lifts to 68 per cent.

These results seem then to suggest that common macro shocks are not the sole source of bank risks and that the dynamics of EU banks' fragility are largely accounted for by banking system specific factors and that these factors are becoming increasingly important. Of course this outcome may also be due to the fact that we were unable to correctly identify all macro shocks. However, the finding we obtained does not come as a total surprise if one takes into account the fact that since around 2001 there has been an increasing detachment between the results of banks and the performance of the EU economy: while the latter has progressively stagnated, the former have been able to keep their profitability at rather satisfactory levels.

Moving to the decomposition of what we have labelled the banking system specific component, the results (Table 13.8) show that the EU-wide part – now at the banking sector level – remains still relevant and is increasing in time even once we have removed the influence of common macroeconomic shocks. Taking the post-1999 period the EU-wide component accounts on average for 50 per cent of the variance in the banking system specific source of fragility (or 34 per cent of the whole dynamic in monthly DD changes) up from 35 per cent in the 1995–8 time interval. Hence, in the second part of the sample EU-wide banking sector common shocks seem to have become more important than common macro shocks in explaining banks' fragility.

Conclusions

With this work we aspired to measure the extent to which the fragility of EU banks is subject to common shocks. We did this by resorting to a methodology which has recently been extensively applied in the analysis of economic cycles, namely the dynamic factor model, which allows us to decompose an indicator of bank fragility, the distance to default, into three main mutually orthogonal components: an EU-wide, a country specific and a bank-level idiosyncratic component.

The results of our model can be summarized as follows. First, the weight of EU-wide shocks appears not to be negligible since they explain around 42 per cent of the variance in bank risk (as measured by monthly changes in the distance to default indicator). The relevance of the EU component is also significantly increasing over time, perhaps reflecting greater banking integration among EU banks. Second, as one would probably expect, the EU component is much greater for large banks, explaining in a number of cases more than 80 per cent of the variance in bank risk. Further, this set of banks constitutes the transmission channel of common shocks. Third, even once we take into account the influence of common macroeconomic shocks, the dynamics of EU banks' fragility is largely accounted for by banking system specific factors and these factors are becoming increasingly important at the EU-wide level. Fourth, by analysing co-movements in the frequency domain, we found that common EU-wide shocks are more relevant at cyclical and/or long-term frequencies, which is in line with increasing banking integration. However, we notice that co-movements at very high frequencies (i.e. in the very short term) are relevant for large banks, which might be indicative of some form of contagion.

We believe our results have quite important implications as regards the monitoring of financial stability conducted by central banks and supervisory authorities in Europe. In particular, that developments in the fragility of large banks are largely affected by common EU-wide shocks constitutes a clear justification for macro-prudential surveillance at the EU level, a field which has been recently developed by some central banks (like the European Central Bank (ECB)).

More importantly, our findings provide some indications as to the split of supervisory competencies between national and EU-wide authorities. The large weight of the idiosyncratic component indicates that banking supervision at the domestic level is still important. However, its scope should be limited to small to medium-sized banks, whilst for large banks our results suggest, at a minimum, an increased scope for supervisory co-operation at the EU-wide level. This is further motivated by the growing relevance of a banking system specific source of risk at the EU-wide level.

The results obtained lend themselves also to a number of potential extensions and applications. First, the finding of the emergence of common shocks stemming from EU banking system specific factors suggests that the sources of such shocks should be investigated. This means opening the 'black box' and measuring, for instance, the extent to which developments in EU-wide fragility are related to common exposures and/or interbank exposures. Second, a result of the dynamic factor model is the calculation of an EU-wide fragility indicator, which is cleansed of country specific or idiosyncratic shocks. In this respect, a potential application consists of conducting stress testing exercises on the fragility of EU banks by showing what happens to the EU-wide fragility indicator in the case of changes in the DD of one bank or a set of banks.

Notes

1 The authors would like to thank Fabio Braga, Kenneth Kuttner, Francesco Meucci, Kjell Bjørn Nordal, Chiara Oldani, Andrea Sironi and Cristiano Zazzara, as well as participants at the Lisbon Conference on Money and Finance (Lisbon, 10 September 2004), at the First Italian Congress of Econometrics and Empirical Economics (Venice, 24–25 January 2005), at the International

Conference on Finance (Copenhagen, 2–4 September 2005) and at the 2nd DG ECFIN Research Conference 'Financial Stability and the Convergence Process in Europe' (Brussels, 6–7 October 2005) for their useful comments and suggestions. Excellent research assistance by Lucio De Angelis is gratefully acknowledged. The usual disclaimer applies.

2 The monthly DDs are obtained as a simple average of the weekly.

3 Stock and Watson (1998, theorem 1 at p. 16) show that the approximate dynamic factor model yields estimated factors that are asymptotically efficient in forecasting out of sample for any joint sequences (N, T).

4 Statistically significant correlations are those above or below the threshold $\pm 2/\sqrt{T}$. Economically significant correlations are defined as those greater than 30 per cent or 50 per cent for the weekly and monthly changes, respectively.

5 We used the Matlab code provided by Croux, Forni and Reichlin, which is available at www.dynfactor.com. All the other programmes and routines were prepared by the authors.

6 The figures report the cohesion for frequencies ranging from 0 (low frequencies corresponding to medium- to long-term cycles) to 3.14 (high frequencies corresponding to very short dynamics). This means that with weekly data having, for example, 210 observations a frequency of 1.55 corresponds to a cycle of approximately four weeks.

7 These results are also confirmed by a spectral analysis of the three components extracted with the dynamic factor model. We do observe, in particular, that in the short term (high frequencies) the idiosyncratic component tends to dominate over the other two, while in the long run the EU-wide component starts to become relevant. For the period 1999–2003, there is also the emergence of an EU-wide factor at cyclical frequencies. In particular, the figures noticeably suggest a cycle of slightly more than two years that can be associated with the industrial cycle in EU countries in the last years. Further, the presence of a national cycle at four months frequency in the first sub-sample seems to have been absorbed by the EU component in the second period.

8 Nothing prevents the use of a dynamic principal components approach like the one proposed in various papers by Forni, Hallin, Lippi, Reichlin (2000). We resort here to the simpler approach proposed by Stock and Watson and quite common in the literature (Angelini *et al.* 2001; Camacho and Sancho 2003).

9 See the discussion in Stock and Watson (1998: 8, 23).

References

Angelini, E., J, Henry and R. Mestre (2001) *Diffusion Index-based Forecasts for the Euro Area*, ECB Working Paper no. 61, April.

Bai, J. and S. Ng (2002) 'Determining the number of factors in approximate factor models', *Econometrica* 70(1): 191–221.

Billio, M. and L. Pellizzon (2002) *Contagion and Interdependence in Stock Markets: Have They Been Misdiagnosed?*, GRETA Working Paper no. 02.08, December.

Bongini, P., L. Laeven and G. Majnoni (2002) 'How good is the market at assessing bank fragility? A horse race between different indicators', *Journal of Banking and Finance* 26(5): 1011–28.

Cabral I., F. Dicrick and J. Vesala (2002) 'Banking Integration in the Euro Area', ECB Occasional Paper, no. 6, November.

Camacho, M. and I. Sancho (2003) 'Spanish diffusion indexes', *Spanish Economic Review* 5(3): 173–203.

Croux C., M. Forni and L. Reichlin (2001) 'A measure of co-movement in economic variables: theory and empirics', *Review of Economics and Statistics* 83(2), May: 232–41.

De Bandt, O. and P. Hartmann (2000) *Systemic Risk: A Survey*, ECB Working Paper no. 35, November.

De Nicolò, G. and M. Kwast (2002) 'Systemic risk and financial consolidation: are they related?', *Journal of Banking and Finance* 26: 861–80.

De Nicolò, G. and A. Tieman (2006) 'Economic integration and financial stability: a European perspective?', IMF Working Paper No. 06/296.

Emiris, M. (2002) *Measuring Capital Market Integration*, BIS papers no. 12, August.

Fama, E. and K. French (1993) 'Common risk factors in the returns on stocks and bonds', *Journal of Financial Economics* 33: 3–56.

Forni, M. and L. Reichlin (1998) 'Let's get real: a dynamic factor analytic approach to disaggregated business cycles', *Review of Economic Studies* 65: 453–73.

—— (2001) 'Federal policies and local economies: Europe and the US', *European Economic Review* 45: 109–34.

Forni M., M. Hallin, M. Lippi and L. Reichlin (2000) 'The generalised dynamic factor model: identification and estimation', *Review of Economics and Statistics* 82: 540–54.

Galati, G. and K. Tsatsaronis (2001) *The Impact of the Euro on Europe's Financial Markets*, BIS Working Papers no. 100, July.

Gropp, R. and G. Moerman (2003) *Measurement of Contagion in Banks' Equity Prices*, ECB Working Paper no. 297.

Gropp R., J. Vesala and G. Vulpes (2004) 'Market indicators, bank fragility and indirect market discipline', *Federal Reserve Bank of New York Policy Review* 10(2): 53–62.

—— (2006a) 'Equity and bond market signals as leading indicators of bank fragility', *Journal of Money Credit and Banking* 38(2), March: 399–428 (an earlier version is ECB Working Papers Series no. 150, June 2002).

Gropp, R., M. Lo Duca and J. Vesala (2006b) *Cross-Border Bank Contagion in Europe*, ECB Working Paper No. 662.

Hartmann P., A. Maddaloni and S. Manganelli (2003) 'The euro-area financial system: structure, integration and policy initiatives', *Oxford Review of Economic Policy* 19(1): 180–213.

Hawkesby C., I. Marsh and I. Stevens (2003) 'Large complex financial institutions: common influences on asset price behaviour?', *Financial Stability Review* 15, December: 124–34, Bank of England.

—— (2005) *Comovements in the Prices of Securities Issued by Large Complex Financial Institutions*, Bank of England Working Paper no. 256.

KMV (2003) *Modelling Default Risk*, San Francisco: KMV Corporation.

Krainer, J. and J. Lopez (2003) 'Forecasting bank supervisory ratings using securities market information', Paper presented at the RTF Workshop on Applied Banking Research, Rome, March.

Lehar A. (2003) 'Implementing a portfolio perspective in banking supervision', mimeo, University of Vienna, June.

Merton, R. (1977) 'An analytic derivation of the cost of deposit insurance and loan guarantees', *Journal of Banking and Finance* 1: 3–11.

Nickell, P. and W. Perraudin (1999) 'How much bank capital is needed to maintain financial stability?', unpublished ms.

Pain, D. and J. Vesala (2004) 'Driving factors of credit risk in Europe', mimeo, Frankfurt: European Central Bank.

Pesaran, M., T. Schuermann, B. Treutler and S. Weiner (2003) 'Macroeconomic dynamics and credit risk: a global perspective', Center for Financial Institutions Working Papers 03-13, Wharton School Center for Financial Institutions, University of Pennsylvania.

Sargent, T.J. and C.A. Sims (1977) 'Business cycle modelling without pretending to have too much a priori economic theory', in C.A. Sims (ed.) *New Methods in Business Research*, Minneapolis: Federal Reserve Bank of Minneapolis.

Schinasi, G.J. and P.G. Teixeira (2006) *The Lender of Last Resort in the European Single Financial Market*, IMF Working Paper no. 06/127, May.

Schoenmaker, D. and S. Osterloo (2005) 'Financial supervision in an integrating Europe: measuring cross-border externalities', *International Finance* 8(1): 1–27.

Stock, J. and M. Watson (1998) *Diffusion Indexes*, NBER Working Paper no. W6702.

—— (2002) 'Macroeconomic forecasting using diffusion indexes', *Journal of Business and Economic Statistics*, 20(2), April: 147–62.

Stiroh, K. (2004) 'Diversification in banking: is noninterest income the answer?', *Journal of Money Credit and Banking* 36(5): 853–82.

Stiroh, K. and A. Rumble (2006) 'The darkside of diversification: the case of U.S. financial holding companies', *Journal of Banking and Finance* 30: 2131–61.

Upper, C. and A. Worms (2002) *Estimating Bilateral Exposures in the German Interbank Market: Is There a Danger of Contagion?*, Deutsche Bundesbank Discussion Paper No. 09/02.

14 Challenges to banking stability in the EU

A survey

Christoph Walkner

Introduction[1]

Of all the policies pursued in the frame of EU financial market integration, the fostering of cross-border banking linkages is one which will have some of the most significant consequences. EU economies are mainly bank based, and the sector has therefore a crucial role to play in providing financing for investment and economic growth. The industry has until recently often been regarded as mercantilist and subject to considerable public sector interference. Opening domestic banking sectors to foreign competition might therefore result in a significant change regarding the way banking sector services are provided as financing decisions will henceforward be purely based on economic profitability criteria without public interference. The policy of EU cross-border banking integration is therefore likely to have strong consequences in terms of economic growth (see Appendix).

Yet there is another dimension, equally crucial: macro-financial stability, the focus of this chapter. In economies where banks do not cross borders, the fate of an economy and that of its banks are closely tied, as an economic downturn affecting non-financial companies would also affect the profitability and stability of the country's banking sector, thereby deepening recessions due to non-financial companies' collateral loss and banks' capital losses. Foreign bank entry can have rather different consequences for macro-financial stability, in that foreign bank subsidiaries (or branches) may behave not as completely autonomous businesses but as part of a larger bank holding company. Another stability aspect derives from increased competition, which might lead to reduced profitability of domestically owned banks rendering weaker banks more vulnerable to stress.

After surveying the literature on macro-financial stability risks, this chapter examines the development of cross-border banking integration in the EU, its facilitating factors and progress to date. Empirical analysis indicates contrasting developments within the pre-enlargement EU-15 and the recently acceded EU-10. Cross-border banking linkages are relatively uncommon among the EU-15, when compared to linkages between EU-15 and EU-10, suggesting that integration in the EU banking sector has progressed to a larger extent outside the EU regulatory framework than within. Exploring this apparent paradox, the chapter then examines the more typical avenues for banking integration within the EU, namely organic growth through greenfield investments, cross-border mergers and acquisitions (M&As), and the cross-border provision of banking services. In the course of this discussion, barriers are identified as relating to economics, national considerations, and legal and institutional factors. Following that the chapter examines the factors responsible for the high level of foreign ownership in the banking sector of the EU-10. Based on the above analysis, the chapter assesses the stability challenges resulting both from the current arrangement of EU supervision and from broader macroeconomic stability considerations.

Macro-financial stability effects of cross-border bank integration

The effects of foreign bank lending

On a theoretical level foreign bank entry could be either stabilizing or destabilizing for an economy. A positive effect on macro-financial stabilization can arise from foreign bank entry when a bank operating in different countries can provide capital to a subsidiary or branch where capital is under pressure but lending opportunities are favourable – thus protecting the domestic economy from bank-specific shocks. In that sense, geographic bank diversification smooths the respective overall bank holdings' business volatility and thus stabilizes borrowing conditions for the respective bank clients. In contrast, it is possible that a bank would divert capital away from a subsidiary operating in a weak economic environment in favour of outlets in a more promising environment – thus aggravating a local economic downturn. Whatever the economic conditions, capital might also be repatriated in the event that the home bank were to experience financial fragility, which would cause lending restrictions for foreign subsidiaries. To obtain greater clarity regarding the net effect in macro-stabilization, it seems advisable to turn to empirical investigations.

Most empirical studies find foreign bank lending to have a net positive macro-financial stabilization effect. Following the deregulation of the US banking sector in recent years, where states have opened their borders to non-state banks, Morgan *et al.* (2003) discover reduced business volatility as integration allowed banks to diversify against shocks to their own capital. The authors find a de-linking of bank capital growth and employment growth within states, as state banks became increasingly interlinked with non-state banks. In addition, they demonstrate falling state-specific variation in employment and personal income growth, even when taking into account different growth rates or aggregated business cycles. Overall the benefits of bank integration are most pronounced in the least diversified states. The smaller and more correlated state business cycles lead the authors to speculate that banking integration might be one factor behind the recently observed decline in aggregate US economic volatility.

Similarly, Hughes *et al.* (1999) demonstrate that US interstate consolidation improved bank efficiency, particularly when the objective of the consolidation was to diversify macroeconomic risk and so to reduce insolvency risk. Although these papers draw mainly on US experience, the conclusion seems to be that banking integration results in reduced business volatility and enhanced overall macro-financial stability due to geographical risk spreading.

De Haas and Van Lelyveld (2003) study whether foreign-owned banks have reacted differently than domestically owned banks to prevalent business cycle conditions and a host-country banking crisis. The authors look at the effects of foreign bank entry into Central and Eastern Europe. Their dataset panel comprises data on more than 300 banks for the period 1993–2000 with detailed bank ownership information. During crisis periods, domestic banks contracted their credit and deposit bases, whereas foreign banks did not. Additional evidence for this thesis comes from Peek and Rosengreen (2000), Crystal *et al.* (2002) and Goldberg *et al.* (2000). All three papers – focusing on developments in an emerging market context in Latin America – agree that foreign-owned banks were better able to absorb losses than domestically owned banks and have thereby strengthened the financial systems of their host countries.

Another finding of De Haas and Van Lelyveld is that deteriorating home-country conditions lead holding companies to encourage their foreign subsidiaries to increase their lending activities in order to compensate for the lack of profitable investment conditions for their mother banks in the home country. This is taken as an indication that the parent bank allocates scarce capital among its subsidiaries on the basis of expectations of national risk/return characteristics.

While Peek and Rosengreen (2000), Montgomery (2003) and Clarke *et al.* (2001) stress the overall stabilization effects of the presence of foreign banks, the authors find that, in an emerging market context, the stability of foreign bank lending varies by method of entry, with foreign cross-border lending most volatile. In contrast, branch lending is more stable and foreign subsidiaries' credit seems to be the most reliable. However, the latter two papers cite limited empirical evidence on this matter and call for further research.

An interesting perspective is offered by Martinez Peria *et al.* (2002), who suggest that cross-border lending might represent the first phase of a bank's foreign expansion. A more stable lending behaviour is found as branch and subsidiary lending becomes more important and grows to higher relative importance over time. However, the apparently more volatile offshore lending might point to a role for banking supervision in maintaining financial stability.[2]

In contrast, a destabilizing effect of foreign banks is revealed by Peek and Rosengreen (1997a), who find that – following the Japanese stock market decline – binding risk-based capital requirements resulted in reduced lending activity by Japanese banks in the United States. Goldberg (2001) finds that US foreign bank claims are highly correlated with US GDP growth, but not with foreign demand conditions of other industrial countries and of emerging Asia. While Martinez Peria *et al.* confirm that banks transmit shocks from their home countries, an increasing overall exposure of a foreign bank to a host country is found to result in a reduced shock transmission effect.

Although a foreign bank's ability to follow different lending cycles from domestically owned banks seems to result in much-needed stabilization effects during crisis periods, there is also evidence of destabilizing effects, which would suggest a role for efficient and properly designed supervisory and regulatory structures. Overall, though, the presence of foreign banks appears to exert a stabilizing effect on the domestic economy.

Integration fostering competition

Foreign bank entry forces domestic banks to compete and improve their services. This, in turn, increases overall bank efficiency, which allows the sector to contribute to economic growth via better resource allocation. However, reduced profitability of initially weaker domestic banks might also lead to increased banking vulnerabilities.

Lensink and Hermes (2004) note that foreign banks entering a domestic market increase competition, thus lowering the costs for clients and enhancing service quality, and bring with them innovative financial services and practices, which force the domestically owned banking community to adapt and equally engage in innovation, a costly process in the short term. In developing countries, due to the often considerable gap in terms of financial development between foreign-owned and domestically owned banks, costly innovation – the so-called spill-over effect – is more significant than the competition effect. In contrast, the spill-over effect is much less significant than the competition effect in more developed countries, where foreign bank entry leads to overall lower margins, profits and costs.

The effect of foreign bank competition on domestic bank margins is demonstrated by Levine (2003). A study of almost 1200 banks in 47 countries shows that restricting foreign bank entry boosts bank net interest margins. Claessens *et al.* (2001), using 7900 observations from 80 countries for the 1988–95 period, observe that for most countries the share of foreign-owned banks is correlated with a reduction in profitability and margins of domestically owned banks. Another finding is that it is the number of foreign bank entries rather than foreign bank market share that makes a difference. This finding suggests that the impact of foreign competition is felt immediately upon foreign bank entry, with domestically owned banks reacting within a very short period of time. While foreign bank entry seems to improve overall welfare, reduced profitability of domestically owned banks would make weaker ones more vulnerable to distress, suggesting that strong and efficient supervisory structures are needed.

Cross-border banking integration in the EU

Facilitating factors

Several factors have combined to facilitate integration and consolidation within the EU banking sector over the past quarter of a century. These include the globalization of the international financial system due to the liberalization of international capital movements and financial deregulation within countries; major technological advances, particularly in the field of data processing; a diminishing effect of so-called natural barriers such as language and culture; improvements in the regulatory environment; and specific advances in the EU linked to the Single Market Programme.

Globalization is a broad phenomenon, encompassing social, cultural and technological integration. Economic factors – notably the consensus on the benefits to international trade and investment – have played a major part in promoting the globalization process. In a narrower context, the liberalization of capital movements – to finance the growth of international trade and investment – has had a specific impact in integrating the international financial system. An important feature of integration in the international financial system (IFS) has been the internationalization of the banking sector. In consequence, an increasing number of banks have chosen to hold significant assets outside their home jurisdiction.[3]

Globalization of the international financial system has been associated with a shift from bank-centred to market-based financing. This shift has been reflected in the asset composition of banks, as higher-rated borrowers have turned to direct financing via the markets for commercial paper and corporate bonds. The result has been a dramatic change in the income profile of banks, with the proportion of interest income declining relative to income from more fee-based activities. On the liability side, a search for yield has prompted an outflow of depositor funds from banks to a range of competing financial products. The relative decline in banks' core business areas, combined with an increasing focus on shareholder value, has encouraged banks to look for attractive consolidation opportunities both domestically and abroad.

Technological change has fostered bank consolidation, particularly to the extent that advances in information technology have led to declining costs for information collection, storage, processing and transformation. An obvious consequence of advanced information technology for banking has been the substitution of paper-based methods with computer and powerful telecommunication systems. The resulting centralization of many services has yielded significant cost savings – not only in the back office but also in trading, brokerage, etc. Internet and automated lending technologies have shaped new electronic delivery channels, enabling banks to enlarge their delivery capacity, and thereby facilitating the distribution of a wider array of products/services to a larger number of clients over a wider geographical area.[4] The harnessing of information technology has allowed tailored products to be targeted directly at specific clients. In consequence, new technologies are likely to have increased the optimum bank size, providing a powerful rationale for consolidation.

So-called 'natural' barriers to banking consolidation emerge in the form of national-based market differences, which relate to language, cultural preferences and considerations of geographical proximity. While such barriers are very difficult to overcome completely, developments in recent years have mitigated their effect. For example, barriers related to geographical distance or a high cost of cross-border information and communication have been eased by advances in information technology (e.g. wider internet access) and by lower telecommunication prices due to liberalization. In this way, many natural barriers now represent management challenges rather than insurmountable obstacles.[5]

Another key factor facilitating banking integration and consolidation has been regulatory reform. In the 1980s, there was a marked shift in government attitudes toward banking, resulting in a move away from a 'government knows best' approach and a relaxation of many constraints on the banking sector. Market discipline and risk-based capital guidelines were the hallmarks of the new era, replacing the extensive focus on safety and security concerns and protective regulations. The new regulatory style supported a reorientation towards more efficiency through competition, and encouraged a relaxation of a number of barriers previously hindering banking consolidation.[6]

In an EU context, efforts to promote an EU internal market in financial services intensified from the mid-1980s onwards, holding out the prospect of a much larger and more liquid 'domestic' market for banks operating in the EU. In that respect, the introduction of the euro – together with the accompanying payment system infrastructure such as TARGET – signalled a step change in financial integration and, by eliminating exchange rate risk on the bulk of intra-EU financial flows, created the potential for economies of scale and scope within the financial sector – and more specifically banking. This development might have also enhanced the attractiveness of EU Member States' banking markets for foreign-country banks. One major feature in that regard has been the EU Capital Adequacy Directive, ensuring that banks encounter a level playing field in terms of capital requirements.[7]

Another major development has been the introduction of home-country supervisory control and the single licence, which raised hopes for EU banking sector integration and consolidation. The respective Directive states that a credit institution (a bank for the purposes of this chapter) is allowed to open *branches* in the other EU Member States, so long as it is authorized to do so by its home-country supervisor.[8] In this way, a single banking licence opens the possibility for the bank to do business throughout the EU while the home-country supervisor retains responsibility for its financial health. The home-country supervisor has the power to scrutinize the adequacy of the institution's administrative structure and financial situation and, if appropriate, to prohibit the bank from opening a branch in another Member State. However, the justification for any negative decision must be disclosed, allowing the bank to contest the supervisor's decision in court.

Once the home-country supervisor has authorized the bank to open branches in another Member State, it may not interfere except to require the foreign-owned branches to report periodically on their activities for statistical purposes. It retains responsibility for supervision of branch liquidity, however, and may interrupt the provision of services by the branch if any legal provisions in this regard are being violated. Moreover, in emergency situations, the host-country supervisor may – subject to ex post control by the European Commission –

take any precautionary measures necessary to protect the interests of depositors, investors and others to whom services are provided. Given this division of responsibility between home- and host-country supervisors, close co-operation is required between the two agents. A number of memoranda of understanding have been signed to that effect, although none of these is legally binding.

A second possibility for a bank to expand across borders within the EU would be via the establishment of a *subsidiary* in another Member State.[9] In this case, the foreign-owned subsidiary must report primarily to the host-country supervisor, although the home-country supervisor remains responsible for supervising the subsidiary and its parent bank on a consolidated basis. Although originally seen by many as less important than the single licence, expansion via subsidiaries remains an important integration avenue (see pp. 313–14).

Progress to date

While domestic bank consolidation has progressed rapidly in the EU-15 since the introduction of the euro, cross-border retail banking integration is lagging behind, with the partial exception of the Benelux and Nordic countries. In contrast, the banking system is largely foreign owned in most of the recently acceded EU Member States (EU-10).

An examination of trends in consolidation within Member States of the EU-15 reveals a sharply declining number of credit institutions. Between 1997 and 2003, the number of credit institutions fell by almost 35 per cent in Germany, over 25 per cent in France and the Netherlands, and in excess of 20 per cent in the United Kingdom. In Belgium the number of institutions has declined by more than 17 per cent. Running counter to this generalized trend, the number of credit institutions in Ireland increased by almost 13 per cent, while

Table 14.1 Number of credit institutions, change in %

	Year							
Country	*1997*	*1998*	*1999*	*2000*	*2001*	*2002*	*2003*	*1997–2003 change in %*
Belgium	131	123	117	118	112	111	108	−17.6
Denmark	213	212	210	210	203	178	203	−4.7
Germany	3420	3238	2992	2742	2526	2363	2225	−34.9
Greece	55	59	57	57	61	61	59	7.3
Spain	416	404	387	368	366	359	348	−16.3
France	1258	1226	1158	1099	1050	989	939	−25.4
Ireland	71	78	81	81	88	85	80	12.7
Italy	909	934	890	861	843	821	801	−11.9
Luxembourg	215	212	211	202	194	184	172	−20.0
Netherlands	648	634	616	586	561	539	481	−25.8
Austria	928	898	875	848	836	823	814	−12.3
Portugal	238	227	224	218	212	202	200	−16.0
Finland	348	348	346	341	369	369	366	5.2
Sweden	237	223	212	211	211	216	222	−6.3
UK	537	521	496	491	452	451	426	−20.7
Euro area 12	8637	8361	7954	7521	7218	6906	6593	−23.7
EU-15	9624	9337	8872	8433	8084	7751	7444	−22.7

Source: European Central Bank (2004: Table 1); own calculations.

the respective numbers advanced as well in Greece (7.3 per cent) and Finland (5.2 per cent). Calculating EU and euro-area aggregates based on these national numbers, the number of credit institutions declined by 23.7 per cent in the euro area and by more than 22 per cent in the EU-15 according to the most recent data available (see Table 14.1).

Further evidence of bank consolidation can be found by examining the number of local banking units adjusted for population changes. Here, the number of banking units declined by 47.7 per cent in the Netherlands, by over 33 per cent in Belgium and by slightly more than 26 per cent in Germany. In contrast, the number of local units increased significantly in Greece (30.4 per cent), Italy (15.6 per cent) and Portugal (10.6 per cent). For the euro area and EU-15 the number of units declined by 10.0 per cent and 9.3 per cent, respectively (see Table 14.2).

An examination of trends in cross-border banking linkages between the EU-15 reveals a certain degree of integration at the wholesale level (bank to bank or bank to large companies) but very little evidence of consolidation at the retail level.[10] No truly 'pan-European bank' has emerged at the retail level and the market share of foreign branches and subsidiaries in other Member States is low, especially in larger Member States. Integration on a limited scale has been achieved, though, in some smaller Member States such as the Benelux and the Nordic region. Evidence of fragmentation in the retail market is found in the dispersion of company loan and household interest rates, although the dispersion has trended downwards in recent years (with the exception of consumer loans). Differences in bank profitability across countries are another indication of fragmentation. Direct cross-border provision of traditional banking services remains small in absolute terms and seems relevant only for large clients.

In contrast to the limited extent of cross-border banking integration in the EU-15, most of the EU-10 have a high level of foreign ownership in their banking systems (see Figure

Table 14.2 Number of local banking units per 100,000 inhabitants, change in %

	Year							
Country	*1997*	*1998*	*1999*	*2000*	*2001*	*2002*	*2003*	*1997–2003 change in %*
Belgium	72	70	68	65	60	54	48	−33.3
Denmark	43	43	43	44	44	40	39	−9.3
Germany	77	73	71	69	65	62	57	−26.0
Greece	23	26	26	28	29	30	30	30.4
Spain	97	99	99	98	97	96	97	0.0
France	43	42	42	42	43	43	42	−2.3
Ireland	26	28	26	23	25	24	23	−11.5
Italy	45	46	47	49	51	52	52	15.6
Luxembourg	76	76	80	76	62	61	60	−21.1
Netherlands	44	43	40	38	32	29	23	−47.7
Austria	59	58	57	57	57	55	54	−8.5
Portugal	47	49	53	55	54	52	52	10.6
Finland	25	24	23	23	24	24	24	−4.0
Sweden	28	25	24	23	23	23	23	−17.9
UK	28	27	26	25	25	24	24	−14.3
Euro area 12	60	59	59	58	57	56	54	−10.0
EU-15	54	53	53	52	51	50	49	−9.3

Source: European Central Bank (2004: Table 3); own calculations.

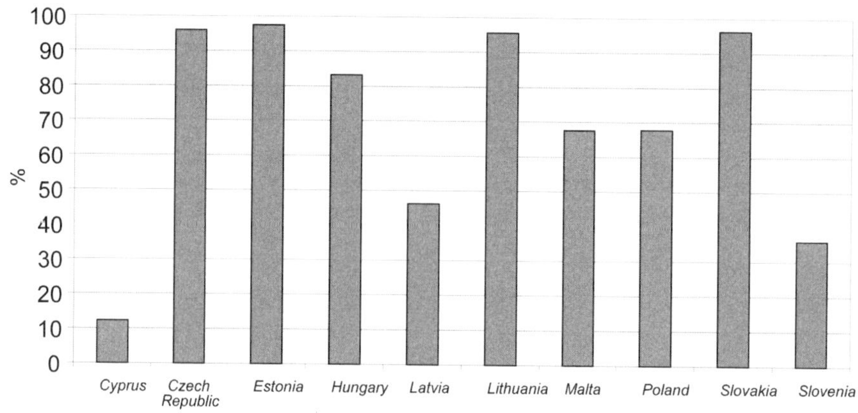

Figure 14.1 Market shares of foreign banks in per cent, as measured in assets.

14.1). The share of foreign-owned banks is especially high in Estonia (97.5 per cent), the Czech Republic (96 per cent), Slovakia (96.3 per cent) and Lithuania (95.6 per cent). The market share of foreign-owned banks amounts to 83.3 per cent in Hungary, 67.8 per cent in Poland and 67.6 per cent in Malta. In contrast, the share of foreign banks is below 50 per cent in Latvia (46.3 per cent), Slovenia (36.0 per cent) and Cyprus (12.3 per cent).

Explaining the differences in cross-border integration and consolidation between EU-15 and EU-10

The following explains the lagging cross-border banking integration within the EU-15 and compares that development with the more internationalized EU-10.

Why cross-border consolidation is lagging in the EU-15 ...

Integration of the EU banking sector can proceed along three different avenues, namely through organic growth in the form of foreign branches and subsidiaries; consolidation via cross-border mergers and acquisitions; and the provision of services on a cross-border basis, allowing customers to choose banking products freely from their country of choice. The following analysis will point to a number of obstacles in each of these avenues, some related to economics, but others related to exogenous institutional factors. As the focus is here on obstacles specifically relating to cross-border integration, other barriers, equally relevant for purely domestic M&As, are not explicitly mentioned.

As explained before, current EU legislation on banking aims to facilitate organic growth by granting each bank a licence valid in all of the Member States, enabling it to establish a foreign branch which is subject to home-country supervision. The objective is to allow a bank from one Member State to enter the domestic market of other Member States via a greenfield investment without the need to report to multiple supervisors. As a bank operating across borders via subsidiaries is subject to host-country supervision in each and every Member State – in addition to home-country supervision on a consolidated basis – it would be expected that organic growth across borders would occur mainly via branches and not subsidiaries.

However, cross-border bank integration has taken place substantially through the establishment of subsidiaries. The number of subsidiaries of other European Economic Area (EEA) countries (that is, EU Member States plus Iceland, Norway and Liechtenstein) in EU Member States reached 333 in 2002 with a market share (based on assets) of 19 per cent when compared with overall EU GDP in 2001 (latest figure available for EU-15); and 23 per cent in the euro area (in 2002).

While the corresponding number of cross-border branches in the EU is clearly higher at 571, the market share in terms of assets amounted to only 24 per cent of GDP in the EU, only slightly above the share recorded for subsidiaries (and surprisingly most of the branches added since 1997 seem to have been concentrated in the non-euro-area Member States).[11]

The relatively even split between the use of foreign-based branches and subsidiaries in terms of GDP share is surprising, given the apparent advantages of a branch-based structure in terms of supervisory compliance costs. Several factors may explain this outcome. For example, Dermine (2002) presents a list of possible explanatory factors, such as the fact that the creation of a subsidiary would help to insulate the mother company from business risk, thereby avoiding investor worries about risk shifting towards faraway places; that the probability of a consolidated branch defaulting would be lower when compared to a subsidiary structure; a subsidiary structure would therefore allow the deposit insurance put option to be exploited in the event of a subsidiary facing difficulties; and the possibility of a separate stock market listing.

More fundamentally, however, the idea that banks would rush to establish branches in other Member States may have been illusory in view of the fact that banks require local knowledge to screen clients, resulting in the need for a proprietary information accumulation.[12] As each loan applicant presents a specific adverse selection problem, banks already active in a specific market have an informational advantage over new entrants, not only in respect of potential clients but also in respect of local market characteristics.

Supporting those arguments, economic research suggests that foreign banks have lower interest margins and lower profitability than their domestic rivals in developed countries (in contrast to emerging markets, see p. 318).[13] Banks would therefore be expected to hesitate in establishing greenfield operations in other Member States – especially for retail clients – and may prefer to enter a foreign banking market through mergers or acquisitions.[14]

Cross-border mergers and acquisitions are another possible avenue for integration in the EU banking sector. Mergers can be defined as the combination of two organizations (with comparable size) into one legal entity. Acquisitions are transactions where one firm purchases a controlling stake in another one, without necessarily combining the involved firm's assets. According to the available data, cross-border mergers and acquisitions have not been a major feature of the EU banking sector. In terms of numbers, mergers and acquisitions among domestic credit institutions represent about 80 per cent of total consolidation activity in the EU in each year since 1991[15] (see Figure 14.2). The only clear pick-up in cross-border mergers and acquisitions is evident in the run-up to the creation of the single market in 1992, when the share of domestic mergers fell to about 60 per cent in 1989 and 1990. However, cross-border mergers and acquisitions have never come close to exceeding domestic mergers and acquisitions.

The dominance of domestic consolidation is even more remarkable in terms of value (see Figure 14.3), accounting for a share of about 80 per cent or more in fourteen out of the last seventeen years and falling below 70 per cent only in 1989. A possible explanation for the different outcomes in terms of numbers and value may be that EU banks pursue modest cross-border value deals in order to escape the involvement of national politicians and regulators.[16]

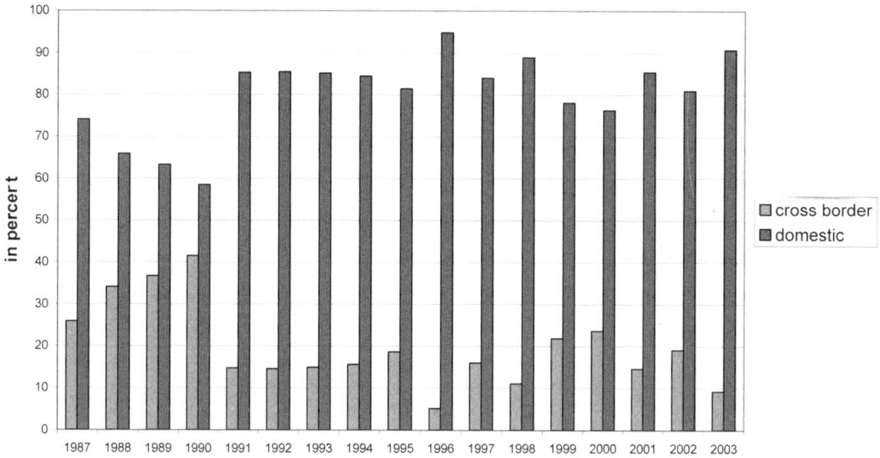

Figure 14.2 Share of domestic, cross-border depository institutions on overall M&As in numbers.

Although national banking systems may have evolved differently due to deeply rooted cultural and political preferences, possibly preventing full EU banking integration even in the absence of any kind of barriers,[17] there are a number of specific reasons potentially explaining the low number of cross-border M&As within the EU, rooted in political considerations leading to investment restrictions and in other institutional barriers related to taxation and a lack of common financial reporting.[18]

The divergence between bank consolidation at the domestic and cross-border levels may be explained by the existence of political resistance to foreign bank entry. For example, some have argued that economic openness and international financial integration pose a threat to the domestic corporate establishment, which is able to finance most of its projects through retained earnings and so does not need a competitive banking system.[19] It has also been suggested that domestic banks may oppose foreign entry in an effort to limit competition. As government authorities are involved in the banking sector – often as bank owners and more often as supervisors – powerful vested national interests pressuring the political class for their purposes cannot be excluded.[20] In this context, some observers have pointed to 'state-induced' barriers to integration, such as explicit and implicit rules against foreign competitors which are sometimes accompanied by strategies to create national champions.[21, 22] One observer sums up the EU situation in the banking sector with the following words:

> The domestic banks in Europe were – and are – protected as domestic flagships. A fundamental belief that financial institutions should not be controlled by foreigners has (so far) almost prevented any cross-border merger ... central banks, ministries of finance and the banks operate in close concert. This is not very surprising: a very homogenous group of executives is in charge of the financial sector, central bank and government ministries guaranteeing a clear national identity of domestic institutions. In countries with explicit government involvement ... foreign control over domestic institutions is even more unlikely ... unless banks become so inefficient and weak that involvement of foreigners becomes almost inevitable.
>
> (Boot 1999: 610f.)

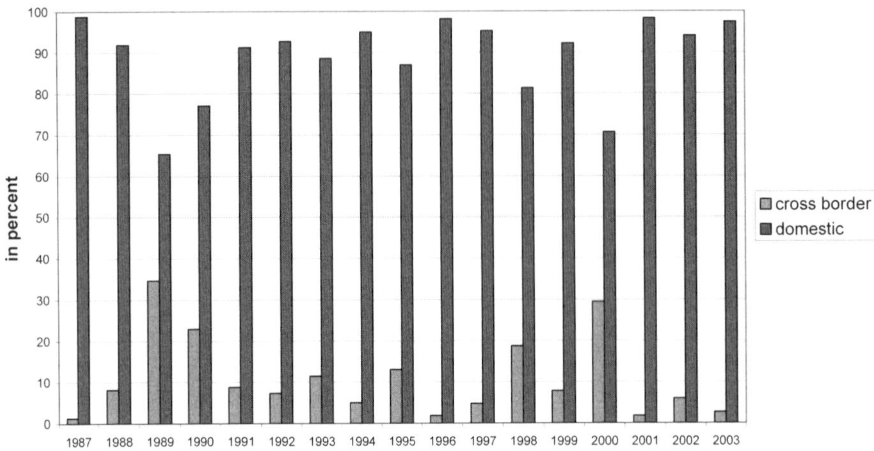

Figure 14.3 Share of domestic, cross-border depository institutions on overall M&As in value.

Political fear mongering about a sell-out of 'national' banks may meet a receptive broader audience as – already – domestic banking sector consolidation can be controversial, with proponents stressing the benefits of increased synergies and cost-savings and opponents warning of job losses and the regularity of failure among business strategies. Cross-border integration can be particularly controversial because of the inevitable foreign dimension in any transfer of ownership (see the Appendix for the effects of banking integration and consolidation).

Inward investment restrictions are one of the most obvious examples of government intervention to protect national companies and thus potentially impede cross-border consolidation. These restrictions can take several forms, the most important of which are special public control rights of Member States, restrictions deriving from company law and restrictions deriving from prudential considerations.[23]

Many cross-border barriers still derive from tax legislation and from different financial reporting requirements. The major tax related barriers are:[24]

Income flows between associated companies: income flows between company groups – mainly dividends, interest rate payments and royalties – are not subject to double taxation, if covered by EU Directives. However, the narrow scope of the Directives and implementation problems at Member State level often render the provisions inapplicable, thereby undermining incentives for cross-border consolidation.

Cross-border restructuring operations: in order to guarantee equality of treatment, the taxation of cross-border restructuring operations following mergers and acquisitions is partially harmonized at EU level through the 'Merger Directive'. However, diverging national merger rules, a narrow scope and transposition problems hamper its application.

Loss compensation: while losses incurred by foreign branches may usually be offset at the level of the parent company (subject to special conditions and maximum thresholds), an offset from subsidiaries is often not allowed. In addition, diverging national loss compensation rules generate – even in the case of branches – interpretational divergences detrimental to their recognition by tax authorities.

The calculation of transfer prices: in practice, companies encounter several problems with the concept of transfer pricing, which is significant for tax authorities as it affects the tax allocation between different jurisdictions.

Shortcomings in double taxation treaties: Member States have concluded a number of agreements with the aim of avoiding double taxation of companies operating on a cross-border basis. However, this goal is not always achieved.

In addition, an international framework of rules and regulations on financial reporting is necessary, not least to ensure that the information disclosed by banks is comparable across the EU.[25]

Another barrier to the achievement of M&A gains consists of stifling labour laws thwarting gains from post-M&A restructuring, although this would presumably equally apply to domestic consolidation. If banks were able to supply products and services on an EU-wide basis, the EU banking market could become integrated from the consumer side. However, apart from bank-to-bank transactions and services offered by investment banks, this avenue of integration on a retail level has not been exploited significantly to date in the EU-15.

One reason for the absence of foreign lending to retail clients may simply relate to asymmetric information and the significance of having a local presence and local knowledge. Guiso *et al.* (2002) find that it is financial institutions' local presence which boosts entrepreneurial activity, especially among the young, increases the formation of new firms, augments product competition leading to smaller profit margins for non-financial companies, results in higher growth of firms and enhances overall economic growth. In addition, Berger *et al.* (2002) show that even foreign affiliates of large multinational corporations opt in most cases for cash management services provided by a local bank, rather than taking the – supposedly – more convenient step of sticking with 'their' host bank.

Another rationale, though – although possibly related to the first – is the absence of sufficiently consolidated European private law, which creates – for example – difficulties for enforcing cross-border collateral pledges. One prominent manifestation of this more general problem is the diverging levels of consumer protection and bankruptcy laws, making the introduction of EU-wide retail banking products (mortgages, loans, pension products, saving vehicles) impossible, thus denying banks operating on a cross-border basis the possibility of reaping economies of scale.[26]

... while consolidation has progressed in the EU-10

Although today the EU-15 and the EU-10 face similar barriers to cross-border banking integration and consolidation, these barriers were presumably higher for the EU-10 before their accession to the EU in legal and regulatory terms. Paradoxically, however, banking integration has advanced much further outside the regulatory structures of the EU than within.

An explanation for the high level of foreign banks in the EU-10 might be found in the combination of a number of factors related to special historical circumstances. Banks previously operating under a centrally planned regime were ill prepared to meet the challenges of the transition to a market-based economy, lacking the necessary risk management skills and a capability for effective scrutiny of lending. In consequence, many governments decided to embark on major privatization processes by actively inviting foreign institutions to enter – with foreign banks bringing with them the necessary know-how and experience and enabling a rapid transformation towards the establishment of an efficient banking system.

In consequence, the level of national resistance to foreign bank entry – through the cited integration avenues – was presumably much lower than in the EU-15. In addition, governments were presumably also willing to address foreign entrants' concerns regarding existing legal and regulatory barriers.

As a result, cross-border banking M&As were much easier and more politically welcome. Even the case for greenfield investments would seem different for the EU-10 when compared to the Member States of the EU-15 due to special factors. First, foreign banks would not have faced the information disadvantages usually encountered in more mature economies as local banks previously operating under the auspices of a centrally planned economy would not have historical credit-related knowledge either. Second, a greenfield entry might have the additional advantage of avoiding the heritage of bad loans from past – largely plan-driven – lending decisions. As a result, foreign banks have used the entrance avenue provided by organic growth on a much larger scale.[27]

Although there is significant cross-border lending recorded between the EU-15 and the recently acceded Member States – reaching 42 per cent of EU-10 GDP in 2003 – this seems to reflect primarily bank-to-bank lending in the form of group funding via parent banks. The high share of cross-border lending between the EU-15 and the EU-10 might also relate to the heightened role of foreign currency lending, reflecting the more benign funding conditions in foreign currencies and the anticipation of membership of the euro area.[28]

Foreign banks were attracted to the EU-10 for a variety of reasons. First, the relatively strong economic performance of the EU-10 provided an attractive growth opportunity. Second, empirical findings suggest that foreign banks report significantly higher net interest margins than domestic banks in emerging markets due partly to their more efficient business practices but also to their ability to ignore political pressures to lend to inefficient sectors.[29] Third, many of the foreign banks seemed to have entered those countries with long-term strategic goals in mind. For example, Nordic banks are active in the Baltic States and Austrian and Italian banks operate in many neighbouring Central European countries. In contrast, the role of non-EU banks is rather limited.[30] In addition, the possible anticipation of EU membership will have played a significant role also.

Stability challenges linked to EU banking integration

The following analysis points first to the risks related to the current EU supervisory arrangement and then to broader macroeconomic stability risks.

The EU supervisory arrangement

The current arrangement

The EU supervisory framework has been regarded until recently as a convenient means to facilitate market entry without the need for a major change in Member State arrangements. As outlined above, a bank operating across borders via subsidiaries is subject to host-country supervision in each and every Member State – in addition to home-country supervision on a consolidated basis. A pan-EU bank can therefore be required to deal with a plethora of supervisors from different jurisdictions, each operating in accordance with different rules and distinct procedures. Consequently, there might be an issue of co-ordination between the large numbers of authorities involved.

In the case of a crisis the situation would be even more complex as not only the supervisors, but also the central banks and the ministries of finance may be involved in raising co-ordination issues at the national as well as cross-border level. While channels for co-ordination on a national level would seem sufficiently well developed, cross-border co-ordination between home- and host-country authorities or between different host-country authorities in the case of a subsidiary would seem more cumbersome. Although it can be expected that supervisory authorities would in general share the common goal of redressing a crisis situation effectively, there might be some delicate cases. One example might be philosophical and political differences leading to conflicts as some authorities could favour a bail-out of the whole group while others would be inclined to let the bank subsidiary in their jurisdiction fail.

Emergency liquidity assistance through a domestic central bank would be another issue, possibly involving similar problems. The supranational character of the monetary authority responsible for the euro might raise the additional matter of how effectively diverging views between participating central banks might be resolved.

In the case of a bank expansion via branches the home-country supervisor bears the cost of supervising the foreign-branch activities of its domestic banks, while the host country receives most of the possible benefits (and risk) in terms of a healthy (or frail) domestic financial system. Consequently, the home-country supervisor may face suboptimal incentives in performing its duties vis-à-vis the host country. This problem of incentives would be most pronounced in circumstances where the foreign-branch business of the home-country bank is relatively small in terms of its total activity but relatively large in terms of the host country's banking system. In such a situation, financial distress in the bank's foreign branches would have only limited consequences for the home country but would have more significant implications for the financial system of the host country (Schüler 2003).[31]

In that case, there is a risk that national interests might discourage the home-country supervisor from declaring a bank insolvent as this would put pressure on the home-country taxpayers to provide funds for bail-out payments or restructuring costs, while benefiting the home country only to a limited degree. In the case of a pan-European bank, pre-agreed procedures to follow in any bank bankruptcy proceedings and/or agreements regarding potential banking bail-outs might become necessary in order to avoid an undue burden on a (possibly small) home country.

In that context, the responsibilities of a home-country supervisor in relation to foreign branches can be a cause of concern for the host-country supervisor. While the host country retains some emergency powers, these can be used only in extremis, if a spirit of co-operation and trust between home and host supervisor – as well as the confidence of foreign banks operating in the host country – is to be maintained.[32] In these circumstances, the host-country supervisor has very limited possibilities to influence the behaviour of foreign banks within its domestic financial system.

Another issue might arise if a bank's overall balance sheet is healthy enough to permit further lending, domestically as well as abroad, while considerations related to the business cycle or the exchange rate would warrant tightening lending conditions in a host country. As a result, a special type of conflict could arise between home-country prudential control related to specific banks' solvency ratios and host-country concerns relating to overall financial stability.

Different national deposit guarantee arrangements can become another source of concern in a cross-border context. Diversity is said to exist in terms of national arrangements' scope (what is covered), cover (up to what amount), funding (ex post v. ex ante funding) and contributors (depositors v. banks). If a foreign bank with branches in another country were to fail, irritation and deception might result in certain cases for retail consumers as the unfamiliar guarantee arrangements of the bank's home country would apply.

Other problems can arise for the host-country supervisor in the operational phase of a cross-border banking M&A, when operational risk and managerial risk can be high. Unintended credit and liquidity risks might emerge due to a technical failure, especially in an early transition phase where management might not yet be in full control of a newly created entity. Risks stemming from operational failures might be relevant in the consolidation of back office operations. Organizational problems in the context of complex mergers and acquisitions can be another hazard, particularly if the management lacks experience in some activities of the new entity.

Proposals to improve EU supervisory arrangements

Further banking integration might fuel a possible reform of the EU supervisory framework, possibly propelled by the EU entry of the ten new Member States, where some banking systems are largely foreign owned. The matter is gaining increased attention from competent political bodies, allowing further progress to be made. It is noteworthy in this context that a number of proposals for developing the EU supervisory structure further are under discussion.

For efficiency reasons, the cross-border operating commercial banking sector is increasingly calling for a lead supervisor to deal with the split of work between home- and host-country supervisors, although the exact role and competences are not yet very well defined. A variation would be the delegation of certain powers currently held by a home supervisor to a host supervisor, or – in the case of a pan-European operating bank – the delegation of supervisory powers to a selected supervisor, or a supervisory network. While such a model would have to overcome the diverging incentive structures of home and host authorities, a lead supervisory structure would presumably also imply the need for a lead central bank and a lead finance ministry.

A second possible modification to the current supervisory arrangements would be the constitution of a single supervisory authority, either as a centralized institution or organized in a more decentralized way. A variation would be a single supervisory authority exclusively devoted to banks operating on a cross-border basis. Although the advantages of such a model would be that a unified structure could presumably better overcome the diverging incentive structures mentioned above, effective prudential supervision would still be hampered by the unsolved issues inherent in the life-cycle of a bank such as cross-border liquidity assistance and potential taxpayer-financed bail-outs.[33] This idea would therefore be difficult to implement in the current environment as it would also require a single central bank (or a functioning emergency liquidity provision arrangement) for the whole EU and a single pre-agreed bail-out fund administered by a single EU financial authority.

Broader macroeconomic stability issues

Broader macroeconomic stability risks deriving from cross-border banking integration relate to the strong links between the EU-10 and the EU-15, the weak links within the EU-15 and other more general risk considerations.

The link between the EU-10 and the EU-15

The significant market share of foreign banks in the EU-10 raises a number of stability-related issues as foreign bank entry could be either stabilizing or destabilizing. Although experience in the EU-10 seems to have been more positive than negative,[34] the relatively strong links between their banking systems and those of the EU-15 Member States could also transfer instability, affecting both sides. However, in practice, the much larger size of the EU-15 banking system implies that that of the EU-10 is currently much more vulnerable. In the future, though, the faster-growing EU-10 markets might render this stability risk increasingly applicable to the EU-15 as well. A possible consolidation wave between EU-15 originated banks, also active inside the EU-10, would heighten their vulnerability in the event of a home-country banking problem within the group; and perhaps also the vulnerability of group earnings in the event of problems in the EU-10.

The suboptimal incentive structures for banking supervisors and unclear issues in the provision of emergency liquidity and in any taxpayer-financed bail-out, as outlined above, might therefore – for the moment at least – affect the largely foreign-owned EU-10 to a much larger degree than the EU-15. In the current political climate, however, home-country fiscal authorities might find it very difficult to justify to their electorate a transfer of funds to bail out a failed bank with a significant branch network in other Member States. Yet a failure to act might result in general calls at the political level to retreat from European arrangements in the light of their apparent failure to deliver.

Another consideration would relate to the potential widespread take-off of EU banking integration, which might mean heightened competitive pressure on the banking system of the EU-10, as the comparatively high margins – and the corresponding elevated level of profitability – may erode. The resulting diminishing bank capital buffers might lead to stability risks, requiring vigilance on the part of supervisors, if not accompanied by cost restructuring. Given that some foreign banks seem to go rather aggressively for market share in the EU-10, therefore heightening banking competition, there is a worry that some of the weaker banks might be tempted to engage in more risky business activities.

Risks related to weak links within the EU-15

In contrast, the risk for the EU-15 is different and originates from the lack of cross-border banking integration, which is isolating national retail banking markets. As a result, asymmetric shocks within an individual Member State's economy or its banking system might *not* spill over into the banking system of the other EU-15 countries, but instead aggravate economic downturns purely locally. This lack of risk sharing and contagion would lead to frictions and would make it politically difficult for the Union as a whole to counteract such an adverse development with existing policy instruments, which are mostly designed for multi-country groupings – such as monetary policy for those Member States participating in the euro area. In extremis, the difficulties of setting an adequate interest rate for such an area, divided by economic fortunes, might mean excessively high rates for slow-growing countries – leading to distressed banks – and result in too low rates for fast-growing countries – leading to asset bubbles.

Under the euro regime a national financial system's stability cannot be insulated from the stresses caused by the slow adjustment in real sector markets and an overextended – i.e. weak – fiscal policy. It is therefore likely that the strain caused by a negative shock originating in the real sector might impact on banks' stability, leading either to a withdrawal of funds (potentially from both domestic and cross-border lenders) or to adverse consequences for those depositors not withdrawing theirs – with the latter hitting consumer and business confidence. Even if banking defaults can be avoided, though, more widespread fragility in the national banking sector might lead to suboptimal lending opportunities for the non-financial sector, given the absence of cross-border banking links. As a consequence, this could lead to a mutually reinforcing vicious cycle between weak banks and the suboptimal funding of the non-financial sector.

In addition, the lack of EU-15 cross-border banking linkages means the continued absence of a valuable tool to smooth the often observed large differences in economic cycles across Member States and the overall cyclical volatility of the EU economy.

More general risk considerations

Apart from these more specific concerns relating to either the EU-10 or the EU-15 there is also another, more general, concern: namely that national pride and stifling labour laws could keep inefficient and unprofitable banking institutions in operation longer than economically justified, making them either increasingly vulnerable to failure or – alternatively – providing incentives for them to seek risky business strategies in a gamble for resurrection.

Currently, foreign bank ownership is a reality for the EU-10 and to a more limited degree in the Nordic Countries and the Benelux, but also in other smaller countries such as Austria. These dozen or more countries are thus already alert to the benefits and risks of foreign bank ownership on a relatively small scale. Before integration spreads on a larger scale to big economies – as now may be beginning to happen – the stability challenges must be addressed.

Appendix: effects of banking integration and consolidation on growth and economic performance

The role of the banking system

The financial system as a whole, and the banking sector in particular due to its significant size in Europe, plays an essential role in the economy by transforming assets, facilitating risk management, financing trade, enabling capital accumulation and spurring technological innovation.

Banks fulfil two important functions which contribute to a more efficient resource allocation:

A monitoring function for investors: the financial system is characterized by an information asymmetry between those wishing to borrow at the lowest possible cost and those wishing to invest at the highest possible return. This asymmetry creates risk for the investor, as the borrower cannot be relied upon to be entirely transparent about his creditworthiness. Verification of the creditworthiness of each potential borrower is costly and, while it may be feasible for larger-scale investors to undertake their own credit analysis, smaller investors typically lack the required resources. Here, a bank fulfils the role of monitoring credit quality on behalf of individual investors, so ensuring a high level of funding available for investment.

A gatekeeper function for companies: in the absence of a monitoring intermediary, investors would tend to apply an average value to all possible investment opportunities. This would imply over-investment in lower-quality projects and under-investment in higher-quality projects.

Through their capacity to rank investment opportunities in order of quality, banks ensure that savings are channelled to those projects with the highest (risk-adjusted) rate of return, thereby ensuring higher productivity from investment.

This section surveys first the effects of cross-border banking integration on the performance of the banking sector and, by extension, on economic performance and growth in the whole economy via the wider opportunities available for firms and households located in less developed financial systems. Then, the efficiency effects derived from consolidated banking systems and the finance–growth nexus are considered.

Financial integration as opportunity for less developed financial countries

Rajan and Zingales (1998) start with the hypothesis that – within countries – industries which are more dependent on external financing (as opposed to financing from retained profits) will have relatively higher growth rates in countries that have more developed financial markets. Utilizing a proxy for financial dependence on a sample of publicly listed companies, the authors find that financial development influences economic growth rates via the reduction of the cost of external finance to financially dependent firms. It is also suggested that a developed financial system may play a crucial role in the rise of new firms, while a lack of financial development may favour incumbent firms – able to fund themselves through retained profits – over new entrants.

Applying those results to EU financial integration it could be argued that banking integration among countries with varying levels of financial development might especially benefit firms and households in financially less developed countries, and increase their growth opportunities in particular. This argumentation is utilized by Guiso *et al.* (2004), who point to the large diversity of national financial systems and their differing degree of sophistication where – for example – the GDP ratio of bank claims ranges from 40 to 50 per cent in Greece and Italy to over 100 per cent in Sweden and the Netherlands. According to the authors, most of the EU-10 countries score at or below the least financially developed member of the EU-15. Financial integration starting from such a range of diverse initial conditions is therefore to be regarded as a great opportunity for the less developed countries as integration improves the access for firms and households located there to the credit and securities markets of the more financially developed countries. Based on several scenarios, the authors conclude that it would be reasonable to expect financial integration to result in a 'growth dividend'.

In addition, access to an efficient banking system benefits the development of the entire financial services by fostering the evolution of a money market through increased interbank lending, bond and equity markets through underwriting services and more efficient risk pricing through securitization programmes.

Consolidation and banking sector performance

A significant consequence of EU banking integration will be – in a first step – primarily domestic consolidation reflecting adjustments to a more competitive environment and the availability of increased scale and scope economies.[35] It is therefore useful to examine the relevant effects of consolidation on client welfare, operating efficiency, profit efficiency and overall efficiency. Although most of the following analysis is related to consolidation within a country, it might become – over time – equally relevant for banking consolidation across countries.

Client welfare

The impact of consolidation on banking sector performance remains controversial.[36] A number of empirical papers indicate that banking consolidation – if successful – increases client welfare by improving lending rates and increasing credit access for borrowers, as well as raising deposit rates but over longer time periods. For example, Bonaccorsi di Patti and Gobbi (2002) show that bank consolidation improves the availability of credit for (high-quality) corporate borrowers.

Using a set of Italian banks with a large number of small and privately held companies as clients, Sapienza (2002) discovers that in-market mergers (involving banks operating previously in the same geographical area) benefit borrowers if such mergers involve the acquisition of banks with small market shares, as rates charged by the consolidated bank decline. However, this effect is reversed if the merged banks increase their combined market share significantly, possibly due to competition problems. The positive interest rate effect is equally found in out-of-market mergers (involving banks previously operating in another geographical area), but to a lesser extent.

In contrast, some studies, e.g. Sapienza (2002), indicate that smaller borrowers are disadvantaged by bank consolidation to the extent that longstanding bank–client relationships and lending policies are disrupted, and the transfer of information from the target institution to the acquiring bank is not smooth. Moreover, evidence suggests that the problems for small borrowers increase with the size of the acquiring bank, with larger acquiring banks tending to cut off many more small borrowers. In an emerging market context, Berger *et al.* (2001) find large size and foreign ownership of banks to be statistically significant barriers for providing relationship lending services in Argentina. The effect seems to be most pronounced for small businesses with delinquencies in repaying loans. While Scott and Dunkelberg (2003), surveying a sample of small US firms in the mid-1990s, find that banking consolidation has no significant effect on small firms' ability to obtain loans, they seem to increase non-price loan costs (e.g. service fees) as well as leading to a deterioration in service quality and an increase in the frequency of small companies changing banks.

Peek and Rosengreen (1997b) argue that bank consolidation need not always curtail small business lending. They stress that an acquiring bank tends to recast the target bank in its own image, which leads the new consolidated bank to have a similar portfolio composition of small business clients to that of the acquiring bank. In this respect, bank consolidation would be problematic for smaller enterprises if the acquiring bank was not already a significant lender to such enterprises. They point out that in roughly half of the commercial and savings bank mergers in the United States, the acquirer had a larger small business loan portfolio than the target bank. In addition, the most common acquirer of a small bank had been another small bank. Karceski *et al.* (2000) assess the impact of bank consolidation on borrowers' welfare by analysing share price reactions of corporate borrowers to a merger announcement using a Norwegian data set. They find that smaller borrowers of target banks seem to benefit from small banking mergers, as reflected in a gain in their share prices, while their share prices fall when two large banks merge.

With respect to deposit holders, Focarelli and Panetta (2002) find strong evidence that banking consolidation leads to rising deposit rates in the long run, thus overcoming possible adverse price changes immediately following a merger or acquisition. However, retail banking markets are overwhelmingly local and evidence suggests that strongly rising local bank concentration rates tend to be associated with lower interest rates on deposits (see Simons and Stavins 1998). Prager and Hannan (1998) demonstrate that a more pronounced decline in deposit rates is observable in those local markets where substantial horizontal banking mergers have taken place when compared to markets where no such mergers have occurred. Therefore, a disproportionate domestic consolidation may impact negatively on client welfare due to rising national banking concentration rates and consequently rising prices. Cross-border bank integration in segmented markets, though, could strengthen competition.

Operating efficiency

While the balance of evidence suggests that – in the absence of strongly concentrated banking markets – consolidation leads to welfare gains for clients, evidence of efficiency gains within consolidated banks seem to be much less clear cut. In a meta-examination, Rhoades (1994) considers thirty-nine empirical studies of bank consolidation and efficiency that were undertaken between 1980 and 1993. About half of the studies use an 'operating-performance' approach, thus observing the financial performance of banks following a merger or acquisition. The other half comprise 'event' studies, measuring the reaction of stock prices of acquirer and target banks, subsequent to a merger or acquisition announcement.

The findings of the operating-performance studies point to a lack of improvement in bank efficiency or profitability as a result of mergers, while results from the event studies fail to find rising stock prices – when prices of bidders and targets are combined – in response to mergers.

Pilloff and Santomero (1997) fail to establish statistically significant post-merger gains, either in share value gains or via improved performance indicators as derived from accounting data. Investigating consolidation benefits for banks in various industrialized countries, Amel *et al.* (2002) find economies of scale mainly for mergers and acquisitions involving smaller banks, while convincing evidence for economies of scope or gains in managerial efficiency is not found. However, Huizinga *et al.* (2001) discover improved cost efficiency for consolidating banks, both for large and small bank mergers, often especially pronounced when both banks portray poor pre-merger cost efficiency.

The frequent absence of observed efficiency gains from bank consolidation may be explained by various efficiency barriers in bank mergers and acquisitions. In respect of cross-border EU merger and acquisitions, Vander Vennet (2002) points out that the typical deal is characterized by the takeover of a poorly performing bank by a relatively efficient foreign bank. The study finds evidence of an increase in realized profits, but not in operational efficiency, at least in the short term. The author explains these findings by reference to different legal and tax systems, which prevent the full exploitation of synergies in cross-border bank consolidation.

Hughes *et al.* (2003) argue that the key to successful banking mergers is efficient bank corporate governance structures. This study finds that an increase in acquired assets improves the financial performance of banks with less entrenched management – defined as a low proportion of the bank owned by management. On the other hand, an increase in acquired assets tends to worsen performance of banks with a more entrenched management, which may prefer to 'build empires' rather than seek the most valuable acquisitions. The analysis suggests that acquisitions might allow an entrenched management to increase its consumption of agency goods (defined as perks) and also to avoid effort and risk. The authors explain their result by suggesting that managers owning banks are better able to resist the pressure of market discipline, while a larger share of outside owners results in a better monitoring of management performance.[37]

A number of analyses argue that efficiency gains from bank consolidation are understated due to measurement problems. Unlike most studies, which use financial data or estimates of managerial efficiency, Haynes and Thompson (1999) examine the impact of acquisitions on the productivity of building societies and banks over the period 1981–93 using a Cobb–Douglas production function approach. The authors find evidence of productivity gains from consolidation, whereby the effect is steadily increasing over a period of six or more years subsequent to an acquisition. This is explained by the gradual dismissal of initial retained staff, who had received employment assurances for an immediate post-acquisition period. This observation shows also that a short-term oriented assessment – such as possibly reflected in share price changes – might not always take longer-term efficiency effects into account.

Another reason for understating gains from banking sector consolidation in US studies might be found in accounting rules, as discussed by Kwan and Wilcox (1999). Two methods exist in the US General Accepted Accounting Principles (GAAP) to account for banking mergers and acquisitions – purchasing accounting and pooling of interest.

In purchasing accounting, the difference between the (usually higher) purchasing price and the book value of the target bank's equity (including its premises and equipment) is recorded as goodwill, an intangible asset. As intangible assets must be amortized and expensed, the consolidated bank's depreciation charge and amortization expense will rise instantly, even if there is no change in performance of the consolidated bank after the merger.

On the other hand, in pooling-of-interest accounting, the reported assets of the new consolidated bank would be equal to the sum of the reported assets of the two merging banks. The authors argue that a significant use of the purchasing accounting approach for reporting results and rising share prices after M&As (as was the case in the 1990s) would aggravate the negative effect on reported expenses. With data corrected for these factors, bank consolidation leads to significant efficiency gains and reduced operating costs, in terms of both labour costs and other expenses.

Profit efficiency

Cost efficiency is defined as a cost reduction per unit of output for a given set of output quantities and input prices. However, Akhavein *et al.* (1997) investigate profit efficiency, which is taking cost considerations *and* revenue considerations into account. Profit X-inefficiency is the failure to produce the highest value of output for a given set of input quantities and output prices. One example would be a profit X-inefficient firm which produces too few outputs for a given set of inputs, being inside its production possibilities frontier.[38] Another example would be a firm operating on the production possibilities frontier but responding inadequately to relative prices and therefore producing too little of a high-priced output and too much of a low-priced output.

In case customers prefer services that can only be provided by a larger firm or that are complementary to each other (one-stop shopping), profit efficiency can also be the function of scale or scope economies. For overall economic welfare, an increase in the value of output – associated with higher profits – is equally beneficial to a decrease of costs.

In their data set, merging banks tend to shift their output mixes towards high-profit products, possibly because the new consolidated bank may have improved risk diversification opportunities allowing for a higher loan/asset ratio. Consequently, the authors demonstrate that their sample of merged banks significantly improved profit efficiency on average.

Two alternative hypotheses – on why profit efficiency increases following bank mergers – are advanced on the basis of available evidence: the relative efficiency hypothesis, which states that the acquiring bank tends to bring the acquired bank towards its own level of efficiency, and the low efficiency hypothesis, where the merger event would act like a 'wake-up event' (possibly also used as an excuse), causing substantial restructuring and efficiency improvements, increasing the profitability of both parts of the combined institution.

Overall efficiency

Banking mergers may also improve the sector's overall efficiency and resilience to economic shocks. Beck *et al.* (2003) look at banks in seventy countries from 1980 to 1997 and find a higher resilience to economic shocks in more consolidated banking systems with better diversified banks, which are also easier to monitor. On the other hand, a too concentrated banking system might be subject to other forms of idiosyncratic risks undermining the financial system such as in the case of scandals or fraud.

One area where consolidation can clearly bring efficiency gains is in the elimination of excess capacity, particularly as the alternative method is through bank defaults. DeYoung and Whalen (1994) find that since failed banks are significantly less efficient than their peers, consolidation can be a means to eliminate inefficient banks.

The finance–growth nexus

While the above relates mainly to micro-sector analysis, a more efficient banking sector affects also the macroeconomic performance. Although theoretical and empirical work in the field of financial development and economic performance is ongoing, the overall evidence confirms the importance of a developed – hence efficient – banking sector in boosting economic performance.

Using a macro approach, King and Levine (1993) find a positive correlation between a developed banking sector, productivity growth and output per capita in studies of eighty countries over the period 1960–89; the experience of financial sector reforms in five countries; firm-level evidence on the allocative effects of financial reforms; and the success of general policy reforms depending on financial development. Levine *et al.* (2000) demonstrate a strong positive link between financial intermediary development and economic growth, using a range of indicators of intermediation such as overall size of intermediaries and the extent to which financial institutions funnel credit to private sector activities.

The authors apply a variety of econometric techniques to a panel dataset of seventy-four countries covering the period from 1960 to 1995. The possibility of reverse causality is rejected. They further demonstrate that the development of financial intermediation is fostered by laws that give a high priority to secured creditors receiving the full present value of their claims against defaulted firms; legal systems that rigorously enforce contracts; and high-quality accounting standards, which deliver comprehensive and comparable corporate financial statements.[39] Similarly, Beck *et al.* (2000) find a robust and positive link between financial intermediary development and total factor productivity growth which feeds through to overall GDP growth.

Other empirical analysis using a macro approach broadens the concept of financial development to give financial markets a more prominent role next to intermediaries. In a survey article, Levine (1997) documents a strong positive link between the functioning and development of the financial system as a whole and long-run economic growth. Levine and

Zervos (1998) complement their measure of banking sector development (using the value of loans made by commercial banks and other deposit-taking banks to the private sector corrected for GDP) with a proxy for the development of the stock market. They show that banking/financial market development is positively and robustly correlated with current and future economic growth, as capital accumulation and productivity increase. Beck and Levine (2004) find that both banks and stock markets independently boost growth.[40] Research in this field is at present very lively.

Notes

1 This chapter originates from a version of Walkner and Raes (2005). Comments from John Berrigan and Maxwell Watson are gratefully acknowledged.
2 Caution should be used in applying those results too literally in an EU context, which differs fundamentally from offshore lending to emerging markets in institutional, economic and political terms.
3 In a study published in 2000, 38 out of the top 50 international banks are found to have at least 30 per cent of their assets abroad. See *The Banker* (2000).
4 Berger (2003) finds that technological advances have increased productivity and scale economies in processing electronic payments and have as well reduced costs, in some cases by more than 50 per cent.
5 Berger and DeYoung (2000) suggest that efficient organizations can overcome distance effects and there may be no optimal geographic scope for banking institutions.
6 For example, Stiroh and Strahan (2003) argue that in competitive environments, like manufacturing and in the telecommunications industry, capacity has the tendency to go to high-productivity plants, making thus the overall sector more productive. The study provides evidence that deregulating banking markets may have had a similar effect on US banks with the link between performance and market share increasing significantly over time.
7 Basel II will be also transposed via a new Directive.
8 A branch is understood to be a legally dependent part of a credit institution (a bank, for the purpose of this chapter), fully allowed to carry out all of the transactions inherent in the business of banks. It is worth noting that any number of legally dependent parts set up in the same Member State by a single non-domestically authorized credit institution are regarded as a single branch.
9 A subsidiary can be defined as any undertaking over which a parent company effectively exercises a dominant influence.
10 See European Commission (2004a, 2004b). Other papers discussing EU banking integration include: Baele *et al.* (2004), Cabral *et al.* (2002), Corvoisier and Gropp (2001), Dermine (2002), Kleimeier and Sander (2002) and Vander Vennet (2002). See also Manna (2004).
11 European Commission (2004b).
12 See Marquez (2002) and also Kaas (2003) for models on bank entry.
13 See Claessens *et al.* (2001).
14 The banking group Nordea provides an interesting – and unusual – example as it pursued first cross-border M&As, only later trying to convert the group's legal structure through a Societas Europeae into branches (Nordea 2003).
15 Source of Figures 14.2 and 14.3: Competition Databases of DG ECFIN Unit E2 based on Thomson Financial Services: General Statistics on Mergers and Acquisitions; extraction 3 March 2004; data comprise completed as well as announced M&As and include all EU financial firm mergers from any of the depository institutions, non-depository institutions and security and commodity brokers sectors as bidders into the depository banks as target sector; own calculations. A number of sources confirm a low level of banking cross-border M&As, for example Schich and Kikuchi (2003) and Buch and DeLong (2001).
16 *Wall Street Journal* (2003).
17 In addition, a case could be constructed whereby a specific economic and institutional environment led to a special banking model in a particular country. Over time, though, the environment would change, for example due to policies pursued by the EU regarding banking integration. While this changed environment could render the original bank–client relationship inefficient from

the point of view of a *new* client seeking funds, switching costs for *existing* clients would prolong the current banking model and prevent its termination. If history matters to this extent, there might be little demand for a foreign bank even if its lending methods were superior. This scenario is a rather free interpretation – perhaps the original authors would consider it too free? – of the arguments applied to financial structure by Monnet and Quintin (2005). See also Hartmann *et al.* (2003: 189).

18 For a more detailed exploration of the issues, see Walkner and Raes (2005).
19 See Rajan and Zingales (2001, 2003).
20 Similarly to state-owned banks, banks might also be owned by regions or municipalities, syndicates or trade associations.
21 See Berger *et al.* (2000).
22 See, for example, Standard & Poor's (2001): 'The influence of domestic ... regulators should not be underestimated. Political intervention has played a big part in countries such as Italy, Portugal, and France, where governments have intervened to block outside predators. In these countries, the priority remains the emergence of national champions, strong enough to compete on an international basis' (p. 5).
23 See Walkner and Raes (2005).
24 See Walkner and Raes (2005).
25 A remedy to this situation might be at hand in the forthcoming application of the International Accounting Standards (IAS) in the EU.
26 See Walkner and Raes (2005).
27 See European Central Bank (2005).
28 See European Central Bank (2005).
29 See Claessens *et al.* (2001).
30 On this point, see European Central Bank (2005).
31 See also Group of Ten (2001, ch. III: 152f.).
32 A further complication in the use of those 'emergency' instruments would be that banking crises are often characterized by both developing and spreading rapidly, making swift supervisory action necessary as well as opaque (even for supervisors). However, quick unilateral pre-emptive action within an obscure environment might make it difficult for the host supervisors to clearly demonstrate the justification for that action ex post.
33 More detailed cross-border issues to be addressed would include the provision of bank liquidity provision, emergency liquidity assistance, crisis management, lender of last resort clarification, deposit guarantee schemes and bank liquidation.
34 On this, see European Central Bank (2005).
35 Integration and consolidation are expected to coincide (at least over the long term), although – theoretically – it would be possible to observe integration without consolidation.
36 For example, Schenk (2000) declares most banking mergers to be economic failures.
37 A similar point is made by Bertrand and Mullainathan (2003) observing that managers prefer to have quiet lives if they are insulated from takeovers.
38 The concept of X-efficiency was introduced by H. Leibenstein.
39 While Leahy *et al.* (2001) find financial development related to economic growth, they judge the direction of the causation in these relationships to be unclear.
40 However, Andrés *et al.* (1999) do not find a significant growth–finance relationship for developed countries. For one overview confirming that financial development is related to economic growth even in industrial countries, see Thiel (2001).

References

Akhavein, J.D., A.M. Berger and D.B. Humphrey (1997) 'The effects of megamergers on efficiency and prices: evidence from a bank profit function', *Review of Industrial Organisation* 12: 95–139.

Amel, D., C. Barnes, F. Panetta and C. Salleo (2002) *Consolidation and Efficiency in the Financial Sector: A Review of the International Evidence*, Federal Reserve Board, Finance and Economics Discussion Series, No. 47.

Andrés, J., I. Hernando and J.D. Lopez-Salido (1999) *The Role of the Financial System in the Growth–Inflation Link: The OECD Experience*, Banco de España, Servicio de Estudios, Working Paper No. 9920, October.

Baele, L., A. Ferrando, P. Hördahl, E. Krylova and C. Monnet (2004) *Measuring Financial Integration in the Euro Area*, European Central Bank, Occasional Paper Series, No. 14, April.

The Banker (2000) 'Globalisation takes hold', *The Banker*, internet edition, 1 February.

Beck, T. and R. Levine (2004) 'Stock markets, banks, and growth: panel evidence', *Journal of Banking & Finance* 28: 423–42.

Beck, T., R. Levine and N. Loayza (2000) 'Finance and the sources of growth', *Journal of Financial Economics* 58: 261–300.

Beck, T., A. Demirguc-Kunt and R. Levine (2003) *Bank Concentration and Crisis*, NBER Working Paper 9921, August.

Berger, A.N. (2003) 'The economic effects of technological progress: evidence from the banking industry', *Journal of Money, Credit, and Banking* 35(2), April: 141–76.

Berger, A.N. and R. DeYoung (2000) *The Effects of Geographic Expansion on Bank Efficiency*, FEDS Working Paper No. 1–03, November.

Berger, A.N., R. DeYoung and G.F. Udell (2000) *Efficiency Barriers to the Consolidation of the European Financial Services Industry*, Federal Reserve System, Finance and Economics Discussion Series, No. 37, June.

Berger, A.N., L.F. Klapper and G.F. Udell (2001) *The Ability of Banks to Lend to Informationally Opaque Small Businesses*, World Bank Working Papers, No. 2656, August.

Berger, A.N., Q. Dai, S. Ongena and D.C. Smith (2002) 'To what extent will the banking industry be globalized? A study of bank nationality and reach in 20 European nations', paper presented by S. Ongena at the Workshop of the ECB-CFS Research Network 'European Debt Market Structures' and 'Financial Linkages between Europe, the US, and Japan', Frankfurt am Main, 29–30 April.

Bertrand, M. and S. Mullainathan (2003) 'Enjoying the quiet life? Corporate governance and managerial preferences', *Journal of Political Economy* 111(5): 1043–75.

Bonaccorsi di Patti, E. and G. Gobbi (2002) 'Winners or losers? The effects of banking consolidation on corporate borrowers', preliminary version December 2002; presented at the second workshop at the ECB-CFS Research Network on 'Capital Markets and Financial Integration in Europe', Helsinki, March 2003.

Boot, A.W.A. (1999) 'European lessons on consolidation in banking', *Journal of Banking & Finance* 23: 609–13.

Buch, C.M. and G.L. DeLong (2001) *Cross-border Bank Mergers: What Lures the Rare Animal?*, Kiel Working Paper, No. 1070, August.

Cabral, I., F. Dierick and J. Vesala (2002) *Banking Integration in the Euro Area*, European Central Bank, Occasional Paper Series No. 6, December.

Claessens, S., A. Demirgüç-Kunt and H. Huizinga (2001) 'How does foreign entry affect domestic banking markets?', *Journal of Banking & Finance* 25: 891–911.

Clarke, G., R. Cull, M.S. Martinez Peria and S.M. Sanchez (2001) *Foreign Bank Entry: Experience, Implications for Developing Countries, and Agenda for Further Research*, World Bank Policy Research Working Paper, No. 2698, October.

Corvoisier, S. and R. Gropp (2001) *Bank Concentration and Retail Interest Rates*, European Central Bank Working Paper No. 72, July.

Crystal, J.S., B.G. Dages and L.S. Goldberg (2002) 'Has foreign bank entry led to sounder banks in Latin America?', Federal Reserve Bank of New York, *Current Issues in Economics and Finance* 8(1), January: 1–6.

De Haas, R. and I. Van Lelyveld (2003) *Foreign Banks and Credit Stability in Central and Eastern Europe: Friends or Foes*, De Nederlandsche Bank, MEB Series No. 2003–04, Research Series Supervision No. 58, May.

Dermine, J. (2002) 'Banking in Europe: past, present and future', in *The Transformation of the European Financial System*, Second ECB central banking conference, pp. 32–95, October.

DeYoung, R. and G. Whalen (1994) 'Banking industry consolidation: efficiency issues', paper presented at the Jerome Levy Economics Institute Conference, 14–16 April 1994.

European Central Bank (2004) *Structural Analysis of the EU Banking Sector – Year 2003*, November, Frankfurt: ECB.

—— (2005) *Banking Structures in the New EU Member States*, January, Frankfurt: ECB.

European Commission (2004a) 'EMU and the process of financial integration', in *EMU after 5 Years*, European Economy Special Report, Part III, No. 1, Brussels: European Commission, Directorate General for Economic and Financial Affairs.

—— (2004b) *Financial Integration Monitor*, Commission Staff Working Document, Directorate General Internal Market, Brussels: European Commission.

Focarelli, D. and F. Panetta (2002) *Are Mergers Beneficial to Consumers? Evidence from the Market for Bank Deposits*, Banca d'Italia Working Paper, No. 448, July.

Goldberg, L. (2001) *When Is US Bank Lending to Emerging Markets Volatile?*, NBER Working Paper, No. 8209, April.

Goldberg, L., B.G. Dages and D. Kinney (2000) *Foreign and Domestic Bank Participation in Emerging Markets: Lessons from Mexico and Argentina*, NBER Working Paper, No. 7714.

Group of Ten (2001) *Report on Consolidation in the Financial Sector*, January, posted simultaneously on the websites of the BIS, IMF, and OECD, which are the three organizations that provide the secretariat for the Group of 10.

Guiso, L., P. Sapienza and L. Zingales (2002) 'Does local financial development matter?', paper presented at the Workshop of the ECB-CFS Research Network 'European Debt Market Structures' and 'Financial Linkages between Europe, the US, and Japan', Frankfurt am Main, 29–30 April.

Guiso, L., T. Jappelli, M. Padula and M. Pagano (2004) *Financial Market Integration and Economic Growth in the EU*, Centre for Economic Policy Research, Discussion Paper Series, No. 4395, June.

Hartmann, P., A. Maddaloni and S. Manganelli (2003) 'The euro-area financial system: structure, integration, and policy initiatives', *Oxford Review of Economic Policy* 19(1): 180–213.

Haynes, M. and S. Thompson (1999) 'The productivity effects of bank mergers: evidence from the UK building societies', *Journal of Banking & Finance* 23: 825–46.

Hughes, J.P., W. Lang, L.J. Mester and C.-G. Moon (1999) *The Dollars and Sense of Bank Consolidation*, Wharton Working Paper No. 04.

Hughes, J.P., W.W. Lang, L.J. Mester, C.-G. Moon and M.S. Pagano (2003) 'Do bankers sacrifice value to build empires? Managerial incentives, industry consolidation, and financial performance', *Journal of Banking & Finance* 27: 417–47.

Huizinga, H.P., J. Nelissen and R. Vander Vennet (2001) *Efficiency Effects of Bank Mergers and Acquisitions in Europe*, Tinbergen Institute Discussion Paper, No. 088/3.

Kaas, L. (2003) 'Financial market integration and loan competition: when is entry deregulation socially beneficial?', version 11 November, presented at the Third Workshop of the ECB-CFS Research Network on 'Capital Markets and Financial Integration in Europe', 20–21 November, Athens.

Karceski, J., S. Ongena and D.C. Smith (2000) *The Impact on Bank Consolidation on Commercial Borrower Welfare*, Board of Governors of the Federal Reserve System, International Finance Discussion Papers, No. 679, August.

King, R.G. and R. Levine (1993) 'Finance, entrepreneurship, and growth – theory and evidence', *Journal of Monetary Economics* 32: 513–42.

Kleimeier, S. and H. Sander (2002) *Towards a Single Retail Banking Market? New Evidence from Euroland*, Maastricht Research School of Economics of Technology Organization, METEOR, Research Memoranda, No. 0061.

Kwan, S.H. and J.A. Wilcox (1999) *Hidden Cost Reductions in Bank Mergers: Accounting for More Productive Banks*, Working Papers in Applied Economic Theory, No. 10, Federal Reserve Bank of San Francisco.

Leahy, M., S. Schich, G. Wehinger, F. Pelgrin and T. Thorgeirsson (2001) *Contributions of Financial Systems to Growth in OECD Countries*, Economics Department Working Papers, No. 280, March, OECD.

Lensink, R. and N. Hermes (2004) 'The short-term effects of foreign bank entry on domestic bank behaviour: does economic development matter?', *Journal of Banking & Finance* 28: 553–68.

Levine, R. (1997) 'Financial development and economic growth: views and agenda', *Journal of Economic Literature* 35, June: 688–726.

—— (2003) *Denying Foreign Bank Entry: Implications for Bank Interest Margins*, Central Bank of Chile Working Papers, No. 222, August.

Levine, R. and S. Zervos (1998) 'Stock markets, banks, and economic growth', *American Economic Review* 88(3), June: 537–58.

Levine, R., N. Loayza and T. Beck (2000) 'Financial intermediation and growth: causality and causes', *Journal of Monetary Economics* 46: 31–77.

Manna, M. (2004) *Developing Statistical Indicators of the Integration of the Euro Area Banking System*, ECB Working Paper Series, No. 300, January.

Marquez, R. (2002) 'Competition, adverse selection, and information dispersion in the banking industry', *Review of Financial Studies* 15(3): 901–26.

Martinez Peria, M.S., A. Powell and I. Vladkova-Hollar (2002) *Banking on Foreigners: The Behaviour of International Bank Lending to Latin America: 1985–2000*, World Bank Policy Research Working Paper Series, No. 2893.

Monnet, C. and E. Quintin (2005) *Why Do Financial Systems Differ? History Matters*, European Central Bank, Working Paper Series, No. 442, February.

Montgomery, H. (2003) *The Role of Foreign Banks in Post-crisis Asia: The Importance of Method of Entry*, ADB Institute Research Paper Series, No. 51, January.

Morgan, D.P., B. Rime and P. Strahan (2003) *Bank Integration and State Business Cycles*, NBER Working Paper, No. 9704, May.

Nordea (2003) 'Nordea reduces complexity in its legal structure by forming one European company', press release, 19 June.

Peek, J. and E.S. Rosengreen (1997a) 'The international transmission of financial shocks: the case of Japan', *American Economic Review* 87(4), September: 495–505.

—— (1997b) 'Bank consolidation and small business lending: it's not just bank size that matters', paper prepared for the conference 'The Economics of Small Business Finance', at New York University Stern School of Business, 22–23 May.

—— (2000) 'Implications of the globalization of the banking sector: the Latin American experience', *New England Economic Review*, September/October.

Pilloff, S.J. and A.M. Santomero (1997) *The Value Effects of Bank Mergers and Acquisitions*, Wharton Working Paper Series, No. 07.

Prager, R.A. and T.H. Hannan (1998) 'Do substantial horizontal mergers generate significant price effects? Evidence from the banking industry', *Journal of Industrial Economics* XLVI(4), December: 433–52.

Rajan, R. and L. Zingales (1998) 'Financial dependence and growth', *American Economic Review* 88(3), June: 559–86.

—— (2001) *The Great Reversals: The Politics of Financial Development in the 20th Century*, NBER Working Paper, No. 8178, March.

—— (2003) *Banks and Markets: The Changing Character of European Finance*, NBER Working Paper, No. 9595, March.

Rhoades, S.A. (1994) *A Summary of Merger Performance Studies in Banking, 1980–93, and an Assessment of the 'Operating Performance' and 'Event Study' Methodologies*, Federal Reserve Board, Staff Studies, No. 167, July.

Sapienza, P. (2002) 'The effects of banking mergers on loan contracts', *Journal of Finance* LVII(1), February: 329–67.

Schenk, H. (2000) 'On the performance of banking mergers – some propositions and policy implications', paper presented at the UNI conference on 'Mergers and Takeovers: Implications on Employment, Consumers and Shareholders', London, 23–24 October.

Schich, S. and A. Kikuchi (2003) 'European banking and stock market integration', in *Financial Market Trends*, OECD, No. 84, March.

Schüler, M. (2003) *Incentive Problems in Banking Supervision – The European Case*, Mannheim: Centre for European Economic Research (ZEW), October.

Scott, J.A. and W.C. Dunkelberg (2003) 'Banking mergers and small firm financing', *Journal of Money, Credit and Banking* 35(6), December: 999–1017.

Simons, K. and J. Stavins (1998) 'Has antitrust policy in banking become obsolete?', *New England Economic Review*, March/April: 13–26.

Standard & Poor's (2001) 'European banking consolidation: time-out?', commentary by Yves Burger, 25 October.

Stiroh, K.J. and P.E. Strahan (2003) 'Competitive dynamics of deregulation: evidence from US banking', *Journal of Money, Credit, and Banking* 35(5), October: 801–28.

Thiel, M. (2001) *Finance and Economic Growth – a Review of Theory and the Available Evidence*, European Commission, Directorate General for Economic and Financial Affairs, Economic Paper, No. 158, July.

Vander Vennet, R. (2002) *Cross-border Mergers in European Banking and Bank Efficiency*, Universiteit Gent Working Paper, No. 152, September.

Walkner, C. and J.P. Raes (2005) *Integration and Consolidation in EU Banking – an Unfinished Business*, European Commission Directorate-General for Economic and Financial Affairs, Economic Papers, No. 226, April 2005.

Wall Street Journal (2003) 'Europe's banks expand by taking small bites', *Wall Street Journal Europe*, 10 November.

Part IV

Policy challenges

15 Financial supervision in Europe

A proposal for a new architecture

Dirk Schoenmaker and Sander Oosterloo

Introduction[1]

After the successful establishment of the EMU, the debate on the need for a 'European System of Financial Supervisors' is intensifying in the literature (e.g. Vives 2001; Schoenmaker and Oosterloo 2005) as well as in the policy arena (e.g. Economic and Financial Committee 2002; Committee of European Securities Regulators 2004; Financial Services Committee 2005).

The basic argument in favour of moving to a European structure is that it might be difficult to achieve simultaneously a single financial market and stability in the financial system, while preserving a high degree of nationally based supervision and crisis management with only decentralized efforts at harmonization (Thygesen 2003). This is an application of the classical trilemma in macroeconomic policy. Policy-makers are confronted with three desirable, yet contradictory, objectives: fixed exchange rates, capital mobility and independent national monetary policy. Only two out of the three objectives can be pursued at the same time, leaving policy-makers with the decision of which one they wish to give up: the 'trilemma' (Rose 1996). Figure 15.1 illustrates the three incompatible objectives in our case: (1) a stable financial system; (2) an integrated financial market; and (3) independent national financial supervision and crisis management. An argument against moving to a European solution for financial supervision at the present time could be that the degree of integration in financial markets does not yet justify such a move.

The integration of financial markets is thus the key driver for possible changes. In particular, the capacity of the financial services groups to span different EU financial markets fosters integration. Emerging pan-European banks and insurers give rise to cross-border externalities arising from the potential failure of these banks (and insurers). The increasing presence of financial groups from other EU countries undermines the capacity of host authorities to manage effectively the stability of their financial system. Host authorities are thus dependent on the action, or lack of it, of home authorities. Moreover, increased linkages between banks, insurers and pension funds may raise the potential vulnerabilities of the wider European financial system. If these trends continue, it may become necessary to give up the third objective of the trilemma: national financial supervision and crisis management. To maintain the stability of an integrated EU financial system, arrangements for financial supervision and stability may have to be anchored at the EU level.

This chapter identifies the trends in the European financial landscape. The first trend is centralization of risk management functions at the headquarters of financial groups. This reinforces the role of the home supervisor as the consolidating supervisor. The second trend is increasing cross-border penetration of banks and insurers. New evidence on emerging pan-European banks and insurers is provided. We are moving from a landscape with primarily

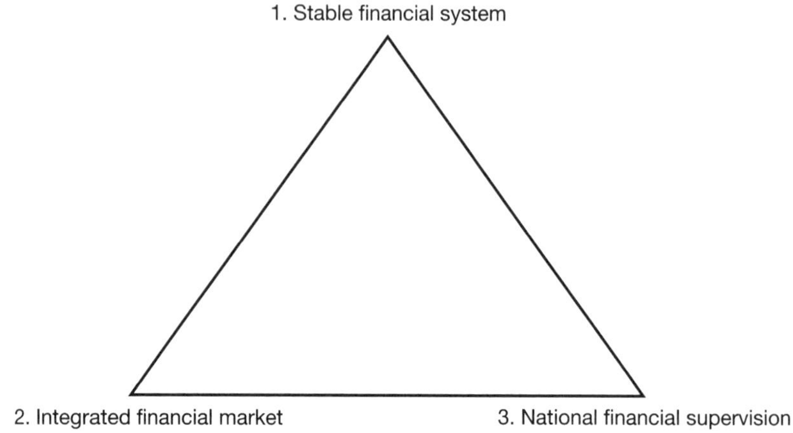

Figure 15.1 The trilemma in financial supervision.

domestically operating financial firms to a small group of large European-wide operating financial firms. Some of these large firms even operate on a global scale.

To create an internal market for financial services, regulations are based on a European footing to ensure their effectiveness as well as a European level playing field. However, supervisory authorities, who enforce these regulations, are still nationally rooted with some elements of European coordination. The national base of supervisors is related to political sovereignty (Herring and Litan 1994). In a more practical sense, it also related to the issue of jurisdiction. One needs a jurisdiction for enforcement of regulations, liquidation and winding-up procedures and taxation. As a European jurisdiction is (or can be made) available, policy-makers have the choice to organize financial supervision and crisis management on a national or a European basis.

We review the different policy options. Coordination arrangements between national supervisors will cultivate duplication of supervisory efforts by home and host supervisors and multiple reporting by financial groups (Schüler and Heinemann 2005). In this chapter, we propose a prospective European System of Financial Supervisors to be created by a European Financial Agency working in tandem with the national financial supervisors. Key elements are decentralized day-to-day supervision close to financial institutions and centralized policy-making to foster a uniform execution of supervision. Such a European System could combine the advantage of a European framework (to incorporate cross-border effects in the decision-making) with the expertise of national supervisors.

Current supervisory arrangements

The current system of prudential supervision in the European Union (EU) is based on the principle of home-country control combined with minimum standards and mutual recognition. A financial institution is thus authorized and supervised in its home country and can expand throughout the EU (via offering cross-border services to other EU countries or establishing branches in these countries) without additional supervision. The host country has to recognize supervision from the home-country authorities.

The arguments for home-country control are twofold. First, it promotes the effectiveness of supervision, as the home supervisor is able to make a group-wide assessment of the risk profile and the required capital adequacy of financial institutions (i.e. the concept of consolidated supervision). The concept of consolidated supervision is well established in banking.[2] The recently adopted Directive on Financial Conglomerates introduces a single coordinator who is responsible for group-wide supervision of financial conglomerates (in addition to supervision of the separate entities of conglomerates).[3] However, the concept of solo-plus supervision is applied in insurance. The primary focus of supervision is on the separate legal entities (the solo element), with some limited attention for group-wide supervision (the plus element).[4] A broader use of group supervision is discussed in the negotiations on a new supervisory regime for insurance (Solvency II).

Second, home-country control promotes the efficiency of supervision, as financial institutions are not confronted with different supervisors possibly resulting in duplication of efforts and a higher regulatory burden. Home-country control is applicable to financial institutions that offer cross-border services to other EU countries or establish branches in these countries. In practice, however, financial institutions also operate through subsidiaries (separate legal entities) in other countries for reasons of taxation and limited liability. These subsidiaries are separately licensed and supervised by the host-country authorities (*de jure* control). The scope for control by host countries of these subsidiaries is limited in practice, as key decisions are often taken at the parent company in the home country and the financial health of the subsidiary is closely linked (via intra-group transactions and/or joint branding) to the well-being of the financial group as a whole. The effective control of large financial groups is to some extent in the hands of the consolidating supervisor in the home country (*de facto* control).

While home-country control may be useful for the effectiveness and efficiency of prudential supervision, home-country authorities are not responsible for the financial stability in host countries (Mayes and Vesala 2000). Stability of the financial system is the remit of the host country. Increasing integration within the EU gives rise to cross-border spill-over effects or externalities. A failure in one country may cause problems in other countries. The policy question is whether home-country control for supervision and host-country responsibility for financial stability are sustainable in an integrating market.

Industry developments

Growing cross-border externalities

Both aggregate data and data on individual banking groups suggest that cross-border externalities within the EU have been rising since the late 1990s. The level of cross-border penetration within Europe is gradually increasing, rising from 11 per cent in 1995 to 18 per cent in 2005 (Figure 15.2). Cross-border penetration is measured as the share of business of banks from other EU countries as a percentage of a country's total banking assets. This quantity-based integration measure suggests that banking integration is progressing. Looking at the country level, it is clear that the degree of cross-border penetration is uneven across Europe. Table 15.1 provides an overview of cross-border penetration in the different countries. While the accession countries have experienced a strong inflow from West European banks (60 per cent of total banking assets in the NMS-10, the ten new member states of the EU (as of 2004)), the cross-border penetration is more limited at 17 per cent in the EU-15. Within the latter group, Luxembourg has a strong presence of EU banks, which is primarily driven by a favourable tax regime. France, Germany, Italy, the Netherlands and Sweden have a low degree of cross-border penetration (less than 10 per cent).

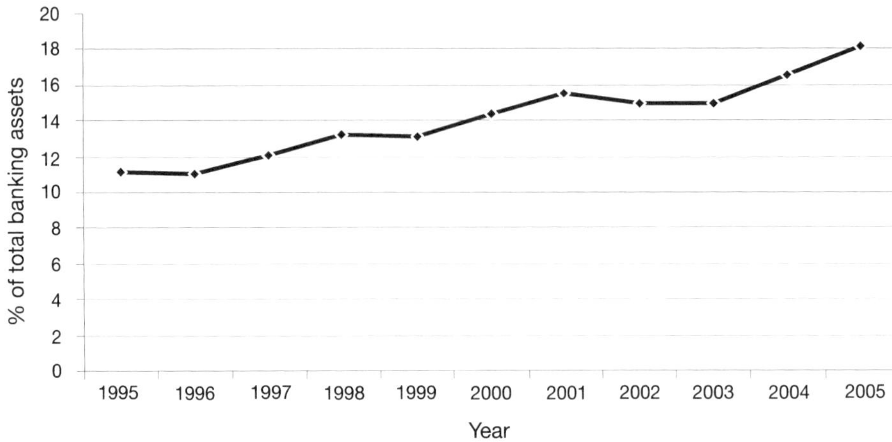

Figure 15.2 Cross-border penetration in European banking.
Sources: Authors' calculations based on Report on EU Banking Structure (ECB, 2004) and EU Banking Structures (ECB, 2006).

Note: Share of assets from EU countries measured as a percentage of total banking assets. The share is calculated for the EU as a whole.

Ongoing financial integration fostered by the advance to EMU and the nearly full completion of the Financial Services Action Plan gives rise to increasing cross-border penetration of interbank markets and payment systems, which are important channels for cross-border contagion. Although the vast majority of the 8,684 credit institutions in the EU are mainly domestically oriented, pan-European and regional banks are emerging with a sizeable cross-border presence. The 14 largest of these cross-border banking groups already account for almost one-third of total banking assets in the EU (Papademos 2005). The level of cross-border business of banking groups is an appropriate measure for the cross-border impact of the (potential) failure of these groups ('cross-border externalities'). While there is a consensus that the need for European arrangements ultimately depends on the intensity of cross-border spill-over effects or externalities within the EU, there has been little or no attempt to measure these cross-border externalities (exceptions are Schoenmaker and Oosterloo 2005; Hartmann *et al.* 2006).

Schoenmaker and Oosterloo (2005) have collected a new data-set on cross-border penetration (as a proxy for cross-border externalities) of large banking groups. The top 30 EU banking groups are selected according to Tier 1 capital. The geographical segmentation of the business of these 30 banks is based on the Transnationality Index calculated as an unweighted average of (1) foreign assets to total assets, (2) foreign income to total income and (3) foreign employment to total employment. The definition of a significant cross-border presence within Europe is twofold. First, a bank conducts more than 50 per cent of its business abroad (outside its home market). Second, a bank conducts more than 25 per cent of its business in the rest of Europe. Figure 15.3 shows that the internationalization of the banking sector is increasing. The number of international banks (European and Global banks) increased from 12 in 2000 to 14 in 2005. It is interesting to see that within the group of International banks, the number of European banks increases (from 7 to 11), while the number of Global banks decreases (from 5 to 3). We conclude that the number of banks

Table 15.1 Cross-border penetration of banking at the country level (2005 figures)

	Number of banks	*Total banking assets (€ billions)*	*Business from domestic banks (%)*	*Business from EU countries (%)*	*Business from third countries (%)*
Austria	880	721	80	19	1
Belgium	100	1,055	77	21	2
Cyprus	391	60	72	22	5
Czech Republic	56	105	7	89	5
Denmark	197	722	79	19	2
Estonia	11	12	1	99	0
Finland	363	235	42	58	0
France	854	5,090	88	10	1
Germany	2,089	6,827	89	9	1
Greece	62	281	72	28	0
Hungary	215	75	41	56	3
Ireland	78	942	57	35	8
Italy	792	2,509	91	9	0
Latvia	23	16	47	50	3
Lithuania	78	13	25	75	0
Luxembourg	155	792	5	87	7
Malta	18	27	68	32	0
Netherlands	401	1,698	98	1	1
Poland	739	152	33	59	8
Portugal	186	360	77	22	1
Slovakia	23	36	3	97	0
Slovenia	25	30	78	22	0
Spain	348	2,151	89	11	0
Sweden	200	653	91	9	0
United Kingdom	400	8,320	48	26	26
EU-15	7,105	32,356	75	17	8
NMS-10	1,579	526	35	60	5
EU-25	8,684	32,882	74	18	8

Source: EU Banking Structures (ECB 2006).

Notes: Share of business from domestic banks, share of business of banks from EU countries and share of business of banks from third countries are measured as a percentage of the total banking assets in a country. The shares add up to 100 per cent. Figures are for 2005. EU-15, NMS-10 and EU-25 are calculated as a weighted average (weighted according to assets).

that have the potential to pose significant cross-border externalities within the European context is substantial and increasing. Within a six year period (2000–5), a statistically significant upward trend of emerging European banking groups is found.

Figure 15.4 depicts the geographical segmentation of the top 25 European insurance groups from 2000 to 2005. The choice of the top 25 insurance groups is based on the top 25 composed by the Comité Européen des Assurances (2007) and ranked on the basis of total group premium. Figure 15.4 indicates that the insurance industry is very internationally oriented. About half of these 25 large insurance groups had an international focus in 2005. Thirteen out of the sample of 25 insurance groups operate on an international scale (more than 50 per cent of their business abroad). Of this international group, 10 operate on a European scale (more than 25 per cent of their business in the rest of Europe). Cross-border insurance is thus widespread in Europe among the large insurers.

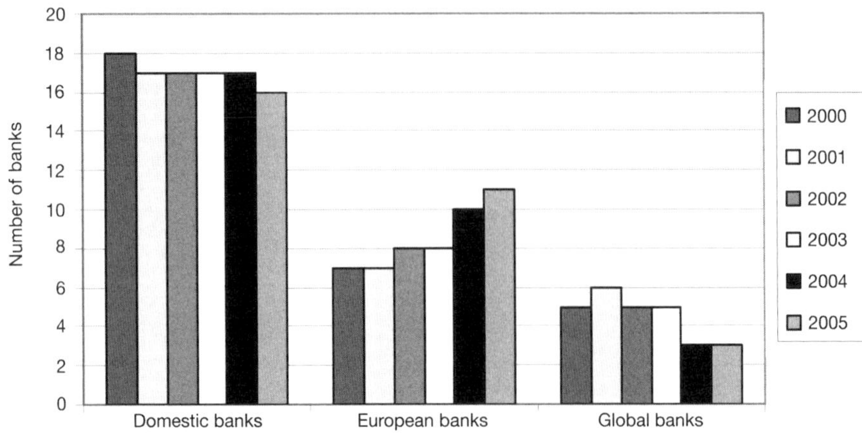

Figure 15.3 Classification of top 30 EU banks.
Source: Schoenmaker and Van Laecke (2006) based on annual reports 2000–2005.

Notes: National banks conduct more than 50% of business in the home market. International banks (more than 50% of business abroad) are divided into European banks (more than 25% of business in other European countries) and global banks (less than 25% of business in other European countries).

This is supported by Van der Zwet (2003), who examines the geographic distribution of revenues of the 38 largest financial groups worldwide in 2000. European financial groups (26 out of the total sample of 38) earn on average 45 per cent of their revenues in their home country, 25 per cent in other European countries and 30 per cent in foreign non-European countries. Van der Zwet (2003) shows that insurance companies are significantly more internationally oriented than banks. Whereas the banks in her worldwide sample have a clear home-country bias, insurance companies have a foreign bias. Taken together, the largest financial groups appear to focus equally on home and foreign markets. Furthermore, Van der Zwet (2003) argues that European financial groups are most strongly internationally diversified.

Integration of risk management functions

The organizational structure of international financial firms is moving from the traditional country model to a business line model with integration of key management functions. The growing integration and centralization of management functions, such as risk management, internal controls, treasury operations (including liquidity management and funding), compliance and auditing greatly affect the scope for control of supervisory authorities. One of the most notable advances in risk management is the growing emphasis on developing a firm-wide assessment of risk. These integrated approaches to risk management aim to ensure a comprehensive and systematic approach to risk-related decisions throughout the financial firm. Although it is costly to realize, Flannery (1999) argues that once firms have a centralized risk management unit in place, they should expect to reap economies of scale in risk management. Nevertheless, these centralized systems still rely on local branches and subsidiaries for local market data. The potential capital reductions that can be achieved by applying the advanced approaches of the new Basel II framework encourage banking

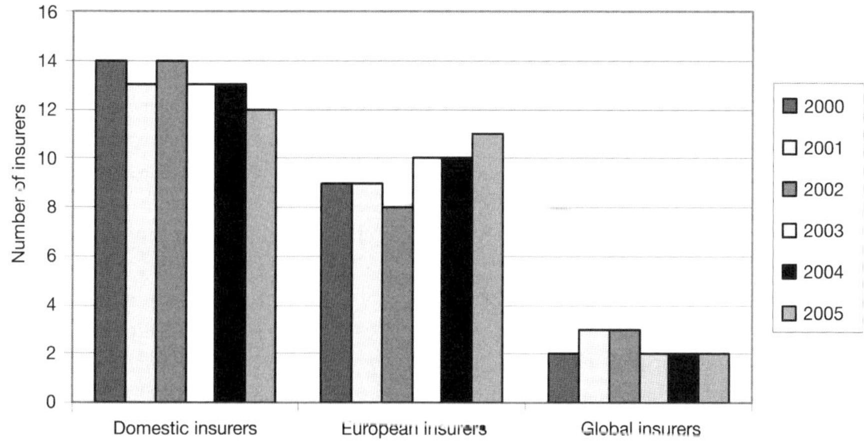

Figure 15.4 Classification of top 25 EU insurers.
Source: Schoenmaker, Oosterloo and Winkels (2007) based on annual reports 2000–2005.

Notes: National insurers conduct more than 50% of business in the home market. International insurers (more than 50% of business abroad) are divided into European insurers (more than 25% of business in other European countries) and global insurers (less than 25% of business in other European countries).

groups to organize their risk management more centrally. The same could also be true for the future Solvency II framework for the European insurance industry. Drzik (2005) argues that, as insurers consider how to implement new ways to measure and manage their business, they would do well to heed the lessons learned in the banking industry, which has been on a similar path since the late 1990s. Firms that implement a well-constructed risk and capital management framework can derive significant near-term business benefits, and substantially strengthen their medium-term competitive position. The emergence of Chief Risk Officers at the headquarters of large insurance groups confirms this trend towards centralization.

Kuritzkes, Schuermann and Weiner (2003) provide evidence that internationally active financial conglomerates are putting in place centralized risk and capital management units. The dominant approach is to adopt a so-called 'hub and spoke' organizational model. The spokes are responsible for risk management within business lines, while the hub provides centralized oversight of risk and capital at the group level. Activities at the spoke include the credit function within a bank, or the actuarial function within an insurance subsidiary or group, each of which serves as the frontline manager for most trading decision-making. These managers are familiar with the local conditions such as the business cycle (relevant for credit risk) and the legal and social security framework (relevant for actuarial risk) in a country. Moreover, aggregation across risk factors within a business line also typically takes place in the spokes, often in a finance unit that is responsible for funding and business reporting for the subsidiary. While the hub is dependent on risk reporting from the spokes, in many cases it is also responsible for overseeing the methodology development of an integrated economic capital framework that is then implemented within the spokes. The specific roles of the hub vary, but tend to include assuming responsibility for group-level risk reporting; participating in decisions about group capital structure, funding practices and target debt rating; liaising with regulators and rating agencies; advising on major risk transfer transactions, such as collateralized loan obligations and securitizations; and, in some institutions, actively managing the balance sheet. A case in point for insurance firms is group-wide asset and liability management done at the headquarters (hub).

In sum, there is clear trend to centralize key management functions that previously belonged with the separate entities of a financial group. Centralization implies that strategic decision-making is transferred from the functional or sectoral entities of the group to the level of the group as a whole (that is, the holding level). The centralization of activities (such as asset management) and key management functions results from the drive of financial groups to reap the benefits of synergy. The prospect of cooperation between different entities of a financial group is an important part of the rationale for the group. During this process, the legal structure and the operational structure of the group will increasingly diverge (see, for example, Dermine 2006; Schoenmaker and Oosterloo 2007). In consequence, it becomes harder to attribute activities to the legal entities on which the division of supervisory responsibilities is based. A large difference between the legal structure and organizational structure will complicate the execution of supervision, since supervision is based on statutory power to supervise legal entities (legal structure) and this may not correspond to where activities actually take place (organizational structure). This tension between operationally integrated financial groups looking for synergies and legally constrained supervisors looking for an effective lever on key decision-makers of these financial groups poses a challenge for policy.

Summing up, we see two diverging industry trends:

- cross-border penetration by large financial groups (groups headquartered in one EU country conducting business in other EU countries) – this trend undermines the capacity of host authorities to maintain financial stability in their country
- centralization of risk management functions of large financial groups – this trend reinforces the role of the home supervisor (as consolidating supervisor) to control the group-wide activities of these financial groups.

Future policy options

The newly emerging European financial landscape confronts the home and host authorities with complex coordination issues. In the face of these challenges, it is questionable whether cooperation between different national authorities will be an adequate arrangement in an integrating market. As a European jurisdiction is (or can be made) available, policy-makers have the choice to organize financial supervision on a national or a European basis. The main challenges for a future supervisory framework are twofold: first, how to deal with integrated financial groups; second, how to incorporate the cross-border externalities arising from the failure of EU-wide operating financial groups. While addressing these challenges, an efficient and effective supervisory framework for locally operating financial firms should be kept.

We develop three criteria to judge the different policy options. The first criterion is effectiveness of the arrangements for financial supervision and stability. More precisely, could the arrangements take an EU-wide view? The second criterion is efficiency. Efficiency implies no duplication by supervisors. Supervisors should also operate as closely as possible to the supervised institution to know what is really going on. The third criterion is a level playing field. The Single Financial Market promotes a level playing field. While the EU regulatory framework (Directives and Regulations) is largely harmonized, a real level playing field would only be achieved by a consistent and common application of the harmonized rules by the supervisors.

Given the importance of financial conglomerates in the EU, we assume that prudential supervisors operate on a cross-sector basis. Cross-sector supervision can be carried out by an integrated agency (the Financial Services Association (FSA) model) or by separate agencies for prudential supervision and conduct of business (the twin peaks model). See Kremers, Schoenmaker and Wierts (2003b) and Schoenmaker (2005) on the different models of cross-sector financial supervision.

On a conceptual level, the most obvious policy options for the structure of financial supervision are:

1 *Enhance cooperation between home and host authorities*: this can be regarded as maintaining the current supervisory system in the EU. In the current system, the home supervisor is responsible for a financial group and its EU-wide branch network and is the consolidating supervisor as well. The host country is responsible for a group's EU subsidiaries and controls the stability of its financial system. The home and host authorities have to cooperate for financial supervision and stability.
2 *Appoint a lead supervisor for prudential supervision of cross-border financial groups*: in practice, this will mean that the home-country authority of a pan-European financial group is given full responsibility for the EU-wide operations, both branches and subsidiaries.
3 *Establish a central agency that works in tandem with the national supervisors*, some form of a European System of Financial Supervisors: there are two basic forms. First, the central agency in the System is responsible for prudential supervision of cross-border financial groups at the European level. This central body will be given full responsibility for the EU-wide operations, both branches and subsidiaries, of pan-European financial groups. Second, the role of the central agency is to foster cooperation and consistency among members of the System, but to leave the day-to-day supervision of cross-border financial groups with the consolidating or lead supervisor.

Cooperation between home and host countries

In the area of banking supervision, two important policy initiatives have recently been taken to enhance the cooperation between home and host authorities and to strengthen cross-border arrangements for the supervision of large and complex banking groups. First, the recently adopted Capital Requirements Directive (CRD) introduces an improved legal framework for supervisory cooperation for banking groups with foreign subsidiaries. In particular, the CRD entrusts the consolidating supervisor (i.e. the home supervisor) with coordination responsibilities. The consolidating supervisor should together with the host supervisors aim at reaching a joint decision on the approval of a bank's internal model. If and when a joint decision cannot be reached within six months, the consolidating supervision can decide. The CRD also strengthens and clarifies the requirements for information sharing and cooperation between all authorities responsible for the supervision of group entities. This improved framework should promote and facilitate effective supervisory cooperation, especially for large groups that are active in several countries. Second, the Ecofin Council has adopted proposals to enhance coordination between national supervisors in the EU. The European structure is thus moving from cooperation to coordination with the implementation of the Lamfalussy approach to speed up the regulatory process and to foster supervisory convergence in the EU. A new committee structure was first proposed by Lamfalussy for securities supervision and subsequently implemented. This committee is a form of European coordination between national supervisors. The Ecofin Council has decided to extend the Lamfalussy structure for securities to banking, insurance and financial conglomerates (Economic and Financial Committee 2002). The goal of these new regulatory and supervisory committees is to streamline the preparation of regulation and to foster supervisory convergence.

It is, however, questionable whether improved cooperation will end the existing duplication and overlap of supervision. Cross-border expansion through branches can be done without extra supervision (only some minor notification procedures), but subsidiaries in the host country still experience duplication in supervision from the supervisor in the host country and the consolidating supervisor in the home country. In particular, the new Member States have a large presence of banks from other EU countries. Taking EU-wide figures, the division between branches and subsidiaries for cross-border business is about 50/50 (see ECB 2006: Tables 11 and 13). However, the subsidiary form is the primary vehicle for cross-border penetration in new Member States. Host authorities of new Member States have an incentive (as well as a legal basis) to keep on supervising these subsidiaries with EU parents, because of the importance of these subsidiaries for the stability of their financial system.

Efficient supervisory structures are also important for the competitive position of EU financial institutions. A system with duplication by different supervisor authorities with (slightly) different requirements and reporting formats places a high burden on financial institutions and hampers further cross-border expansion within the EU. As a result European banks may fall behind their counterparts from the US, where the remaining barriers to interstate banking and branching were lifted in 1994.[5] Schüler and Heinemann (2005) have calculated the cost of fragmentation of financial supervision in the former EU-15. Their results indicate increasing economies of scale in supervision.[6] Comparing the current structure with 15 national supervisors with a cost-efficient European supervisory framework, they predict cost savings of some 15 per cent. Although they only calculate the institutional costs of running supervisory agencies, Schüler and Heinemann (2005) suggest that the results could be generalized to other types of supervisory costs, such as the compliance costs of regulated firms (reporting requirements, etc.).

Enhanced cooperation and coordination will also not address the issue of how to deal effectively with integrated financial groups. In this supervisory system home and host authorities work together to maintain financial stability. However, coordination failure is possible during a crisis, as resolving cross-border externalities relies on voluntary cooperation. In line with the allocation of supervisory responsibilities, the responsibility for decision-making in crisis situations regarding an individual institution and its branches rests with the home-country authorities. However, home-country authorities are not responsible for the financial stability of host countries. Moreover, the home-country taxpayer may not be prepared to pay for cross-border spill-over effects of a failure. The issue of cooperation and loss sharing has hardly been touched upon in the literature. Freixas (2003) is among the first to explore incentive-compatible mechanisms to allocate the fiscal costs of a possible bail-out among national authorities. He shows that in the current situation nationally based arrangements underestimate the externalities related to the cross-border business of financial institutions. As a result insufficient capital will be contributed and the financial institution will not be bailed out. Freixas (2003) pinpoints the public good dimension of collective bail-out and shows why improvised cooperation between national authorities will lead to an underprovision of public goods, that is, to an insufficient level of bail-outs.

Lead supervision

According to the European Financial Services (EFR) Round Table (2004) a clearly defined lead supervisor (usually the home supervisor) for prudential supervision of cross-border financial institutions would be an important step towards a more coherent and efficient supervisory framework in the EU. The EFR argues that the lead supervisor should in particular be the single point of contact for all reporting schemes, validate and authorize internal models, approve capital and liquidity allocation, approve cross-border set-up of specific functions and decide about on-site inspections. Furthermore, the lead supervisor should be responsible for supervision not only on a consolidated level, but also on the solo and sub-consolidated level.

The EFR agrees that host countries should be involved in the supervisory process, as local supervisors generally have a better understanding of the local market conditions. The EFR suggests forming colleges of supervisors (one for each specific group) that advise the lead supervisor and discuss proposals of involved local supervisors, but would not have the power to delay decisions of the lead supervisor. As the role and the powers of the host supervisor in these colleges are non-committal,[7] the actual involvement of host authorities can be limited in practice.

In comparison with the current situation, both the efficiency of supervision and competitiveness of the financial sector are enhanced under this option (responding to the first industry trend). Nevertheless, the lead supervisor does poorly with respect to financial stability, as its national mandate does not induce the lead supervisor to incorporate the cross-border externalities of a failure of a financial institution in its decision-making (not responding to the second industry trend).

In a follow-up report, the EFR (2005) acknowledges the importance of cross-border crisis-management arrangements, such as the lender of last resort and guarantee schemes, to deal with the second industry trend. The EFR suggests a European System of Financial Supervisors (see next section) as a medium-term option.

A European System of Financial Supervisors

To respond to the increasing integration within the EU and to have a supervisory system that incorporates the cross-border externalities of a failure of a financial institution, an option is to establish a European System of Financial Supervisors with a European Financial Agency (EFA) at the centre of the system and national supervisors in the different countries. In this context, Breuer (2000: 9) proposes that 'it may also be sensible to have those banking groups that operate on a truly European scale supervised directly by the central agency' (see Figure 15.5). However, a two-tier system (with a central supervisor and national supervisors) as proposed by Breuer could create an un-level playing field between pan-European banks and domestically oriented banks, while both are competing in the same market.

Another question that comes to the forefront is related to the appropriate level of (de)centralization of a putative central agency. Supervision is primarily a micro-policy as day-to-day supervision should be conducted close to supervised institutions (see pp. 348–49). Nevertheless, there may be some merit in centralizing policy-making and pooling information, allowing effective market surveillance of European-wide systemic risks. The drawback of a central European supervisor could be that the distance between the central agency and the supervised institutions may be too large – physically and in terms of familiarity with local circumstances.

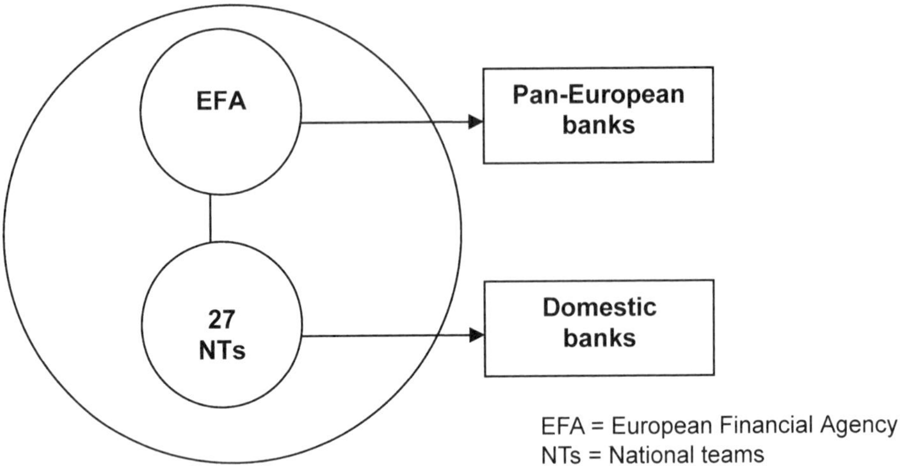

Figure 15.5 A centralised European system of financial supervisors: the Breuer Model.

But would the possible establishment of a pan-European supervisor necessarily result in a predominantly centralized system of supervision? There is a strong case for decentralization. First, there are many small and medium-sized financial institutions which operate mainly within national borders. There is no need for involvement at the European level for these institutions. Padoa-Schioppa (2004) draws an interesting picture from Italian experience:

1 Small banks are supervised by the respective regional branch of Banca d'Italia.
2 National banks are supervised by the respective branches but key decisions are taken at the headquarters of Banca d'Italia in Rome.
3 Pan-European banks are supervised by a group of national supervisors working collectively in a multilateral mode as a single consolidating supervisor.

Second, prudential supervision should be executed at the local level where the financial institutions are based. The use of field inspections is an important tool of prudential supervision. By being close to the coal face, supervisors would get a feeling for what is going on at an institution and would also be more familiar with local market conditions in which an institution is operating. For pan European financial institutions, the 'lead supervisor' should thus remain located near the head office of the financial institution.[0]

In our view a decentralized European System of Financial Supervisors could combine the advantages of a European framework with the expertise of local supervisory bodies (Schoenmaker and Oosterloo 2007). One could think of a European System of Financial Supervisors with a body at the centre (EFA) working in tandem with the 27 decentralized national auxiliary branches (see Figure 15.6). In such a system the following applies:

- Small and medium-sized banks which are primarily nationally oriented are supervised by one of the 27 national teams. In practice not much will change for these banks as they will be supervised by the respective national branch of the European System of Financial Supervisors (ESFS) and there will be no involvement at the European level.
- Pan-European banks are supervised by the consolidating or lead supervisor (usually the supervisory team of the home country). In accordance with the wish of the EFR, this

national team will be the single point of contact for all reporting schemes (no reporting to the host authorities), validate and authorize internal models, approve capital and liquidity allocation, approve cross-border set-up of specific functions and decide about on-site inspections.[9] With respect to the latter, the lead supervisor can ask host authorities to perform on-site inspections on its behalf. The lead supervisor is compelled to inform host authorities about its activities and host authorities should have access to all reporting schemes (i.e. a common database of the ESFS). In case a host authority feels the lead supervisor does not take account of its interests and no mutual concessions can be reached, it can present its concerns to the EFA. If necessary, the EFA can overrule the lead supervisor.

- Crisis management is also done on a European basis. While the national team in the home country takes the lead during a crisis at an individual institution (gathering information, making an assessment of the situation), the System is involved to ensure an adequate EU-wide solution. When a crisis hits more (large) financial institutions at the same time, the involvement of the EFA (in close cooperation with the European Central Bank) will be intensified.
- Key supervisory decisions (for example the assessment of potential cross-border mergers and acquisitions or crisis management decisions) as well as the design of policy are made at the centre by the Governing Council consisting of the Executive Board of the EFA and the chairs of the 27 national teams (in the same way as the European System of Central Banks (ESCB) takes decisions on monetary policy).[10] In this way, host-country authorities are fully involved and the interests of their depositors are fully taken into account (i.e. potential cross-border externalities are incorporated). Day-to-day supervision is conducted by one of the 27 national teams close to the financial firms. The EFA will be responsible for information pooling and is therefore best equipped to perform EU-wide peer group analysis of large European financial groups.
- The EFA is responsible for the correct and uniform application of supervisory rules (level playing field) and it can also act as a mediator in case of problems between home- and host-country authorities. In doing so, it may give instructions to the 27 national teams. This mediation role for the EFA could evolve from the mediation mechanisms which are currently set up for the European supervisory committees at level 3 (Financial Services Committee 2005).
- Accountability is an important element of the System. On behalf of the ESFS, its chair will report periodically to the Ecofin Council and the European Parliament. Crucial elements such as the legal basis of the System, the way in which the System will provide information on its activities, and the formal relationship between the System on the one hand and the European Commission, the European Parliament and the Ecofin Council on the other need to be elaborated (see Lastra 2006: ch. 11 for a good overview). It should be noted that there are similarities and differences between the accountability of central banks and financial supervisors. Whereas for independent central banks there should be no political interference in any case, for financial supervision there should be no interference in individual supervisory cases. On the other hand, political authorities are responsible for an adequate functioning of the financial system and an adequate achievement of the objectives of financial stability and consumer protection. Political authorities therefore retain responsibility for overall policy-making for financial supervision.

In order to make this system work, policy rules (e.g. the rulebook and reporting requirements for institutions under supervision) and information pooling (e.g. reporting format and

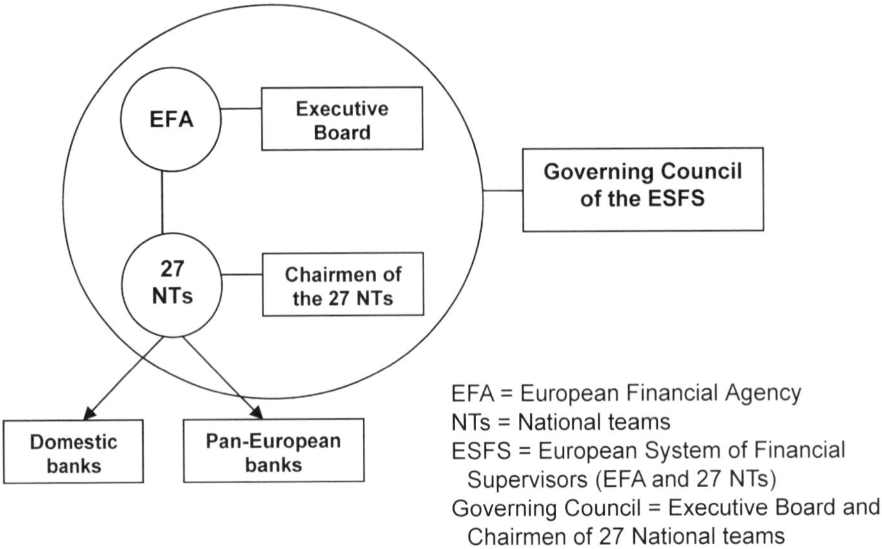

Figure 15.6 A decentralised European system of financial supervisors (ESFS).

computer systems) need to be made uniform. Such a uniform policy framework would very much be built on the unified regulatory regime established by EU Directives. It can, however, be questioned whether EU Directives are sufficient, because Directives often allow national discretion. In contrast, EU Regulations have a direct application throughout the EU and thus establish a uniform framework. The introduction of the euro and the application of the International Accounting Standards (IAS) in the EU are, for example, governed by Regulations to ensure a uniform framework. Next, appropriate decision-making and incentive mechanisms should be designed to ensure that the national teams adhere to this policy framework. In game-theoretic terms, national teams operate in a repeated-game setting. There should, therefore, be sufficient incentives for the lead supervisor to incorporate the interests of host countries to avoid the (embarrassing) possibility of being overruled by the centre (too often). Furthermore, information pooling will allow effective market surveillance of systemic risks by the EFA (including a peer group analysis of large pan-European financial institutions).

There is also the question whether a European System of Financial Supervisors should continue to build on the existing structure of national supervisors or should be built up from scratch. Anecdotal evidence seems to suggest that one of the reasons for banks' failure to consolidate extensively on a cross-border basis may be partly due to the intervention of national authorities (European Commission 2005). When building on the existing structure, the existing national biases remain relevant and are most likely to persist. By replacing the existing national structures with a totally new European structure, the risk of national biases could well be restricted.

However, to substitute the existing supervisory structure in the different Member States for another seems to be a very costly operation, which also entails the risk of a drain of local knowledge. Arguments in favour of using existing, but transformed, national authorities are based on experience, expertise and continuity. According to Hartmann (2007), a way in which a European System of Financial Supervisors, based on the principle of subsidiarity, could be made to work is to mix non-nationals of the home country into examination teams. While not strictly comparable, the example of International Monetary Fund (IMF) article IV or programme missions could provide some lessons. Whatever solution is chosen, there seems to be a clear need for ex ante rules to prevent national biases.

There are two comparative, but differing, examples of creating a European system. The first is the revolutionary option. The role of DG Competition in competition law enforcement started from scratch at the time of the creation of the European Coal and Steel Community (ECSC), because many Member States did not have a competition authority at the time. It is interesting to see that Member States have now established their own competition authority. This has led to the *ex post* creation of the European Competition Network in 2004 to introduce decentralized elements of competition law enforcement (Smits 2005).

The second is the evolutionary option. As all Member States had a fully functioning central bank at the time, the ESCB was created on top of the national central banks from the start. It should be noted, however, that Member States had to adjust their Banking Act to ensure full independence (as well as legal convergence) for their central bank as enshrined in the Maastricht Treaty. The route towards the creation of the ESCB was in different stages. The Committee of EU Central Bank Governors (stage 1) was turned into the European Monetary Institute (EMI) (stage 2) to prepare the ground for a single monetary policy. The EMI was subsequently turned into the ESCB, comprising the European Central Bank at the centre and the national central banks of the participating countries (stage 3). In a similar vein, a European System of Financial Supervisors could evolve from the current European supervisory committees at level 3 (Schoenmaker 2005).

Finally, European supervision raises the thorny issue of who should bear the fiscal costs of a possible bail-out. The first-best solution is to keep decision-making on supervision and fiscal bail-outs at the same level. However, there is no meaningful European budget which can be drawn upon for such cases. Goodhart and Schoenmaker (2006) explore possible *ex ante* mechanisms for fiscal burden sharing in a banking crisis in Europe. The first mechanism could be a general fund to shoulder the burden of recapitalization. This general fund could be financed directly by the participating countries, which would pay their relative share (e.g. based on GDP) in the fund. The main advantage of this system is that the cost of recapitalization is smoothed over countries. There are, however, serious problems with this approach, not least that there is little (political) enthusiasm for cross-border fiscal transfers. The second mechanism involves specific burden sharing. In this scheme, only countries in which the problem bank is conducting business contribute to the burden sharing. A country's contribution can be related to the share of the problem bank's business in that country. In this way, cross-border transfers are largely avoided. Both schemes are subject to the free-rider problem. Countries that do not sign up to burden sharing nevertheless profit from burden sharing, as the stability of the European financial system is a public good. Further research is needed to explore mechanisms for cooperation between a putative European System of Financial Supervisors and national tax authorities to deal effectively with pan-European threats to financial stability.

Conclusions

Supervisory structures should, in our view, adapt to market developments and not the other way round. The chapter therefore starts by identifying the key industry trends. The first trend is centralization of key management functions, such as risk and capital management, at the headquarters of financial groups (banking groups, insurance groups, as well as financial conglomerates). This reinforces the role of the home-country supervisor as consolidating supervisor. The role of the consolidating supervisor is acknowledged in the recently adopted Capital Requirements Directive (Basel II) for banks. The current revision of the Insurance Directives (Solvency II) should, in our view, also establish adequate group supervision of large insurance firms. Although the risk profile of banks and insurers differs, supervisors have to find a way to respond to centralization of key management functions at banking and insurance groups.

The second trend is ongoing integration of EU financial markets fostered by the completion of the Financial Services Action Plan and the advance to EMU. This integration gives rise to increasing cross-border penetration of interbank markets and payment systems, which are important channels for cross-border contagion. Furthermore, emerging pan-European banks give rise to cross-border externalities arising from the (potential) failure of these banks. The data indicate that cross-border presence is even larger for insurance firms. The increasing presence of banks (and insurers) from other EU countries undermines the capacity of host authorities to manage effectively the stability of their financial system.

Due to these market trends, it is increasingly difficult to organize financial supervision and crisis management on a predominantly national basis. In the current national setting, home supervision will remain important, and possibly expand, because of group-wide internal models run from the head office of financial groups. At the same time, host supervision of subsidiaries will continue because of financial stability concerns in the host country. Duplication of supervisory efforts and multiple reporting by financial groups is therefore not likely to diminish in the near future. This raises the question of the appropriate division of responsibilities between home and host authorities.

In our view a European System of Financial Supervisors could combine the advantages of a European framework for financial supervision and crisis management with the expertise of local supervisory bodies. Such a System can be created by the establishment of a European Financial Agency working in tandem with the national financial supervisors. The focal point would remain at the national level, as the home supervisor would conduct the day-to-day supervision. Key supervisory (and crisis management) decisions as well as the design of policy are carried out at the centre (governed by a council with executive directors of the new European Financial Agency and the chair of the national supervisors). In this way, host-country authorities are fully involved and the interests of their depositors are fully taken into account.

How and when to get there? We believe in an evolutionary process (see also Papademos 2005). The recently created level 3 supervisory committees can form the nexus for a new European System of Financial Supervisors. In the next five years we expect further discussions on the desirability and workings of a putative European System of Financial Supervisors and then another five years to implement a new System. Market developments will no doubt dictate the exact speed of the evolution.

Notes

1 The opinions in the paper are those of the authors and not necessarily those of the Netherlands Ministry of Finance.

2 The revised Basel Concordat on international banking supervision introduced the concept of consolidation in 1983. In Europe the concept was adopted in the Consolidated Banking Supervision Directive 92/30/EEC (replaced by the Codified Banking Directive 2000/12/EC).

3 Financial Conglomerates Directive 2002/87/EC.

4 Insurance Groups Directive 98/78/EC.

5 See Barth *et al.* (2000) for a review of the liberalization of the US financial system. Though the US supervisory framework is characterized by multiple state and federal supervisors with overlapping jurisdictions, the Federal Financial Institutions Examination Council has developed harmonized reporting requirements, such as the call report (Kremers *et al.* 2003a: 9).

6 This is consistent with Goodhart, Schoenmaker and Dasgupta (2002), who also find evidence for economies of scale in supervision.

7 In cases of lasting differences of opinion, the EFR proposes to refer cases to the level 3 committees (Committee of European Banking Supervisors (CEBS), Committee of European Insurance and Occupational Pension Supervisors (CEIOPS) or the Conglomerate Committee), which can either act in an appeal procedure or could organize a mediation process.

8 If necessary, the lead supervisor could engage local supervisors to visit branches and subsidiaries located in other EU countries, while keeping full responsibility. This would create a team that consists of the lead supervisor in the home country and the supervisors in the host countries.

9 The EFR (2005: 43) warns rightly 'that the ESFS model could lead to overregulation if it merely added all existing national practices instead of establishing a new, streamlined and efficient system'.

10 The efficiency of decision-making is an important issue. If the number of participating national central banks (NCBs) exceeds 15, the governors will vote on a rotating scheme. See Smits (2003) on decision-making in the Governing Council of the ECB.

References

Barth, James, Dan Brumbaugh and James Wilcox (2000) 'The repeal of Glass–Steagall and the advent of broad banking', *Journal of Economic Perspectives* 14: 191–204.

Breuer, Rolf (2000) 'Convergence of supervisory practices – a banker's view', speech at the Conference of European Banking Supervisors, Copenhagen.

Comité Européen des Assurances (2007) *European Insurance in Figures*, Paris.

Committee of European Securities Regulators (CESR) (2004) *Which Supervisory Tools for the EU Securities Markets? Preliminary Progress Report (Himalaya Report)*, Paris.

Dermine, Jean (2006) 'European banking integration: don't put the cart before the horse', *Financial Markets, Institutions & Instruments* 15(2): 57–106.

Drzik, John (2005) 'At the crossroads of change: risk and capital management in the insurance industry', *The Geneva Papers on Risk and Insurance – Issues and Practice* 30: 72–87.

Economic and Financial Committee (EFC) (2002) *Final Report on Financial Regulation, Supervision and Stability*, Brussels.

ECB (2004) *Report on EU Banking Structure*, Frankfurt am Main: ECB.

—— (2006) *EU Banking Structures*, Frankfurt am Main: ECB.

European Commission (2005) *Cross-border Consolidation in the Financial Sector*, Commission staff working document, Brussels: European Commission.

European Financial Services Round Table (EFR) (2004) *Towards a Lead Supervisor for Cross Border Financial Institutions in the European Union*, Brussels: EFR.

—— (2005) *On the Lead Supervisor Model and the Future of Financial Supervision in the EU*, Brussels: EFR.

Financial Services Committee (2005) *Report on Financial Supervision (Thierry Francq Report)*, Brussels.

Flannery, Mark (1999) 'Modernising financial regulation: the relation between interbank transactions and supervisory reforms', *Journal of Financial Services Research* 16: 101–16.

Freixas, Xavier (2003) 'Crisis management in Europe', in Jeroen Kremers, Dirk Schoenmaker and Peter Wierts (eds) *Financial Supervision in Europe*, Cheltenham: Edward Elgar.

Goodhart, Charles and Dirk Schoenmaker (2006) 'Burden sharing in a banking crisis in Europe', *Economic Review* 2: 34–57, Stockholm: Sveriges Riksbank.

Goodhart, Charles, Dirk Schoenmaker and Paolo Dasgupta (2002) 'The skill profile of central bankers and supervisors', *European Finance Review* 6: 397–427.

Hartmann, Philipp (2007) 'Comments on cross-border issues in European financial supervision', in David Mayes and Geoffrey Wood (eds) *The Structure of Financial Regulation*, London: Routledge.

Hartmann, Philipp, Stefan Straetmans and Casper de Vries (2006) 'Banking system stability: a cross-Atlantic perspective', in Mark Carey and Rene Stulz (eds) *The Risks of Financial Institutions*, Chicago: University of Chicago Press.

Herring, Richard and Robert Litan (1994) *Financial Regulation in a Global Economy*, Washington, DC: Brookings Institution.

Kremers, Jeroen, Dirk Schoenmaker and Peter Wierts (2003a) *Financial Supervision in Europe*, Cheltenham: Edward Elgar.

—— (2003b) 'Cross-sector supervision: which model?', in Richard Herring and Robert Litan (eds) *Brookings–Wharton Papers on Financial Services: 2003*, Washington, DC: Brookings Institution.

Kuritzkes, Andrew, Til Schuermann and Scott Weiner (2003) 'Risk measurement, risk management, and capital adequacy in financial conglomerates', in Richard Herring and Robert Litan (eds) *Brookings–Wharton Papers on Financial Services: 2003*, Washington, DC: Brookings Institution.

Lastra, Rosa (2006) *Legal Foundations of International Monetary Stability*, Oxford: Oxford University Press.

Mayes, David and Jukka Vesala (2000) 'On the problems of home country control', *Current Politics and Economics of Europe* 10: 1–26.

Padoa-Schioppa, Tommaso (2004) *Regulating Finance – Balancing Freedom and Risk*, Oxford: Oxford University Press.

Papademos, Lucas (2005) 'Banking supervision and financial supervision in Europe', speech given at a conference organized by the European Banking Federation on 'Supervision of International Banks: Is a Bank Crisis Still Possible in Europe?', 28 October, Brussels.

Rose, Andrew (1996) 'Explaining exchange rate volatility: an empirical analysis of "the holy trinity" of monetary independence, fixed exchange rates, and capital mobility', *Journal of International Money and Finance* 15: 925–45.

Schoenmaker, Dirk (2005) 'Central banks and financial authorities in Europe: what prospects?', in Donato Masciandaro (ed.) *The Handbook of Central Banking and Financial Authorities in Europe*, Cheltenham: Edward Elgar.

Schoenmaker, Dirk and Sander Oosterloo (2005) 'Financial supervision in an integrating Europe: measuring cross-border externalities', *International Finance* 8: 1–27.

—— (2007) 'Cross-border issues in European financial supervision', in David Mayes and Geoffrey Wood (eds) *The Structure of Financial Regulation*, London: Routledge.

Schoenmaker, Dirk and Christiaan van Laecke (2006) *Current State of Cross-Border Banking*, FMG Special Paper, No. 168, London: London School of Economics.

Schoenmaker, Dirk, Sander Oosterloo and Otto Winkels (2007) *The Emergence of Cross-Border Insurance Groups in Europe with Centralised Risk Management*, FMG Special Paper, No.176, London: London School of Economics.

Schüler, Martin and Friedrich Heinemann (2005) *The Costs of Supervisory Fragmentation in Europe*, ZEW Discussion Paper, No. 05–01, Mannheim: Mannheim University.

Smits, René (2003) *The European Central Bank in the European Constitutional Order*, Utrecht: Eleven International Publishing.

—— (2005) 'The European Competition Network: selected aspects', *Legal Issues of Economic Integration* 32: 175–92.

Thygesen, Niels (2003) 'Comments on the political economy of financial harmonisation in Europe', in Jeroen Kremers, Dirk Schoenmaker and Peter Wierts (eds) *Financial Supervision in Europe*, Cheltenham: Edward Elgar.

Van der Zwet, Annemarie (2003) *The Blurring of Distinctions between Financial Sectors: Fact or Fiction?*, Occasional Study No. 2, Amsterdam: De Nederlandsche Bank.

Vives, Xavier (2001) 'Restructuring financial regulation in the European Monetary Union', *Journal of Financial Services Research* 19: 57–82.

16 Cross-border banking

Challenges for deposit insurance and financial stability in the European Union

Robert A. Eisenbeis and George G. Kaufman

Introduction

It is generally argued that foreign ownership of banks increases competition and efficiency in the banking sector of the host country, reduces risk exposures through greater geographical and industrial diversification, and enlarges the aggregate quantity of capital invested in the banking sector. Indeed, foreign entry through direct investment is widely recommended by researchers and analysts as a means of strengthening weak and inefficient banking structures, particularly in emerging economies. This is because banks that are willing and able to enter a foreign country, especially developing economies, through direct investments are generally larger, in healthier financial condition, more professionally managed and more technically advanced than the average host-country bank, and may therefore be expected to raise the bar for all banks.

Foreign ownership of banks varies greatly among countries. In the European Union, for example, Table 16.1 shows that foreign ownership averages 58 per cent in the 10 new EU Member States as compared with a weighted average of 16 per cent for the older EU members.[1]

Despite the benefits that might accrue to foreign ownership, cross-border banking through either branching or subsidiaries raises a number of important policy issues when financial instability threatens. These concerns are particularly important with respect to the provision of deposit insurance, the effectiveness of prudential regulation, the strength of market discipline, the timing of declaring an insolvent institution officially insolvent and placing it in receivership or conservatorship, and the procedures for resolving bank insolvencies.

Because the actual or perceived adverse externalities of bank failures may be large, it is important to evaluate how banking regulatory structures are likely to function within and across countries at times of financial strain as well as at times when banks are performing well financially. An effective regulatory structure should not only foster competition and efficiency in good times, but also aim to minimize the cost of any adverse externalities associated with insolvencies. This would include avoiding the probability of adopting hasty, *ad hoc*, automatic reflex public policy measures once a crisis emerges that protect most if not all stakeholders against loss. While expedient solutions may appear to minimize the cost of insolvencies in the short run, they may do so only at the expense of even higher longer-term costs because the necessary actions were not taken much earlier. In addition, in the case of cross-border banking, competing interests of stakeholders in the home country versus those in the host country can raise important agency problems that may affect how financially distressed banking organizations are resolved, the incidence of possible externalities associated with failure, and both the magnitude and the distribution of the costs among affected parties when failures do occur.[2]

Table 16.1 Cross-border penetration of banks as a percentage of assets

	Year					
Country	*1997*	*1999*	*2001*	*2002*	*2003*	*2004*
Austria	3	2	19	21	19	19
Belgium	23	20	23	22	21	21
Denmark	4	4	17	18	17	15
Finland	8	9	7	9	7	59
France	7	6	11	11	10	9
Germany	2	3	3	5	5	5
Greece	11	10	4	6	19	25
Ireland	46	50	48	37	35	36
Italy	6	7	5	5	5	6
Luxembourg	83	88	88	89	89	89
Netherlands	5	4	10	9	10	11
Portugal	13	13	24	24	26	25
Spain	9	7	8	9	10	11
Sweden	15	29	6	6	7	8
United Kingdom	25	26	25	23	23	26
EU-15	*13*	*13*	*15*	*15*	*15*	*16*
Cyprus			16	17	18	23
Czech Republic			68	90	92	87
Estonia			91	90	89	98
Hungary			55	53	56	56
Lithuania			47	56	51	74
Latvia			24	21	22	39
Malta			49	42	40	39
Poland			60	59	59	59
Slovenia			14	16	18	19
Slovakia			na	81	82	88
New EU-10			*47*	*53*	*53*	*58*

Source: Schoenmaker and Oosterloo (2005); includes subsidiaries and branches.

While the benefits of cross-border banking conducted through foreign-owned banking offices have been analysed intensely, the implications that alternative regulatory structures have for resolving problems, should these institutions experience financial distress, have been analysed far less. This chapter extends the literature by examining these latter issues in greater depth.[3] Emphasis is on the European Union (EU), which is both economically and financially large and has several features relating to cross-border banking in the form of direct investment that may heighten the problems we consider. These features include the provision of a single banking licence, reliance upon the home country as the primary provider of deposit insurance and application of the bankruptcy processes and host-country responsibility for financial stability and lender of last resort. It should be emphasized that the issues being faced by the EU are not unique and are common to most countries subject to cross-border banking. Indeed, the EU has at least attempted to harmonize policies, and for this reason may be ahead of other parts of the world in facing the problems. Nevertheless, the sooner all countries face up to the problems that crises bring, the less vulnerable their financial systems will be.

In the next section we describe the EU cross-border banking regulatory structure in greater depth to set the background for subsequent analysis. Subsequent sections discuss agency problems that may arise in the supervision and regulation of cross-border banking institutions in the EU, focus on the problems of providing deposit insurance for institutions operating in that environment and look at insolvency resolution; then examine issues concerning the payout from deposit insurance plans and resolving large bank failures and then suggest ways to solve the problems. A further section argues for modification of the new European Company Statute as it applies to banking organizations to require agreement by banks desiring to establish branches across borders both to be subject to a system of prompt corrective action and to be encouraged to give up their charter at a positive capital-to-asset ratio. The last section is a summary and conclusion.

Key features of EU financial regulatory and deposit guarantee systems

The European Union is in the midst of an economic transition from a collection of separate country economies into a single economic market. As part of this integration, the Maastricht Treaty of 1992 established the groundwork for the introduction of the euro in 1999 and establishment of the European Central Bank (ECB). But it left to the individual member countries responsibility for banking supervision and regulation, financial stability, lender-of-last-resort functions and the provision of deposit insurance guarantees.[4]

As part of an effort to encourage the development of a single economic market, the Second Banking Directive (1988) (as modified in 1995 and consolidated into Directive 2000/12/EC of the European Parliament and of the Council of 20 March 2000) established three principles – harmonization, mutual recognition and home-country control. Harmonization requires that a minimum set of uniform banking regulations be adopted across the Union. Mutual recognition means that during the transition to a single market, member countries would honour the regulations and policies of the other Member States. Finally, regulation and supervision by the 'home country' (country of charter) have precedence over regulation and supervision by a 'host country'. Together with the concept of a single licence, these three principles mean that, once a banking institution receives a charter from an EU Member State, it would be permitted to establish branches anywhere within the EU without the necessity of review by the regulators in the host countries into which it expanded. When entry takes place in a host EU country by way of a separately chartered subsidiary, rather than through a branch office, the host country is responsible for supervision and regulation of that entity, since it is the home country for that subsidiary. At the same time, supervision of the consolidated entity remains the responsibility of the home country of the parents.

While minimum prudential standards have been established and roughly comparable rules provided for, substantial latitude on numerous dimensions for regulatory differences continues to exist. For example, while Directive 2006/49/EC of the European Parliament and of the Council lays out how to implement Basel II, numerous national discretions exist as to how Basel II may actually be applied in practice.[5] This raises concerns about incentives to engage both in regulatory arbitrage by regulated institutions and in regulatory competition by country regulators.

One logical implication of the home-country approach is that over time, as the competitive climate increases and more and more cross-border banking evolves, regulatory competition becomes more likely, which in turn should facilitate and drive Europe toward a truly single market environment. To the extent that it does, regulatory competition and the marketplace may serve as a lever in achieving the EU's objective of a single market. Individual country self-interest in promoting their own institutions will also be an inducement to compete through deregulation of financial services. Countries offering more attractive charter options or accommodative regulatory regimes would expect to see domestically chartered institutions gain market share in the EU. The logical consequence of allowing home-country regulation would, as the result of regulatory competition, be a less regulated and homogeneous marketplace.[6]

Mayes and Vesala (2005) argue that the sharing of responsibilities between home- and host-country regulators during the movement toward a single market objective is a viable policy precisely because harmonization of regulation and supervisory policies has taken place and official memoranda of understanding (MoUs) between and among the individual country regulators have been put in place to share information.[7] However, others have argued, as will be seen in the next section, that such a structure is fraught with problems and conflicts that may erupt when significant intuitions experience financial difficulties. Indeed, Mayes (2006) suggests it is just these concerns that have prompted the Nordic countries to lay out specific responsibilities in advance of the onset of a financial crisis, should the dominant institution in those countries – Nordea Bank – get into financial difficulties.

Putting these issues aside for the moment, the EU regulatory structure anticipates the need for supervisory efforts to head off the insolvency of a 'systemically important' bank. Should an institution experience financial difficulties requiring lender-of-last-resort assistance in amounts greater than a given, but confidential, threshold, then approval is required by the Governing Council of the ECB, presumably because a large injection of liquidity might have implications for monetary policy.[8] While the ECB does not at present have formal lender-of-last-resort authority, Gulde and Wolff (2005) suggest that there is a window of opportunity through the ECB's payments system responsibilities to provide such funding.

The EU regulatory system relies on common principles and coordinated approaches that will be followed when institutions experience financial difficulties. Within this general framework, however, substantial differences exist in terms of the details of how the safety net is structured across countries as well as in terms of the types of deposits and amounts that would be insured. These differences contain substantial incentives for institutions to engage in regulatory arbitrage, and create important differences in how nations might respond should substantial institutions get into financial difficulty. These will be detailed in the next sections.

Agency problems and conflicts

Cross-border banking through foreign-owned branches or subsidiaries can subject the entering institutions to multiple regulatory jurisdictions and regulators, as well as to many different legal systems. As a consequence, operating across borders presents potential problems for such banks beyond the fact that there are just more regulations to follow or regulators who may have different incentives.[9] Bank laws can differ greatly and may even be conflicting across the different countries. Therefore, regulatory compliance may be uncertain and difficult for banking organizations with multiple-country operations. Furthermore, bank supervisors and regulators in both home and host countries typically operate in what they consider is the best interest of their country, however defined or perceived (Bollard 2005).[10] This can lead to significant agency problems to the extent that the incentives of the regulators, deposit insurance providers and/or failure resolution entities are typically aligned with the interests of the residents of the regulators' home or host country rather than with the interests of the bank's customers or customers in the whole market or geographic area within which the institution operates.

Schüler (2003) points out that the incentive conflicts actually have two dimensions – a home-country dimension and an international or cross-border dimension. First, with respect to the home-country issues, self-interest and incentive problems of the classical principal/agent type exist between the banking supervisors and taxpayers. Regulators have incentives to pursue policies that preserve their agencies. In addition, they also pursue their own private self-interest to ensure their jobs, their future marketability and employment in the banking industry.[11] These conflicts may lead to the adoption of more accommodating policies in the form of lower than appropriate capital requirements and to regulatory forbearance when institutions get into trouble, thereby shifting risk and any associated costs to taxpayers as regulators attempt to ingratiate themselves with constituent banks.

Second, with respect to cross-border banking, in areas such as the European Union, as foreign banking organizations begin to increase their market share and dominance through the establishment of branches (as distinct from expansion via subsidiaries) in the host country, host-country regulators face a loss of constituents to supervise and regulate. As noted, EU policy specifies that home country regulators are responsible for supervision and regulation of institutions chartered in their country regardless of the location of their branches. At the same time, the host country is responsibility for financial stability within its boundaries. One consequence of this structure is that individual country regulators have a country-centric focus which may be manifested in several dimensions. As noted, nationalistic concerns may lead to a home-country bias. They may favour domestic over foreign institutions and attempt to limit the acquisitions of indigenous banks, or move to create 'national' champions which would be protected from outside takeover.[12] Over time institutions with the more favourable home-country regulatory environment will likely expand at the expense of those institutions with more stringent operating environments, especially when the restrictions impose costs rather than lead to healthier institutions. Thus, different regulatory and supervisory regimes, whether de jure or de facto, create regulatory arbitrage opportunities.[13]

Adding to the problem is the fact that the quality of host-country monitoring and supervision may be reduced with the entry of foreign branches or subsidiaries. Both host-country regulators and the markets in these countries are generally less able to obtain useful financial information from foreign-owned institutions than they are from domestically owned banks (Committee on the Global Financial System 2004).[14] This concern is especially acute for foreign branches which do not have meaningful balance sheets or income statements separate from the bank as a whole. This makes monitoring difficult for the host-country regulator. High-quality and timely information is critical when foreign branches come to control a large share of the host country's deposits, as is the case for many of the accession countries, because the host country is still responsible for financial stability and the lender-of-last-resort function. In the case of subsidiaries, since they are separate legal entities, they would have balance sheets and income statements that would be available to the regulator in the country in which they were chartered. However, in the EU, because the home country is responsible for the consolidated supervision of the parent banking entity, the chartering agency for the subsidiary will still experience information problems to the extent that it may be unaware of, or have difficulty in obtaining information on, problems in other parts of the banking organization that may have implications for the viability of either the parent or its subsidiary.

Schüler (2003) argues that this problem of information access constitutes a form of agency problem between the home- and host-country regulator. The home-country regulator, particularly if its monitoring and performance is weak, may have an incentive to disguise its poor performance by either producing disinformation on the performance of foreign branches or being less than diligent in supplying the host-country regulator with timely information. Without adequate and timely information, the host country may be in a poor position to assess the potential risks or externalities its citizens and economy may be exposed to from its foreign branches. These incentive conflicts may be especially acute in host countries with a large foreign banking presence. This is an especially important issue in small economies where a foreign bank may be a significant player, but where those operations are relatively small compared to those in either its home country or elsewhere. Many of the new EU entrants face this problem since they have a very large proportion of foreign banks, as Table 16.1 shows.

The information problems are likely to become increasingly significant as banking organizations expand and consolidate many of their management and record keeping functions to achieve cost efficiencies. In the electronic age, institutions are increasingly being managed on a consolidated or integrated basis from the home country. Niemeyer noted recently that 'banks are progressively concentrating various functions, such as funding, liquidity management, risk management and credit decision-making, to specific centres of competence in order to reap the benefits of specialization and economies of scale' (Niemeyer 2006: 6–7). Furthermore, data and records are usually kept centrally at the home offices or at sites not necessarily in the host country. Large complex banking organizations in particular are actively centralizing activities and either outsourcing or maintaining separate operating subsidiaries whose functions are to provide critical infrastructure or other functions to their bank subsidiaries.[15]

The logistics and costs to host-country regulators of quickly accessing information on these arrangements, or even finding it, can be daunting, even when the foreign banking organization enters by way of a bank subsidiary rather than a branch. Should a foreign-owned institution become insolvent and be legally closed, it may not be possible to keep those portions of the institution's operations in the host country physically open and operating seamlessly during the resolution process in an attempt to limit any adverse consequences that may accrue to deposit and loan customers. The necessary senior management, operating records and computer facilities may be physically located in the home rather than in the host countries or in separately owned and operated affiliates and subsidiaries in third countries. For these reasons, regulatory oversight and discipline is likely to be more difficult and less effective in host countries with a substantial foreign bank presence than in countries without this presence. The resolution process is also less effective. Perception of these problems is likely to heighten incentives on the part of host-country regulators to seek to protect their own citizens, even at the expense of home-country or other host-country citizens.[16]

With respect to the international dimension to the agency problem, home-country regulators may take insufficient account of how the externalities of a failure, and the way that it is resolved, may affect the host country. That is, because all the regulators in countries in which a banking organization operates may have different objective functions and incentives, they may not all be pulling in the same direction at the same time with respect to prudential supervision and regulation. And these conflicts may be important, even when there exist coordinating bodies or agreements and understandings as to principles, such as in the European Union. As noted earlier, the home country is responsible for monitoring the performance of its chartered institutions, including the foreign branches of those institutions operating in other countries, but the host country is responsible for financial stability.[17] When a crisis arises, responsible parties may not have had a clear delineation ex ante of responsibilities between the home and host country nor any way of enforcing those agreements that may have been made ex ante. EU MoUs are merely agreements and lack enforceability under law. Regulators may take conflicting actions to benefit their own country's residents or institutions, say with respect to the nature and timing of any sanctions imposed on a bank for poor performance, the timing of any official declaration of insolvency and the associated legal closing of the bank, the resolution of the insolvency, or the timing and amount of payment to insured and uninsured depositors.[18, 19]

We would expect that the incentives are for a host-country regulator to favour indigenous institutions and customers. Hence the potential agency problems are likely to become more significant in markets and economic areas that are becoming increasingly integrated, as in the European Union, or that may be experiencing an influx of outside entry. Indeed, the incentives may also vary depending upon simply the differing degree of cross-border activities that may exist, as between the new and original members of the European Union.

Until recently, cross-border banking has proceeded at a rather slow pace, especially within the EU, but as financial integration accelerates, more cross-border mergers are likely to take place, and many institutions will be bought by institutions from other countries.[20] To date, Table 16.1 shows that the degree of cross-border penetration within the EU rose at a modest pace from an average of 13 per cent of banking assets in the 15 old Member States in 1997 to only about 16 per cent in 2004. Penetration varied significantly from a high of 89 per cent in 2004 for Luxembourg to a low of 5 per cent for Germany. The admission of 10 new countries changes the landscape and potential cross-border issues significantly, since the degree of foreign penetration is much greater on average for the new Member States. Table 16.1 shows that foreign ownership in the accession countries averaged 58 per cent of assets in 2004, with a high of 98 per cent for Estonia and a low of 23 per cent for Cyprus. These countries are typically small in terms of GDP relative to the original EU countries (see Table 16.2). The largest of these new entrants is Poland, which accounts for only 4 per cent of the EU's GDP. Of course, several of the older EU members are relatively small as well – seven have less than a 2 per cent GDP share each. Because of the relative importance of cross-border banking to the accession economies, and the relatively smaller size of their economies, compared to the rest of the EU, the potential externalities of the failure of large banks operating within these host countries could be very significant.

From the home-country perspective, the incentives are not only to pay less attention to the externalities that failure may impose on host countries, but also to protect home-country residents from possible costs of failure. These incentives may be especially significant with respect to the provision of deposit insurance, which in the European case is primarily the responsibility of the home country. These issues are considered in the next section.

Deposit insurance

In the European Union the Deposit Guarantee Schemes Directive (DGD) (94/19/EC) provides the basic framework for the structure of how deposit insurance guarantees will be provided. The DGD endorsed a decentralized approach to deposit insurance, despite the fact that depository institutions are authorized to operate within any of the member countries. The design leaves the responsibility of providing coverage to depositors and the particulars of the scheme adopted at all branches, domestic and foreign, to the member home countries where a bank is chartered. The DGD specifies the basic features that an acceptable deposit insurance should have. Most specifically, the system should provide deposit

Table 16.2 Relative size of old and accession economies

Country name	*Income group*	*GDP 2005 (purchasing power parity basis)*	*EU GDP share 2005 (purchasing power parity basis)*	*GDP per capita 2005 (purchasing power parity basis)*
Old Members				
Austria	High income	$269,400,000,000	2.22%	$32,900
Belgium	High income	$329,300,000,000	2.71%	$31,800
Denmark	High income	$182,100,000,000	1.50%	$33,500
Finland	High income	$158,400,000,000	1.31%	$30,300
France	High income	$1,816,000,000,000	14.97%	$29,900
Germany	High income	$2,446,000,000,000	20.16%	$29,700
Greece	High income	$242,800,000,000	2.00%	$22,800
Ireland	High income	$136,900,000,000	1.13%	$34,100
Italy	High income	$1,645,000,000,000	13.56%	$28,300
Luxembourg	High income	$29,370,000,000	0.24%	$62,700
Netherlands	High income	$500,000,000,000	4.12%	$30,500
Portugal	High income	$194,800,000,000	1.61%	$18,400
Spain	High income	$1,014,000,000,000	8.36%	$25,100
Sweden	High income	$266,500,000,000	2.20%	$29,600
United Kingdom	High income	$1,867,000,000,000	15.39%	$30,900
New Members				
Cyprus	High income	$16,820,000,000	0.14%	$21,600
Czech Republic	Upper middle income	$184,900,000,000	1.52%	$18,100
Estonia	Upper middle income	$21,810,000,000	0.18%	$16,400
Hungary	Upper middle income	$159,000,000,000	1.31%	$15,900
Lithuania	Upper middle income	49,410,000,000	0.41%	$14,100
Latvia	Upper middle income	$29,420,000,000	0.24%	$12,800
Malta	High income	$7,485,000,000	0.06%	$18,800
Poland	Upper middle income	$489,300,000,000	4.03%	$12,700
Slovak Republic	Upper middle income	$85,140,000,000	0.70%	$15,700
Slovenia	High income	$42,090,000,000	0.35%	$20,900

Source: CIA, The World Fact Book 2005.

insurance coverage of €20,000, should exclude coverage of interbank deposits and may exclude other liabilities at the discretion of the national government. Co-insurance of liabilities is permitted but not required. Coverage of depositors in branches in countries other than the home country is the responsibility of the home country, but these can also be covered by the host country at its option. Additionally, should the host-country account coverage be greater than that available to a branch through its home-country deposit insurance scheme, the foreign branch may purchase top-up coverage to match that available to competing host-country chartered institutions.[21] There may be more than one scheme for different types of institutions. But most terms of the deposit insurance structure are not prescribed, and the details of the schemes are left to the discretion of the individual member countries.[22] These include the funding of the plans, pricing of coverage, who should operate the plan (the private sector or public sector), how troubled institutions should be handled, what too-big-to-fail policies in terms of protecting de jure uninsured claimants might or might not be pursued, or how conflicts would be resolved where two deposit insurance funds might be affected by the failure of an institution with top-up coverage (see Dale 2000 and Garcia and Nieto 2005 for descriptions of the existing arrangements in the EU).

Additionally, it is the responsibility of the home country's central bank to serve as the lender of last resort. However, little attention has been paid to how the responsible agencies decide whether a problem is a limited micro or broader systemic risk problem, although the EU's Council of Economic and Financial Affairs has recently promulgated a structure for the coordination of financial stability efforts for banking supervisors and central banks within the EU. Banking supervisors have also embarked upon a series of crisis simulations to identify issues and problems that may arise.[23]

In establishing the minimal requirements for deposit insurance schemes, the aim was obviously to balance the fact that most but not all original EU members already had deposit insurance plans in place and that many of the key provisions and features of their programmes were different. Presumably, the best that could be hoped for was that the schemes would be harmonized over time. The potential for cross-border problems, at least in the short run, appeared minimal because there were few truly multinational institutions in the EU. The plans that were put in place by individual countries in order to comply with the DGD varied substantially from those already in place. Finally, responsibility for supervision and risk monitoring is apportioned differently across the system and within the different countries.

Whatever the differences, it was not intended that institutional detail and plan features would serve as a source of competitive advantage within host or home countries. However, Huizinga and Nicodeme (2002) demonstrate that within the guidelines established by the EU, the discretionary differences in insurance system design have affected international depositor decisions as to the placement of their funds. In particular, countries with schemes with low premiums, co-insurance and private administration are more attractive to international depositors. But, more relevant to this study, they also suggest that 'countries can in principle tailor their deposit insurance systems to allow their banks to capture a larger market share in the international deposit market. This could lead to international regulatory competition in the area of deposit insurance policies' (Huizinga and Nicodeme 2002: 15).

Hence it is reasonable to be concerned that the structure of these systems, including their financing and the way that claims will be settled, creates agency problems between host- and home-country citizens and the management of deposit guarantee schemes that may significantly impact the efficiency of resolving insolvent banks at minimum cost to the host country. Going forward the patchwork set of deposit insurance schemes, when coupled with the bifurcated approach to controlling systemic risk, seems fraught with the potential for agency and conflict of interest problems (see Kane *et al.* 2003). These arise from several sources, including:

- uncertainties about the funding of the deposit insurance plans
- differences in deposit insurance coverage and pricing of coverage
- reliance upon the home country, as opposed to the host country, should institutions get into financial difficulties
- differences in treatment with respect to the lender-of-last-resort function
- differences in approaches to bankruptcy resolution and priority of claims in troubled institutions
- differences in European monetary union v. non-European monetary union participants.

EU countries must establish policies for how foreign banks operating in the country will be treated. In addition, EU Directives require that host-country chartered or licensed subsidiary banks of foreign parents receive treatment equal to that accorded chartered domestic banks in the country. But Eisenbeis and Kaufman (2006) suggest that it may not be appropriate to provide the same treatment for branch offices of foreign banks as for subsidiaries, especially when top-up insurance is provided or the branches themselves are also insured in the host country.[24] Host-country monitoring, for reasons discussed earlier, is not likely to be as effective as home-country monitoring, because less meaningful financial reporting information from domestic branches of foreign banks is available. Even if information from the home country about the entire legal entity were available, host countries are unlikely to be able to take action against any banks outside their own jurisdiction. Finally, the potential losses to uninsured creditors and to the deposit guarantee fund depend as much upon the home-country closure and resolution policies as on the financial condition of the institution.

The more insolvent an institution is before it is legally closed, the greater are the losses to the insurance funds and possibly taxpayers. For this reason, host countries may become more reluctant to provide insurance for foreign branches. Despite this, several EU countries not only have either an insurance option for EU and/or branches of institutions chartered in non-EU member countries but also offer top-up options when the home-country deposit guarantee plan is less than in the host country. This exposes host-country insurance funds to 'regulatory risk' because the closure decision and any losses to the host-country insurance fund depend upon actions of the home-country regulator.

Table 16.3 suggests that while there are some differences across EU countries in their insurance treatment of foreign branches and deposits, most countries do enable foreign branches to elect to be insured by their deposit insurance funds, and some provide insurance of foreign deposits as well, with most, but not all, being limited to foreign currency deposits of other EU member countries. Some countries also permit foreign-operated branches to purchase additional insurance, when insured in their home country, if the host country's insurance scheme is more generous. Table 16.4 details the differences that exist in insurance coverage across the euro area. Several countries, including France, Italy and Germany, are substantially more generous in their coverage than the minimum coverage of €20,000, Tables 16.5 and 16.6 also suggest that many of the attributes that Huizinga and Nicodeme (2002) found to be important to international depositors, such as private administration and co-insurance, do vary substantially across EU countries.

Table 16.7 shows that there are substantial differences not only in the legal requirements for when depositors are to be paid but also when they have actually been paid.[25, 26] But even if the countries use the same currency, e.g. euros for Euroland countries, if taxpayers in the home country are required to fund some or all of the insurance, they may be reluctant to make payments to depositors in foreign countries. Despite EU Directives which require universality in the treatment of all EU citizens, the Sveriges Riksbank noted recently that

> if a cross-border [branch bank] were to fail, it is improbable that either politicians or authorities in the respective countries would be willing to risk taxpayers' money to guarantee stability in countries other than their own. This could prompt the concerned countries to try to ring-fence the bank's assets in their own country with a view to minimizing the costs to the domestic economy, or not to intervene at all in the hope that other countries in which the bank has a bigger presence feel forced to act. The result could be a suboptimal resolution of the crisis that proves more costly or that produces greater adverse effects for all the countries involved.
>
> (Sveriges Riksbank 2003: 87)

Table 16.3 Deposit insurance characteristics by country

Country name	*Deposit insurance coverage of foreign institutions and deposits*
Old members	
Austria: Einlagensicherung der Banken & Bankiers Gesellschaft m.b.H.	Only accounts denominated in euros and currencies of other EEA countries
Belgium: Deposit and Financial Instrument Protection Fund	Only accounts denominated in euros and currencies of other EEA countries
Denmark: The Guarantee Fund for Depositors and Investors	Foreign currency deposits are covered if made in Denmark
Finland: Finnish Deposit Guarantee Fund	Foreign currency deposits are covered if made in Finland
France: Deposit Insurance (warranty) Fund	Yes, but only accounts denominated in euros and currencies of other EEA countries
Germany: The German Private Commercial Banks Compensation Scheme for Depositors and Investors (there are other schemes in Germany as well)	Yes, if made in Germany
Greece: Hellenic Deposit Guarantee Fund	Yes, covers deposits in branches in the EU and in branches of non-EU countries unless equivalent coverage is available to those branches
Ireland: Deposit Protection Scheme	All deposits made in Ireland
Italy: Interbank Deposit Protection Fund	Yes; the Interbank Deposit Protection Fund also compensates the depositors of foreign branches of Italian banks; in the case of Italian banks operating in EU countries, the amount of compensation cannot exceed the protection guaranteed by the host country
Luxembourg: The Luxembourg Deposit Guarantee Association	Yes
Netherlands: Collective Guarantee Scheme (CGS)	Yes, but only accounts denominated in euros and currencies of other EEA countries
Portugal: Deposit Guarantee Fund	Yes, deposits are guaranteed regardless of the currency in which they are denominated, and whether the depositor is resident or non-resident in Portugal
Spain: Deposit Guarantee Fund for Banking Institutions	Yes, deposits in Spain or in institutions from another Member State of the European Union, whatever the currency in which they are denominated, with the exclusion of those deposited by financial institutions, public administrations and certain other persons linked to credit institutions in any of the ways envisaged in the regulations
Sweden: Deposit Guarantee Board	Yes, all deposits made in Sweden
United Kingdom: Financial Services Compensation Scheme (FSCS)	Yes, all deposits in euros or EEA currencies
New members	
Cyprus: Deposit Protection Scheme	No
Czech Republic: Deposit Insurance Fund	Yes, but compensation for foreign exchange deposits is disbursed in the Czech currency.

continued on next page

Table 16.3 (continued)

Country name	*Deposit insurance coverage of foreign institutions and deposits*
Estonia: Deposit Guarantee Fund	Deposits of foreign credit institutions are guaranteed
Hungary: National Deposit Insurance Fund of Hungary	Yes
Lithuania: State Company 'Deposit and Investment Insurance'	Yes, deposits of branches of EU-headquartered institutions are eligible for insurance; excluded depositors' deposits are deposits held with the daughter banks of Lithuanian banks or divisions of these banks operating beyond the territory of the Republic of Lithuania; deposits in currencies of foreign countries that are not members of the European Union, with the exception of the USA, are non-insurable
Latvia: Deposit Guarantee Fund	Yes
Malta: Depositor Compensation Scheme	Yes
Poland: Bank Guarantee Fund	Yes
Slovak Republic: Deposit Protection Fund (DPF)	Yes
Slovenia: Deposit Guarantee Scheme	Yes

Source: Hall (2001) and deposit insurer websites.

Notes: Austria has 4 different funds, Germany has 6 funds, Italy has 3 funds, Portugal has 2 funds, Spain has 3 funds. In each case the main insurance funds for commercial banks or credit institutions are listed.

When a large number of foreign branches from different home countries co-exist in a host country, bank customers in that country may encounter a wide variety of different insurance plans. These plans are likely to differ, at times significantly, in terms of account coverage, premiums, insurance agency ownership (private v. government) and operation, ex ante funding and credibility.[27] Table 16.8 provides a general tabulation of the kinds of differences that can and do exist within the EU, despite the attempts to ensure uniformity. At the same time, host-country regulators encounter banks operating under a wide array of different foreign banks and different rules and regulations.

If the home country provides the insurance and pays the losses in branches operating in other countries, it is likely to demand at least some prudential regulatory jurisdiction over the activities of those branches in host countries, regardless of what may or may not be permitted in the host country. If this authority is exercised, this may imply different regulatory regimes with different sanction schedules co-existing for a branch in a host country. Moreover, if a branch has top-up insurance, then depositors of the branch will face potentially different rules and availability for those portions of their deposits covered by the home-country deposit guarantee scheme than for those deposits covered by the host-country scheme. In the EU, many but not all members require or permit topping up. But even here provisions differ. Some countries, such as Malta, only cover the difference between coverage provided in the home country, while others provide duplicate insurance.

The situation becomes more complex and confusing as the number of countries with banks operating branches in a host country increases. Host countries may face quite different situations if home-country A bank failed versus home-country B bank.

Table 16.4 Insured deposits coverage by country in the EU

Country name	*Deposit insurance coverage*
Old members	
Austria	€20,000
Belgium	€20,000 on deposits and €20,000 for financial instruments for a total of €40,000
Denmark	DKK 300,000 deposits covered net of loans (about €40,000)
Finland	FIM 150,000 – up to €25,000, deposits will be covered in full if depositor demonstrates that the deposit represented the sale of a residence
France	€70,000
Germany	30% of bank's equity capital (all non-bank deposits are covered up to a limit of 30% of the liability capital with a minimum limit is €1.5 million, and given that the average equity size of a commercial bank is €295.5 million, the average limit is around €90 million); official coinsurance 90% to €20,000
Greece	€20,000
Ireland	90% of €20,000
Italy	ITL 200 million – equivalent to €103,291
Luxembourg	The total amount of the guarantee will in no case exceed €20,000 (deposit guarantee) + €20,000 (investor compensation) = €40,000 per customer
Netherlands	€20,000
Portugal	€25,000
Spain	€20,000
Sweden	SEK 250,000
United Kingdom	100% of first £2000 and 90% of next £33,000
New members	
Cyprus	Cyprus equivalent of €20,000
Czech Republic	90% with max coverage of €25,000 equivalent
Estonia	From €20,000/EEK313,000 effective from 31 December 2007
Hungary	€20,000/HUF 6,555,555 at EU accession
Lithuania	From 1 January 2008 coverage is €20,000
Latvia	€12,802/9000 lats from 31 December 2007, €18,492/13000 lats from 31 December 2008
Malta	€20,000, about 8600 Maltese lira
Poland	Since 2003 the Fund's guarantee has covered 100% of monies up to a sum of PLN equivalent of €1,000, and 90% of the sums between the value of €1,000 and €22,500 (as counted inclusively regardless of the number of contracts concluded between the depositor and the bank)
Slovak Republic	90%, not to exceed €20,000
Slovenia	5,100,000 tolars (per depositor per institution)

Table 16.5 EU deposit insurance fund governance and funding

Country name	*Funding*	*Premiums*	*Administration*
Old members			
Austria	Government/Private Funding – no permanent fund – ex post	Not risk based – pro rata, ex post assessments on protected deposit base	Managing directors elected by General Assembly with representation from each trade association; are accountable to General Assembly
Belgium	Government/Private Funding State can provide limited funding – permanent fund	Not risk based – flat rate of 0.02% but if fund liquid assets fall below critical level premiums may be raised by 0.04%	Joint Private Official
Denmark	Capital must be at least DKK 3.2 billion (thousands of millions). Any of three separate funds may, if necessary and within prescribed limits, borrow from the other sections; in addition, the Fund may raise loans if its capital is insufficient – permanent fund	Not risk based – flat rate levy with max. rate of 0.2% of covered deposits	Joint Private Official
Finland	Fund members pay an admission fee equal to one-tenth of the total amount of the expenses of actual operations of the Fund for the previous financial period, but at least €17,000. The Fund may borrow from members if funding is insufficient in proportion that their liabilities were of covered liabilities – permanent fund	Not risk based – fixed 0.05% charge and a variable premium that can range up to 0.25% depending upon need for funds	Privately administered by elected representatives from member banks (both domestic and foreign) according to rules set by Ministry of Finance and supervised by FSA
France	Ex post assessments as needed; Fonds de Garantie des Dépôts can borrow funds from members and/or call for additional funds determined by a ruling of the Comité de la réglementation bancaire et financière (French Banking and Finances Committee) – no permanent fund	Not risk based – ex post levy – on demand but limited; contribution may not be less than €2,000 for a half-yearly contribution and €4,000 for the subscription of certificates of association	Private

Country name	*Funding*	*Premiums*	*Administration*
Germany	Private Funding; there is no public funding; Bundesbank may not by law be lender of last resort for the deposit insurance schemes; one-time payment of 0.09% – permanent funds	Not risk based (but hybrid) – mixture of ex ante and ex post premiums; base rate of 0.03% but may range from 0.0 to 0.06% of covered liabilities basis; there can also be an extraordinary premium of up to 100% of a regular premium in case the funds are not sufficient; banks that have paid for more than 20 years and are classified in the lowest risk category (A), can be exempted from premium payment; banks that are classified as higher risks (B or C) are required to pay an additional premium of up to 250% of the regular premium	The scheme is managed by a commission of 10 bank representatives that are accountable to the General Assembly of the Association
Greece	3,000 million GDR with 60% provided by Bank of Greece and 40% provided by Hellenic Banks' Association – permanent fund	Not risk based – annual premiums are graduated (decreasing) as size of deposits increases from 1.25% for smallest size class up to 0.025% for largest size class	Administered jointly between Bank of Greece, Hellenic Bank Association and Ministry of Finance by seven-member board chaired by one of the Deputy Governors of the Bank of Greece. The other six members shall be selected from the Bank of Greece (2), the Ministry of National Economy (1) and the Hellenic Banks' Association (3)
Ireland	Private funding – permanent fund	Not risk based – annual premiums of 0.20% of covered deposits	Public
Italy	Government/Private Funding – Bank of Italy can make low-interest loans to facilitate payout of large bank – no permanent fund	Risk based (levied ex post) – premiums based on sliding scale of protected deposits with marginal premiums increasing as size increases from 0.4% to 0.8%	Private, but decisions must be approved by Central Bank
Luxembourg	Private Funding – no permanent fund	Not risk based – ex post premiums	Private
Netherlands	Government/Private Funding – with government providing interest-free bridge financing – no permanent fund	Not risk based – ex post as needed, up to a max. of 5% of proportion of bank's deposits to total protected deposits in scheme	Jointly managed by central bank and banking sector trade organizations

continued on next page

Table 16.5 (continued)

Country name	*Funding*	*Premiums*	*Administration*
Portugal	Government/Private Funding – permanent fund	Risk based, 0.1% to 0.2% + more in emergencies; the annual contributions are defined according to the monthly average of the deposits made in the previous year and to the fixed contribution rate, weighted by the solvency ratio of each institution (the lower this ratio, the higher the contribution); the payment of the annual contributions may be partly (up to a limit of 75%) replaced by an irrevocable contract, guaranteed where necessary by securities having a low credit risk and high liquidity; if the resources are insufficient to comply with its commitments, the Deposit Guarantee Fund may ask for special contributions or resort to loans	Public
Spain	Government/Private Funcing – central bank can make loans to fund – permanent fund	Not risk based – 0.6% for CBs, 0.4% for SBs and 1% for credit cooperatives, extraordinary contributions may be required, and, exceptionally, extraordinary contributions made by the central bank when they are authorized by law	Joint Private Official – board comprised of four members from Bank of Spain and four from member institutions
Sweden	Government/Private Funding – permanent fund	Risk based, 0.5% now, 0.1% later (future date is not available)	Public
United Kingdom	Private Funding – no permanent fund	Not risk based – fees determined on basis of projections of next year's losses – for banks fees are limited to 0.3% of protected deposits each year	Government legislated and privately administered; board appointed by FSA
New members			
Cyprus	Private Funding – permanent fund	Not risk based – levies determined by the fund after initial contribution is made	Joint and Private Official by Central Bank and five-member Management Committee consisting of the governor of the Central Bank, the head of the Banking Supervision and

Country name	*Funding*	*Premiums*	*Administration*
			Regulation Division of the Central Bank and two representatives of the banks nominated by the Association of Commercial Banks and one representative of the Minister of Finance nominated by the Minister of Finance
Czech Republic	Government/Private Funding – governent provides 50% of funds for compensation of depositors, central bank and government will provide loans to cover shortfall; in case the Fund's reserves are not sufficient to disburse compensation, the Fund has to acquire any and all funds on the market; there is no government guarantee for its borrowing – permanent fund	Not risk based – 0.1% of insured deposits including accrued interest and 0.05% for building and savings banks.	Fund is independent institution managed by a five-member Board of Administration; at least one member of the board is appointed from among employees of the Czech National Bank and at least two members are appointed from among members of the boards of directors of banks
Estonia	Government/Private Funding – government provided initial funding and banks paid EEK 50,000; fund can borrow without government guarantee and can ask the government to borrow a limited amount on its behalf; initial contribution for Deposit Guarantee Sectoral Fund – 50,000 kroons – permanent fund	Not risk based – quarterly contributions for Deposit Guarantee Sectoral Fund – 0.07% of guaranteed deposits for Investor Protection Sectoral Fund	Eight-member supervisory board: two members appointed by the Riigikogu; one by the government on recommendation of Minister of Finance; one by the President of the Bank of Estonia; one by the Financial Supervision Authority; one by the organizations representing credit institutions; one member appointed by the organizations representing investment institutions; one member appointed by the organizations representing pension management companies
Hungary	Government/Private Funding – one-off admission fee on entry (0.5% of the member's registered capital) – permanent fund	Not risk based – 0.5% of deposits up to 1 million HUF, 0.3% between 1 and 6 million HUF and 0.05 above 6 million HUF	Board of Directors consists of Central Bank president, administrative secretary of Ministry of Finance, president of inspections, two delegates from insured institutions and managing director of DIF

continued on next page

Table 16.5 (continued)

Country name	*Funding*	*Premiums*	*Administration*
Latvia	Government/Private Funding with initial contribution of 50,000 lats; if funds are insufficient, then payments will be made by the government	Not risk based – 0.2% of deposits	Public
Malta	Private Funding – permanent fund	Not risk based – ex post assessments, administrative fees and income from investments	Management Committee appointed by the MFSA made up of persons representing MFSA, the Central Bank of Malta, investment firms, the banks and customers
Poland	Permanent fund – joint gcvernment private funding	Not risk based – fees determined yearly and levied on deposits and off-balance sheet liabilities separately	Fund Council and Fund Management Board; the Fund Council consists of a chairman and ten members having appropriate university degrees and professional experience; the Fund Management Board shall consist of five members, including the President and his deputy; the Management Board is appointed by the Fund Council from among persons having the appropriate university degree and five years of service in the banking industry
Lithuania	Funded by banks and by government	Not risk based; commercial banks and branches (departments) of foreign banks pay the Insurance Company insurance premiums, annually amounting to 0.45% of all insurable deposits	Public – the Council is comprised of six members appointed by the government of the Republic of Lithuania; the Ministry of Finance proposes three candidates, the Bank of Lithuania two candidates, the Securities Commission one candidate
Slovak Republic	Government/private – permanent fund	Not risk based – and range from 0.1% to 0.3% for banks	Joint Private Official
Slovenia	Private Funding – no permanent fund	Not risk based – fee calculated on the basis of each bank's share of guaranteed deposits	Public, Bank of Slovenia

Table 16.6 Deposit insurance provisions and characteristics

Country name	*Top-up permitted*	*Co-insurance*	*% co-insurance percentage*
Old Members			
Austria	Yes – both EU and institutions from non-EU countries may join and obtain supplemental insurance	Co-insurance	10%
Belgium	Yes – EU member chartered institutions may join and obtain supplemental insurance	Co-insurance	10%
Denmark	Yes – EU member chartered institutions may join and obtain supplemental insurance	No co-insurance	0
Finland	Yes – EU member chartered institutions may join and obtain supplemental insurance	No co-insurance	0
France	Yes – EU member chartered institutions may join and obtain supplemental insurance	No co-insurance	0
Germany	Branches of foreign banks have several insurance options which may be as high as €1.5 million	Co-insurance	10%
Greece	Yes – EU member chartered institutions may join and obtain supplemental insurance	No co-insurance	0
Ireland		Co-insurance	10%
Italy	Yes – EU member chartered institutions may join and obtain supplemental insurance	No co-insurance	0
Luxembourg	Yes – EU member chartered institutions may join and obtain supplemental insurance	No co-insurance	0
Netherlands	Yes – EU member chartered institutions may join and obtain supplemental insurance	No co-insurance for first €20,000 and 90% for second €20,000	10%
Portugal	No	No co-insurance	0
Spain	Top-up is permitted	No co-insurance	0
Sweden	Yes – EU member chartered institutions may join and obtain supplemental insurance	No co-insurance	0
United Kingdom	Top-up is permitted	Co-insurance	10%
New members			
Cyprus	No	Co-insurance	10%
Czech Republic	Yes – EU member chartered institutions may join and obtain supplemental insurance	Co-insurance	10%

continued on next page

Table 16.6 (continued)

Country name	*Top-up permitted*	*Co-insurance*	*% co-insurance percentage*
Estonia	Yes to extent not covered by home country guarantee system in EU area	Co-insurance	10%
Hungary	Yes – EU member chartered institutions may join and obtain supplemental insurance	Co-insurance	10%
Lithuania	Yes – EU member chartered institutions may join and obtain supplemental insurance	Co-insurance	10%
Latvia	Top-up is mandatory but only for difference between insurance provided by home country	No co-insurance	0
Malta	Effectively yes, since all foreign branches are required to participate regardless of coverage in home country	No co-insurance	0
Poland	Branches of EU banks when guarantee is lower than provided in Poland may join fund to increase coverage	Co-insurance	10%
Slovak Republic	Foreign bank can join fund if its deposits are not insured or available insurance is less than provided by Fund	Co-insurance	10%
Slovenia	Participation is required unless home country has equivalent scheme	No co-insurance	0

Insolvency resolution

As financial integration proceeds, and in particular as cross-border bank expansion increases, even what may appear to be small differences between schemes may be magnified. Equally important, differences in the guarantee arrangements may generate significant cost shifting when a troubled institution needs to be closed or resolved. There are generally two different models for dealing with banking insolvency, and these hinge generally on the special role that deposit insurance and banking supervisors play and the supervisor's ability to intervene in a bank's activities before failure occurs. In the US, special bankruptcy laws apply, whereas in Europe the general bankruptcy statutes apply. The EC Directive 2001/24/EC of 4 April sets forth EU policy for how failed banks (credit institutions) are to be resolved.[28] The intent is to create a common approach to insolvency resolution. It leaves the actual closure decision to each home country and its applicable bankruptcy procedures, but the Directive attempts to promote equal treatment for creditors, regardless of where they are located. Harmony is to be achieved through mutual recognition of both home- and host-country bankruptcy procedures and coordination among authorities. Krimminger (2005) indicates that conflicts are supposed to be resolved through a mediation process that conveys that responsibility to the home country. As for differences in treatment of financial institutions, Hüpkes (2003) indicates that in most countries in the EU bank insolvencies are covered under the general bankruptcy statutes, but several countries provide exceptions. Some give the banking supervisory agency the right to petition for bankruptcy. A few EU countries have separate bankruptcy statutes for banks.

Table 16.7 EU insolvency resolution provisions

Country name	*Closure decision controlled by*	*Claim notification and verification*	*Authority controlling resolution*	*Legal payment requirements for insured deposits*
Old members				
Austria	Financial Market Authority	NC	Financial Market Authority and bankruptcy court	Within 3 months
Belgium	Bankruptcy Court Notice is published in the Moniteur belge	Claimants have two months to file claim,	Bankruptcy court	2 months
Denmark	Closure is by The Danish Financial Supervisory Authority (DFSA)	Must request another institution to file claim. Depositors of failed bank will be notified within one month of failure	The Danish Financial Supervisory Authority (DFSA)	Shall be effected as soon as possible and not later than 3 months after the commencement of the suspension of payments or compulsory winding-up
Finland	FSA declares that the bank had failed to meet its obligations. The FSA has 21 days to make this decision	The fund will notify depositors and also publish notice of its decision to pay out funds	Courts and/or FSA	3 months – failure to receive payment within the required time limit gives the depositor a claim against the fund in court
France	Commission Bancaire's notice prior court's declaration	Customers notified by Fund and have 15 days to respond	Resolution overseen by banking supervisor	3 months with the possibility for the Supervisory Commission to extend by 3 months again
Germany	Petition filed by Financial Supervisory Authority to court	Creditors are notified by German compensation scheme within 21 days of notification of insolvency and claims must be filed in writing by creditors with the German compensation scheme within one year	Financial Supervisory Authority	Payments must be made within 3 months
Greece	Bank of Greece and courts, 21 days after an institution has failed to make payment on contractual obligations, then failure will have occurred	Notification will take place in the press	Bank of Greece and court	HDGF pays compensation in respect of unavailable deposits within three months of the date when the deposits became

continued on next page

Table 16.7 (continued)

Country name	*Closure decision controlled by*	*Claim notification and verification*	*Authority controlling resolution*	*Legal payment requirements for insured deposits*
				unavailable. This time limit may be extended by no more than two further 3 month periods.
Ireland	Determination by either the Irish Central Bank and Financial Services Regulatory Authority or a court ruling	Claims must be filed by depositors	General Insolvency Laws	3 months
Italy	The Courts have the legal power to declare the insolvency status. However, the Bank of Italy, independently of the Courts' declaration, can propose to the Minister of the Economy and Finance the compulsory administrative liquidation of a bank in each of the following cases: exceptionally serious violations of prudential requirements, exceptionally serious irregularities in the bank's administration, exceptionally serious financial losses.	FITD subrogates in the right of depositors and carries out pay-offs directly.	The 1993 Banking Law Bank of Italy appoints liquidator	The reimbursement of depositors shall be made, up to the equivalent of €20,000 (twenty thousand) within three months of the compulsory liquidation order. The Bank of Italy may extend this term in exceptional circumstances or special cases, for a total period not to exceed nine months.
Luxembourg	Petition filed by bank regulator – Commission de Surveillance du Secteur Financier (CSSF) – or institution itself to the court	Claims must be made by depositors to the AGDL and declaration to be made through the liquidators of the establishment	Law on the Financial Sector of April, 1993 Court will appoint a bankruptcy judge who will appoint a liquidator	Reimbursement starts as soon as claims have been verified and must be finished three months after the occurrence of in-availability of funds. The Luxembourg supervision authority may grant 3 extensions of 3 months each of this deadline.

Country name	*Closure decision controlled by*	*Claim notification and verification*	*Authority controlling resolution*	*Legal payment requirements for insured deposits*
Netherlands	Nederlandsche Bank, which is the supervisor, must petition the court	De Nederlandsche Bank can declare insolvency and advertises in the newspapers for depositors to apply for compensation. Victims of the bank failure can then register with De Nederlandsche Bank during a period of five months.	Act of the Supervision of the Credit System 1992, Bankruptcy Act	As soon as possible but in any case no later than three months of the date on which the creditor or investor duly submitted his claims, recompense that creditor or investor for the amount of the claims covered by the scheme. In very exceptional circumstances, decide that the period of three months shall be extended by a maximum of another three months.
Portugal	The Banco de Portugal, as the banking supervisory authority management, is required to notify the Banco de Portugal of the bank's inability to meet its obligations, but Banco de Portugal may also intervene.		Banco de Portugal may force a winding-up pursuant to Credit Institutions and Financial Companies: Legal Framework (approved by Decree-Law No. 298/92 of 31 December and amended by Decree-Laws No. 246/95 of 14 September, No. 232/96 of 5 December, No. 222/99 of 22 June, No. 250/2000 of 13 October, No. 285/2001 of 3 November, No. 201/2002 of 26 September, No. 319/2002 of 28 December and No. 252/2003 of 17 October)	Repayment shall take place within a maximum of three months of the date on which deposits became unavailable; in exceptional circumstances and on a case-by-case basis, the Fund may apply to the Banco de Portugal for a maximum of three further extensions of the time limit, neither of which shall exceed three months. Without prejudice to the period of limitation set forth in the general law, the expiry of the time limit prescribed in the foregoing paragraph does not affect the depositors' right of compensation.

continued on next page

Table 16.7 (continued)

Country name	*Closure decision controlled by*	*Claim notification and verification*	*Authority controlling resolution*	*Legal payment requirements for insured deposits*
Spain	Bank of Spain petitions court	Depositors are not required to file a claim. The insurer makes a record of the depositors who are entitled to compensation and informs depositors of the events through ordinary mail of their right to compensation.	General insolvency laws and Discipline and Intervention of Credit Institutions Law 26/1988, of 29 July (BOE day 30) (Correction of errors, BOE of 4 August 1989), Authority to impose sanctions for very serious infractions shall rest with the Minister of Economy and Finance, at the proposal of the Bank of Spain, except for revocation of authorization, which shall be imposed by the Council of Ministers.	Will start as soon as possible and shall take place within a maximum of three months of the date on which deposits became unavailable; the Funds may apply to the Banco de Espana for a maximum of three further extensions of the time limit, neither of which shall exceed three months.
Sweden	Finansinspektionen	NA	Companies Act	Reimbursements will start as soon as possible. They have to be made no later than 3 months after the institution is declared bankrupt.
United Kingdom	Bank files with court	If a bank or building society becomes insolvent the depositor will be contacted by the liquidator or by Financial Services Compensation Scheme and file a claim form	Insolvency Act 1986, Banking Act 1987	All claims should be paid within 3 months (can be extended by a further 3 months or by actions of the court)
New members				
Cyprus	Bank Supervision Dept, Central Bank of Cyprus or a court order determines if bank unable to repay deposits	Deposit Protection Scheme will collect information on depositors eligible for claims	Banking Law specifies that upon declaration by a court or revocation of the banking license by the Central Bank constitutes grounds for its winding up by the	Publish an announcement in the Official Gazette. The Fund's Management Committee must proceed with the compensation from the date deposits became

Country name	*Closure decision controlled by*	*Claim notification and verification*	*Authority controlling resolution*	*Legal payment requirements for insured deposits*
			Court on the application of the Central Bank and the appointment of a receiver	unavailable, unless the Central Bank of Cyprus approves an extension in accordance with the provisions of the Regulations.
Czech Republic	Banking Supervision of CNB can impose conservatorship. Bank management responsible for notifying CNB of impending insolvency.	Compensation for an insured deposit claim shall be paid from the Fund to an eligible person after the Fund receives notification in writing from the Czech National Bank	General bankruptcy statutes and Act No. 21/1992 Coll. of 20 December 1991, on Banks as amended. If a bank is wound up and liquidated, the Czech National Bank shall have exclusive authority to submit a proposal for the nomination of the liquidator. In addition, the Czech National Bank shall have exclusive authority to submit a proposal for the dismissal of the liquidator and for the nomination of a new liquidator or a proposal for the winding up of the joint-stock company if the bank's license has been revoked. The court shall rule on the Czech National Bank's proposal within 24 hours of the proposal being submitted.	Reimbursement starts within 3 months after deposits become unavailable (may be prolonged twice by 3 months), ends within 5 years
Estonia	Banking Supervision Department of Estonia Central Bank can withdraw a banking licence	Within three working days after the date on which deposits become unavailable, the Fund shall publish a notice in at least two daily national newspapers on	Bankruptcy Act, Act on Credit Institutions – A bank may be wound up by the central bank (Eesti Pank) or on the basis of a court order under the Bankruptcy Law.	Payment must begin not later than thirty days after the date on which deposits become unavailable and completed within three months. The Fund

continued on next page

Table 16.7 (continued)

Country name	*Closure decision controlled by*	*Claim notification and verification*	*Authority controlling resolution*	*Legal payment requirements for insured deposits*
		at least two occasions setting out the name of the bank, the term and procedure for payment and a list of the documents required upon the payment of compensation	When legal insolvency is declared, the Liquidation Board or trustee in bankruptcy takes over	may extend the term by up to three months at a time, but not for more than a total of nine months
Malta	Malta Financial Services Authority	According to rules established by MFSA	Receiver appointed by bankruptcy court and a liquidator	Within 3 months
Latvia	Insolvency petition to Bankruptcy Court or to the Finance and Capital Market Commission or by that Commission	Guaranteed compensation after the occurrence of a case of unavailability of deposits have submitted their claims to the liquidator or administrator or Commission	Liquidator appointed under the Credit Institutions Law under the control of the Finance and Capital Market Commission	Payment within 3 months with up to 3 extensions of 3 months each
Slovak Republic	National Bank of Slovakia files petition	Failed bank or conservator must announce in media and publicize inside the bank	Conservator	Within 5 days after deposits are inaccessible (frozen, become unavailable) the DPF decides a start of reimbursement; reimbursement ends within 3 months (may be prolonged twice by 3 months), special cases may be reimbursed within 3 years
Slovenia	Bank of Slovenia	If bank or savings bank is declared bankrupt guaranteed deposits will be repaid by a bank designated by the Bank of Slovenia to act as successor. This bank will provide the funds necessary for repaying guaranteed deposits.	Bankruptcy court appoints trustee recommended by Bank of Slovenia	Liability for guaranteed deposits will be assumed by Bank of Slovenia Payment must be made within 3 months

Country name	*Closure decision controlled by*	*Claim notification and verification*	*Authority controlling resolution*	*Legal payment requirements for insured deposits*
Hungary	Hungarian Financial Supervisory Authority	Claim filed by customer. Bank and fund are obliged to inform depositors through daily press and announcements which provide information on where indemnity claims can be submitted and when the payments start	The consent of the Minister of Finance and of the President of the NBH is required for the HFSA to withdraw a credit institution's operating licence (CIFE Section 30 (4)). When it withdraws a licence, the HFSA shall make a resolution for winding up the credit institution or initiate liquidation. The HFSA shall initiate the liquidation of the credit institution if the operating licence is withdrawn because the credit institution fails to pay any of its undisputed debts within five days of the date on which they are due or no longer possesses sufficient own funds (assets) for satisfying the known claims of creditors. In any other case, an order for the winding up of the institution may be issued. The special rules laid down in Section 176/A–185/H of the CIFE are applicable to the winding up and liquidation of credit institution, in addition to the rules of the Bankruptcy Act and the Companies Act. As a general rule, the winding up and liquidation proceeding of financial institutions may be conducted only by the HFSA's nonprofit company	Payments must start within 15 days after deposits were frozen or after the bank's operational licence was withdrawn, or after the bank's liquidation was announced, and complete the proceedings within three months. Two 3-month extensions are permitted

continued on next page

Table 16.7 (continued)

Country name	*Closure decision controlled by*	*Claim notification and verification*	*Authority controlling resolution*	*Legal payment requirements for insured deposits*
Poland	Commission on Supervision, which is part of the Polish National Bank, files a petition with the bankruptcy court. Petition must be considered by the court within one month of receipt	Payouts are made on the basis of a list of depositors of the bank, for which bankruptcy has been declared by a court. A list of depositors is drafted by the trustee in bankruptcy within 30 days from the date of announcing bankruptcy and is presented to the Fund Management Board. After checking the list of depositors, within 7 days the Fund Management Board assumes and issues to the public information for a written nationwide announcement, as well as informs the entities covered by the guarantee system of the resolution on transferring to the trustee in bankruptcy the sum of guaranteed funds which is to be paid out	Receiver appointed by bankruptcy court	The trustee in bankruptcy executes payment of the guaranteed funds according to the schedule accepted by the Fund Management Board, but not later than 30 days from receiving the sums from the Fund for payment for the guaranteed deposits
Lithuania	The Central Bank of Lithuania as banking supervisor is empowered to close a bank	The Council of the Insurance Company announces the procedure for paying insurance compensations in the Valstybės Žinios. The Co. announces the place and time of paying insurance claims in at least 2 Lithuanian daily newspapers. To be paid, a depositor must submit a personal identification document	Administrator appointed by the Central Bank of Lithuania is empowered to initiate bankruptcy proceedings which are in turn administered by a court appointed receiver	Payment must be made within 3 months after funds are unavailable or bankruptcy declared. May be extended 3 months twice by the Council of the Insurance Company

Notes: NC = not clear

Table 16.8 Possible deposit insurance systems differences in different countries

Account coverage	*Claim filed*
• Maximum amount	• Automatically
• Type of account, e.g. inter-bank	• By claimant
• Foreign currency deposits	*Pre-insolvency intervention*
• Co-insurance	• Prompt correction action (PCA)
• Netting	*Declaration of insolvency*
Ownership	• Private creditors or government agency
• Private v. public (government)	• Insurance agency v. other
Funding (premiums)	• Closure rule v. discretion (forbearance)
• Ex ante v. ex post	*Insolvency resolution*
• Magnitude	• Administered by insurance agency, other agencies or bankruptcy court
• Risk based v. flat	• Least cost resolution (LCR)
• Regular v. 'topping up'	• Insurer serves as receiver/conservator
Reserve fund	• Too big to fail
• Minimum magnitude	*Membership*
• Voluntary or required	• Mandatory or voluntary
Government support	*Other*
• Explicit (official) v. implicit	• Co-insurance
• Credibility of private funding (premiums)	• Offsetting
Speed of payment if insolvency	
• Insured depositors – to par value	
• Uninsured depositors – to market (recovery) value	
• Advance dividends v. as assets sold	

A number of questions arise concerning cross-border insolvencies. Because both the timing of the official declaration of insolvency and the process by which an insolvency is resolved have important effects on the host country of a branch or subsidiary, should the host country share in the prudential regulation with the home country and, if so, in what way? In the EU, the home country is responsible for a foreign branch but the host country is responsible for any subsidiaries chartered therein.

How far can and does inter-country regulatory cooperation go? Inter-country cooperation tends to operate best when things are going well but deteriorates rapidly as conditions in the countries involved deteriorate and generate conflicts arising from an incentive for a home-country regulator to give preference to its own citizens even at the expense of host-country residents or other host-country citizens. In the EU, substantial efforts have been devoted to cooperative arrangements and understandings about information sharing. In addition, crisis simulations have been undertaken and memoranda of understanding have been struck in many instances. However, cooperation works best when there is no crisis, and the results of simulations can often be misleading since they don't always involve the same cost–benefit calculations that real crises entail.

Does it matter whether the absolute or relative size of the branches or subsidiary is much larger in the host country than in the home country? Would home countries be more or less likely to declare a bank insolvent sooner or later given that this decision may impact the home and host countries differently? Would host countries permit home countries, whose branch banks comprise a large percentage of the banking assets in that country, to be the final determiner of the insolvency decision or 'pull the plug' on their banks in the host countries when the host country has to suffer any excess damage from either overly hasty or overly slow action? In the EU, systemic risk resolution is the responsibility of the local supervisory agencies and central banks. However, in the case of use of the lender-of-last-resort function, large transactions (at present unspecified or at least not publicly available) must be approved by the Governing Council of the ECB. The specifics, however, of the home-country treatment of banks whose failure might present systemically important implications for a host country are not explicitly addressed in EU Directives. Indeed, it is for this very reason that Nordic countries have structured their own arrangements specifically designed to deal with Nordea Bank should it experience financial difficulties.

Should countries be able to impose depositor preferences in favour of deposits at their own home office relative to deposits at foreign host offices, as the United States and Australia do? In Europe, EU Directives specifically require that EU citizens and claims be treated equally in the event of a bank failure.

Accounting rules are also likely to differ among countries. Thus, the timing of when accounting insolvency occurs is likely to differ in different countries. Solvency in one country may be recorded as insolvency in another and vice versa. This alone, even if the regulators in different countries move to resolve official insolvencies at the same speed, will result in different timing of resolutions. Accounting for profitability is also likely to differ among countries. This is likely to result in the transfer of activities within a banking organization and across subsidiaries to countries where the activity receives the most favourable accounting treatment (Cardenas *et al.* 2003). To the extent that such shifts may not only interfere with the efficient allocation of resources in the host-country branches, but also adversely affect the financial condition of subsidiaries in particular countries, they are of concern to the prudential regulators in those countries. Some analysts have argued that requiring foreign bank subsidiaries to have equity outstanding and minority (independent) directors may lessen the likelihood of shifts that impact the host country adversely, in addition to providing additional signals about significant changes in the financial health of the subsidiary or organization as a whole. Despite these concerns, the fact that all EU firms must abide by the International Financial Reporting Standards should serve to at least constrain countries from applying vastly different valuation procedures to some degree.

The effectiveness of home-country prudential regulation of its foreign branches and subsidiaries in most countries depends on a number of factors, including the strength and credibility of the home country's deposit insurance scheme and the relative and absolute sizes of the banks in each country.[29] Host countries logically would prefer home-country prudential regulation of foreign branches particularly when the home-country deposit insurance scheme is strong and host-country branches are large. Home-country regulation is least satisfactory to host countries when its deposit insurance scheme is weak and branches in the host country large.

As noted earlier, for subsidiary banks in financial difficulties, host-country regulators need to be concerned whether the parent will or will not rescue the sub, and for solvent subsidiary banks of troubled foreign parents, whether or not the parent will attempt to strip assets from the sub, whether the sub's solvency is threatened through reputation risk from the parent's insolvency or whether the parent could continue to supply important services.[30] This suggests that the severity of the agency problems are dependent on a number of factors including the absolute and relative sizes of the parent and subsidiary and the countries involved. Some host countries require capital maintenance agreements between the parent and its foreign subsidiary banks' regulators requiring parental support if the sub gets into financial trouble. But enforcement of such provisions across borders can be difficult. The greatest chance of parents walking away from insolvent subsidiaries is when the parent is small and solvent and the sub is insolvent regardless of size. The least chance is when the parent is large and solvent and the sub is insolvent, again regardless of size. Size matters most when the parent is solvent. Small parents are less likely to rescue insolvent foreign subs of any size.

EU member countries have different structures for deposit insurance as well as for financial institution supervision and regulation. Some have split supervision and regulation according to function, while others have consolidated supervision and regulation into a single agency. In some instances, the central bank is involved in prudential supervision and regulation and in other countries it is not. One implication of the different structures is that policy tradeoffs for regulatory agencies faced with the same set of policy issues may differ. This both sets up many opportunities for individual institutions to pit the countries' agencies against each other and fosters potential regulatory arbitrage on the part of financial institutions seeking a competitive advantage.[31]

However, relying upon regulatory competition to level the playing field also risks creating a more lax supervisory system and may open the system up to unintended systemic problems should major financial institutions get into financial difficulty. To be sure, the EU has set minimum supervisory standards for the region through Directives and agreements in order both to set a lower bound as far as safety and soundness risks are concerned and to promote cooperation and information sharing among the individual country supervisors.[32] While these Directives and guidelines are an attempt to limit excessive regulatory competition, except at the margin, there is no EU-wide bank supervisor or other agency responsible for providing Euro-wide deposit insurance or for resolving the failure after declaring an institution insolvent (and establishing and enforcing a common closure rule). This is a major weakness of the current design. It results in one that may seemingly work well during good times, but, as noted earlier, is filled with risks, conflicts and potential delays in resolving problems in bad times. Indeed, these risks are likely to prove more significant over time, as the EU financial system becomes more integrated and more countries with different economic and financial systems at different stages of development join. That is, one of the biggest threats to lasting EU financial stability hinges upon the design of deposit insurance systems within the EU countries and the structure of bankruptcy resolution in the event that institutions get into financial difficulties.

Deposit insurance payout coordination problems for the EU

Numerous practical issues arise if a large cross-border institution should experience financial difficulties and have to be legally closed and resolved. Cross-border coordination and decision-making would be extremely difficult, especially in the absence of explicit ex ante plans.[33] Consider an extreme case in which a cross-border institution operated both branches and separately chartered subsidiaries in each of the current 25 EU countries. In this case there would be 25 home-country regulators (one for the parent institution and each of the separately chartered subsidiaries), 25 different deposit insurance funds (with primary responsibility for the home chartered subsidiaries but with overlapping responsibilities for branches in each host country and foreign branches in their own country to the extent that the institution might have chosen to top up its coverage) and 25 separate central banks possibly involved if emergency liquidity had to be provided to keep the institution operating while claims against it were resolved. In the extreme, there could be 75 separate entities that would have a role in some part of the resolution of this institution.

With different deposit insurance coverage, sorting out who would be responsible for what claims would be a daunting task, especially when it comes to the top-up coverage claims for cross-border branches. In addition, because of different laws governing claims in bankruptcy across the different countries, there would be the added complication that depositors' claims might be treated differently if held in a branch than in a subsidiary. Imagine the difficulty for a depositor, especially a corporate customer, who might have multiple accounts across countries, in choosing an account in his/her own country among say branches of banks headquartered in 24 other countries with different insurance and resolution systems. Any claims might be settled differently depending upon which bank or country the account was held and whether the account was in a branch or subsidiary. Imagine also depositors in a member country with branches of banks chartered, say, in all of the other 24 countries. The depositors would be faced with options involving 25 deposit insurance schemes and 25 insolvency resolution schemes. To make the guarantee system work smoothly, there would have to be no risk that one or more country deposit insurance funds might default or might not be able or unwilling to meet its obligations, particularly when many of the deposits of the insolvent bank are at branches in host countries. While this may, in good times, be viewed by the responsible authorities as an unlikely event, there is ample evidence that commitments are not always kept in bad times (see Appendix for a discussion of the failures of US-sponsored non-federal government deposit insurance systems). For this reason, Goodhart and Schoenmaker (2006) argue for the establishment of explicit ex ante commitments to share the burden should losses occur.

Possible solutions to the deposit insurance problems and difficulties in resolving problems in foreign-owned banks

It is well understood that poorly designed deposit insurance, safety nets and regulatory structures encourage (a) both moral hazard behaviour by banks and (b) poor bank regulator performance in resolving troubled banks can lead to excess forbearance on problem institutions. These effects increase both the likelihood and costs of a banking crisis.

In the EU, there is little uniformity in the underlying legal structure for resolving bank failures. Only a few regulators have legal closure authority, and failure resolution is covered under general bankruptcy laws. This is in stark contrast to the US, for example, where there is a separate bankruptcy and administrative process for banking mergers administered by the Federal Deposit Insurance Corporation (FDIC).

Some of the difficulties with efficient resolution of foreign-owned bank insolvencies lie in the heterogeneity of both the closure rule and the deposit insurance structure across countries. These difficulties include: differences in both provisions and enforcement; overlapping of legislation, regulation and supervision between home and host countries; and inherent incentives for regulators to favour the welfare of their home countries, possibly at the expense of the host country. These problems are complex and do not lead to easy or simple lasting solutions. Moreover, they become increasingly significant as more and more banks operate banking offices in foreign countries.

Coordination and cooperation among home and host countries, which have become the focal point for European efforts to deal with troubled institutions, are a necessary but not sufficient condition to solve the problem.[34] What appears to be required is greater harmonization and homogeneity, particularly in closure policies and claims resolution and, most likely, eventual EU-wide deposit insurance, bankruptcy laws and resolution agencies. Indeed, centralized multinational regimes for deposit insurance and insolvency declaration (closure rule) and resolution, in terms of both provisions and enforcement, appear to be the most promising way to ensure that bank failures are resolved efficiently and without creating undue uncertainty.[35] This would eliminate the differences that make multiple individual home/host-country regulatory regimes and cross-border enforcement a severe problem. But such a system raises numerous questions: which countries should be included in the arrangement; how to deal with those excluded; how to organize the governing board; how countries are to be represented on the board; what authority and enforcement power such a board would have; what funding would be available, especially given the lack of a fiscal taxing authority at the pan-European level; and whether the conflicts discussed above are eliminated by a single structure or primarily only internalized and hidden from view. These issues are significant enough that it is unlikely that a single, multinational structure for either deposit insurance or insolvency resolution could be adopted in the near future. We put forward a four-point programme for efficiently resolving insolvent banks so that both their credit losses and the widespread fear of bank failures are minimized and the adverse moral hazard incentives inherent in deposit insurance become benign. Indeed, with efficient insolvency resolution, deposit insurance provides desirable built-in redundancy in case specific resolutions turn out ex post not to be effective, much like aeroplanes that have two or even three brake systems in case the first system fails. But this is a second-best solution. The preferred solution is to prevent the occurrence of bank insolvencies through effective market discipline and appropriate regulatory prompt corrective actions.

The proposal is based on a fundamental understanding of the nature of bank failures and where their costs occur. Banks become economically insolvent when the market value of their assets declines below the value of their deposits and other debt funding so that the value of their capital turns negative. At this point, a bank cannot pay out all its debts, including deposits at par, in full and on time, and the depositors and other creditors share in the losses according to their legal priority.

These claimants may experience both credit and liquidity losses in the resolution process. Credit losses may occur when the recovery value of the bank as a whole or in parts falls short of the par value of its deposits or other debt on their respective due dates. Liquidity losses may occur for two reasons. First, depositors may not have immediate (next business day or so) and full access to the par value of their insured claims or to the estimated recovery value of their de jure uninsured claims. In the case of insured deposits, the insurer must have a fund to provide eligible depositors with immediate and full access before the insurer may collect the proceeds from the sale of the bank or its underlying assets and, in case of losses, to fill the difference between the par value and the recovery value. In the case of uninsured claims, liquidity can be provided either by a direct injection of funds or through a liquid and active secondary market for receivership certificates given to uninsured claimants by the insurance agency. Second, qualified borrowers may not be able to utilize their existing credit lines immediately. Insolvent banks may be said to be resolved efficiently with least cost to society when the sum of aggregate credit losses and aggregate liquidity losses, or total losses, is at or close to zero.

Insolvent banks in a country may be resolved efficiently if the process employed by bank regulators in the country in which a bank is chartered or licensed can satisfy the following four rules or principles.[36] Each principle focuses importantly on the term 'prompt':

- prompt legal closure when the bank's equity capital declines to some pre-specified and well-publicized positive minimum that is greater than zero (legal closure rule)
- prompt estimate of the recovery values and assignment of credit losses ('haircuts') to de jure uninsured bank claimants when equity is negative to avoid protecting de jure uninsured claimants

- prompt reopening (e.g. next workday), particularly of larger banks, with full depositor access to their accounts on their due dates at their insured or estimated recovery values and full borrower access to their pre-established credit lines provided they are current
- prompt re-privatization in whole or in parts with adequate capital.

Adoption of these four principles and the necessary infrastructure to make them work would largely eliminate most of the agency problems, negative externalities, insurance fund losses and coordination problems associated with the current EU system that has been identified here and by others as well.

The next subsections review how each principle is or could be satisfied in bank insolvencies in the United States. We argue that, while not without flaws and not focused on foreign-owned banks, the current system in the US may serve as a useful model for other countries in designing their insolvency resolution policies. The US system was developed largely in response to the widespread and costly bank and thrift institution insolvencies of the 1980s.

Prompt legal closure

The Federal Deposit Insurance Corporation Improvement Act (FDICIA) of 1991 introduced a bright line bank closure rule that is triggered when the ratio of book value tangible equity capital to total on-balance-sheet assets declines to a minimum of 2 per cent.[37] If this is not corrected within 90 days, the bank must be declared legally insolvent, closed by the appropriate federal or state regulator, and placed in receivership or conservatorship.[38] Its charter is revoked. Shareholder controlling interests are terminated and senior management is changed. If the institution can be successfully resolved before its market value capital declines below zero, losses are confined to shareholders. Depositors and other creditors are fully protected and kept whole, and deposit insurance is effectively redundant. Thus, any adverse spillover effects, which occur primarily when capital turns negative and losses are imposed on counterparties, are minimized.

Because the closure rule is specified in terms of book value capital rather than the market value of capital, there is no guarantee that the institution will be resolved before its economic capital is depleted or that creditors will be fully protected against losses. As a bank approaches insolvency, book values tend to increasingly overstate market values for assets. Thus, there is a risk that use of the book value closure rule may result in de facto forbearance.[39] Nevertheless, specifying a closure rule based on a capital ratio that is greater than zero provides some protection against losses due to the deviation of book from market value and losses due to errors in measuring asset values.

Legal closure according to a well-specified, publicized and credibly enforced closure rule has several desirable attributes. There are no surprises. All players know the rules in advance and base their actions accordingly. It treats all depositors and other creditors in the same priority class more fairly. Because banks tend to have a larger percentage of demand deposits and other short-term deposits and debt than other firms, bad news, impending insolvency or uncertainty about how creditors would be treated in the event of insolvency typically increases the incentives of those who can withdraw their funds to do so while there are still assets available to satisfy their claims. Uncertainty thus raises the probability of a run, with the initial runners receiving full payment and those unable, or unwilling, to run receiving less. However, the presence of a strong perception of an enforced closure rule at positive capital would greatly reduce the incentive to run. All debt claimants, regardless of the date of maturity of their claims, would know that they would not suffer credit losses.

Reducing the incentive for runs also increases the time regulators have to act to deter insolvency or bring about an efficient resolution if the closure trigger is breached. At the same time, equity holders would have greater incentive to attempt to address problems promptly as capital ratios declined, since they would know with greater certainty that they would stand to lose their claims. They would have less incentive to engage in excessive risk taking or moral hazard behaviour.

Table 16.9 Federal deposit insurance corporation improvement act of 1991

			Capital ratios (%)		
			Risk based		*Leverage*
Zone	*Mandatory provisions*	*Discretionary provisions*	*Total*	*Tier 1*	*Tier 1*
1 Well capitalized			>10	>6	>5
2 Adequately capitalized	1 No brokered deposits, except with FDIC approval		>8	>4	>4
3 Under-capitalized	1 Suspend dividends and management fees 2 Require capital restoration plan 3 Restrict asset growth 4 Approval required for acquisitions, branching and new activities 5 No brokered deposits	1 Order re-capitalization 2 Restrict inter-affiliate transactions 3 Restrict deposit interest rates 4 Restrict certain other activities 5 Any other action that would better carry out prompt corrective action	<8	<4	<4
4 Significantly under-capitalized	1 Same as for Zone 3 2 Order re-capitalization* 3 Restrict inter-affiliate transactions* 4 Restrict deposit interest rates* 5 Pay of officers restricted	1 Any Zone 3 discretionary actions 2 Conservatorship or receivership if fails to submit or implement plan or re-capitalize pursuant to order 3 Any other Zone 5 provision, if such action is necessary to carry out prompt corrective action	<6	<3	<3
5 Critically under-capitalized	1 Same as for Zone 4 2 Receiver/conservator within 90 days* 3 Receiver if still in Zone 5 four quarters after becoming critically under-capitalized 4 Suspend payments on subordinated debt* 5 Restrict certain other activities				<2

Source: Board of Governors of the Federal Reserve System.

Notes: * Not required if primary supervisor determines action would not serve purpose of prompt corrective action or if certain other conditions are met.

Banks become insolvent in the US and need to be legally closed because another provision of FDICIA – prompt corrective action (PCA) – has failed to give an incentive to financially troubled banks to turn around before insolvency. PCA established a series of five capital tranches ranging down from 'well capitalized' to 'critically under-capitalized'. Progressively harsher and more mandatory sanctions are applied by the bank regulators on weak financial institutions as their net worth declines through these tranches to discourage their insolvency (Table 16.9). The sanctions are similar to those that the market imposes on firms in non-regulated industries. Sanctions include change in senior management, reductions in dividends, restrictions on growth and acquisitions, adoption of capital restorations plans and, if the bank is a subsidiary of a financial holding company, loss of its parent's status as a financial holding company with the associated wider range of powers.[40] The tranches effectively serve as 'speed bumps' to slow a bank's deterioration and to force regulators to become more involved with troubled banks well before insolvency, so that they may be ready to close them legally when necessary and not be caught by surprise and delayed. Thus, PCA effectively 'buys time' for the regulators to act efficiently. PCA also grants regulators some discretion to apply appropriate sanctions and actions as a bank's capital position deteriorates, depending upon the individual circumstances, to turn the bank around to profitability. This is in contrast to the supervisory actions employed prior to FDICIA when intervention was less frequent and discretion was often focused on ways to keep institutions operating after they had become economically insolvent without forcing improvements. This latter policy tended to result in losses to both uninsured creditors and the FDIC.

While PCA has not prevented all bank failures, it has contributed significantly to turning troubled banks around before insolvency and reducing both the number and the aggregate cost of failures.[41] However, it is important to note that PCA and a closure rule at positive capital are not intended to prevent all failures. As in other industries, inefficient and/or unlucky banks should be permitted to fail and inept management replaced. But, because the adverse externalities of bank insolvencies are widely perceived to be substantially greater than for other firms, such failures should occur only at low cost with minimal losses to creditors.

Prompt estimate and allocation of credit losses

Because the regulators should be scrutinizing troubled banks under PCA well before they approach the capital ratio closure trigger, the recovery value of the institution as a whole or in parts should be able to be estimated quickly upon legal closure for most banks. If the present value of the estimated recovery value falls short of the par value of the deposits and other debts, pro rata losses (haircuts) should be allocated to these claimants in their order of legal priority to avoid protecting de jure uninsured claimants. In the US, the FDIC has equal standing with depositors at domestic offices and higher standing than other depositors and creditors.[42] The FDIC stands in the shoes of the insured depositors at domestic offices and is obligated to make them whole. It also shares proportionally in any losses with uninsured depositors at these offices beyond the losses charged first to other creditors and deposits at foreign offices. FDICIA requires the FDIC to share any losses in the insolvency with uninsured claimants and resolve the institution at least cost to the insurance fund. The only exception is when doing so is likely to 'have serious adverse effects on economic conditions and financial stability', the so-called 'systemic risk exemption' or successor to 'too-big-to-fail'. Requiring parties besides the FDIC to share in any losses is necessary to minimize moral hazard excessive risk-taking behaviour by banks and to enhance market discipline by reinforcing the ex post at-risk nature of de jure at-risk claimants. This should, in turn, reduce the number of bank failures.

Prompt reopening of large banks

Liquidity losses to depositors can occur through delayed access to or freezing of deposit accounts. This process in effect transforms demand deposits and short-term time deposits involuntarily into longer-term time deposits or even bonds. Liquidity losses also result when credit lines cannot be relied upon or drawn down by borrowers to meet business needs. When regulators close a bank legally they often also effectively close it physically, at least partially, until funds are recovered from the sale of assets to start paying depositors on their claims. In many countries the lack of access to deposits and credit lines is more feared than credit losses to depositors and generates as great, if not greater, adverse externalities. The inability to use deposits to make immediate payments greatly reduces the efficiency of the payments system. Additionally, the more likely depositors are to have prompt access to their funds, the less likely they are to engage in runs.

Regulators often are unable or unwilling to avoid, at least briefly, closing banks physically when they close them legally, e.g. because of insufficient information on depositors or recovery values or insufficient funds to advance payments. In some countries, both insured and uninsured depositors first need to file claims with the deposit insurance agency after notification in order to obtain access to their funds. In others, it is left to depositors to monitor newspapers and file claims. This is a time-consuming and costly process during which the funds are effectively frozen. Thus, there is considerable pressure on regulators to avoid legally closing banks promptly. By delaying legal closure, the regulators not only avoid liquidity losses; delay also postpones, at least temporarily, explicitly recognizing underlying implicit credit losses and provides additional time in which the bank may try to regain solvency and thereby avoid altogether the unpleasant task of legal closure. But evidence in many countries strongly suggests that, on average, such forbearance increases the costs in the long run over what they would have been had the insolvent institution been legally closed promptly. To reduce the incentive for regulators to forbear, FDICIA made prompt legal closure mandatory, and to increase the efficiency of the resolution required it be at least cost to the FDIC.

Liquidity losses may be minimized or eliminated entirely by legally reopening the insolvent bank the next business day with full access to all accounts. This would provide insured depositors near-immediate and seamless access to the par value of their accounts, uninsured depositors and other general creditors to the estimated recovery value of their accounts on due dates, and borrowers to their credit lines.[43] Thus, legal closure is separated from physical closure.

Potential payments to depositors and other debt claimants, either directly or through assumption of these claims by another bank, require an immediate sale of the bank by the FDIC or access to a source of funds, either its own or through a pre-designated source of borrowing. The FDIC may also operate the bank temporarily through a newly chartered bridge bank that assumes most or all of the assets and liabilities of the failed bank, generally at market values. The bridge bank is either capitalized with equity by the FDIC or its deposits are fully guaranteed by the FDIC during its operation until it is re-privatized. The bridge bank provides the FDIC with additional time to find qualified private buyers for the bank and wind down its operations efficiently.

It should be noted that minimizing liquidity losses is not a traditional deposit insurance function, which is to protect targeted depositors against credit losses. Less attention has been paid to the problem of the timing of when depositors gain access to their funds. This depends both on when the insurance agency receives the proceeds from the sale of the bank as a whole or in parts and whether the agency has access to a fund or borrowing facilities to make advance payments to the depositors of both the estimated recovery amount and, for insured depositors, also of the amount necessary to make them whole.

In the US, the FDIC usually pays insured deposits at the failed bank at par the next business day even though it may not yet have collected from the sale of the insolvent bank's assets. This occurs either through a transfer of the insured deposits to another solvent bank, which assumes the liabilities, generally with an offsetting financial payment from the FDIC, or, less frequently, through a payout.[44] The FDIC can generally make such speedy payments as they have been monitoring problem banks carefully under PCA and have access to the bank's records on eligible insured deposits.[45] In contrast, uninsured depositors and other creditors generally receive receivership certificates and are paid in order of their legal priority as proceeds are received from the sale of the bank assets. Unless there is an active secondary market for these certificates, uninsured creditors receiving these certificates may suffer liquidity difficulties. To maximize efficiency, these depositors should share in any credit losses but not suffer liquidity losses. To achieve this, the FDIC has the authority to make advance payments to these claimants on the basis of estimated or average recovery amounts before it has actually collected the proceeds (Kaufman and Seelig 2002). If payments are made at the time of legal closure, this procedure is essentially equivalent to not having physically closed the institution. Advance dividends also permit the estimated recovery value of uninsured deposits to be transferred to a newly chartered bridge bank with immediate access by depositors. In bridge banks, performing borrowers generally may maintain access to their existing credit lines. This further reduces any liquidity losses.[46] The FDIC is able to make advance dividends as it has access to a pool of funds provided by premiums paid by banks and can borrow a limited amount from the US Treasury.

Estimates of the recovery value of the funds advanced as dividends tend to be on the conservative side because the FDIC absorbs the loss if it overestimates the recovery amounts. If it underestimates the recovery amounts, it makes additional payments to the claimants later. The FDIC, in its capacity of receiver, can borrow the necessary funds to make advance dividend payments from its corporate capacity, which has access to the FDIC accumulated fund.

The FDIC used advance dividends briefly in a number of resolutions in the early 1980s and early 1990s, when it did not fully protect most or all uninsured debt claimants. But, probably because most bank failures in the US since the mid-1990s have involved small banks, the FDIC has not used advance dividends often since.

Use of bridge banks and advance dividends to minimize liquidity losses, especially in combination with the previous principle of preventing or, at least, minimizing credit losses, should eliminate much of the fear of bank failures. It should permit efficient resolutions of large banks without strong negative reactions by the affected depositors and without having to invoke the idea that some banks are 'too-big-to-fail'.

Prompt re-privatization and re-capitalization

FDICIA requires that insolvencies be resolved at least cost to the FDIC. This also reduces losses to depositors at domestic offices who share the same priority. The requirement encourages rapid sale of bank assets after legal closure and is an attempt to deal with the fact that experience suggests, on average, that assets lose value the longer they are held in receivership. Re-privatization can be more difficult when banks are publicly owned, including bridge banks. Public ownership of banks is not always rooted in the desire to allocate resources efficiently. Nor do publicly owned institutions necessarily seek to maximize profits. Rather, the intention may be to reallocate funds for socially desirable purposes or for political purposes. Thus, when a government-sponsored bank becomes insolvent, the government is likely to keep the institution in operation regardless of its financial condition, and its return to solvency is likely to be slower. The consequence is that losses are likely to continue and the ultimate cost of resolution to the taxpayer is likely to be larger than it otherwise would be.

To minimize government forbearance and its attendant costs, insolvent banks should be sold to the private sector, in whole or parts, as soon as this can be done efficiently. Indeed, in the US, the maximum life of a bridge bank is specified by law to be no longer than two years, with three one-year extensions (which is probably longer than necessary). Moreover, the sale should be on terms that provide sufficient private capital to ensure that, after adjusting for any guarantees to the buyers, the resulting institution will attain, at minimum, 'adequately capitalized' status, if not 'well-capitalized' status, to guard against a quick return to insolvency. Again, because under PCA the FDIC is aware of most pending insolvencies, it can begin the bidder search process for most banks before legal closure and the actual bidding at closure. As noted, larger banks may need to be bridged to give the FDIC additional time to sell to the highest bidders without having to resort to fire-sale losses or otherwise being forced to unwind the bank inefficiently.

Proposed solution to cross-border branching in the EU

To date, little progress has been made to deal with the supervisory and failure resolution issues raised by cross-border banking organizations. The principle focus has been on obtaining cooperation and data sharing among responsible supervisory agencies within the existing decentralized regulatory framework. For example, the major financial public policy authorities of the European Union member countries have recently signed a Memorandum of Understanding on Cooperation in Financial Crisis Situations, announced in a press release (14 May 2005).[47]

Largely motivated by inquiries by the Nordea Bank about the feasibility of taking advantage of the new European Company Statute in order to reorganize itself, the Nordic countries have pushed ahead and established formal memoranda of understanding on joint supervisory policies and agreements governing the treatment of institutions in financial distress (Mayes 2006).[48] The bank considered replacing its cross-border subsidiaries, which are currently supervised by regulators in the countries where they are chartered, with branches to be supervised by Swedish authorities, where Nordea would remain headquartered. The converted subsidiaries' deposits would be insured by the Swedish deposit guarantee system. But financial stability and lender-of-last-resort functions would remain the responsibility of host countries, where Nordea is often more significant than in Sweden.

Mayes (2005) describes in detail the contingency efforts of the Nordic country supervisors to plan and assign supervisory activities and sort out ex ante how they might respond to a crisis should the new Nordea organization experience financial difficulties. While Nordea's plan appears to be stalled at this point, the problems and issues that Nordic country regulators and insurers began to focus on deal with what is likely to become the dominant issue for large European banks in the future. The discussions highlight the complexities in structuring shared regulatory responsibility within the current European framework.

We are sceptical that voluntary cooperative arrangements will work when put to the test in a crisis, especially if substantial commitment of a country's treasury funds should prove necessary either to pay out depositors or to rescue the institution should it experience financial difficulties. However, the efficiency advantages of cross-border branching are too large to discard, and the supervisory issues will arise again.

In lieu of cooperation, we would propose an alternative, which, when combined with the four-point proposal for efficient resolution of trouble institutions discussed earlier, would significantly reduce the home/host-country conflict and loss-sharing problems and enhance financial stability, while co-existing within the current regulatory framework. We propose creating financial incentives through the establishment of differential deposit insurance charges to induce banks or their subsidiaries that operate cross-border branches to accept a system of PCA and structured early intervention and resolution (SEIR) with a legal closure rule at positive capital implemented by the respective home country. Specifically, those banks choosing to be subjected to PCA and SEIR would be offered an effective discount on their deposit insurance premiums. The exact implementation might depend upon the structure of how insurance charges are levied (as detailed in Table 16.5). In cases where an ex ante premium, risk based or otherwise, is charged, PCA banks could be offered a discount on their charges or, alternatively, non-PCA banks could be charged a surcharge on the premiums. In cases where premiums are levied on an ex post basis, PCA banks would be charged less than non-PCA banks. Lower relative premiums for PCA banks are justified because of the lower expected losses that would accrue to the insurer under a well-run PCA structure.

While we leave the ultimate legal structure of such an arrangement to the lawyers, necessary provisions would include a critical, positive capital ratio that would trigger resolution. In the event that this trigger capital threshold was breached, the institution's shareholders would be required to return its charter to the appropriately designed supervisory regulator (presumably the home country) and be put into a statutory receivership to be resolved.

The numerical value of the capital–asset trigger ratio could be determined in a couple of ways. It could be set uniformly across the euro area. Alternatively, it could be determined by the home country and would be the same for all banks chartered in the country. Competition among countries would prevent this ratio from being chosen inefficiently. If it was set too high, banks would not choose the country for their charter. If it was set too low, the deposit insurer would be liable for larger payments to other countries.

The home-country or designated supervisor would have several options to resolve the problems. It could liquidate the bank by selling the assets separately, sell the bank as a whole or operate it temporarily as a bridge bank. For large entities, the bridge bank would mean that it could be opened immediately and services would be maintained almost seamlessly. Liquidity losses would be minimized. The bank would not be liquidated, thus avoiding the negative externalities that have caused so much concern.

If the regulator is able to resolve an institution before its capital turns negative, there is no insolvency or bankruptcy and no losses to depositors and other creditors. Only if regulators fail to catch an institution before its capital turns negative and it becomes insolvent would it be necessary to invoke bankruptcy resolution procedures and assign losses to depositors and other creditors. To deal with an insolvent institution efficiently, it would be useful over the longer term for the EU to require member countries to adopt a separate bankruptcy resolution code for banks. Such a statute could be based on that applicable to banks in the United States that gives regulators the power to legally close banks and assign pro-rata losses to depositors and other creditors (Bliss and Kaufman 2006).

The proposal would have several advantages. If the bank is successfully put into resolution before its capital is depleted, the home country does not impose losses on depositors in either the home or host countries. Thus, the differences in deposit insurance schemes among countries discussed earlier decrease in importance except with respect to the size of the differential premium advantage that would accrue to a PCA bank. The rule requiring the institution to voluntarily give up its charter may be seen as a cost imposed on the banks that would be offset by lower deposit insurance costs for going concerns. Since the shareholders, as a condition of obtaining lower deposit insurance premiums, ex ante have agreed to give up their charter, there are no issues of 'taking of property'.[49] Furthermore, any residual value will be returned to the shareholders. This is similar to conditions any insurance company imposes on its insurees in their contracts. Indeed, shareholders who are unwilling to re-capitalize a troubled institution to bring it up to regulatory standards indicate by their lack of action their belief that the institution as currently organized and operated is no longer a going concern. Finally, there would be less incentive on the part of regulatory authorities to engage in forbearance. Both managers and creditors of the institution would clearly understand when and under what conditions a troubled institution would be forced into resolution mode and this would tend to reinforce market discipline. Finally, regulatory agency problems associated with overlapping jurisdictions and deposit insurance schemes would be eliminated, because the scope and nature of regulatory responsibilities would be specified ex ante and be perfectly clear.

Conclusions

The focus of this study has been on the structure of supervisory and deposit insurance systems in cross-border banking through branching with particular emphasis on the EU and the related aspects of failure resolution and coordination when financial problems arise. The issue is of importance and deserves attention because the costs of any resulting crisis may more than offset the efficiency benefits of the branching. We have identified a number of issues and concerns about the present system design that are likely to result in higher than necessary costs of insolvencies in cross-border banking. To date, little progress appears to have been made in the EU in dealing with them. Indeed, as cross-border branches and subsidiaries increase in importance in host EU countries, the resulting potential dangers of the current structure are likely to become large and may not only substantially reduce aggregate welfare in the affected countries when foreign banks with domestic branches or subsidiaries approach insolvency, but also threaten financial stability. Serious doubts are cast on the longer-term viability of the single passport concept for cross-border branch banking in the existing institutional environment.

To provide a more efficient arrangement, we propose four principles to ensure the efficient resolution of bank failures, should they occur, with minimum, if any, credit and liquidity losses. These include: prompt legal closure of institutions before they become economically insolvent; prompt identification of claims and assignment of losses; prompt reopening of failed institutions; and prompt re-capitalizing and re-privatization of failed institutions. Implementing these proposals would go a long way towards mitigating or possibly even eliminating many of the potential agency and related problems inherent in the current multiple and confusing EU crisis resolution and deposit insurance regimes across countries. Finally, we propose a mechanism to put such a scheme into place quickly in the case where a cross-border banking organization seeks to take advantage of the cross-border banking opportunities in the single banking licence available to banks in the EU using a financial incentive in the form of lower deposit insurance costs. In return for lower premiums, the bank agrees to be subject to PCA and a legal closure rule as a positive capital ratio established by the EU or the home country.

Appendix

The US has experimented extensively with decentralized deposit insurance systems that were not creatures of the federal government.[50] Most of these systems failed within a few years. In every case, the insurance systems were unable to meet unusual demands for a payout when either a very large institution got into financial difficulty or many smaller institutions failed at the same time. The same fate befell funds quite recently in Ohio in 1985 and Rhode Island in 1991 (see Kane 1987; Pulkkinen and Rosengren 1993).

There were several design flaws in these deposit insurance systems (see Pulkkinen and Rosengren 1993) that could have significant implications for the EU. First, the systems tended to be critically under-funded. Second, they tended to be undiversified in one of two ways. Either they were undiversified because the institutions being insured were not geographically disbursed and hence were vulnerable to regional business cycles or economic shocks, or they were undiversified because the failure of one or two large institutions was sufficient to bankrupt the funds. Third, they often had poorly designed governance systems, and this was particularly the case in the privately sponsored plans. Finally, when threatened with collapse, there was not the recognition that what provided the credibility of the plan was not so much the size of the fund, but the willingness of the sponsoring entity – the particular state legislature – to make good on the guarantees the fund offered.

Many of the same design flaws in these state-sponsored systems appear to be potentially inherent in many of the systems being put in place in the European monetary union. Any fund whose insured base is not adequately diversified or that does not have the ability or willingness to use taxpayers' resources, should fund resources be depleted, will not likely stand up to the costly failure of a few large banks. These diversification issues are especially important in those EU countries with only one or two major institutions, where the failure of even one might endanger the entire fund. Smaller countries, in particular, with only a few relatively large institutions are more likely to experience funding problems than larger countries. At a minimum, this means that reliance upon private deposit insurance systems, which the EU Directive permits, seems extremely risky. Moreover, the fact that the fund is private may still not insulate taxpayers from fiscal responsibility, especially when the fund is jointly managed by both private and public officials from either the central bank, ministry of finance or supervisory authority. This government involvement raises the perception of implicit government backing, even without official recognition of that responsibility.

What most architects of deposit insurance schemes seem to miss is that it is nearly impossible to determine ex ante whether or not a fund is adequately funded. More importantly, what gives the fund credibility, especially when the financial problems in one institution threaten to spill over to others, is not the size of the fund per se but rather the willingness to make good on the guarantees should the fund run out of resources. The differences in arrangements within the EU raise considerable questions about how responsibilities will be handled in the event that a fund gets into trouble. For example, Table 16.5 shows that some schemes are supposedly fully funded, some are only funded with ex post premiums or levies, some can make special assessments on their members over and above normal contributions, some can borrow from the public or central bank, and some funds, such as in Latvia, have an explicit provision committing the government to provide funds.

Kane (1987) argues that waffling and legislative delay were a major problem in the case of the Ohio Deposit Guarantee Fund (ODGF) that was in part political posturing, but tendency to delay and avoid recognition of losses applies to federally sponsored programmes as well. The events surrounding the eventual collapse of the Federal Savings and Loan Insurance Corporation (FSLIC) in the US demonstrate the propensity of legislators to avoid facing up to the problem.

The circumstances surrounding the ODGF crisis also point to another problem related to the split of responsibilities for systemic risk between the member countries of the EU and the ECB. Specifically, the longer the delay in attempting to deal with the problem, the more likely it is that runs or systemic problems would develop that would convert what might be a problem in one institution into a problem for the deposit system itself. Individual member nations' regulatory and legislative authorities, to the extent that they may be reluctant to impose costs on their own taxpayers, have incentives to delay and gamble that a broader authority would step in and assume the responsibilities for a crisis.[51]

In Ohio, the losses to the ODGF amounted to about $170 million, which was more than the state legislature was willing to appropriate to make good on the guarantees implicit in its state sponsorship. This episode illustrates two facts. First, it is the ability to tap into taxpayer resources as needed rather than the size of the fund that provides the credibility of the deposit insurance guarantee. The initial reluctance of the State of Ohio to live up to its commitment provides an interesting comparison with many of the countries currently in or entering the EU. Ohio's state gross domestic product (GDP) in 1985 was 176 billion. This is larger than the GDP of eight of the original EU countries, including: Austria, Belgium, Finland, Greece, Luxembourg, the Netherlands, Portugal and Spain. It is also larger than the real GDP of all the newly admitted countries to the EU.

It is not clear why countries with even smaller resources would be more willing than a relatively richer state like Ohio to honour their deposit insurance liabilities, especially if payments were to be made to resident depositors in other, larger EU countries. The temptation on the part of poorer countries and their politicians to gamble, in the hope that they will be bailed out by the ECB, should a major crisis arise. A chief difference, of course, between the resolution of the ODGF crisis and a potential deposit insurance crisis in the EU is that there is no federal deposit insurance fund in the EU to which losses could be shifted. We conjecture based on past experience that these problems would be greatest in countries (1) that are smaller, (2) that have unfunded plans, (3) that have highly concentrated banking systems, (4) that have a large number of foreign banks operated in the system and (5) where there are strong perceptions of implicit guarantees or there exist government guarantees for the insurance fund.

Notes

1 See European Commission (2005).
2 See Dell'Ariccia and Marquez (2001).
3 Reviews of the benefits appear in Caprio *et al.* (2006), Committee on the Global Financial System (2004), Goldberg (2007) and Soussa (2004). Brief previous warnings about the unsettled state of affairs in cross-border banking appear in Goodhart (2005), Eisenbeis and Kaufmann (2005), and Mayes (2005). See in particular the analysis of the Nordea Bank, which is headquartered in Sweden but operates in a number of other countries, in the appendix to Mayes (2005).

4 See Mayes and Vesala (2005)
5 Regardless of the form of entry, however, the Core Principles for Effective Banking Supervision (Basel Committee on Banking Supervision 1997) clearly indicate that supervision is to be 'effective' within the EU, regardless of whether it is provided under the auspices of the home or host county
6 The recent discussions over where a merged Barclay's/ABN AMRO would be headquartered centre on differences in regulatory climate and oversight as a key determinant.
7 Others argue vigorously that only a single regulator at the EU level, like the ECB is situated for monetary policy, will be effective (see Walter 2001; Di Giorgio *et al.* 2000).
8 See Gulde and Wolf (2005) for a review of the financial stability responsibilities in Europe.
9 See Eisenbeis and Kaufman (2005) for a detailed discussion of these issues.
10 This problem has arisen in France with the country's attempt to preserve Credit Lyonnais with injections of governmental funds in more than three separate instances in the past several years. More recently, an editorial in the *Wall Street Journal Europe* (2005) entitled 'Spaghetti banking' pointed out that the governor of the Bank of Italy had refused to approve the acquisition of a single Italian bank by a foreign institution for the last 12 years. The governor indicate his desire to 'preserve the banks' Italianness also in the future'. This protectionism was challenged by the European Union's Internal Market Commission in connection with the proposed acquisitions of two Italian banks by ABN Amro and Banco Bilbao Vizcaya Argentina, and the governor of the central bank was ultimately forced out amid criminal investigations associated with the blockage of the proposed transactions.
11 See Kane (1991, 1989), Schüler (2003) and Lewis (1997).
12 The French and Italian authorities have, in the past, attempted to limit acquisitions of their large institutions.
13 Kane (1977).
14 Differences in quality can exist simply because countries fund their banking regulators differently or because they have had only limited experience in supervising market entities.
15 Schoenmaker and Oosterloo (2006) and Goodhart and Schoenmaker (2006) make similar observations about this centralization trend and include, in addition to functions mentioned above, internal controls, treasury operations, compliance and auditing.
16 New Zealand addressed this problem by requiring subsidiaries to be structured in such a way that if the parent becomes insolvent, solvent subsidiaries can be operated effectively without interruption in terms of capabilities and management. This may deny them the full benefits of economies of scale, scope and risk management.
17 The Sveriges Riksbank (Bank of Sweden) recently raised the question of how much responsibility home countries are willing to take for financial stability in other countries where a bank operates. For example, the Nordea Group is a Swedish bank that has its largest market share in Finland. Would the Swedish authorities be willing and able to judge Nordea's impact on stability in Finland? And would the Finnish authorities be prepared to transfer responsibility for a considerable part of its financial system to Sweden? Similar problems exist in other countries (Sveriges Riskbank 2003: 2).
18 A classic case of just such a decision occurred in the Herstadt Bank failure, in which German authorities closed the institution at the end of the business day in Germany, but before all the bank's foreign exchange transactions had been settled with counter parties in other time zones. While not affecting the total amount of loss, the timing of the legal closure did shift losses, either intentionally or not, from holders of mark claims on the bank, primarily German depositors, to those expecting to receive dollars from the bank, primarily US and UK banks, later in the day.
19 In the US, such conflicts have existed among state regulators and among federal banking regulators despite a national mandate to coordinate regulatory and supervisory policies and the existence of the Federal Financial Institutions Examination Council.
20 In New Zealand, for example, there are effectively no indigenous banks at all.
21 This also means that if home-country insurance is superior in other features to that provided generally in the host country, then the branch would have a competitive advantage relative to institutions chartered in the host country.
22 For a brief review, see European Commission (2005) and European Parliament (1994).
23 Nieto and Penalosa (2004) describe the proposed structure in great detail and discuss recent efforts to deal with the problems of coordination. See Kane (2003) for a discussion of how schemes should be structured.
24 Eisenbeis and Kaufman (2005) discuss in detail differences in the implications of entry by branches as opposed to through the establishment of subsidiaries.

25 Because many countries permit several extensions of the payment deadlines, this probably explains the difference between the legal payout requirements and actual performance.

26 Within the European Union, of course, there are countries that have the euro but others that aren't part of the Economic and Monetary Union and have their own currencies.

27 Many of the specific differences are detailed in Tables 16.3–16.6.

28 Krimminger (2005).

29 See Mayes (2004) and Eisenbeis (2004).

30 A similar matrix is developed in Goodhart (2005). A more detailed analysis of the decision to expand across borders through branches or subsidiaries appears in Dermine (2006) and Eisenbeis and Kaufman (2005).

31 Kremers, Schoenmaker and Wierts (2003) recognize the importance of the existence of certain of these conflicts involving systemic supervision (the lender of last resort) and prudential supervision in comparing the supervisory structure adopted in the Netherlands and the United Kingdom.

32 One of the more important of these Directives sets policy towards capital adequacy through the Capital Adequacy Directive, which led to the Basel I capital standards for EU supervisors to follow. Basel I has now been refined by the Basel Bank Supervisors Committee now known as Basel II. Unfortunately, concentration of supervisory efforts on capital standards substitutes supervisory judgement for market-based risk weights to determine if an institution has sufficient capital. Wall and Eisenbeis (2002) argue that this focus is misplaced and misdirects supervisory attention from prompt corrective action and least cost resolution of the troubled institution.

33 The European Commission is engaged in a review of its Deposit Insurance Directive 94/19 and surveys are still being conducted to provide an up-to-date compendium of the exact provisions of each country's scheme.

34 This issue has also been addressed by Denmark's Nationalbank (Danmarks Nationalbank 2005).

35 Kane (2005) considers another alternative which involves the sale of options on insolvency losses.

36 See Kaufman (2004). Similar plans have been proposed by Mayes (2005) and the Reserve Bank of New Zealand (Harrison 2005), among others.

37 Banks and thrift institutions in the US are not subject to the corporate bankruptcy code but to a special code in the Federal Deposit Insurance Act (FDIA). The bank act is considerably more administrative and less judicial, considerably more creditor friendly, and potentially faster in the declaration of insolvency ousting the shareholders and in-place senior management, and payments to creditors. Bank and financial holding companies are, however, subject to the general corporate bankruptcy code (Bliss and Kaufman 2006).

38 Two 90-day extensions are permitted.

39 While regulators in the US may also declare a bank insolvent for a number of other reasons, such as unsafe and unsound banking, they must do so when the closure rule capital ratio is breached. Wall and Eisenbeis (2002) demonstrate that, on average, institutions in the US have been legally closed long after the market value of equity became negative.

40 Price-Waterhouse Coopers (2003).

41 See OCC (2003) and Salmon *et al.* (2003). Kaufman (2004) and Wall and Eisenbeis (2002) both suggest, however, that losses in individual cases have been significant.

42 Under the Depositor Preference Act of 1993, claims of general bank creditors, including sellers of Fed funds, and deposits at foreign offices are subordinated to deposits at domestic offices. See Kaufman (1997) and Marino and Bennett (1999).

43 Fear of the adverse consequences of liquidity as well as credit losses have at times induced the regulators not to give haircuts to uninsured debt claimants, particularly at large banks, after failing the institution by revoking its charter and ousting shareholders and management. This is often incorrectly termed 'too-big-to-fail' (TBTF). This has proven highly costly and inefficient. Losses tend to increase and ultimate resolution is only postponed, at which time losses are borne by the FDIC or taxpayer.

44 Recent surveys of deposit insurance practices indicate that few countries (only about 15 per cent) pay insured depositors within 3 months (see Demirgüç-Kunt *et al.* 2005 and Kaufman and Seelig 2002). In large part this reflects the fact that the insurance agency has insufficient information on the identity of the insured depositors and the amount of deposits insured, and requires the claimant to file a claim. In the US, the FDIC generally has the necessary information and typically does not require depositors to file claims.

45 The FDIC currently does not have information on all insured depositors at the largest banks but has issued a proposal for obtaining this information.

46 FDIC chairman Bair (2007) recently discussed ways to deal with this liquidity problem by putting holds on a portion of funds that may not be insured while making funds available to depositors.

47 Press Release, 'Memorandum of Understanding Between the Banking Supervisors, Central Banks and Finance Ministries of the European Union in Financial Crisis Situations', 14 May 2005; available at http://www.ecb.int/press/pr/date/2005/html/pr050518_1.en.html. The MoU is not a public document.

48 The bank is headquartered in Sweden and operates subsidiary banks in that country as well as in Norway, Denmark, Finland and Sweden. In addition it has branches in Estonia, Poland, Singapore and New York City. According to Mayes (2006), Nordea holds the dominant market share in Finland, with a 40 per cent market share; 25 per cent of the market in Denmark; 20 per cent in Sweden; and 15 per cent in Norway.

49 It should be pointed out that giving up a charter, once the institution is no longer viable, is a small cost relative to the value of lower deposit insurance premiums to a going concern.

50 These started with the New York State safety fund and culminated with the failure of the Rhode Island Share and Deposit Indemnity Corporation in 1991. Between 1908 and 1917 a total of eight states established deposit insurance systems. These included Oklahoma, Kansas, Nebraska, Texas, Mississippi, South Dakota, North Dakota and Washington. See Thies and Gerlowski (1988).

51 This observation is rooted not only in experience but also in theory. See Kahn and Santos (2004), also Garcia and Nieto (2005).

References

Bair, S. (2007) 'Remarks by Sheila C. Bair, Chairman, Federal Deposit Insurance Corporation at the Exchequer Club', Washington, DC, 21 March; available at http://www.fdic.gov/news/news/speeches/archives/2007/chairman/index.html.

Barth, J.R., G. Caprio Jr and D.E. Nolle (2004) *Comparative International Characteristics of Banking*, Economic and Policy Analysis Working Paper 2004–1, Washington, DC: Comptroller of the Currency, January.

Barth, J.R., G. Caprio Jr and R. Levine (2006) *Rethinking Bank Regulation and Supervision: Till Angels Govern*, Cambridge: Cambridge University Press.

Basel Committee on Banking Supervision (1997) 'Core principles for effective banking supervision, final version', Bank for International Settlements, 22 September.

Bliss, R.R. and G.G. Kaufman (2006) 'A comparison of U.S. corporate and bank insolvency resolution', *Economic Perspectives*, Federal Reserve Bank of Chicago, second quarter.

Bollard, A. (2005) 'Being a responsible host: supervising foreign-owned banks', in D. Evanoff and G. Kaufman (eds) *Systemic Financial Crises: Resolving Large Bank Insolvencies*, Singapore: World Scientific.

Caprio, G., D.D. Evanoff and G.G. Kaufman (2006) *Cross-Border Banking: Regulatory Challenges*, Singapore: World Scientific.

Cardenas, J., J.P. Graf and P. O'Dogherty (2003) *Foreign Bank Entry in Emerging Market Economies: A Host Country Perspective*, Committee on the Global Financial System (CGFS) Working Group paper, Basel, Switzerland: Bank for International Settlements.

Citigroup (2004) *Form 10-q for Citigroup Inc, Quarterly Report*, 4 November, Citigroup.

Committee on the Global Financial System (2004) *Foreign Direct Investment in the Financial Sector of Emerging Market Economies*, Basel, Switzerland: Bank for International Settlements, March.

Dale, R. (2000) *Deposit Insurance in Theory and Practice*, Société Universitaire Europeenne de Recherches Financieres, Amsterdam.

Danmarks Nationalbank (2003) *Financial Stability 2003*, Copenhagen: DK.

Dell'Ariccia, G. and R. Marquez (2001) *Competition among Regulators*, IMF Working Paper 01–73.

Demirgüç-Kunt, Asli, Baybars Karacaovali and Luc Laeven (2005) *Deposit Insurance around the World: A Comprehensive Database*, World Bank, 14 April.

Dermine, J. (2003) 'Banking in Europe: past, present and future', in V. Gaspar, P. Hartmann and O. Sleijpen (eds) *The Transformation of the European Financial System*, Frankfurt: European Central Bank.

—— (2006) 'European banking integration: don't put the cart before the horse', *Financial Markets, Institutions, and Instruments* 15(2), May.

Di Giorgio, D., C. Di Noia and L. Piatti (2000) *Financial Market Regulation: The Case of Italy and a Proposal for the Euro Area*, Wharton Financial Institutions Center, Working Paper 00–24.

Eisenbeis, R.A. (2004) 'Agency problems in banking supervision: the case of the EMU', paper presented at the conference 'The Structure of Regulation', Bank of Finland, 2–3 September.

Eisenbeis, R.A. and G.G. Kaufman (2005) 'Bank crisis resolution and foreign-owned banks', paper prepared for a conference on 'Banking Crisis Resolution: Theory and Practice', 16–17 June 2005, at Norges Bank in Oslo, Norway, and published in the Federal Reserve Bank of Atlanta, *Economic Review*, fourth quarter.

—— (2006) 'Cross-Border banking: challenges for the European Union', in G. Caprio, D.D. Evanoff, and G.G. Kaufman, *Cross-Border Banking: Regulatory Challenges*, Singapore: World Scientific.

European Commission (2005) *Financial Integration Monitor 2005*, Commission Staff Working Document, SEC (2005) 927.

European Financial Services Round Table (2005) 'On the lead supervisor model and the future of financial supervision in the EU: follow-up recommendations of the EFR', position paper of the European Financial Services Round Table, June, Brussels: EFR.

European Parliament (1994) 'Directive 94/19/EC of the European Parliament and of the Council of 30 May 1994 on Deposit-Guarantee Schemes, Brussels: European Parliament.

Garcia, G.H. and M. J. Nieto (2005) 'Banking crisis management in the European Union: Multiple regulators and resolution authorities', *Journal of Banking Regulation* 6(3): 215–19.

Goldberg, L. (2007) 'Financial FDI and host countries: new and old lessons', Federal Reserve Bank of New York, *Economic Policy Review* 13(1).

Goodhart, C.A.E. (2005) 'Multiple regulators and resolutions', in D. Evanoff and G. G. Kaufman (eds) *Systemic Financial Crisis: Resolving Large Bank Insolvencies*, Singapore: World Scientific.

Goodhart, C.A.E. and D. Schoenmaker (2006) *Burden Sharing in Banking Crisis in Europe*, LSE Financial Markets Group, Special Paper Series No. 164.

Gulde, A. and H.C. Wolf (2005) 'Financial stability arrangements in Europe: A review', Oesterreichische Nationalbank, *Proceedings of OENB Workshops* No. 4.

Hall, M.J.B. (2001) 'How good are EU deposit insurance schemes in a bubble environment?', in *Asset Price Bubbles: Implications for Monetary and Regulatory Policies*, vol. 13, Amsterdam: Elsevier Science Ltd.

Harrison, Ian (2005) 'The Reserve Bank of New Zealand's Creditor Recapitalization (BCR) Project: an option for resolving large banks?', in D. Evanoff and G. Kaufman (eds) *Systemic Financial Crises: Resolving Large Bank Insolvencies*, Singapore: World Scientific Publishing, pp. 397–406.

Huizinga, Harry and Gaetan Nicodeme (2002) *Deposit Insurance and International Bank Deposits*, March, CEPR Discussion Paper No. 3244.

Hüpkes, E. (2003) 'Insolvency – Why a special regime for banks?', in *Current Developments in Monetary and Financial Law*, Vol. 3, International Monetary Fund, Washington, DC.

Kahn, C.M. and J.A.C. Santos (2004) 'Allocating lending of last resort and supervision in the Euro Area', in V. Alexander, J. Melitz and G.M. von Furstenberg (eds) *Monetary Union: Why, How and What Follows?*, London: Oxford University Press.

Kane, E.J. (1977) 'Good intentions and unintended evil: the case against selective credit allocation', *Journal of Money, Credit and Banking*, February: 55–69.

—— (1987) 'Who should learn what from the failure and delayed bailout of the ODGF?', *1987 Proceedings of Conference on Bank Structure and Competition*, Chicago: Federal Reserve Bank of Chicago, pp. 306–26.

—— (1989) 'Changing incentives facing financial-services regulators', *Journal of Financial Services Research* 2(3): 265–74.

—— (1991) 'Financial regulation and market forces', *Swiss Journal of Finance* 127(3): 325–42.

—— (2003) 'What kind of multinational deposit-insurance arrangements might best enhance world welfare?', *Pacific-Basin Finance Journal* 11: 413–28.

—— (2005) 'Confronting divergent interests in cross-country regulatory arrangements', in *Guidelines for Cross-Border Banking Proceedings*, December; available at http://www2.bc.edu/~kaneeb/.

Kane, E.J., A. Hovakimian and L. Laeven (2003). 'How country and safety-net characteristics affect bank risk-shifting', *Journal of Financial Services Research*, June: 21–30.

Kaufman, G.G. (1997) 'The new depositor preference act: time inconsistency in action', *Managerial Finance*, 23(11): 56–63.

—— (2004) 'Bank regulation and foreign-owned banks', *Reserve Bank of New Zealand Bulletin*, June: 65–74.

Kaufman, G.G. and S. Seelig (2002) 'Post-resolution treatment of depositors in failed banks', *Economic Perspectives*, Federal Reserve Bank of Chicago, second quarter: 27–41.

Kremers, J.J.M., D. Schoenmaker and P.J. Wierts (2003) *Cross-sector Supervision: Which Model?*, ed. R.E. Litan and R. Herring, Brookings–Wharton Papers on Financial Services.

Krimminger, M.H. (2005) 'Deposit insurance and bank insolvency in a changing world: synergies and challenges', *Current Developments in Monetary and Financial Law*, vol. 4, Washington, DC: International Monetary Fund.

Lewis, D. (1997) 'Incongruent incentives in banking supervision: the agent's problem', *Journal of Economics* 23(1): 17–31.

Marino, James A. and Rosalind L. Bennett (1999) 'The consequences of national depositor preference', *FDIC Banking Review* 12(2): 1–38.

Mayes, D.G. (2004) 'An overview of the issues', in D.G. Mayes and A. Liuksila (eds) *Who Pays for Bank Insolvency?*, New York: Palgrave Macmillan.

—— (2005) 'The role of the safety-net in resolving large financial institutions', in D. Evanoff and G. G. Kaufman (eds) *Systemic Financial Crises: Resolving Large Bank Insolvencies*, Singapore: World Scientific.

—— (2006) 'Financial stability in a world of cross-border banking: Nordic and Antipodean solutions to the problem of responsibility without power', paper presented at the Annual Meetings of the Allied Social Science Associations, Boston, MA, 6 January.

Mayes, D.G. and J.M. Vesala (2005) *On the Problems of Home Country Control*, Bank of Finland Working Paper.

Merton, R.C. and A.F. Perold (1993) 'Management of risk capital in financial firms', in S.L. Hayes III (ed.) *Financial Services: Perspectives and Challenges*, Boston, MA: Harvard Business School Press.

Murton, A.J. (2005) 'Resolving a large bank: The FDIC's perspective', in D. Evanoff and G.G. Kaufman (eds) *Systemic Financial Crises: Resolving Large Bank Insolvencies*, Singapore: World Scientific.

Niemeyer, J. (2006) 'The regulatory framework for banks in the EU: An introduction', Riksbank, *Economic Review* 2.

Nieto, M.J. and J.M. Penalosa (2004) 'The European architecture of regulation, supervision and financial stability: a central bank perspective', *Journal of International Banking Regulation* 5(3): 228–42.

Office of the Comptroller of the Currency (2003) *Annual Report: Fiscal Year 2003*, Washington, DC, November.

Osterloo, S. and J. de Haan (2005) 'Arrangements for financial stability in OECD and EU countries', in D. Evanoff and G.G. Kaufman (eds) *Systemic Financial Crises: Resolution of Large Bank Insolvencies*, Singapore: World Scientific.

Peek, J. and E.S. Rosengren (1997) 'The international transmission of financial stocks: the case of Japan', *American Economic Review*, September: 495–505.

Price Waterhouse Coopers (2003) *A Regulatory Guide for Foreign Banks in the United States*, Washington, DC.

Pulkkinen, T.E. and E.S. Rosengren (1993) 'Lessons from the Rhode Island banking crisis', Federal Reserve Bank of Boston, *New England Economic Review*, May/June.

Salmon, Richard, Lisa Anston, Jeanne McBride, Dennis Trimpea, Elvis Nelson, Debbie Barr, Bent Armond, Gwen Hudson, Donna Kinser and Vicki Robinson (2003) *Costs Associated with Bank Failures*, Federal Deposit Insurance Corporation Working Paper, 10 October.

Schoenmaker, D. and S. Oosterloo (2005) 'Financial supervision in an integrating Europe: measuring cross-border externalities', *International Finance* 8(1): 1–27.

—— (2006) 'Financial supervision in Europe: do we need a new architecture?', *Cahier Comte Boël*, no. 12, Brussels: European League for Economic Co-operation.

Schüler, Martin (2003) *Incentive Problems in Banking Supervision: The European Case*, Discussion Paper, No. 03–62, Mannheim: Centre for European Economic Research, November.

Soussa, F. (2004) *A Note on Banking FDI in Emerging Markets: Literature Review and Evidence*, Committee on the General Finance System (Basel, Switzerland) Working Paper, March.

Strum, J. and B. Williams (2004) 'Foreign bank entry, deregulation, and bank efficiency', *Journal of Banking and Finance*, July: 1775–99.

Sveriges Riksbank (2003) *Financial Stability Report, 2/2003*, Stockholm: Sveriges Riksbank.

Thies, C.F. and D.A. Gerlowski (1998) 'Deposit insurance: a history of failure', *Cato Journal* 8(3), winter.

Vives, X. (2001) 'Restructuring financial regulation in the European Monetary Union', *Journal of Financial Services Research*, February: 57–82.

Wall, L.D. and R.A. Eisenbeis (2002) 'Reforming deposit insurance and FDICIA?', *Economic Review*, Federal Reserve Bank of Atlanta, first quarter: 1–16.

Wall Street Journal Europe (2005) 'Spaghetti banking', *Wall Street Journal Europe*, Friday/Saturday, 1 April: A8.

Walter, N. (2001) 'The banking supervision issue in Europe', Briefing Paper for the Committee on Economic and Monetary Affairs (ECON) of the European Parliament, May.

17 The search for the elusive twin goals of monetary and financial stability

Claudio Borio

Introduction[1]

Looking back, economic historians will probably consider the early 1980s a defining moment. It was then that central bankers started in earnest their successful fight against the Great Inflation of the postwar era. Since then, another concern, financial instability, has been gaining ground and risen to the top of national and international policy agendas.

There is much that we have learnt since that defining moment about how to make progress on these two fronts. Price stability, in the form of low and stable inflation across much of the world, has been achieved and there is a broad consensus about how to preserve it. While financial stability has remained more elusive, by now we all know that one key to success is strengthening the financial infrastructure. Ever since the Asian crisis, the international community has made major efforts to develop the outline of a comprehensive approach to achieving this goal, articulated through a number of codes and standards. The Basel-based community, not least through the Basel Committee on Banking Supervision, has played a prominent role here. Likewise, countries have made major efforts to implement those codes and standards.[2]

In this chapter, I would like to explore not what is known, but what is still largely unknown; to ask questions that might help us push out the envelope of our understanding. In Richard Feynman's words, I would like to 'leave the door of the unknown ajar'. The issue I would like to address is the relationship between monetary and financial stability; the policy question is how to achieve the two simultaneously. Clearly, strengthening the financial infrastructure is a necessary condition for the achievement of this goal. It is not, however, sufficient, nor was it ever intended to be. From this perspective, you may think of my remarks as exploring the 'missing pillar' of the international financial architecture, more broadly defined to encompass the realm of liquidity creation.

So posed, the question is a much more ambitious one. For, as I shall argue, even though some countries have been more successful than others, on balance the simultaneous attainment of monetary and financial stability has remained rather elusive in modern history. And if we just look at the last twenty years or so, while monetary stability has finally been secured through most of the globe, lasting financial stability has remained harder to attain. Indeed, since the 1980s financial instability has emerged as a major policy concern, forcing its way to the top of the international agenda. One battlefront opened up just as another was victoriously being closed.

My main conjecture is that we may be closer to achieving lasting monetary and financial stability than ever before. The opportunity is there for the taking. But doing so may call for some refinements to current monetary and prudential frameworks.

This conjecture is based on the hypothesis that changes in the financial and monetary regimes worldwide have been subtly altering the dynamics of the economy. On the one hand, financial liberalization may have made it *more likely* that financial factors in general, and booms and busts in credit and asset prices in particular, act as drivers of economic fluctuations. On the other hand, the establishment of a regime yielding low and stable inflation, underpinned by central bank credibility, may have made it *less likely* that signs of unsustainable expansion show up first in rising inflation and *more likely* that they emerge first as excessive increases in credit and asset prices. The bottom line is that the current environment may be more vulnerable to the occasional build-up of financial imbalances, by which I mean overextensions in (private sector) balance sheets that herald economic weakness and disinflation down the road, as they unwind. This unwinding can in turn raise the risk of financial strains and possibly broader financial instability. The unwinding may occur either because inflation eventually does emerge and the central bank is forced to tighten, or because the boom falters under its own weight.

In previous work, some of my colleagues and I have referred to the property of the economy that makes the emergence of financial imbalances more likely as increased 'elasticity' or, in another context, increased 'procyclicality'.

The main policy implication of this analysis is the need for closer co-operation between prudential and monetary authorities. For prudential authorities, the task would be to strengthen the macroprudential orientation of current arrangements. This would mean shifting the focus somewhat from individual institutions and towards the system as a whole while at the same time recognizing explicitly in the calibration of their policy instruments the endogenous interaction between the financial system and the real economy. This would set the technical basis for using prudential instruments to increase cushions during booms so as to run them down, up to a point, in the downswings. For monetary authorities, the task would be to lengthen the policy horizon beyond the one to two years typical of some inflation targeting regimes while at the same time paying more attention to the balance of risks. These modifications would set the technical basis for using monetary policy as a kind of insurance device, leaning against the financial imbalances as they build up even if near-term inflationary pressures remain benign. Through these mutually reinforcing policies, the two sets of authorities could limit the unwelcome consequences of the subsequent unwinding of the imbalances on financial stability, output and inflation, with each authority still focusing on its main objective. This could contribute to the achievement of monetary and financial stability on a lasting basis.

The main concern is that this issue may fall through the cracks. Prudential authorities may be reluctant to address problems that, from their perspective, appear to have exclusively a macroeconomic origin, and be tempted to leave it exclusively to the monetary authorities. Monetary authorities may feel that as long as near-term inflation appears under control, addressing the build-up of imbalances is a task that should be left exclusively to their prudential counterparts, in so far as the imbalances raise threats to financial stability.

In the rest of my remarks I will elaborate on this conjecture, drawing extensively on research carried out with my colleagues at the Bank for International Settlements (BIS).[3] I will first consider in more detail the role of changes in the financial and monetary regimes. I will then provide some empirical support for the basic hypothesis. I will do so by sketching a broad-brush historical overview of the elusive search for monetary and financial stability across regimes before taking a closer look at the more recent experience. I will finally turn to the policy implications.

The basic hypothesis

The role of the financial regime

What, then, is the role of changes in the financial regime? The key here is the remarkable process of *financial liberalization*, both within and across national borders, that the world has witnessed over the last twenty years or so. Industrial countries typically began partial liberalizations in the mid-1970s, and then pushed such reforms considerably further in the 1980s and 1990s. By the early 1990s, liberalization efforts were virtually complete. Developing countries generally followed somewhat later, but made substantial progress in freeing their relatively repressed financial systems in the 1990s. By then, to use Padoa-Schioppa and Saccomanni's (1994) phrase, to all intents and purposes the shift from a government-led to a market-led international financial system had been accomplished.

There is no question that a liberalized financial system is essential to reach a better trade-off between economic efficiency and stability. Repressive financial arrangements had resulted in serious misallocation of resources and inefficiencies. Moreover, by making it easier to raise 'seigniorage' revenue through the inflation tax, the various constraints on financial institutions' portfolios and cross-border flows actually attenuated the incentive of governments to fight inflation.

At the same time, a liberalized financial environment can more easily accommodate, and reinforce, fluctuations in economic activity. It can do so by lending strength to the procyclical[4] forces inherent in financial arrangements and in their two-way interaction with the real economy.

The financial system is inherently procyclical (Borio *et al.* 2001). Perceptions of value and risk move procyclically. And so does the willingness to take on risk. Aside from obvious minor lead and lag relationships, asset prices and credit spreads move procyclically. There is a growing body of evidence indicating that, despite their intended design, the ratings of rating agencies exhibit significant sensitivity to the cycle (e.g. Amato and Furfine 2003). Internal bank risk ratings are considerably procyclical (Lowe 2002). And accounting measures of expected losses, such as bank provisions, and profits, too, move procyclically. Because the availability and pricing of external funding are intimately related to perceptions of value and risk, as well as to the willingness to take on risk, they move in sympathy with economic activity as well. Thus, for instance, the ratio of credit to GDP tends to move procyclically.

The inherent procyclicality of the financial system tends to interact with the real economy in ways that can amplify economic fluctuations. During booms, self-reinforcing processes can develop, characterized by rising asset prices, loosening external financing constraints, further capital deepening, rising productivity and profits. These processes operate in reverse during contractions.

Clearly, these behavioural patterns are part of the physiology of a properly functioning economy. The elasticity of external funding during booms tends to reflect a genuine improvement in the outlook. It can also allow the economy to take better advantage of growth opportunities. And as long as the system retains sufficient cushions, it can continue to act as a shock absorber in the face of unforeseen unwelcome developments. This elasticity is the oil that lubricates the system.

The concern is not with this 'physiological' procyclicality, but with those occasional 'pathological' episodes of excessive procyclicality that lie at the root of some of the more costly cases of financial distress. On these occasions, the procyclical processes can go too far and the system is unable to build sufficient cushions in good times so as to act as an effective shock absorber in bad times. When this occurs, masked by benign conditions, financial imbalances and associated distortions in the real economy build up during the boom phase. Fostered by genuine uncertainty in interpreting available evidence, cyclical developments are mistaken for more fundamental improvements in long-run growth prospects. The built-in stabilizing mechanisms in the economy are not sufficient to prevent it from becoming overstretched. This sows the seeds of potentially damaging headwinds down the road, as the economy, having grown at an unsustainable pace, finally slows down and the procyclical forces go into reverse. Some of the headwinds arise from the demand side, as households and firms struggle to restructure their balance sheets, caught between declining profits and incomes, falling asset prices and levels of indebtedness that prove excessive. Others stem primarily from the supply side, as financial markets and institutions become more cautious in extending finance. In extreme cases, broader financial crises can arise and exacerbate the downturn further.

But why should the financial system be prone to behave, occasionally, in an excessively procyclical way? I think that the reason has to do with two 'gaps' (Borio 2003; Knight 2003). There is a 'risk perceptions gap'. Economic agents are better able to measure the cross-sectional dimension of risk than the time dimension of risk, especially of system-wide risk. In fact, a careful look at the literature on the effectiveness of market discipline indicates that much of it is of a cross-sectional nature (e.g. Flannery 1998). There is also an 'incentives gap'. That is, actions that are rational from the perspective of individual economic units can result in undesirable collective outcomes. Familiar notions like prisoners' dilemma, herding and co-ordination failures are key. For instance, is it reasonable to expect a bank manager to trade off a sure loss of market share in a boom against the distant hope of regaining it in a future potential slump? Or to fail to retrench in slump only because, if everyone did the same, the slump would be worse? Short horizons are at the heart of some of these distortions. And short horizons can themselves be grounded on the contractual mechanisms designed to overcome 'asymmetric information' obstacles, which may thus have unintended consequences. The frequent monitoring of performance based on short-term benchmarks is one such example.

Three implications follow. First, in a liberalized environment risk perceptions and time-varying risk tolerance become more important factors driving the economy.[5] Second, markets typically behave as if risk fell in booms and rose in recessions. And yet, there is a sense in which *risk rises in booms*, as imbalances build up, *and materializes in recessions*, as they unwind. Finally, the Achilles heel of market discipline may not be so much indiscriminate reactions to idiosyncratic shocks, as highlighted in the analysis of contagion. Rather, it may be failing to prevent *generalized* overextension.

Against this background, it is easy to see how a liberalized financial environment can raise the elasticity of the financial system and make the occasional overextension more likely. Such an environment multiplies the potential sources of funding, making it easier to accommodate imbalances on those occasions in which they do arise. Heightened competitive pressures increase incentives to take on risks and, by reducing quasi-rents, narrow the scope for absorbing losses, especially when they interact with comparatively rigid cost structures. And they might also tend to increase the value of any subsidies associated with explicit or implicit safety nets in place. After all, ceteris paribus, as option theory makes clear, guarantees become more valuable once the environment becomes riskier.

The likelihood of such episodes of excessive procyclicality is especially high during the transition towards a liberalized environment. For the lasting legacy of financial repression is bloated cost structures and a limited capacity to assess, price and manage risks, on the part of both market participants and official authorities.

The role of the monetary regime

What about the role of the monetary regime? Here the argument is necessarily more speculative, as the establishment of low and stable inflation underpinned by central bank credibility is of more recent vintage, with only a handful of countries reaching this stage already in the 1980s. More generally, by the late 1990s, the signs indicated that the process had reached full maturity, in the sense that the credibility of the central banks' anti-inflationary commitment had been established.

It is hard to imagine that financial imbalances could build up without some form of monetary accommodation. When financial instability arises in an inflationary climate, as it often has, the source of monetary accommodation is easily identifiable.

What might be harder to imagine is how monetary accommodation could take place if the authorities pursued a vigilant anti-inflation policy. I would argue, however, that this can in fact happen. The argument is quite simple: in today's fiat money regimes the only exogenous *monetary* constraint on the otherwise endogenous credit expansion is the reaction function of the central bank. Therefore, if that reaction function responds exclusively to short-run inflation pressures, it may unwittingly accommodate the build-up of the imbalances.

More specifically, one can identify at least three reasons for this.

First, long expansions of the type that encourage the build-up of financial imbalances would most likely develop following favourable developments on the supply side. Improvements in productivity or, especially in emerging market countries, the establishment of credible policy frameworks are obvious examples. These developments would naturally tend to attenuate price pressures. They would do so directly, by cutting production costs, and indirectly, by encouraging additional capital accumulation and the appreciation of the currency, as financial capital chased perceived higher returns.

Second, for a given aggregate demand, unsustainable asset price increases could themselves play a role in dampening inflation. For one, they could artificially boost accounting profits, allowing firms to follow more aggressive pricing strategies. Just think of the impact of lower contributions to pension funds and of financial gains on firms' investments. During the boom of the 1980s, for instance, Japanese companies derived a sizeable share of earnings from their now notorious 'Zaitech' (or financial engineering) activities; and during the more generalized equity boom of the 1990s, pension fund surpluses played a major role. Likewise, large financial gains by employees could also partly substitute for higher wage claims. And unsustainable asset price increases would also tend to increase tax revenue and hence strengthen fiscal positions, crowding in capital accumulation and hence productivity gains.

Finally, the very success in establishing an environment of low and stable inflation, underpinned by greater central bank credibility, could further dampen the inflationary process. If so, underlying excess demand pressures would tend to take more time to show up in overt inflation. In part, this could result from fixed ('menu') adjustment costs, which would lead to stickier wages and prices. Above all, however, with inflation expectations better anchored around inflation objectives, supported by the authorities' commitment to keep inflation in check, agents would be less likely to adjust wages and prices upwards. And the belief that inflation was no longer a threat could itself contribute to the build-up of imbalances, by removing the prospects of a recession induced by a monetary tightening to bring inflation under control.

The bottom line is that, given unusually muted near-term inflation pressures during much of the expansionary phase, policy rates could fail to rise sufficiently promptly to help restrain the build-up of financial imbalances.

Several additional points are worth highlighting.

First, from this perspective, developing financial imbalances, if they appear to be fairly large, could provide critical additional, and hence complementary, information about the likely future evolution of the economy. This information would not be available from traditional indicators of inflation pressures, since those indicators generally focus on the current and near-term degree of pressure on resources rather than on the pressures that might develop further out in the future, as financial imbalances unwind. Indeed, because of the demand-depressing effect of the unwinding, the real risk to which large financial imbalances would point is economic weakness. And with inflation initially low, deflation could be a greater risk than inflation.

Second, during expansions of the type described here, applying more traditional paradigms to the interpretation of developments could lead policymakers astray. Interpreting rapid monetary and credit expansion as a sign of upward pressures on the price level down the road would be inappropriate. Likewise, a misleading approach would be to calibrate estimates of potential output, and hence of the sustainability of the expansion, by cross-checking them with actual inflation performance (e.g. Gerlach and Smets 1999). It is not uncommon, for instance, to take stable or falling inflation as an indication that slack may be larger than could be surmised from more direct estimates. This can be justified within the traditional models used to describe the economy. In particular, given the considerable uncertainty surrounding estimates of potential output and long-term productivity at times of possible structural breaks, it would make sense to pay more attention to actual inflation, which is measured with less error (Smets 1998). However, from the perspective of the paradigm stressed here, such a procedure would tend to bias upwards the estimates of potential.

Third, the credibility of the central bank's anti-inflation commitment can be a double-edged sword. On the one hand, the credibility reinforces other structural factors that may put a lid on inflationary pressures. On the other, by helping to anchor longer-term inflation expectations around the central bank's inflation objectives, that credibility makes it more likely that unsustainable booms could take longer to show up in overt inflation. This 'paradox of credibility' means that the central bank can be a victim of its own success (Borio and Lowe 2002a).[6] Conquering inflation can contribute to changes in the dynamics of the system that could mask the risks arising in the economy.[7]

The evidence

Having laid out the basic hypothesis in some detail, let me now turn to the empirical evidence. I will first look at the historical record and argue that it is broadly consistent with the stylized interpretation of the relationship between monetary and financial stability across monetary and financial regimes just outlined (Borio and Crockett 2000; Borio and Lowe

2002a). I will then turn to the experience since the 1970s, and examine the empirical evidence more closely and formally.

A historical perspective: monetary and financial stability across regimes

Table 17.1 summarizes the relationship between monetary and financial stability since the Gold Standard regime. Under the classical Gold Standard a liberalized financial regime coexisted with monetary arrangements that resulted in a good measure of price stability over longer horizons (e.g. Borio and Filardo 2004). One can think of convertibility into gold as acting as the single anchor for monetary and financial stability. Monetary stability was defined in terms of maintenance of convertibility. In turn, the convertibility constraint would typically give way at times of financial instability, when deposits could no longer be turned into gold at par. Few, if any, constraints existed on banks' balance sheets and cross-border financial transactions. And the current framework of prudential regulation was non-existent or in its infancy in a number of countries. The convertibility constraint was highly visible and explicit. It was not sufficient, however, to prevent waves of financial instability in the wake of excessive credit expansion (Goodhart and De Largy 1999; Bordo *et al.* 2001).

In the interwar years, still against the background of liberalized financial markets, the progressive emergence of fiat standards clouded the tight link between monetary and financial stability and loosened the constraints on credit expansion. Monetary stability became increasingly identified with price stability per se. The acceptance of a currency was increasingly based on the power of the state to tax. With the domestic currency acting as the basis for the measurement of value and with convertibility of deposits into currency being assured, financial instability was decoupled from convertibility into gold. At the same time, the emerging regime made credit more endogenous. With initially little change in arrangements in the financial sphere, the system became more vulnerable to financial cycles. Financial imbalances built up either in the wake of the re-establishment of monetary stability, as in some continental European countries, or against the background of low and stable inflation, as in the United States.

The major financial instability that characterized the Great Depression was the catalyst for the introduction of the strict regulation of commercial banking, including through a variety of liquidity, maturity matching and solvency requirements (Allen *et al.* 1938; Giannini 2001). A separate anchor was thus put in place in the financial sphere. This anchor, however, went hand in hand with the establishment or major strengthening of safety nets; explicit deposit insurance in the United States is the best-known example. Inadvertently, by weakening financial discipline, ceteris paribus, safety nets added to the potential for the build-up of imbalances.

Table 17.1 The empirical record: the broad picture

	Regime		*Stability*	
	Financial	*Monetary*	*Financial*	*Monetary*
Gold Standard	liberalized	credible	no	yes
Bretton Woods–1970s	repressed	non-credible	yes	no
1980s–early 1990s	liberalization	non-credible(generally)	no	no (generally)
Mid-1990s–present	liberalized	credible	no	yes

The Bretton Woods regime quickly developed into a fiat standard coupled with financial repression. The de jure convertibility constraint for official transactions gave way to a de facto dollar standard. At the same time, a complex web of regulations of a monetary nature (e.g. ceilings on loan growth and interest rates) was superimposed on, and largely superseded, previous prudential arrangements. This web of controls heavily constrained balance sheets as well as cross-border and foreign exchange transactions. By typically favouring government over private sector financing, these restrictions limited the scope for financial cycles. Central banks' common tendency to focus on bank credit played a reinforcing role (Borio and Lowe 2004). For a while, the system did deliver monetary and financial stability, but at increasing costs in terms of resource allocation. And starting in the late 1960s to early 1970s, greater willingness to use money to finance deteriorating fiscal positions and increasingly ambitious macroeconomic policies led to runaway inflation. Monetary stability was lost and the Great Inflation era was ushered in.

Eventually, the costs of financial repression led governments to deregulate the financial system, loosening the exogenous constraints on private sector credit expansion; initially, this took place in the context of a monetary regime that was not credibly ensuring price stability, but over time it coexisted to varying degrees with the successful fight against inflation. This is the period that goes roughly from the 1980s to the early to mid-1990s. Financial instability re-emerges, often coexisting with inflation. The authorities begin to strengthen prudential safeguards.

The subsequent phase takes us to the present day, in which credible anti-inflation monetary regimes coexist with a liberalized financial environment. In the monetary sphere, after a protracted battle in the 1980s inflation has been conquered. And institutional arrangements have been put in place to consolidate these gains. At the same time, financial liberalization has gathered pace, nationally and internationally, and is largely complete. Financial cycles appear, if anything, to have grown in amplitude and financial instability is still a major policy concern. Efforts to upgrade prudential safeguards have intensified and broadened geographically.

This brief review highlights four points:

1 Arguably no regime in history has simultaneously achieved sustained monetary and financial stability. The search for appropriate anchors in the monetary and financial sphere has proved elusive.
2 Financial and monetary stability are inextricably intertwined. To address the policy issues satisfactorily, a consensus is needed between monetary and prudential authorities regarding the genesis of, and possible remedies for, financial instability.
3 The configuration of monetary and financial regimes has come to resemble in some significant respects that prevailing in the pre-World War I period (Borio and Filardo 2004). This was the last time when liberalized financial markets coincided with a monetary regime seen as guaranteeing a good measure of monetary stability. In the early decades of the twentieth century, this was the Gold Standard; nowadays, it is a monetary framework that, while based on fiat money, is structured so as to secure the control of inflation.
4 There are, however, some significant differences with respect to that period; the concept of 'elasticity' can help us to understand them. In the financial sphere, prudential regulation now reduces the system's elasticity, by constraining overextension in balance sheets. At the same time, safety nets can work in the opposite direction, by increasing moral hazard. In the monetary sphere, the external convertibility constraint imposed

under the Gold Standard has been replaced by the reaction function of the monetary authorities that is essentially discretionary.[8] Which of the two regimes is more elastic? The answer presumably depends on the specifics of the arrangements and policy strategies.

A closer look: specific empirical findings

Drilling through the broad picture, four pieces of evidence can be seen as consistent with the basic hypothesis about the relationship between monetary and financial stability put forward in this chapter. First, cycles in credit and asset prices have become more prominent since the early 1980s. Second, measures of 'financial imbalances' have useful predicting content for subsequent widespread banking distress. Third, those same measures also contain useful information about subsequent output and inflation performance. Finally, a closer look at the empirical record confirms that 'financial imbalances' can easily build up in the context of comparatively low and stable, or even declining, inflation. Let me address each point in turn.

More prominent booms and busts in credit and asset prices

Since the mid-1980s, many countries have seen larger medium-term fluctuations in asset prices. This is illustrated for a selected sample of countries in Figure 17.1, based on the evolution of equity as well as commercial and residential property prices. Their behaviour is captured by an aggregate asset price index, which weighs the various asset prices by rough estimates of their shares in private sector wealth (Borio *et al.* 1994).

Abstracting from some cross-country differences, the graphs in Figure 17.1 illustrate that since the 1970s two major cycles have taken place and a third is underway, in sympathy with real economic activity. They correspond to the early to mid-1970s, the mid-1980s to the early or mid-1990s, and the second half of the 1990s to the present. Japan did not take part in the latest upswing following the bust in asset prices at the turn of the 1990s and the subsequent 'lost decade'. The data indicate that, if anything, the size and amplitude of the cycles may be growing.

These cycles have typically coexisted with similar fluctuations in credit. Since the 1980s, the ratio of credit to GDP has risen markedly in most countries. In addition, the evolution of this ratio has tended to exhibit a generally positive correlation with medium-term swings in asset prices, as further confirmed by more detailed econometric evidence (Borio *et al.* 1994). Importantly, the same formal empirical work indicates that this correlation appears to have become tighter following financial liberalizations. More recent studies suggest that the correlation is especially close with real estate prices, as might be expected (Hofmann 2001; Davis and Zhu 2004).

Financial imbalances herald financial instability

A look at the empirical record indicates that financial imbalances, in the form of unusually strong and sustained credit and asset price expansion, have preceded most of the episodes of serious financial instability and strong financial 'headwinds' that have become more common since the 1980s, in industrial and emerging market economies alike. This retraces a pattern that was quite familiar under the Gold Standard (Kindleberger 2000; Goodhart and De Largy 1999).

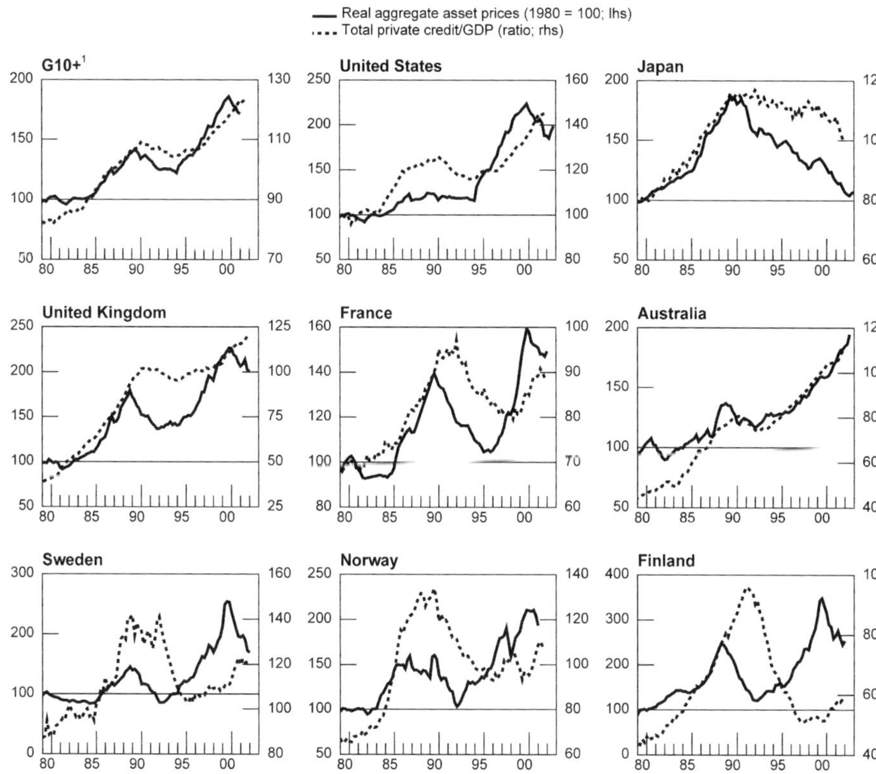

Figure 17.1 Large medium-term swings in asset prices and credit.
Sources: Private real estate associations; national data; BIS calculations.

Note: 1 GDP-weighted average of the Group of Ten countries, plus Australia, Denmark, Finland, Norway and Spain; weights based on 2000 GDP and PPP exchange rates.

This observation has been confirmed by more formal statistical work. With Phil Lowe, for instance, we have shown that it is possible to 'predict' fairly well episodes of major banking distress based on very simple proxies of 'financial imbalances' (Borio and Lowe 2002a, 2002b, 2004). The proxies are based on two key variables. The first is a measure of *misalignment in some key asset prices*, which can be taken as an indicator of the likelihood and size of a reversal. The second is some measure of the private sector *leverage* (here private sector credit in relation to GDP), which can be taken as an indicator of the likely damage caused to the economy by the reversal in asset prices. Both of these elements measure deviations from the 'normal' range of historical experience, or 'gaps', defined in terms of deviations that exceed certain critical thresholds.

Given the limited time available, let me just highlight a few points about this empirical evidence, summarized in Tables 17.2–17.4.

First, the gap variables are constructed based exclusively on information available at the time when the predictions are made; technically, the trends are calculated recursively based on ex ante information only. This is important to make sure that they can be useful for policy in real time.

Table 17.2 Composite indicators of banking distress, industrial countries[1]

Horizon (years)	*Credit (4) and asset price (40)*		*Credit (4) and exchange rate (4)*		*Credit (4) and (asset price (40) or exchange rate (20))*	
	Noise/signal	*% crises predicted*	*Noise/signal*	*% crises predicted*	*Noise/signal*	*% crises predicted*
1	0.09	50	0.11	44	0.09	50
2	0.06	56	0.10	44	0.06	56
3	0.04	63	0.10	44	0.04	63

Source: Borio and Lowe (2002b).

Note:
1 See Table 17.4 for how to interpret this table and Borio and Lowe (2002b) for the specifics due to the use of annual frequencies.

Table 17.3 Composite indicators of banking distress, emerging market countries

Horizon (years)	*Credit (4) and asset price (40)*		*Credit (4) and exchange rate (5)*		*Credit (4) and (asset price (40) or exchange rate (13))*	
	Noise/signal	*% crises predicted*	*Noise/signal*	*% crises predicted*	*Noise/signal*	*% crises predicted*
1	0.23	38	0.15	58	0.16	67
2	0.12	54	0.11	58	0.12	71
3	0.08	58	0.10	58	0.09	75

Source: Borio and Lowe (2002b).

Table 17.4 Composite indicators of banking distress, industrial countries

Horizon (years)[2]	*Combined gaps*[1]											
	Money[3] *(2) and credit*[4] *(4)*		*Money (2) and output*[5] *(2)*		*Money (2) and asset price*[6] *(60)*		*Credit (4) and output (2)*		*Credit (4) and asset price (60)*		*Credit (4), asset price (40) and output (1.5)*	
	Noise/ signal	*% crises predicted*	*Noise/ signal*	*% crises predicted*	*Noise/ signal*	*% crises predicted*	*Noise/ signal*	*% crises predicted*	*Noise/ signal*	*% crises predicted*	*Noise/ signal*	*% crises predicted*
3	0.21	60	0.21	47	0.09	47	0.13	53	0.06	47	0.05	27
3,4	0.20	60	0.17	53	0.07	53	0.07	73	0.02	73	0.02	47
3,4,5	0.19	60	0.16	53	0.06	53	0.06	73	0.02	73	0.01	60

Source: Borio and Lowe (2004).

Notes:
1 A gap is measured as percentage points from an ex ante, recursively calculated Hodrick–Prescott trend; the size of the threshold is shown in brackets.
2 A signal is correct if a crisis takes place in any one of the years included in the horizon ahead. Year 3 means the year starting 12 quarters ahead; 'year 3,4' means either year 3 or year 4; etc. Noise is identified as mistaken predictions within the same horizon. Given the data frequency and difficulties in assigning crises to a specific date, banking stress is arbitrarily assigned to the last quarter in any given year.
3 Money is measured as the ratio of money to GDP (lambda = 400000). The monetary aggregate used is roughly equivalent to M2 or M3 depending on the country.
4 Credit is measured as the ratio of private sector credit to GDP (and lambda = 400000).
5 GDP (and lambda = 1600).
6 Real equity price index (and lambda = 400000).

Second, they are calibrated based on developments during the boom only. Thus, they can be thought of as helping to distinguish sustainable from unsustainable economic expansions. This is reinforced by the fact that the proxy for financial imbalances contains information well beyond that contained in traditional output gaps (Tables 17.2–17.4).

Third, it is the requirement that the thresholds be exceeded *simultaneously* by the indicators of price misalignment and leverage that helps to improve the accuracy of the prediction. It does so by eliminating a lot of 'noise', namely by not predicting too many crises. This underscores the point that what matters are financial imbalances, not asset price misalignments per se.

Fourth, the financial imbalance proxies contain information that extends beyond short horizons, with the accuracy of the predictions improving as the horizon is lengthened. On annual data, we have shown that this is the case if one extends the horizon from one to three years ahead (Tables 17.2 and 17.3). More recently, based on quarterly data for industrial countries, we have shown that this is also the case if the forecasting horizon is three to five years ahead. This highlights the significant time that the build-up and unwinding of imbalances can take and that the information content goes beyond the typical horizons used for monetary policy.

Finally, the financial imbalance indicators capture most of the episodes with clear macroeconomic significance during our sample. In industrial countries, these include the banking crises in the Nordic countries and Japan as well as the serious financial strains experienced in the early 1990s in the United States, United Kingdom and Australia. In emerging market countries, they include most of the banking crises that have occurred in Latin America and Asia since the late 1980s.

Financial imbalances herald output weakness and disinflation

Not surprisingly, given the close association of banking distress with output weakness, recent empirical evidence suggests that financial imbalance proxies also help to predict weak economic activity and disinflationary pressures. And, as with banking distress, they do so beyond traditional horizons employed for monetary policy.

The evidence, so far available only for industrial countries, is summarized in Tables 17.5 and 17.6, and is drawn from recent work with Phil Lowe (Borio and Lowe 2004). It is based on probit regressions, which predict the probability of negative output gaps below 1 per cent and year-on-year declines in inflation over a horizon of between two and four years ahead. The financial imbalance proxies are the same as those calibrated to predict banking distress in the previous analysis. Without going into details, four findings stand out.

First, the information content of the composite indicator is particularly strong with respect to the output gap, and is additional to that contained in lagged values of the output gap itself (Table 17.5). The unconditional probability of observing such economic slack in the sample is 40 per cent, but it increases to 66 per cent and to 75 per cent, respectively, in the third and fourth year following the quarter in which the financial imbalance proxy flashes red. On their own, high output gaps have little predictive power about the future. This is consistent with the evidence that suggests that booms do not simply die of old age (e.g. Filardo and Gordon 1998). But if one adds the composite financial imbalance indicator to

Table 17.5 Financial imbalances as indicators of the output gap[1]

Conditional probabilities of an output gap of less than minus 1%[2] (unconditional = 39)							
Single indicators				*Composite indicators*			
Gaps	*Year 2*	*Year 3*	*Year 4*	*Gaps*	*Year 2*	*Year 3*	*Year 4*
Output (2)	37	42	49**	Credit (4) and equity (60)	41	66**	75**
	(−0.53)	(0.94)	(2.92)		(0.50)	(5.54)	(7.00)
Credit (4)	54**	47**	37	Credit (4) and output (2)	56*	60**	53
	(6.43)	(3.36)	(−0.63)		(2.34)	(2.74)	(1.78)
Equity (60)	35	53**	59**	Equity (60) and output (2)	34	63**	77**
	(−1.25)	(4.61)	(6.68)		(−0.69)	(3.19)	(4.71)
Money (2)	42	42	40	Credit (4), equity (60) and output (2)	55	99**	1.00[3]
	(1.42)	(1.52)	(0.53)		(1.06)	(2.91)	–
				Money (2) and credit (4)	50**	44	37
					(4.11)	(1.78)	(−0.64)
				Money (2) and output (2)	31	39	40
					(−1.44)	(0.11)	(0.19)
				Money (2) and equity (60)	37	61**	65**
					(−0.41)	(4.39)	(5.46)

Source: Borio and Lowe (2004).

Notes:

1 Results of probit regressions in which the variable predicted and the predictors are treated as zero/one dummies depending on whether the corresponding conditions defining the event are met; z-statistics in brackets. The sample is 1974 Q1–1999 Q4. Two and one asterisks correspond to statistical significance at the 1% and 5% levels respectively.

2 Ex ante output (lambda = 1600, throughout the table). The prediction relates to the ex ante output gap satisfying the condition (here, less than minus 1) in any one of four successive quarters (year). Thus, if the prediction is made in Q1 of, say, 1980, in the case of year 2 ahead the negative output gap of minus 1 relates to any one of 1982 Q1, Q2, Q3 and Q4, i.e. any one of 8, 9, 10 or 11 quarters ahead. Thus, the two-year horizon is only approximate. The same applies to the other horizons.

3 Conditional probability calculated by counting the frequency of events; the econometric routine does not converge.

the positive output gap, then the probability of economic weakness increases further to 99 per cent and 100 per cent, respectively.

Second, the indicator also contains information about inflation which is additional to that of the output gap, with a clear time pattern as the horizon is lengthened. The predictive performance, however, is not quite as good as that with respect to output (Table 17.6). The findings suggest some slight upward pressure on inflation one year ahead, turning into downward pressure by the fourth year, as imbalances unwind. For instance, the unconditional probability of observing a decline in inflation in any given year is 50 per cent. If the financial imbalance proxy is combined with a positive output gap in excess of 2 per cent, this raises it to over 90 per cent in the fourth year ahead compared with 60 per cent for predictions based on the output gap alone.

Finally, the same tables suggest that, based on the same criteria, the performance of money is on balance inferior to that of credit aggregates. This is especially the case with respect to predictions of output weakness; there is less to choose between the two as regards inflation. The finding is consistent with the close association of credit with asset prices discussed above

Table 17.6 Financial imbalances as indicators of inflation[1]

Conditional probabilities of a decline[2] (unconditional = 50)							
Single indicators				*Composite indicators*			
Gaps	*Year 2*	*Year 3*	*Year 4*	*Gaps*	*Year 2*	*Year 3*	*Year 4*
Output (2)	47	60**	58*	Credit (4) and equity (60)	41*	53	63**
	(−0.71)	(2.64)	(2.11)		(−2.08)	(0.58)	(2.69)
Credit (4)	50	51	54	Credit (4) and output (2)	29**	68*	62
	(0.17)	(0.27)	(1.70)		(−2.84)	(2.46)	(1.53)
Equity (60)	41**	52	56*	Equity (60) and output (2)	41	56	71**
	(−2.99)	(0.68)	(2.11)		(−1.35)	(0.87)	(2.79)
Money (2)	45*	52	54	Credit (4), equity (60) and output (2)	36	55	92*
	(−2.16)	(1.02)	(1.92)		(−1.07)	(0.31)	(2.38)
				Money (2) and credit (4)	49	52	52
					(−0.20)	(0.63)	(0.92)
				Money (2) and output (2)	46	62*	59
					(−0.75)	(2.28)	(1.56)
				Money (2) and equity (60)	42	54	63**
					(−1.73)	(0.99)	(2.85)
				Money (2), equity (60) and output (2)	47	56	74
					(−0.23)	(0.50)	(1.80)

Source: Borio and Lowe (2004).

Notes:

1 Results of probit regressions in which the variable predicted and the predictors are treated as zero/one dummies depending on whether the corresponding conditions defining the event are met; z-statistics for the underlying regression coefficients in brackets. The sample is 1974 Q1–1999 Q4. Two and one asterisks correspond to statistical significance at the 1% and 5% levels respectively.

2 Inflation is defined as an average year-on-year change over four quarters. Thus, if the prediction is made in Q1 of, say, 1980, in the case of year 2 ahead the decline in inflation relates to the average year-on-year change between 1982 and 1981.

and the importance of leverage to capture the possible costs of the reversal of asset price booms. It suggests that for the type of phenomena considered here monetary aggregates alone are unlikely to be an adequate substitute for private sector credit.

Financial imbalances do build up in low inflation environments

What about the role of inflation per se in encouraging the build-up of financial imbalances and sowing the seeds of subsequent financial distress? It is of course possible to find examples of imbalances built in an inflationary environment. For instance, in industrial countries a clear example is the credit and commercial real estate boom that preceded the secondary banking crisis in the mid-1970s in the UK, following the lifting of credit constraints. The inflation-hedge demand for real estate and tax provisions that encourage leverage as inflation increases are well-known mechanisms that can explain the positive association between inflation and financial imbalances.

At the same time, it is equally possible to find examples of low and stable inflation coexisting with the build-up of financial imbalances as harbingers of subsequent banking crises accompanied by serious economic weakness. Most recently, the experiences of Japan and some East Asian countries, notably Korea, immediately spring to mind (Figure 17.2).

In fact, experiences of this kind were quite common in the interwar years or before World War I, when the environment was one of comparative price stability. For instance, the case of the United States in the 1920s and that of Australia in the 1880s are just two examples out of several (Figure 17.2).

In fact, even confining the analysis to the period since the 1970s, the relationship between inflation and the build-up of financial imbalances is not quite the one that classical monetarists might have expected (e.g. Schwartz 1995; Bordo *et al.* 2000) (see Figure 17.3). The evidence from both industrial and emerging market countries indicates that while, on average, inflation falls with a lag after a banking crisis, it does not pick up systematically in the years prior to it. The short-lived inflation spike after the crises reflects primarily the sharp currency depreciations that accompany twin crises. Indeed, and more revealingly, the

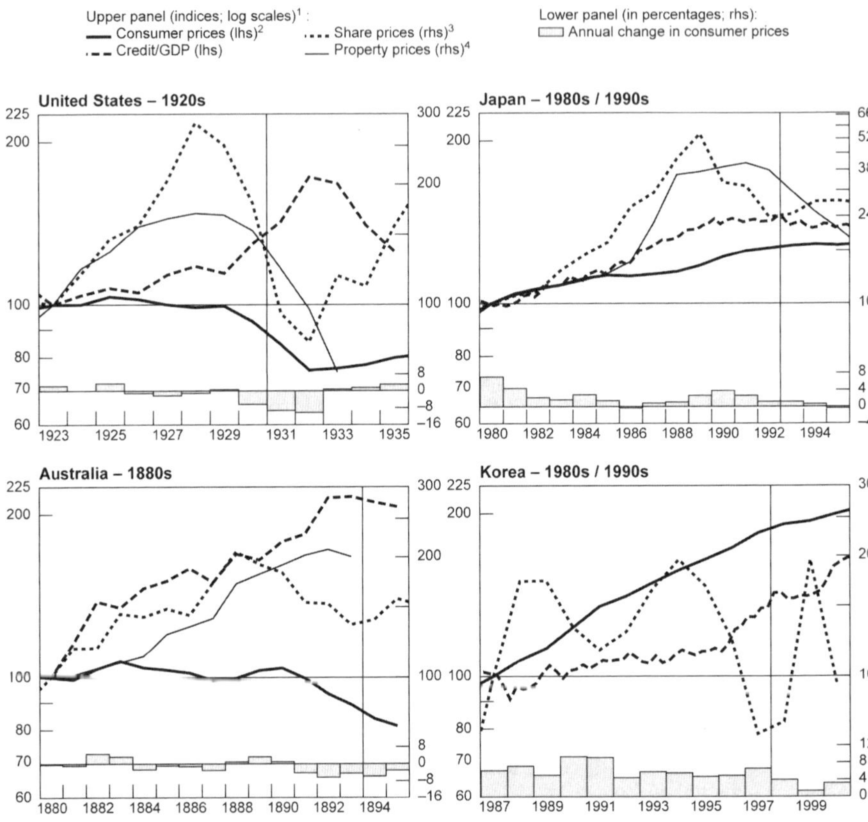

Figure 17.2 Low and stable inflation and financial instability: selected episodes.

Sources: For property prices: Tokyo National Land Agency and local governments; Chicago, Hoyt (1933); Melbourne, Kent and D'Arcy (2001); otherwise, B. Taylor 'Global Financial Data' (database) and national data.

Notes:

1 Base year: for the United States, 1923; for Japan, 1980; for Australia, 1880; for Korea, 1987.
2 For Australia, GDP deflator.
3 For the United States, SP 500; for Japan, Nikkei 225; for Australia, All Ordinaries.
4 For the United States, Chicago land value; for Japan, Tokyo commercial land prices; for Australia, Melbourne capital value of rateable property.

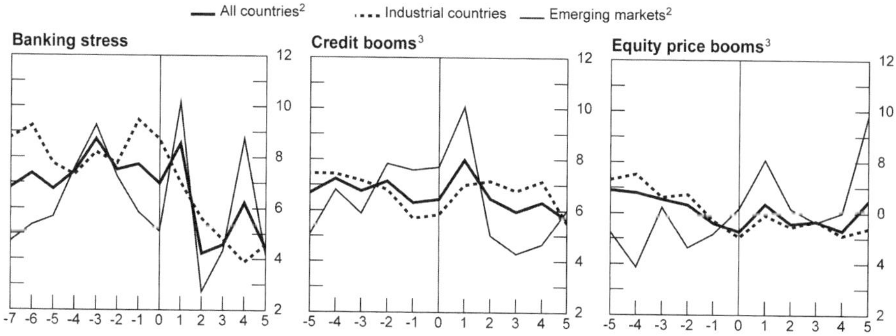

Figure 17.3 Inflation around financial imbalances and banking stress.[1]

Notes:

1 Simple arithmetic means of annual percentage changes of consumer prices across all countries in the individual country groups. Based on annual data for all the series.

2 Except Latin America.

3 Defined as the year in which the credit/GDP gap (equity price gap) first exceeds 4 (40) percentage points.

evidence also indicates that, if anything, lending and equity price booms tend to develop against the background of disinflation. Thus, *judged on the basis of the performance of inflation*, during these booms a central bank could hardly be accused of following an easy monetary stance.

More generally, looking back at the experience in recent years, it is possible to detect increasingly common signs of an intensified interaction between credit and asset prices in an environment of stable and low inflation. The experiences in Japan, some countries in East Asia and, in several respects, recent developments in the United States and hence in the global economy share a common characteristic: investment-led booms that were reinforced by financial developments and that did not end up with rapidly rising inflation (Borio *et al.* 2003). These tended to coincide with periods during which sustainable growth prospects were overestimated. In those cases where financial imbalances grew sufficiently large and unwound in a disruptive way, financial strains emerged, helping to put further downward pressure on prices. And in contrast to much of the postwar experience, the global slowdown that began in the autumn of 2000 was not fundamentally triggered by a tightening of monetary policy to restrain inflation pressures. Rather, it was mainly the result of the spontaneous reversal of the previous investment boom and of the collapse of equity prices, which had reached unsustainable heights. Likewise, the current boom in China shares several of the same characteristics.

The policy options

If one accepts the broad thrust of the basic hypothesis outlined in this chapter, what are the policy implications? Let me sketch the implications for prudential and monetary policy in turn.

Prudential policy

Given the prominent role that financial instability plays in the basic thesis, it is only natural to think of prudential policy as the first line of defence. This is the typical answer that those concerned with macroeconomic stability would immediately give. Ensuring that the financial system is sound would at least limit the risk that financial strains would seriously exacerbate economic weakness.

Indeed, the well-known efforts to strengthen the financial infrastructure in the context of the broader strategy to improve the international financial architecture are a way of addressing this issue head on. These necessary and important steps have been making a vital contribution to strengthening financial systems, in industrial and emerging markets alike. Moreover, a welcome trend has been to structure the policy response so as to work as far as possible with, as opposed to against, the grain of market forces. In sharp contrast to the financial repression era, by seeking to enlist the disciplinary market mechanisms, these steps have promoted a better balance between financial stability and an efficient allocation of resources. Examples abound. Attempts to narrow the scope of safety nets, enhance transparency and disclosure (Borio and Tsatsaronis 2004) and mould safeguards so as to rely more on financial institutions' own risk management systems are obvious cases in point. Through these policies, the authorities have helped to reinforce, spread and hard-wire the significant improvements in risk management that have taken place since liberalization and to hone a credit culture. Arguably, the resilience exhibited by the financial system in the recent slowdown owes significantly to such efforts (Bank for International Settlements 2003).

Strengthening the macroprudential orientation

At the same time, putting adequate defences in place would arguably call for going beyond current efforts and strengthen the 'macroprudential orientation' of current frameworks (Crockett 2000; Borio 2003). What this means is probably best understood by comparing this orientation with its more traditional microprudential counterpart (Borio 2003; Tsatsaronis 2004) (see Table 17.7). The more familiar microprudential dimension focuses on limiting financial distress at individual institutions, calibrates prudential instruments with respect to their individual risk profiles and hence ignores correlations in exposures across them. In addition, it treats risk as fundamentally exogenous. By contrast, its macroprudential counterpart focuses on limiting the risk of system-wide distress with potentially serious consequences for the real economy, calibrates prudential controls with respect to the risk profile of the system as a whole and hence pays close attention to correlations in exposures across individual financial institutions. Naturally, it treats risk as endogenous with respect to the collective behaviour of institutions. The microprudential perspective can best

Table 17.7 The macro- and microprudential perspectives compared

	Macroprudential	*Microprudential*
Proximate objective	limit financial system-wide distress	limit distress of individual institutions
Ultimate objective	avoid output (GDP) costs	consumer (investor/depositor) protection
Model of risk	(in part) endogenous	exogenous
Correlations and common exposures across institutions	important	irrelevant
Calibration of prudential controls	in terms of system-wide distress; top-down	in terms of risks of individual institutions; bottom-up

be rationalized in terms of depositor or investor protection; its macroprudential counterpart in terms of limiting systemic risk.

Thus, in a nutshell, a 'macroprudential' orientation would stress the system-wide perspective of risk in terms of objectives and of the way of achieving them (Borio 2003, Table 17.7). For the purposes of the discussion here, it would, in particular, highlight the mutual interaction between the financial and real economy. Consequently, it would also pay greater attention to the procyclical mechanisms in financial arrangements that tend to amplify the business cycle and make the financial system more sensitive to downturns. A core element of a macroprudential framework would be to ensure that defences, or protective cushions, are built up in booms in order to run them down in downswings. This would make institutions stronger to weather deteriorating economic conditions, when access to external funding becomes more costly and constrained. And by leaning against the wind, it might also reduce the amplitude of the financial cycle, thereby limiting the risk of financial distress in the first place.

Several possible options can be envisaged (Borio *et al.* 2001; Borio and Lowe 2002b; Borio 2003). One might be to adjust minimum capital requirements or provisioning practices. Another might be to rely on loan-to-value ratios, either adjusting the ratio itself or the way in which, for prudential purposes, valuations are calculated (Tsatsaronis and Zhu 2004). A better assessment of financial vulnerabilities, going beyond the simple proxies for financial imbalances described here, could form the basis for such policies. In all of these cases, issues concerning the balance between rules and discretion would need to be carefully considered.

While encouraging steps have been taken in recent years to strengthen the macroprudential perspective, there is still a long road ahead. First, culturally, prudential authorities still remain rather reluctant to address financial instability through the instruments at their disposal if the origin is somehow seen to lie with broader macroeconomic developments, regardless of what the contribution of financial factors might be. Such a response tends to be seen as beyond their remit and comparative advantage. Second, the proposed solutions, while feasible, raise technical difficulties. For example, supervisors still feel that they do not yet have adequate tools to assess how system-wide risk evolves over time. Similarly, countercyclical adjustments to prudential instruments, be these discretionary or rule based, may be thought to be too intrusive and inconsistent with the current trend towards relying increasingly on firms' internal risk management systems. These systems hardly incorporate cyclical considerations and, to the extent that they do, may even exacerbate procyclical forces, partly because of the short horizons used and the tendency simply to extrapolate current conditions.[9] And in some cases remedies would require the co-operation of other authorities, such as those in charge of taxation or accounting, with quite different perspectives; the heated debate about the role of forward-looking provisioning is one such example. Indeed, broader questions arise about the proper co-ordination and roles of prudential policies, on the one hand, and accounting policies, on the other (Borio and Tsatsaronis 2004).

A macroprudential orientation may not suffice

Let us imagine for a moment, however, that these cultural and technical obstacles could be overcome. Even then, it could be argued that this might not be sufficient to prevent significant macroeconomic costs from the build-up and unwinding of imbalances. There are at least two reasons for this.

First, the mechanisms that generate financial instability with macroeconomic costs can operate just as much through open capital markets as they do through financial institutions. Markets, too, are strongly procyclical and are just as capable of seriously constraining the availability of external funding. Similarly, they can freeze under stress, as liquidity evaporates (Borio 2000, 2004; Committee on the Global Financial System 1999). A narrow focus on financial institutions, notably banks, would not be sufficient to address these potential shortcomings. Moreover, if countercyclical constraints were to be applied to banks, regulatory arbitrage would simply encourage market funding to step in. As a result, risks could migrate elsewhere.

Second, the costs of financial overextension for the macroeconomy can be serious even if they fall short of materializing in a full-blown financial crisis. Indeed, even if the financial sector was still capable of and willing to provide external funding, the real constraint might be on the demand side. For, after a long period of overextension, businesses and households could come under pressure to rebuild their balance sheets and cut spending.

The bottom line is simple: there are limits to what prudential instruments can do. Some of them are of a political economy nature, reflecting interpretation of mandates and public expectations. Others are rooted in intellectual perspectives. But others still relate more closely to inherent limitations of the instruments themselves. The raw material on which they operate is based on perceptions of risk and value that may be less than fully adequate. In turn, these perceptions are intimately linked to the availability of liquidity, which allows them to be translated into purchasing power or hard funding.[10] But prudential authorities have only limited influence on the liquidity generated in an economy. This brings us to the importance of monetary policy.

Monetary policy

From this perspective, the role of monetary policy would be to anchor the liquidity creation process and hence the availability of external finance; credit extension plays a key role here. The anchoring would help to reduce the elasticity of the economy, thereby providing critical support to prudential policy. The authorities could implement it by being prepared to lean against the build-up of financial imbalances by tightening policy, when necessary, even if near-term inflation pressures were not apparent.

The motivation for such a policy would be twofold. It would seek to limit the downside risks for the macroeconomy further down the road. And, by the same token, it would take out some insurance against the risk of monetary policy losing effectiveness. As experience indicates, economic weakness associated with balance sheet adjustments following the build-up of imbalances is arguably less amenable to a monetary policy cure. If imbalances are generalized, headwinds could be considerable, arising from both the demand for, and the supply of, external finance. If they are unevenly distributed across sectors, the short-term policy stimulus may become more lopsided than usual, and potentially achieve short-run success but at the risk of contributing to sectoral financial imbalances of its own (see pp. 422–23). And if the worst scenario materializes, central banks may need to push policy rates to zero and resort to less conventional measures, whose efficacy is less certain.

Nevertheless, even if the prima facie case for a preventive tightening is accepted, a number of significant implementation problems remain. These have led many observers and policymakers to eschew such a course of action.

First, it has been argued that financial imbalances cannot be identified with a sufficient degree of comfort. The burden of proof is simply too high. And by the time they might be identified, it would be too late. Given the lags involved in the transmission mechanism, the economy could easily find itself labouring under the joint effect of the unwinding of the imbalances and of the policy tightening.

Second, it has been stressed that it is very difficult to calibrate the tightening. The response of imbalances may be very hard to predict, not least since they tend to be associated with speculative activities and hence grounded in investor psychology. On the one hand, a mild tightening might even boost the imbalances further if it is taken as a sign that the central bank will guarantee non-inflationary sustainable growth. On the other hand, if market participants perceive expected returns to be particularly high, their response could be very muted. If so, a strong tightening might be needed, shifting the brunt of the adjustment to the more interest rate sensitive sectors. The policy could thus trigger the very recession it was supposed to avert.

Finally, it has been noted that the political economy constraints are daunting. A central bank tightening even as near-term inflation pressures remained subdued or non-existent would be regarded as going beyond its remit. Its action would probably be seen as aborting a sustainable expansion and fully justified increases in wealth. Nor could the central bank, ex post, prove that its action was appropriate. The actual loss in wealth would be all too apparent, but the counterfactual, even larger, loss would remain invisible.

These objections are powerful and well grounded. At the same time, they do not seem sufficient to rule out a tightening of monetary policy altogether.

The objections concerning identification sound especially convincing when couched in terms of 'bubbles'; they appear less daunting, however, once the focus is more fruitfully placed on financial imbalances. That is, the more relevant question is whether it is possible to identify the set of conditions that are harbingers of future serious strains for the real economy. The forward-looking indicators presented in this chapter and in related work are just one step in that direction. Given that this type of work is in its infancy, the scope for further progress is encouraging. Nor do the measurement difficulties appear to be qualitatively different from those associated with more traditional concepts, such as economic slack or potential output.

Likewise, the objection regarding calibration draws part of its appeal from references to 'bubbles' as opposed to broader financial imbalances. The objective of a tightening is not to attempt a kind of surgical removal of the 'bubble', which would leave the real economy untouched. This is clearly unrealistic. From the perspective developed in this essay, financial imbalances are seen as inextricably linked to the real economy. They contribute to, and reflect, underlying disequilibria that undermine sustainable growth. In the absence of overt inflation pressures, they are symptoms of a 'disguised overheating'. The objective of the tightening is precisely to slow the economy down in the near term in order to avoid a more costly contraction further down the road. From this perspective, the conditions for the effectiveness of policy, or the mechanisms through which it operates, are not that different from those associated with a traditional tightening to quell inflationary pressures. Moreover, if the authorities are seen to be reacting to the imbalances, the agents may be more responsive to the tightening. Indeed, communicating a reaction function of this type ex ante might even diminish the likelihood of imbalances developing in the first place, much as the credibility of the anti-inflation commitment nowadays tends to anchor inflation expectations. By contrast, being seen to react asymmetrically, by easing only when imbalances unwind, might inadvertently contribute to their build-up. In a way, such a policy could also be thought of as being subject to a 'time inconsistency' problem: a sequence of accommodating responses to current conditions that seem compelling in the short run might not be the most appropriate when its cumulative effect is taken into account.

Finally, while serious, political economy constraints are not immovable. They depend crucially on perceptions of trade-offs between policy choices and hence on views about the workings of the economy and the role of policy. Such views change over time, in the light of evolving circumstances. It was, for instance, the recognition of the absence of a long-run trade-off between inflation and unemployment during the global inflationary phase that laid the basis for the adoption of the current mandates and policy rules. Likewise, a view of economic processes that stressed the role of financial imbalances could help promote the necessary intellectual and political consensus for action. Indeed, several central banks have recently been moving in this direction (e.g. Bank of England 2002; Stevens 2003).

How far would current policy frameworks need to be modified in order to accommodate the occasional pre-emptive tightening of policy in view of evidence of developing financial imbalances? The answer is 'probably not much' (Borio and Lowe 2002a; Borio and White 2004).

There is no real need to change the *ultimate objectives*, typically couched in terms of inflation and output. While the costs can be more immediately understood in terms of output, the unwinding of imbalances could also have a potentially significant impact on inflation, raising the risk of an undershooting as the imbalances unwind, and possibly even deflation (Borio and Filardo 2004). From a macroeconomic perspective, financial instability is relevant only to the extent that it has undesirable consequences for the real economy. Moreover, as argued, the processes at work can have serious costs even if they fall short of materializing in full-blown financial crises.

At the same time, operationally the shift in perspective has somewhat different implications for specific monetary frameworks. The reconciliation is easier where the central bank is not pinned down to any numerical objective for inflation over an explicit short-term horizon. At least for communication purposes, in strict inflation targeting regimes with up to two-year horizons the justification of policy actions in response to imbalances may not be straightforward. To be sure, it should be well understood by now that inflation targeting is by no means oblivious to output fluctuations. This objective is implicitly incorporated into the framework through features such as the length of the horizon and the width of the target band. But it may be hard to rationalize a tightening in the absence of obvious inflation pressures, especially if the outcome is likely to be inflation below target over the usual horizon, even if the risk is in fact a larger shortfall down the road.

Arguably, at least two modifications would be called for in this case. First, policy decisions should be articulated on the basis of *longer horizons*. While the precise timing of the unwinding of imbalances is rather unpredictable, the processes involved tend to be drawn-out ones.[11] For example, the notion of ensuring price stability on a 'sustainable' basis or over the medium term might be useful in capturing the prospect of future downward pressure on prices linked with the unwinding (Okina *et al.* 2001). The second modification would be to assign *greater weight to the balance of risks* in the outlook, as opposed to central scenarios or most likely outcomes. This would highlight the role of monetary policy actions in providing insurance against costly outcomes. Central banks are already used to thinking in these terms. But the nature of the problem would put a premium on considerations of this kind. In fact, the two modifications are closely related. Given the uncertainties involved, the extension of the horizon cannot be done mechanically. Simply extending a point forecast would make little difference or even sense. Rather, the longer horizon would more naturally be used as a device to better assess and communicate the balance of risks facing the economy.

Beyond this, the precise implementation would depend on the specifics of the arrangements. These could vary from monitoring ranges for the variables of particular interest, such as credit and asset prices, to less formalized ways of assessing developments. For instance, the monetary analysis component of the ECB strategy would be an obvious vehicle for incorporating concerns about financial imbalances, especially now that it has been modified to give less prominence to a specific variable (M3) (Issing 2003). Indeed, the ECB has been rather explicit about this possibility in recent statements.

Having said this, the differential behaviour of various asset prices can complicate the picture further. One such asset price is the exchange rate. In particular for small open economies, credit expansion tends to be fuelled by capital inflows and a tightening of monetary policy might encourage those inflows further. Another asset price is that of real estate, which is arguably even more relevant than equity prices, owing to the large component of wealth tied up in property and to its extensive use as collateral. Reductions in interest rates to soften the unwinding of equity markets may risk contributing to the build-up of imbalances in real estate markets. The experience in the late 1980s (Borio and Lowe 2004) and the more recent one (Borio and McGuire 2004) share some of these characteristics.

These complications highlight the uncomfortable dilemmas raised by business cycles in which financial imbalances play a salient role. They also put a premium on pre-emptive action. And they suggest that the relative weight to be placed on monetary and prudential arrangement should vary with circumstances, based on the comparative effectiveness of the instruments. For instance, in highly open small economies, a larger weight on prudential instruments may be justified.

Conclusions

The search for lasting monetary and financial stability has proved rather elusive through history. We are probably closer than ever before to achieving this goal. In this chapter, I have tried to explore the reasons for this elusiveness and sketched a possible way forward. In doing so, following Feynman's advice, I have tried to 'keep the door of the unknown ajar'. As a result, the informed conjecture and main thesis on which this way forward is based are testing the limits of our current knowledge. What would be the implications if the basic thesis was regarded as sufficiently promising? I would summarize them in 'four needs'.

First, we need much more analytical work. This work is required to see how the processes outlined in this chapter can be incorporated into proper models, with rigorous foundations. Such models could help us better understand the interaction between the financial system and the real economy and hence the appropriate calibration of policy instruments. Developing such models will certainly be very challenging. While a number of building blocks do exist, they have so far not been assembled together into a consistent whole. Technical difficulties are not trivial, as the processes envisaged are fundamentally non-linear.[12] My guess is that success will require blending three lines of enquiry that have been evolving largely independently, dealing respectively with macroeconomic issues, financial crises and risk measurement and management. In the process, it will also call for a rediscovery of the classical intellectual tradition stressing endogenous business cycles (Borio *et al.* 2003; Borio and White 2004; Filardo 2003).

Second, we need much more empirical work. This work would be designed to improve our ability to identify financial imbalances in good time, based on a more comprehensive assessment of vulnerabilities (Borio 2003; Borio and Tsatsaronis 2004). This is likely to bring together measures of the likelihood of distress, such as the indicators described here, with measures of the costs given distress. Macro-stress tests could play a prominent role here. The work should also seek to help us to understand better the relationship across key asset classes, notably equity prices, property prices and, if one may refer to it as an asset price, the exchange rate. Real estate prices, in particular, have been neglected for too long. It should allow us to quantify theoretical models. And it should help us understand in more depth the costs of financial instability. My guess is that these are only partly captured by short-run deviations of output from trend or even output volatility, and that they are much longer lasting, given the potential longer-term misallocation of resources that financial imbalances can generate.

Third, we need educational efforts to communicate clearly how the policies outlined here are consistent with existing mandates and hence to build the required support for them. In the case of prudential authorities, educational efforts are necessary to explain to the public how a stronger macroprudential focus is also conducive to stronger financial soundness of individual institutions (Borio 2003). In the case of monetary authorities, they are essential to explain to the public how a policy response to the build-up of financial imbalances even if near-term inflation appears under control is consistent with the pursuit of inflation objectives; indeed, it is more conducive to sustainable price stability (Borio and Lowe 2004). This is especially difficult in the context of inflation targeting regimes, given the rhetoric employed until recently. But even in less restrictive regimes, there is a risk that the authorities may incorrectly be seen as pursuing policies that go beyond their mandate.

Finally, we need a much more intense dialogue between prudential and monetary authorities. The goals they pursue are arguably much more tightly linked than they may appear at first sight. Their attainment calls for closer co-operation, based on a common understanding of the problems and a common strategy to address them. Ultimately, this dialogue is probably the most solid foundation on which to build for the future. It is the best way to ensure that the quest for lasting monetary and financial stability will turn out to be less elusive than in the past.

Notes

1 This chapter largely reproduces the inaugural keynote address delivered at the 6th Money and Finance Conference, 'Money and Finance in the Indian Economy', IGIDR, Mumbai, 25–27 March 2004. A shorter version of this lecture has appeared as Borio (2005). All errors are my sole responsibility. The views expressed are my own and do not necessarily reflect those of the Bank for International Settlements.
2 William White from the BIS has developed this important theme (see White 1998; 2000).
3 Correspondingly and deliberately, the reference list consists almost exclusively of BIS research, so as to highlight this work. Those papers include comprehensive bibliographies.
4 In what follows, to avoid confusion, a variable is said to behave procyclically if its co-movement with economic activity is such as to tend to amplify it. For instance, if credit spreads fall during expansions and rise during contractions, they are said to move procyclically.
5 For some recent attempts to measure time varying risk aversion, see Tsatsaronis (2000) and Tarashev *et al.* (2003).
6 For an analysis consistent with this paradox, based on the absence of common knowledge, see Amato and Shin (2003).

7 Just as with financial liberalization, the likelihood of the build-up of financial imbalances is especially high during the transition from a high to a low inflation environment, for a different reason from the one highlighted in the main text. This is because of the possible existence of money illusion, often strengthened by institutional arrangements that are slow to adjust to lower inflation (e.g. actuarial discount rates etc.). The classic reference here is Modigliani and Cohn (1979), who note the obverse phenomenon: how rising inflation led to undervaluation of equities in the 1970s (see also McCauley *et al.* 1999). For instance, arguably, the repeated episodes of search for yield we are observing these days result in part from the pursuit of unrealistic nominal target rates of return, still based on an environment of higher inflation.

8 In fact, in some respects the resemblance may be closer with the first phase of the interwar period. This phase had seen either successful efforts to re-establish monetary stability by returning to the Gold Standard, as in a number of central European economies, or experimentation in how to conduct monetary policy in a context of price stability but weakened exogenous constraints on credit expansion, as in the United States.

9 In this context, a pertinent question is whether the New Basel Capital Accord, by making minimum capital requirements on a given portfolio a function of its perceived riskiness, could contribute to the procyclicality of the financial system. Probably the best answer is that its net effect is unclear at this stage. Admittedly, minimum capital requirements are likely to be more procyclical, as suggested by some empirical evidence (e.g. Segoviano and Lowe 2002; Jordan *et al.* 2002 and Catarineu-Rabell *et al.* 2003). At the same time, a number of factors could mitigate or more than compensate for this mechanical effect. For one, the New Accord will result in major improvements in risk management, so that problems could be identified and corrected earlier. In addition, Pillars 2 (supervisory review) and 3 (disclosure) can underpin this shift. For instance, supervisors could induce higher than minimum requirements during booms, not least by relying more on stress testing. And markets could become less tolerant of banks whose (disclosed) internal ratings fluctuated suspiciously strongly during the cycle. Of course, quite apart from these considerations, one should never lose sight of the fact that the positive contribution of the Capital Accord to financial stability goes well beyond its impact on procyclicality. For further analysis of these issues, see Bank for International Settlements (2001, 2002), Lowe (2002), Borio (2003) and Greenspan (2002).

10 Indeed, as argued in Borio and Crockett (2000), liquidity may be best defined as the ability to realize perceived value. Perceived value can be as transparently intangible as the future earning stream from capital or labour, or as deceptively tangible as a piece of property or financial asset. And value can be realized perceived either through the sale of the asset or by obtaining external finance against it. Credit creation is a core element of liquidity creation.

11 For views broadly sympathetic with this point, see King (2002), Bean (2003), Bäckström (2002) and Gjedrem (2003). See also Dodge (2003) and Issing (2003).

12 See, e.g., Filardo (2003) for a discussion of these issues and an attempt to address them in a very simple reduced-form model.

References

Allen, A.M., S.R.L Cope, L.J.H. Dark and H.J. Witheridge (1938) *Commercial Banking Legislation and Control*, London: Macmillan.

Amato, J. and C. Furfine (2003) *Are Credit Ratings Procyclical?*, BIS Working Papers, 129, February.

Amato, J. and H.S. Shin, (2003) 'Public and private information in monetary policy models', paper presented at BIS Conference on 'Monetary Stability, Financial Stability and the Business Cycle', BIS Working Papers, no. 138, September.

Bäckström, U. (2002) 'Financial cycles', speech at the Philadelphia Fed Policy Forum on 'Crises, Contagion and Coordination: Issues for Policymakers in the Global Economy', Philadelphia, *BIS Review*, no. 68, November.

Bank for International Settlements (2001) 'Cycles and the financial system', *BIS 71st Annual Report*, Chapter VII, June: 123–41.

—— (2002) 'The interaction between the financial sector and the real economy', *BIS 72nd Annual Report*, Chapter VII, June: 122–40.

—— (2003) 'The financial sector', *BIS 73rd Annual Report*, Chapter VII, June: 120–41.

Bank of England (2002) *Minutes of Monetary Policy Committee Meeting*, 6 and 7 November, London: Bank of England.

Bean, C. (2003) 'Asset prices, financial imbalances and monetary policy: are inflation targets enough?', paper presented at the BIS Conference on 'Monetary Stability, Financial Stability and the Business Cycle', BIS Working Papers, no. 140, September.

Bordo, M., M. Dueker and D. Wheelock (2000) *Aggregate Price Shocks and Financial Instability: An Historical Analysis*, NBER Working Paper, 7652, April.

Bordo, M., B. Eichengreen, D. Klingebiel and M.S. Martinez-Peria (2001) 'Is the crisis problem growing more severe?', *Economic Policy* 16(32), April: 51–82.

Borio, C. (2000) 'Market liquidity and stress: selected issues and policy implications', *BIS Quarterly Review*, November: 38–48.

—— (2003) *Towards a Macro-prudential Framework for Financial Supervision and Regulation?*, *CESifo Economic Studies* 49(2): 181–215. Also available as BIS Working Papers, no. 128, February.

—— (2004) 'Market distress and vanishing liquidity: anatomy and policy options', in A. Persaud (ed.), *Liquidity Black Holes: Understanding, Quantifying and Managing Financial Liquidity Risk*, Risk Publications, December. Also available (revised and updated) as BIS Working Papers, no. 158, 2004.

—— (2005) 'Monetary and financial stability: so close and yet so far?', *National Institute Economic Review* 192, April: 84–101.

Borio, C. and A. Crockett (2000) 'In search of anchors for financial and monetary stability', *Greek Economic Review* 20(2), autumn: 1–14.

Borio, C. and A. Filardo (2004) 'Looking back at the international deflation record', *The North American Journal of Economics and Finance*, 15: 287–311. A more extensive version is also available as *Back to the future? Assessing the deflation record*, BIS Working Papers, no. 152, March.

Borio, C. and P. Lowe (2002a) 'Asset prices, financial and monetary stability: Exploring the nexus', BIS Working Papers, no. 114, July. An abridged version of this paper is 'Financial imbalances or "bubbles"? Implications for monetary and financial stability', in W. Hunter, G. Kaufman and M. Pomerleano (eds), *Asset Price Bubbles: The Implications for Monetary, Regulatory, and International Policies*, MIT Press, January 2003, 247–70.

—— (2002b) 'Assessing the risk of banking crises', *BIS Quarterly Review*, December: 43–54.

—— (2004) 'Securing sustainable price stability: should credit come back from the wilderness?', paper prepared for ECB Workshop on 'Asset Prices and Monetary Policy' in December 2003, BIS Working Papers, no. 157, July.

Borio, C. and P. McGuire (2004) 'Twin peaks in equity and housing prices?', *BIS Quarterly Review*, March: 79–93.

Borio, C. and K. Tsatsaronis (2004) 'Accounting and prudential regulation: from uncomfortable bedfellows to perfect partners?', *Journal of Financial Stability*, 1(1), September, 111–35. A more extensive version, covering in addition to the microprudential aspects, the macroprudential dimension, is available as 'Accounting, prudential regulation and financial stability: elements of a synthesis', BIS Working Papers, no. 180, September 2005.

Borio, C. and W. White (2004) 'Whither monetary and financial stability? The implications of evolving policy regimes', in *Monetary Policy and Uncertainty: adapting to a changing economy*, Proceedings of symposium sponsored by the Federal Reserve Bank of Kansas City, Jackson Hole, 28–30: 131–211. Also available as BIS Working Papers, no. 147, February 2004.

Borio, C., B. English and A. Filardo (2003) *A Tale of Two Perspectives: Old or New Challenges for Monetary Policy?*, BIS Working Papers, no. 127, February.

Borio, C., C. Furfine and P. Lowe (2001) 'Procyclicality of the financial system and financial stability: issues and policy options', in *Marrying the Macro- and Micro-prudential Dimensions of Financial Stability*, BIS Papers, no. 1, March, 1–57.

Borio, C., N. Kennedy and S. Prowse (1994) *Exploring Aggregate Asset Price Fluctuations across Countries: Measurement, Determinants and Monetary Policy Implications*, BIS Economic Papers, no. 40, April.

Catarineu-Rabell, E., P. Jackson and D.P. Tsomocos (2003) *Procyclicality and the New Basel Accord – Banks' Choice of Loan Rating System*, Bank of England Working Papers, no. 181, March.

Committee on the Global Financial System (1999) 'A review of financial market events in autumn 1998', *CGFS Report*, no. 12, October.

Crockett, A (2000) 'Marrying the micro- and macro-prudential dimensions of financial stability', *BIS Speeches*, 21 September.

Davis, P. and H.B. Zhu (2004) *Bank Lending and Commercial Property Cycles: Some Cross-country Evidence*, BIS Working Papers, no. 150, March.

Dodge, D. (2003) 'A coherent monetary policy framework and asset prices', remarks presented to researchers at the Bank of Canada and elsewhere in regard to the potential role of asset prices in the conduct of monetary policy, *Bank of England Speeches*, February.

Filardo, A. (2003) 'The enduring core of business cycles', paper prepared for a conference honouring the contributions of Victor Zarnowitz to the study of business cycles – theory, history, indicators and forecasting at the Rheinisch-Westfalisches Institut für Wirtschaftsforschung (RWI) in Essen, Germany, 27–28 June, forthcoming BIS Working Papers.

—— (2004) 'Should monetary authorities prick asset price bubbles?', paper presented at the EEA meetings, BIS Working Papers, no. 155, June.

Filardo, A. and S.F. Gordon (1998) 'Business cycle durations', *Journal of Econometrics* 85(1), July: 99–123.

Flannery, M. (1998) 'Using market information in prudential bank supervision: a review of the US empirical evidence', *Journal of Money, Credit and Banking*, 30, August: 273–305.

Gerlach, S. and F. Smets (1999) 'Output gaps and monetary policy in the EMU area', *European Economic Review* 43: 801–12.

Giannini, C. (2001) 'Broad in scope, soft in method. International cooperation and the quest for financial stability in emerging markets', paper presented at the Seventh Dubrovnik Economic Conference on 'Current Issues in Emerging Market Economies' organized by the Croatian National Bank, 28–29 June.

Gjedrem, S. (2003) 'Financial stability, asset prices and monetary policy', speech at the Centre for Monetary Economics/Norwegian School of Management, *BIS Review* 25, June.

Goodhart, C. and P. De Largy (1999) 'Financial crises: plus ça change, plus c'est la même chose', LSE Financial Markets Group, Special Papers, no. 108, January.

Greenspan, A. (2002) 'Cyclicality and banking regulation', remarks given at the conference on Bank Structure and Competition, Federal Reserve Bank of Chicago, 10 May.

Hofmann, B. (2001) *The Determinants of Bank Credit to the Private Sector in Industrialised Countries*, BIS Working Papers, no. 108, December.

Issing, O. (2003) 'Monetary and financial stability: is there a trade-off?', presentation at the policy panel of the BIS Conference on 'Monetary Stability, Financial Stability and the Business Cycle', BIS Papers, no. 18, September, pp. 16–23.

Jordan, J., J. Peek and E. Rosengren (2002) 'Credit risk modeling and the cyclicality of capital', paper presented at the BIS Conference on 'Changes in Risk through Time: Measurement and Policy Options', Basel, 5–6 March.

Kindleberger, C. (2000) *Manias, Panics and Crashes*, Cambridge: Cambridge University Press, 4th edn.

King, M. (2002) 'The inflation target ten years on', speech presented at the London School of Economics, *Bank of England Speeches*, 19 November.

Knight, M.D. (2003) 'Three observations on market discipline', speech delivered at the BIS-Federal Reserve Bank of Chicago Conference on 'Market Discipline' in Chicago, *BIS Speeches*, 30 October.

Lowe, P. (2002) 'Credit risk measurement and procyclicality', paper presented at the Conference on 'Banking Supervision at the Crossroads' on the occasion of the 50th Anniversary of the Dutch Act on the Supervision of Credit Systems, BIS Working Papers, no. 116, August.

McCauley, R., J. S. Ruud and F. Iacono (1999) *Dodging Bullets: Changing US Corporate Capital Structures in the 1980s and 1999s*, Cambridge, MA: MIT Press.

Modigliani, F. and R. A. Cohn (1979) 'Inflation, rational valuation and the market', *Financial Analysts Journal*, 35(2): 24–44.

Okina, K., M. Shirakawa and S. Shiratsuka (2001) *Asset Price Bubble and Monetary Policy: Japan's Experience in the Late 1980s and the Lessons*, IMES Discussion Paper, no. 2000-E-12, Institute for Monetary and Economic Studies, Bank of Japan.

Padoa-Schioppa, T. and F. Saccomanni (1994) 'Managing a market-led global financial system', in *Managing the World Economy: Fifty Years After Bretton Woods*, Washington, DC: IIE, pp. 235–68.

Schwartz, A. (1995) 'Why financial stability depends on price stability', *Economic Affairs*, autumn: 21–5.

Segoviano, M.A. and P. Lowe (2002) 'Internal ratings, the business cycle and capital requirements: some evidence from an emerging market economy', paper presented at the Federal Reserve Bank of Boston Conference on 'The Impact of Economic Slowdowns on Financial Institutions and Their Regulators', BIS Working Papers, no. 117, August.

Smets, F. (1998) *Output Gap Uncertainty: Does It Matter for the Taylor Rule?*, BIS Working Papers, no. 60, November.

Stevens, G.R. (2003) 'Structural change and the conduct of monetary policy', remarks at Federal Reserve Bank of Kansas City Economic Symposium, Jackson Hole, 30 August.

Tarashev, N., K. Tsatsaronis and D. Karampatos (2003) 'Investors' attitude towards risk: what can we learn from options?', *BIS Quarterly Review*, June: 57–66.

Tsatsaronis, K. (2004) 'Systemic financial risk and macroprudential supervision', paper presented at the Bocconi University Centennial conference on 'Risk and Stability in the Financial System: What Roles for Regulators, Management and Market Discipline?', in BIS Working Papers, forthcoming.

—— (2000) 'An indicator of investors' attitude towards risk', *BIS Quarterly Review*, February: 12–13.

Tsatsaronis, K. and H. Zhu (2004) 'What drives housing price dynamics: cross-country evidence', *BIS Quarterly Review*, March: 65–78.

White, W.R. (1998) 'Promoting international financial stability: The role of the BIS', in *Regulatory and Supervisory Challenges in a New Era of Global Finance*, Forum on Debt and Development (FONDAD).

—— (2000) *What Have We Learned from Recent Financial Crises and Policy Responses?*, BIS Working Papers, no. 84, January.

Index

Abel, A. 58
Abiad, A.G., Leigh, D. and Mody, A. 235
ABN Amro 398n6, 398n10
Abreu, Marta 81n1
accession: adaptation to full EMU membership, dimensions of 44–45; adjustment to stage 3, living with 43–46, 52; approaches to adjustment on 42; challenges of stage 3, 32–35, 50; participation and the 'j-curve' concept 5, 33–34, 36, 39, 40, 42, 46, 50, 52; *see also* RAMs
accountability 349
accounting rules on insolvency 384
Adalid, Ramon 81n1
Adam, K. *et al.* 261–62
Adjaouté, K. and Danthine, J.-P. 262, 268
adjustment in EMU, model-based analysis of experiences 127–160; competition, exposure to (demand) 135; composition of investment (costs) 134–135; country dynamics 135–154; current account imbalances 131–132; DSGE model 127, 132–135, 138, 141, 144, 147, 150, 153, 158n5; exchange risk premia 132; Germany, adjustment scenario for 154, 156–157; Germany, adjustment simulation results 137–139; Germany, demand and supply shocks 136–137; Germany, stylized facts 136; Germany, summing up on adjustment exercise 139; households in standard macro models 158n6; housing price developments 130–131; industrial structure differences 158n7; inflation differentials 128–129; inflation dispersion 129–130; Ireland, adjustment simulation results 140–142; Ireland, demand and supply shocks 140; Ireland, stylized facts 139–140; Ireland, summing up on adjustment exercise 142; Italy, adjustment simulation results 143–145; Italy, demand and supply shocks 143; Italy, stylized facts 142–143; Italy, summing up on adjustment exercise 145; mortgage debt 159n20; Netherlands, adjustment simulation results 147–148; Netherlands, demand and supply shocks 146; Netherlands, stylized facts 145–146; Netherlands, summing up on adjustment exercise 148; Portugal, adjustment simulation results 149–151; Portugal, demand and supply shocks 149; Portugal, stylized facts 148–149; Portugal, summing up on adjustment exercise 151; productivity and wage trends 129; Spain, adjustment scenario for 154–156; Spain, adjustment simulation results 152–154; Spain, demand and supply shocks 151–152; Spain, stylized facts 151; Spain, summing up on adjustment exercise 154; stylized developments (and stylized facts) 128–132
adjustment to euro, exploration of implications of entry 56–82; appreciation in real exchange rate 63–64, 79–80; Blanchard-Yaari households, habit formation in endowment economy 65–75, 79; Blanchard-Yaari households, numerical simulations for two-good economy 75–79, 80–81; credit growth and household debt 61, 64, 79–80; current account deficits 63, 64, 79–80; dynamics, sensitivity to parameter values 76; GDP growth differentials 62–63, 64, 79–80; household expenditure and debt 56–57; household expenditures 61, 64, 79–80; interest rate convergence 56–57; interest rate convergence, impact of 58–65, 79–80; nominal convergence 58–65, 79–80; non-housing investment 61–62, 64, 79–80; participation in union, consequences of 56; stylized facts 58 65; *see also* Blanchard-Yaari households; booms and busts, adjustment experiences
Afonso, A. *et al.* 105
Afonso, Antonio 108n1
agency problems and conflicts 358–61
Aglietta, M. *et al.* 36
agricultural employment 45, 223
Ahearne, A. *et al.* 168
Akhavein, J.D. *et al.* 326
Albania 120

Alfaro, L. *et al.* 222
Allen, A.M. *et al.* 410
Allen, M. *et al.* 86
Allsopp, Chris 81n1
Alves, Nuno 81n1
Amato, J. and Furfine, C. 406
Amato, J. and Shin, H.S. 426n6
AMECO database (European Commission) 79–80
Amel, D. *et al.* 325
Andrés, J. *et al.* 329n40
Angelini, E. *et al.* 304n8
Angeloni, I. *et al.* 191n7
anti-inflationary commitment 408–9, 423
anticipatory OCA endogenicity 35
architecture revision 337–53
Argentina 36, 54n6, 124n8
Arora, N. *et al.* 278n6
Arratibel,O. *et al.* 109n14
Artis, Michael J. 11–12, 242–57, 278n2, viii
Artis, M.J. and Hoffmann, M. 242, 247, 251, 253, 257
Asdrubali, P., Sørensen, B.E. and Yosha, O. 22, 243, 244–45, 250, 257n4
Asia 415, 417–18, 419; Asian 3 (Korea, Malaysia, Thailand) 95, 96, 98, 108n10; financial crisis in 404; South-East Asia, analysis of boom-bust episodes 95–98
asset markets 20, 21; credit and asset prices, booms and busts in 412; price increases, unsustainability in 408; total assets, banking and insurance 277–78
Assurances, Comité Européen des 341
asymmetric shocks 214, 215
Australia 89, 120, 124n8, 415, 418; housing wealth effects 171, 172–173; international risk sharing 245
Austria 56, 59, 60, 62, 64, 80, 81n2, 119, 124n8, 131, 322; banking integration progress 311–13; deposit insurance characteristics 365, 367, 368, 373; insolvency resolution 375; international risk sharing 245; risk profile sensitivity to shock 274; short-term interest rates 163
Ayuso, J. *et al.* 183

Backé, P. and Zumer, T. 109n15
Backé, P. *et al.* 102
Bäckström, U. 427n11
Backus, D. *et al.* 244
Baele, L. *et al.* 261, 268, 328n10
Bagehot, Walter 212
Bai, J. and Ng, S. 296–96
Bair, S. 400n46
Balassa-Samuelson (BS) effect 40, 50, 63
Balcerowicz, Leszek 36
Baldwin, R. *et al.* 45
Baltic states 32, 38, 39, 45, 47, 50, 103, 104, 121, 123
Banca d'Italia 159n16
Banco Bilbao Vizcaya Argentina 398n10
Banco de Portugal 80
bank credit, GDP ratio to 47–48
bank fragility: co-movements in 301–2; co-movements in, results of modeling 302, 303; common macro-shocks, role of 301–2, 303; *see also* DD (distance-to-default) measurement
bank lending in RAMs 48
Bank of England 209, 424
Bank of Spain 183
bank ownership 37
banking crisis (US, 1893) 208–9, 214
banking disruption, potential sources in move to EMU 44
banking fragility: fragility indicator 283–84
banking integration 281–304; bank fragility, co-movements in 301–2, 303; bank fragility, common macro-shocks, role of 301–2, 303; banking stability, challenges to 306–29; descriptive analysis, contemporaneous correlation analyses 288–89; descriptive analysis, correlation at leads and lags 290–91; descriptive analysis, dynamic correlations and cohesion 292–94; descriptive analysis, preliminary 288–94; dynamic factor model 295–300, 303; dynamic factor model, description 295–96; dynamic factor model, estimation procedure 296–96; dynamic factor model, results 297–300, 303; fragility indicator 283–84; sample of banks 285–86; *see also* cross-border bank integration
Banking Sector Stability Report, 2003 (Czech National Bank) 31–32
banking sector stress 111
banking stability: assessment of 115–17, 117–20; challenges to 306–29
banking supervision *see* supervision
banking system: architecture revision 337–53; borrower indebtedness 117; budgetary ratios 40–41; client welfare 324–25; consolidation and banking sector performance 323–27; cooperation between home and host authorities 338, 345–46; costs and logistics of cross-border banking 360; crisis situations, domestic and foreign banks' reactions 307–8; defaults and bank failures 48; delegation of supervisory powers 320; domestic consolidation, dominance of 314; efficiency of 325–27; foreign bank lending, effects of 307–8; foreign currency lending 118, 120; gatekeeper function for companies 322–23; geographical segmentation of institutions 341–43; home and host-country regulatory

sharing 358; home-country supervisory controls 310–11; identification of booms and busts 87; incentive conflicts 358–59; inter-country cooperation on insolvency 383–83; legislation and reporting requirements 316–17; lending fervour of banks 43; lending volatility 308; local currency, inability to borrow abroad in 43; loss compensation
316–17; market developments, adaptation to 351–52; market developments, impact on economic adjustment 20; market imperfections 111; monitoring by host countries 359, 364; monitoring function for investors 322; national-based market differences 310; objective functions of regulators, differences in 360–61; operating efficiency 325–26; opportunities of integration for less-developed financial countries 323; pace of cross-border penetration 361; patterns of boom-bust, similarities in 84; penetration of banks cross-border 355–56; post-merger gains 325; procyclicality of 406–8; profit efficiency 326–27; provision of services, cross-border 317–18; reopening of large banks, promptness in 388, 391–91; restructuring operations 316; role in cross-border bank integration 322–23; stability of, challenges to 306–29; synchronization of economic cycles 38; trends in cross-border linkages 312–13
Barker, K. 191n10
Barnes, Sebastian 190n1
Barro, R.J. and Sala-i-Martin, X. 31, 231
Barros, P.P. *et al.* 261
Barth, J. *et al.* 353n5
Basel Committee on Banking Supervision 404
Basel II Capital Accord 120, 159n9, 182, 328n7, 342–43, 352, 357, 399n32, 427n9
Bates, D.S. 59
Baunkjoer, C. 176
Bayoumi, T. and Eichengreen, B. 35
BEA (Bureau of Economic Analysis) 225–27
Bean, C. 427n11
Beck, T. and Levine, R. 328
Beck, T. *et al.* 327
Becker, S.O. and Hoffmann, M. 253
Begg, D. *et al.* 109n18
Begg, Ian 4–5, 31–53, viii
Bekaert, G., Hodrick, R.J. and Zhang, X. 273
Belgium 56, 59, 60, 62, 64, 80, 81n2, 124n8; banking integration progress 311–13; deposit insurance characteristics 365, 367, 368, 373; housing cycles, soft landings in 167; insolvency resolution 375; international risk sharing 245; mortgage market in 174; risk profile sensitivity to shock 274; short-term interest rates 163
Benalal, J. *et al.* 61
Benelux countries 311, 322
Berben, R.-P. *et al.* 59
Berger, A.N. 328n4
Berger, A.N. and DeYoung, R. 328n5
Berger, A.N. *et al.* 317, 324, 329n21
Bernanke, B. *et al.* 85
Berrigan, John 328n1
Bertrand, M. and Mullainathan, S. 329n37
Bikker, J.A. and Metzemakers, P.A.J. 183
BIS (Bank of International Settlements) 406, 420, 426n2, 426n3, 427n9
Black, F. and Scholes, M. 269, 270, 283
Blanchard, O. 57, 65, 69
Blanchard, O. and Fisher, S. 65, 69
Blanchard, O. and Giavazzi, F. 57, 62, 233, 235, 256
Blanchard-Yaari households 57; demographics and insurance markets 65–66; dynamics of the aggregate economy 68–69; habit formation in endowment economy 57–58, 65–75; numerical simulations for two-good economy 58, 75–79, 80–81; representative household intertemporal problem 66–68; single good with habits 71–72; single good without habits 69–71; traded and non-traded goods without habits 72–75
Bland-Allison Silver Purchase Act (US) 208
Blattner, Tobias 108n1
Bliss, R.R. and Kaufman, G.G. 395
Blomstrom, M., Lipsey, R.E. and Zejan, M. 222
Bollard, A. 358
Bonaccorsi di Patti, E. and Gobbi, G. 324
booms and busts, adjustment experiences 84–109; analysis of past boom-bust episodes 89–102; CEE (Central and East European) Member States 102–6; competitiveness and trade channel 91–92, 96–98, 101, 105; country choice and discussion parameters 87–89; credit transmission channel 85; current account developments 101; data and sources 107–8; domestic financial environment 90, 96, 100–101, 103–5; emerging markets, analysis of past boom-bust episodes 95–98; exchange rate developments 89–90; exchange rates, unit labour costs and real effective rates 92–93; external adjusters 84–85, 106; external adjusters, internal adjusters compared 87; financial policies, boom exacerbation through 86; fiscal balances 101–2; fiscal channel 86; fiscal developments 105; fiscal policies, role of 93; identification of booms and busts 87; industrial countries, analysis of past boom-bust episodes 89–95; inflation performance 90–91; internal adjusters 84–85,

106; internal adjusters, external adjusters compared 87; international capital flows, boom exacerbation through 86; international financial channel 86, 93, 98, 105; international trade vulnerability 101; Netherlands, analysis of recent boom-bust episodes 98–102; patterns of boom-bust, similarities in 84; Portugal, analysis of recent boom-bust episodes 98–102; public debt 93–94; public finances, developments in 98; real economic environment 90; real economic growth of CEE 102–3; real effective exchange rate in CEE 102–3; sectoral channels, interlinkages between 86–87; South-East Asia, analysis of past boom-bust episodes 95–98; statistical tests, evidence from 94–95; stylized facts (and shortcomings of) 84, 85, 88, 89, 94, 99, 105, 106, 107; trade channel 85–86, 91–92, 96–98, 101, 105; transmission channels 85–87; triangular methodology 108n5; variable choice and discussion parameters 87–89
Boot, A.W.A. 315
Bordo, M. *et al.* 418
Bordo, M.D. and Jeanne, O. 85, 87
Borghijs, A. and Kuijs, L. 42
Borio, C. and Crockett, A. 409, 427n10
Borio, C. and Filardo, A. 410, 411, 424
Borio, C. and Lowe, P. 120, 409–10, 411, 413, 414, 415, 416, 417, 421, 424
Borio, C. and McGuire, P. 425
Borio, C. and Tsatsaronis, K. 420, 421, 426
Borio, C. and White, W.R. 424, 425
Borio, C. *et al.* 406, 410, 412, 419, 421, 425
Borio, C., Kennedy, N. and Prowse, S.D. 87
Borio, Claudio 7, 16–17, 85, 182, 404–27, viii
borrower indebtedness 117
Bosnia-Herzegovina 114, 120, 122
Brada, J.C. *et al.* 38–39, 47
Braga, Fabio 303n1
Brasili, Andrea 13–14, 281–304, viii
Brazil 124n8
Bretton Woods 410, 411
Breuer, Rolf 347–48
Broadbent, B. *et al.* 137, 159n9
Brouwer, H. *et al.* 42
BSI (Banking System Indicator) 117–20
Buch, C.M. and DeLong, G.L. 328n15
budgetary ratios 40–41
Bulgaria 102, 109n17, 113, 120, 121, 122
Bulíř, A. and Šmidková, K. 46
Bundesbank 47

Cabral, I. *et al.* 283, 295, 328n10
Calvo, G.A. *et al.* 86, 87
Camacho, M. and Sancho, I. 304n8
Campbell, J. and Cochrane, J. 58
Canada 89, 124n8; Bank of Canada QPM 184; housing wealth effects 171, 172–173; international risk sharing 245; taxation of residential property 177
capital flows 222–41; BEA (Bureau of Economic Analysis) 225–27; capital-abundant regions 223; catch-up growth 223–24, 233–34; Cobb-Douglas production function 224, 225; country-level data, deviations in 222; current account, growth and 225; entry costs and 224, 238, 240; equilibrium level, adjustment to 225; EU patterns 222–23; farming advantages 223; Feldstein-Horioka correlation 235; inflows 45; institutions and 237–40; marginal product of capital 222; MPK (capital stock/marginal product relation) 224; patterns in US of 222–23; productivity and 222; SPI (state-level personal income) 227; US-EU comparison 224–37; US-EU comparison, EU results 232–37; US-EU comparison, model 224–25; US-EU comparison, US results 225–31; US patterns 222–23
capital insufficiency in CEE 118
capital market linkages in housing 170
Caprio, G. and Klingebiel, D. 87, 95
Caprio, G. *et al.* 397n3
Cardenas, J. *et al.* 384
Carroll, C., Overland, J. and Weil, D. 58, 67
Caselli, F. and Coleman, W.J. 223, 231
Caselli, F. and Feyrer, J. 222
Caselli, F. and Tenreyro, S. 38, 235
Casolaro, L. *et al.* 174
Catarineu-Rabell, E. *et al.* 427n9
catch-up growth 223–24, 233–34
Catte, P. *et al.* 171, 172, 176
Catte, Pietro 190n1
CEBS (Committee of European Banking Supervisors) 353n7
CEE (Central and East European) Member States 33, 40, 42, 84, 85, 87, 95, 98, 108n2, 120, 121, 122, 123, 235; booms and busts, adjustment experiences 102–6; financial sector transformation 112; foreign bank entry into 307
CEIOPS (Committee of European Insurance and Occupational Pension Supervisors) 353n7
central authority and regional interest rates 200–207
Central Bank of Ireland Quarterly Bulletin 80
central banks and booms in house prices 180
Chan, N. *et al.* 96
Chile 124n7, 124n8
China 419
Chiuri, M.C. and Jappelli, T. 175
Christiano, L., Eichenbaum, M. and Evans, C. 82n13

Christophe, André 190n1
Cihak, M. and Holub, T. 42
CIS-3 (Kazakhstan, Russia, Ukraine) 111, 115, 120, 121, 123; financial sector transformation 112
Civil War (US, 1861–65) 207
Claessens, S. *et al.* 309, 328n13
Clark, G. and Feenstra, R. 222
Clarke, G. *et al.* 308
Cobb-Douglas production function 66, 224, 225, 326
Cochrane, J.H. 257n3
Coconuts (Marx Brothers movie) 211
competitiveness: exposure to (demand) 135; fostering of 308–9; and interest rate channels 162–170; and interest rate channels, illustrative simulation 187–188; and interest rate channels, model simulations of 168–170; trade channel competitiveness 91–92, 96–98, 101, 105
concentration risks 120
construction employment 45
consumer debt 37
consumption risk sharing: globalization and 242, 245–50; measurement of 243–45
consumption-smoothing 20, 22–23
convergence: 'convergence boom' 34; cooperation between home and host authorities 338, 345–46; cross-country convergence 262; intra-country convergence 37; money prices and bond markets 261–62; new members as optimum currency area candidates 35–36, 50–51; nominal and real convergence, challenges of 23–24; nominal convergence 58–65, 79–80; nominal convergence criteria 31; policy rethinking for stage 3 adjustment 43–46; prior adjustment in stage 2 39–42; real convergence experience 23–24; towards reality in transition within EMU 38–39, 51–52
Corker, Bob 278n1
Corvoisier, S. and Gropp, R. 328n10
costs and benefits, debate on 32–33, 47
costs and risks of financial supervision 350–51
Cottarelli, C. *et al.* 48, 109n16, 111, 113–14
country-specific development 21
Cournède, B. *et al.* 169
CPI (consumer price index) 87; CPI-based REER (real effective exchange rate) 84, 89, 95–96, 99, 101, 102
CRD (Capital Requirements Directive) 345–46
credit and asset prices, booms and busts in 412
credit growth: household debt and 61, 64, 79–80; rapidity in CEE 111, 114
credit-induced effects on stability 48
credit loss, estimation and allocation of 387, 390–90
Credit Lyonnais 398n10
credit prices 20
credit transmission 85
crisis management 349
Croatia 111, 113, 114, 120, 121, 122
Crockett, A. 420
cross-border bank integration: CEE, foreign bank entry into 307; client welfare 324–25; competition, fostering of 308–9; consequences of 306; consolidation and banking sector performance 323–27; crisis situations, domestic and foreign banks' reactions 307–8; cultural and political preferences 315; delegation of supervisory powers 320; domestic consolidation, dominance of 314; double taxation treaties, shortcomings in 317; efficiency of banking system 325–27; emergency liquidity assistance 319; EU-10 and EU-15 linkages 321; EU-15 consolidation hold-ups 313–17; EU-10 progress towards 317–18; EU consolidation and 313–18; EU perspective on 306–7, 309–13; EU supervision 318–20; EU supervision, current arrangement 318–20; EU supervision, proposals for improvement 320; exchange rate risk 310; facilitating factors in EU 309–11; finance-growth nexus 327–28; foreign bank lending effects of 307–8; gatekeeper function for companies 322–23; globalization 309; growth, economic performance and 322–28; home-country supervisory controls 310–11; income flows between associated companies 316; inward investment, restrictions on 316; legislation and reporting requirements 316–17; lending volatility 308; loss compensation 316–17; macro-financial stability, effects of 307–9; macro-financial stability, importance of 306; macroeconomic stability issues 320–22; mergers and acquisitions 306, 313, 314, 315, 316, 318, 326, 328n14, 328n15; monitoring function for investors 322; national-based market differences 310; operating efficiency of banking system 325–26; opportunity for less-developed financial countries 323; political resistance to foreign-bank entry 315–16; post-merger gains for banking system 325; profit efficiency in banking system 326–27; progress to date in EU 311–13; provision of services 317–18; regulatory reform 310; restructuring operations 316; risk considerations, macroeconomic stability 320–22; role of banking system 322–23; single banking licenses 310; special banking models 328–29n17; stability challenges linked to 318–22; subsidiaries, establishment of 311; supervision authority, constitution of single

authority 320; tax-related barriers 316–17; technological innovation 309–10; transfer price calculation 317; trends in cross-border linkages 312–13; US interstate consolidation 307; weak links within EU-15, risks related to 321–22
cross-border banking, problems and solutions: accounting rules on insolvency 384; agency problems and conflicts 358–61; Basel II 357, 399n32; challenges for 355–400; costs and logistics 360; credit losses, promptness in estimation and allocation of 387, 390–90; cross-border branching, problem of 359; cross-border branching, solution to problem of 393–94, 395–95; deposit guarantee system 357–58; deposit insurance 361–74, 383, 385; deposit insurance, payout coordination problems 385–85; deposit insurance, solutions to problems of 386–92, 395–95; DGD (Deposit Guarantee Schemes Directive) 361–63; ECB (European Central Bank) 357; EU deposit guarantee system 357–58; EU financial regulatory system 357–58; financial regulatory system 357–58; harmonization, requirements for 357; home and host-country regulatory sharing 358; incentive conflicts 358–59; incentives of regulators, differences in 360–61; information access, problem of 359–60; insolvency resolution 374–84; insurance system design, discretionary differences in 363; inter-country cooperation on insolvency 383–83; legal closure, promptness in 387, 388–89; Maastricht Treaty 357; monitoring by host countries 359, 364; objective functions of regulators, differences in 360–61; pace of cross-border penetration 361; payout coordination problems, deposit insurance 385–85; PCA (prompt corrective action) 390, 392, 393, 394, 395; penetration of banks cross-border 355–56; prudential regulation on insolvency 384–84; prudential standards, establishment of 357; re-privatization and re-capitalization, promptness in 388, 392–92; regulatory competition, likelihood of 357–58; regulatory compliance, uncertainty in 358; reopening of large banks, promptness in 388, 391–91; SEIR (structures early intervention and resolution) 394
cross-border externalities, growth in 339–42
cross-border penetration of financial supervision 340–41, 342, 344
cross-border supervision arrangements in housing 179–182
cross-country convergence 262
Croux, C., Forni, M. and Reichlin, L. 292, 304n5
Crucini, M. 244, 246
Crystal, J.S. *et al.* 307
cultural preferences 315
currency mismatch 43
current account: deficits in 63, 64, 79–80; developments in 101; growth and capital flows 225; imbalances in 131–132; trends 20, 21
Cyprus 32, 53n1, 81n3, 109n12, 120, 121, 122; deposit insurance characteristics 365, 367, 370, 373; foreign banking penetration in 361; foreign-owned banks in 313; insolvency resolution 378
Czech National Bank 31–32, 47
Czech Republic 32, 37, 40, 45, 46, 48, 49, 51, 81n3, 102, 113, 119, 122, 123; deposit insurance characteristics 365, 367, 371, 373; foreign-owned banks in 313; insolvency resolution 379

Dale, R. 362
Danmarks Nationalbank 399n34
Datastream Europe 274, 279n9
Davis, P. and Zhu, H.B. 412
DD (distance-to-default) 268–74, 279n8, 282, 284–84, 288–300, 301–2, 303, 304n2
De Angelis, Lucio 304n1
De Grauwe, P. and Mongelli, F.P. 34–35
De Haas, R. and Van Lelyveld, I. 307, 308
De Nicolò, G. and Kwast, M. 261, 282
De Nicolò, G. *et al.* 261
De Nicoló, G., Hayward, P. and Vir Bhatia, A. 270
De Nicolò, Gianni 12–13, 261–79, 281, 282, viii–ix
debt intolerance 43
defaults and bank failures 48
Dell'Ariccia, G. and Marquez, R. 397n2
demand deposits 118
Demirgüc-Kunt, A. *et al.* 399n44
Denmark 32, 121n8; banking integration progress 311–13; deposit insurance characteristics 365, 367, 368, 373; housing policies 162; housing supply elasticities and constraints 179; insolvency resolution 375; international risk sharing 245; mortgage market in 172
deposit concentration 118
deposit guarantee system 357–58
deposit insurance 361–74, 383, 385; payout coordination problems 385–85; proposed solutions to problems of 386–92, 395–95; systems in United States 396–96
Dermine, Jean 314, 344, 399n30
Deroose, S. *et al.* 190n2
descriptive analysis of integration 288–94; contemporaneous correlation analyses

288–89; correlation at leads and lags 290–91; dynamic correlations and cohesion 292–94
Detken, C. and Smets, F. 87
Deutsche Bank 285
DeYoung, R. and Whalen, G. 324
DG ECFIN (Directorate General fir Economic and Financial Affairs) 3, 19, 108n1, 136, 158n1, 240n1, 257n1, 278n1, 303–4n1, 328n15
DGD (Deposit Guarantee Schemes Directive) 361–63
Di Giorgio, D. 398n7
Dickey, D.A. and Fuller, W.A. 202
diversification opportunities 261
Djankov, S. *et al.* 240
Dobson, W. and Hufbauer, G.C. 182
Dodge, D. 427n11
domestic credit 47
domestic financial environment 90, 96, 100–101, 103–5
double taxation treaties, shortcomings in 317
Drew, A. *et al.* 169
Drzik, John 343
DSGE (dynamic stochastic general equilibrium) model 8, 20–21, 23, 127, 132–135, 138, 141, 144, 147, 150, 153, 158n5
Duan, J.-C., Gauthier, G. and Simonato, J.-G. 270
Duval, R. *et al.* 169
dynamic factor model 295–300, 303, 304n7; banking integration 295–300, 303; description of 295–96; estimation procedure for 296–96; results of running 297–300, 303

EBRD (European Bank for Reconstruction and Development) 114, 120, 121, 122
ECB (European Central Bank) 36, 47–49, 53n4, 61, 63, 81n1, 109n15, 181, 303, 351, 384; Convergence Reports 109n19; cross-border banking, problems and solutions 357; establishment of 357–58; financial supervision in Europe 351; monetary analysis of 425; Statistics Pocketbook 45; systemic risk, trends in 270
Ecofin Council 345–46, 349
econometrics: financial stability, emerging Europe and CIS-3 114–15; regional interest rates 202–9
economic activity: evolution of 39; history of financial market integration 19; monetary union, economic perspective on 39–40; real economic environment 90; real economic growth of CEE 102–3; structural change in geometry of 45
Economic and Financial Committee 337
economic integration and financial stability 261–79; convergence, money prices and bond markets 261–62; countervailing effects on stability 261; cross-country convergence 262; diversification opportunities 261; environment, structural change in 261; equity market integration 266–68, 276; real activity, synchronization of 262–66, 276; systemic risk and integration 268–76; systemic risk and integration, convergence of measures 270–73; systemic risk and integration, measures of systemic risk 268–70; systemic risk and integration, sensitivity of measures to real and financial shock 273–76; systemic risk and integration, trends in systemic risk 270; total assets, banking and insurance 277–78
ECSC (European Coal and Steel Community) 351
educational effort, need for 426
EFA (European Financial Agency) 338, 347, 352
EFR (European Financial Services), Round Table on 347, 348–49, 353n7, 353n9
Eichengreen, B. 36, 54n6
Eichengreen, B. and Choudhry, O. 86
Eichengreen, B. *et al.* 43
Eisenbeis, R.A. and Kaufman, G.G. 191n13
Eisenbeis, Robert A. 16, 355–400, ix
Ekinci, M. *et al.* 222, 240
Ekinci, M., Kalemli-Ozcan, S. and Sørensen, B. E. 236–37
El-Khoury, Marianne 278n1
Elliot, G. *et al.* 202
Els, P.J.A. van *et al.* 159n19
emergency liquidity assistance 319
emerging markets, analysis of boom-bust episodes 95–98
EMI (European Monetary Institute) 351
Emiris, M. 282
entry costs and capital flows 224, 238, 240
equilibrium level, capital flow adjustment to 225; *see also* DGSE
equity market integration 266–68, 276
Erlandsen, E. *et al.* 179
ERM II 42, 46, 102
ESCB (European System of Central Banks) 181, 349
Eschenbach, F. and Schuknecht, L. 94, 179
ESFS (European System of Financial Supervisors) 337, 338, 345, 347–51, 352
Estonia 35, 42, 48, 81n3, 102, 113, 121; deposit insurance characteristics 366, 367, 371, 374; foreign banking penetration in 361; foreign-owned banks in 313; insolvency resolution 379
European Banking Congress, Frankfurt 36
European Commission 20, 24, 81n1, 109n14, 115, 136, 158n1, 310–11, 328n10
European Competition Network 351

European Economic Area (EEA) 313–14
European Mortgage Federation 174
European Securities Regulators, Committee of 337
European Union (EU): Banking Directive (1988) 357; banking supervision 318–20; banking supervision, current arrangement 318–20; banking supervision, proposals for improvement 320; capital flows, EU patterns 222–23; Council of Economic and Financial Affairs 363; CRD (Capital Requirements Directive) 345–46; cross-border bank integration, EU consolidation and 313–18; cross-border bank integration, EU perspective 306–7, 309–13; cross-border banking 355–400; cross-border banking regulatory structure 356–57, 357–58; deposit guarantee system 357–58; *Economy Review* 20, 23; EU-10 14, 308, 313, 314, 315, 319–20, 322, 323, 324, 325, 358; EU-10, EU-15 linkages 323; EU-10, progress towards cross-border bank integration 319–20; EU-15 7, 13, 14; EU-15, banking integration and co-movements of banks 283, 287, 303–4, 305; EU-15, challenges to banking stability 308, 313, 314, 315–20, 322, 323, 324, 325; EU-15, consolidation within, hold-ups in 315–19; EU-15, cross-border banking 358; EU-15, diversification benefits 272; EU-15, economic integration and financial stability 272; EU-15, financial stability in emerging Europe 115, 116; EU-15, financial supervision 341, 343, 348; EU-15, international risk sharing 247, 248, 253, 254; EU-15, transition to full EMU participation 31, 32, 35, 37, 39, 45, 48, 49, 50; EU-15, weak links within, risks related to 323–24; facilitating factors in EU cross-border bank integration 311–13; Financial Conglomerates, Directive on 341; financial regulatory system 359–60; GDP of 316, 320, 329; insolvency resolution (Directive 2001/24/EC) 376; integration progress to date 313–15; internal market promotion 312; MoUs (Memoranda of Understanding) 183, 360, 363, 402n47; participation in union, consequences of 56; Single Market Programme 311; Structural Funds 45; US-EU comparison on capital flows 226–39; US-EU comparison on capital flows, EU results 234–39; US-EU comparison on capital flows, model of 226–27
Eurostat 39, 45, 165, 183; Comparative Consumer Price Level dataset 63, 80; *Euro Indicators* 51; Structural Indicators 40
Eurosystem 81n1, 184, 191n7; ESBC model 184; Monetary Transmission Network 191n7
exchange rates: as adjustment instrument 41–42; appreciation in real rate 63–64, 79–80; developments in 89–90; exchange rate premium 21; exchange risk 310; exchange risk premia 132; real effective exchange rate in CEE 102–3; unit labour costs and real effective rates 92–93; value on entry to EMU 46
expectations, role in housing market 188–189
external adjusters 84–85, 106; internal adjusters compared 87
external debt 47
external shocks from global conditions 21–22

F-tests (variance) 94, 108n10
Fagan, G. and Gaspar, V. 56–57, 108n4, 128
Fagan, Gabriel 5–6, 56–82, ix
Fama, E. and French, K. 282
Favero, C. *et al.* 59
FDI (foreign direct investment) 89, 105
FDIA (Federal Deposit Insurance Act, US) 399n37
FDIC (Federal Deposit Insurance Corporation, US) 374–84, 386, 390, 391, 392, 393
FDICIA (Federal Deposit Insurance Corporation Improvement Act, US) 389–89
Federal Deposit Insurance (US) 215
Federal Reserve (US) 180; period (1914–43) 210–12, 214–15, 217; period (1955–2002) 212–14, 215, 218–19; reserve system, establishment of 209, 210
Feldstein, M. and Horioka, C. 256
Feldstein-Horioka correlation 62, 235
Fernández de Lis, S. *et al.* 183
Feynman, Richard 404, 425
Fidrmuc, J. and Korhonen, I. 35
Filardo, A. 425, 427n12
Filardo, A. and Gordon, S.F. 415
finance-growth nexus 327–28
Financial Conglomerates, Directive on 339
financial environment, structural change in 261
financial imbalances: build-up of 408, 409, 423, 427n7; build up of, in low inflation environments 417–19; instability and 412–15; likelihood of 427n7; output weakness and disinflation 415–17
financial intermediation 48
financial landscape, trends in 337–38, 351–52
financial liberalization 406–8, 427n7; key process 406
financial market integration 19–26; asset markets 20, 21; banking supervision 24; benefits of, realization of full benefits 19–20, 23–24, 24–26; consumption-smoothing 20, 22–23; country-specific development 21; credit prices 20; current account trends 20, 21; DSGE (dynamic general equilibrium)

model 8, 20–21, 23; economic history 19; euro, adjustment in euro area 20; euro, messages of first decade 26; exchange rate premium 21; external shocks from global conditions 21–22; financial policies, boom exacerbation through 86; financial sector policies 25; Financial Services Action Plan 19, 20, 25; financial supervision in Europe 337; fiscal analysis 24–25; fiscal policy 24; growth, differences in 20, 21; growth, fostering of 19; housing demand 21; importance of 20; inflation, differences in 20, 21; labour markets 25; Lisbon Strategy 25; macroeconomic change, markets as drivers 20–22; market developments, impact on economic adjustment 20; migration 21; mortgage market integration 20; nominal and real convergence, challenges of 23–24; official policies, interaction with markets 19; product markets 25; public finances, management of 25; *Public Finances in EMU* (European Commission) 24; real convergence experience 23–24; risk premia 21, 24; risk-sharing 20, 22–23; Stability and Growth Pact 24–25; stabilizing role of 22–23; transition within EMU 37; US monetary union 19, 22

financial regime, role of 404–5, 406–8

financial regulatory systems 357–58; incentives of regulators, differences in 360–61

financial sector: dramatic transformation in CEE 111; policies for financial market integration 25; in RAMs 47–50, 52

financial services, spatial concentration of 45

Financial Services Action Plan 19, 20, 25, 170, 340, 352

Financial Services Committee 337, 349

financial stability 337; countervailing effects on 261; crucial nature of 31–32, 50; historical perspective on stability 410–12; links to real convergence from 42–43; monetary transmission and stabilization 46–47; salience of 36–37, 51

financial stability, economic integration and 261–79; convergence, money prices and bond markets 261–62; countervailing effects on stability 261; cross-country convergence 262; diversification opportunities 261; environment, structural change in 261; equity market integration 266–68, 276; real activity, synchronization of 262–66, 276; systemic risk and integration 268–76; systemic risk and integration, convergence of measures 270–73; systemic risk and integration, measures of systemic risk 268–70; systemic risk and integration, sensitivity of measures to real and financial shock 273–76; systemic risk and integration, trends in systemic risk 270; total assets, banking and insurance 277–78

financial stability, emerging Europe and CIS-3 112–25; banking sector stability, assessment of 116–18, 118–21; banking sector stress 112; borrower indebtedness 118; BSI (Banking System Indicator) 118–21; capital insufficiency 119; concentration risks 121; credit growth, rapidity in 112, 115; demand deposits 119; deposit concentration 119; econometric evidence 114–15; financial sector, dramatic transformation in 112; fiscal performance 116; foreign currency lending 119, 121; historical experience, lessons from 115–16; inter-bank positions 118; lending concentration 119; liquidity 119; market imperfections 112; MPI (Macro-prudential Indicator) 121–22; off-balance sheet weakness 119; policy implications 121; regulatory transparency 119, 121; SAIR (System Average Individual Rating) 118, 121; sovereign exposure 119, 121; systemic risk 112; systemic risk matrix 122–23

financial supervision in Europe: accountability 349; architecture revision for 337–53; Basel II (Capital Requirements Directive) 342–43, 352; cooperation between home and host authorities 338, 347 – 8; costs and risks 350–51; crisis management 349; cross-border externalities, growth in 339–42; cross-border penetration 340–41, 342, 344; ECB (European Central Bank) 351; EFA (European Financial Agency) 338, 347, 352; effectiveness of arrangements for 344; efficiency in supervision 344, 346, 347, 348–49; efficiency in supervision, home-country control and 339; EFR (European Financial Services), Round Table on 347, 348–49, 353n7, 353n9; EMI (European Monetary Institute) 351; ESFS (European System of Financial Supervisors) 337, 338, 345, 347–51, 352; evolutionary option 351; financial landscape, trends in 337–38, 351–52; financial market integration 337; Financial Services Action Plan 340, 352; financial stability 337; financial supervision, effectiveness of arrangements for 344; financial supervision, trilemma in 337–38; fiscal burden sharing 351; geographical segmentation of institutions 341–43; harmonization, consistency in application of rules for 344–45, 349; IAS (International Accounting Standards) 350; incompatible objectives 337; industry developments 339–42; Insurance Directives (Solvency II) 339, 343, 352; Italian experience 348; lead supervision of cross-border groups 338, 345, 347, 348–49; macroeconomic policy, trilemma in 337–38; market developments,

adaptation to 351–52; national monetary policy, independence in 337; policy options, future possibilities 344–51, 351–52; prudential supervision 348; risk and capital management, centralization of 343–44; risk management functions, integration of 342–44; Single Financial Market 344–45; supervisory arrangements, current setup 338–39; trilemma in 337–38
Finland 36, 44, 56, 81n2, 81n5, 89, 93–94, 95, 124n8; banking integration progress 311–13; credit losses 191n11; deposit insurance characteristics 365, 367, 368, 373; housing cycles, soft landings in 167; housing policies 162; housing supply elasticities and constraints 179; insolvency resolution 375; international risk sharing 245; monetary transmission mechanisms 170; mortgage market in 172; short-term interest rates 163
fiscal adjustment 41
fiscal analysis 24–25
fiscal balances 101–2
fiscal burden sharing 351
fiscal channels 86
fiscal consolidation 34
fiscal developments 105
fiscal performance 115
fiscal policies: financial market integration and 24; role of 93
fiscal rules, conformity with 46
Fitch Ratings 112, 115, 117, 119–20, 122
Flannery, Mark 342
Flood, Bob 278n1
Flood, R. and Rose, A. 262, 266
Florida land boom 211, 214, 215
Focarelli, D. and Panetta, F. 324
foreign currency lending 118, 120
Forni, M. 304n8
Forni, M. and Reichlin, L. 281, 295–95
Forni, M. *et al.* 282, 304n8
Fox, Richard 7–8, 111–24, ix
France 38–39, 45, 56, 59, 60, 62, 64, 80, 81n2, 89, 90, 124n8, 152; banking integration progress 311–13; cross-border externalities 339; deposit insurance, coverage in 364; deposit insurance characteristics 365, 367, 368, 373; housing wealth effects 171, 172–173; insolvency resolution 375; international risk sharing 245; mortgage market in 171, 172, 174; risk profile sensitivity to shock 274; short-term interest rates 163
Fratzscher, Marcel 108n1
Frazer, W. and Guthrie, J.J. 211
FRB-US macroeconomic model 184
Freixas, Xavier 346
Frenkel, J. and Razin, A. 81n7
Frenkel, M. and Nickel, C. 51
Friedman, M. and Schwartz, A.J. 208–9, 212, 220n9
Friedman, Milton 212
Fries, S. and Taci, A. 50
FSLIC (Federal Savings and Loan Insurance Corporation, US) 397

GAAP (General Accepted Accounting Principles, US) 326
Galati, G. and Tsatsaronis, K. 281
Garcia, G.H. and Nieto, M.J. 362, 400n51
Gaspar, Vitor 5–6, 56–82, ix
GDP (gross domestic product) 225, 351, 397; average growth in 100; bank claims, ratio of 323; bank credit, GDP ratio to 47–48; bank credit ratio to 47–48; capital inflows as proportion of 98; current account balance *versus* per capita GDP 131–132, 133; current account deficits as proportion of 96–98, 105; debt ratios as proportion of 90, 93–94; deflator minus euro-area average 129; domestic credit as proportion of 111; EU GDP 314, 318, 327; export/GDP ratios 92–93, 94; foreign asset ratio to 63, 77–79, 80; gross foreign assets relative to 257n7; growth differentials 62–63, 64, 79–80; growth in Germany 138, 139, 156; growth in Ireland 140, 142; growth in Italy 142, 143, 145; growth in Netherlands 145, 146, 148; growth in Portugal 148, 149, 151; growth in Spain 151, 152, 154, 156; growth in US 308; housing investment as share of 61, 165; primary activities reflected in 45; private sector credit as share of 113, 120, 121; ratio of credit to 406, 412, 413; shares of ‘cohesion’ countries 45; taxation as share of 177; trade relative to 187; trend growth in nominal GDP 41; US GDP growth 308; volatility in 37; weightings 35–36
geographical segmentation of institutions 341–43
Gerlach, S. and Smets, F. 409
Germany 21, 35, 38–39, 44, 45, 56, 58, 59, 60, 62, 64, 80, 81n2, 119, 124n8, 128, 129, 130, 131, 133, 135, 136, 159n10, 159n11; adjustment scenario for 154, 156–157; adjustment simulation results 137–139; banking integration progress 311–13; cross-border externalities 339; demand and supply shocks 136–137; deposit insurance, coverage in 364; deposit insurance characteristics 365, 367, 369, 373; DSGE results for 138; foreign banking penetration in 361; housing wealth effects 171, 172–173; insolvency resolution 375; international risk sharing 245; mortgage market in 171, 172; risk profile sensitivity to shock 274; short-term interest rates 163;

stylized facts 136; summing up on adjustment exercise 139
Gertler, M. and Rogoff, K. 222
GGDC (Groningen Growth and Development Centre) 136
Giannini, C. 410
Girouard, N. and Blondal, S. 191n8
Girouard, N. *et al.* 164, 191n3
Girouard, Nathalie 190n1
Giuliodori, M. 191n7
Gjedrem, S. 427n11
Glaeser, E. *et al.* 191n10
Global Financial System, Committee on the 359, 397n3, 422
globalization 309; and international risk sharing 245–50
Gold Standard 410, 411, 412, 427n8
Goldberg, L. 308, 397n3
Goldberg, L. *et al.* 307
Golinelli, R. and Ravelli, R. 38
Goodhart, C.A.E. and De Largy, P. 410, 412
Goodhart, C.A.E. and Schoenmaker, D. 351, 386, 398n15
Goodhart, C.A.E., Schoenmaker, D. and Dasgupta, P. 353n6
Goodhart, Charles A.E. 53n2, 397n3, 399n30
Gourinchas, P. and Jeanne, O. 222
Great Contraction (US, 1929–32) 211–12, 214
Great Depression 53n6, 210, 215, 410
Great Inflation 404, 411
Greece 31, 45, 56, 57, 58, 59, 81n2, 81n6, 113, 114–15, 116, 124n8; banking integration progress 311–13; current account deficit 233–34; deposit insurance characteristics 365, 367, 369, 373; insolvency resolution 375; international risk sharing 245; risk profile sensitivity to shock 274; short-term interest rates 163
Green, R.K. and Wachter, S. 174
Greenfield, R. and Rockoff, H. 207
Greenspan, A. 427n9
Gropp, R.E. *et al.* 278n6, 281, 282, 283, 284
growth: capital flows and 225; catch-up growth 223–24, 233–34; in cross-border externalities 339–42; differences in 20, 21; economic performance and 322–28; finance-growth nexus 327–28; fostering of 19; real economic growth of CEE 102–3; in TFP 21, 136, 139, 140, 142, 143, 145, 149, 154, 156, 236
Gruber, J. 58
Guiso, L. *et al.* 317, 323
Gulde, A. and Wolff, H.C. 191n13, 358, 398n8

Hallett, M. 41
Hallin, M. 304n8
Hansen, J. and Roeger, W. 159n8
Harding, D. and Pagan, A. 108n5
harmonization: consistency in application of rules 344–45, 349; requirements for 357
Hartmann, P. *et al.* 270, 281, 328–29n17, 340
Hartmann, P., Straetmans, S. and de Vries, C. 270
Hartmann, Philipp 350–51
Hau, H. and Rey, H. 257
Hawkesby, C., Marsh, I. and Stevens, I. 282
Haynes, M. and Thompson, S. 326
Heid, F. *et al.* 54n7
Henley, A. and Morley, B. 191n8
Herring, R. and Litan, L. 338
Herstadt Bank 398n18
Hess, G.D. and Shin, K. 244
Heston, A., Summers,R. and Aten, B. 245
HICP (Harmonized Index of Consumer Prices) 54n9, 80
Hilbers, P. *et al.* 124n10
historical experience, lessons from 114–15
historical perspective on stability 410–12
Hoeller, P. *et al.* 162
Hoeller, Peter 9–10, 161–191, ix
Hoffmann, Mathias 11–12, 242–57, ix–x
Hofmann, B. 412
Hong Kong 95, 96, 98, 108n9, 108n10, 124n8
Honohan, P. and Klingebiel, D. 87, 95
households: debt and expenditure 56–57; expenditures 61, 64, 79–80; in standard macro models 158n6
housing markets, adjustment and 161–191; bank provisioning, pro-cyclical tendency of 182–183, 191n14; capital market linkages 170; central banks and booms in house prices 180; competitiveness and interest rate channels 162–170; competitiveness and interest rate channels, illustrative simulation 187–188; competitiveness and interest rate channels, model simulations of 168–170; cross-border supervision arrangements 179–182; expectations, role of, illustrative simulation 188–189; housing cycles, soft landings in 167; housing demand and financial market integration 21; housing wealth effects 171, 172–173; integration, deepness of 169, 170; Italian mortgage market, small size of 174–175; labour market flexibility 169; monetary transmission mechanisms 170; OECD recommendations 183–184; price developments 130–131; product market flexibility 169; prudential supervision issues 179–183; resilience, housing market as source of 170–183; small country in monetary union, model of 184–187; soft landings? 167; supply elasticities and constraints 179; tax incentives 175–177; trade intensity 170; wealth, influence of, illustrative simulation 189–190; zoning regulations 177–179

Houston, J.F. and Stiroh, K.J. 270
Hsieh, G. and Klenow, P. 222
Huefner, Felix 190n1
Hughes, J.P. *et al.* 307, 325
Huizinga, H. and Nicodeme, G. 363
Huizinga, H.P. *et al.* 325
Hungary 32, 35, 37, 40, 45, 46, 48, 51, 81n3, 102, 111, 113, 120, 121, 123; deposit insurance characteristics 366, 367, 371, 374; foreign-owned banks in 313; insolvency resolution 381
Hüpkes, E. 374

Iacoviello, M. 191n8
IAS (International Accounting Standards) 329n25, 350
Iceland 314; international risk sharing 245
ICRG *(International Country Risk Guide)* 240
IFS (international financial system) 309
Imbs, Jean 248
IMF (International Monetary Fund) 108n7, 111, 278n1, 351; IMF-World Bank Financial Sector Assessment Programmes 180–181
impulse response functions 204, 216, 217, 218–19
income flows between associated companies 316
Indonesia 36, 54n6, 124n8
industrial countries, analysis of boom-bust episodes 89–95
industrial structure differences 158n7
inflation: anti-inflationary commitment 408–9, 423; differentials in 20, 21, 128–129; dispersion of 129–130; inflationary processes, stability in 408–9; performance on 90–91; targeting of 37–38
information access, problem of 359–60
insolvency resolution 374–84; Directive 2001/24/EC 374
institutions and capital flows 237–40
Insurance Directives (Solvency II) 339, 343, 352
insurance system design, discretionary differences in 363
integration and risk sharing 242–57; *see also* banking integration; cross-border banking integration; financial market integration; financial stability, economic integration and
inter-bank positions in CEE 117
interest rates: competitiveness and interest rate channels 162–170; competitiveness and interest rate channels, illustrative simulation 187–188; competitiveness and interest rate channels, model simulations of 168–170; convergence of 56–57; convergence of, impact of 58–65, 79–80; decisions on 36; sensitivity to interest rate shocks 50
internal adjusters 84–85, 106; external adjusters compared 87
international capital flows, boom exacerbation through 86
international financial channels 86, 93, 98, 105
International Financial Reporting Standards 384
international risk sharing 242–57; data on 245; determinants of patterns 253–56; globalization and 245–50; increase in 242–43, 245–50, 256–57; patterns of 250–56
international trade vulnerability 101
interstate consolidation, US cross-border bank integration 307
intra-country convergence 37
intra-euro area trade 45
intra-state and interstate branch banking, US lifting of restrictions on 215
investment: composition of investment (costs) 134–135; inward investment, restrictions on 316; non-housing investment 61–62, 64, 79–80
IPG (industrial production growth) 262–66, 267, 278n3
Ireland 21, 31, 40, 44, 45, 56, 59, 60, 62, 64, 80, 81n2, 113, 114–15, 116, 124n8, 128, 135, 136, 159n12; adjustment simulation results 140–142; banking integration progress 311–13; demand and supply shocks 140; deposit insurance characteristics 365, 367, 369, 373; DSGE results for 141; housing policies 162; insolvency resolution 376; international risk sharing 245; mortgage market in 172; risk profile sensitivity to shock 274; short-term interest rates 163; stylized facts 139–140; summing up on adjustment exercise 142
Issing, O. 37, 46–47, 50, 425, 427n11
IT (inflation targeting) 37
Italy 21, 44, 46, 56, 59, 60, 62, 64, 80, 81n2, 89, 124n8, 128, 135, 136, 159n15; adjustment simulation results 143–145; banking integration progress 311–13; cross-border externalities 339; demand and supply shocks 143; deposit insurance, coverage in 364; DSGE results for 144; financial supervision in Europe, experiences of 348; housing wealth effects 171, 172–173; insolvency resolution 376; international risk sharing 245; mortgage market in 171, 172, 174–175; risk profile sensitivity to shock 274; stylized facts 142–143; summing up on adjustment exercise 145

Jaeger, A. and Schuknecht, L. 86, 87, 93, 108n5, 108n7, 108n8
Japan 86, 89, 90, 95, 105, 120, 124n8, 417–18, 419; financial engineering ('Zaitech') in 408; housing wealth effects 172–173; international risk sharing 245; stock market decline in 308

Jiménez, G. and Saurina, S. 43
Johansen, S. 203
Jokipii, T. and Milne, A. 182, 183
Jonung, L. and Hagberg, T. 36
Jonung, L. and Stymne, J. 93–94
Jonung, L. *et al.* 108n6
Jonung, L., Schuknecht, L. and Tujula, M. 108n7
Jonung, Lars 3–18, 108n1, 257n1, x
Jordan, J. *et al.* 427n9
J.P. Morgan 209

Kaas, L. 328n12
Kahn, C.M. and Santos, J.A.C. 400n51
Kalemli-Ozcan, S. *et al.* 222, 225, 229, 241n8
Kalemli-Ozcan, Sebnem 11, 222–41, x
Kaminsky, G.L. and Reinhart, C.M. 111
Kane, E.J. 396, 397, 398n11, 398n23, 399n35
Kane, E.J. *et al.* 363
Karceski, J. *et al.* 324
Kaufman, George G. 16, 191n13, 355–400, x
Kaufman, G.G. and Seelig, S. 399n44
Kazakhstan 111, 113, 120, 122, 123
Kennedy, N. and Andersen, P. 191n8
Kindleberger, C. 412
King, M. 427n11
King, R.G. and Levine, R. 327
Kleimeier, S. and Sander, H. 328n10
Klöckers, Hans Joachim 108n1
Knickerbocker Trust Company 209
Knight, M.D. 407
Koen, Vincent 190n1
Kok, W. 46
Korea 95, 120, 124n8, 167, 417–18
Korhonen, I. and Fidrmuc, J. 35
Kose, A. *et al.* 278n2
Kose, Ayan 278n1
Kose, M., Otrok, C. and Whiteman, C.H. 247
Kraay, A. and Ventura, J. 222, 240n5
Krainer, J. and Lopez, J.A. 278n6
Kremers, J. *et al.* 353n5
Kremers, J., Schoenmaker, D. and Wierts, P. 345, 399n31
Krimminger, M.H. 374, 399n28
Kuritzkes, A., Schuermann, T. and Weiner, S. 343
Kuttner, Kenneth 303n1
Kuwait 124n7
Kwan, S.H. and Wilcox, J.A. 326
Kwiatkowski, D. *et al.* 202

labour markets: dynamics of 45; financial market integration and 25; flexibility in 169
Lamfalussy regulatory structure 345–46
Landon-Lane, J. and Rockoff, H. 204
Landon-Lane, John 10, 199–220, x
Lane, P.D. 245
Lane, P.D. and Milesi-Ferretti, G.M. 62, 80, 242, 245, 257n7
Lane, P.R. 64, 158n2, 191n5
Langedijk, S. and Roeger, W. 158n3
Langedijk, Sven 8–9, 127–160, x
Larch, M. 159n17
Lastra, Rosa 349
Latin America 120, 307, 415
Latvia 40, 48, 49, 81n3, 102, 113, 120, 122; deposit insurance characteristics 366, 367, 372, 374; foreign-owned banks in 313; insolvency resolution 380
LCFI (large complex financial institutions) 282
lead supervision 338, 345, 347, 348–49
Leahy, M. *et al.* 329n39
legal closure, promptness in 387, 388–89
legislation and reporting requirements 316–17
Lehar, A. 283
lending concentration in CEE 118
lending volatility 308
Lensink, R. and Hermes, N. 308
Levine, R. 308, 327
Levine, R. and Zervos, S. 327–28
Levine, R. *et al.* 327
Lewis, D. 398n11
Liechtenstein 314
Lindquist, K. 183
Lippi, M. 304n8
liquidity and financial stability in CEE 118
Lisbon Strategy 25, 46
Lithuania 45, 48, 54n9, 81n3, 102, 113, 120, 122; deposit insurance characteristics 366, 367, 372, 374; foreign-owned banks in 313; insolvency resolution 382
local currency, inability to borrow abroad in 43
Lombard Street (Bagehot, W.) 212
Lopez Salido, D. *et al.* 128
loss compensation 316–17
Lowe, Phil 182, 406, 413, 415, 427n9
Lucas, R. 222
Lumsdaine, R.L. and Prasad, E.S. 263
Lütkepohl, H. and Krätzig, M. 204
Luxembourg 45, 56, 81n2, 81n4; banking integration progress 311–13; cross-border externalities 339; deposit insurance characteristics 365, 367, 369, 373; foreign banking penetration in 361; insolvency resolution 376; international risk sharing 245

Maastricht Treaty 31, 39, 223, 357; convergence criteria established by 31, 32, 34, 46, 107; cross-border banking, problems and solutions 357; fiscal adjustment ratios 41; fiscal criteria 115; nominal convergence route 50; price inflation criterion 40, 42
McCauley, R. *et al.* 427n7
Mace, B. 257n3

Macedonia 120
MacKinnon, J.G. *et al.* 203
Maclennan, D. *et al.* 177
macro-financial stability: effects of 307–9; importance of 306; macroeconomic stability issues 320–22
macroeconomic acclimatization 44
macroeconomic change, markets as drivers 20–22
macroeconomic policy, trilemma in 337–38
macroeconomic volatility, risk of 42
macroprudential orientation: possible insufficiency of 421–22; strengthening of 420–21
Magyar Nemzeti Bank 54n12
Malaysia 95, 124n8
Malta 32, 53n1, 81n3, 109n12, 119, 121, 122; deposit insurance characteristics 366, 367, 372, 374; foreign-owned banks in 313; insolvency resolution 380
Manna, M. 328n10
marginal product of capital 222
Marin, José 108n1
Marino, J.A. and Bennett, R.L. 399n42
Mark, N.C. and Sul, D. 251
market developments: adaptation to 351–52; impact on economic adjustment 20
market imperfections 111
Marquez, R. 328n12
Marshall, David 268
Martin, Reiner 6–7, 84–109, x–xi
Martinez Peria, M.S. *et al.* 308
MATLAB BVP4C 77
Matthews, A.M. and Eckler, A.R. 211
Mayes, D.G. 358, 393–93, 397n3, 399n29, 400n48
Mayes, D.G. and Vesala, J.M. 339, 358, 398n4
Meltzer, Allan H. 211, 212
mergers and acquisitions 306, 313, 314, 315, 316, 318, 326, 328n14, 328n15
Merton, Robert C. 269, 270, 283
Meucci, Francesco 303n1
Mexico 120, 124n8
migration 21
Modigliani, F. and Cohn, R.A. 427n7
monetary policy 422–25; frameworks for, refinements to 404–5; monetarist approach to union 40; preconditions for sound discretion 38; variables, setting of 35–36
monetary regime: change in 31; choice of 37–38; role of 404–5, 408–9
monetary transmission 46–47; mechanisms for 170
monetary union: economic perspective on 39–40; model of small country in 184–187; national monetary policy, independence in 337
Mongelli, F. and Vega, J.L. 56
Monnet, C. and Quintin, E. 328–29n17
Montenegro 120
Montgomery, H. 308
Monti, P. 159n17
Morgan, D.P. *et al.* 307
mortgage debt 159n20
mortgage market: integration of 20; in US 172, 174
MoUs (Memoranda of Understanding) 181, 358, 361, 400n47
MPI (Macro-prudential Indicator) 117, 120–21
MPK (capital stock/marginal product relation) 224
Muellbauer, J. 177
Mundell, Robert A. 199

Nagy, Piroska, M. 7–8, 111–24, xi
NAIRU (non-accelerating inflation rate of unemployment) 149
Nash, Gerald 211
National Bank of Poland 36
National Monetary Commission (US) 209
Neary, J.P. 45, 74
Nederlandsche Bank 145
Netherlands 21, 56, 59, 60, 62, 64, 80, 81n2, 85, 98–102, 109n11, 124n8, 128, 130, 135, 136, 159n18; adjustment simulation results 147–148; analysis of recent boom-bust episodes 98–102; banking integration progress 311–13; cross-border externalities 339; demand and supply shocks 146; deposit insurance characteristics 365, 367, 369, 373; DSGE results for 147; housing cycles, soft landings in 167; housing policies 162; housing supply elasticities and constraints 179; housing wealth effects 171, 172–173; insolvency resolution 377; international risk sharing 245; mortgage market in 172, 174; risk profile sensitivity to shock 274; short-term interest rates 163; stylized facts 145–146; summing up on adjustment exercise 148
New Deal initiatives in US 211
New-Keynesian-DSGE model 127, 132–135, 138, 141, 144, 147, 150, 153, 158n5
New York City 207, 209, 212, 213, 215, 400n48
New Zealand 124n8, 398n16, 398n20; international risk sharing 245
Nickell, P. and Perraudin, W. 283
Niemeyer, J. 360
Nieto, M.J. and Penalosa, J.M. 398n23
nominal and real convergence, challenges of 23–24
nominal convergence 58–65, 79–80
nominal convergence criteria 31
non-housing investment 61–62, 64, 79–80

Nordal, Kjell B. 303n1
Nordea Banking Group 328n14, 358, 384, 393–93, 398n17, 400n48
Nordic countries 36, 120, 174, 311, 322, 415
Norway 124n8, 314; international risk sharing 245; risk profile sensitivity to shock 274

Obstfeld, M. 58
Obstfeld, M. and Rogoff, K. 57
OCA (optimum currency area) criteria 34–35; anticipatory OCA endogenicity 35
Odell, K.A. and Weidenmier, M.D. 209
ODGF (Ohio Deposit Guarantee Fund) 397
OECD (Organization for Economic Cooperation and Development) 40, 162, 166, 168, 169, 170–171, 179; *Economic Surveys* 183–184; Financial Balance Sheet databank 80; INTERLINK model 184–187; international risk sharing 245, 246, 248, 252, 253, 255; recommendations on housing markets 183–184
off-balance sheet weakness 118
Okina, K. *et al.* 424
Oldani, Chiara 303n1
Oosterloo, Sander 14–15, 337–53, xi
optimality, dimensions of 34–35
Orlowski, L.T. 33
overextension 407

Padoa-Schioppa, T. and Saccomanni, F. 406
Padoa-Schioppa, Tommaso 348
Papademos, Lucas 340
PCA (prompt corrective action) 390, 392, 393, 394, 395
Peek, J. and Rosengreen, E.S. 307, 308, 324
Perron, P.P. 202
Peuckmann, Stefanie 108n1
Phillips, P.C.B. and Moon, H.R. 251
Pilloff, S.J. and Santomero, A.M. 325
Poland 35, 37, 38, 40, 45, 46, 47, 48, 50–51, 81n3, 102, 113, 120, 122, 123; deposit insurance characteristics 366, 367, 372, 374; foreign banking penetration in 361; foreign-owned banks in 313; insolvency resolution 382
policy implications for CEE stability 123
policy options: evolutionary option on financial supervision 351; future possibilities 344–51, 351–52; for monetary and financial stability 419–25; official policies, interaction with markets 19
political preferences 315
political resistance to foreign-bank entry 315–16
Political Risk Services Group 240
Portugal 21, 40, 44, 45, 56, 57, 59, 60, 62, 64, 80, 81n2, 85, 98–102, 109n11, 113, 114–15, 116, 123, 124n8, 128, 130, 135, 136, 151; adjustment simulation results 149–151; analysis of recent boom-bust episodes 98–102; banking integration progress 311–13; current account deficit 233–34; demand and supply shocks 149; deposit insurance characteristics 365, 367, 370, 373; DSGE results for 150; insolvency resolution 377; international risk sharing 245; mortgage market in 172, 174; risk profile sensitivity to shock 274; short-term interest rates 163; stylized facts 148–149; summing up on adjustment exercise 151
Posen, A. 180
Prager, R.A. and Hannan, T.H. 324
Prasad, E.S. *et al.* 222
price convergence, acceleration in 42
price developments in housing 130–131
price levels 40
price stability 404
procyclicality 406–8; of banking system 406–8; in housing market 182–183, 191n14
product markets 25; flexibility in 169
productivity: and capital flows 222; and wage trends 129; *see also* TFP
productivity growth: financial development and 43; labour costs and 38
profit x-inefficiency 326
prudential policy: frameworks for, refinements to 404–5; stability, monetary and financial, twin goals 419–22; standards for, establishment of 357
prudential regulation on insolvency 384–84
prudential supervision 348; housing markets 179–183
public debt 93–94
public finances: developments in 98; management of 25
Public Finances in EMU (European Commission) 24
Pulkkinen, T.E. and Rosengren, E.S. 396
PWT (Penn World Table) 245

Rae, D. and van den Noord, P. 168
Rae, David 9–10, 161–191, xi
Rajan, R. and Zingales, L. 323, 329n19
RAMs (recently acceded members) 31–32, 34–35, 35–36, 37, 38, 40, 41, 43, 45, 46, 47–50, 51–52
Ratto, M., Roeger, W. and In't Veld, J. 158n4
Ravn, M.O. and Uhlig, H. 278n4
re-privatization and re-capitalization, promptness in 388, 392–92
real activity, synchronization of 262–66, 276
real convergence experience 23–24
real economic environment 90
real economic growth of CEE 102–3
real effective exchange rate in CEE 102–3
Reconstruction Finance Corporation (US) 211

reform fatigue 40–41
regional interest rates 199–220; asymmetric shocks 214, 215; central authority and 200–207; econometric exercise 200–207; econometric exercise, statistical tests and analysis used 202–7; impulse response functions 204, 216, 217, 218–19; SBIC (Schwarz Bayesian Information Criterion) 203; structural shocks, identification of 200–202; symmetric shocks 214; US before Federal Reserve (1880–1913) 207–10, 214, 216; US Federal Reserve (1914–43) 210–12, 214–15, 217; US Federal Reserve (1955–2002) 212–14, 215, 218–19; US monetary history 199–219; VaR (Value-at-Risk) analysis 59, 199–204, 252; VEC (Vector Error Correction) model 203; *see also* United States
Regling, Klaus 3–4, 18, 19–26, xi
regulation: compliance on, uncertainty in 358; financial regulatory system 357–58; financial regulatory systems 357–58; reform and cross-border bank integration 310; regulatory competition, likelihood of 357–58; regulatory oversight 37, 52; transparency in 118, 120
Reichlin, L. 304n8
Reinhart, C.M. and Rogoff, K.S. 222
repressive financial arrangements 406
resilience, housing market as source of 170–183
restructuring operations 316
Rhoades, S.A. 325
risk: and capital management, centralization of 343–44; considerations of, macroeconomic stability and 320–22; for emergent economies 43; management functions, integration of 342–44; 'risk perceptions gap' 407; risk premia 21, 24
risk sharing: consumption risk sharing, globalization and 242, 245–50; consumption risk sharing, measurement of 243–45; European integration and 242–57; financial market integration and 20, 22–23; SWYZ (Sørensen, Wu, Yosha and Zu) 242, 251, 253, 254, 255; *see also* international risk sharing
Rockoff, Hugh 10, 199–220, xi
Roeger, Werner 8–9, 127–160, xi
Romania 102, 105, 109n17, 113, 120, 122
Romans, J.T. 225–28
Romer, C.D. and Romer, D.H. 220n10
Rose, Andrew K. 45, 337
Rostowski, J. 42
Rother, Philipp 108n1
Roubini, N. 180
RSR (risk sharing regression) 244
Rubene, Ieva 108n1
Russia 111, 113, 120, 121, 122, 123; crisis in (1998) 54n7; crisis in (1998), repercussions of 31
SAIR (System Average Individual Rating) 117, 120
Saks, R. 191n10
Sala-i-Martin, X. 191n6
Salmon, R. *et al.* 399n41
San Francisco 209
Sapienza, P. 324
Sapir, A. *et al.* 46
Sargent, T.J. and Sims, C.A. 282
Saudi Arabia 124n7
SBIC (Schwarz Bayesian Information Criterion) 203
Schadler, S. *et al.* 40, 46, 102, 113–14
Schenk, H. 329n36
Schich, S. and Kikuchi, A. 328n15
Schinasi, G.J. and Teixeira, P.G. 282
Schoenmaker, D. and Oosterloo, S. 282, 337, 340, 344, 348, 398n15
Schoenmaker, Dirk 14–15, 337–53, xii
Schuermann, Til 278n1
Schuknecht, Ludger 6–7, 84–109, xii
Schüler, M. and Heinemann, F. 338, 346
Schüler, Martin 319, 359–60, 398n11
Schwab, Gerhard 108n1
Schwaegermann, Saskia 108n1
Schwartz, Anna 212, 418
Scott, J.A. and Dunkelberg, W.C. 324
sectoral channels, interlinkages between 86–87
Segoviano, M.A. and Lowe, P. 427n9
SEIR (structures early intervention and resolution) 394
Serbia 120
Simons, K. and Stavins, J. 324
Singapore 124n8
single banking licenses 310
Single Financial Market 344–45
single market, competitive effects of 38
Single Market Programme 309
Sironi, Andrea 303n1
Slovakia 40, 45, 81n3, 102, 113, 120, 122; deposit insurance characteristics 366, 367, 372, 374; foreign-owned banks in 313; insolvency resolution 380
Slovenia 39, 40, 45, 46, 48, 49, 54n9, 81n2, 81n3, 109n13, 111, 113, 119, 122; deposit insurance characteristics 366, 367, 372, 374; foreign-owned banks in 313; insolvency resolution 380
Smets, F. 409
Smets, F. and Wouters, R. 82n13, 158n4
Smits, René 351
Solnik, B. and Roulet, J. 263
solvency, indicators of 49–50
Solvency II (Insurance Directives) 339, 343, 352
Sørensen, B.E. *et al.* 242
Sørensen, Bent E. 11, 222–41, xii
Soussa, F. 397n3

South Africa 124n7, 124n8
South-East Asia, analysis of boom-bust episodes 95–98
sovereign exposure 118, 120
Spain 21, 38, 44, 50–51, 56, 59, 60, 62, 64, 80, 81n2, 89, 113, 114–15, 116, 124n8, 128, 129, 130, 135, 136; adjustment scenario for 154–156; adjustment simulation results 152–154; banking integration progress 311–13; demand and supply shocks 151–152; deposit insurance characteristics 365, 367, 370, 373; DSGE results for 153; housing policies 162; housing supply elasticities and constraints 179; housing wealth effects 172–173; insolvency resolution 378; international risk sharing 245; mortgage market in 172; risk profile sensitivity to shock 274; short-term interest rates 163; stylized facts 151; summing up on adjustment exercise 154
special banking models 328–29n17
special bankruptcy laws (US) 374
SPI (state-level personal income) 227
Sprague, O.M.W. 220n3
stability, monetary and financial, twin goals 404–27; analytical work, need for more 425; anti-inflationary commitment 408–9, 423; asset price increases, unsustainability in 408; Basel II 427n9; credit and asset prices, booms and busts in 412; dialogue between authorities, need for more 426; educational effort, need for 426; empirical findings 412–19; empirical work, need for more 425–26; evidence 409–19; financial imbalances, build up in low inflation environments 417–19; financial imbalances, build-up of 408, 409, 423, 427n7; financial imbalances, instability and 412–15; financial imbalances, likelihood of 427n7; financial imbalances, output weakness and disinflation 415–17; financial liberalization 406–8, 427n7; financial liberalization, key process 406; financial regime, role of 404–5, 406–8; historical perspective 410–12; hypothesis 406–9; inflationary processes, stability in 408–9; macroprudential orientation, possible insufficiency of 421–22; macroprudential orientation, strengthening of 420–21; monetary policy 422–25; monetary regime, role of 404–5, 408–9; opportunity beckons 404–5; overextension, failure to prevent 407; policy options 419–25; procyclicality of system 406–8; prudential policy 419–22; refinements to monetary and prudential frameworks 404–5; repressive financial arrangements 406; 'risk perceptions gap' 407; stability across regimes, historical perspective 410–12
Stability and Growth Pact 161; breaches of 46; financial market integration and 24–25
stabilization: monetary transmission and 46–47; stabilizing role of integration 22–23
Standard & Poor 329n22
Stevens, G.R. 424
Stiroh, Kevin J. 270, 281
Stiroh, K.J. and Rumble, A. 270, 281
Stiroh, K.J. and Strahan, P.E. 328n6
Stock, J.H. and Watson, M.W. 247, 263, 278n2, 282, 285, 296–96, 304n3, 304n9
stock market capitalization 49
stock market slide (US, 1903) 209
Stockman, A.C. and Tesar, L.L. 244
Stracca, Livio 108n1
structural shocks, identification of 200–202
stylized facts: adjustment to the euro, exploration of implications of entry 58–65; for CEE member states 107; and shortcomings of 84, 85, 88, 89, 94, 99, 105, 106, 107; stylized developments (and stylized facts) 128–132
subsidiaries, establishment of 311
supervision: authority for, constitution of single authority 320; banking supervision 24; costs and risks of financial supervision 350–51; cross-border penetration of financial supervision 340–41, 342, 344; cross-border supervision arrangements in housing 179–182; dialogue between authorities, need for more 426; efficiency in 344, 346, 347, 348–49; efficiency in, home-country control and 339; EU supervision 318–20; EU supervision, current arrangement 318–20; EU supervision, proposals for improvement 320; evolutionary option on financial supervision 351; incompatible objectives of 337; industry developments 339–42; lead supervision 338, 345, 347, 348–49; prudential supervision 348; prudential supervision issues 179–183; supervision authority, constitution of single authority 320
supply elasticities and constraints in housing 179
Sveriges Riksbank 364, 398n17
Swank, J. *et al.* 177
Sweden 32, 36, 89, 93–94, 95, 124n8; banking integration progress 311–13; cross-border externalities 339; deposit insurance characteristics 365, 367, 370, 373; housing cycles, soft landings in 167; insolvency resolution 378; international risk sharing 245; monetary transmission mechanisms 170; risk profile sensitivity to shock 274
Switzerland 86, 89, 90, 105, 124n8; international risk sharing 245
SWYZ (Sørensen, Wu, Yosha and Zu) 242, 251, 253, 254, 255

symmetric shocks 214
systemic risk 111; convergence of measures 270–73; integration and 268–76; measures of 268–70; sensitivity of measures to real and financial shock 273–76; systemic risk matrix 121–22; trends in 270
Systemic Risk Analysis 118, 119

Taiwan 120, 124n8
Tarashev, N. *et al.* 426n5
Tarashev, Nikola A. 278n6
taxation: of residential property in US 177; tax incentives for housing 175–177; tax-related barriers to integration 316–17
TBTF (too-big-to-fail) 399n43
technological innovation 309–10
TFP (total factor productivity) 140, 156, 159n14, 159n22, 236; demand and supply shocks to 140, 145, 159, 236; growth in 21, 136, 139, 140, 142, 143, 145, 149, 154, 156, 236; trends in 135, 137
Thailand 95, 124n8
Thiel, M. 329n40
Thomson Financial Datastream 285
Thygesen, Niels 337
Tieman, Alexander 12–13, 261–79, 281, 282, xii
Tobin, James 18
total assets, banking and insurance 277–78
Townsend, R.M. 257n3
trade: channels of 85–86, 91–92, 96–98, 101, 105; intra-euro area trade 45
transfer price calculation 317
transition within EMU 31–53; accession, participation and the 'j-curve' concept 5, 33–34, 36, 39, 40, 42, 46, 50, 52; accession to stage 3, challenges of 32–35, 50; adaptation to full EMU membership, dimensions of 44–45; adjustment and full EMU at stage 3, living with 43–46, 52; adjustment approaches 42; agricultural employment 45; anticipatory OCA endogenicity 35; Balassa-Samuelson (BS) effect 40, 50; bank credit, GDP ratio to 47–48; bank lending in RAMs 48; bank ownership 37; banking disruption, potential sources in move to EMU 44; banks, lending fervour of 43; budgetary ratios 40–41; capital inflows 45; change, extent within RAM economies 34; construction employment 45; consumer debt 37; convergence, towards reality in 38–39, 51–52; 'convergence boom' 34; costs and benefits, debate on 32–33, 47; credit-induced effects on stability 48; currency mismatch 43; debt intolerance 43; defaults and bank failures 48; domestic credit 47; economic activity, evolution of 39; economic activity, structural change in geometry of 45; economic perspective on monetary union 39–40; endogenous OCA, new members and 35–36; exchange rate, value on entry to EMU 46; exchange rate as adjustment instrument 41–42; external debt 47; financial intermediation 48; financial market integration 37; financial sector in RAMs 47–50, 52; financial services, spatial concentration of 45; financial stability, crucial nature of 31–32, 50; financial stability, links to real convergence from 42–43; financial stability, salience of 36–37, 51; financial system, monetary transmission and stabilization 46–47; fiscal adjustment 41; fiscal consolidation 34; fiscal rules, conformity with 46; inflation targeting 37–38; interest rate decisions 36; intra-country convergence 37; intra-euro area trade 45; labour market dynamics 45; local currency, inability to borrow abroad 43; longer-term effects 45; macroeconomic acclimatization 44; macroeconomic volatility, risk of 42; monetarist approach to monetary union 40; monetary policies, preconditions for sound discretionary policies 37–38; monetary policy variables, setting of 35–36; monetary regime change 31; monetary regime choice 37–38; monetary transmission 46–47; new members as optimum currency area candidates 35–36, 50–51; nominal convergence criteria 31; OCA (optimum currency area) criteria 34–35; optimality, dimensions of 34–35; policy rethinking for stage 3 adjustment 43–46; price convergence, acceleration in 42; price levels 40; prior adjustment in stage 2, convergence and 39–42; productivity growth, financial development and 43; productivity growth, labour costs and 38; reform fatigue 40–41; regulatory oversight 37, 52; risks to emergent economies 43; Russian crisis (1998), repercussions for 31; sensitivity to interest rate shocks 50; single market, competitive effects of 38; solvency, indicators of 49–50; Stability and Growth Pact, breaches of 46; stabilization, monetary transmission and 46–47; stock market capitalization 49; synchronization of economic cycles 38
transmission channels 85–87
triangular methodology 108n5
Tsatsaronis, K. 420, 426n5
Tsatsaronis, K. and Zhu, H. 421
Tùma, Zdeněk 37, 47
Turan, Belgi 11, 222–41, xii
Turkey 36

Ukraine 111, 113, 120
ULC (unit labour costs) 91–92, 105, 166

Union Financière de France 285
United Kingdom 32, 89, 124n8, 415, 417; banking integration progress 311–13; deposit insurance characteristics 365, 367, 370, 373; HM Treasury 191n8; housing cycles, soft landings in 167; housing wealth effects 171, 172–173; insolvency resolution 378; international risk sharing 245; monetary transmission mechanisms 171; mortgage market in 172, 174; risk profile sensitivity to shock 274; taxation of residential property 177
United States 124n8, 220n1, 400n50, 415, 418, 419; banking crisis (1893) 208–9, 214; Bland-Allison Silver Purchase Act 208; capital flows, patterns of 222–23; Civil War (1861–65) 207; deposit insurance systems in 396–96; FDIA (Federal Deposit Insurance Act) 399n37; FDIC (Federal Deposit Insurance Corporation) 374–84, 386, 390, 391, 392, 393; FDICIA (Federal Deposit Insurance Corporation Improvement Act) 389–89; Federal Deposit Insurance 215; Federal Reserve 180; Federal Reserve (1914–43) 210–12, 214–15, 217; Federal Reserve (1955–2002) 212–14, 215, 218–19; before Federal Reserve (1880–1913) 207–10, 214, 216; Federal Reserve System, establishment of 209, 210; Florida land boom 211, 214, 215; FRB-US macroeconomic model 184; FSLIC (Federal Savings and Loan Insurance Corporation) 397; GAAP (General Accepted Accounting Principles) 326; GDP growth 308; Great Contraction (1929–32) 211–12, 214; housing wealth effects 171, 172–173; international risk sharing 245; interstate consolidation, cross-border bank integration 307; intra-state and interstate branch banking, lifting of restrictions on 215; monetary history of 199–219; monetary union within 19, 22; mortgage market in 172, 174; National Monetary Commission 209; New Deal initiatives 211; ODGF (Ohio Deposit Guarantee Fund) 397; Reconstruction Finance Corporation 211; reserve requirements, doubling of (1936–37) 212; special bankruptcy laws 374; stock market slide (1903) 209; taxation of residential property 177; twin-shock crisis (1896) 209; US-EU comparison on capital flows 224–37; US-EU comparison on capital flows, model of 224–25; US-EU comparison on capital flows, US results 225–31; Volcker disinflation 213; War Finance Corporation 211, 215
Upper, C. and Worms, A. 281
Uruguay 124n8

Van den Noord, P. 177
Van der Zwet, Annemarie 342
van Lemmen, Jan 257n1
Vander Vennet, R. 325, 328n10
Vanderblue, Homer 211
VaR (Value-at-Risk) analysis 59, 199–204, 252
Vartia, L. 179
Vassalou, M. and Xing, Y. 278n6
VEC (Vector Error Correction) model 203
Velculescu, D. 58
Vives, Xavier 337
Volcker, Paul 213
von Hagen, J. and Traistaru, I. 51
Vujcic, Boris 278n1
Vulpes, Giuseppe 13–14, 281–304, xii

Wagner, M. and Hlouskova, J. 109n14
Walkner, C. and Raes, J.P. 328n1, 329n18
Walkner, Christopher 3–18, 306–29, xii
Wall, L.D. and Eisenbeis, R.A. 399n39
Walter, N. 398n7
War Finance Corporation (US) 211, 215
Watson, Max 3–18, 19–26, 87, 108n1, 328n1, xiii
wealth, influence on housing 189–190
Weber, A. and Beck, G. 191n6
White, William R. 426n2
Whitehead, Sarah 108n1
Wicker, Elmus 208
Wilcoxon/Mann-Whitney statistical tests 87, 94, 108n10
World Bank-IMF Financial Sector Assessment Programmes 180–181
Wyplosz, C. 40

Yaari, M.E. 57, 65

Zaitech (financial engineering) in Japan 408
Zazzara, Christino 303n1
zoning regulations for housing 177–179